PLAYERS

By the same author

SPORT: Almost Everything You Ever Wanted to Know

TIM HARRIS

PLAYERS

250 MEN, WOMEN AND ANIMALS WHO CREATED MODERN SPORT

YELLOW JERSEY PRESS
LONDON

Published by Yellow Jersey Press 2009

2 4 6 8 10 9 7 5 3 1

Copyright © Tim Harris 2009

Tim Harris has asserted his right under the Copyright, Designs
and Patents Act 1988 to be identified as the author of this work

First published in Great Britain in 2009 by
Yellow Jersey Press
Random House, 20 Vauxhall Bridge Road,
London SW1V 2SA

www.rbooks.co.uk

Addresses for companies within The Random House Group Limited can be found
at: www.randomhouse.co.uk/offices.htm

The Random House Group Limited Reg. No. 954009

A CIP catalogue record for this book
is available from the British Library

ISBN 9780224082778

The Random House Group Limited supports The Forest Stewardship
Council (FSC), the leading international forest certification organisation. All our
titles that are printed on Greenpeace approved FSC certified paper carry the
FSC logo. Our paper procurement policy can be found at
http://www.rbooks.co.uk/environment

Mixed Sources
Product group from well-managed
forests and other controlled sources
www.fsc.org Cert no. TT-COC-2139
© 1996 Forest Stewardship Council
FSC

Typeset in Fairfield LH Light by Palimpsest Book Production Limited,
Grangemouth, Stirlingshire

Printed and bound in Great Britain by
Clays Ltd, St Ives PLC

For my parents, Sidney and Susan Harris.

'I believe in rules. Sure I do. If there weren't any rules, how could you break them?'

LEO 'THE LIP' DUROCHER

Introduction and Welcome

It may be natural to play games, but the sports we love aren't natural at all. Each and every one of them has been invented, tweaked, pushed and pulled to come up with better rules, cleverer tactics and more effective techniques. There are no prizes for guessing who invented the Cruyff turn or the Fosbury flop – but what about the header or the sliding tackle? The dive pass or the scrum? The lob or the smash? The sand wedge or the tee? The googly or the flipper?

This book introduces 250 men, women and animals, each of whom transformed at least one major world sport. Famous or infamous, remembered or forgotten, god-like or god-awful, the game was never the same after them.

At the top are the 'Rulers' – extraordinary talents such as Muhammad Ali, Michael Jordan or Suzanne Lenglen, who achieved new levels of skill and drew the eyes of the world. Some of them, like Don Bradman in cricket or Babe Ruth in baseball, were so good that the rules or equipment had to be changed to give others a chance. One or two were so brilliant that they even killed off their sport as a genuine contest. Most are attacking players, but not all. Footballer Bill McCracken and cricketer Jack Blackham both changed their sports through their defensive skills.

Next are the 'Rogues', the schemers and scammers, duckers and divers who dreamt up new cheats, dodges and ruses to win. Some of their inventions, such as reverse swing in cricket, the single-handed shot in basketball or the modern racing eight, have become part of the game – but there are some out-and-out villains too. Dopers, cheats and crooks have also played their part in sport's rich pageant, and here we salute their rat-like cunning.

The third group are the 'Revolutionaries' – the inventors of new rules, tactics and techniques that we all take for granted today. A few are geniuses who dreamt up massively popular sports such as tennis, basketball or greyhound racing. Some suddenly turned years of sporting orthodoxy on its head and found different ways to ride horses or motorbikes. Most simply found a new way to win the game. The one-two punch, the three-man defence, the four-wheel drift . . . they're all here.

Writing this book has been a lot of fun. For a start, there's been finding out how and why the great sports stars became so successful. Then the digging out of the more obscure characters and the stories behind the creation of the penalty, the scrum or the marathon. And finally there are the often surprising connections between them all. These links are indicated by underlining in the text and I hope they encourage you to jump around and get thoroughly lost.

In choosing these 250 names, I've tried to strike a balance between the blinking obvious and the deliberately perverse. I hope you have as much enjoyment disagreeing with my choices as I did coming up with them.

Notes and Thanks

Deciding which names to include and which to exclude has meant making a few tough choices. Just being a great player in a major world sport and leaving behind a stack of records wasn't enough. Neither was simply taking a sport from one place to another – so there is no entry for the first man to play soccer in, say, Bulgaria (sorry, George de Regibeaus). Although there are entries on everything from snooker to mountaineering, most names have come from the more popular world sports: football, cricket, rugby, golf, tennis, athletics, cycling and motor sport. I have also tried to favour sportspeople over the promoters, businesspeople and PR men who cluster around them. They're just more interesting.

Cramming 250 biographies into one book – or one author's lifetime – won't go, so I have limited myself to introducing these men, women and animals and how and why they changed the world of sport, rather than providing blow-by-blow descriptions of their careers. If you want to dig deeper, the bibliography contains a number of sources. Covering so many different sports and their stars has often meant relying on secondary sources rather than original materials and I apologise for any myths, lies and half-truths I have fallen for. God knows there are enough of them in sport.

Each entry contains a brief summary of a character's major sporting achievements – if any. In the interest of keeping them short and relevant, different sports and stars have been treated differently. Thanks to the Internet, far more detailed statistics on appearances and scores are just a click – or possibly a frustrating pause – away. In terms of career statistics, all averages are presented in brackets. In the case of baseball, which has its own statistical language, it may help to know that batting averages are the ratio of hits to bats (anything over .300 is something to be very proud of) while RBI – runs batted in – refers to all the runs achieved while that player was 'at-bat'.

Particular thanks go to David Barber at the Football Association, Peter Clare at Snooker Heritage, Adrian McGlynn at Weatherbys, Bill Miller at rowinghistory.com, Ron Palenski at Otago Rugby Football

Union and Neil Rhind at Blackheath Football Club. My thanks also to Tim Waller, Mark Stanton at Jenny Brown Associates, Tristan Jones, Juliet Brooke, Zoe Hood and Jenny Rowley at Yellow Jersey and Lucy, JJ and Al at home.

Finally, my apologies to all those sportspeople who are remembered for a one-off 'rush of blood' rather than a lifetime of honest sporting toil. As the story of John the Goat-shagger reminds us, it's not the hundreds of goats you *don't* shag that get remembered.

Players

Basil D'Oliveira – The great South African all-rounder who helped bring about the boycott of apartheid sport.

Dickie Downs – The inventor of the sliding tackle.

George Eastham – The mercurial winger whose transfer changed British football.

162

Bernie Ecclestone – The man who transformed Formula One from a hobby into a multinational business.

166

Eclipse – The 18th century's superhorse, father of three Derby winners, ancestor of most successful thoroughbreds today.

168

Arthur Elvin – The wheeler-dealing tobacconist who saved Wembley stadium.

170

Manfred Ewald – The joint mastermind of the GDR's hugely successful doping policy.

172

'Felix' – Cricket's pioneer of pads, caps and gloves.

174

Enzo Ferrari – The racer turned team manager turned constructor who became racing's most famous (and dangerous?) character.

182

Bernard Fitzalan-Howard, 16th Duke of Norfolk – The inventor of the Group system of racing and the man who lifted the lid on racehorse doping.

184

Dick Fosbury – The high jumper who went from 48th to 1st in the world by going backwards.

186

William Foulke – The heavyweight goalie who inspired the ballboy and the penalty rules.

188

C.B. Fry – The man who killed off lob bowling.

190

Masaru Furukawa – The human submarine who changed the rules of swimming.

191

Dave Gallaher – The all-conquering All Black who created modern rugby tactics.

194

Mike Gatting – The England captain who brought us neutral umpiring the hard way.

197

Spencer Gore – The inventor of the volley.

199

E.M. Grace – W.G.'s brother, who flouted convention with his leg-hitting.

201

W.G. Grace – The cricketing legend who broke almost every record and every rule.

205

Clarrie Grimmett – Slow bowler who created the flipper.

207

Walter Hagen – Golf's first international star.

556 **Madge Syers** – The skating star who took on and beat the men.

557 **Maurice Tate** – The first seamer.

559 **J.H. Taylor** – The golfer who created the PGA.

561 **Peter Taylor** – The judge whose report changed British football grounds for ever.

563 **Edward Thring** – The headmaster who created modern school sports.

564 **John Thurston** – The creator of the billiard table.

566 **Bill Tilden** – The tactical master of tennis who transformed the image of the game.

568 **Harry Vardon** – Golf's first international star.

571 **Harry Vassall** – Rugby's pioneer of inter-passing.

572 **Willy Voet** – The man behind the Tour de France's greatest scandal.

574 **Wavell Wakefield** – The British rugby captain who brought new skills into the game.

576 **Frederick Wall** – The FA secretary who drove women from the game.

582 **Shane Warne** – The man who brought back leg spin.

585 **Maud Watson** – The tennis player who became Britain's first female sports star.

586 **James Weatherby** – The man whose family have run British horse racing for 200 years.

588 **Johnny Weissmuller** – The perfector of the crawl (and Tarzan).

590 **John Willes** – Cricket's pioneer of round-arm bowling.

592 **Frank Williams** – The man at the heart of British GP racing for 30 years.

595 **J.P.R. Williams** – The first attacking full back.

597 **Tom Wills** – The creator of Aussie Rules.

599 **Edgar Willsher** – Cricket's pioneer of overarm bowling.

600 **Walter Wingfield** – The inventor of lawn tennis.

602 **Katarina Witt** – The skater who was too smart and sexy for her sport.

604 **Tiger Woods** – Golf's mega-earning master of distance and control.

607 **Babe Zaharias** – The extraordinary sporting all-rounder who created the Ladies' PGA.

Illustrations

3 Air Jordan XX Launch Party, 2005; Greg Louganis hitting the diving board during the 1988 Olympic Games (both courtesy of Getty).

4 Ray Mancinni, 1982 WBA Lightweight Title; Ayrton Senna crashes at the San Marino Grand Prix, 1994 (both courtesy of Getty).

5 Johan Cruyff in the World Cup semi-final, 1974 (courtesy of Offside); Jonah Lomu at the graveside of All-Black captain Dave Gallaher, 2000 (courtesy of Getty).

6 Martin Becher in the Grand National Steeplechase, 1839 (courtesy of Getty); Lester Piggott at Newbury racecourse, 1985 (courtesy of PA Photos).

7 Billie-Jean King relaxes before a match, 1980; Ed Moses at the 1984 Olympic Games (both courtesy of Getty).

8 Muttiah Muralithara delivers a ball during a training session, 2009 (courtesy of Getty).

Section 3

1 Illustration of Suzanne Lenglen, circa 1920 (courtesy of Getty).

2 Mick the Miller receiving a massage, circa 1930; Tom Morris, 1880 (both courtesy of Getty).

3 Johnny Weissmuller, circa 1924–1928; Mildred Didrikson wins gold in 1932 (both courtesy of Getty).

4 William Renshaw and H.F. Lawford playing for the Men's Singles title at Wimbledon, 1881; Harry Vardon, circa 1920 (both courtesy of Getty).

5 Kerry Packer, 1978 (courtesy of Getty); Pelé's final match, 1977 (courtesy of PA Photos).

6 Jarno Saarinen, 1972 (courtesy of Action Library); Tazio Nuvolari, circa 1930 (courtesy of Getty).

7 Jackie Stewart in hospital with his wife Helen, 1966; Clive Rowlands talking to his team during a match, 1966 (both courtesy of Getty).

8 Emil Zatopek wins the 10,000 metres in Switzerland, 1954 (courtesy of Getty).

PLAYERS

Giacomo 'Ago' Agostini

Giacomo Agostini, motorcyclist and team manager, born Brescia, Italy 16 June 1942. Career: MV Agusta 1964–74, Yamaha 1974–7, world champion 350 cc 1968, 69, 70, 71, 72, 73, 74, 500 cc 1966, 67, 68, 69, 70, 71, 72, 75. Overall record: 186 Grands Prix, 122 wins, 117 fastest laps. Motorcycle Hall of Fame 1999.

Despite a record number of Grand Prix wins, the most significant race in the world-beating career of Giacomo 'Ago' Agostini was one in which he *didn't* take part.

With 122 GP victories between 1964 and 1977, Agostini was motor-cycling's first superstar. The handsome and wealthy Ago tricked his family into allowing him to race – by implying that he meant to become a cyclist – and soon became the undisputed king of the sport. He very rarely crashed and only Jarno Saarinen's 'hanging-off' style ever really threatened him. In 1974, Ago's move from MV Agusta to Yamaha signalled the final takeover of 500 cc racing by the Japanese manu-facturers – but the race that made the biggest difference to the sport had taken place two years earlier.

On the morning of 9 June 1972, the 125 cc British Grand Prix took place around the Isle of Man TT course in heavy rain, low cloud and mist. The course was dangerous enough in perfect condi-tions – long and hard to learn, with narrow twisting roads, flanked by buildings and stone walls covered by only the most basic padding. Here, on the multiple bends known as Verandah, Agostini's friend Gilberto Parlotti crashed into a concrete post and wire fence and was killed.

After Agostini threatened to withdraw from that afternoon's senior race, conditions improved enough for him to compete and win his tenth TT, but afterwards he declared a personal boycott of the course, and got the backing of other stars, such as British champion Phil Read. The effect was electric – a sport's greatest hero turning his back on its totemic event. Although some changes were made to Verandah, the boycott remained in force and by 1976 the Isle of Man was no longer a Grand Prix course. Other boycotts followed – of Monza, the

Nürburgring and the Yugoslavian Grand Prix – and the sport slowly followed the example of motor racing by switching from races on public roads to purpose-built tracks. Despite this, the TT course remains in use today, having claimed over 200 lives so far. There were seven deaths in 2005 alone and in a health and safety conscious age, question marks hang over traditions like 'Mad Sunday', in which any member of the public can race over a section of the course.

Since retiring, Agostini has managed a number of successful riders including Kenny Roberts. Although in 2008 Valentino Rossi overtook Ago's record of 67 premier class wins, he is still well short of his total of 301 victories in all competitions.

Charles Alcock – 'The Father of Modern Sport'

Charles William Alcock, footballer, cricketer and sports administrator, born Sunderland 2 December 1842, died 26 February 1907. Football career: Forest FC 1859–63, Wanderers FC 1863–75 (FA Cup 1872); England 1875, 1 cap, 1 goal (captain). First-class cricket career: Middlesex 1867, MCC 1862. Administrative career: FA honorary secretary 1868–70, FA secretary 1870–95, FA treasurer 1877, FA vice-president 1896–1907, Surrey CCC secretary 1872–1907. Editor *Cricket* 1882–1905, editor *James Lillywhite's Cricketers Annual* 1872–1900, editor *Football Annual* 1868–1907.

A hyperactive sportsman, promoter, administrator, lawmaker and journalist, Charles Alcock is probably the single most influential figure in British sporting history. As well as being the pioneer of football as a national and international sport and the creator of the FA Cup, he also set up the first English Test match and was the spark for international rugby.

Just as a player Charles Alcock is worth a note. Although he wasn't a great sporting star at Harrow School, he founded the Forest football team in Epping in 1859, which re-formed as the Wanderers four years later and won the first FA Cup final, during which Alcock had a goal disallowed for offside. Robust and tall for his day, Charles was a dribbling forward with a high work rate, a hard shot and a fierce tackle. Team-mate W.G. Grace – a pretty physical player himself – recalled Alcock sending rivals 'flying off like catherine wheels', and he even threw opponents like G.H. Sampson to the ground. Alcock was also one of the first to 'back up' or deliberately 'combine' with other players, and after he persuaded a reluctant FA to visit the North to play Sheffield, his interplay with fellow forwards Chenery and Viney impressed all who saw it – 'as near to perfection as possible,' said the *Sheffield Independent*. As a cricketer he was considered a good fielder, a steady batsman and a fair 'change' fast bowler. As well as captaining Middlesex in their very first match, he played for the MCC and various other gentlemanly sides. (He once even led a 'France' side against 'Germany' at a match in Hamburg.) Alcock also played rugby for the prestigious Blackheath team, umpired when injured and was the first president of the Referees' Association, overseeing two FA Cup finals. However, he didn't just play our big three team sports – he also helped create them.

When Alcock began his sporting career in the 1860s, football was pretty much like fives or rackets today – a minority sport played by a small number of ex-public schoolboys like himself. The rugby style was more prestigious and popular and the FA was simply the London-based organiser of a handful of teams, playing poorly attended, under-strength meetings in Battersea Park and a few other open spaces. Rules varied from team to team and place to place – although this hardly mattered, as there were no national competitions. During the 1860s it was simply a matter of keeping the game alive, but within ten years of Alcock taking over as the FA's secretary, soccer would be well on the way to becoming Britain's favourite sport.

Alcock's brother John had already proposed the 'anti-hacking' motion that first divided soccer from rugby, and at 23 Alcock took over from him as Wanderers' rep. Two years later, as honorary secretary, he oversaw the ending of all handling – except by the goalie in his own half – and hastened the final split with rugby. Unlike other more hidebound footballers, Alcock was open to new ideas, and in December 1871 he persuaded the London FA to play William Prest and Nathaniel Creswick's Sheffield Association – who, although they played to different rules, had more clubs, more players and a longer history than the FA itself. These early matches raised football's profile at a time when the *Daily Telegraph* still felt it necessary to explain that in the FA's version of football, players didn't catch the ball. During the return match in January 1872, Alcock established the idea of half-time – at first to allow matches to be played to different rules in different halves – and the half-time turnaround. Gradually, the FA would adopt the Sheffielders' ideas of free kicks, corners and crossbars, until by 1877 they were willing to merge their rule books and join the FA, making it a truly nationwide organisation.

The Sheffielders' own Youdan Cup competition may also have inspired Alcock's other great scheme – the FA Cup – although another influence was the old Cock House tournament he had played in at Harrow. After mooting the idea in 1871, Alcock hosted the first 1872 final at Wanderers' home ground, the Oval, where he became the first winning captain. The idea of a nationwide knockout competition took a while to catch on. At first only two teams north of Hertfordshire entered and both scratched during the knockout stages. Even by the mid-1870s the Cup was still only attracting about 40 teams – but the number of entrants soon rose and then soared, and by 1893 spectator numbers at the Oval had increased to a 32,000 lockout. By now, football had become the number one game in Britain and was spreading across the world.

As well as making football a national game, Alcock also staged the first 'internationals'. Without a Scottish FA in existence, he used his press and personal contacts to stage a series of five unofficial matches, starting in 1870. While these might not have included many genuine Scots, they did stir up interest and led to the formation of a Scottish FA. However, they also provoked another group of Scottish footballers into staging the first rival rugby international and setting up a Scottish RFU. When the first official soccer international was staged in 1872, Charles was injured and unable to play, but this 'jovial companion' still travelled up overnight on hard seats to umpire a goalless draw at Partick. The following year he received a single England cap at centre forward.

At the same time, Alcock was also masterminding the development of the nation's summer game. From 1872 he was the secretary of Surrey CCC – which made him Britain's first professional sports administrator. At this time Surrey's membership was just 650 and the club had only recently stopped staging poultry shows to pay the rent. Nationally, the game was pretty anarchic, with players like James Southerton popping up all over the place, random touring parties visiting from abroad and a chaotic County Championship that was decided by the newspapers.

From his base at the Oval, Alcock organised the other county secretaries to agree rules for player qualification – even standing up to the MCC when they threatened a rival tournament with looser rules to suit their aristocratic members. The Oval soon became the first national sporting centre. As well as cricket, it staged the first England v Scotland rugby international south of the border, the first rugby match against the Irish and half of the first 14 internationals – until 1879, when the damage to the pitch became too great. As for football, 20 of the first 21 FA Cup finals were held there, until the crowds grew too huge to manage. Lawn tennis, cycling, lacrosse, baseball and Australian rules football were also staged – although a plan to flood the pitch to create an ice rink was, perhaps fortunately, abandoned. By the time of Alcock's death in 1907, Surrey's membership had grown to 4,000 and the club's new pavilion – the best in the country – even boasted hot baths. After his death it remained usual for the Surrey secretary to take the lead in arranging the playing schedule for touring cricket sides, and even today the concluding Test in a full series is still played at the Oval.

Despite all this activity, Charles Alcock considered himself first and foremost a journalist. In 1868, he became editor of the first *Football Annual*, as well as the 'Red' *Lillywhite's Cricketers' Annual* – while also working as assistant editor of *The Sportsman*, at whose offices FA meetings were often held. It was the press that enabled him to operate so effectively – deliberately needling the Scots into a football match by enquiring in the *Glasgow Herald* whether there was a 'spark left of the old fire'. He also published *Football* and *Cricket* – the first weekly magazines devoted to the sports.

By 1880 Alcock was using his powers of persuasion to create cricket's first great international sporting rivalry. At this time the touring Australians in Billy Murdoch's team were in bad odour. A riot in Sydney during <u>Lord Harris</u>'s tour had soured the MCC towards the Australians and Lord's wouldn't entertain them, so their tour was limited to just three county matches. Having managed to get Sussex to postpone their fixture, Alcock persuaded Lord Harris to put together a side and from 6 to 8 September he staged the first English Test match, which proved a huge hit. (After printing 40,000 scorecards they ran out of paper altogether.) With the Aussies' lethal weapon – bowler <u>Frederick Spofforth</u> – out of action and two great catches by Fred Grace, England needed just 57 to win, but fiddled pointlessly with the batting order and lost half their wickets for 31 before they were rescued by W.G. Grace. After these heroics the 1882 Test was even more of a thriller. The tension was so high that one spectator was said to have died of excitement, while another gnawed through his own umbrella handle. After Fred Spofforth had ripped through the English batsmen, the stunned Alcock was found with his head in his hands. These two Tests would inspire another 19 England v Australia tours before the end of the century and the creation of Test cricket as we know it – although the term wasn't in general use until the 1890s. Alcock also organised the schedule for the first Indian touring side – a Parsee team that visited in 1886.

If all that wasn't enough for one man, in 1885 Charles Alcock played yet another crucial role in sporting history, managing football's transition to professionalism. At the time, it seemed that this might tear the game in two, with 36 teams threatening to set up a rival British Football

Association. With his cricket background, Alcock saw no harm in professionalism, as long as it was properly controlled. Backed by other progressives such as Lord Kinnaird, he successfully argued for rules that would allow professionals to play in open competition, provided they lived within six miles of their club and had been resident for two years. (Though they were to be banned from FA meetings and committees.) While not very democratic by modern standards and not very long-lasting, Alcock's move was enough to keep soccer together and prevented the kind of ruinous split that divided rugby into union and league.

Alcock's other great footballing idea was the creation of a selectorial system, which he introduced in 1887. This paid off immediately as England dominated the home internationals. Though it became outdated, it was a definite advance on the old trials system, in which up to 90 players would jockey for inclusion in the national side. Another impact on the game was the suggestion that vertical Harrow stripes be the basic footballer's costume – ever since stripes have predominated over Rugby School-style hoops.

For all his innovations, Alcock was not a revolutionary. Although he was a keen 'backer up', as late as 1879 he still doubted that 'a wholesale system of passing pays'. Off the pitch, his successes were based on diplomacy, persistence and energy. A businessman rather than an idealist, he paid his star Surrey professionals well, but paid himself far better and stood out against their demands for £20 per Test in 1896 – roughly the same as the already wealthy 'amateurs' received. When the MCC, in a rare fit of energy, suggested a cricket cup – just like the FA Cup he had founded – Alcock was determinedly against the idea, as he didn't want a rival to the County Championship.

Exactly how important Charles Alcock is in sporting history depends on whether you believe that he was a far-sighted genius or, like W.G. Grace, that he was simply 'the right man at the right time'. He was certainly the right man at a crucial time. It was only after he created an open nationwide contest with clear universally accepted rules that football began to boom, and by smoothing the way to professionalism, he helped the sport avoid the split that left rugby in second place as Britain's winter sport. Though not a visionary in the style of Olympic founder <u>Baron Pierre de Coubertin</u>, it was Charles Alcock, a practical man of action, who created the first truly global game and much else besides. No wonder his wife complained that she hardly ever saw him.

After his death in 1907, few seem to have had a bad word to say about Charles Alcock. He was buried in West Norwood – where his grave was recently restored. Today it is estimated that all the lines on all the world's football pitches would stretch around the planet 11 times. That is perhaps his real monument.

Muhammad Ali – 'The Greatest'

Cassius Marcellus Clay Jnr, boxer, born Louisville, Kentucky 17 January 1942. Olympic light-heavyweight champion 1960, world heavyweight champion 1964–7, 74–8, 78–9. Overall record: 61 fights, 56 wins, 37 KOs, 5 losses. BBC Sports Personality of the Century.

'I am the King! I am the King! The King of the World! Eat your words! Eat your words!'

Voted the Greatest Sportsman of the 20th century by both *Sports Illustrated* and the BBC, Muhammad Ali dances into any list of sporting greats and revolutionaries. A global icon, it is easy to lose sight of just how extraordinary he was and in how many ways. For a start, his first heavyweight championship victory, celebrated with these words, came as a total, numbing surprise to everyone – especially his opponent, the feared Charles 'Sonny' Liston.

Ali was an unusual boxer from the beginning, coming from a more comfortable background than most fighters – even though as a black man in racially segregated Kentucky he was still a second-class citizen. (Ali's attempts to be 'blacker than thou' didn't play well with fighters like Joe Frazier, who had come from a far tougher background, and this helped turn 'Smoking Joe' from an Ali supporter to an Ali hater.) Whatever his history, there was no doubting Ali's extraordinary dedication, speed and reflexes, or his unusual coolness in a crisis. From the age of 12, as Cassius Clay, he put together a series of amateur victories, including the Golden Gloves, which he won after first being knocked down, before taking the gold medal at the Rome Olympics – a medal that, for a while, he wore continuously. After turning pro, he put together 19 victories, including 15 KOs, but his light weight, lack of any kind of guard and neglect of body punches all suggested a sacrificial victim for the feared Liston. Craziest of all, Ali pulled back to avoid punches rather than ducking from side to side in the usual way. This was a basic boxing 'no-no' that only he and fellow champion Jack Johnson got away with. To quote light-heavyweight champion José Torres, 'the train never caught up with them.'

At the time of the Liston fight there was little to suggest that Ali

was a serious threat, having scored inconclusive victories over Doug
Jones and Henry Cooper, who, like Sonny Banks, had even put him
down. At the weigh-in Ali was like no boxer ever seen before. In place
of the usual ritualised posturing, he began taunting Liston and deliberately freaked out to unsettle him. Even so, Liston was still 7–1 on for
victory before Ali defeated him, dancing, dodging punches and in round
five withstanding the pain of having his eyes burned by a liniment-like
substance on Liston's gloves. (Not the first time the champion's corner
had used this trick.) Having survived all this, Ali came back so strongly
that Liston quit on his stool, claiming a shoulder injury – which was
later proved to be genuine.

As Ali leapt about, yelling at a hostile press, it was clear that this
was no meek and deferential black star in the Joe Louis/Floyd Patterson
mould. In fact, the very next day Ali spoke of his membership of the
Nation of Islam – then also known as the 'Black Muslims' – a separ-
atist political group that eventually took over his management, protecting
and promoting him as the Mafia had Sonny Liston. Later, Ali would
speak out against mixed marriages and in favour of the separate
development of the races, while the Nation would rename him and
fictionalise parts of his history – for example, the incident in which,
terrorised by a white gang and refused service in a diner, he threw his
Olympic medal in the Ohio river. (It seems more likely that it was
simply lost.)

Having defeated Liston a second time with a punch so fast that few
saw it properly, Ali went on to make eight defences in rapid succession, often predicting – with some accuracy – in which round he would
win. As a fighter he was unique. Not only was he genuinely funny –
claiming Liston was so ugly that his tears ran down the back of his
head – he was such a kidder that opponents didn't know whether he
was faking injury or not, an approach that more than once got him out
of jail. Though he was not the first boxer to make up verses about his
opponent – William 'Bendigo' Thompson had done so in the 19th century
– Ali was certainly a 'rapper before rap'. As he gained size and power,
he also became one of the most talented champions in history – a 'four-
way fighter' able to move in, back or side-to-side with ease. The third
biggest and tallest heavyweight champion to date, his speed, anticipation, reflexes, timing and power were irresistible. Above all, he was
his own man and his fiercest fights were also the most political. When

the ex-champion, Christian integrationist Floyd Patterson, set up a 'moral crusade' against Ali, he was rewarded with a vicious and prolonged beating. So too was Ernie Terrell, who had taken on Ali's WBA title after he was stripped of it on a technicality. Terrell had pointedly called Ali by his 'slave name', and in their 1967 match he received 15 rounds of terrible punishment including, he claimed, a thumbed eye, as Ali repeatedly demanded, 'What's my name, Uncle Tom?'

Although he had already toured Africa to publicise the Nation of Islam, Ali became a global rather than a racial hero after an almost chance remark. Having been classified '1Y' for the Vietnam War in 1964 ('I said I was the greatest, not the smartest'), he was reclassified '1A' two years later and was required to fight as 'Cassius Clay'. When asked why he was avoiding the Vietnam draft, Ali replied that 'I ain't got no quarrel with them Vietcong'. This refusal to fight for a nation that regarded him as second-class polarised America at a time when the Vietnam War was already becoming less popular. Unlike former champ Joe Louis, who had enlisted in World War II and fought segregation from the inside, Ali delivered 200 anti-war speeches and became a hero for the anti-Vietnam War movement in America and abroad. Now under Army and FBI surveillance, he was stripped of his titles in 1967, and lost about $10 million in purses – plus his best years in the sport – as well as receiving hate mail that included a dead dog. Eventually he received a $10,000 fine and a five-year suspended sentence, but only ever served time for a driving offence.

After a Supreme Court decision in 1971 that the FBI had spied on him illegally, Ali was allowed to fight again against a new crop of far more serious contenders – Joe Frazier, George Foreman, Larry Holmes and Ken Norton. By now he was the biggest star on the planet. Ali and Frazier earned $2.5 million apiece for a non-title fight, and politicians – usually dictators – vied to stage his globally broadcast fights. Unable to dance through an entire 15 rounds, Ali began boxing in bursts, showing both his ability to take a punch and his tolerance of pain after getting his jaw broken by Ken Norton.

It wasn't until 1974 that Ali regained his heavyweight championship title in Zaire at the 'Rumble in the Jungle'. Here he benefited from the extra training time created by George Foreman's pre-fight injury and used it to acclimatise to the heat. Knowing that he couldn't dance through the bout and that Foreman would go for an early victory, Ali changed his tactics – to the great alarm of his corner – allowing Foreman to punch himself out by the fifth round. Using his 'rope-a-dope' technique, Ali exhibited his ability to absorb and deflect some shattering blows. This was a two-edged sword and in 1977 his doctor Ferdie Pacheco quit in protest at his decision to carry on fighting. He fought on until 1980, winning some disgracefully bent decisions before losing and regaining the title once more. By this time his general slowing down and the damage being caused by the fights was quite obvious and the promoters' decision to allow him to box on was a disgrace. After the final bout – a defeat by Trevor Berbick – his record stood at 56 wins and five losses.

Despite his global standing, the limits to Muhammad Ali's power were shown by his failure to persuade black African nations to join the US boycott of the 1980 Olympic Games, but he still remained a massive star, helping to negotiate the release of hostages before the 1990 Gulf War. By 1996, he was diagnosed with 'Pugilist Parkinson's disease' and billions witnessed his battle to light the Olympic flame at Atlanta, while wearing a replacement medal. In money terms, his name and image rights were still worth $50 million in 2006.

Only the damage to his health made Muhammad Ali like other boxers. Because of his truncated career, comparisons with other fighters are difficult, but at his dazzling mid-1960s best, with 24 out of 30 fights won by a knockout or technical knockout, he was pretty much untouchable. Today, as boxing remains splintered and becomes increasingly low-profile and even anachronistic, it seems unlikely that any fighter will ever rival The Greatest.

Robert Barclay Allardice

Captain Robert Barclay Allardice, 6th Laird of Ury, athlete and trainer, born Ury, Scotland 25 August 1779, died 8 May 1854.

Generally known as 'Captain Barclay', the sturdy Robert Barclay Allardice was one of the most famous athletes of his day. Born into a family renowned for their strength, he specialised in epic pedestrian matches, including a successful bid to walk 1,000 miles in 1,000 consecutive hours for 1,000 guineas. This feat, on which an estimated £40 million in today's money was wagered, made him nationally famous, but his most lasting contribution to sport was probably his recognition of the importance of training.

By the 18th century, backers of sporting matches might allow their performers some cash for training, but the whole thing was regarded as the athlete's business and a kind of black magic. It was Barclay who, by personally taking control of his training, raised up Tom Cribb, an ordinary prizefighter, to became British sport's first world champion.

Known as the 'Black Diamond' because of his history as a coal porter, Cribb was an ex-bellhanger and docker who had a thunderous punch and could take a hit. To become Champion of the Ring, he twice beat Jem Belcher – a talented counter-puncher handicapped by the accidental loss of an eye – but was frustrated by the black American boxer Bill Richmond, and it was 20 minutes before he could land a punch. Against Richmond's countryman, the freed slave Tom Molineux, Cribb was out on the ropes and had to be rescued by the crowd who held him up, stalled the fight and apparently broke Molineux's fingers. Though Cribb was judged the eventual winner after 39 rounds and 55 minutes, most observers recognised that Molineux should have been champion.

Before the 28 September 1811 rematch, Cribb was badly out of condition until Allardice carted him off to Scotland and put him through a brutal training regime, which Cribb later joked was tougher than the fight itself. Though some of Barclay's theories might seem odd to us ('yes' to stale bread, biscuits, beefsteak, mutton and chicken, 'no' to veal, lamb, pork, fish or vegetables), he was in deadly earnest as he trained his man to a peak of performance with gruelling runs and sweats, tying his arm into position to get him to keep a consistent guard and teaching him the new skill of 'milling on the retreat'. At Thistleton Gap in Leicestershire, a transformed Cribb finished the fight in 11 rounds thanks to his new ring sense and two thunderous punches, one of which broke Molineaux's jaw.

After this championship victory, boxing standards rose fast and Cribb became a national hero, retaining his title for ten years by reputation and setting a sky-high purse of 1,000 guineas. On his eventual retirement he was presented with a lion-skin belt – a tradition that lasts in boxing today.

As for Barclay, he kept his strength and even in his seventies was still able to lift a man on the palm of his hand. Though his methods have been superseded, the value of training for sporting victory has never been seriously disputed since.

Jacques Anquetil – 'Maître Jacques'

Jacques Anquetil, road and track cyclist, born Mont-Saint-Aignan, Normandy 8 January 1934, died 18 November 1987. Career 1950–69. Major wins: Tour de France 1957, 61, 62, 63, 64, world hour record 1956, Giro d'Italia 1960, 64, Vuelta a España 1963, Grand Prix des Nations 1953, 54, 55, 56, 57, 58, 61, 65, 66, Liège–Bastogne–Liège 1966. BBC International Sports Personality of the Year 1964.

Jacques Anquetil, the first man to win the Tour de France five times and the first to win all of Europe's big three stage races, won a bronze medal at Helsinki in 1952 aged 18 and burst onto the professional cycling scene the following year, winning the Grand Prix des Nations – the world time-trialling championship – at an unheard-of 42 kph, six minutes ahead of the field. It was to be the first of nine victories. Three years later, Maître Jacques broke Fausto Coppi's 14-year-old world hour record at over 46 kph. Without a serious rival after Roger Rivières broke his back in a crash, Anquetil would still be setting world hour records eight years later.

A farmer's son from Normandy, Anquetil was also the first modern racing cyclist, riding in a way that seemed odd at the time, but has since been proved to be the 'perfect' style. He rode with a high saddle, back parallel to the crossbar, and drove an unheard-of 54 x 13 gear ratio at an extraordinary 88–92 rpm. Unlike his flat-footed, propped-up rivals, Jacques rode toes-down with hardly any use of the ankles, pulling on the upstroke – a style that he claimed added 5 kph to his speed. Above all, 'Monsieur Chrono's' style remained perfect even when he was suffering badly. British rider Tom Simpson recalled hearing the great gulps of breath as Anquetil attacked from behind. His 1962 average speed in the Tour would remain the record until 1981.

An expert at disguising his own suffering on the road, he was a master of bluff off it – once demolishing a plate of seafood and a bottle of Muscadet during a Tour to demonstrate his iron stomach. Though he exaggerated the effect for the media, he had amazing powers of recuperation, once winning the eight-day Dauphiné Libéré and then the epic Bordeaux–Paris race the following night. He was wily too, and on the

1963 Tour he faked a brake cable failure at the foot of a climb in order to bend the rules and switch to a lighter model.

During his career Anquetil bridged the 'old world' of filmed races and national teams and the 'new world' of commercially sponsored teams and TV cameras. With his icy blue eyes and perfect style – he usually visited the hairdresser before a big time trial – he became cycling's first small-screen star.

As a rider he had his limits. He excelled in the heat but hated the cold and wet, and though he was rarely dropped on a climb, he couldn't drop a rival either. A famously poor tactician, he drove his team-mates nuts by trailing along at the back of the bunch and often had to be told when to attack by his manager Raphaël Géminiani. Another quirk was a profound lack of interest in the technical set-up of his bike.

Most of Jacques's victories were based on his excellence in time-trialling, a photographic memory for the course and fine calculations of what he needed to do to win – an approach that would later help Greg LeMond to three Tour victories. Once, when dropped by his great rival Raymond Poulidor on a crucial mountain stage, the barely conscious Anquetil was told that he was just 14 seconds ahead overall. 'That's 13 more than I need,' he replied. The uncertainties of one-day classic races had little appeal for him and he won just three in his career.

More popular abroad than in his own country, Anquetil won *Sportsnight*'s International Sports Personality of the Year – a remarkable achievement given the BBC's total lack of interest in cycling. Within France he was never as popular as his rival Raymond Poulidor, and in 1961 he was heckled on his Tour win – this after delivering on his promise to wear yellow throughout and also capturing the green jersey and team trophy. Later, he alienated the fans by publicly turning his back on the one-day classics. On TV and in press articles he also broke the racer's code of silence by explaining that he rode for money rather than glory, that rivals were sometimes bought off and that drugs were used. In fact, Jacques believed that stimulants made only a marginal difference – worth about 1½ kph – but they were useful in enabling racers to compete in more races. 'Only an imbecile imagines that a professional rider who rides 235 days a year can do so without stimulants. Let's not be hypocrites. You don't do that on fizzy water and salad,' he wrote. Today racing without drugs is still termed 'racing on mineral water'. His 46 kph world hour record was never ratified, as he refused to take a urine test in a tent in front of the crowd, arguing that drug testing was only acceptable if it was done consistently and with dignity. Ruthless on a bike, Anquetil had a reputation for generosity off it, although he could be a pointed commentator on races. After his death from stomach cancer in 1987, the funeral crowds at his home city of Rouen spilled out of the cathedral.

Roone Arledge

Roone Pinckney Arledge, broadcaster, born Queens, New York 8 July 1931, died 5 December 2002. President ABC Sports 1968–86, chairman of ABC News 1977–98. Winner of 37 Emmy Awards. Television Academy Hall of Fame 1989.

In 1994 *Sports Illustrated* declared that the third most important figure in US sport, after <u>Muhammad Ali</u> and <u>Michael Jordan</u>, was not a sports star or coach but a TV producer with the unusual name – even for America – of Roone Arledge. Soon afterwards, *Life* magazine went further, ranking him among the 20th century's 100 most important Americans. The reason was simple. Roone Arledge had done more than any other man to create modern sports coverage on TV, and in doing so had changed professional sport for ever.

The crucial moment occurred in 1960, when Arledge, then a junior sports producer for the struggling ABC network, wrote an internal memo that was to revolutionise sports broadcasting. At the time, he was attempting to persuade advertisers to back his planned *Wide World of Sports* – a sports magazine show that would paper over ABC's lack of major US sports events by showcasing college football and athletics, plus a variety of cheap international contests – many of which were already out of date but hadn't had their results reported in the US. In his memo Arledge promised 'to bring show business to sports broadcasting'. In fact, what *WWS* actually brought to sports broadcasting was journalism, using every trick they could possibly think of to bring background, colour, story, heroes and villains to the screen – just as a good journalist would in print. As Arledge later put it, the idea was to grab a US audience's interest even if Liechtenstein were playing Andorra.

At the time, this approach was unheard of. Even the NFL, which had embraced TV in the 1950s, was usually filmed by static cameras on the halfway line, commentated on by paid announcers who treated every play – however unsuccessful – with uncritical admiration. As for the less TV-friendly sport of baseball, Commissioner Ford Frick had demanded that the view on TV be that from the worst seat in the park, so that the crowds didn't stay at home.

With minutes to spare, ABC scraped together enough advertising dollars to fund *Wide World of Sports*, which was to become a huge success – despite featuring such obscure, low-scoring minority sports as the FA Cup final. Anchored by Jim McKay, *WWS* brought 'the thrill of victory and the agony of defeat' with new camera angles and the first hand-held cameras – then known as 'creepy-peepies' – to get 'up-close and personal' with the coach, players or crowd. By 1965 the flying-in of film from around the world was being replaced by the use of the 'Early Bird' satellite to send live pictures of European sports events across the Atlantic.

Having broadcast college football from 1960, the ABC approach was also applied to Lamar Hunt's ramshackle American Football League, with the pioneering use of video replays, post-match analysis and even slow motion. This was first achieved in a Texas v Texas A&M match in 1961 by filming the TV screen with a double-speed camera. Other innovations included a camera in the huddle and even a radio mic – until it picked up too many obscenities – as well as the first use of player profiles and highlights of previous plays and games. With tiny crowds at AFL matches, ABC learned to keep the cameras off the stands and concentrate instead on dynamic fast-cutting close-ups of the action. ABC ruled the AFL so completely that after one team kicked off during an ad break, the producer simply marched onto the field and respotted the ball.

As ABC's executive producer for ten Olympic games, Arledge was to transform their TV coverage too. After losing the 1960 Winter Games at Squaw Valley because ABC's finances were so ropey, Arledge was determined to do better than CBS's paltry 15 minutes of footage per day. At Innsbruck he struck TV gold (though not Olympic gold) with the glamorous skater Peggy Fleming, and by the following 1968 Mexico City games, ABC was ready to revolutionise coverage with live colour TV, an army of 450 producers and a mic on the Olympic torch to capture the whoosh of the flames. Their snappy journalism was rewarded when they zoomed in on 200 metres champ <u>Tommie Smith</u>'s Black Power protest, then chased him down and interviewed him. 'The cardinal error,' declared Roone, 'is to be there with a camera and miss what is happening.'

Two years later, Arledge finally had NFL–AFL matches to cover, as NFL commissioner Pete Rozelle relaunched *Monday Night Football*.

As well as innovations like the reverse angle (pioneered by director Chet Forte) and split screens to show both offence and defence in action simultaneously, *Monday Night Football* also broke with convention by having one ball-by-ball commentator – most famously Frank Gifford – plus two studio 'colour' commentators, usually the laid-back Don Meredith and the spiky Howard Cosell. Renowned for his aggressive questioning and photographic memory, Cosell would become both the 'most liked' and 'most hated' man on US TV, and one Georgia bar hired a new TV every Monday night for patrons to fire their guns into. The show itself soon drew massive audiences, leading to a decrease in crime on Monday nights, the cancellation of social clubs and even an attempted ban on Monday-night births at one Seattle hospital.

Famous for his long lunches, tall tales, odd fashion sense and conspicuous jewellery, Roone married three times – once to a former Miss Alabama – and finally wrecked one marriage after quitting a family holiday to film a football game.

In 1972, ABC kept their lock on the Olympics, making a star of Olga Korbut and dominating the news with their coverage of the Munich hostage crisis. So great was Arledge's success that he was placed in charge of ABC's news division as well as sport. By the following Winter Games, ABC were willing to invest $250,000 on cameras to line the entire rutted Innsbruck ski course and captured Franz Klammer's near-suicidal 80 mph descent – an event judged the most exciting TV sports coverage since the legendary 1958 Colts–Giants championship game. In 1984, the LA Olympics achieved the highest ratings and largest audience ever, thanks largely to ABC's pioneering work. Although Roone was carpeted by the International Olympic Committee for excessively pro-American footage, ABC would keep the games until 1988, when they overbid for the Calgary winter games and lost an estimated $75 million.

By creating modern sports coverage and turning sportspeople into stars, Arledge had let the genie out of the bottle. As the Olympics and other events expanded endlessly, sucking in more and more TV money, he recognised some of the negative effects that TV had had on sport, such as the concentration on good looks rather than ability and the general bloating of the schedules. Even so, anyone who has ever been gripped by a sporting event on TV – and that is most of the world – owes a big debt to Roone Arledge.

Arthur Ashe

Arthur Robert Ashe Jnr, tennis player, team manager and author, born Richmond, Virginia 10 July 1943, died 6 February 1993. Wins include: US Open 1968, Australian Open 1970, Wimbledon 1975. ATP president 1979.

In 1977, a small group of demonstrators were gathered outside the US Open, protesting against US tennis's continuing sporting links with apartheid South Africa. Suddenly it was announced that Arthur Ashe, the first black US Open champion, wanted to speak to them live on camera. Their hearts probably sank. Arthur Ashe was a walking poster for integration – a black player who had risen to the top by playing the white game both on and off the court. (Billie Jean King once joked that *she* was blacker than Arthur Ashe.)

Growing up in racially segregated Richmond, Virginia, Ashe played in the parks where his father was superintendent and became the first black child to play in the citywide tennis tournament. Sponsored by Dr Robert Walter Johnson, who had also supported Althea Gibson, the first black Wimbledon champion, Arthur moved to a high school in St Louis, where he made a similar breakthrough at the previously segregated Interscholastic Tournament. At UCLA, he won the 1965 NCAA singles, though he was banned from several country clubs because of his race, became the first black US Davis Cup player in history and later the first to head the rankings, spending 12 years in the top ten and amassing 80 victories. With his lightning first serve, extraordinary deception and control, and 'go for broke' attitude, he was popular with the press and fellow players alike. In 1968, he won both the US Amateur and Open titles – the first home-grown Open winner since 1955. This was the last hurrah of the $24 per diem amateur, as tennis opened up to big money. After Arthur had played in the first victorious US Davis Cup side for ten years, two rival promoters – Lamar Hunt and George McCall – both made offers of up to $40,000, but when he did turn pro he signed with Donald Dell, preventing any single promoter getting a lock on the game. The following year's semi-final clash with Rod Laver was reckoned to have included the two most exciting sets in tennis history. Arthur also helped set up the Association of Tennis Professionals (ATP), steering it through various showdowns with the tennis authorities and becoming the first player to earn $100,000 in a season.

While other sports stars such as Muhammad Ali were advocating separate development for the black race, Arthur Ashe was arguing for integration, founding a junior tennis league that encouraged inner-city kids to play the game and seeking the right to play in the South African 'Open'. When he was refused, he campaigned for South African expulsion from the ILTF, until in 1973 he became the first black player to compete in the republic, winning a doubles title. He continued to earn big money, promoting Howard Head's first big-headed racket and would become ATP president in 1979. In 1974 he had won Wimbledon despite a night of blackjack at the Playboy Club, beating the favourite, the nine years younger Jimmy Connors, with a serene display of controlled tennis. ('Come on, Connors!' called a fan. 'I'm trying, for Chrissake!' Jimmy yelled back.)

Having wrong-footed opponents both on and off the courts, Arthur Ashe did so again at the 1977 US Open protest, publicly declaring that he had been wrong about South Africa and that only a full-scale boycott would end apartheid. After joining the protesters at the following year's Davis Cup, he succeeded in persuading US tennis to end its sporting links with the apartheid regime and helped talk John McEnroe out of accepting an invitation to a $1 million pay day in a South African 'homeland'. After retiring from tennis with heart problems, Arthur coached the US to two more Davis Cup victories in 1981 and 1982, wrote studies of the progress of black athletes in US sports, and continued to amass directorships and honorary degrees while protesting against apartheid and being arrested at one demo in 1985.

In 1992, with the sporting battle against apartheid won, Arthur Ashe made more headlines with the news that he had contracted HIV from a blood transfusion after a heart operation – news which made even hardened New York sports journalists cry. By now seriously ill, he might have been expected to accept the plaudits – such as Sports Illustrated's 'Man of the Year' – and fade away. Instead, he was arrested again for demonstrating outside the White House at the treatment of Haitian refugees, and praised the energising effect of making a protest. After his death the following year, he became the first Virginian since

Stonewall Jackson to lie in state in the Governor's mansion and later had a statue raised among the Confederate Generals on the city's Memorial Avenue. Since 1997, the US Open has been played at the Arthur Ashe Stadium.

Sydney Barnes

Sydney Francis Barnes, cricketer, born Smethwick, Staffordshire 19 April 1873, died 26 December 1967. First-class career: Warwickshire 1894–5, Lancashire 1902–3, 133 matches, 1,573 runs (12.78), 719 wickets (17.09); 27 Tests 1901–14, 242 runs (8.06), 189 wickets (16.43). Wisden Cricketer of the Year 1910. Giant of the Wisden Century (1963).

In his day the dark, gaunt and brooding Sydney Barnes was regarded as the most skilful bowler to have walked the planet and many still rate him the best ever. Only Australian paceman Jack Marsh could match his bowling threat and Marsh, as an aboriginal Australian, was kept out of Test sides.

With a brisk medium pace and a high action that whipped the ball down and even tore out chunks of turf, Barnes was the first bowler to combine swing, spin and cut to make the ball go any way he chose. Rather than target the wicket itself, he bowled at the batsman's weaknesses. Especially deadly on matting or wet turf, Barnes could make the ball break and swing on any wicket in any weather in any country. His most lethal delivery would first swerve then straighten up, and although he could bowl a googly, he claimed never to have needed it. With a career total of 6,229 wickets, he was probably right. No respecter of batsmen, Barnes forced a new caution in play, and was credited with personally ending the 'Golden Age' of free-scoring cricket.

Barnes's total wicket haul vastly exceeds his Test and county totals because S.F. Barnes and Test and county cricket didn't get on. Born in Staffordshire, he was messed about and then frozen out by Warwickshire and preferred the greater financial security of the leagues. He might never have played Test cricket had he not been talent-spotted in the Old Trafford nets by England captain Archie MacLaren. Despite Barnes taking 6 for 70 in Lancashire's last match of the season, his inclusion in the Ashes touring party was a total surprise to the cricketing establishment, but one that was to prove astonishingly successful.

In Australia, Barnes caught and bowled star batsman Victor Trumper with only his second delivery, going on to record 5 for 65 in the first Sydney Test and take 13 wickets in Melbourne, before breaking down with a knee injury. Never a ray of sunshine, he considered himself to be the captain when he was bowling and was one of the first bowlers to set his own field. When the tourists' boat suffered a terrible crossing to New Zealand, MacLaren consoled himself with the thought that if the ship did go down, so would 'that bugger Barnes'. Needless to say, the relationship with Lancashire didn't last and after two seasons Barnes returned to Staffordshire, where he wouldn't get 'bowled into the ground for a pittance'. In a 1902 Sheffield Test he had taken 6 for 49 in a single innings, but was frozen out of home Tests until 1909, although he returned to Australia to bowl out Trumper with a ball that swung away and then broke back. Non-striker Charles Macartney declared it the sort of delivery 'a man might see if he was dreaming or drunk'.

Always experimenting, Barnes remained in and out of Test sides until 1911/12, when he and Frank Foster secured England's greatest Ashes triumph, with Barnes taking 34 wickets at under 23 runs apiece to win the last four Tests. At one stage, despite a fever, he took five top-order wickets for six runs. In the following 'Triangular' series against Australia and South Africa, he took 39 wickets at just over ten runs each and in 1913/14, aged 40, was still capable of magic, taking 49 wickets against South Africa – an all-time Test series record – though he played in just four matches. Regarded as the best in Britain as late as 1928, he was still averaging under nine runs per wicket at the age of 56 and bowled until he was 67, having taken all ten wickets in a match 12 times.

When he was fit and well, the man *The Times* called 'the embodiment of hostile action' won every Test he played in, setting records unmatched by any regular bowler since – and he did so when he was only allowed one narrow-seamed ball per innings or (from 1907) 200 runs. God alone knows what he might have achieved under present rules.

'Captain' Martin Becher

Captain Martin William Becher, steeplechaser, born Hillington, Norfolk 18 May 1799, died 12 October 1864. Winner Liverpool Grand Steeplechase 1836.

Once famous for his astonishing animal impersonations, ability to leap high enough to kick a ceiling and to circle a room by balancing on the skirting boards, Martin Becher's fame now rests on, or rather in, the eight foot-wide Becher's Brook. It was here that he was dumped by Conrad during what was then the Liverpool Grand Steeplechase, but was to become the Grand National. (Becher remounted, only to be dumped into another ditch, and later joked, 'Water's no damn good without brandy.') In fact, he deserves to be remembered as the inspiration behind this most famous steeplechase and a race that, for a long period, kept the sport going.

An honorary captain who had acted as a storekeeper for Wellington's army, Becher became a professional rider, distinguished by his bushy hair and piercing eyes. Having competed in the first big steeplechase, the 1830 Great St Albans Chase, which was set up to entertain the 1st Life Guards billeted in the town, Becher's tales of derring-do inspired Aintree hotelier William Lynn to stage his own 'Grand Race of the North'. Despite steeplechasing's bad reputation – some racing journalists regarded it as a 'bastard amusement' between racing and hunting – Lynn attracted a good crowd, who on 29 February 1836 saw the captain come home on second-favourite The Duke to win by a length. He rode for another 11 years before becoming an 'Inspector of Sacks' for a railway company.

In 1839, the year of Becher's historic tumble, the race really took off, as the newly arrived railway brought in record crowds. The race was a pretty harum-scarum affair, incorporating ploughed fields and a loose stone wall, which claimed the life of Dictator, while the Irish challenger Rust was manoeuvred off the course by his rivals. The *Liverpool Mercury* dismissed the whole affair as 'wanton torture', but the crowds kept coming, the sport grew in popularity and by 1845, when it got a recognised calendar, there were over 60 courses listed.

However, most meetings had little prestige or prize money, and naturally there was next to no bloodstock market. It was 1866 before the Jockey Club recognised the National Hunt Committee and 1884 before the National first attracted royal patronage, with the Prince of Wales entering The Scot. After the prince won the race in 1900 with Ambush II, the National finally became firmly established, but without those big Liverpool crowds, steeplechasing might not have survived – and without Becher's exploits and ideas, they wouldn't have been there in the first place. The brook itself was filled in in 1990, but the name remains.

Franz Beckenbauer – 'der Kaiser'

Franz Anton Beckenbauer, footballer and coach, born Munich 11 September 1945. Playing career: Bayern Munich 1964–77 (league champions 1969, 72, 73, 74, cup winners 66, 67, 69, 71, European Cup 74, 75, 76, Cup Winners' Cup 1967, Intercontinental Cup 1976), New York Cosmos 1977–80 (Soccer Bowl 1977, 78, 80), Hamburger SV 1980–2 (league champions 1982), New York Cosmos 1983; West Germany 1965–77, 103 caps, 14 goals (World Cup 1974, European Championships 1972). Management career: Germany 1984–90 (World Cup 1990), Olympique Marseille 1990–1 (league champions 1991), Bayern Munich 1994, 96 (league champions 94, UEFA Cup 1996). Vice-president DFB 1998–.

The footballing 'libero' started off as a free-ranging defensive clogger, clearing balls upfield or into Row Z. The man who reinvented the position as a fluid attacking player was converted winger and midfielder Franz Beckenbauer. Beckenbauer, a football-mad boy from a working-class family, had to start playing soccer in cut-off ski boots, and when he got his first proper Adidas boots, he was so excited that he even wore them in bed. As a midfielder he was in the German national squad by 19, and he and Bobby Charlton cancelled each other out in two World Cup tournaments, until <u>Alf Ramsey</u> substituted Charlton in 1970 ('a mistake I will always regret') and Germany broke through to win. Even with him playing with a dislocated arm in a sling, Beckenbauer's side still took the Italians to extra time in the semi-finals, but they would have to wait until the next tournament to win the trophy.

From 1968 to 1969 Beckenbauer, now also captaining Bayern, was playing as a new-style sweeper. Having been encouraged into the new role by Bayern's Yugoslavian coach Zlatko Cajkovski, Beckenbauer's pace, vision and passing ability helped the club win three European Cups on the bounce and keep the trophy. In the 1974 World Cup, 'der Kaiser' showed his leadership skills both on and off the field. After the squad confronted manager Helmut Schoen with demands for 100,000 DM each and were threatened with mass dismissal, it was Beckenbauer who negotiated a compromise and calmly explained away a shock defeat to East Germany before a transformed squad went on to win the trophy.

Beckenbauer's good business sense was obvious both from this episode and his later decision to play in the American Soccer League. Less obvious were his close and profitable links with <u>Adi</u> and <u>Horst Dassler</u>, which led to his company ROFA controlling the marketing rights for the 1982 World Cup.

Reinforced by his coolness, style and arrogance, Beckenbauer's 'Kaiser' nickname has been attributed both to a supposed resemblance to mad King Ludwig of Bavaria and the caption of a photo-shoot next to a bust of Franz Joseph I. However, the favourite explanation was Beckenbauer's regal unconcern after a foul on Reinhard Libuda, the Schalke 04 player known as 'The King of Westphalia'.

Such was the aura around Beckenbauer that, despite lacking coaching qualifications, he was called to lead the national squad. In 1986, Germany reached the final, playing a similar system to the 1974 squad, but with Willi Schultz in the sweeper role, and in the following tournament Beckenbauer became the only man in history to win the World Cup as both captain and coach.

Today the president of Bayern Munich, Franz Beckenbauer has converted the club into a limited company, which in 2002 was revealed to have taken secret payments from the broadcaster Kirch. Der Kaiser, who had previously dismissed the German Federation as 'brainless', was as unabashed as ever and went on to chair the winning bid for the 2006 World Cup, run the organising committee and become a federation vice-president. Variously voted the second or third best footballer of the century behind <u>Pelé</u> and <u>Johan Cruyff</u>, he is also the honorary captain of the German team.

Lord George Bentinck – 'The Leviathan of the Turf'

Lord (William) George Frederick Cavendish-Scott-Bentinck, racehorse owner and Jockey Club steward, born Welbeck, Nottinghamshire 27 February 1802, died 21 September 1848. Wins include: St Leger 1836, 2,000 Guineas 1838, 40, 1,000 Guineas 1840, 42, Oaks 1840.

As the second 'Dictator of the Turf', Lord George Bentinck fitted in between Charles Bunbury and Admiral Rous and was a major force in organising and cleaning up racing at a time when it was thoroughly corrupt. On the other hand, there was a strong element of self-interest in most of Bentinck's reforms. An aristocratic dandy who wore a new cream satin scarf every day, he was renowned for his volatile temper and heavy betting, and one unpaid debt nearly cost him his life in a duel. After Bentinck fired his pistol into the air, his opponent, Squire Osbaldestone, an expert marksman, put a shot through Bentinck's hat as a warning. When other lesser men started using the chaotic laws of the day to pursue him for unpaid debts and the Jockey Club formally withdrew from control of gambling, Bentinck helped bring about a new Gaming Act that gave control of racing to the club and gambling to the Tattersall's club committee. One unintended consequence was a sudden boost in the number of bookmakers, most of whom went underground when they were made illegal soon afterwards.

Bentinck was keen to increase the prestige of the club and from 1835 was careful to add D for Duke, E for Earl etc after the 150 Jockey Club names in the *Racing Calendar*. He virtually controlled Goodwood, having paid to have 16,000 tons of turf brought in, and by 1845 his annual investment in racing was up to £45,000. While he was not above sharp practice himself, Bentinck did crack down on some of the various schemes and ploys that had been used to win races and unsettle winners like his own mare Preserve. A formal parade in the paddock was introduced, as well as the numbering of horses, the weighing-in and -out of jockeys and their saddles, the lowering of a flag to signal the off, fines for late starting, the confining of the crowds into priced enclosures and the ending of the old tradition of winning owners giving prizes to judges.

To further proof his horses against rival owners' ploys, he employed local people to wave flags and bang drums until the animals got used to the rumpus. Another of his ideas was the first horse-drawn horsebox, in which Elis and Drummer were taken to Doncaster by six post horses. The former won the 1836 St Leger, beating the bookies, who had assumed the long walk would wear him out, but Bentinck soon switched to faster and easier rail travel.

Famous for his dogged pursuit of welchers and shysters, Bentinck was far less inclined to go after the rich and powerful, despite great doubts over the age and identity of the 1839 and 1840 Derby winners, to name just two. Some cases were easily solved – such as when jockey Billy Day wrote to him and a bookie, offering differing advice on backing a horse, but put the letters in the wrong envelopes. On the other hand, Goodman Levy, the brains behind the operation that won the 1844 Derby with four-year-old Maccabeus masquerading as Running Rein, was never caught.

Although conditions were improved for spectators, most racing was still run for the benefit and convenience of Jockey Club members and the new enclosures were intended to prevent interference with the horses, rather than to please the punters. It was 1847 before the club allowed a railway line into their Newmarket stronghold – and that was only because the town was losing trainers to better-connected places.

In 1846, Bentinck suddenly sold his massive bloodstock holdings for a pittance. Despite not having spoken in Parliament for 18 years, he made an alliance with Benjamin Disraeli and brought down the government of Robert Peel over the repeal of the Corn Laws. In return, Disraeli lauded Bentinck as the 'Napoleon and Lord Paramount of the Turf' who was 'incapable of deception'. In racing terms the decision was poorly timed, as the duke's old horse Surplice promptly won the Derby for his new owner – although Bentinck did still collect £15,000 on the win. After Bentinck's mysterious death, discovered sprawled in his own grounds, he was commemorated with a statue on his home turf of Cavendish Square Gardens and a benevolent fund for the families of jockeys and trainers. His eccentric brother William succeeded to the dukedom and also went on to fame and notoriety, excavating a series of underground chambers beneath the family seat at Welbeck.

Carlos Bilardo

Carlos Salvador Bilardo, footballer, coach and sports administrator, born Buenos Aires 16 March 1939. Playing career: San Lorenzo 1958–60, Deportivo Español 1961–5, Estudiantes 1965–70 (league champions 1967, Copa Libertadores 1968, 69, 70, Intercontinental Cup 1968). Management career: Estudiantes 1971–5, Deportivo Cali 1976–8, San Lorenzo 1978–9, Colombia 1979–81, Estudiantes 82–3, Argentina 83–90 (World Cup 1986), Sevilla FC 92–3, Boca Juniors 1996, Libya 1999–2000, Estudiantes 2003–4. Buenos Aires Secretary of Sport 2007–.

Carlos Bilardo, who coached Argentina to one World Cup final win and came close to a second, created the last great tactical change in football – one that led to a style so negative that the rules of the game had to be changed to compensate for it.

El Narigón ('Big Nose') first came to fame in the 1960s as the defensive midfield anchor for Osvaldo Zubeldía's notorious Estudiantes – 'The Killer Juveniles'. The Estudiantes style, known as '*antifútbol*', aimed to break up attacks with tight marking and closing-down, scoring from set-piece trickery that used secret signs and languages. In fact, the work of breaking up attacks began well before the match itself as Estudiantes planned how to goad their opposite numbers. On the pitch they dived, disputed decisions and time-wasted. Though Bilardo probably didn't actually stick pins in opponents, as some have claimed, he pulled shirts and faked injury. As a doctor – actually a gynaecologist – he was well placed to prey on opponents' fears and neuroses, accusing one of 'murdering' his recently deceased mother. Tormenting another about his wife's health earned him a kick in the stomach. Against Manchester United in the 1968 Intercontinental Club final, one of Bilardo's fouls left Bobby Charlton needing stitches and eventually the Argentinian public grew sickened of their style.

As a coach, Bilardo preferred a balance of seven defensive players to three attacking ones, but instead of adding defenders, as had happened throughout football history, he took one away. Reasoning that wingers were no longer being used in most matches, the newly redundant full backs became midfielders in his new 3-5-2 formation, although they could be pulled back to create an ultra-defensive 5-3-2 – a complete reversal of football's original formation. To compensate for the lack of attacking options, the front three were allowed maximum flexibility.

As an international coach Bilardo started off with just three wins in 15, but won enough matches on a 1984 tour to retain his job, perfecting his tactics for the 1986 World Cup in which 3-5-2 would be his secret weapon. In the finals, Bilardo's front three were Jorges Valdano and Burrachaga and Diego Maradona. In the quarter-final against England, Maradona displayed both the cynicism and skill of the team by punching in one goal and then scoring the other with a breathtaking dribble that even England fans once voted the best ever. Though England's wingers nearly undid them in the latter stages, the Argentinians reached the final, before which Bilardo was so concerned about the set pieces that he crept the corridors of the team hotel, pouncing on sleeping players and demanding to know who they would be marking.

After Argentina won the 1986 final, Bilardo's 3-5-2 formula spread internationally, helping to produce a sterile 1990 tournament in which penalty shoot-outs encouraged teams to shut up shop and chance their luck from the spot after extra time. (From 1952 to 1982, there were no shoot-outs and less than ten percent of matches in the knockout stages even went to extra time.) The Argentinians were once again finalists against Germany, having had more men red-carded than they won games or scored goals. After a time-wasting bore, the Germans outdived them to win 1–0. Two years later, the European Championships averaged just 2.13 goals per game, and in response FIFA outlawed the back pass and tackle from behind to help rekindle the attacking game and reduce injuries.

In the longer term, Bilardo's 3-5-2 carried the seeds of its own destruction. By targeting the playmaker, the front man could be isolated, which made a nonsense of having three defenders opposing him. Although Bilardo was being mooted as a national coach as late as 2006, the tactical pendulum has swung towards more attacking formations and away from the man who once declared, 'Football is played to win. Shows are for cinema and theatre.'

'Black Jack' Blackham – 'The Prince of Wicketkeepers'

John McCarthy Blackham, batsman and wicketkeeper, born Fitzroy North, Victoria 11 May 1854, died 28 December 1932. First-class career: Victoria 1874–94, 275 matches, 6,395 runs (16.78), 455 dismissals; 35 Tests, 800 runs (15.68), 61 dismissals. Wisden Cricketer of the Year 1891. Australian Cricket Hall of Fame 1996.

Nicknamed after his thick beard, 'Black Jack' Blackham dominated Australian wicketkeeping, toured with the first eight sides to visit England, and is usually credited with being the first to stand close behind the stumps no matter who was bowling – raising wicketkeeping to such a level that the traditional longstop behind him was no longer needed.

In fact, Blackham did back off to fast bowlers such as Frederick Spofforth – who boycotted the inaugural 1877 Test in protest at the Melburnian's inclusion – and the title 'Prince of Wicketkeepers' was already held by Richard 'Dick' Pilling of Lancashire, a Bedford-born stonemason who stood up to the fastest bowlers. Reckoned 'a perfection of neatness and rapidity', Pilling played 250 first-class matches between 1877 and 1889, plus eight Tests, touring Australia with Alfred Shaw and Arthur Shrewsbury's sides. Unfortunately, he never enjoyed good health and died aged 35. (Other early longstop-free keepers were George Pinder of Yorkshire, Tom Plumb of Buckingham and the Hon Alfred Lyttelton of Middlesex.)

Despite these competing claims, Jack Blackham was regarded as the best ever and after 1878 he ruled the roost for 18 years. His catching, in thin gloves, was utterly reliable and he perfected the skill of catching the ball and sweeping off the bails in a single movement. On a tricky pitch against 'Eighteen of Stockport', he once stumped six and caught four.

A useful, though not particularly stylish, batsman, Jack played some crucial innings, but oddly for such a calm man on the field, he was an inveterate worrier off it – unable even to watch a close finish. He found captaincy a particular strain and it was all too much after Andrew Stoddart's 1894/5 tourists, forced to follow on, made the most of a rain-affected wicket to record the last 'follow-on victory' before Headingley in 1981. After muttering about 'cruel luck', he quit the captaincy, Test cricket and wicketkeeping for good.

Many sportsmen have defined a role, but Blackham made one – that of longstop – obsolete, freeing up an extra fielding position, a change which in England led to protests from a group of cricketing clergymen, angry at the loss of this easy billet.

'Fanny' Blankers-Koen – 'The Flying Housewife'

Francina Elsje Blankers-Koen, runner, hurdler, high jumper, long jumper and pentathlete, born Lage Vuursche, Netherlands 26 April 1918, died 25 January 2004. Olympic champion 100 m, 200 m, 80 m hurdles, 4 x 100 m relay (all 1948). European champion 80 m and 4 x 100 m relay (1946), 100 m, 200 m, 80 m hurdles (1950). IAAF Female Athlete of the Century.

The greatest all-round female athlete in history, Fanny Blankers-Koen (pronounced 'koon') laid to rest the idea that motherhood represented the end of an athlete's competitive life. Born to a farming family, the blonde, long-legged Fanny was naturally athletic and after just a year of serious training finished fifth in the high jump and sixth in the relay at the 1936 Berlin Olympics. Initially a middle-distance runner and jumper, her coach, triple-jump champion Jan Blankers – previously an opponent of women's athletics – steered her towards sprinting and hurdling, as there was little middle-distance racing for women. Women's track and field had only made it to the Olympics in 1928 and female competitors were caught in a 'Catch 22'. Low standards in events like the high jump and discus were derided, but when Lina Radke and Kinue Hitomi drove for the line in the 800 metres, the event was deemed too strenuous and banned. As late as 1984, the longest Olympic race for women was the 3,000 metres.

Having set her first 100 yards world record in 1938, Fanny married Jan in 1940 and gave up athletics after her son was born. However, after her second pregnancy she resumed training, despite the disapproval of some of her stuffier neighbours. While her children played in the long jump pit, she trained to equal the world 80 metres hurdle record, set new high and long jump records in 1943 and cut a fifth of a second off the 100 yards record the following year. Having survived the bitter 'Hunger Winter' of 1944/5, she anchored the Dutch team to victory in the 1946 Oslo European Championships and, in the run-up to the 1948 London Olympics, set new 100 metres and hurdle records. However, by the time of the London games, Fanny was 30 and Jack Crump, the leader of the British squad, told his female athletes she was 'too old to make the grade'. In fact, she was still the pre-eminent female athlete, with seven world records. Not only was she fast (100 metres in 11.5 seconds), but she was the first really good female long jumper, achieving 20 feet 6 inches, but also reached 5 feet 7½ inches in the high jump.

The success of the 'Dutch housewife' came as a total surprise to the British public, whose attention had been diverted away from the world of track and field between 1939 and 1945. With 11 races in 17 days and the Olympic 80 metres finals and long jump clashing, Fanny opted out of the latter, which was won by a leap two feet shorter than her best. On a muddy cinder track, she ran 11.9 to win the 100 metres final, but was only just persuaded to compete in the 80 metres hurdles. In the final, she made a bad start, ran so fast that she hit the last two hurdles and, 'staggering like a drunkard', dived so low for the line that the tape cut her neck. Only a photo could place her ahead of Maureen Gardner. After a good 200 metres heat Fanny broke down, wanting only to go home and see her children. Only Jan was able to persuade her to at least try to reach the final. Clearly it was a cathartic weep, as she went on to run a good semi and beat Audrey Williamson by seven-tenths of a second in the rain-soaked final – the largest margin in Olympic history. More drama followed, when a shopping expedition in search of a new beige coat caused her to arrive late for the sprint relay. Anchoring the team, she started in last place but snatched victory by inches. 'See,' said Jan, 'you aren't too old after all!' Only later was it discovered that she was also in the early stages of pregnancy.

Returning home with four golds, Fanny's only concern was to see her children and to get her new coat through customs, but instead she was scooped up by an open-topped coach and drawn through cheering crowds by four white horses to meet the mayor of Amsterdam. 'All I did was win a few footraces,' she said modestly, though those around her knew how fiercely she competed. The neighbours gave her a bike – 'so that you won't have to run so much'. Further world records followed in the 80 metres hurdles and pentathlon, but the 1952 Olympics was a contest too far. Troubled by a blood infection, she withdrew or failed to finish in three events. She acted as a team leader until 1968, before which both she and Jan were implicated in the disqualification of her young rival Foekje Dillema, who was judged to be 'intersex' – although under present rules she would have been allowed to compete.

Had the planned 1940 Tokyo and 1944 Helsinki games been held,

Fanny would almost certainly have amassed vast numbers of medals. It seems unlikely that her single Olympics haul will ever be beaten. Already as her career ended, more specialist training methods were ending the era of the all-rounder. In later life she toured Australia and America, introduced to thousands of young girls as 'Fanny Blankers-Koen, who got married, had two children and won four Olympic gold medals'. It was a nice irony that this new model of liberated sporting womanhood had cried for her children and been distracted by a spot of clothes shopping.

Jan Boklöv

Jan Boklöv, ski jumper, born Koskullskulle, Sweden 14 April 1966. World Cup winner 1988/9.

Ski jumper Jan Boklöv pioneered the V-style that revolutionised ski jumping in the late 1980s and early 1990s.

What is considered 'good' ski jumping style has varied throughout the sport's history. In the early days, jumpers simply did a standing jump, waving their arms around to stay upright, but by the 1950s the arms were being held out in front in a Superman-style. By the time Boklöv entered competition in the 1980s, the convention was that the body leaned forward with the arms clamped to the sides and the skis held parallel. Boklöv accidentally discovered that a V-style, with the ski tips held apart, felt better and produced a longer glide. (In fact, this was a rediscovery, as the Polish jumper Miroslaw Graf had been penalised for doing the same thing years earlier.) After wind-tunnel experiments, it was found that this created a 'wing' shape, in which the air currents over the top of the ski produced low pressure and 28 per cent more lift. The downside is that the air turbulence makes the skis harder to control.

At first, Boklöv's wobbly style was seen as a hideous aberration and he lost points for it, never finishing better than seventh in the 1988 Winter Olympics. However, having won the World Championships the following season, his better aerodynamics began to be appreciated and the sport became split until both styles were accepted. Today it is almost universal, and new, aerodynamically shaped skis are being developed to enhance the effect.

Bernard Bosanquet

Bernard James Tindal Bosanquet, googly bowler, born Enfield 13 October 1877, died 12 October 1936. First-class career: Oxford University 1898–1900, Middlesex 1900–8, 11,696 runs (33.42), 629 wickets (23.81); 7 Tests 1903–5, 147 runs (13.36), 25 wickets (24.16). Wisden Cricketer of the Year 1905.

In July 1900, Sam Coe of Leicestershire, playing against Middlesex at Lord's and just two runs short of a century, spotted an obvious leg break being bowled by a tall and rather effete-looking Old Etonian amateur. This lame ball hopped four times down the wicket, but just as Coe was preparing to smack it into the next parish, it suddenly veered towards him and he heard the unmistakable clatter of his wicket. The supposed leg break had suddenly turned the other way. The 'goggling' Coe had fallen victim to Bernard Bosanquet, the inventor of the 'googly'.

In the past both W.G. Grace and A.G. Steel had bowled an apparent leg break that straightened up, but never one that went the other way. For the first time a batsman couldn't read the type of ball simply from the position of the bowler's fingers. 'It's unfair,' Bosanquet's Test colleague Arthur Shrewsbury complained. 'Not unfair, just immoral,' replied the inventor.

Bernard Bosanquet was more of an athlete than he at first appeared, a university hammer thrower and billiards ace who also captained an ice hockey team. A bit of passion could creep into his cricket too – in 1903 he called a New Zealand batsman who stayed put a 'bloody cheat'. His trademark ball had been invented at Oxford University while playing a game called 'twisty-grab', in which a tennis ball was spun off a table so that the opponent seated opposite could not catch it. By delivering the ball from the back of his hand and turning his wrist at the moment of delivery, the axis of spin and the eventual path of the ball was altered. From 1899 Bosanquet was able to make a cricket ball do the same thing, disguising an off break as a leg break.

In 1903 Bosanquet took the googly to the world after a surprise call-up for the 1903/4 tour of Australia led by his county captain Pelham Warner, who claimed that Bosie bowled more bad balls than any other man. He didn't cut an impressive figure in the team photo, wearing a floppy hat and looking in the wrong direction, but the first use of his invention on Australian soil skittled ace batsman Victor Trumper and in the Sydney Test he took 6 for 56 to secure a series victory. The following year Bosanquet took 8 for 107 in one innings at Trent Bridge – still a Test record for the ground – but was never consistent and stopped bowling soon afterwards. Variously named the 'googly' (by the press), the 'twisti twosti' (by Bosanquet himself) and the 'bosie' (by the Australians), his delivery was picked up by the South Africans, who found it especially effective on their matting wickets and used it to take 106 wickets over two series wins in 1905/6 and 1909/10. In Australia, the delivery was perfected by Dr Herbert 'Ranji' Hordern, whose superior length and consistency enabled him to take 32 wickets across the 1911/12 Test series, including 12 wickets in the first.

By ending the old certainties, the googly briefly shifted the balance of power towards the bowler, until batsmen like Jack Hobbs and Wilfred Rhodes learned to read the signs of an incoming googly. Mandatory turf wickets from 1926 helped end its dominance, although it was a googly-style delivery that skittled <u>Don Bradman</u> in his final Test appearance, robbing him of a 100+ Test average. Soon afterwards, the Australian 'Big Jack' Iverson developed a 'front of the hand' googly that took 6 for 27 in one innings on the 1950/1 Ashes tour.

Jean-Marc Bosman

Jean-Marc Bosman, midfielder, born Liège 30 October 1964. Playing career: RFC Liège, St Quentin, St Denis, Olympique Charleroi, Vise.

In 1995, Jean-Marc Bosman, a Belgian midfielder invariably described as a 'journeyman', won a landmark EU court case which, like Curt Flood's case in US basketball, created 'free agency' in European soccer. By allowing out-of-contract footballers to move freely and negotiate their own terms, the Bosman ruling helped open the door to a new world of multinational squads and huge wages.

Jean-Marc's case was against now-defunct Belgian side RFC Liège, who first slashed his wages, then raised the fee they were demanding for him from French side Dunkerque, even though he was now out of contract. In Britain, a deal hammered out by <u>Alan Hardaker</u> in 1978 allowed free transfer for any out-of-contract player not offered the same deal or better, but Bosman had to fight through the courts. His case involved both players' contracts and the freedom to work across EU borders, so the European Court of Justice ruling was a double shock to clubs, which were used to controlling their players, and to UEFA, who had a 'gentleman's agreement' limit of three 'foreigners'. (This meant any federation, so Welshman Ryan Giggs was a 'foreigner' when he played for Manchester United.)

After the ruling, enforced by the EU's Competition Directorate, Ajax promptly lost six top players to wealthier EU leagues. After four years, it was agreed that foreign players only needed to satisfy immigration policy – hence a flood of cheap and talented African footballers into European sides. Another effect of the ruling was to give top players more exit options and negotiating clout. The money previously spent on transfers now shifted to wages and bonuses. With new TV cash, sponsorship and shareholder money pouring into big-league football, and no US-style salary caps or effective shareholder controls in place, clubs spent to the max. Top players' wages leapt by 30 per cent year on year, and by 2005 £1 million salaries were normal. In one famous case, Winston Bogarde of cash-happy Chelsea collected £8 million for just four starts in four years. Naturally, the players' agents also made out like bandits.

Internationally, the ruling has encouraged a core of wealthy EU-based leagues, while the poorer ones suffer as their best players leave. Post-Bosman wage inflation has also exaggerated the difference between rich and poor within the top divisions, thus reducing their 'competitiveness' – the ability of smaller clubs to beat bigger ones. Lower-league sides also began to make less money through transfers to the top sides, although this has sometimes encouraged them to innovate and attract more spectators. The Bosman ruling does not affect the four-year residential qualification to play for national sides, but the lack of top-flight opportunities for local players is supposed to have led to a weakening of some national squads, although smaller, less wealthy footballing nations like Scotland may have improved by having more cohesive squads.

In 2005, UEFA announced a plan to try to boost local representation in football. A possible solution would be a US-style system where players have a fixed long-term contract for their first club. On the other hand, US sports have specific legal exemptions and don't have to cope with ultra-free marketeers like the EU Competition Directorate.

Overall, the players who have seen the least benefit from Bosman are those playing for smaller sides in smaller nations – like Bosman himself who, having seen his marriage break up during the court cases, ended up playing in front of tiny crowds for Belgian fourth division side Vise. Although his court battles made other players stinking rich, efforts to get the millionaires to stage a fundraiser for him have not been successful.

Don Bradman – 'The Don'

Sir Donald George Bradman, cricketer, born Cootamundra, New South Wales 27 August 1908, died 25 February 2001. First-class career: New South Wales 1927–33, South Australia 1934–49, 28,067 runs (95.14); 52 Tests 1928–48, 6,996 runs (99.94). Member Australian Board of Control 1945–80, chairman 1960–3, 1969–72.

Don Bradman's Test average of 99.94 is probably the most famous single statistic in sport – and also the most dominant performance by any single player. (His average was 110.19 across all Sheffield Shield matches.) To quote Jack Hobbs, the Don was simply 'too good', scoring so many runs that he upset the balance of the game. He scored fast too – on only twelve occasions did he stay at the wicket for over six hours – and this aggressive scoring was especially lethal after 1930, when Tests were limited to four days. The need to defeat him – somehow, anyhow – led cricket into the bodyline crisis and a number of important rule changes. Afterwards, as an administrator, he continued to direct the game for three decades.

Despite being only 5 feet 7 inches tall and having – it was later revealed – poor eyesight, Bradman was a natural athlete with phenomenal speed, aggression and will to win, who honed his cricketing reactions by striking a golf ball against a curved wall with a single stump. After narrowly rejecting tennis for cricket in 1926, the 'Bowral Boy' compensated for his lack of height on high-bouncing matting wickets with horizontal-bat techniques and a baseball-style grip that enabled him to roll his wrists, keeping the ball down and denying catching chances. His habit of resting the bat between his feet, a late and crooked backlift and his 'cross-bat' strokes were criticised by purists like England captain Percy Fender as 'brilliant but unsound'. However, by keeping his hands close to his body, he was able to vary his shots and was hugely mobile, moving up and down the wicket to control the game. Above all, he had unrivalled patience and concentration – more so than batsmen like Stan McCabe, who Bradman regarded as his technical superior. If that wasn't enough, he also had complete mastery of the laws, passing his umpire's test after just six years in the game.

The Don's first Test series came in 1928/9, with just ten first-class matches behind him, and included a century, his only Test run-out and a stuttering performance on a sticky wicket, the one surface he never fully mastered, which resulted in him being dropped for one match. When in 1930 an unfancied Australian side arrived to play on unfamiliar English wickets, there were greater hopes of team-mate Archie Jackson, but Bradman made a double century on his debut and devastated bowlers like <u>Maurice Tate</u>. By the end of May, he had 1,000 runs and went on to score 254 at Lord's, with *The Cricketer* noting that he played his first bad shot after scoring 200 runs. At Headingley, he scored 100 by lunch and 309 in a day, before signing off at the Oval with 232 – averaging a shade under 140 for the series. His batting dominance would continue for twenty years, with the highest average in five Test series, the second four times and the third just once. Though he was rarely popular with all his team-mates, in a national side that often split between ex-Irish Catholics and Freemason-Protestants like Don, as a captain he would never lose a series.

Don became a massive star in a depressed Australia, where one in three men was unemployed. Many would gather in the city streets to watch mechanical signs tick up his scores, and when he was persuaded to make a solo return tour, he was mobbed by the crowds. His team-mates, who hadn't had a sniff of the £1,000 Don had been given by an admirer, reckoned that bowler <u>Clarrie Grimmett</u> had been more valuable. For Bradman, who badly needed the money, the attention was a real burden and in 1934 he moved to Adelaide to try to escape it – having come close to abandoning Test cricket for journalism and the better-paying Lancashire League. With one son afflicted by polio and a daughter with cerebral palsy, he too would be affected by illness and depression, growing more taciturn and ruthless, and only reluctantly accepted a knighthood in 1949 – the first for a sportsman still in action.

By overturning the balance between batsman and bowler, Bradman's dominance helped lead to an optional increase in wicket size from 1931, though he was unaffected by this. His only weakness seemed to be against fast, short-pitched balls, and after Surrey's <u>Douglas Jardine</u> replaced Percy Chapman as England's captain, this inspired the body-line tactics which limited 'the little bastard' – as Jardine termed him – to a series average of just 56 and led to a lull in form afterwards. The tactic was later judged to have made the Don's batting more cautious.

In general, 1930s bowlers gave up direct attacks on the wicket and looked for catches by bowling wider. In the longer term, there would also be an increase in bouncers and dangerous bowling, slightly limited by the MCC's 1934 condemnation of bowling at the 'batsman standing clear of his wicket'. Without a baseball-style outlawing of balls over a certain height, injuries would gradually worsen until players padded and helmeted up in the 1970s.

After Bradman returned to Britain in 1934, securing a series win with a record 451 stand at the Oval, he was hospitalised with appendicitis and even reported dead. An appeal for blood donors led to the infirmary being besieged by admirers, with the King himself asking for updates on the Don's health as he was treated with the new wonder drug penicillin. After missing the 1935/6 season, an easy Ashes win followed for Bradman in 1936/7, despite the latest attempt to rein him in – a change to the lbw law which allowed a ball that pitched outside the off stump – as well as directly between the wickets – to be given out. This change favoured speed and containment, with seamers and off-spinners dominating at the expense of leg spin, which was almost dead before <u>Shane Warne</u> revived it in the 1990s. In 1938, despite exhaustion, Bradman had his most consistent season, scoring six successive centuries.

Invalided out of the forces in 1941, Bradman was robbed of some feeling in his hand by fibrositis, and the bankrupting of the brokerage he worked for led him to strike out on his own. Reckoned to be a ghost of his former self before the 1946/7 Ashes series, he failed to walk at Brisbane after what even some of his team-mates thought was a fair catch, and went on to score 187. 'A fucking fine way to start a Test series' was Walter Hammond's verdict, and some trace a general reluctance to 'walk' – unless ordered to do so – from this one occasion. In 1948, on his final tour, Bradman was uncharacteristically relaxed and witty and drew vast crowds, with Glamorgan deliberately easing up their attack to guarantee a bank-holiday sell-out the following day. Against Essex, Bradman's 'Invincibles' scored 721 in a day until Keith Miller tired of the turkey shoot. Among the English bowlers, only Alec Bedser threatened him and caused Bradman to eliminate leg glances from his repertoire. At his final appearance at the Oval, with a Test average of 101.39, Eric Hollies's second delivery caught him out for a duck. An 'unbelievable hush of calamity' was reported by ex-team-mate Jack Fingleton – although Jack was believed to have celebrated secretly. An England collapse ensured there would be no second innings.

As an administrator and selector, Don Bradman wanted to prevent the negative containing tactic of bowling wide of the leg stump and in 1957 helped bring about a ban on more than two fielders between the wicket and square leg. To its critics this was an unprecedented intrusion on a captain's right to set his field. Three years later the taciturn Don offered more encouragement for attractive cricket, urging Richie Benaud to go for victory against Frank Worrell's West Indians. He immediately recognised the resulting tie as a victory for the game, reigniting enthusiasm after a series of dour battles. From 1959 an initially reluctant Bradman was also instrumental in introducing the new front-foot bowling rule, eliminating 'chuckers and draggers' such as Ian Meckiff. At the end of the 1960s he avoided enormous trouble for Australian cricket by ruling out a tour of apartheid South Africa and in 1970/1, after the cancellation of the third Melbourne Test, sanctioned the first one-day international. This wasn't quite the 'big hits fest' it later became, with Geoff Boycott scoring just eight off 33 balls, but it drew 46,000 enthusiastic fans and was the start of a revolution. Though it was 20 months before there was another ODI, it provided a template for the first 1973 World Cup. Although the poorly paid players who joined Kerry Packer's World Series Cricket felt that the thrifty Bradman should have had more sympathy and understanding with them, he was credited with pragmatic handling of the crisis which led to official cricket embracing the new world of cash and excitement.

Although he continued to protect his privacy, Bradman remained the dominant personality in Australian cricket. In 1958, he wrote the highly rated *The Art of Cricket*, and afterwards fired off occasional salvos in the press against ideas such as altering the ball or pitch. Having managed his press contacts to build his legend, he founded a museum in 1987 to honour the 'greatest living Australian'. In 1993, the man the journalist Neville Cardus had termed 'a genius with an eye for business' sold the intellectual rights to his name. Today there are Bradman stands at the SCG and Adelaide Oval, and his baggy green cap sold for £172,000.

Described as a 'solitary man with a solitary aim' by cricket writer R.C. Robertson-Glasgow, Bradman still holds batting records today, although his Test average was theoretically beaten by Andy Ganteaume of Trinidad's one-off 112. Even Bradman's sworn enemy Douglas Jardine, with whom he never exchanged more than two words, later admitted 'the little man was bloody good'. His view is shared. When in 2000 *Wisden* asked a panel of cricketing experts to choose five Players of the Century, every single one picked him. Given the general rise in sporting standards, it seems unlikely that any player will ever again dominate a game the way Don Bradman did cricket.

James Braid

James Braid, golfer and course designer, born Elie, Fife 6 February 1870, died 27 November 1950. Wins include: British Open 1901, 05, 06, 08, 10, News of the World Match Play 1903, 05, 07, 11, French Open 1910.

The dominant golfer of the years 1901 to 1911, James Braid not only played with what *Country Life* golf editor Horace Hutchinson termed 'a kind of divine fury', but became one of the most important course designers of the interwar years.

Though he was born in 'golf country' in Fife, Braid received little encouragement in playing the game from his family. After caddying as a boy, he started work as a joiner, which helped him when in 1893 he suddenly moved to London to make clubs at the Army and Navy store. (An accident with some lime caused him an eye injury which worsened in later life.) These were boom times for golf and in 1895 the tall, thin Braid became the pro at the Romford club, remaining English-based thereafter. A long driver, he was renowned for his ability to tear the ball out of bad lies, but his putting let him down until he switched to the 'new technology' of an aluminium-headed putter. With a deep dislike of ships, he didn't travel as much as <u>Harry Vardon</u> and <u>John Henry Taylor</u>, the other members of golf's 'Great Triumvirate'.

In 1914 Braid, Vardon and Taylor were all involved in a scientific test of the old guttie ball versus <u>Coburn Haskell</u>'s new rubber-wound ball. This confirmed the Haskell ball's superiority and changed British golf forever. The improvements in equipment and standards of play led by the Triumvirate meant that a good round came to mean one in the low 70s, rather than the 80s.

Braid was also president of the PGA, which had been born out of the poor pay and low prize money that many competitions offered. Habitually togged out in a tweed cap, Norfolk jacket and collar and tie, he was praised for his diplomacy, moderation and dignity, and helped win acceptance for the organisation. During 25 years as club pro at Walton Heath, he never once used the front door, yet played rounds with royalty, prime ministers and superstars such as <u>W.G. Grace</u>. Both

Walton Heath, where there is a room named in his honour, and the R&A later gave him membership.

From 1910, Braid's skills as a player went into decline, but he went on to design or work on over 200 courses – notably the King's and Queen's courses at Gleneagles, which were famed for their variety and dangers, drawing golfers into shots they really didn't want to have to play. Braid also remodelled Troon and, in 1926, the demanding Carnoustie – nicknamed 'Car-nasty' – which was an Open venue within five years. While concentrating on fundamentals such as good drainage, Braid is also credited with the first deliberately designed dog-leg holes and the use of stepped 'bench' greens, cut into a slope.

Michel Bréal

Professor Michel Jules Alfred Bréal, philologist, born Landau, Bavaria 26 March 1832, died 1915. Commandeur de la Légion d'honneur.

When the first modern Olympics were held in Athens in 1896, they introduced two new athletic events, both inspired by ancient Greece. The first was the discus, which was based on the ancient pentathlon, while the other was the marathon – a symbolic race dreamt up by Michel Bréal, a friend of Olympic founder <u>Pierre de Coubertin</u>.

Bréal, an expert in ancient myths and languages and the founder of modern semantics, had suggested a re-enactment of the legendary non-stop 490 BC run from the plain of Marathon, where the Athenians had defeated 20,000 Persians, to the Athenian Senate, where the runner was supposed to have cried, 'Rejoice, we have won,' before dropping dead on the spot. As Bréal would have known, rival candidates include Pheidippedes (Herodotus), Phiddippus (Cornelius Nepos), Philippides (Lucian) Thersipus (Heraclides Ponticus) and Eukles – although both Pliny and Herodotus claimed that he had in fact travelled the far longer distance from Athens to Sparta in search of help before the battle.

Whatever the facts, the Greeks took the 40-kilometre race very seriously, staging two trials and having their 17 entrants guarded by police escorts. When local man <u>Spiridon Louis</u> entered the Panathenaic Stadium in first place, there was bedlam among the packed crowd. The highlight of the first games, it was said by de Coubertin to be one of his 'most extraordinary memories'. The marathon cemented the games' popularity in Greece and after two disastrous Olympics, the Greeks helped revive them with another successful games in 1906. The marathon was now established as the ultimate athletic test, although the precise distance would vary between 40 and 42.75 kilometres until 1924, when it finally settled down at 42.195 kilometres. By this time, Portuguese Olympic runner Francisco Lázaro had truly 'done a Pheidippides', covering his body with wax to ward off the sun so that his pores became clogged and he died of overheating. Despite Lázaro's exit, Bréal's idea is more popular than ever as a mass athletic challenge.

Mike Brearley

John Michael Brearley OBE, cricketer, journalist and administrator, born Harrow 28 April 1942. First-class career: Cambridge University 1961–8, Middlesex 1961–83 (county champions 1976, 77, 80), 455 matches, 25,186 runs (37.81); 39 Tests 1976–81 (31 as captain), 1,442 runs (22.88); 25 ODIs, 510 runs (24.28). Wisden Cricketer of the Year 1977. MCC president 2007–8.

Famed as the most cerebral of cricketers, Mike Brearley made two very practical impacts on the game. The first was establishing head protection for batsmen. (Fellow cricketer Pat Pocock described the experience of batting with and without helmets as 'chalk and cheese'.) The other was banishing the aluminium bat.

The great cliché/truth about Brearley is that his achievements as a captain greatly exceeded those as a batsman-wicketkeeper. Although he scored 4,310 runs for Cambridge University and a triple century for an MCC junior side in 1966/7, his Test record of 29.79 runs per 100 balls is one of the slowest. (Fellow batsman-wicketkeeper Adam Gilchrist achieved 82.29.) However, this hardly mattered when Brearley was leading England to seven victorious Test series out of nine.

From 1977, Brearley, with his First in Classics from Cambridge, top marks in the Civil Service Exam and PhD thesis on 'Emotion and Reason', was protecting his famous brain with a skullcap. After braving the press scorn ('looking like an affronted turkey-cock,' said one writer), he pioneered a more dignified full-face helmet that improved his batting confidence. Although Dennis Amiss had been the first cricketer to wear a helmet in one of <u>Kerry Packer</u>'s Supertests, and Graham Yallop of Australia had modelled a motorcycle-style version against the West Indies, it was Brearley's design that showed the way forward, while Amiss's obsolete titfer led to Andy Lloyd spending five days in hospital after a crack on it. By developing this new helmet, Brearley had finally made top-level cricket reasonably safe to play – something that the sprawling cricket bureaucracy had signally failed to achieve in over forty years.

Cricket has always been a dangerous game – in 1870 George Summers of Nottinghamshire was killed on the notoriously dangerous Lord's wicket – but it was during the 1970s that non-stop pace attacks, financial incentives to finish off the tail-enders, and umpires who were unwilling to intervene made the sport even more perilous, and in 1972 Graeme Watson required 40 pints of blood to keep him alive. Australia's fast bowlers Dennis Lillee and Jeff Thomson were notorious for their speed and aggression, with the home crowd chanting 'Kill! Kill! Kill!' behind them, but it was Peter Lever who came closest to taking a life, when Ewen Chatfield's heart stopped. Luckily, Brearley's invention arrived just before the unnerving reverse swing of Sarfraz Nawaz.

In 1979, Brearley changed the history of bats as well as hats when he protested against the aluminium ComBat, which its endorser Dennis Lillee had just used to straight-drive Ian Botham. In fact, Lillee had used the bat without protest two weeks before against the West Indies (scoring 0) and there was no rule against it. Brearley protested that it was taking an unfair toll on the ball and in the dispute that followed Lillee threw the bat some 30 metres in the direction of Greg Chappell. Soon afterwards an 'all wood' rule was passed, ensuring that willow didn't go the way of persimmon in golf clubs – but not before Brearley had inscribed the offending bat 'To Dennis. Good luck with the sales.'

In cricket politics Brearley had already made an impact, risking his own career to support Basil D'Oliveira. At a time when most English cricketers saw South Africa simply as a good winter billet, he seconded an MCC motion against apartheid. During the war with Kerry Packer's World Series Cricket, Brearley again kept a level head, refusing to victimise Packer players and keeping them in the squad. Those who downplay his achievements against Packer-weakened opponents fail to appreciate that he was one of the reasons England remained strong enough to win.

As captain of Middlesex, with three championships between 1976 and 1980, Brearley's use of reason led to some innovative play. In 1977, Middlesex tied the County Championship by declaring after just one ball against Surrey, bowling them out twice in a single day to secure victory after a nail-biting run chase. Two years later at the Oval, even England keeper David Bairstow was sent to the perimeter to prevent the West Indies making the three runs they needed off the last ball. As for the use of emotion, Brearley's return to the England captaincy in 1981 included the legendary third Test at Headingley, credited with reviving the fortunes of the game in Britain. After being 133 for 6 and needing 94 simply to avoid an innings defeat, Brearley masterminded

an extraordinary turnaround, particularly of the previously demoralised
ex-captain Ian Botham, who was inspired to 'give it some humpty' with
the bat before taking five wickets for one run to achieve the first 'follow-
on' victory in 905 Tests. (Two of Brearley's reported gambits were 'my
aunt bowls faster than you' and, perhaps more lethally, 'Chris Old has
the edge over you today.') Inevitably, not all cricketers were enthusiastic members of his fan club – Phil Edmonds and Fred Titmus being
two notables.

Brearley retired for good in 1983 to work as a journalist, academic
and speaker. His 1985 book *The Art of Captaincy* is still pretty much
the last word on a subject for which he gained such recognition. After
becoming president of the MCC in 2007, he was spotted waiting for
the bus home after his inaugural dinner – evidence that the lack of
pretention, like the brains, remains intact.

John 'Jack' Broughton – 'The Father of Boxing'

John Broughton, boxer, born Cirencester or London 1703, died 8 January 1789. Champion of the Ring 1734–50. International Boxing Hall of Fame 1992.

Perhaps the most significant fight in boxing history lasted 35 minutes at Taylor's Booth in London between Champion of the Ring Jack Broughton and George 'the Coachman' Stevenson in 1741. Before the fight Stevenson had threatened Broughton with death, and on the day he got in three or four times as many hits, but it was Broughton's blow over the heart that proved fatal to Stevenson.

At first, Broughton swore never to fight again, but on 16 August 1743 a group of gentlemen based at his amphitheatre in Hanway Yard off Tottenham Court Lane produced a set of seven laws which were to last virtually intact for over a century and still influence boxing today. Until this time, the boxing rules had been unwritten, but included no kicking, biting or gouging or blows below the waist, rounds that ended when a man was down and eight seconds to get 'up to scratch' – a line in the middle of the ring – before the start of the next round.

Broughton's new rules gave control to two umpires representing each side, plus a referee if the umpires couldn't agree. The square ring was restricted to the fighters and their seconds. Thirty seconds' recovery time was allowed after a knock-down and failure to come up to the scratch in the ring, or surrender by the seconds, would end the match. The other rules allowed no hitting when down and no hair-grabbing and stated that a man on his knees was judged down – which gave rise to years of long drawn-out fights, as contestants dropped to their knees again and again. The Broughton Rules, which also covered stake money, survived virtually intact until 1838, when the London Prize Rules made going down without a blow an offence and banned more unorthodox forms of reviving a downed fighter – such as biting through his ear. The core of Broughton's Rules survived two further redrafts in 1853 and 1866, which detailed more fouls. They also heavily influenced the 1867 Queensberry Rules, and the last old-fashioned prize-ring fight was held as late as 1889.

Like the previous great Champion of the Ring, Jemmy Figg, Broughton was an intelligent, ambitious man who had worked as a lighterman on the Thames, winning 'The Glory of the River' – Doggett's Coat and Badge rowing race – in 1730 while he worked his way up through the fight game. By 1737, Broughton's fights were such a draw that a barber was squeezed to death while trying to get a look, and in 1743 the Duke of Cumberland lent Jack £3,000 to set up his own amphitheatre and an academy in the Haymarket. This helped boxing become a fashionable sport, although from 1750 prizefights were declared illegal and the press declared it 'a nursery for Tyburn'.

To extend the appeal of amateur boxing, Broughton introduced 'mufflers' – gloves named after the protective coverings used in cockfights, which were made of lambswool or horsehair to prevent what Jack termed the 'inconveniency of black eyes, broken jaws and bloody noses'. Given that a ten-ounce glove is necessary to limit blunt trauma, he must have pulled a lot of punches.

As well as the first protection for boxers, Jack also developed the sport's tactics. Famous for his precision, counter-punching, perfect defence, parrying and blocking, he was also the first to box on the retreat – then known as 'hitting away'. His signature punch, a KO to the solar plexus, was known as his 'projectile'. Although he finally separated boxing from the all-in fighting and sword and cudgel fights of the past, he incorporated the best of the old traditions, including the lunges, sidesteps and stop-blocks of fencing and the use of the left arm to act as a shield or buckler.

Jack's reign came to an end in 1750, after a fight with butcher Jack Slack, who was apparently Figg's grandson. The Duke of Cumberland had wagered £1,000 at 10–1 on the 46-year-old Broughton, but Slack defeated him with a range of moves including 'the cleaver', with which he was supposed to kill rabbits – a possible origin for the phrase 'rabbit punch'. Temporarily blinded by Slack's blows, Broughton fought on for 14 minutes before finally surrendering. In revenge, Cumberland is supposed to have had Jack's amphitheatre closed down, though the evidence suggests it wasn't. In any case, Broughton was a determined and diplomatic man and a useful supplier of muscle at elections, and won back the duke's favour. He made a good living through the antiques trade and was appointed to the Yeomen of the Guard, probably accompanying the King to the Battle of Dettingen. Broughton lived to 86, left a very substantial £7,000 in his will and was buried in Westminster Abbey in a coffin that he had invested in some years previously. The authorities objected to inscribing his stone 'Champion of England', but in 1988 he finally got the epitaph he deserved.

Avery Brundage

Avery Brundage, athlete and administrator, born 28 September 1887, died 8 May 1985. President American Amateur Athletic Union 1928–34, president US Olympic Committee 1929–33, vice-president International Amateur Athletic Federation 1930–52, member IOC 1936–73, vice-president 1945–52, president 1952–72.

Candidly described by the official Olympic history as a 'despotic, moralising bulldozer', Avery Brundage saw his own version of 'Olympism' as a religion or moral crusade and himself as its true defender. Never afraid of a fight, his name crops up in virtually every major Olympic row over 60 years – the last 20 spent as IOC president. Though his relentless energy and enthusiasm kept the Olympics going in the post-war period, it later threatened to tear it apart as the world changed and Brundage didn't.

The son of an absentee stonemason father, Brundage qualified as an engineer and became a self-made success in construction, founding a company in his own name that survived the Depression and helped fund the US Olympic movement. Although he remarried in his eighties and allowed his new 37-year-old wife to hammer through his fortune, he was still able to donate a vast collection of Asian art to the San Francisco Museum.

As an athlete, Brundage was US all-round champion in 1914, 1916 and 1918 – although this was in the absence of Jim Thorpe, to whom he'd finished sixth in the 1912 Olympic pentathlon and a distant 16th in the Swedish version of the decathlon. The press revelation that Thorpe had earned a little money from baseball led to an investigation that ignored all the other athletes and soon robbed Jim of his medals. This probe is believed to have been orchestrated by Avery 'Ignorance is no excuse' Brundage. It wasn't until after Brundage's death that Thorpe's family got his medals back from Olympic president Juan Antonio Samaranch. Brundage was also implicated in the suspension of the great Finnish distance runner Paavo Nurmi for offending Olympic amateurism. Completing his trio of scalps of the three greatest athletes of the half-century, Brundage also had Jesse Owens suspended from athletics within two weeks of his 1936 Berlin Olympics triumph. This came after Owens, who had signed no contract, quit a money-spinning post-Olympics tour that Brundage was running to fill the AAU coffers. (Brundage had already relieved Owens of $159 he had earned as a lift attendant.) After Jesse left for home and the European promoters cut the AAU's share of the gate money from 15 per cent to 10 per cent, he was thrown out of track and field and reduced to running in novelty races against horses.

The 1936 Berlin games at which Owens starred demonstrated Brundage's relentless determination that Germany should continue 'pursuing the spirit of the Olympics' despite the 'Jewish–Nazi altercation'. With a contract to build a new German embassy in his pocket, Brundage smeared all the opponents of the Berlin games as 'Communists', silenced AAU members and forced out IOC member Ernest Lee Jahncke, whose IOC seat he took. He was also fingered for the sudden removal of Jewish runners Marty Glickman and Sam Stoller from the US relay squad, and by 1941 even the America First movement, to which Brundage belonged, had disowned him as a little too pro-Nazi. Another Brundage bugbear was female athletes. En route to Berlin he expelled swimmer Eleanor Holm for unseemly partying and lobbied to have the 'ineffective and unpleasing' female athletes banished from the track. As late as 1952, he was still trying to remove women's athletics from the games.

Post-war, Brundage rushed to Europe to press for the resumption of the Olympics in 1948, and at Helsinki in 1952 he welcomed the Soviets, turning a blind eye to the state-sponsored professionalism of their athletes, while coming down hard on US athletes such as miler Wes Santee, who was thought to be profiting from his efforts. It was only in 1962, when the Eastern bloc were threatening to win everything, that Brundage reluctantly accepted broken-time payments for Western athletes. He also took the first step against drugs with the creation of the IOC Medical Commission.

In a turbulent political era, Brundage caught a lot of flak when the Olympics recognised 'Red China'. He was highly suspicious of the idea that each National Olympic Committee should enjoy a vote and feared that this kind of democracy would make the Olympics more political and encourage 'pork-barrel politics' designed to please smaller nations – a fear that was to be proved entirely correct.

Though a capable politician, Brundage was short-sighted in his attitude to TV, expressing no interest in this financial lifeline at a time when the IOC was heading towards bankruptcy. Brundage saw TV as a necessary evil at best, which meant that negotiations were left to local organisers and no effort was made to brand or even archive coverage – an attitude that would put the IOC on the back foot until the 1980s. Another blind spot was the growing protest against South African apartheid. After at first ignoring the problem, then kicking it into the long grass with various commission reports, Brundage was finally forced to expel South Africa, although he fought tooth and nail to retain a mixed-race Rhodesian squad. He also rode out the political storms surrounding the 1968 invasion of Czechoslovakia, pointing out that if the USSR was excluded because it fought wars then soon there would be no nations competing. By this time, Brundage had become a hate figure for black US athletes, who toyed with the idea of a boycott to remove him from the IOC. Never a man to take a backward step, he tried to have sprinters Tommie Smith and John Carlos's medals taken from them after their Black Power protest, and in 1972 had Wayne Collett and Vince Matthews expelled for slouching through their medal ceremony.

Another Brundage bugbear was the Winter Olympics, where professional or sponsored athletes were commonplace. After personally boycotting the 1964 Innsbruck games, he threw out Austrian skier Karl Schranz in protest at his commercial activities. Avery was also thoroughly suspicious of judged artistic sports like ice dancing with their obvious potential for corruption and after the planned 1976 Denver Olympics were cancelled, he was only narrowly persuaded not to ban the whole thing.

A bulldozer to the last, Brundage was determined that the 1972 Munich Olympics should go on despite the killing of 11 Israeli athletes and coaches in the village. This was arguably the correct decision, but he lost much support by bracketing the terrorists with those nations who had opposed Rhodesia's entry.

As an absentee president, Brundage allowed the IOC to become sclerotic and bureaucratic and develop a legendarily high staff turnover under de facto leader Monique Berlioux. He had a low opinion of his successor Lord Killanin ('not a leader'), but talent-spotted Juan Antonio

Samaranch, a man of similar political views, for whom he bent the rules of IOC membership to appoint him Head of Protocol.

IOC chiefs have praised Brundage as a sophisticated politician who managed a particularly difficult period in Olympic history, but many athletes felt he deserved his nickname – 'Slavery Bondage'.

Frank Bryan

Frank Bryan, inventor and businessman, born Turnham Green 1847, died 1931.

The origins of table tennis, the world's biggest participation sport, are not terribly clear, as they arose from various attempts to sell a tabletop version of lawn tennis. In Britain, several different versions were marketed by rival games makers, including Jaques's and Hamley's 'Ping Pong' – a name that came from the different sounds the ball made when hitting the table and the tambourine-style bats of stretched vellum. Ping Pong gained popularity after distance runner James Gibb visited the US and brought back some new celluloid balls, which bounced much better than the cloth-covered rubber then in use. Despite the new balls, the game remained a harmless pat-a-cake diversion, and although the papers carried letters worrying that it was undermining the nation's morals, the craze might have gone the way of deely-boppers and the hula hoop until Frank Bryan invented the rubber-faced bat.

In December 1901 Bryan, a sporting goods manufacturer, put in a patent for his 'Atropos' (Greek for 'no turn') bat, which he advertised with the memorable slogan 'A Wonderful Bat for Screwing'. Its surface of dimpled rubber – rather than bare wood, cork, leather or sandpaper – allowed new levels of spin and control and helped transform an after-dinner diversion into an athletic sport. By the end of the 1930s the rules had to be changed, requiring that the ball be tossed up from the flat of the palm before serving, to prevent extra finger spin.

For some reason, credit for the rubber-faced bat was given to one E.C. Goode, who was supposed to have been inspired by the rubber mat on a pharmacist's counter while buying headache pills. However, it seems clear that Bryan was the true inventor. (Back in 1886, Frank had also made footballs bouncier by patenting a proper valve instead of the party balloon-style tying of a long rubber neck.)

Despite the new surface, something of the 'ping pong' sound remained until the 1950s, when the Japanese popularised an earlier invention by Jaques and English player Ivor Montagu – a sponge rubber sandwich to soften the bat.

Phil Bull

Philip Bull, publisher, racehorse owner, breeder and administrator, born Hemsworth, West Yorkshire 9 April 1910, died 11 June 1989. Publisher *Best Horses* 1943–7, *Racehorses* 1949–68, *Timeform* 1948–69, *Timeform Racecards*. Chairman Horseracing Advisory Council 1980.

Sometimes you can tell a lot from a man's car. Racing radical Phil Bull's motor was a Rolls-Royce as red as his hair.

The reason for a miner's son turned socialist playwright driving a Roller and smoking cigars was that Bull had used his mathematical ability to devise a new and original method of assessing and recording a horse's merit – a system which is now almost universal. Having made the equivalent of £5 million betting in the late 1940s, the grumpy bow-tied Santa Claus set up his own stud at Halifax and became the most successful owner-breeder in Yorkshire, though a third place in the 1,000 Guineas was his greatest success in what he termed 'the great irrelevance'.

Bull's great insight was the importance of speed as a measurable quantity that a horse could reproduce in other races. He also had a far clearer grasp of genetics than many of the witch doctors of the Turf with their mythic 'bloodlines' and 'tap roots'. Focusing on horses' performance rather than race results and taking his own timings, Bull started a mail-order tipping service under his playwriting nom de plume William Temple. His Time Test Service produced weekly raceform analysis sheets from 1937 to 1947 and highlighted under-appreciated horses such as Nasrullah. Bull encouraged punters to avoid ante-post betting and racecourse gossip and instead look for good-value odds on proven fast horses. By 1942 he was struggling to complete the annual 1,100-plus-entry *Best Horses*. His odd hours and occasional verbosity didn't help and the books often came out late. Today even his 2s6d books can sell for thousands.

The great breakthrough occurred when Bull combined his timings with naval officer Dick Whitford's creation of a single composite handicap for every horse. Whitford had stripped out the effect of weight for age to create the first independent assessment of merit, with all horses rated on the same scale. From 1947 the new Timeform figures appeared weekly, although Whitford soon left the irascible Bull to work as a handicapper. Their 'marriage of time and form' was accompanied in the annual *Racehorses* by terse summaries of the kind racegoers had never seen before ('Good-looking wastrel: usually tailed off'). By 1952 these ratings had replaced Bull's old timing figures and proved their value by highlighting great horses like Dante. When William Hill closed the accounts of some of his customers, Bull stormed his office – a confrontation that led to a lasting friendship.

With more competitive racing in the 1950s, the big coups became less frequent, despite elaborate betting schemes that used Timeform employees. The introduction of betting tax in the mid-1960s virtually ended Bull's betting (never 'gambling') exploits, but Timeform extended into National Hunt racing and was computerised by the mid-1970s.

A not-always-popular voice in the sport, Bull regarded betting as its main purpose and the punters as the most important interest group. He argued in turn for covered stands, clear display of odds, overnight declarations, camera patrols, photo finishes, Sunday betting and mass ownership of horses, and was usually well ahead of the ruling Jockey Club. Bull had an especial dislike of the club's more peremptory, devious and arbitrary ways – especially their 'Star Chamber' courts, which he considered to be more concerned with discipline than justice. His 40,000-word submission to Lord Rothschild's commission led to better betting shops, but failed to persuade the government to topple the Jockey Club. He criticised the club for holding too few handicaps, skewing those that did exist in favour of 'better horses' and funnelling unfair amounts of prize money towards favoured events. Bull considered Epsom 'unsuitable for racing', while the <u>Duke of Norfolk</u>, who opposed sponsored races, was 'talking through his coronet'. (In response, the authorities banned Bull from naming a horse after Vietnamese communist leader Ho Chi Minh.) Keen to encourage two-year-old stayers, Bull invented the group one Timeform Gold Cup, the richest two-year-old race and, anticipating the threat posed by a national lottery, campaigned for a big racing event every Saturday. However, his greatest bugbear was Rule 153, under which a horse, its owners and backers could be penalised for a jockeying offence that didn't affect the race result. As part of his 30-year campaign against the rule, Bull arranged a private 'first past the post' deal with bookmakers who paid out whatever 153 said. Prickly with his staff, but also willing to support the family of a man he had sacked for embezzlement, he didn't last long as chairman of the Horseracing Advisory Council.

Sir Charles Bunbury – 'The King of the Turf'

Sir Thomas Charles Bunbury, 6th Baronet, racehorse owner, sports administrator and politician, born Mildenhall, Suffolk May 1740, died 31 March 1821. Jockey Club steward 1768–84, 1790–1812. Wins include: Derby 1780, 1801, Oaks 1801, St Leger 1813.

Today Sir Charles Bunbury is best known – if at all – as one of sport's most famous 'what-ifs', the man who lost the coin toss to name what became the Epsom Derby, at first a dog-leg mile with a prize of £1,065. However, as Jockey Club steward from 1768, one of three from 1770 and de facto boss when not in office, Bunbury oversaw the transformation of the sport and, partly by accident, set the club on the way to controlling British racing.

When Bunbury lost the coin toss in 1779, it was to his friend <u>Edward Smith Stanley, 12th Earl of Derby</u>, as they celebrated the success of the inaugural Oaks, a race for three-year-old fillies and one of the thrilling new 'sweepstakes' that were replacing traditional matched races for four- or five-year-olds. Bunbury had already been a steward for 11 years and was to remain one almost all his life, becoming the first 'Dictator of the Turf'. Since 1771, the three stewards had been given powers over racing at Newmarket, including stakes and forfeits. Bunbury employed and championed <u>James Weatherby</u>, who produced the *Racing Calendar*, the club's official mouthpiece, from 1773 and whose family firm produced the *General Stud Book* to keep track of thoroughbred pedigrees. As well as the founding of the two remaining classics, the 2,000 Guineas (1809) and 1,000 Guineas (1814), Bunbury's reign also included the arrival of the first races for two-year-olds in 1769, the first on-course bookmakers in 1790 and the first official handicap – Ascot's Oatlands the year after.

Ironically, the greatest boost Bunbury gave to the Jockey Club arose from the 1791 dispute with the Prince of Wales – later George IV – over jockey Sam Chifney's supposed 'inconsistent' running of Escape against Bunbury's Diomed. After the Prince refused to sack Chifney and left Newmarket for good, Bunbury, who had only ever intended to get rid of the jockey, was downcast and sold most of his horses, but his actions accidentally increased the prestige of the club, which would gradually assume complete power over British racing.

As well as winning the first Derby with Diomed, Bunbury also owned Eleanor, the first filly to win both the Oaks and the Derby, Smolensko, the first to do a Derby and 2,000 Guineas double, plus Highflyer, who when sold to auctioneer Richard Tattersall, helped fund a business that lasts to this day. Diomed, who at one stage was down to a two-guinea stallion fee, was later exported to the US and proved a huge success, breeding dozens of winners. His death in 1808 was said to be as mourned as that of George Washington himself.

Beryl Burton

Beryl Burton (née Charnock) OBE, road and track cyclist, born Leeds 12 May 1937, died 8 May 1996. World road race champion 1960, 67, world individual pursuit champion 1959, 60, 62, 63, 66, holder of 122 national titles, including best all-round time-trialler 1959–83. Bidlake Memorial Prize 1959, 60, 67.

Despite their progress in sport, it was not until 1967 that a British woman set an overall national endurance record, as Beryl Burton over-took Mike McNamara during an amateur time trial in her native Yorkshire. Feeling that the occasion should be marked in some way, she was reported to have offered him a Swiss roll-shaped liquorice allsort, which McNamara accepted. At the end of the race she had covered 446 kilometres – 9 kilometres more than any other Briton in history.

The woman who proved that women could more than match men for guts and endurance was an unlikely candidate as an all-conquering athlete. As a child, Beryl suffered from rheumatism and nervous prob-lems, including St Vitus's dance, which left her partially paralysed, but after taking up swimming she was turned on to cycling by her husband Charlie and was up to international standard by 1957 – the beginning of a quarter of a century of racing dominance. Beryl considered herself mainly a time-triallist, and set national records at every distance from 1 to 100 miles, plus a world 20-kilometre record. Her 100-mile record lasted for 28 years and her 12-hour record still stands today. She would have won even more titles had there been more events and were it not for her aggressive pace-setting style, which left her vulnerable to late attacks. (And there was no women's cycling at the Olympics until 1988.) Even so, she was given the rare honour, for a woman, of an appear-ance at the Grand Prix des Nations and was awarded cycling's top award, the Bidlake Memorial Prize, a record three times.

In her career she came back from a broken leg and shoulder and 56 stitches in her face, and only advanced pregnancy kept her off her bike. Even this had a sporting outcome, as her daughter Denise became a fellow British champion and national squad member, setting a 10-mile tandem record with her mother in 1982. It is perhaps no surprise that

Beryl's record-breaking 1960s heyday coincided with the decision of many sporting authorities to allow women to compete in endurance events, such as the Olympic 1,500 metres, first held in 1972. She carried on competing until the age of 58, when she died of a heart attack during a training run, and is commemorated with a trophy and a cycle way.

Walter Camp – 'The Father of American Football'

Walter Chauncey Camp, American footballer, coach and journalist, born New Britain, Connecticut 7 April 1859, died 14 March 1925. Playing career: Yale 1876–80. Coaching career: Yale 1888–91, Stanford 1892, 94–5. Overall record: 81 wins, 5 defeats, 3 draws. College Football Hall of Fame 1951.

Not many men are being described as 'the father' of their sport at the age of 33, but Walter Camp arrived at just the right time and place to create a new 'American football' and was to remain a huge influence on the game for the rest of his life.

Camp appeared at Yale in 1876, just as new football rules were being agreed between the big East Coast colleges. (There would be no professional club football for nearly 20 years.) At both Yale and Harvard, various violent football games had been played and banned during the 1860s, leaving Rutgers and Princeton to tough it out on tiny pitches with 25-a-side teams playing versions of the London FA's rules. These round-ball games included 'innings' with either side in possession, while butting and limited carrying of the ball was also allowed. After Harvard created its own 'Boston Rules' game in 1871, an intercollegiate association was formed, still based on the London rules, but with different scoring, 20-a-side teams and larger pitches and goals. The following year, Harvard was the first to switch to an oval ball game, having played a rugby-style match against Canada's McGill University. Camp's Yale, who had played a touring Eton soccer side in 1873 and lost 1–2, still preferred a more open 11-a-side game, but two years later they also changed to the rugby style, and by the following year all five major East Coast colleges were playing it, effectively killing off soccer in the US.

It was now that Camp, Yale's halfback and future captain, made his first impact on the game, steering his side to a series of huge wins. As a coach he was the first to use pictures and illustrations of play as he led the team to a series of championships. In 1888 Yale were invincible, winning all 13 games and racking up 698 points without conceding a single one, and between 1891 and 1894 they lost just one match.

Their dominance attracted big crowds to watch the slaughter and by 1914 they would be able to build the 70,000-seater Yale Bowl – the first large sports stadium in the US. Camp was so in demand that he also coached at Stanford in California, helping football's national spread, and from 1889 was cooperating with Caspar Whitney of *The Week's Sport* magazine to put together 'All American' teams. For the rest of his life inclusion in Camp's sides would be a badge of greatness, though he moved first to *Harper's Weekly* and then to *Collier's Weekly*.

Despite 30 books and over 250 articles, Camp's greatest influence was on the football rules themselves. As early as 1880 he had persuaded the other colleges to do away with massed scrummages in favour of orderly possession, with two Yale-sized teams on either side of a 'line of scrimmage'. After two years of deadly dull blocking games against Princeton, Walter came up with the idea of 'downs' – a traditional cry on the rugby pitch when a ball or player was grounded. These downs allowed three attempts to move the ball forward five yards, tightened the game up and gave rise to the use of a quarterback, who used agreed signals and tactics, supported by two halfbacks and a full back. For a while, a squared system of markings was used to judge progress on the pitch, hence the nickname 'gridiron', which dates from 1897. Although the centre still heeled the ball back in a rugby style, this was the beginning of American football as we now know it.

The following year, Camp agreed a new points system although, as in rugby, a field goal still counted for more than a touchdown. In 1885 he got the other colleges to allow referees on the field and three years later persuaded them to allow tackling below the waist, which ushered in an amazingly violent period in sporting history. Between 1888 and 1893 massed tactics like Amos Alonzo Stagg's 'Turtleback' or Harvard's 'Flying Wedge' caused death and destruction, and in 1894 inter-college games nearly ended, before a shorter 70-minute game and a limit on the number of players running in from behind the line was agreed. From 1903 the minimum number on the line was seven when playing between the 25-yard lines. The following year, a minimum of six players were required to be on the line at all times and a touchdown finally counted for more than a goal. Despite this, there were another 18 deaths on football fields in 1905 before President Theodore Roosevelt himself threatened to shut down the game for good.

In response, Camp and his committee recreated themselves as the

Intercollegiate Athletic Association, later to become the all-powerful NCAA. The ICAA opened up football by allowing a forward pass, although at first this had to be thrown from within five yards of the line and travel no more than 20 yards. At first seen as a desperate last-ditch move, it was months before it was even used in a game and only after 1912, when the 20-yard restriction was lifted, did Knute Rockne and Gus Dorais of Notre Dame use it to defeat the Army. Other 1906 rule changes, also intended to make the game less violent, were a time cut to 60 minutes, the establishment of a neutral zone between the teams on the pitch and a ban on 'hurdling', so that all tackles happened on the ground. Despite these moves, another six tackles died in 1909.

The following year, Camp's rule-makers required another player on the line and finally banned massed assaults, ending such tactics as interlocking and dragging or pushing the ball carrier along. As a result, defences grew so powerful that a fourth down to reach ten yards was agreed, plus an increase in the points value of touchdowns and a standard 100-yard pitch with end zones. Unlike rugby, Camp's game also allowed points for a 'safety' – a tackle behind the opposition's goal line. With these changes, American football had nearly become the game we know today.

As well as masterminding US college football, Camp also promoted exercise generally, and his fitness regime 'The Daily Dozen' was cleverly marketed with a set of wind-up gramophone records. Eventually, he would train the armed forces themselves, while keeping up the flow of articles that made him not only the greatest lawmaker in US football but also its greatest mythmaker.

Tullio Campagnolo

Gentullio 'Tullio' Campagnolo, racing cyclist and inventor, born Vicenza, Italy 26 August 1901, died 3 February 1983.

Perhaps the most significant bike race of the 20th century was the 1927 Gran Premio della Vittoria. It was here that a talented amateur rider and Olympic hopeful named Tullio Campagnolo found himself stuck on the snowy Croce d'Aune pass, unable to free the frozen wing-nuts of his bike with his numbed fingers. At the time, changing gear on a racing bike meant taking the back wheel off and flipping it around to engage the second cog. With chattering teeth, Campagnolo watched his chances of victory slip away, and declared, *'Bisogno cambiar qualcossa de drio!'* ('Something has to change at the back!'). Change it did, as Campagnolo, whose family owned a hardware business, created first the quick-release hub (1933) and four years later the first practical derailleur gear, which allowed easier switching between a wider range of gears while still keeping moving.

Campagnolo's first 'Cambio Corsa' gear soon helped increase racing speeds and from 1937 it was used by star cyclists like Gino Bartali, although its dual rods and fork-like selector were tricky to operate. As orders rose, Campagnolo hired his first employee and by 1949 had created the Gran Sport, a sprung, single-cable system that was to be universal in bike racing for about thirty years.

At his Vicenza factory, Campagnolo went on to develop lighter bike frames and an expertise in alloys that was employed by the motor car and motorbike industries and even NASA itself. The family business, still concentrating on the production of high-quality parts for racing cycles, remains a prestigious name today.

Francis Campbell

Francis Maule Campbell, footballer and administrator, born Blackheath 1843, died 30 December 1920. Treasurer Football Association 1863.

Had it not been for a young Victorian wine merchant named Francis Campbell, we might not have both Association Football ('soccer') and rugby football today. In the early 1860s Campbell was a founder of the Blackheath club, one of the few sporting organisations open to all-comers – hence its nickname, 'The Club'. He was also Blackheath's representative on the new Football Association, when it first met to agree some compromise rules for the game, and it was at a crucial FA meeting in December 1863 that his great moment came.

Blackheath had already swung to a more rugby style, following an influx of ex-Rugby School boys, although Campbell, now voted in as FA treasurer, was willing to admit that the Cambridge Rules on which the FA were basing theirs were 'worthy of consideration'. However, he began to lose sympathy when the Sheffield clubs started calling for limits on catching and running with the ball. A compromise measure was reached, but Campbell became unhappy with the minuting of previous meetings, and refused to accept the abolition of tripping and shin-kicking, or 'hacking', which, his opponents argued, made the game suitable only for reckless schoolboys. On 1 December, Campbell declared that the abolition of hacking would 'do away with all the courage and pluck of the game, and I will be obliged to bring over a lot of Frenchmen who will beat you with a week's practice'. Only a trio of school clubs supported him, and having lost his anti-hacking motion 13–4, he quit the FA, refusing even to take part in a trial non-hacking period. The Richmond club also left and by 1864 both clubs were playing their own more macho rules.

This historic split was probably unnecessary, as at first the FA carried on with catching and occasional hacking, but it deepened as Blackheath developed inter-passing between their forwards and the FA finally banned catching in 1866. In the same year – either because of the death of a player or the fact that they were unable to put out uninjured sides –

Blackheath and Richmond agreed to stop tripping and hacking in matches. In 1871, both clubs were instrumental in setting up the RFU, which also banned hacking, although it lingered on for a while at some of the more vigorous public schools. Rugby's unnecessary split with football had now set it off on a very different course. Although Campbell's Blackheath Club is one of the seven RFU founder members to have survived to the present day, the man himself died unremarked. No obituary has been found and the only known portrait of him is a team photo of the 1862 side.

Federico Caprilli

Federico Caprilli, equestrian, born Livorno 8 April 1868, died 6 December 1907.

It takes a special kind of genius to appreciate that absolutely everyone is doing something very basic completely wrongly – and such a genius was Lieutenant Federico Caprilli.

Caprilli joined the Italian cavalry at a time when artillery and machine guns had made the traditional battlefield charge a mass suicide note. Instead, cavalry was being developed for surprise attacks over rough country, where there would be plenty of obstacles to leap. At this time everyone believed that horses should land on their back legs, or all four at once, to save their supposedly fragile front limbs. Riders used long stirrups and leant back, hauling at the horse's mouth to steer it up and over the obstacle – hence in old hunting prints the riders are always leaning backwards over the hedges.

Federico, who used high-speed photography to test his beliefs, soon decided that this was wrong in every way. In nature, he discovered, horses *always* landed on their front legs. He argued that by leaning forward and slightly out of the saddle with a shorter stirrup, the rider would not only be more comfortable, but more stable, as he would be over the horse's centre of gravity. As for the horse himself, he would find jumping easier and more pleasant without the idiot on top screwing up his jumping action and hauling away at his mouth.

For this rebellious attitude Caprilli was banished to the south of Italy, until his methods were tried with great success and he was reinstated. Under his tuition, both horses and riders made incredible progress, and could soon complete a jumping course without even using the reins. Caprilli was made chief riding instructor of the Italian Cavalry, published his book *Natural Equitation* in 1904, and drew riders from around the world to the Tor di Quinto and Pinerolo schools to see his world-beating methods in action. He even demonstrated them at the 1906 Athens Olympics, only to die the following year – not boldly leaping over a chasm, but after his horse slipped on some icy cobbles.

Amadeo Carrizo

Amadeo Raúl Carrizo Larretape, goalkeeper, born Rufino, Argentina 12 June 1926. Playing career: River Plate 1945–68 (league champions 1952, 53, 55, 56, 57), Millonarios 1969–70 (Copa Mustang 1969); Argentina 1954–64 (Copa de las Naciones 1964).

Nicknamed 'Tarzán' by his team-mates, the handsome Amadeo Carrizo is often credited as the first modern-style goalkeeper.

Instead of simply watching from between the sticks, Carrizo, a converted forward, had the ball skills and soccer sense to take up advance positions on the pitch. At River, he astonished the crowds by routinely leaving his penalty box to defend. Rather than simply recycling the ball to his backs, he used his goal kicks to launch attacks, and was also one of the first to wear gloves as a matter of course.

During his career, Amadeo played a record 513 consecutive first division matches for the River Plate 'machine' and achieved an unprecedented eight clean sheets in a row. His adventurous style inspired flamboyant Latin American goalies such as René Higuita and José Luis Chilavert, but since the pass back to the keeper's hands was banned in 1992, all goalies have had to become faster and more skilful with their feet and link better with their defenders. They're all 'Tarzáns' now.

Don Catlin

Don H. Catlin, Professor Emeritus of Molecular and Medical Pharmacology at the UCLA David Geffen School of Medicine, Director Olympic Analytical Laboratory, born 1938. 2003 Chicago Tribune Sportsman of the Year. President and CEO Anti-Doping Research 2005–.

In June 2003, IOC Medical Commission member Dr Don Catlin received a test-tube sample that was to change sporting history. The clear liquid inside contained a few drops of an unidentified substance, passed on by an anonymous track coach. Despite the lack of clues and the fact that the substance kept breaking down in testing, Catlin's team not only identified the steroid it contained, but detected it in samples provided by 20 athletes at the recent US National Track and Field trials. The resulting investigation exposed a series of top athletes, footballers and baseball players, leading to the first prosecutions of coaches and a tightening-up of the previously lax US laws on drugs in sport.

Catlin was clearly the right man to send the sample to. Since 1982, he had run America's first accredited drug-testing lab, raising standards throughout the Olympic movement – though he stopped some educational programmes when it became clear that coaches were using them to learn how to dope without detection. In the 1990s, Catlin developed a carbon isotope ratio test to differentiate between natural and artificially introduced testosterone – a big drug in sports since steroid detection had begun in the 1970s. By 1998 he was also calling for the banning of androstenedione, a drug used to boost testosterone by athletes such as record-setting baseballer Mark McGwire, and which 8 per cent of male high-school seniors were using when it was finally banned five years later. In 2002 Catlin's testers had stripped medals from three Olympic cross-country skiers after detecting the blood booster darbepoetin for the first time. In the same year, Catlin's team also 'cracked the code' of norbolethone, a 'dead' steroid first developed in 1966 but brought back into use because it wasn't being tested for.

Despite these achievements, it was the cracking of tetrahydrogestrinone – aka THG or 'The Clear' – that really made history. THG was another tweaked 1960s steroid whose distribution was traced to BALCO, a £60 million business supplying a host of athletes and baseball and football stars. Investigations led to a series of high-profile bans and the prosecution of BALCO founder Victor Conte and coach Greg Anderson. (The journalists who carried out the investigations were threatened with even longer sentences for refusing to reveal their sources.) The BALCO case led to the International Athletic Association Federation threatening coaches as well as athletes with a two-year ban, while baseball commissioner Bud Selig commissioned the Mitchell Report into drug use. This revealed that since steroid testing had begun in 2002, many US baseballers had switched to Human Growth Hormone (HGH).

In 2007, having helped uncover the use of two more steroids – Madol and 6-OXO – and revealed drug use by Olympic gold medallist Justin Gatlin, Catlin announced that he was leaving UCLA to set up Anti-Doping Research, Inc to seek out better tests for the blood booster EPO and the currently untestable HGH.

Vic Cavanagh Snr

Victor George Cavanagh Snr, rugby player and coach, born Dunedin, New Zealand 29 July 1874, died 11 June 1952. Playing career: Caversham and Southern. Coaching career: Southern University.

From the very earliest days of rugby, there were scrums, mauls and line-outs. The great tactical innovation is the ruck, whose home is New Zealand and particularly the Southern Island province of Otago, where it reached its apogee under father and son coaches 'Old' and 'Young' Vic Cavanagh.

New Zealand rugby encouraged rucking from the earliest days by penalising lying on the ball, and it was always a favourite tactic in Otago, an 1860s gold town that by 1877 was capable of beating the capital Wellington. The southerners' reputation was for ferocity and stubbornness, and it took a four-year domestic boycott to persuade them to accept the NZRFU – or as they saw it, rule from the capital. Their refusal to join a combined Australasian side ensured that All-Black rugby remained separate and distinct. In 1905, <u>Dave Gallaher</u>'s all-conquering All Blacks, coached by Otago's Jimmy Duncan, used their 'loose scrum' to tie up the opposition and heel the ball out to their outnumbering backs.

From the turn of the century to the 1950s, first Vic Senior and then his son developed the ruck into a deliberate, devastating weapon – inviting the tackle and then driving a human threshing machine over the top. Instead of having a loose bunch of players forming a ruck, both men devoted themselves to developing body positions and packing patterns until you could throw a blanket over their forwards, charging in fast and low, backs parallel to the ground. Either the opposing backs were drawn in and the overlap exploited, or they just started all over again. Crowds of over 15,000 came to the Vic Junior's 'House of Pain' to watch the 16-legged Otago monster defend the Ranfurly Shield 19 times between 1947 and 1950. (If a first half went badly, the standard half-time speech was 'Out you go again, girls.') Against the Lions, who had thrashed Otago in 1930, there were victories in 1950, 1959 and 1966. 'I have never seen anything like their rucking before in my life,' said centre

Bleddyn Williams. Only the kicking of Barry John and Phil Bennett over-came them in 1971 and 77.

Though it was said that Cavanagh Junior could coach 15 fit bone-heads to victory, neither he nor his father ever ran the national team and without his guidance the 11 Otago players on the 1949 All-Black tour of South Africa lost every match. Always dangerous, the ruck was even more so away from the soft turf of Dunedin, and in 1956 the violence on the South African tour was so bad that the NZRFU censored the footage.

Though Vic Senior died in 1952 the NZ ruck still rolled on. The first World Cup was won in 1987 with what captain David Kirk called 'a discovery that applied violence legally to great effect . . . demoralising and hurting the opposition at the same time'. However, by 2003 coach John Mitchell had declared the ruck 'dead', as playing patterns altered and defences refused to commit to it. Today, continuity of possession is preferred to a series of clashes in which the fastest and lowest win, but a trophy match between University and Southern is still named after the two Vics. As the 1993 Lions found out after a morale-sapping defeat before the first Test – you know when you've been Otago'd.

'Cavendish'

Henry Jones, surgeon, journalist, author and sports administrator, born London 2 November 1831, died 10 February 1899. Cards and pastimes editor *The Field*. All England Club secretary 1871.

Many books on the history of tennis make no mention of Victorian journalist Henry 'Cavendish' Jones, yet he is, arguably, the main reason for the success of the game.

Born into a medical family, Jones qualified as a surgeon and worked as a general practitioner from 1852 to 1869, until he was lured into journalism by his love of card games. Taking his nom de plume from the Cavendish card club, Henry wrote *The Principles of Whist* in 1862 and was soon such an authority that his father wrote to him on a point – unaware that he was addressing his own son. Eventually, Henry became cards and pastimes editor of *The Field*, introducing and debating the finer rules and tactics of games such as billiards and croquet. He also joined *Field* editor John Henry Walsh's Wimbledon-based All England Croquet Club, which had been founded at the paper's offices six years earlier. Cavendish was not only responsible for setting up the first lawn tennis court at Wimbledon in 1875, but also for staging, publicising and sponsoring the first lawn tennis tournament two years later, supposedly to raise funds for a new pony-drawn roller. The question was – to which rules should the competitors play? The existing games of rackets or real tennis, or something entirely different? Cavendish's rules subcommittee included a rackets champion in Julian Marshall and real tennis champion Charles Heathcote, who had persuaded a reluctant MCC to agree a court and issue rules two years previously.

There had been competing scoring systems in lawn tennis since 1873, when its inventor, Walter Clopton Wingfield, first opted for a rackets-style 'first to 15 by a margin of two', in which only the server scored. By 1875 the All England Club was playing to the MCC's rules, which stipulated Wingfield's hourglass-shaped court but used real-tennis scoring with a second service and the server on the baseline. However, the All England Club had lowered the net for a more exciting game and *The Field* had hosted vigorous debates over rival court measurements, scoring systems and net heights.

From all this confusion Cavendish's committee produced two lasting changes – the first was to fix the court dimensions at 78 x 27 feet (23.77 x 8.23 metres), which is how they have remained ever since. The second was to keep real tennis's ancient four-point system and second service, but allow both players to score points in a best-of-five-sets contest in which the first to six games won a set. Whether they realised it or not, Cavendish's group had struck gold, creating a game that could swing on a single point. Even rival paper *The Sportsman* had to admit that Wimbledon's first 1877 final was 'a very exciting struggle'. Over the next ten years, playing styles, equipment, net heights and service lines would all vary, until champion Ernest Renshaw could declare that the game was pretty much perfect, since he only lost a point when he made an error. Although we now have tiebreakers, Cavendish's scoring system still keeps us glued to the game, never knowing if a single dropped point or fluffed service might turn the whole contest.

Cavendish kept up his journalism to the end, but tennis was on a temporary fade when he died in 1899 and the obituaries failed even to mention the whist expert's link to the game.

Neville Chamberlain

Colonel Sir Neville Francis Fitzgerald Chamberlain KCB, KCVO, KPM, snooker player, born Upton, Buckinghamshire 13 January 1856, died 28 May 1944.

Though his claim has been disputed, no one has been able to come up with a more convincing candidate as the inventor of snooker than Lieutenant Colonel Sir Neville Chamberlain.

In 1938, while his namesake the Prime Minister was busily declaring 'peace in our time', the 82-year-old Chamberlain spoke to journalist Compton Mackenzie and described the game's invention. This dated from 1875 when he was a young subaltern, stationed with the 11th Devonshire Foot Regiment at Jubbulpore in India. Here the Devonshires played various billiards-type games – often for a 'pool' of money or an agreed stake per ball. One was Pyramids, in which the aim was to pot 15 red balls on the table. Another was Life Pool, in which rival players attempted to pot each other's balls in turn until three lives were lost, the balls being dyed different colours to identify them. A variant was Black Pool, the regiment's favourite, in which the black was an extra bonus ball.

Chamberlain's genius was to combine the three games, although it was a while before points values were assigned to the various colours, and the notion of break-building didn't exist – the usual tactic being to pot a red and a colour and then hide. The name 'snooker' is said to have arisen after a player fluffed a shot and Chamberlain described him as playing like a 'snooker' – Woolwich barracks slang for a first-term cadet. He then mollified the offended officer by saying that 'they were all snookers in this game'. (The ultimate origin of the word 'snooker' may come from the French 'neux' meaning new, or the Victorian comedy duo Hooker and Snooker.) After leaving Jubbulpore, Chamberlain spread both the name and the game as he joined the Central India Horse. After being wounded in 1878 in the Second Afghan War, he moved to the hill station at Ootacamund, where the Ooty Club drew up the first rules. In 1885, Chamberlain is supposed to have passed on a description of the game to a touring billiards pro – probably John Roberts, although this is disputed and it may have been John Ross or Fred Shorter. It wasn't until 1887 that the game was recorded in Britain as 'Snooker's pool'. The first published rules have been attributed to billiards pro John Dowland and the equipment manufacturers Burroughes and Watts.

In 1938, the origins of the game were still being disputed and some claimed that it had been invented by a 'Colonel Snooker' – just like in hockey, where a 'Colonel Hockey' was sometimes credited. At the age of 82, Chamberlain's recall probably wasn't perfect, but no better candidate has emerged. His reluctance to claim the game as his own might have been due to its low-rent 'boots and corduroys' image. Until the mid-1920s, when Joe Davis popularised it, many billiard players regarded snooker as a 'game for navvies'.

John Graham Chambers

John Graham Chambers, rower, athletics promoter, coach and administrator, born Carmarthenshire, Wales 12 February 1843, died 4 March 1883. Editor *Land and Water* 1871–83.

The credit for boxing's 1867 Marquess of Queensberry Rules, which stipulated gloves, the ten-second count and the three-minute round, should really go to the marquess's old Cambridge University pal, boat club president John Graham Chambers.

After leaving Cambridge, a sudden reversal in his family's fortunes meant that Chambers had to begin chiselling out a living in the booming world of sport. Backed by Victor Villiers, an ex-Oxford miler and future Earl of Jersey, he set up an Amateur Athletic Club, a gentlemanly sporting body based at the Beaufort House ground in west London, but which soon moved to Chambers's own premises at Lillie Bridge. Here, from 1868 he staged athletics, bike races and boxing matches – plus the second FA Cup final.

To encourage more participation in boxing, a sport with a thuggish reputation, Chambers raised the tone by introducing vests instead of bare chests and rewrote the rules, stipulating the use of weighed and examined gloves, weight limits to allow a fair fight, an elevated 24-foot ring to prevent outside interference, no seconds in the ring during rounds, three-minute rounds with one-minute breaks between, and no wrestling or 'hugging'. To help protect the contestants, there was no striking a man who was down or helpless on the ropes and a ten-second count was introduced for clarity. In 1867, Chambers persuaded Queensberry to donate and present the prizes at the first tournament and lend his name to the new rules. Overall, the new style favoured more skill and footwork, although without the risk of breaking bare knuckles, contests could be longer and more brutal.

Despite all these advances, there were still no limits to the number of rounds, which would only gradually reduce from 45 to 15 over the following century. Points decisions and official weight limits would both arrive later and for a quarter of a century both styles of fighting continued side by side. It wasn't until 1889 that a particularly crooked fight between

Frank Slavin and Jem Smith led to the creation of the National Sporting Club, who from 1892 began staging light-, middle- and heavyweight Empire contests under the Queensberry Rules. In the US, champion John L. Sullivan fought an inconclusive fight under them against Dominick McCaffrey in 1885, but it wasn't until his 1892 title fight against James J. Corbett that they were employed in what is now considered the first modern championship contest.

Chambers himself remained a keen rower and in 1875 was in the boat that accompanied Matthew Webb on his historic cross-Channel swim. Though he was part of the committee that banned working men from amateur rowing contests in 1878, Chambers continued to stage all manner of professional and amateur athletic contests, toughing it out with the nearby London Athletic Club, which since 1877 had allowed mere tradesmen to compete and had also moved to a new ground at nearby Stamford Bridge. By the end of the decade, two rival amateur championships were being held. With the northern counties now threatening to break away, Chambers attended a crisis meeting at Oxford in 1880, after which he was forced to agree to a new 'financial' rather than 'social' amateur code. Under the new rules, amateur athletes of all classes could compete together, and a new Amateur Athletic Association was formed with Villiers as president. Olympics founder Pierre de Coubertin would later copy the AAA's strict rules. In theory, they allowed anyone to compete, but in practice, the Olympics were to become a rich man's club, which fought an eighty-year losing battle against professionalism.

Despite the 1880 Oxford agreement, grounds like Lillie Bridge were still free to stage professional-only events and it was at one of these in 1887, that a 'fixed' sprint between two famous pros – Harry Gent and Harry Hutchens – led to an argument and stand-off because neither would 'throw' the race. The crowd, both halves of which thought they were on to a safe bet, rioted and burned down the grandstand. Lillie Bridge never reopened. Chambers himself had died – four years earlier – apparently of overwork.

Colin Chapman

Anthony Colin Bruce Chapman, motor racing driver, chief engineer and team owner, born Richmond 19 May 1928, died 16 December 1982. Constructors' champion 1963, 65, 68, 70, 72, 73, 78. Driver's Championship 1963, 65, 68, 70, 72, 78. Overall record: 72 Grand Prix victories, 88 pole positions, 63 fastest laps. Winner Indianapolis 500 1965.

'If not a genius, then bloody close to one.' That was the verdict on Colin Chapman from driver Innes Ireland, who gained the first Team Lotus victory in 1961. It was all the more generous because it was delivered after Ireland had been fired by Chapman and had plummeted 150 feet into a gorge in one of his fragile, lightweight cars.

The most creative racing car designer in history, Colin Chapman entered the lowest echelons of sport with very little money before producing a stream of inventions over 30 years that helped create the modern Formula One car. When he died in 1982, Lotus were still leading the way and had achieved more Grand Prix wins than any other team, including the longer-established and far wealthier Ferrari.

Trained as a structural as well as a mechanical engineer, the university-educated Chapman brought new thinking into the sport, replacing a craft-based 'black art' with testing and a more scientific style of driving. Though Lotus was small and often overstretched, Chapman's unique position as driver, owner and engineer allowed him to bet the ranch on what he termed 'monumental decisions', an astonishingly high proportion of which turned out to work. As a businessman he was adept in the use of mass-produced components to hurry up production and keep the costs down. An innovator in promotion as well as design, he was one of the first to take advantage of advertising on cars. A £60,000 deal with Player's Gold Leaf saw the green and gold Lotuses repainted red, white and gold, signalling the arrival of the tobacco money which would sustain the sport for 30 years. In 1973 the team even renamed itself JPS Lotus and created the fabulous-looking all-black JPS Specials.

Famous for his analytical thinking, Chapman was also a great spotter of talent, employing bright young engineers including Mike Costin and

Keith Duckworth of future Cosworth fame, while chief accountant Fred
Bushell was recruited – quite innocently – after a chat in a public toilet.
On the track Chapman's greatest partnership was with driver Jim Clark,
who won 19 Grands Prix out of 39. Clark's death in 1968 devastated
Chapman and was reckoned to have changed his character thereafter.

As well as having ambition and motivational skills, Chapman was
also a great reader and lateral thinker, such that when pumped petrol
was banned in place of a gravity feed, he designed a record-breakingly
fast system. Rather than being narrowly car-obsessed, he had interests
in aeronautics and boat design, on which he drew for his lightweight
racing cars. A study of aeroplane fuel tanks led to the monocoque car
construction that is universal today, while De Havilland planes inspired
the idea of putting radiators in the car's wings. (The idea for the Mark
IV's suspension came from a tractor design.) Chapman's interests in
boatbuilding led him to become an expert in composites, producing the
largest-ever pieces of injection moulding. In 1982, Lotus would be joint
first with McLaren's John Barnard in the use of carbon fibre, but Lotus
were able to manufacture their own pieces, rather than having to buy
them in. Another Chapman talent was fastening on the lucky accident
– such as ground-effect aerodynamics – and making the most of it.
Always a man in a hurry, he never stopped working. After a fracas at
the 1965 Dutch Grand Prix, he was discovered in jail, drafting elegant
plans on the back of a writ.

Beneath all this invention, Colin Chapman had an underlying principle – a belief in low weight to boost acceleration and get the most
from smaller, lighter engines. As early as his home-made Mark II, an
adapted 1930 Austin Seven, he was achieving 90 mph from a 750 cc
engine. In 1963 US racers would be astonished by the 143 mph Jim
Clark achieved from a tiny 1.5-litre car.

Though the rear-engine single-seater was John Cooper's idea, Lotus
produced most of the subsequent innovations in materials and design
that defined the look of an F1 car. His use of new technologies was
apparent from his very first Mark I – an earlier souped-up Austin Seven,
made with stressed aluminium-bonded plywood for lightness and rigidity.
The follow-up used a triangulated space frame – an idea that was to
remain standard in racing cars until 1968. The Mark VI used stressed
aluminium panels to match the best the mighty Mercedes could offer,
while in 1954 his Mark VIII was the best 1500 cc car in the world –

despite being made in a modest garage in Hornsey, north London. Having left Roman numerals behind, the 11 was judged the most effective car at the 1957 Le Mans, while the Elite sports car replaced expensive and impractical steel and tubing with a glass-fibre body. By the time of the 18, Lotus were combining aluminium and fibreglass, and their 21 pioneered a new layout, with the driver dropped down into a more streamlined, near-reclining position that is now universal in Grands Prix. In 1962, the 25's monocoque was four times stronger than the space-framed 24, and the quest to maximise strength and minimise weight continued with the full monocoque 38, after which yet more weight was saved by bolting the engine onto the back of the 42 and 43 cockpit. By the time of the 1967 Lotus 49, the engine itself was a body part – an elegant, weight-saving solution that enabled Jim Clark to gain a lap on the field at Monza. Most influential of all was the wedge-shaped 72 – the father of all subsequent GP cars. Its side radiators saved weight on pipes and prevented the driver being roasted alive, while traction was improved by moving the weight back. Over six seasons, the 72 won 20 GPs, before the less-successful 76 pioneered another new idea – adjustable tracking, wheelbase and centre of gravity, to improve perform-ance on different circuits. Again, this is now universal. In 1977, the 78 used side-pods to improve its handling, then the 88 employed lighter, stronger carbon fibre, which could handle the stresses of more powerful engines and be moulded to the optimum shape.

Less obvious, though just as important, were Lotus's innovations in suspension. As early as the Mark II, Chapman was using independent front suspension, while the Mark VI had the coil spring and telescoping dampers used in most cars today. 1956's double wishbone design remains the F1 standard. Lotus was also the first to 'tune' the chassis, and the 18's road-holding amazed drivers. Later innovations included the inboard torsion-bar suspension on the 72, which smoothed the ride, increased traction and reduced the unsprung weight to increase speed. Most ingenious of all was the double chassis 88, in which the rock-hard suspension of the primary chassis kept the car glued to the road, while an independent inner one prevented the driver and engine being shaken to bits. After the shock of the 88's rejection by the stewards, Chapman pioneered active suspension, in which computer-aided devices compen-sated for the effects of braking and cornering to keep the car perfectly level. This was so effective that it was later banned.

As for aerodynamics, as early as the Mark VII Frank Costin was being employed to cloak the car in an aerodynamic shell. Lotus invented the driver's air deflector and limited the frontal area of the car to help Jim Clark lap the entire field at Zandvoort in 1963. The 49B had aerofoil fins either side of the nose cone and a scoop out of the engine bay that used the air flowing over the car to hold it down, rather than just trying to 'cheat the wind'. It was Clark who first used an inverted helicopter rotor blade to force the car down, but once Chapman seized on the idea, his cars had flimsy biplane wings operating straight onto the suspension and generating 400 lb of downforce. True to form, they were tensioned with rubber bands. After a bit of wing from a Brabham landed at the feet of the ruling CSI president, wings were at first banned, then only allowed if fixed to the chassis – creating the F1 'look' ever since. 1975 brought another 'monumental decision' as Chapman embarked on a study of 'ground effects'. By using a wind tunnel (another first) he discovered that the car body itself could function as an inverted wing, generating less downforce than wings, but also less drag. To maintain low air pressure, brushes and skirts were used around the car, with special side-pods on the 78. The improved 79 was said to stick to the road 'like a white line' by its driver Mario Andretti, but the wily Chapman distracted attention from the venturi tunnels that did the trick by using the gearbox as a decoy and he had his engineers rush to cover it up whenever it was in the pits. The belief that he had 'cracked' aerodynamics caused Chapman to set off in other directions with the unpredictable 80, while Frank Williams won the 1980 championship with his FW07 – pretty much a copy of the 79.

Aerodynamics was about transmitting more power to the tyres and here too Lotus were the leaders, being the first to switch to wider tyres in the 1950s and adopting the US idea of temperature-testing them at all points to see how well the car was handling. Though a 'kit constructor' rather than a grand engine-maker, Chapman was also partly responsible for the creation of the Cosworth engine, once he and PR man Walter Hayes convinced the Ford hierarchy to invest $100,000 in Mike Costin and Keith Duckworth's new engine. This 400 bhp masterpiece of power and reliability won 154 Grands Prix and 10 championships. Designed as an integral part of the Lotus 49, it went straight to pole position at Zandvoort in 1967, but the team failed to capitalise due to technical problems and it was soon available to anyone, allowing the rise of new teams like Brabham and Tyrrell. Other products of Colin Chapman's 'fertile-plus' mind were inboard brakes, used on the 72 to reduce the unsprung mass. Of course not every invention was a triumph. The two-pedal 76 had an electric clutch to allow left-foot braking, but never worked properly. Another abandoned project was the turbine car. Although a 56B turbine car nearly won the Indy 500, the 63 was heavy, hard to control and unresponsive, requiring drivers to accelerate and brake at the same time – plus it had no engine braking, was 'set' for 80 mph and was complicated by being combined with four-wheel drive.

A Lotus turbine car was to claim the life of Mike Spence – just one in a series of disasters made worse by Lotus's questionable engineering standards and Chapman's obsession with lightness. In just one race at Spa in 1960, Stirling Moss broke his legs after a wheel flew off a defect-ive hub (something that happened 'several times'), Alan Stacey was killed outright at virtually the same spot and Mike Taylor was thrown from his car after the steering column came away in his hands, demol-ishing a tree with his body and breaking his back. Afterwards he gained a substantial sum in compensation from Lotus. Stirling Moss's manager Rob Walker frequently replaced faulty drive shafts, and two years later an 18/21 hybrid ended Moss's career. Jackie Stewart refused to drive for the slapdash Lotus, while defective washers and oil lines cost Jim Clark two world championships. (The 49's brakes weren't great either.) Clark's death at Hockenheim in 1968 shocked the sport, but Chapman still favoured lightness over strength and at Montjuich his 'Superteam' of Graham Hill and Jochen Rindt both crashed at the same place on the circuit as their flimsy wings failed. Convinced that the cars would go even faster without wings, Chapman bullied his drivers into dropping them. John Miles refused, but Jochen Rindt, who had written open letters to Chapman pleading for a little more bulk and safety, crashed fatally at Monza, winning a posthumous championship. In 1971, Lotus had to enter as Worldwide Racing to dodge prosecution over Rindt's death. With his 'take it to the limit' approach, it was no surprise that Chapman's boat hulls were also prone to fail at sea.

Despite his poor record on safety, Colin Chapman was widely respected in the sport. From 1961 his team manager Andrew Ferguson helped set up the first version of FOCA, at the time a cost-saving travel agency for the teams, which Bernie Ecclestone would later forge into a powerful marketing body. During the height of Ecclestone's war with F1 boss Jean-Marie Balestre, Balestre offered Chapman the opportunity to seize control of FOCA, which he rejected. A long-term consequence of this rejection would be the eventual banning of many of Lotus's 'gizmos'.

The innovative Chapman was always coming up against, and then wriggling through, the rules – a quality that his rival <u>Enzo Ferrari</u> greatly admired. In his early 750 cc racing days, he had won everything by redesigning the air intake in a way the rule-makers had never envisaged, and in the 1172 cc formula he changed the camshaft timing to become 'preposterously fast'. Again the rules had to be changed. Chapman's clear vision of Formula One was as the pinnacle of racing design, a proving ground for new ideas with a limited number of parameters and a crash test, rather than a 'quagmire of plagiarism, chicanery and petty rule interpretation forced by lobbies manipulated by people for whom sport has no meaning', which is pretty much what it would become. Chapman was smart enough to guess that his planned turbo car would be banned, and even joined in the decrying of Gordon Murray's Brabham 'fan car', but despite warnings, he persevered with the double chassis 88. When rival teams threatened to boycott it, the stewards caved in, commending the design even as they banned it. It was a shattering blow, and even though he bounced back with more innovations and won in Austria in 1982 after four lean years, Chapman noticeably preferred the world of microlight aircraft, where anything went.

After Chapman's death in 1982, the Lotus brand and heritage were strong enough for it to carry on until 1994, but the production-car finances were always suspect and quality controls and construction standards were variable. (Early Elites were prone to parting company with their axles.) Financial demands increased after a share sale, and high taxation, VAT, oil crises and the three-day week all damaged the company, as did crooked distributors in the US, such that output fell from 3,000 to 500 cars a year. These pressures led to some questionable involvement in the fraudulent DeLorean scheme and, had he lived, Chapman might have had some hard questions to answer. (Though he was lucky with lawyers – one brief, chasing him for unpaid fees, accidentally electrocuted himself with a faulty shaver socket.)

What Colin Chapman might have created given more time and money and a more sympathetic business and sporting culture is a mystery. As is the name Lotus. He never let on where it came from.

Herbert Chapman – 'Football's Napoleon'

Herbert Chapman, inside forward and manager, born Kiveton Park, Sheffield 19 January 1878, died 6 January 1934. Playing career: 1897–1909. Managerial career: Northampton Town 1907–12 (Southern League champions 1909), Leeds City 1912–18, Huddersfield Town 1921–5 (league champions 1924, 25, FA Cup 1922), Arsenal 1925–34 (league champions, 1931, 33, FA Cup 1930).

Herbert Chapman was the original football manager – the first to organise an entire club to serve his vision, and thus the most influential in history. If that wasn't enough, he also revolutionised soccer with his counter-attacking style and new team formation and brought branding into sport for the first time.

Chapman's entry into management was, like his playing career, low-key. Candidly described by the *Tottenham Herald* as 'hardly in the first flight of footballers', the tubby Spurs striker's main distinguishing features were the vast number of poor, disorganised teams he had played for, his part-time studies as a mining engineer and his yellow boots. Tipped off by team-mate Walter Bull, who didn't want the job, Chapman was hired by lowly Northampton Town as secretary-manager. No one else wanted to run an impoverished club in a rugby town.

In retrospect, the signs of Chapman's future greatness were all there – the yellow boots, designed to make him easier to pick out, showed imagination and original thinking while the mining studies proved his work rate, management abilities and desire to improve himself. He had also learned from bitter experience in bad and fractured clubs, where the directors picked and punished the team, trainers concentrated on fitness rather than ball work and knots of players worked out ad hoc tactics just before the match. He knew there had to be a better way.

After a short-lived honeymoon, Northampton soon slid down the table to fifth from bottom. It was now that Chapman showed his first big tactical insight, arguing after a game against Norwich that one could attack for too long. In place of the usual tactic of trying to dominate the midfield and pack the box, Northampton began to draw back, soaking up pressure, creating space at the back and looking to counter-attack with fast running and low accurate passes rather than what he termed 'senseless centring into a packed box'. As results improved, Chapman won the trust of the players with his open team talks and a policy of encouragement rather than the usual 'hire and fire'. Good cup results against Newcastle, Sheffield Wednesday and Nottingham Forest encouraged the directors to spend up to £200 on better players and embark on a pioneering tour of Germany, and the team topped the Southern League with record totals of points, wins and goals.

Second Division Leeds City were the next struggling soccer club in a rugby town to buy into the Chapman method. After helping them secure re-election and a best-ever league position, Chapman was fined for illegal payments that he himself had brought to the FA's attention, and he turned to running a wartime munitions factory – which he did with great success. This probably helped saved his football career after a second scandal over claims of illegal payments at Leeds. These were common throughout the League, but led to the FA making an example of Leeds, with its players sold off and Chapman banned from the game. Once the FA relented, he made a low-key return to football in 1921, initially as assistant manager of Huddersfield, where he soon took full charge, implementing two more tactical innovations. The first was using veteran Clem Stephenson as a withdrawn centre forward, able to launch attacks from behind the halfway line and avoid the tighter offside laws of the day. The second was using centre half Tom Wilson, not as a traditional playmaker, but as a withdrawn 'stopper', breaking up attacks. This helped win the FA Cup – although the press and purists decried these negative tactics. Once again, progress on the pitch was marked by progress off it, with better facilities and the encouragement of women spectators, who the gentlemanly Chapman hoped would curb some of the excesses of the crowd.

Chapman's last move was to The Arsenal in 1925. This was another struggling, indebted club ruled over by interfering chairman Sir Henry Norris, who insisted on cheap, tall players and seemed to be getting rid of Chapman's predecessor Leslie Knighton to avoid paying him a bonus. Chapman negotiated a promise of full control and, although he declared that it would take five years to create a winning side, reached an FA Cup quarter-final in 1926.

The 1925/6 season was the first with a two-man offside rule and led to Chapman conceiving his famous 'WM' formation. After a 7–0 defeat by a Newcastle side bolstered by withdrawn centre half Charlie

Spencer, Chapman's big signing, captain and striker Charles Buchan threatened to leave unless The Arsenal developed a plan to deal with the new law. The more obvious part of the plan was to use their own centre half as a third back, marking the opposing centre forward. The less obvious move was to swap the defensive duties of the full backs and wing halves, with the former spreading wide to mark the wingers, while the wing halves turned their attention to the opposing inside halves. Thus was born the defensive 'M', anchored by new centre half Herbie Roberts, a flame-haired bargain from Oswestry Town. As the first 'policeman centre half', the intelligent but phlegmatic Roberts abandoned playmaking for breaking up attacks and passing out fast to his counter-attacking forwards.

Up front, The Arsenal were also remodelled into what gradually became an attacking 'W'. Instead of withdrawing Buchan from inside half to midfield as he had requested, Chapman used reserve player Andy Neil as a withdrawn inside forward, linking the defence with his 'flying columns' – the centre forward and wingers. Instead of old-fashioned mazy dribbles and crossing into a packed box, they cut inside to attack the goal direct. From 1928 the team turned striker Alex James into an inside forward and really flew. A first FA Cup was secured and the following season Arsenal became the first southern side to win the League Championship, with 66 points – a record that stood for 30 years. Other club managers found it easier to emulate Arsenal's defence than their attack and their overall legacy was one of stopper centre halves and 'bull at a gate' number nines.

Chapman's success, and Norris's suspension by the FA in 1927, gave 'Football's Napoleon' a degree of control which other ambitious managers such as Billy Walker at Wednesday could only dream of. Soon Chapman was creating a brand as well as a team, as he renamed the team simply Arsenal and got the London Electric Railway to do the same for nearby Gillespie Road tube station. He also invented a catchy new nickname – 'The Gunners'. On the pitch he pioneered shirts rather than jerseys, squad numbering (though the League took until 1939 to accept it) and, from 1933, more distinctive white sleeves. The man with the yellow boots also experimented with rubber studs for frosty pitches and hooped blue socks to make team-mates instantly recognisable when looking down at the ball. Recognising that greyhounds and speedway were challenging football's popularity, and having seen floodlights in use in Belgium in

1930, he installed the first set at Highbury and used a more visible white ball – although the FA insisted on carrying on playing winter games in unlit afternoon gloom.

Above all, in 1931 Arsenal started building a magnificent new art deco West Stand in gleaming Snowcrete – the design of architect Claude Waterlow Ferrier. Though conventional in construction and seating only 4,000, it was a landmark that soon attracted international matches. With the turnstiles monitored by an automatic 'enumerator' to avoid crushes, Chapman arranged music at half-time and a motorised cart bearing team news. Having seen referees mistime matches, he had a giant countdown clock installed at one end, until the FA insisted it be replaced with a conventional one. It was Chapman who insisted that the team should applaud all four sides of the ground when they emerged from the tunnel, and later suggested that the teams at the FA Cup final should march out together and dine together afterwards. Another suggestion – that of having referees on each half of the pitch – was overtaken by Stanley Rous's 1934 diagonal system. Meanwhile Arsenal and Chapman's fame were spread with the first radio broadcast against Everton in 1927 and Herbert's own lively *Sunday Express* column.

While he was a visionary and a showman, Chapman was also an operator. Arsenal cast their net wide for bargains and one player was literally signed at the pithead, while Eddie Hapgood came from lowly Kettering and Cliff Bastin, renowned for his evasive runs and hard shots, was signed aged just 17. In the case of the elegant David Jack, Chapman knocked £1,500 off the price by getting the Bolton directors tipsy while he drank ginger ale from a whisky glass. A favoured ploy was to bid for an unobtainable player, and then put in a cheap offer for the man he really wanted. Of course, not every signing worked, and he recruited several star forwards before 1932, all of whom failed to displace veteran striker Jack Lambert. Meanwhile, the reserves or 'spare men' played to the same pattern as the first team so that they could be easily slotted in. In an age when players were deprived of the ball 'to keep them keen', Arsenal introduced head tennis as well as a range of experimental exercise machines, while trainer Tom Whittaker became Britain's expert on treating sports injuries.

Chapman was justly famous for his man management, convincing George Male that he would become the League's finest full back, and converting Alex James from a scorer to a maker of goals. Chapman once dragged James from his sickbed to play, in the knowledge that this would bring out the best in him, but also once promised him a cruise and packed him off in a trawler to work as a deckhand. There was steel behind the cheery team talks and chummy photo-ops. Chapman disliked excessive goal celebrations and foul play; dissent and independence all led straight to the exit. After a shock cup defeat to Walsall in 1933, a number of players were got rid of fast.

Internationally, Chapman was well aware of the progress being made by foreign coaches like Vittorio Pozzo, who had assimilated his tactics. A proponent of a European league, Chapman wanted the Austrian Rudy Hiden as a goalie but was blocked by League and players' union opposition to foreign players. He also became the first de facto national manager, although the team and formation was chosen for him and all he could really contribute was the team talk and the suggestion that the number of selectors be reduced from 12 to a more sensible three. His England team drew against Pozzo's Italy and beat Switzerland.

Chapman's career at Arsenal was ended by his sudden and unexpected death from pneumonia after defying illness to check out opponents Sheffield Wednesday and attend a reserves match. His coffin was carried by a 2-2-2 of David Jack, Eddie Hapgood, Joe Hulme, Jack Lambert, Cliff Bastin and Alex James. Art and football don't normally mix well, but a fine bust of Chapman was commissioned from Jacob Epstein, and is now on display at the Emirates stadium. (Fittingly, both Arsenal and Huddersfield have two of the best and most modern stadiums.)

Just as Huddersfield had gone on winning without him, so Arsenal prospered too, building a second matching stand in 1936 and going on to more success under Tom Whittaker. In 1937, eight years after he made the suggestion, the FA implemented the penalty circle, which Chapman had seen in Italy. Tactically, many clubs didn't catch up with Arsenal until the 1950s, when the League and FA also finally sanctioned floodlighting. Chapman's idea of artificial pitches wouldn't come about until the 1960s, while in British football his notion of an enclosed, roofed stadium would have to wait for the Millennium Stadium in 1999. Today, artificial means of detecting goals are being developed in place of the 'goal judges' he called for. Seventy years after his death, it seems that British football is finally catching up with Herbert Chapman.

William Clarke

William Clarke, cricketer, born Nottingham 24 December 1798, died 25 August 1856. First-class career: Kent 1854, Nottinghamshire 1835–55, Surrey 1852, Suffolk 1847, Sussex 1854, MCC 1846–53; 143 matches, 795 wickets (10.06), 2,133 runs (10.13).

In the early summer of 1846, a new and rather unlikely-looking bowler presented himself at Lord's to work as a hired hand, bowling for their aristocratic members. William Clarke had only one eye and was tall and sombre-looking, a former bricklayer and publican from Nottingham, a northern outpost of the game that was usually well off the MCC's radar. Already aged 47, Clarke hadn't played his first big match until 37 and, if that wasn't odd enough, he still bowled with the out-of-date underarm style, producing a gently turning leg break. Little did the MCC suspect that they were letting in a leg-spinning incubus, a player who between 1847 and 1853 would average 340 wickets a season with what J.F. Sutton termed his 'deceitful twisting peculiars', and then blow apart their cosy world of dining, law-making and prestige matches, turning cricket into a truly national sport. Had they guessed his intentions, the MCC certainly wouldn't have let him in.

Having played cricket from the age of 17, Clarke had used his bowling skill to leave the building trade and buy a pub, and from 1830 was captain of the Nottingham Old Team. Five years later they became a county club, twice beating Sussex. A judicious second marriage to Mrs Chapman of the Trent Bridge Inn in 1837 enabled him to open an enclosed ground instead of playing on the racecourse, but with few teams good enough to draw a crowd, Clarke seemed to have failed, his best years now behind him. In fact, they were just starting.

As a bowler he might be slow, but William Clarke could vary pace, length and flight at will, combining all three with spin and a sudden high kick. Attritional, economical and subtle, he forced batsmen to take risks to score and soon got the measure of them – even star batsman <u>Felix</u> – using his lobs to 'think his opponents out'. Clarke was also one of the first bowlers to go for catches, a technique that had been regarded as little better than run-outs by some, and for which bowlers were credited only from 1836. At the time 'correct' style encouraged batsmen to stay within their crease and rely on fast footwork, an approach that, Clarke declared, 'was ready money to him'. Another ruse was unsettling batsmen with an early form of sledging. 'We shall have an h'accident, sir, in a minute' was a favourite.

Clarke had also come to Lord's with a plan – to cash in on the growing popularity of cricket across the country. Having mothballed his Nottinghamshire side, he waited until the MCC scattered for the grouse moors before amassing the best pros, whose seasonal wages the MCC had just cut, and announcing a late-season tour of the North, playing '22 of Sheffield', '18 of Manchester' and '18 of Yorkshire'. The response was so good that the following year, having skittled the Gentlemen for 42 and 58, he staged a tour of 17 venues that took in such unheard-of spots as Liverpool, Leeds and Newcastle. As he departed Lord's, he told equipment-maker Robert Dark that he would soon be selling balls by the cartload. With his All England XI, Clarke made money right, left and centre with £65 appearance fees, gate money and hospitality, and enjoyed 'sodas, duck and cigars', though he kept a lid on players' wages and made no allowance for expenses. In revenge, Felix produced a leaflet on 'How to Play Clarke'.

The following season Clarke was gone from Lord's, playing over 20 games a season with All England and picking up new talents like John Jackson, the original 'demon bowler' whose deliveries were so fast that one batsman, declared 'not out', announced that he'd like to leave the crease anyway. William's careful attitude to money caused a 'United England' breakaway led by John Wisden and Jemmy 'Ploughboy' Dean, but rather than return to the MCC, they formed their own United England side in 1852. Soon there were nearly a dozen such sides and the number of cricket pros had shot up from a handful to hundreds. New county clubs were springing up in cities such as Manchester, which, to quote his critic James Pycroft, Clarke had 'inoculated with cricket'. Though the MCC banned the new professionals from Lord's, they couldn't prevent their more impoverished and talented members from playing for these barnstorming sides.

Despite a broken wrist and a growing stoutness from all the duck and sodas, Clarke played on to the age of 56 and took a wicket with his last ball, although by that time he was clearly second best to John Wisden. Clarke had proved that a non-revolutionary could create a revolution. All he really wanted to do was take wickets and earn a living, but in the new railway era of mass travel and big crowds he had turned cricket into a national game. From 1850, the reinstated Nottingham were playing Surrey, breathing new life into the county game, and their North–South rivalry created a strong professional, northern 'backbone' for the national side. In 1859, three years after William Clarke's death, his successor George Parr would join up with Wisden to stage the first overseas tour to the US, which in turn encouraged tours of Australia and the first great international sporting rivalry.

Today there is a stand named after Clarke at his old stomping ground, Trent Bridge.

Harry Clasper

Harry Clasper, rower, coach and boatbuilder, born Dunston, Gateshead 5 July 1812, died 13 July 1870. Winner of the Thames Fours 1845, 48, 49, 56, 57, 59, 62.

Rowing's big annual outing may be on the Thames tideway, but it was on the 'coaly Tyne' that modern boat racing was invented by a surprisingly small and light oarsman named Harry Clasper.

The crucial moment came on 16 July 1842 when Clasper and a local crew, including two of his brothers, took on the London watermen for £150 and lost the lot badly in front of a vast and hugely disappointed crowd. Clasper had been their sporting hero, a miner's son who had survived an explosion in the notorious Jarrow pit to become a boat-builder, wherryman and publican. Since 1840 he had been winning in his new racing boat *The Hawk*, built in the traditional 'lapstrake' style, with oak planks nailed over an elm frame. In designing it, Clasper had made the usual trade-offs – too long and the drag would increase, too short and it would always be climbing its bow wave, too heavy and it wouldn't win, too light and it wouldn't survive the trip. As for width, a wider boat slowed you down, but gave you more leverage on the oar, hinged between traditional thole pins on the side.

After his humiliating and expensive defeat, Clasper declared that 'We weren't beaten by the rowing, we were beaten by the boat,' noting that the Londoners' lighter boat had sat higher in the water – sacrificing stability for lower drag, while its curved oars made a clean exit harder, but gave more grip. In the Paradise boatyard, Clasper set out to build a revolutionary new boat to win what was then regarded as the championship of the world.

Harry's new boat – *The Five Brothers* – looked like nothing ever seen before. It was more like half a gun barrel than a boat. Long and narrow, with the rowers seated directly behind each other, it was smooth-skinned, its polished mahogany planks fitted side by side and it had an internal keel. (Local rival Robert Jewitt and London oarsmen the Pococks both claimed that this was industrial espionage, copying their designs.) To compensate for the narrowness of the craft, Harry had extended iron outriggers from the hull, perfecting an idea first tried out in wood by Anthony Brown in 1828 and improved upon by Frank Emmet's 1830 *Eagle*. Rowing such an unstable craft required expert oarsmanship and Clasper, who stroked the boat, drilled his four brothers in what became known as the Derwenthaugh crew, rowing with a 'Tyne stroke' that used the legs to push across the fixed seats. At first, their bizarre-looking design was seen as unmanly and was laughed at, but soon they were local champions and ready to take their revenge against the cockneys.

On 26 June 1845 Clasper's crew took on two London crews on the Thames in an even lighter boat, the *Lord Ravensworth*, with Harry at stroke, brother Richard coxing and William, Robert and Uncle Ned supplying the power. (Ned was filling in for recently deceased brother Edward.) This time they won by 1½ lengths and returned to a tumultuous welcome – minus the canny Harry, who had stayed on to sell the boat for £80 and pick up more orders. Back in Newcastle, Harry profited from his sales and expanded his pub chain to eight, while remaining a champion rower. In 1851, he became the only pro ever invited to Henley and won a career total of £2,600. As well as building a prototype smooth-skinned eight in 1848, he also trained the next great local hero and world champion, Robert Chambers.

Harry's ideas of lightness would be taken still further by Tyne oarsman Matthew Taylor, who in 1854 built *The Victoria* with a 'shell' hull over an internal skeleton. The following year, one of his fours won at Henley, the year after which a Taylor-made eight carried off the Grand Challenge Cup at Henley, despite an inexperienced crew. In 1857, one of his shells even won the Boat Race. (This was the same year that J.C. Babcock of New York's Nassau Rowing Club started work on a sliding seat.) The shape of the modern racing eight was now in place, although there were still some important inventions to come – notably from US rower and boatbuilder Michael Davis.

After Harry's death from 'congestion of the brain', 100,000 mourners jammed the streets and his body had to be ferried up the Tyne to St Mary's Church in Whickham. The *Newcastle Daily Chronicle* remarked that a 'lowly artisan' had gained 'a pathway to fame and a sepulchre kings might enjoy'. A final sporting legacy had come eight years earlier at a testimonial dinner for him at Balmbra's Music Hall when entertainer Geordie Ridley tried out a new tune, 'The Blaydon Races', a theme tune for Newcastle United ever since.

Brian Close

Dennis Brian Close CBE, cricketer and footballer, born Rawdon, Yorkshire 24 February 1931. Cricket career: Yorkshire 1949–70 (county champions 1959, 60, 62, 63, 66, 67, 68, Gillette Cup 1969), Somerset 1971–7. Football career: Leeds United 1948–9, Arsenal 1951–2, Bradford City 1952–3. First-class record: 786 matches, 34,994 runs (33.26), 1,171 wickets (26.42). Test career 1949–76, 22 matches, 887 runs (25.34). Test selector 1979–81. Wisden Cricketer of the Year 1964.

Whether fielding suicidally close at square leg, standing up to intimidatory bowling, or going toe to toe with the cricket 'authorities', the tall, balding Brian Close was charismatic, teak-hard and never far from controversy. One of his many run-ins with the men in blazers bequeathed us the first rules on over rates – a change that addressed the age-old problem of slow play in county matches.

Close, an excellent student and all-round sportsman, was an England youth international at football, but found it impossible to combine playing for both Yorkshire and Arsenal and concentrated on cricket from 1949. His time at Bradford City ended with a career-threatening injury and signalled the end of the 'two-season player', with pressure on him and another Yorkshire cricketer, Fred Trueman of Lincoln City, to give up the winter job.

As a cricketer Close was a prodigy, the first and only player to do the double (1,000 runs and 100 wickets) in his debut season. Unconventional in his stroke-making – his sweep offended the purists – he batted left-handed but bowled right-handed off-spinners. Despite getting into trouble for failing to 'mister' an opponent when playing for the Players against the Gentlemen, he became England's youngest Test cricketer and was called up while on national service – actually while confined to barracks for absenting himself from an Army match. Probably selected too young, Close fell out with his team-mates, became injured, gave up his wicket cheaply and was never a regular Test player thereafter. At county level, however, he had great success and was captain from 1962. Unselfish and pragmatic, he favoured quick runs rather than big totals, and disliked the new one-day matches, which he felt encouraged negative tactics.

In 1963, he became a hero after standing up to the West Indies bowlers unprotected, even advancing down the wicket to make 70. Chosen as the replacement captain for an England side already 3–0 down against the West Indies, he caught Gary Sobers for a duck to win the final Test. His record as captain stood at seven wins from eight matches before his Test career juddered to a halt, sacked after refusing to apologise for slow play against Warwickshire while chasing a third County Championship in five years. Having bowled just two overs in 15 minutes, Fred Trueman was reported to have been attacked by an enraged umbrella-wielding Warwickshire supporter, while Close had to be protected from the crowd. The result was a new regulation stipulating 20 overs in the last hour of a first-class match, plus penalties for slow over rates. This could penalise a hard-working team with tired bowlers, and allowed teams to time-waste in the last hour but one, but it did help to end the slow-play problem in county matches, though Test captains could continue to run down the clock.

Sacked from Yorkshire for offending Lancashire's chairman Lionel Lister, the supposedly xenophobic Close accepted a non-captain's role at Somerset but was soon leading a successful multinational side that specialised in one-day wins. According to county team-mate Ian Botham, Close was the toughest player he ever saw. Struck on the head by a speeding ball, the pole-axed Close is supposed to have cried 'Catch it!' as he fell. Having toured apartheid South Africa and Rhodesia, he made his final Test appearance aged 45 at Old Trafford where, in poor light on a cracked, hard wicket, he and John Edrich stood up to a prolonged and brutal battering from Clive Lloyd's West Indians. During the 162-minute assault, both men suffered cracked ribs, bruises and lacerations for the sake of 20 runs. In theory Law 42.6 dealt with intimidation, but it was (as usual) loosely worded. There was no inter-vention from umpire Lloyd Budd and only one from Bill Alley. After calls to outlaw the bouncer, the lawmakers responded with another marginal strengthening of the laws.

Close played until 55, giving up his own wicket for the last time when just six runs short of a 35,000 total. As chairman of Yorkshire's cricket committee in the 1980s, Close fought many battles with Geoff Boycott, whose individualistic run-amassing style was anathema to him. A selector from 1979 to 1981, he carried on coaching into his seventies.

John Cooper

John Newton Cooper CBE, racing car racer and designer, born Kingston, Surrey 17 July 1923, died 24 December 2000. Constructors' championship 1959, 60. Driver's championship 1959, 60. Overall record: 16 Grand Prix victories, 11 pole positions, 14 fastest laps. President British Racing Sports Car Club.

In 1946 the future of motor racing was drawn out in chalk on a garage floor in Surbiton by the father-and-son team of Charles and John Cooper. Cooper junior, whose father's business included sports-car mainten- ance, had been driving cars since the age of eight and by 12 was clocking up 87 mph around Brooklands, until the stewards intervened. After a wartime spent working on experimental engineering projects, he set to work designing a home-made car to race in Formula 500, the most junior formula, in which tiny-engined cars drove round improvised tracks on unused airstrips.

Charles's thrift and practicality and John's ebullience and inventive- ness turned a single-cylinder JAP bike engine and clutch, two Fiat Topolino chassis and some struts from an air-raid shelter into a car, but instead of placing the engine in front of the driver, they put it at the back, driving the wheels by a chain. This was not the first time the driver had been put in front of the engine – Ferdinand Porsche had done so before the war – but the car reversed all current thinking. For example, Enzo Ferrari, whose team dominated motor sport, was emphatic that 'the ox pulls the cart' and that success came through clever engine design that maximised power.

The rear-engine Cooper soon proved to have huge advantages over conventional layouts. The driver wasn't cooked by the engine, the low overall weight improved acceleration and the weight distribution was easier on the tyres, improving traction and making it easier to handle – especially as the diminishing fuel load didn't affect the handling so badly. Unable to afford to make an engine themselves, the Coopers had to use what they could find, but were soon clocking up 93 mph laps and impressed a whole new generation of drivers with their cheap 'ugly bugs', finished in dark green and white. By 1951, John was already winning Formula Three races on Germany's perilous Avus track.

By this time the Coopers were formally in the racing business, and although there were rows between father and son over Charles's reluctance to spend and invest, they upped the power by boring another 800 cc out of a 1.1-litre Coventry Climax engine, originally designed for a fire pump. Untroubled by the costs and complexity of engine design, the Coopers were able to adjust and refine their cars, developing better streamlining, disc brakes and rear coil suspension – unlike the power-obsessed continentals. This would create a lasting tension in the sport between the continental grandees and the British 'garageistes', as Ferrari termed them.

From 1954, a new 2.5-litre limit favoured smaller cars in Formula One, as did a requirement to use pump petrol, which limited the power advantage of more conventional racing cars. Driver 'Black' Jack Brabham made Coopers' F1 debut in a 2.2-litre Bristol-engined car and achieved fifth place in the 1957 British GP at Aintree. The following year, Rob Walker's team flew Stirling Moss's lightweight Cooper to Argentina – another first for a sport where cars had always been shipped. Though it cost just one-tenth of the price of the other cars on the track, Moss drove the Cooper to victory. Knowing that its four-bolt wheels would make any pit stop fatal, mechanic Alf Francis pretended to be getting ready for a stop to fool the chasing Ferraris and Moss drove his tyres down to the canvas to clinch victory by two seconds.

The 1959 and 1960 seasons brought successive F1 drivers' and constructors' championships for Brabham and Cooper, while other manufacturers copied their engine layout. In the latter season, Jack achieved five wins on the bounce in a low-lying Cooper T53 and John Cooper celebrated by turning somersaults in the pit lane. Ahead of the pack thanks to a new five-speed gearbox, Brabham himself was a racing revolutionary, driving in a new head-down opposite-lock style, and at Indianapolis he set a 144 mph first lap – silencing the critics who had laughed at his spindly car. In America too, the writing was on the wall for the big front-engined racer.

In 1961, the Cooper revolution was confirmed by a new 1.5-litre formula that required lighter, more compact cars, although the engineering innovations were now coming from Colin Chapman's Lotus, to which Stirling Moss switched. Although Bruce McLaren won for Cooper at Monaco in 1962, Charles's excessive caution limited the firm's growth and development. John crashed spectacularly while testing on the Kingston bypass and his father died the following year. Better-funded and resourced teams had overtaken the Surbiton '*garageistes*' and the racing business was sold. Although the Cooper name continued in F1 until 1969, there were to be no more Grand Prix wins after South Africa in 1967. In the meantime, the inventor of rear-engined Grand Prix cars turned to front-engined rallying. Despite the doubts of designer Alec Issigonis, John created a souped-up Mini that was so effective that other teams campaigned to get it disqualified. Though British Leyland stopped production in 1971, the company carried on turning out kit cars until the model was revived in 1985. When Mini was bought by BMW, the Cooper name was still valued and retained.

Henry Cotton

Sir Thomas Henry Cotton MBE, golfer, born Congleton, Cheshire 28 January 1907, died 22 December 1987. British Open Champion 1934, 37, 48. World Golf Hall of Fame 1980.

Henry Cotton was not only Britain's greatest player between World War I and the early 1980s – when Nick Faldo began winning major tournaments – but he also raised the status of the golf professional from a mere club servant, actually getting him into the clubhouse.

Talent-spotted as a boy by J.H. Taylor, who recognised his determination and concentration, Henry Cotton was always an exceptional professional – a middle-class public schoolboy, rather than a promoted greenkeeper. At Alleyn's School in Dulwich, Cotton refused a caning, was banned from cricket and announced that he was going to play golf instead. After leaving school at 16, he became an assistant professional at Fulwell, despite the low prize money and rules that made it possible to earn cash as an amateur. Quickly recognised as a talent, and remarked on for actually practising between rounds, Cotton became the youngest ever club pro at Langley Park aged just 19 and was eighth in that year's Open.

With his Jermyn Street shirts and aloof and self-reliant manner, Cotton was a new type of player who attracted the attention of the press, public and manufacturers. His first Open win at Sandwich included a round of just 65, commemorated by Dunlop with their '65' ball. As a player he was said to be 'equal parts Hagen and Hogan'. Like Walter Hagen, he was witty, immaculately and expensively dressed and used a limousine to change in, rather than the tent the organisers provided. With two houses and a suite at the Grosvenor, he was a natural showman who carried out trick-shot demonstrations at the Coliseum Theatre, endorsed 'anti-shank' clubs with offset heads, charged high fees for lessons and wrote books and articles in a journalistic career that lasted 30 years. The 'Ben Hogan' element in his character was that he practised until his hands bled, was intolerant of fools or failure and recommended that ambitious young golfers avoid distractions like marriage. Cotton and Hogan rarely met. Ben's dislike of Britain and its links courses usually kept him on the other side of the pond.

As a player, Cotton's greatest year was 1937, when he won his second Open at Carnoustie in heavy rain, with the entire US Ryder Cup team in pursuit. However, his most lasting contribution was undoubtedly the new status he gave to professionals, who had traditionally entered the clubhouse (if at all) by the back door. Cotton insisted on honorary membership as a condition of his joining the Ashridge Club, where a spacious pro's shop was also created for him.

Invalided out of the war in 1943, Cotton earned an MBE for his fund-raising exhibition matches. The war took a huge bite out of his career, but he was still captaining Ryder Cup teams in 1947 and 1953, and created the Golf Foundation to promote junior golf. He made enemies during his career and, though never a great putter himself, was particularly critical after the young Peter Alliss fluffed a 15-foot chip and three-putted on the 18th to help lose the 1953 Ryder Cup. Cotton's sharp tongue may be one reason why it was not until 1969 that he was made an R&A member. Playing competitively until 1977, he settled in Portugal, where he transformed a series of paddy fields into the Penina course. Although he was temporarily exiled by a coup in 1974, he returned and carried on designing courses and promoting new gadgets such as a lorry tyre that could be struck to build strength in the wrists. It was only just before his death that he was awarded a knighthood.

Pierre de Coubertin

Pierre de Frédy, Baron de Coubertin, sportsman and administrator, born Paris 1 January 1863, died Lausanne 2 September 1937. General secretary International Olympic Commission 1894–6, president 1896–1924, honorary president 1925–37.

Baron Pierre de Coubertin was a small, slim man with a very big moustache and some even bigger ideas – notably that of re-establishing the ancient Greek Olympic games as an independent, universal and all-embracing sporting contest, at a time when such a thing seemed quite preposterous. Today, the Olympic games remain the world's greatest sporting occasion. Much of their success, as well as many of their quirks and past difficulties, can be attributed to the baron and his influence.

Born into an ancient but fairly minor French noble family that supposedly included Rubens and Cyrano de Bergerac, de Coubertin was a recreational rower, boxer and fencer who also refereed the first French rugby final in 1892. However, his real interest was in the philosophy and sociology of sport. As a liberal educational reformer, he admired the way that sports-loving British schools embraced games as a way of building up character as well as bodies. De Coubertin thought that sports-shunning France could adopt the same ideas to build itself up and help prevent another military disaster like the Franco-Prussian war, in which Alsace and Lorraine had been lost and the Emperor and much of the army rounded up. In years to come, one of the Olympics' many quirks would be that it featured individuals representing nations. More than one athlete has asked why it can't just be man against man, but of course it is the national interest that keeps the public more interested in it than in any other sporting tournament. As a spectator remarked to de Coubertin at the first games in Greece in 1896, 'I see your internationalism does not kill national spirit, it strengthens it.'

By the age of 20, de Coubertin was touring British schools, universities and sports clubs, where he admired their independence and shunning of cash prizes. When his International Olympic Committee was set up, it would be a self-elected club like Henley, which would future-proof it against attempted raids from rival organisations like

UNESCO or takeovers by political power blocs. On the other hand, de Coubertin was blind to the social exclusivity of these clubs. When the IOC established its rules on amateurism, it broadly followed those of the British Amateur Athletic Association, which in theory meant that anyone could compete, but in practice made it very difficult for working people. The rules on amateurism were never very clear and de Coubertin's own sport of fencing immediately bent them to allow professional instructors to compete.

De Coubertin founded his first national Physical Education Committee in 1888 – five years before the first France v England athletic contest – and began to gather around him impressive-sounding aristocrats as well as loyal supporters like Henri Didon, who invented the Olympics' 'Faster, Higher, Stronger' motto. A copious essayist who wrote 60,000 pages during his lifetime, de Coubertin recognised the power of the written word, and in the years to come it was often only his control of the *Olympic Bulletin* that kept the games out of the hands of the Greek government, who felt they owned them, and the Americans, who thought they could run them more profitably. Control of the *Bulletin* also enabled de Coubertin to downplay previous attempts to resuscitate the Olympics – notably Evangelis Zappas's earlier games.

Having assembled 79 delegates from 12 countries around the world to kick-start the IOC, de Coubertin showed its intended international scope by immediately planning follow-up games in Paris in 1900 and a US city in 1904. This would make the Olympics a global games and keep it out of the hands of national governments, but would also leave it at the mercy of the local organisers, over which it had imperfect or no control. Though de Coubertin worked on the plan and budgets, it was Demetrius Vikelas who did most of the organising work for Athens in 1896. De Coubertin nearly resigned in 1895 and only turned up for the contest 12 days beforehand. From the beginning, the intention was to recreate an ideal rather than the ancient games itself, and the stadium chosen was the Panathenaic, rather than wrecked and remote Olympia. Had it not been for donor George Averoff, even these under-funded games, in which the 'swimming pool' was the Bay of Zea, would have foundered. Runner Spiridon Louis's success in the marathon set the seal on their success, and also showed how the Olympics could begin to create new sports and standardise existing ones. Over the years to come, rules for events like the discus and triple jump would all be sorted out at the games, after the very first title was won by triple jumper James Connolly with a hop, hop and jump. The notion of any women competing seemed extraordinary to de Coubertin, whose liberalism extended to education for women, but not athletics. When the Greek female athlete Stamata Revithi ran a solo marathon to get to the stadium, she was left outside and treated only with pity and amusement.

Over the next three Olympics, the problems of funding were solved by making the games an add-on to trade fairs – with fairly disastrous results. At the chaotic 1900 Paris games, fencing was conducted as part of the Cutlery Exhibition and swimming as part of Lifesaving. Lost in the politics, de Coubertin resigned from the organising committee of a contest so fragmented that many athletes never even realised they had been in an Olympic Games. On the plus side, this lack of organisation meant that women were admitted into the golf and tennis tournaments and also crewed yachts. It would be left to local organisers and sports federations to admit female competitors rather than de Coubertin's IOC, and he later fretted in print about the 'The Crisis in Marriage and the New Women'. The baron also fell for various non-scientific theories about the difficulties female athletes experienced in childbirth. He may have been particularly sensitive on the subject because his own son Jacques suffered brain damage after being left in the sun too long and daughter Marie suffered from emotional problems. (Two beloved nephews both died in the war.)

Worse followed at the 1904 St Louis games, from which de Coubertin, regarded by the US organisers as a freak and a nuisance, absented himself. In fact, it was the St Louis games themselves that were, for all the highfaluting baloney spouted by organiser James Sullivan, at worst a glorified freak show. De Coubertin, who had toured the US, was impressed by its vigour but horrified by its racism, and was shocked by reports that the hucksters in charge had staged exhibitions in which various 'primitive people' were invited to fight or climb greasy poles. On this occasion, de Coubertin was abundantly clear: 'That outrageous charade will lose any appeal when black, red and yellow men learn to run, jump and throw and leave the white men behind them.' Luckily, he had gathered about him sufficient loyal Brits, Germans, Czechs, Swedes and New Zealanders to keep the show on the road. It is a testimony to this anglophile Frenchman that he managed to keep even the

British interested in a sporting event outside their own islands. In fact, de Coubertin's faith in British fair play led the games into their next controversy. After downplaying the very successful 1906 Athens games, which he regarded as a sop to the Greek government, and deciding to award the first gold medals, there were numerous complaints over the judging decisions at London in 1908. From this emerged the present policy of having the IOC own the Olympics, the local organisers run them, the National Olympic Committees select the athletes and the federations judge the events. After the 1908 and 1912 Olympics, a host of international sporting federations, such as the IAAF in athletics and FINA in swimming, would spring up – many of them run by French officials keen to emulate de Coubertin's success. Again, this was something of a hostage to fortune, leaving the games open to abuse by incompetent or corrupt officials over whom they had no control.

After making the best of a bad job on four occasions, the 1912 Stockholm games, complete with cultural events and the mixing of the athletes, finally saw de Coubertin's Olympic ideal come alive. He even won a gold medal himself for an anonymously entered 'Ode to Sports'. Keen to heal the rift between France and Germany, de Coubertin had eagerly anticipated the 1916 Berlin games (cancelled for obvious reasons), and after World War I he hurried to re-establish the Olympics, inventing a five-ring flag that symbolised the unity of the continents, with every nation's national colours represented by at least one ring. Today, de Coubertin's flag is said to be the world's most recognised symbol and selling the rights to use it provides much of the finance he always struggled to raise. However, his internationalism did not extend as far as actually inviting the defeated powers to compete, and it wasn't until Juan Antonio Samaranch's time in charge that the IOC started issuing the invitations rather than leaving it to the organisers – another frequent source of political trouble in years to come. The 1920 Antwerp games were also the first outing for the modern pentathlon, a sport de Coubertin himself invented as a test of character and military skills and which, for a while, was administered by the IOC itself. Sadly, his other pet sport, rugby, disregarded the games and was dropped after a series of no-shows.

In 1921 his worsening finances caused de Coubertin to hand control to an IOC executive board on which he neglected to place himself. At a time when workers' sports fairs were being held across Europe, de Coubertin, an enthusiast for universal education, found that the aristocrats with whom he had surrounded himself had no interest in welcoming working people to the Olympics. This helped lead to a split with the Soviets in particular that would last until 1950. Matters might have been helped in 1925, had a move to allow broken-time payments for working men and women not been narrowly defeated. As it was, there were to be years of disqualifications, rows over money and secret payments before professional athletes were finally admitted in the 1980s. As for costly, time-consuming team games like football, the 1932 LA organisers were free to dump them from the programme, which helped give rise to the World Cup – while tennis also left after stars such as de Coubertin's favourite Suzanne Lenglen turned professional. By now the games were clearly destined for success, with more and more countries competing, and this brought the first limits on the number of entrants per nation.

De Coubertin's last Olympics were the German games he had always wanted to see – the 1936 Berlin games. On the one hand, these were the 'Nazi games', taken over by Hitler for prestige purposes, but such was the power of the Olympics that de Coubertin could still announce, 'We are in Olympia' and the IOC was able to get the Nazis to respect its rules. In the years to come, the IOC would maintain a quasi-diplomatic role for itself and argue that its contests, to quote Jesse Owens, 'lead not to Berlin or Moscow, but the best in all of us'. De Coubertin also lived to witness an Olympic regional spin-off – the first Asian games.

The Baron died of 'apoplexy' in 1937, having spent his fortune on the Olympics and been reduced to living in lodgings. His heart was buried at Olympia and today there is a Pierre de Coubertin medal for fair play, supporting his notion that 'what matters is not to have won but to have fought well'. (This is one of the few awards that the IOC hasn't been able to devalue by awarding to semi-criminal cronies, wealthy sponsors and tin-pot dictators.) Curiously neglected by his home nation, de Coubertin never received a Nobel Prize for Peace, perhaps because the backing for it came from Hitler's government. Since de Coubertin's death, various scandals have shown the fallibility and occasional corruption of IOC members, as well as the greed and incompetence of the organisers. On the other hand, they have also repeatedly shown the power of the Olympics to grab and hold the attention of the world. The baron's money was well spent.

Danie 'Doc' Craven

Dr Daniel Hartman Craven, scrum half, rugby coach and administrator, born Lindley, South Africa 11 October 1910, died 4 January 1993. Test career: 16 Tests 1931–8, 6 points. South African coach 1949–56. President South African Rugby Board 1956–93. Chairman IRB. IRB Hall of Fame 2007.

Aged just 45, Danie Craven became the seventh and last president of the South African Rugby Board. For the next 37 years he would rule the sport, seeing it gradually excluded from international competition and then suddenly brought back in.

As a player, Craven's selection at the age of 22 was so unpopular that his father cancelled the papers to avoid having to read the criticism. However, he soon proved to combine good handling and kicking with solid tackling and was so versatile that in consecutive Tests he played at fly half, scrum half, number 8 and centre. At scrum half he introduced <u>Oubass Markötter</u>'s high-speed dive pass to international rugby. Though it has since been displaced by the more accurate spin pass, which leaves the scrum half on his feet, Craven created time and space for master kicker Bennie Osler, when not triggering sneak attacks with the first specialist number 8, André McDonald. (Craven also had the privilege of playing alongside Ebbo Bastard, often introduced by radio broadcasters as 'a player I shall call Smith'.) The 1930s Boks, who Craven would eventually captain, defeated England, Australia, the Lions and the All Blacks. Danie was usually in the thick of the action, but he was fast enough to escape without a single broken bone.

After the war Craven returned to his old university, Stellenbosch, as director of physical education and rugby coach – guiding the 'Maties' to 25 championships during his 43 years in charge. He was national coach from 1949 – officially described as the 'assistant manager', as coaching was banned. Craven was one of the first coaches to look at every position in detail – choosing different flankers for particular sides of the scrum. His tactic of twisting the ball into the scrum was the beginning of the end for it as a genuine contest for the ball, while at line-outs Craven's Boks were the first to place blockers in front of and behind the jumper. They won ten internationals in a row, and in 1949 Danie insulted the All Blacks by publicly offering to coach them. Forwards like Hennie Muller were so disruptive that Craven himself became an advocate of changing the laws to give opposing backs more room.

Having won 17 out of 23 tests, including a 44–0 massacre of the Scots at Murrayfield, Craven secured the presidency of the white South African Rugby Board (SARB) thanks partly to the influence of the Broederbond, the secret Afrikaner society whose members surrounded him. As SARB president, Craven continued to coach and manage the Springboks, arranging the first short jet-age tour by France in 1958 and building up Argentinian rugby through Springbok tours. He was particularly effective in stamping out rugby league, ensuring it never got a foothold in South Africa, and even tried to get South Africa into the Five Nations. Within the IRB, Craven was a progressive, favouring the 'Australian Dispensation' which penalised direct kicks into touch outside the 25-yard line, the introduction of 10 yards space between forwards and backs at line-outs, and, in 1976, the Welsh move to allow substitutes.

A tougher nut to crack was the growing opposition to apartheid. Long ignored by the white rugby world, apartheid became harder to overlook after 4 September 1965, when Prime Minister Verwoerd made it clear that no Maori players would be allowed to tour South Africa. Trying to wriggle round this, Craven was attacked as a racist by anti-apartheid protesters and as a traitor by conservative whites. For the rest of his life he would be fighting on two fronts, knowing that change was essential, but never able to move fast enough to satisfy the outside world.

Craven used his scrum half's determination and guile to keep up international contacts. Despite demonstrations in Ireland in 1965, a near vote to ban South Africa by the Welsh Rugby Union and the cancellation of an All Black tour in 1967, Craven persevered through the violent 'demo tours' of Britain in 1969/70 and Australia in 1971, and persuaded his government to allow multiracial touring sides as well as 'multinational' tours against South Africa's various racial 'nations'. However, the Boks themselves remained all-white. Both Lion John Taylor and All Black Ken Gray boycotted South African tours, where the police permanently injured some white anti-apartheid protesters.

In 1975 Craven held the first 'illegal' multiracial trial and fielded a multiracial President's XV. Trials for the Boks were also multiracial from 1977, and in 1980 fly half Errol Tobias became the first black Springbok. Official tours – which led to the 1976 Montreal Olympics boycott – carried on until violent protests wrecked the 1980 tour of New Zealand. Thereafter, the Springboks only had paid-for 'rebel' opposition – a mockery of Craven's amateur ethos, which weakened his standing in the IRB and at home.

Though heavily in debt (thanks to an absconding business partner and his first wife's debt-financed share deals), Craven built up the SARB's funding and staged racially integrated rugby clinics across South Africa, repeatedly risking his life as he hedge-hopped across the veldt in all conditions. Visiting small towns and mines to stage multiracial clinics didn't do much to spread the rugby gospel to black South Africans in the townships, but Craven felt it helped break white resistance to apartheid within sport, and his integrated Craven Week youth tournament even split the National Party itself. By 1991, when the SARB and the black SARU finally merged, Craven could claim 200,000 non-white players.

In 1988, Craven had persuaded the SARB to let him talk to the exiled ANC, striking up a friendship with future president Thabo Mbeki and head of sport Steve Tshwete, who as a prisoner had been secretary of the Robben Island Rugby Club. Four years before the end of white rule, Craven was already talking about a 'new South Africa', and the opportunity to see international rugby again was a powerful incentive for many whites to vote for change. After 1992, Craven recommended an easy return for the new SARFU Boks against weaker opposition, but instead they suffered a series of defeats to the strongest nations.

Danie Craven never lived to see the awarding of the 1995 Rugby World Cup finals to South Africa, or Francois Pienaar and Nelson Mandela hoisting the trophy. Though he died when his international prestige was at its lowest, he is commemorated by various awards and tournaments, plus the Stellenbosch University stadium and the South Stand at Cape Town's Newlands stadium. At his funeral, the *dominee* (pastor) likened him to Moses – a complicated, driven man, guiding his people, but destined never to see the Promised Land.

Alfred Critchley

Brigadier General Alfred Cecil Critchley CMG, CBE, DSO, sporting promoter, born Calgary 1890, died 9 February 1963.

Setting up British greyhound racing in 1926 was only one incident in the packed life of Alfred Critchley. That 'Critch' had even lived that long was something of a miracle, as his life was a catalogue of adventures, including plane crashes, near shipwrecks, amoebic dysentery, kidnap attempts, spying on him by the US secret service plus various scrapes in ranching and oil exploration. On the Western Front, he became the youngest brigadier general in the imperial armies. Placed in charge of aircrew training, where the death rate was a scarcely credible 50 per cent, he sacked all the old instructors before introducing fitness training and the use of live ammunition.

By 1926, the well-connected Critch had begun to rationalise the cement industry and create the Blue Circle brand when he was inspired by American Charlie Munn to set up the Greyhound Racing Association with capital of £14,000. Critch reasoned that the sport would appeal to working men like his valet George Barton who were unable to watch the horse races they bet on. After a slow start opposite the Belle Vue grounds in Manchester, crowds totalling 330,000 were being attracted within the first year, drawn by the first weekday evening sport, which offered exciting races and a fair gamble in convenient urban stadiums. In London, the GRA took over the abandoned White City Olympic stadium, where the grass was waist high, and invested £300,000, installing 32 million candle-power floodlights, restaurants and a car park, and drawing nightly crowds of over 40,000. As well as seeking to bring rugby league to the capital by importing Wigan Highfield, Critch's GRA built a second London track at Harringay, followed by New Cross, Leeds, Birmingham, Liverpool and White City Manchester. They also built the Harringay Arena – for many years the home of British showjumping and the site of the first televised boxing and ice hockey matches. Along the way, the GRA had to fight racketeers and rioters as well as gambling reformers who wanted to close the sport down.

Along with his father, Critch wrote the rule book for racing, specifying strict security to prevent the dogs being 'got at'. By 1947, when it was hit by punitive taxes, greyhound racing was attracting more fans than football itself.

By this time, Critchley had been elected MP for Twickenham, after campaigning in an autogyro and a coach and four. Never a great parliamentarian, he did succeed in getting the Tote legalised for greyhound racing, and the world's largest 640-booth mechanical Tote computer was installed at the White City. Here his son John – later to die in service – experimented with the UK's first photo-finish camera. In wartime, Critch returned to aircrew training and helped turn round the fortunes of BOAC and establish Heathrow, which, if he had had his way, would have been properly planned, named 'Churchill Field' and equipped with a lake for flying boats. After the war, he set up the pioneering Skyways airline, which was closed down by his political enemies in the Labour government and taken over by loss-making state-subsidised carriers.

Despite his successes with the dogs, Critch's favourite sport was golf. He won amateur tournaments across Europe, touring by plane or in his own unique articulated Buick-drawn caravan, complete with a telephone link to the chauffeur up front. Despite sudden blindness in 1953, he was captain of Wentworth for three years and helped organise the Canada Cup – golf's World Cup equivalent. He died in 1963, with greyhound racing in decline because of more TV viewing and betting legalisation that gave handouts for well-connected horse racing but nothing for the 'poor man's racecourse'.

Hansie Cronje

Wessel Johannes Cronje, cricketer, born Bloemfontein 25 September 1969, died 1 June 2002. First-class career: Orange Free State 1988–2000, Leicestershire 1995; 184 matches, 12,103 runs (43.69); 68 Tests 1992–2000 (53 as captain), 3,714 runs (36.41); 188 ODIs, 5,565 runs (38.64).

'I'm sorry, Doc, I haven't been honest with you.'

It was this 4 a.m. call to South African cricket boss Dr Ali Bacher from his national captain Hansie Cronje that revealed that cricket corruption was not, as many fondly hoped, restricted to the Indian subcontinent and that absolutely anyone might be involved.

Within South Africa the April 2000 revelations were, to quote writer Tim de Lisle, like 'discovering the Queen had been fiddling her expenses'. Cronje was post-apartheid South Africa's greatest sporting son, a first-class player since the age of 18, Orange Free State captain at 21 and acting national captain within three years. Renowned for his slog sweep, Hansie was a dogged batsman who batted for seven hours to record his first century. An especially good player of spin, he successfully took on Shane Warne, the most dangerous bowler of the day. As a bowler Cronje was naggingly accurate, and as well as being tactically astute, he was determined – once playing with a broken finger. As early as 1992, South Africa had come close to defeating the West Indians, then the world's best team, and by 2000 they had beaten all bar the Australians and thrashed the West Indies 5–0. Cronje's record as a captain – 11 losses from 50 Tests and 99 wins out of 138 One Day Internationals (ODIs) – ranked just behind Australia's Ricky Ponting and Allan Border.

Complaints about Hansie's uneven batting and an over-cautious approach were usually regarded as griping – as were reports of his growing aloofness and a money and power obsession. With a declared salary of 1.6 million rand and four sponsors contributing A$3 million, his success was generally admired. So too was his record of having opposed apartheid before majority rule; but he then fought against having racial quotas imposed on the national team. His conversion to Christianity came about after he killed a six-year-old girl in bad visibility on Natal's North Coast road. On the other hand, his worsening temper had led him to deliberately step on a ball, pressurise umpires and even ram a stump through one official's door.

Given his caution on the pitch, it seemed odd that in 2000 Cronje sacrificed an innings to make a game of the fifth Test against England at Centurion and that his generous declaration helped them to win by two wickets. Another peculiarity was opening a game against India with off-spinner Derek Crookes. It wasn't until 7 April that news broke that he had been caught selling information to bookie Sanjay Chawla for $10–15,000. Purely by chance, an Indian police phone tap had caught them, and after some less than convincing denials, the truth came out – resulting in an investigation by retired judge Edwin King.

During the King investigation it soon became clear how Cronje had been enmeshed in cricketing corruption. In India and Pakistan, where cricket attracts ten times as much money as horse racing, gamblers will bet on a single ball, while the endless, pointless made-for-TV one-day internationals meant little to the players and were ripe for exploitation. As early as January 1995, Hansie was offered $10,000 to throw a Mandela Cup match and the following year was introduced to bookie Mukesh Gupta by subsequently disgraced Indian captain Mohammad Azharuddin. In December that year, Gupta paid him $30,000 to throw a Test – although Hansie didn't – and the whole South African team came close to throwing a benefit match for a fee which Cronje negoti-ated up to $350,000. Within a month Hansie was supplying Gupta with Test match information in return for a commission on wins, though he turned down $300,000 to throw a Test. By March 2000, fielding up to 20 calls a day from bookies, he thought he had persuaded Herschelle Gibbs to score 20 runs max and Henry Williams to allow 50 runs off ten overs in a Pepsi Cup game in Nagpur, while double-crossing the bookies into believing that two other team-mates were also involved and needed paying. He was selling information about the England Test series when the trap closed.

Offered immunity from prosecution, Cronje confessed that 'in a moment of weakness . . .' (actually several moments) '. . . I allowed Satan to dictate terms to me.' The use of off-spinner Crookes was shown to have been a minor betting coup, while the 'sporting' Centurion Test had been worth 53,000 rand plus a leather jacket from bookie Marlon Aronstam. Overall, Cronje admitted pocketing $140,000 over five years, variously smuggled into the country, placed in 72 accounts or stashed around his house. Gibbs and Williams collected six-month bans, while Hansie was banned for life – as were Azharuddin and Pakistan captain Saleem Malik. The charming fantasist was soon on the comeback trail, appealing against the decision and supported by the nation's cricket fans. However, in June 2002, his sense of thrift caught up with him after he hitched a lift home on a cargo plane that crashed into Craddock Peak in bad weather. Given his gambling links with organised crime, this produced the anticipated number of conspiracy theories.

Although there has been crookedness and gambling throughout cricket's history, the King revelations, plus the revelation that Australia's Shane Warne and Mark Waugh had received cash for information, showed that corruption might occur anywhere. Perhaps the last word on the subject is also one of the first. Writing in *The Cricket Field* in 1851, the Reverend James Pycroft noted, 'The constant habit of betting will take the honesty out of any man.'

Johan Cruyff

Hendrik Johannes Cruyff, footballer and manager, born 25 April 1947 Bettendorp, Holland. Playing career: Ajax 1964–73, 1981–3 (league champions 1966, 67, 68, 70, 72, 73, 82, 83, cup winners 1967, 70, 71, 72, 83, European Cup 1971, 72, 73, Uefa Super Cup 1972, 73, Intercontinental Cup 1972), Barcelona 1973–8 (league champions 1974, cup winners 1978), Los Angeles Aztecs 1978, Washington Diplomats 1979, Levante 1980, Feyenoord 1983–4 (league champions 1984, cup winners 1984); Holland 1966–77, 48 caps, 33 goals. Managerial career: Ajax 1985–8 (cup winners 1986, 87, Cup Winners' Cup 1987), Barcelona 1988–96 (league champions 1991, 92, 93, 94, cup winners 1990, Cup Winners' Cup 1989, European Cup 1992, Uefa Super Cup 1992). European Footballer of the year 1971, 73, 74.

Deep-lying, stick-thin and wearing number 14, the extraordinarily talented Johan Cruyff was never going to be a conventional attacker. In fact, he became football's most original star – the only player to have a move named after him.

When 'Jopie' Cruyff was growing up in the shadow of the Ajax stadium, his grocer father Manus boldly claimed that his son's speed, skills and anticipation meant he would be a '£10,000 player' one day. Sadly, Manus never lived to see his son's first-team debut at 17. Within two years, Johan had achieved mastery of the game – able do things naturally that other players simply couldn't be taught. Cruyff's biographer Nico Scheepmaker credits him as the first 'four-footed' player, equally happy to use the inside or outside of either foot. The most obvious example of his exceptional control and balance was his trademark turn, shaping as if to pass or cross, but then using the inside of his foot to drag the ball back behind his standing leg and wrong-foot the defender. After seeing Cruyff play, Rudolf Nureyev said he should have been a dancer.

By 19, Cruyff was an international, and announced the arrival of Dutch football with the 'Match in the Mist' against Bill Shankly's Liverpool. Twice he came from nowhere to score in front of a bemused Kop, and the 5–1 scoreline finally persuaded Shankly that Ajax was more than just a scouring powder.

Like his hero Alfredo di Stéfano, Cruyff covered much of the pitch, attacking from deep to score goals and make assists no other player

could attempt. Perhaps his most extraordinary goal was in an early 1970s
friendly when, having been one-on-one with the keeper, he turned his
back to the goal and ran away, backheeling the ball into the goal without
breaking stride. The pursuing goalie had almost reached the halfway
line before he realised Cruyff had scored.

Having mastered the game – he could judge a pass by sound alone –
Cruyff developed a fascination for tactics, 'falling and failing' as he questioned everything and worked to make the team around him play even
better. His commitment to attacking football would lead to a triumph over
the defensive orthodoxy, which at the time seemed the only way to win.

Cruyff was fortunate in playing for Ajax, a team with an attacking
tradition since the days of expat trainer Jack Reynolds. First selected
by Vic Buckingham, from 1964 Cruyff played under <u>Rinus Michels</u>,
developing a unique style which combined the Dutch traditions of hard
work (up to four training sessions a day) and individual freedom, as
players were encouraged to express themselves on the pitch. Cruyff
built an almost telepathic understanding with players such as left winger
Piet Keizer, and the team began covering for each other, developing
multiple passing options to flummox defences and getting the ball to
either the player in space, or the one who could create it.

From this understanding emerged the idea of 'total football', with
Cruyff at the head of a central spine of goalkeeper, two central defenders,
an attacking defender, a central midfielder and an attacker. Typically,
the keeper got the ball out fast to the attacking defender, who then
combined with the central midfielder and the deep-lying Cruyff,
preventing him becoming isolated. Meanwhile, the rest of the team
created space and stretched defences used to more conventional play.
Should an attack break down, the front men immediately switched to
defence, harrying the ball carrier while the four-man defence moved
up to compress the space available and catch the opposition offside.
The tactic helped conserve the Ajax players' energy, but required great
understanding and concentration. They dominated European football
in the early 1970s, unpicking the defences of Juventus and Inter Milan,
and at one point held five different championships. Despite the departures of Michels for Barcelona in 1971 and Cruyff for a world-record
fee in 1973, the system was robust enough to win two more European
Cups, before the loss of players such as Johan Neeskens, Johnny Rep
and Gerry Muhren finally undermined it.

In what should have been their greatest hour, Cruyff's Dutch national side reached the 1974 World Cup final and scored the fastest-ever goal but, as Johnny Rep put it, 'forgot to score the second' and paid for their decision to play an injured Rob Rensenbrink at left wing, so that he could fulfil his boot contract. The team were defeated by Germany, who combined their usual grit with their own innovative system – two attacking wingers in Uli Hoeness and Jurgen Grabowski, an attacking defender in Paul Breitner and the 'libero' <u>Franz Beckenbauer</u>. Cruyff himself played so deep that his marker Berti Vogts got in more attacks than he did. At the following World Cup, Cruyff was absent for a tangle of reasons, including his distaste for the murderous Argentinian junta. Without him the team reached the final but lost to Argentina.

At Barcelona, Cruyff and Michels reawakened a 'sleeping giant', achieving a first league win in 14 years. They later reunited in LA after Cruyff, who had lost money on a pig-farming business, returned to the game. In 1983, he ruffled feathers by becoming player-manager at Ajax's great rivals Feyenoord without a coaching diploma, but won the league championship through flexible, attacking play. (For example, Ruud Gullit was irregularly switched from right wing to sweeper.) Back at Ajax, Cruyff adapted his ideas to create a 1-3-3-3 formation, designed to overcome the defensive, counter-attacking style of the time. In his first match as technical director, he descended the stands to reorder the team on the pitch and transform a 1–3 scoreline into a 5–3 win. He was carefully vague when describing winning tactics: 'If I wanted you to understand, I'd have explained it better.' After falling out with Ajax, he returned to Barcelona as coach, achieving a first European Cup win and four league championships in eight years – more than the club had managed in 30 years. Though he came close to taking over the Dutch national side in 1992, the deal fell through, thanks to one of his recurring arguments over pay, and four years later he left Barcelona, where he had never got on with president Josep Lluís Núñez.

A great believer in the value of sport for all, Cruyff's Welfare Foundation promotes games amongst people with physical and mental disabilities and has founded a school in India.

Stan Cullis

Stanley Cullis, footballer and manager, born Ellesmere Port 25 October 1916, died 28 February 2001. Playing career: Wolverhampton Wanderers 1933–47, England 12 caps, 20 wartime internationals. Management career: assistant manager Wolves 1947–8, manager 1948–64 (FA Cup 1949, 60, league champions 1954, 58, 59), Birmingham City 1965–70.

'There they are. The champions of the world!' Those were the words attributed to Stan Cullis as he presented his exhausted, exhilarated Wolves players to the press. Cullis's Cubs' 3–2 win over the Hungarian masters Honvéd in 1954 seemed all the more significant as six of the defeated side had previously beaten England 3–6 and 7–1. Their floodlit match, followed by the nation on BBC TV and radio – until the Beeb switched over to *The Show Band Show* with 90 seconds left to play – restored national footballing pride and seemed to usher in a new era of floodlit, broadcast soccer. Stan's quote, probably misreported, would also lead directly to the creation of the European Cup.

The Wolves victory was really a triumph for 'physique over technique', as their apprentices (including a young Ron Atkinson) had been instructed to water the pitch into a strength-sapping quagmire. Wise heads also noted that Red Star Belgrade, well adrift in the Yugoslav League, had also beaten Honvéd without being declared 'Champions of the World'. Former French international and editor of *L'Equipe* Gabriel Hanot called for a midweek championship to settle the issue, gaining the support of Juan Touzón of the Spanish FA and Santiago Bernabeu of Real Madrid. Despite FIFA and UEFA's objections, within nine months a midweek club tournament was in place, using Cullis's floodlit fiestas as a template and setting European football on the road to riches.

The 1954 victory for traditional British grit fitted the style of Cullis, a tough player toughened still further by military service. As a manager, the balding Stan favoured rigorous training and strict discipline, and his dressing-downs were famous, though he never swore, preferring 'flipping' and 'flopping' to more conventional obscenities. In fact, his whole life exemplified personal honour, hard work and self-improvement. Born into poverty, with a severely disabled mother and a father who refused to let him go to grammar school, he taught himself French, Esperanto and shorthand as well as football. He was Wolves' captain at 20 and England's youngest ever at 22, though he was briefly dropped for refusing to do a Nazi salute at Berlin in 1938. By 1947, he had been warned off playing because of the effect of repeatedly heading hard leather balls. In his final match as a player he could have brought down Liverpool's Albert Stubbins to secure the League Championship, but his principles wouldn't let him do it.

Wolves claimed the FA Cup within two years of Cullis becoming manager – their first trophy since 1908 – and became the team of the 1950s, succeeding through teamwork, fitness, high-tempo play and close marking at the back. Up front, Cullis favoured long, accurate passes, crosses into goal and pressure from the halfbacks, which produced 100+ goals in four consecutive seasons, but was derided by some as 'kick and rush'.

Supported by Wolves' chairman Joe Baker, Cullis, who studied European sides and favoured a world club championship, set up one of the first organised youth and scouting systems, created a 'nursery side' in Wath Wanderers, and argued for the televising of football to bring in more fans, a mid-season break and a smaller first division. After staging his first 'floodlit fiestas', complete with fluorescent shirts and illuminated linesmen's flags, he helped persuade the FA to allow floodlit cup matches – despite the complaints of cinema owners who feared losing business and residents who didn't like the new pylons. Wolves even contemplated a futuristic new double-decker stadium with curved, cantilevered stands, concourses and undercover parking, which would have been quite revolutionary in British football.

Though Wolves came within a point of the double in 1959/60, their 1960 FA Cup marked the end of the good times and some supporters threw rubbish in protest at their rough tactics. More tellingly, the team never did better than the European Cup quarter-finals, where they were beaten 9–2 on aggregate by Helenio Herrera's Barcelona. Herrera declared that Wolves, with their outdated reliance on strength, had 'no method, no technique'. The end of the maximum wage, led by Cullis's admirer and fellow West Midlands manager Jimmy Hill, gave players more freedom to move and Cullis wasn't prepared to countenance the illegal payments they now demanded. As his team fell apart, old soccer injuries may have contributed to his mini-stroke, and Joe Baker was replaced as chairman by ex-second-hand car dealer John Ireland, who came close to making Stan swear. In 1964, Stan's was the first high-profile managerial sacking in British football – an event so seismic it shared top billing with the calling of a general election. Ireland rewarded thirty years of service from a manager who had 'kicked every ball' by requesting that he return the £4 the club had advanced against his phone bill. Fans boycotted matches in protest, tore up their season tickets and wrote letters of sympathy. Apart from a mid-1970s purple patch, when they won the League Cup, Wolves have never again threatened the top of the league.

Cullis's return to management with Birmingham City brought two good cup runs and near promotion in 1968, but a poor 1969/70 season ended his career, while Don Revie's Leeds prospered with a similarly tough but intelligent style. A benefit organised by Villa's Doug Ellis raised funds for his retirement and nursing care, and the rebuilt Molineux now has a statue and a Stan Cullis stand. It is on the site of the old North Bank, where tens of thousands of Black Country fans once stood in the cold night air, roaring on Cullis's Cubs.

'Adi' Dassler

Adolf Dassler, shoemaker and businessman, born Herzogenaurach, Germany 3 November 1900, died 6 September 1978.

Adolf 'Adi' Dassler not only founded a huge sports business but also created dozens of innovative new shoe designs to help athletes win Olympic gold medals and World Cups. His business, founded after World War I in the small Bavarian town of Herzogenaurach, would eventually kill off the amateur tradition in athletics and usher in a new world of professionalism, endorsement and sponsorship.

Having survived the Western Front, Adi and his brother Rudolf founded their sports shoe company at a time when such a thing was unknown in Germany. Adi, the shorter, quieter and younger of the two, was a keen athlete and a striver for perfection who was to register 700 patents in his life. At first using bike-powered machinery, the Dasslers made lighter running shoes than ever before, with Adi using scales to shave the weight down and signature strips of leather to reinforce the shoe. Contacts with German track coach Jo Waitzer helped the spread of these lighter shoes and soon many athletes were wearing Waitzer-endorsed spikes. Another boost was the Gleichschaltung, which involved compulsory reorganisation of sport by the Nazis, which boosted the sports market. At the 1936 Berlin Olympics both brothers recognised the value of having their shoes worn by an outstanding athlete and managed to get Jesse Owens to wear them.

During the war the Dasslers produced 'Kampf' and 'Blitz' models until wartime pressures led to them switching to army boot production, while Rudolf ended up working for the Gestapo. The two brothers, both sharing a single home with their families, fell out bitterly over the drafting of employees and after the war Rudi spent a year in jail while Adi's wife Kathe personally saved the factory from destruction by the American forces. Adi himself was able to escape most of the charges against him and was soon supplying US troops with ice hockey, base-ball and basketball boots made from scrounged materials. When Rudolf returned from his incarceration, he soon took half the staff (mostly sales people) to set up a rival company on the other side of the river Aurach. This was named Ruda, although 'Puma' was soon preferred. As 'Addas' was already in use by a children's shoe company, Adi chose 'Adidas', and after debating two or four stripes settled on three for better visibility in photos and on screen. The Finnish shoe company Karhu bartered away their rights to three stripes for a few deutschmarks and a bottle of schnapps. (Emil Zátopek removed one stripe when running, as he didn't want to appear a capitalist lackey.) Meanwhile, Puma chose a reinforcing 'formstripe' as their symbol.

In 1954, Adi's shoes received a huge publicity boost after Sepp Herberger's West German team used his new varying-length screw-in studs to win the World Cup and provoke mass jubilation. 'What a Dassler!' read one UK headline as Adidas became 'Der Sportschuh der Weltbesten' – 'The Sports Shoe of World Champions'. Adidas had already followed the South Americans by removing the toecap to make a football boot that was lighter and more sensitive – a real contrast with the old-style British boots made by firms like Manfield of Stockport, which could take two years to break in. Kathe and Adi continued to welcome potential distributors to their door – including the Humphries Brothers of Wilmslow, who distributed Umbro clothing alongside Adi's shoes. From the 1956 Melbourne Olympics, Adi's son Horst Dassler took charge of promotion, eventually setting up a parallel marketing operation in France.

While lawsuits and allegations of spying flew between Puma and Adidas, the market boomed. Adidas used new plastics and rubbers, as well as materials like kangaroo skin, which stretched in one direction only, for a better fit. Before the 1966 World Cup, Bukta offered the England team just 20 per cent off list price to wear their kit and Umbro swooped, offering a free uniform. Meanwhile, Bobby Moore did a deal that saw most of the team wearing Adidas rather than Puma. Before the final, each player received an unprecedented £1,000 in a brown envelope, which some threw around in their rooms like confetti. By 1974 the financial demands of the German team led by Franz Beckenbauer would lead to a break between Adi and the team he had accompanied to victory twenty years earlier.

Despite losing a finger to a leather-punching machine, Adi continued to perfect his shoes, creating a special non-matching pair to suit the action of high jumper Dick Fosbury and a pair of rear-lacing boots for soccer star Uwe Seeler, who was recovering from a tendon injury. Adi was even able to diagnose running faults by watching athletes on TV and sent a special pair by air to 400 metres and 800 metres Olympic gold medal winner Alberto Juantorena after he spotted a flaw in his style.

Adidas operations eventually reached a peak of 180,000 pairs a day and supplied 144 countries, but the company was dogged by chaotic ordering and distribution, amateurish advertising and a legacy of secret payments and family squabbles between Puma, Adi, Horst and the Dasslers' four daughters – all of whom were involved in the business with their families. The company was unable to fight back effectively against new rivals such as Phil Knight's Nike, and Herzogenaurach was late to enter the clothing market. When they eventually started trying to catch up with the jogging boom, their shoes were better suited to German-style runs through the woods than US pavement pounding.

Adi lived until 1978, still concentrating on the shoes and sometimes avoiding business callers by passing himself off as the gardener. After he died, he was buried in a corner of the Herzogenaurach cemetery – as far away from Rudi as possible. Although Horst took over the whole business after Kathe's death in 1984, he lived only until 1987, when the failing business was sold off for just 550 million deutschmarks. Even so, it was 2004 before the first executive dared cross the Aurach from one company to the other.

Horst Dassler

Horst Dassler, businessman, born Herzogenaurach, Germany 1936, died 9 April 1987.

'Everything is a matter of relationships,' said Horst Dassler, the sporting goods millionaire who would happily sit in the lobby of a luxury hotel on the off chance that someone important might come through. Though he appeared quiet, modest and friendly and was never a great speaker, Dassler was a workaholic with a vast appetite for intrigue that took him from promoting his father Adi's shoes to building his own secret sporting goods empire. Later, he would use his contacts to go from writing endorsement contracts to creating the modern world of sports marketing, selling the rights to the Olympics and World Cup.

The young Horst Dassler's keen eyes and hawk nose first appeared on the international sporting scene at the Melbourne Olympics in 1956. After a harrowing trip, Horst arrived to find all his shoes impounded. Undeterred, he managed to get the goods out of customs before his rivals and then announced to the astonished Australian distributor that he was going to *give them away* – a practice unknown at the time. News of Dassler's free spikes spread like wildfire among the unpaid Olympic athletes, for whom running shoes were a significant expense. Instead of paying top dollar at G.L. Law of Wimbledon for titanium spikes, UK athletes got better, lighter shoes for nothing and were happy to wear them. Dassler also made friends with the photographers to make sure his shoes got featured. Although the convention of the time was that faces were blanked out in advertisements, this didn't include press photos, where the Adidas stripes stood out so well. As a junior javelin champion and hockey player, Horst built relationships with future multiple gold champions such as Al Oerter and Bobby Morrow – a sprinter with an action so smooth he could run with a full glass balanced on his head. Other less famous athletes such as Australia's Kevan Gosper would later rise to be Olympic vice-presidents.

After returning home, Horst was soon given his own French factory to run in parallel with his father's business. The more dynamic and open-minded son soon identified new markets such as footballs, as well as cheaper means of production – having the balls sewn by prisoners of General Franco's fascist regime. He began 20 years of concerted schmoozing when he bought the Auberge de Kochersberg, a centre for wining and dining sportspeople from every nation. Horst, who spoke five languages, was eventually able to offer a cellar with 90,000 bottles, plus cigars, limousines and as much free Adidas product as you could carry.

During the 1960s, the conflict between Adidas and Puma intensified and in 1960 and 1964 gold medal sprinters Armin Hary and Bob Hayes both auctioned their endorsement rights, beginning a process that would finally overwhelm Olympic amateurism. In soccer, where Puma were stronger, Adidas used contacts such as Bobby Moore to do deals with most of the England team. As shoes were 'technical equipment', the England squad, who would receive only a £100 bonus for winning the World Cup, were able to negotiate freely. As Horst's influence spread, he was even able to quash the 400 metres record set by Lee Evans while wearing Puma's revolutionary 'brush spikes', and although at the 1968 Mexico games Puma signed up star athletes Tommie Smith and Bob Beamon, Adidas were the official supplier in the village. Horst's cousin Armin, who was attending on behalf of Puma, had his room raided, while his US agent Art Simberg was even arrested.

Elsewhere in sport, Adidas's non-slip herringbone soles and stronger leather uppers ousted old-style canvas shoes such as Converse basketball boots and Dunlop tennis shoes. By the late 1960s, 85 per cent of US basketballers had switched to Adidas, especially after Kareem Abdul-Jabbar signed a headline-grabbing $25,000 deal. In tennis, the new Robert Haillet shoe, rechristened the Stan Smith, sold 40 million pairs as a fashion item, and soon Adidas were able to offer £50,000 to win over Nike's first endorsee, Ilie Nastase, who had signed up for one-tenth the amount. A joint Adidas-Puma deal was supposed to prevent a potentially ruinous auction for Pelé, but when Puma broke the agreement, Horst deliberately bid up the price to damage his competitor. Afterwards, Adidas co-founded the Golden Boot competition for Europe's best striker, although irritatingly it was first won by the Puma-wearing Eusébio. In smaller sports such as weightlifting, friendly federations were persuaded to amend their rules so that only Adidas boots could be worn, but in general athletes were still able to choose their own 'technical equipment'. Horst used his money to first support and then control the sports federations' new organisation, the GAISF, which had been set up to grab a bigger share of Olympic TV rights. Even when IOC boss <u>Avery Brundage</u> was on the warpath, seeking to banish professional sports and those athletes who received free shoes, he didn't dare touch Adidas. (It was at Brundage's own wedding that Dassler first met <u>Juan Antonio Samaranch</u>, who would bring in a far more business-minded Olympic regime.)

From 1972, Horst was using his Olympic influence and a new trefoil design to market the first Adidas clothing. As the new sports fashion market grew, Horst's empire – still kept secret from his parents – would expand to include Pony, Arena and Coq Sportif. Having backed <u>Stanley Rous</u> for re-election as FIFA president and swung many votes behind him, Dassler gained the respect of the victor, <u>João Havelange</u>, and soon built a strong relationship with him. Dassler's influence now spread among the African nations, who were Havelange's main supporters, funding more teams and federations and publishing a cheerleading magazine named *Champion d'Afrique*. The endlessly accommodating Horst once supplied 3,000 free footballs to the deposed dictator of Burkina Faso, did production deals with East German leader Erich Honecker and supplied 10,000 pieces of free kit for the 1976 Montreal games. As Horst's power grew, some Puma representatives even began receiving death threats from unknown sources.

With the growth of global TV, Dassler reached a new peak of power with a worldwide network of political operators who would help him promote sympathetic officials such as Juan Antonio Samaranch and depose awkward ones such as FIFA's Helmut Kaser. Horst had grasped the fact that non-sporting manufacturers might want to buy into sports advertising and sponsorship and that this could be even more profitable than the sports-equipment business itself. It was time to move from paying teams and athletes to profiting from sporting federations and events. Horst teamed up with <u>Patrick Nally</u> to build up the first modern sports marketing operation – one that would eventually take over the marketing of athletics, the Olympics and the World Cup – all without any need for awkward tenders. In 1974, Adidas's involvement with the World Cup had been limited to a bidding war with Puma over the German and Dutch teams, who ended up wearing a compromise two-stripe kit, but for 1978, the plan was different. With Dassler supplying the political influence, Coca-Cola the finance and Nally the sales ability, they began marketing the 1978 Argentina World Cup to businesses – a tough sell, given that the main tournament

organiser had been assassinated by his own side, while political prisoners were being tortured within earshot of the main stadium. Despite
these presentational difficulties, the employment of a large PR company
helped make the tournament a commercial success.

At the 1980 Moscow Olympics, Nally and Dassler's new agency SMPI
smoothed their way with the organisers by supplying 32,000 free items,
particularly jeans, which were in great demand in the Eastern bloc, and
helped cement their relationship with ex-Moscow diplomat Samaranch.
During this time, there were endless intrigues and escapades – including,
it was thought/joked, the gift of a 'bugged' dog. The American government's blackout of the Moscow games was a near-disaster for the
Olympics, and Samaranch realised that the sort of funds Nally and
Dassler promised to raise were essential if the games were to continue.

In 1982 SMPI was struggling to make money from the Spanish World
Cup, battling within FIFA for exclusive rights to use its logos, while
the organisation demanded ever more money to support Havelange's
enlarged 24-team tournament. More investment was needed and secret
funding vehicles were set up, supported by Franz Beckenbauer and
other unnamed investors. Looking to the future, Horst recruited ex-
Longines PR man Sepp Blatter, and became increasingly paranoid, firing
staff and using long-range mics to monitor conversations. Dassler also
fell out with Nally, who, after negotiating to buy the company himself,
was bought out by Japanese advertising agency Dentsu. At the following
1986 World Cup, the renamed ISL would make a 30 per cent commission on the 200 million Swiss francs they raised.

By the time of the 1984 LA Olympics, Dassler was important enough
to persuade the Romanians to break the Eastern bloc boycott and attend,
while the businesslike sponsorship programme implemented by the LA
organiser Peter Ueberroth finally convinced the IOC members that big
money could be made from official sponsorships. Ueberroth himself
was unacceptable to the IOC and ISL got the gig instead. Though
forbidden from promoting Adidas, Dassler's ISL was able to negotiate
with the most important National Olympic Committees, who still
controlled the use of the rings in their own nations, and managed to
set up The Olympic Programme (TOP) as a new global sponsorship
programme. By offering up to 30 exclusive worldwide deals by product
category, ISL was able to raise $95 million in 1988 for the IOC Olympic
movement and its growing numbers of sporting hangers-on.

By this time, Adidas was losing out badly to Nike, and Dassler's lieutenants such as US distributor Angelo Anastasio used new techniques to shift product and raise the brand's profile. Even if real boxers like <u>Muhammad Ali</u> were no longer wearing customised tasselled Adidas boots, screen boxers like Sylvester Stallone ('Rocky') could still wear the stripes, while performers such as Ziggy Marley and Run DMC also promoted and sang about them.

By the mid-1980s, Horst had taken over the whole Adidas operation, which had always been riven by family quarrels. Having sold 180,000+ pairs of shoes a day at its peak, the firm was weakened by bad distribution and supply problems, and was being eaten alive by Nike and Reebok, with their lower-cost Far Eastern manufacture and better design and advertising. A takeover of their UK and US distributors landed Adidas with $120 million of unsold stock. While Nike made a fortune selling fashion gear as sports equipment, Adidas made the disastrous mistake of trying to do the reverse – using a sports name to sell city shoes – some of which bizarrely featured flavoured laces. To buy out his sisters, Dassler had to sell most of his ISL holdings, only to die of cancer in 1987 while still struggling to right the ship. Adidas was then sold to Bernard Tapie, who didn't have the money to pay for it, before being offloaded on very favourable terms to Robert Louis-Dreyfus and Christian Tourres, who continued the work Horst had started, rebuilding relationships with crucial teams/brands like AC Milan, Real Madrid and Bayern Munich. David Beckham was signed up for £4 million a year and Adidas returned to profitability, swallowing Reebok in 2004.

Without Horst Dassler's political influence, ISL folded in 2001. By this time, the IOC had quit as a client, signing up ex-ISL executives to create Meridian Marketing, but the collapse hit FIFA and the Association of Tennis Professionals hard – a reminder of how completely global sport now relied on sponsorship and advertising.

Today, highly paid lawyers and executives tread the corridors of vast sports management agencies, inventing competitions and signing up stars to keep still-vaster corporations happy. For all the excess and occasional corruption, few sports could manage without the money they bring. Even the Olympics would struggle if forced to rely on unreliable host cities and their cheesed-off taxpayers. With his cigars, 90,000 bottles and bugged dogs, Horst Dassler was their angel in disguise – although at times it was a very good disguise indeed.

Herman David

Herman David CBE, tennis administrator, born 26 June 1905, died 25 February 1974. Davis Cup captain 1953–8. International Tennis Hall of Fame 1998.

In 1968, famously a year of unrest and uprisings, tennis had its own revolution as Herman David's All England Club dumped nearly a century of tradition on its head and went 'open' to professionals and amateurs alike. This would bring a huge influx of money into the game, set rival federations against each other and create the modern world of tennis.

David, an expert on industrial diamonds, was a good enough player to take sets off <u>Fred Perry</u> and was the non-playing captain of the Davis Cup team. As early as 1959, he was campaigning for an open game, arguing that it was fairer to players, who either earned nothing for their work or were forced to earn their money surreptitiously as 'shamateurs'. He stated that amateurism had become a 'living lie' and that open competition would bring back lost stars and prevent the grand-slam championships being made irrelevant by new professional tournaments. At the time, official tennis was so traditional that even exchanging your £15 Wimbledon winner's voucher for food rather than an ornament was seen as 'bad form'. A ballot on open competition might have been won, had one proponent not been in the toilet when the crucial vote was taken. Instead, the pros became demonised and within two years only David was still holding out for open competition, with another vote comfortably defeated in 1964.

As Herman had feared, only Wimbledon still retained its prestige in 1967 when he, Bryan Cowgill of the BBC and promoter <u>Jack Kramer</u> staged an open tournament after the 1967 championships. 14,000 fans including royalty attended the (colour) televised contest, with Rod Laver beating Ken Rosewall 6–2, 6–2, 12–10. The 'old' Wimbledon now seemed ridiculous and the following December, with the support of the entire All England Committee, the LTA voted 205–5 to open up the championships – a rare example of British leadership in sport. David had a massive grin on his face, though the decision set the LTA on a collision course with the International Lawn Tennis Federation, and risked British players being expelled from foreign tournaments. In practice, the ILTF capitulated the following year, allowing national federations to make their own decisions. As the big stars returned, David became one of the first to plan a Grand Prix series to bring structure to the tennis year.

Most of the big contests soon followed Wimbledon's lead in going open, but the ILTF produced pointlessly elaborate rules for the Davis Cup, which set it in opposition to the pros. National federations who relied on Davis Cup revenues insisted on their right to suspend players who didn't show up, and when the ILTF forced the issue in 1973 there was a boycott of Wimbledon. Few of the pros would have wished such a thing on David, who was powerless to act. Players' leader Jack Kramer considered David a 'terrific fellow' and noted the distress the boycott caused him so soon before his death.

In the event, the boycott led to a surge in interest in that year's Wimbledon and opened the door for new players, but the aftermath left the game split between rival federations and promoters – all of which might have been avoided had the ILTF been as bold in its acceptance of the new era as Herman David's All England Club.

Joe Davis – 'The Sultan of Snooker'

Joe Davis OBE, billiards and snooker player and promoter, born Whitwell, Derbyshire 15 April 1901, died 10 July 1978. World professional billiards champion 1928–32, UK professional billiards champion 1934–9, 47, world professional snooker champion 1927–40, 46.

Few sportspeople have ruled and changed their game as completely as Joe Davis did snooker, dragging it up from working-class 'clogs and corduroy' obscurity to overtake and then replace its parent billiards.

It was in 1921 that Davis arrived on the billiards scene. A short, unsmiling, thickset man, Joe had learned the game in the family pub, worked in billiards halls since he was 14 and turned pro at 18. It was usual for billiards players to come from playing families and start early, but Joe was unlike most others. His cue was two ounces heavier than most, his style aggressive, crisp and accurate. Instead of long, graceful, flourishing shots, he had a short back movement and a dead level cueing action. After scoring 147 on his first visit to the table as a pro, he was second division champion by 1923, but unable to afford the £200 needed to challenge for a spot on the 'magic circle', playing in the hushed opulence of Thurston's Hall in Leicester Square. After first reaching the finals in 1926, he finally beat Tom Newman in 1928, a title he held on four occasions but twice lost to the Australian master Walter Lindrum.

It was billiards' new nursery cannon that would spawn professional snooker. The shot led to such rapid scoring that the traditional 666 points per session were soon reached and demonstration snooker matches were held to pad out the last half-hour. Though billiards champions like Tom Reece saw snooker as a game 'for navvies in their lunch hour', Joe realised that as well as requiring greater accuracy of potting and more cue ball control, it offered more excitement to the spectator with its snookers, duelling qualities and long pots. Only the aficionado could enjoy Lindrum's remorseless break-building or the complex angles, minute touches and ever-changing rules of billiards.

Good though he was at billiards, Joe was made for snooker. He practised all kinds of shots rarely seen before, mastered screw and stun to kill the ball on the unreliable nap of the tables, and thought many moves ahead, working out snooker strategy for the first time. In 1923, he played at the first tournament, organised by billiards hall owner Bill Camkins, and two years later helped originate the 'play again' rule for touching balls. In 1927, he promoted, organised and won the first Snooker World Championship, winning just £6 10s and gaining four paragraphs in *The Billiard Player*. Despite billiards champion Willie Smith's view that 'they'll never fall for this', the crowds did, particularly because the game was easier to bet on, being faster and simpler to handicap. Even so, it was hard going in the depression, when matches might offer just £1 prize money. In 1931, there were only two entries for the snooker championship, but by 1935 it had widened out. The *Daily Mail* Gold Cup contest switched from billiards, Con 'The Canadian Crasher' Stanbury demonstrated the first power shots and Thurston's was soon overflowing, as week-long sessions were held.

Joe would keep the snooker championship until 1946, before retiring undefeated. During this time he set five record breaks and his only real challenger was brother Fred, who he played in the 1940 final. In wartime, Joe raised over £125,000 for charity, playing trick shots under a mirror, and after the war moved into promotion, running the game from the old Thurston's site, the hall having been destroyed by bombing. As chairman of the Professional Billiards Association, his approval was needed to break into the game, and with his *News of the World* column to influence opinion, only Fred was unafraid to beat him, which he did just four times.

Despite his other interests, Joe dominated the sport for the first 15 years of his 'retirement' and in 1955 finally achieved the first official 147 break with regulation pockets. When the BBC and ITV began to televise contests they dealt with Joe, and most games consisted of five frames between him and AN Other. (The fixing of games to last the full five frames was not uncommon.) With his withdrawal from competition, interest went out of it and the championship became defunct between 1957 and 1964. Joe responded by trying to launch 'snooker plus' with mauve and orange balls added. In fact, it was colour TV that changed the game's fortunes from 1968, with *Pot Black* appearing on screen the year afterwards and the World Professional Billiards and Snooker Association setting up two years later. By now a new generation of players, led by John Spencer, were overtaking Joe's super-accurate control through sheer potting ability.

Davis's end came at The Crucible in 1978 after a collapse while watching brother Fred in action. Accused of running a closed shop and excluding new pros in the past, Joe simply pointed out the dangers of running poorly organised events for no money, especially when the pros were so often in dispute with the ruling Billiards Association and Control Club. Rather than having any masterplan, he said, 'All we were doing was scraping and scratching for a living.'

Michael Davis – 'The Leonardo da Vinci of Rowing'

Michael F. Davis, rower and inventor, born Ireland 1851, died (?).

There can't be many candidates for the title 'Leonardo da Vinci of Rowing', but if anyone deserves it then it must be Michael Davis. The eldest of six sons, Davis, who trained as a pharmacist in Portland, Maine, joined the local Emerald Boat Club and between 1874 and 1884 produced a series of innovations, many of which have been used ever since, while others have been forgotten and then resurrected.

In Davis's time, rowing was a big spectator sport in New England and thousands travelled to Silver Lake in 1878 to watch him take on the Boston champion Patrick 'Patsy' Regan. (After losing to Davis, Regan and 18 other passengers were killed on their way home in New England's worst train disaster.) After this victory, Davis was described by national newspaper *The Spirit of the Times* as the 'most noteworthy oarsman of the time' and would soon coach the Yale crew.

By now J.C. Babcock had perfected the sliding seat, which allowed rowers to employ their leg muscles properly, while the Troy, New York firm of Waters, Balch were producing revolutionary, though hard to repair, shells made from paper and resin. Soon Davis was producing a stream of new inventions, including a light, three-stay tubular steel outrigger in place of the old heavy solid iron. Other inventions included a steering foot stretcher to allow coxless racing, but the greatest impact was the creation of the swivelling rowlock, which allowed rowers to reach farther round for a longer stroke. Though popular in the US, it wasn't until 1905 that a Belgian crew won at Henley with them, and as late as 1949 the diehards at the Leander Club were still rowing with fixed rowlocks.

After Davis's inventions, there were no truly revolutionary changes in rowing until 1971, when the German federation and Empacher Bootswerft began creating the first fibreglass and resin shells – the modern equivalent of the old Waters, Balch boats. Ten years later, Empacher came up with another radical idea – a fixed seat with a sliding rigger and foot stretcher to stop the boat pitching backwards and forwards with each stroke. After taking the first five places at the 1982 championships, this design was banned by the authorities on grounds of cost. It was the latest in a series of fixed-seat designs dating back – surprise, surprise – to Davis himself in 1877.

In 1991, just before the Barcelona Olympics, the authorities did allow a big change in the sport, with Dick and Pete Dreissigacker's asymmetric hatchet blades, which were so effective that one crew switched to them between the Olympic semi-final and final. Had anyone before ever had the idea of a more effective asymmetric blade? You bet. Michael F. Davis of Portland, Maine – back in 1880.

Ron Dennis

Ron Dennis CBE, racing engineer and team owner, born Woking 1 June 1947. Chairman and CEO McLaren Group 1981–. Constructors championship 1984, 85, 88, 89, 90, 91, 98. Drivers championship 1984, 85, 86, 88, 89, 90, 91, 98, 99, 2008. Overall record: 162 Grand Prix victories, 141 pole positions, 137 fastest laps.

Ron Dennis, who was to bring new levels of professionalism and investment into motor sport, had a meteoric rise within it. After joining the Cooper garage aged 18, he was working on Formula Two and Three cars within two years and, after moving to Brabham with Jochen Rindt, was chief mechanic by 21. Ten years younger than most of his peers, he was already effectively running the team at US races.

At the age of 24, Dennis formed Rondel with Neil Trundle, signed up Graham Hill as a driver and even managed to extract cars on credit from Brabham. A serious accident in 1972 and the oil crisis hit the team hard, but their high standards on a low budget had impressed sponsors Philip Morris, who backed a new venture in 1975. The following year brought a new 'Project Three' with BMW and bought-in March cars, followed by success in Formula Two and Three in what was now Project Four. In 1980, Philip Morris funded a reverse takeover of the McLaren team, then languishing after the death of its founder ten years earlier. By 1981, a first victory had been secured and Dennis became a team owner at just 34.

Ron Dennis's first great impact on Formula One design was probably the carbon-fibre MP4/1, built after hiring Lola engineer John Barnard. Despite spotting new talents like Ayrton Senna (who turned down the team's first offer in 1983), ultimate success required an engine that would do justice to the new chassis. Investments from Saudi-funded TAG, who had been rebuffed after trying to buy Williams, allowed McLaren to order a new turbo engine from Porsche that was fast and frugal enough to meet the new fuel limits. In 1984, team drivers Niki Lauda and Alain Prost shared 12 out of 16 wins and scored over twice the points of the nearest competitor. By 1987, McLaren's advantage over the rest of the field was being whittled away, but it was regained by persuading Honda to quit Williams and supply engines that were

40 bhp ahead of the competition. In 1988, Alain Prost and Ayrton Senna won 15 out of 16 races and Prost clinched the 1989 title after a deliberate collision at Suzuka. Keeping two such intense rivals together proved impossible, despite a policy of equal treatment, and after Prost quit Senna broke the $1 million-a-race barrier in 1993. On one occasion, Dennis apparently concluded pay negotiations by flipping a coin for the final disputed million and reportedly clinched another deal by winning a chilli-eating challenge.

The loss of Honda engines in 1993 led to a series of short-lived deals, before signing with Mercedes the following year. Fuelled by new TV revenues and sponsorship, no advantage was too small, and during the ageing Nigel Mansell's short stay with the team, his cockpit was modified at a cost of £12,000 per extra millimetre of space. McLaren's deep pockets would enable them to survive shocks like the banning of driver-aiding 'gizmos' in 1994 and the abandonment of asymmetric/retarded braking systems in 1998, but the loss of Honda engines led to a fallow period in the early 1990s, during which Dennis attempted to purchase the entire Ligier team to secure Renault engines – a deal vetoed by Ligier's sponsor ELF. Three years later, a new alliance with Mercedes left their works team Sauber high and dry. In 1996, Williams designer Adrian Newey was hired and McLaren opened up a new HQ where over 250 employees worked on projects including the F1 supercar.

In 2000, Mercedes took a 40 per cent stake in what Dennis observed was 'a business that turns into a sport for 16 afternoons a year'. They invested an unprecedented £40 million in engine development over five seasons and poured 12,000 man-hours into aerodynamic development in just one year – a rate of spend that caused many other smaller teams to fall behind and then give up. After narrow defeat in the 2005 season, McLaren's determination to win caught up with them two years later, after Ferrari's chief engineer was discovered feeding them technical data. (This would have been a masterpiece of espionage had the documents not been taken to a Woking copy shop.) As a result, they lost all their constructors' points, and were fined $100 million but, with a reported £800 million of Vodafone sponsorship, were able to shrug off the reverse. After winning a thrilling 2008 season by a whisker, Dennis stood down as team manager in 2009. He remains famous for 'Ronspeak', a style of address that is, depending on one's viewpoint, either cautious and verbose, or careful and informative. Though Mercedes may take over the entire operation and Dennis has reduced his stake to 15 per cent, McLaren remain a big fish in the small piranha-filled pool that is F1.

Henri Desgrange – 'le Patron'

Henri Desgrange, cyclist, journalist, promoter and sports administrator, born 31 January 1865, died 16 August 1940. World hour record 1893. Tour de France president 1903–36.

Henri Desgrange didn't invent the idea of long-distance bike racing, or even of a Tour de France, but it was his force of personality that created the world's most popular annual sporting event and the sport of bicycle stage racing. Today the leader's yellow jersey still bears his initials and the colour of *Auto*, the magazine he edited.

It was *Auto* writer Géo Lefevre who first came up with the idea of linking a series of one-day classic races into a giant circuit – one of a host of promotional ideas designed to boost the failing paper, which was flatlining at 25,000 copies. *Auto* had been founded by a group of right-wing industrialists from the Auto Club de Paris, angered by Pierre Giffard's more successful green-tinted *Vélo*, which also sponsored long-distance races. Giffard had enraged them by supporting Captain Dreyfus, a Jewish-French officer unfairly convicted of treason. The Anti-Dreyfusards, who had even attacked the president of France himself at Auteuil races, were determined to have their revenge, and in 1900 even named their new paper *Auto-Vélo* as a spoiler, until the courts insisted they stop.

Desgrange, the man they had appointed editor, was an entrepreneurial keep-fit fanatic who had shifted from track to endurance racing and bought a share of the Parc des Princes velodrome. Throughout his life, Desgrange would push himself to the limit on daily cross-country runs and set up Audax – a set of timed endurance races for walkers, swimmers or skiers that puns on the French for 'audacious'. He would later declare that in his ideal Tour only one rider would manage to finish, and though he never achieved this state of perfection, he came bloody close. For 40 years he would pit himself against the riders, technical progress and team tactics, keeping the Tour so tough that during his reign the average speed only increased from 25 to 30 kph.

At first, Desgrange was unsure about Lefevre's Tour, and he avoided the start in 1903, failing to attend the race until success seemed assured.

He even announced the end of the Tour after the second running. Thanks to Desgrange's epic night-time stages, this had turned into a riot of violence in which riders were menaced by men in cars, had their fingers broken, were attacked by mobs, had their bikes sabotaged, drinks spiked and fouled and nails spread on the road, caught trains, got tows from cars and tipped emery into rivals' shorts. (After all of which, the UVF, the French cycling federation, belatedly banned the first four home for illegal feeding.) A tripled *Auto* circulation persuaded Desgrange to seize full control of the Tour and cut free from the UVF. Until 1936, riders would have to cope with both the physical challenge of the race and the mental torments created by a capricious, dictatorial *patron* addicted to excessive regulation.

After the chaos of 1904, Desgrange had to abandon night starts and adopted a policy of more shorter stages, which generated extra content for his paper. By the sixth Tour, the total distance had doubled and only 14 out of 96 riders managed to complete it. The total Tour distance would peak in 1926 at a massive 5,745 kilometres and the climbs grew steadily more demanding. Although the third Tour had introduced hill stages, it wasn't until 1910 that Alphonse Steinès, who had been pushing for mountain stages, persuaded Desgrange to include them by issuing an encouraging message from near the summit of the Tourmalet – where he had nearly died of exposure. Characteristically, Desgrange stayed away from the mountains until success was assured.

Though a famously poor race tipster, Desgrange had a flair for flamboyant prose, which could tip into apparent madness, such as in 1914 when he enthusiastically encouraged his readers to sign up and 'bayonet the Prussian bastards'. (Aged over 50, he volunteered as a private soldier, won the Croix de Guerre and was promoted to officer.) In peacetime he invented humiliating nicknames for the riders and ghosted or invented columns in their names, making light of this epic of endurance. One column entitled 'Dirty Feet' criticised the hygiene of athletes who caught his eye – or nose. Cyclists who quit the Tour or refused to sign up for it caught his full wrath and when Maurice DeWaele won despite being ill, his name was kept out of the headline, which instead read 'Victoire d'un Moribond'. In 1911, Desgrange dismissively termed Maurice Brocco a 'domestique' or servant, creating a lasting bit of cycling lingo. Typical of Desgrange's character was his *Private Eye*-style refusal to correctly spell the name of Émile Mercier, a manufacturer and sponsor who had criticised him. The yellow jersey to identify the winner appeared only belatedly and intermittently from 1919.

The success of the Tour, which drove circulation of his magazine to a claimed 854,000 in 1933, was mainly because it was a free spectacle, and Desgrange had to juggle sponsorship, entry fees and prize money to persuade enough top riders to enter. Despite having a commercial caravan of sponsors from the off, the Tour organisation was famously careful with its money, requiring riders to return every single stamped item of kit, including the Tour-approved suitcase and rain cape. Since then, commercial sponsors have remained an essential part of the Tour, with spectators scrapping in the gutter for promotional tat as the caravan zooms by. In the race itself, various cash bonuses were offered in Desgrange's time, including prizes for ascending mountains on heavy two-gear bikes without dismounting. The polka-dot King of the Mountain jersey dates from the days when Poulain chocolate presented the winner with his own weight in sweets.

In terms of the evolution of bikes and riding, Desgrange set himself against technical progress and only gave ground slowly and erratically. Starting off with wooden rims, no freewheels and just two gears, he at first required riders to repair their own bikes, so that in 1913 Eugène Christophe battled for four hours to drag his wrecked machine to a blacksmiths and repair it himself, dropping from second to fifth and acquiring an extra ten-minute penalty for the crime of allowing a boy to operate the bellows for him. Technical improvements were often only introduced when there were sponsors to fund them, and as late as 1930 the Tour was insisting on standardised yellow bikes. Freewheels were still being penalised in 1914, and though the requirement to repair rather than replace parts was dropped in 1923, it was briefly brought back. It was the mid-1930s before Tullio Campagnolo's derailleur gear ended the sight of riders dismounting to remove their back wheel, turn it around and engage a different cog, and they remained festooned in replacement inner tubes for years to come.

Though the obvious way to win in cycling is to compete as a team, sharing the work of pace setting, Desgrange fought another ultimately unsuccessful battle against this logic. By 1906, his 'no assistance' principle had already bitten the dust and he was forced to accept trainers and sponsored teams, although these were banned from 1919 to 1924. In 1927–8, in an effort to stop riders collaborating on the road, Desgrange

introduced a time-trial style of racing for several stages, which led to
excessively high dropouts and general confusion about who was actually
winning. A new regional team structure was also put in place, eliminating
the old solo *touriste-routiers* about whom Henri had so often waxed lyrical.
Official approval of teams didn't arrive until 1930 and this established
the modern pattern of domestiques sacrificing their chances for the team
leader, with poor René Vietto,who never won a Tour, forced to cycle back
along the course to donate his bike to his team leader. Despite promising the poor confused punters no changes in 1931, new time bonuses
and disqualifications appeared, and two years later the King of the
Mountains competition arrived. A 1939 rule that the final rider in every
stage would be eliminated was dropped without explanation. In the meantime, Desgrange's myriad extra rules covered feeding, drinking, tyre
changing and even taking off jerseys. Enraged riders frequently quit,
including the entire 1937 Belgian team and Sylvère Maes while wearing
yellow. In years to come, some rules – such as the limit on drinking water
– caused serious damage to the health of riders and arguably helped lead
to the death of <u>Tommy Simpson</u>.

A fervent patriot (and racist), Desgrange chose and managed the
French team, favoured red, white and blue François bikes and even
rigged the rules in favour of French riders – although his points system
actually robbed them of victory and was dropped in 1913. Even his
Tour route had a political message. The second significant hill that the
Tour climbed was the Ballon d'Alsace, then on the border with Germany,
and after Alsace-Lorraine was returned to France in 1919, the Tour was
credited with popularising the restored hexagonal shape of the country.

Desgrange remained at the helm of the Tour until 1936, when he
made the mistake of following the race over bumpy roads shortly after
a prostate operation. After handing over to Jacques Goddet, he died in
1940. Although he was against holding official wartime Tours, *Auto* was
taken over by German backers and used as a propaganda mouthpiece,
while the Velodrome d'Hiver cycling stadium, in which Desgrange had
had a stake, was used to incarcerate Jewish men, women and children
before they were deported to the concentration camps. After the war,
the collaborationist *Auto* was reborn as *L'Équipe*, which regained ownership of the Tour, though it was banned from using yellow paper.

Today Desgrange has a memorial stone on the Col du Galibier and
there is a prize for the first Tour rider to reach it – although some riders

have emptied their bladders on it instead. Despite many changes, the Tour remains the toughest major sporting event in the world. To quote le Patron, 'It is necessary to keep the Tour's inhuman side. Excess is necessary.' Since his death, this excess has continued to place insane demands on riders in all conditions with the continual threat of the elimination of backmarkers. The legacy has inevitably been one of drug use, which has repelled sponsors, come close to ending the Tour more than once and, as in 1904, even left it with no clear winner. Many of its problems, as well as its glories, can still be traced straight back to the half-deranged 'HD'.

Peter Dimmock

Peter Harold Dimmock CBE CVO, TV controller, producer and commentator, born Wandsworth 6 December 1920. BBC Controller Outside Broadcast 1946–72. Presenter *Sportsview* 1954–64. Head of BBC Enterprises 1972–7.

Noted for his 'Mr Cholmondley-Warner' appearance and delivery, Peter Dimmock probably had more influence on the development of UK sports broadcasting than any other man. An ex-RAF flight lieutenant, he was recruited to the BBC via the Press Association in 1946 and within two years was covering the London Olympics with just three cameras. By 1953 he had helped persuade the Westminster Abbey authorities to allow the cameras in for the coronation, which he himself produced and directed, creating a huge boost for TV ownership in Britain. The year after that he also persuaded the Postmaster General that key sporting events should be safeguarded for the BBC – provided that they paid a suitable fee – having raised the fearful spectre of these 'crown jewels' being seized by the then London-only commercial broadcasters. This was a complete masterstroke, as it was not long since the BBC itself had been a London-only broadcaster. With this move, Dimmock protected BBC Sports for years to come and hobbled ITV, though it began to pick up major events as early as the 1957 St Leger.

Dimmock was also involved in the jockeying for the broadcast rights for the Melbourne Olympics, which was also to have long-term consequences for both the games and the Beeb. Having once again spiked the guns of commercial TV, which had hoped to cover the event, the BBC and the US broadcasters insisted on extended free coverage as a 'news event', until the Melbourne organisers refused and the principle of Olympic sporting rights – albeit at a minuscule level – became established.

As well as fronting the first two episodes of *Grandstand*, Dimmock also presented the sports magazine *Sportsview* (later *Sportsnight*) and championed and hosted the first, rather rushed, *Sports Personality of the Year*, despite opposition from the press and internal complaints about the cost of the trophy. This showed the new power of TV in shaping sporting heroes, as favourite Roger Bannister was passed over in favour of Chris Chataway, whose run against Vladimir Kuts had been televised live rather than filmed.

As well as using his powers of persuasion to extend the BBC empire to include the Grand National from 1960, Dimmock also arranged the first live Europe-wide broadcasting of the Rome Olympics and used his relationship with Sir Stanley Rous to secure the 1962 Chile World Cup with a long-term contract that also included the 1966 finals.

From 1972, Dimmock ran BBC Enterprises, charged with selling its footage worldwide. However, there was stern criticism from the likes of Phil Bull at the 'peppercorn' fees the BBC offered, including a 'derisory' £716 for a Doncaster meeting in 1971. Dimmock knew that sports events needed the BBC to give TV exposure to their sponsors, but soon a steady stream of broadcasting events were leaving the BBC and its 'Enterprise' arm, realising that they could do better elsewhere. (In 1976, the Grand National raised more money by itself in one year than the BBC had made for it in the previous fifteen.)

Although all UK sports have grown more commercial in their outlook, the notion of 'crown jewel' events that should be broadcast free of charge has lasted for over half a century.

Reggie ('RF') and Laurie Doherty – 'Big Do' and 'Little Do'

Reginald Frank Doherty and Hugh Lawrence Doherty, tennis players. Reggie born Wimbledon 14 October 1872, died 29 December 1910; Laurie born 8 October 1875, died 21 August 1919. Wimbledon doubles champions 1897, 98, 99, 1900, 01, 03, 04, 05, Wimbledon singles champions (Reggie) 1897, 98, 99, 1900, (Laurie) 1902, 03, 04, 05, 06, US men's doubles champions 1902, 03, US singles champion (Laurie) 1903, Olympic doubles champions 1900, 08, mixed doubles (Reggie) 1900, singles champion (Laurie) 1900.

Brothers Reggie and Laurie Doherty not only changed the tactics of doubles tennis, but re-energised the game in Britain and internationally by making a genuine contest of the Davis Cup.

In 1895, Wimbledon was running at a loss and, having dropped 'croquet' from its title in 1882, was forced to bring it back, due to the slump in tennis's popularity. Two local boys, both Trinity College, Cambridge-educated, saved the game. Reggie was tall and skinny and frequently ill, while the much shorter, younger Laurie had the better tennis sense and became the first non-American winner of the US singles. In doubles tennis they transformed tactics by 'parting the pair', with the receiver's partner coming up to the net on his own.

The brothers were the best of champions for Wimbledon: gentlemanly, instantly recognisable with their wavy centre-parted hair and not too crushingly successful, which kept the crowds interested. After a tough doubles match in 1906, they promised their mother that they would quit the game and Reggie died not long afterwards. Having brought back the fans and saved the sport, they are commemorated today by the Doherty gates.

Basil D'Oliveira

Basil Lewis D'Oliveira, cricketer and coach, born Cape Town, South Africa 4 October 1931. First-class career: Worcestershire 1964–79, 367 matches, 19,490 runs (40.26); 44 Test matches 1966–72, 2,484 runs (40.06). As coach: county champions 1974. Wisden Cricketer of the Year 1967.

Basil D'Oliveira was a South African Sportsman of the Year, a dangerous seam bowler, a relaxed but powerful batsman capable of scoring 225 runs in 70 minutes and captain of a successful multiracial touring side to East Africa. However, after 1958 he was, like all non-white South Africans, forbidden from representing his country or playing multiracial sport. Instead, he had to play on wasteland, trudging for miles with matting wickets or watching elite matches from the Newlands cage.

Like many other sports, international cricket ignored apartheid and D'Oliveira would probably have ended his career in obscurity had it not been for his persistence, the good work of broadcaster John Arlott and an offer from Lancashire League side Middleton. They took a punt on an unknown player and supported him as he learned to cope with soggy grass wickets until he eventually topped the averages, ahead of even Gary Sobers. In 1964, Tom Graveney's Worcestershire signed him just ahead of Lancashire and D'Oliveira's debut 106 plus five other centuries helped them to the County Championship. Having wisely lopped three years off his actual age, he topped the averages in 1965, took 35 wickets and made his England Test debut the following year.

On 13 March 1968, the South African leader John Vorster made it clear to the MCC selectors (one an ex-fascist and most supporters of South Africa) that D'Oliveira would not be welcome on the planned 1968/9 tour. Being a wily old bird, Vorster made this statement indirectly, misled the Foreign Office about his intentions, muddied the waters by suggesting that New Zealand Maori rugby players would be welcomed in 1970 and encouraged tobacco company boss Tiene Oosthuizen to buy D'Oliveira off with a £40,000 coaching deal that would rule him out of any future tour. Being spineless, the selectors concealed the truth and tried to edge D'Oliveira out of the squad. A recent bad run of form against the West Indies helped, but after being recalled for the final Ashes Test at the Oval, D'Oliveira walked out to huge applause and showed his mettle by scoring 158 in the first innings and taking the crucial wicket that helped draw the Ashes with five minutes to spare. Even the *Telegraph*'s E.W. Swanton, who would have preferred D'Oliveira to rule himself out, declared that his exclusion was 'inconceivable'. Instead, after a meeting of which the notes later vanished, he wasn't selected. 'Bastards' was Tom Graveney's comment as the team – including his own name – was read out on the radio. D'Oliveira, an emotional man, first cried, then wrote eloquently for the press wishing the tourists good luck without him.

Though most of his fellow pros were unconcerned, many MPs and MCC members were outraged, and of the 2,000 letters D'Oliveira received 1,999 were supportive. David Sheppard, an ex-Test player and future Bishop of Liverpool, arranged a special MCC meeting and a protest motion was seconded by rising star <u>Mike Brearley</u>, while others pointed to the damage the decision would do to British sport. 'It is difficult to think of any step taken by the cricket establishment more likely to mar the image of the game,' wrote John Arlott. When Tom Cartwright ruled himself out, the selectors backtracked and included D'Oliveira. In response, Vorster stopped the tour, arguing that D'Oliveira's selection for a team of 'anti-apartheid movement and pink ideals' was 'political'. (As if his exclusion hadn't been.)

A crisis point had been reached and many Britons could no longer accept a system that prevented so many South Africans from even competing in sport. A 1969 Springboks rugby tour turned into a series of riots and protests, but the MCC still tried to pretend that nothing had happened and invited the South Africans, then the best team in the world, to tour in 1970. After 12 grounds were sabotaged in a single night and with the Commonwealth Games put in jeopardy, Home Secretary Jim Callaghan had to can the tour in favour of a replacement Rest of the World side, which included South African stars Barry Richards, Mike Procter and Graeme Pollock.

D'Oliveira received an OBE in 1969, but the selectors continued to regard him as a nuisance and he only helped to regain the Ashes after Ray Illingworth held them to an earlier false promise. In Britain too, D'Oliveira suffered occasional abuse and at Hull in 1974 he retaliated by thumping the offending Yorkshire side for 277 runs. Having coached

Worcestershire to the county championship that year, he collected a large county benefit in 1975, and retired four years later with a simultaneous ovation at every county ground.

Since 1971 cricket had accepted the inevitable and the ICC had excluded South Africa. A meaningless promise to 'select on merit' was never good enough, because non-whites were denied the chance to display any merit. Although white South African players wanted change and their authorities gradually reformed the game, the improvements were overtaken by riots and repression at the national level. The result was years of isolation and a series of rebel tours by players from many nations. The irony was that the 'D'Oliveira Affair', which brought about the sporting boycott, arose from a man committed to gradual change, who simply wanted to play the game he loved. Today there is a D'Oliveira stand at Worcester, and England and South Africa now play for a trophy in his name.

Dickie Downs – 'The India Rubber man'

John Thomas Downs, defender, born Middridge, Durham 13 August 1886, died 24 March 1949. Playing career: Barnsley 1909–12 (FA Cup 1912), Everton 1920–3, Brighton and Hove Albion 1923–5; England 1920, 1 cap.

In 1956, looking back on fifty years in the game, England international Charlie Buchan concluded that no player had altered soccer more than full back Dickie Downs, the inventor of the sliding tackle.

A sturdy, combative player, Downs was singled out in press reports of the 1910 and 1912 FA Cup finals, the second of which his club Barnsley won in a replay. After a career interrupted by war he was signed for £3,000 by Everton, a team he had helped beat in the cup semis, and delighted the crowds with his overhead kicks and 'flying' (later 'sliding') tackles, which allowed an ageing defender to catch an attacker. Until this time, a defender who had been passed or turned could be safely ignored by a speedy winger, but Downs's invention denied forwards the time to shoot, dribble or pick their spot. Buchan argued that the sliding tackle had led to a faster though less accurate and elegant game, plus more serious injuries because of unexpected tackles from behind – something that was finally made illegal in 1990.

George Eastham

George Edward Eastham OBE, inside forward, midfielder and manager, born Blackpool 23 September 1936. Playing career: Ards 1953–6, Newcastle United 1956–60, Arsenal 1960–6 (captain 1963–6), Stoke City 1966–73; England: 19 caps, 2 goals. Managerial career: Stoke City 1977–8.

George Eastham, a slim, blond playmaker usually referred to as 'mercurial', played in two World Cup squads, captained Arsenal for four years, took Stoke City into Europe, went 18 years without a booking and was the first son of an England international to become an international himself. However, he is most significant for winning the court case that ended the hated 'retain and transfer' system.

For over sixty years this system, often referred to as the 'slave contract', had allowed clubs to treat players as possessions. At the end of each season they could choose to keep a player, sack him, sell him or, worst of all, 'retain' him – which meant he was unpaid but unable to play for another team. Not only were 1950s footballers earning little more than the man on the terrace, they also lacked his right to quit. (In theory, they could request a transfer, but a club could simply set too high a price to attract any offers.) At its worst, this meant families thrown out of tied homes at a week's notice, players suspended without pay as a punishment, or forced to work as labourers because their club wouldn't release them. (Ex-Manchester United centre half Ronnie Cope ended up shovelling cement after one dispute.) In 1947, future Conservative Cabinet Minister Walter Monckton described the footballers' as the worse contract he'd ever seen.

Because the system made money for the clubs, the League clung to it, though secretary <u>Alan Hardaker</u> later admitted that they knew it was probably illegal. Most players knuckled under and even Wilf Mannion of Boro, who staged a one-man strike, was ground down in the end. Under new leader <u>Jimmy Hill</u>, the Professional Footballers' Association got League president Joe Richards to agreed to amend the contract, but he soon backtracked and not even complaints in Parliament could shake the League. In the end, Jimmy Hill and PFA secretary Cliff Lloyd decided to go to court, backing George Eastham against Newcastle United at a cost of £15,000.

Eastham had transferred to Newcastle from Ulster side Ards for £10 a week back in 1956. Though United had a reputation as free-spending cup winners, they were riven between chairman Stanley Seymour and vice chairman Alderman William McKeag, who between them undermined a series of managers. Eastham incurred McKeag's wrath after a series of disagreements about his dilapidated club-owned house, the part-time job he was offered, his England under-23 duties, a missed train and his fiancée getting a lift on the team coach. His request for a transfer was denied and one director told him he'd see him go down the pit rather than play again. Eastham quit football, and though at one time he was down to his last fiver, he stuck with his case, buoyed by PFA and press support, plus a job offer from businessman Ernie Coles. Eventually, Newcastle grudgingly sold Eastham to Arsenal for £47,000 – their second biggest signing – but still retained his loyalty bonus, or 'benefit money', plus unpaid wages.

In court, Eastham sued the FA, the League – who had refused to arbitrate – plus United's board and manager Charlie Mitten. In a 16,000-word judgment Mr Justice Wilberforce agreed that the system was unfair and incongruous and a blatant restraint of trade. This decision brought about new contracts for all players and marked the beginning of the end of the retain-and-transfer system, though the clubs still found enough 'wiggle room' to hold off free transfers until 1978 and it took the Bosman ruling of 1995 to finally break the chains.

1978 marked George Eastham's departure from the English game, having survived further disagreements over pay to captain Arsenal. After being sold to Stoke City, he scored his first goal in 18 months to win the 1972 League Cup while aged 35 and get the club into Europe. Having already collected an OBE for services to football, he emigrated to South Africa to set up a sports business and, as an opponent of apartheid, coached a new generation of black players.

Bernie Ecclestone

Bernard Charles Ecclestone, racing driver, team owner and promoter, born St Peter South Elmham, Suffolk 28 October 1930. Owner Brabham 1971–87, (Drivers championship 1981, 83), president and CEO Formula One Management and Formula One Administration 1987–, chief executive Formula One Constructors' Association 1978–, vice-president FIA 1987–.

Instantly recognisable with his white hair and dark glasses, Bernie Ecclestone almost single-handedly turned Formula One from a collection of racing enthusiasts into a marketing arm of the world's car industry. Though he claims to 'make deals rather than money', his personal fortune has been estimated at £2.4 billion and in 2008 he and fellow rights holders CVC Capital Partners were reported to be keeping half the sport's revenues – to the chagrin of the teams.

Ecclestone's early career was similar to that of many other team owners. After his family moved to Bexleyheath he began racing motorbikes on the grass track at Brands Hatch before switching to Formula Three, where, with a reputation for either winning or crashing, he once shot off the circuit and into the car park. Always entrepreneurial, he is said to have traded cakes and biscuits at school and pens and watches at weekends, before building up London's second-biggest motorbike dealership, where he displayed another F1 trait – obsessive neatness and tidiness. With money from real-estate, credit and car-auction businesses, he bought the Connaught team and even attempted qualification for the 1958 Monaco GP himself. When star driver Stuart Lewis-Evans moved to Vanwall, Ecclestone remained his manager until a fiery crash at the Moroccan Grand Prix left Lewis-Evans with 70 per cent burns. With his driver propped in a chair, Ecclestone and team owner Tony Vandervell chartered a plane to take him to the burns unit at East Grinstead Hospital, but to no avail.

After Lewis-Evans's death, both Vandervell and Ecclestone dropped out of the sport until Ecclestone returned to manage Jochen Rindt and his F2 team in 1970. After Rindt's death at Monza that year, Ecclestone stayed in the sport, buying first half then all of Brabham. Although he claimed it was a 'retirement project', he transformed the team, concentrating entirely on racing rather than car production, and employed Gordon Murray as chief designer. Murray created the triangular-profile BT-42 and in 1978 ex-champion Niki Lauda was hired. Ecclestone also attracted sponsorship from Parmalat and Alfa Romeo, whose powerful but heavy and unreliable engines limited the team's progress. (In the same year, Ecclestone also brought in Professor Sid Watkins as the sport's first medical adviser.)

As a team owner, Ecclestone took over the Formula One Constructors' Association (FOCA) and began the long campaign for control of the sport. Founded in 1964 by Lotus's Andrew Ferguson as FICA (which apparently had unfortunate meanings in some languages), it was little more than a glorified travel agency, but Ecclestone and March owner Max Mosley began to deal with promoters, demanding more prize money – partly to get them to organise themselves better – before parcelling out the funds to guarantee the teams' attendance at all races. The next move was to secure the TV rights, and from 1978, as chief executive, Ecclestone led FOCA into conflict with the volatile but astute Jean-Marie Balestre, newly elected president of the CSI – later renamed FISA. A drawn-out war spilled over into various battles about technical regulations, as the English aerodynamicists toughed it out with the continental 'grandees' at Ferrari, Renault and Alfa Romeo, with their heavier but more powerful turbo engines. During these battles the ban on ground-effect cars, Murray's inventiveness, Ecclestone's political influence, Nelson Piquet's driving ability and a switch to Ford Cosworths followed by BMW turbos won Brabham the drivers' championships in 1981 and 1983. A fuel irregularity on the way to the 1983 title was soon forgotten about.

In 1981, after tit-for-tat boycotts of events, Ecclestone and Mosley called Balestre's bluff by staging a FOCA-only 'World Federation of Motor Sport' event in South Africa. Though they could never have afforded to run them, they announced grand plans for a rival series of events, which would imperil the official US Grand Prix, which was crucial for Renault's commercial interests. A nightclub meeting between Ecclestone, Balestre and the head of sponsors Philip Morris turned into an extended redrafting exercise near the Place de la Concorde in Paris, where Ecclestone 'lost the battle to win the war' – conceding overall authority to FISA, but keeping a hand in technical regulations and taking control of the all-important commercial rights. Having raised $313m in eight hours, Bernie gained a 100-year lease on the right to negotiate with advertisers, sponsors, broadcasters and race promotors, and is believed to have since earned $3bn from their sale. At first the revenue split was: Teams 47 per cent, FIA 30 per cent, Ecclestone's companies 23 per cent. Since this original Concorde agreement, there have been three others and their super-secret technical and financial agreements have dominated the sport ever since. In 1997, when Williams and McLaren led protests on the eve of the flotation of Ecclestone's Formula One Holdings, the agreement is supposed to have gone through 60 drafts.

Ecclestone's hand was strengthened in 1982 when he settled a drivers' strike over new FISA licences and led a partial boycott of the San Marino Grand Prix over a ban on water-cooled brakes that got round the weight restrictions. After Max Mosley was elected to head first FISA and then the FIA, they improved the sport's safety record through direct control of 'sporting regulations' such as tyres – which managed speeds downwards – and were able to squeeze teams like Tyrrell and Toleman that hadn't supported FOCA's San Marino strike.

As a power broker, Ecclestone helped engineer moves like Michael Schumacher's controversial extraction from Jordan in 1991. Driven by German TV and marketing interests rather than promises, handshakes and signed heads of agreements, this marked another stage in the sport's 'loss of innocence', and even Ayrton Senna, no mean politician himself, claimed to be disgusted by it. After Senna's death at Imola, the bringing-in of Nigel Mansell was another Ecclestone deal, as was Jacques Villeneuve's move to Williams. A Contracts Recognition Board was later brought in to try to introduce some order to proceedings.

Under Ecclestone's control, F1 was claimed to employ an estimated 40,000 people by 2001, was valued at $7.5 billion and attracted some 500 million TV viewers. As early as the 1980s, promoters were being asked for £10 million to stage events, which enriched the teams but impoverished many circuit owners. The public were cleared out of the paddocks, with electronic turnstiles and passes introduced, and Paddock Club corporate hospitality was established, making £50 million p.a. Though the teams gain only one-fifth of their income from their share of the TV rights, much of the remaining 80 per cent comes from sponsorship generated by that exposure.

Ecclestone himself has admitted that there was never a masterplan in his transformation of the sport. Instead, decisions and judgements

Muhammad Ali shocked the world with his first world championship win
and just carried on shocking it.

Two fathers of football: Charles Alcock (*left*) created the rules of the modern game, founded the FA Cup and helped establish both Test cricket and international rugby. Lancashire-born Jimmy Hogan (*below*) masterminded and spread a more fluent continental style.

Newcastle United's Bill McCracken (*right*) helped produce the most fundamental football rule change of the twentieth century. Carlos Bilardo (*below*, with Diego Maradona) created the 3-5-2 formation – the most defensive ever seen.

Joe Davis mastered snooker strategy and used his crisp, accurate new cueing style to replace billiards as the number one game.

were made along the way – shifting the Australian GP from Adelaide to Melbourne despite protests, then ditching both ITV and Silverstone in favour of the BBC and Donnington Park. The huge investment in digital TV is questionable, but there is no doubt that the sport is a global attraction. Ecclestone continues to come up with new ideas such as limiting testing to allow more races and dropping old circuits for new ones, but has stood against some cost-cutting measures like an open market in chassis, arguing that F1's 'design and build' requirement ensures a team's commitment to the sport.

Probably only Ecclestone could have managed this circus, handling UK and EU politicians, rival promoters and the fractious 'Piranha Club' of team owners. Known for his straightforwardness, humour and hands-on approach (he once got down on the pit lane to show just how he wanted the marking tape laid out), he has bailed out many teams in the past and has an unrivalled collection of favours owed. And of course he is too rich to corrupt. How can you bribe a man who once put the King of Spain on hold?

Eclipse

Eclipse, dark chestnut stallion by Marske out of Spilletta, foaled Windsor Park, Berkshire 1 April 1764, died 26 February 1789. 18 wins, 0 defeats, including 11 King's Plates.

In 1768 a Smithfield sheepdealer named William Wildman decided not to geld (castrate) a large and temperamental chestnut colt, which he had recently bought for just 75 guineas. It was perhaps the single most important decision in the long history of horse racing.

Wildman's feisty beast was a long chestnut with a thin blaze on his large head, a white 'sock' on its off hind leg and black spots on its rump. Bred at Windsor by the Duke of Cumberland, the King's third son, it was a great-great-grandson of the Darley Arabian, later recognised as a founding thoroughbred sire, and was named after the great solar eclipse which had occurred during its birth.

Eclipse's first public race was at Epsom in May 1769 in the Noblemen and Gentlemen's Plate, a best-of-three-heats contest run over four miles for a £50 prize. The five-year-old won the first heat so easily that the renowned Irish blackleg (gambler) 'Colonel' Dennis O'Kelly made the most famous bet in history: 'Eclipse to win – the rest nowhere'. Under the rules of racing, a horse that hadn't reached the distance post when the race was won was 'nowhere', and when Eclipse thundered home in the second heat the rest were still over 240 yards back. O'Kelly collected and a month later had reportedly bought a half share from Wildman for 650 guineas. (After another successful gamble, O'Kelly is believed to have secured the other 50 per cent of Eclipse.) Following the most famous racing bet, it was the greatest racing bargain. Over 18 races, including 11 four-mile King's Plates, Eclipse was never stretched or headed and never needed to be whipped or spurred.

Eclipse became a legend and has remained one ever since. With jockey John Oakley, the only one who could cope with his head-down style, Eclipse was so intimidating that eight of his victories were walkovers. As a sire he produced three of the first five Derby winners, although it was his ex-stablemate (King) Herod who was the champion sire. This was partly due to snobbery over O'Kelly's origins. The

'Colonel' had been by turns a jailbird, sedan-chair man, gigolo, billiard marker and tennis pro, while his partner Charlotte Hayes was an ex-prostitute and brothel-keeper. Another factor may have been O'Kelly's reputation for trickery. In the end, however, quality won out and Eclipse sired 344 winners. Lord Grosvenor's offer of £11,000 was turned down and the horse earned O'Kelly some £25,000 in stud fees – worth perhaps £1.5 million today – which he spent and gambled away as he attempted to ingratiate himself with the aristocratic Jockey Club, only to be blackballed by them.

After Eclipse's death from colic in 1789, an autopsy by the renowned veterinarian Professor Charles Vial de Sainbel reported powerful back legs and a huge heart and lungs – and helped to give the impetus to the founding of the Royal Veterinary College. On the other hand, a more scientific RVC investigation in 2005 suggested that Eclipse was not a freak, but 'just right in every possible way'. Various hooves – as many as five – were preserved, including one mounted on a gold platter, which ended up as a private trophy for those Jockey Club members light and brave enough to ride their own horses.

Quite how fast Eclipse really was is debatable. Contemporary reports of a mile in a minute can't possibly be correct, and in the 1850s Admiral Rous claimed that Eclipse would now struggle in a £50 plate. However, his progeny included Gladiateur and St Simon, who won the 1884 Ascot Gold Cup by 20 lengths. In 1886, the richest race in the kingdom, worth £10,000, was named after Eclipse – and Sandown's Eclipse Stakes remains the most prestigious Group One race over 1¼ miles. Since 1971, the US racing industry's own 'Oscars' has also been named after the 18th-century wonder horse. More to the point, an estimated 80 to 95 per cent of all thoroughbreds now trace their parentage back to him – and rising, thanks to the success of Northern Dancer. In 2006, every single runner in the English, French and Kentucky Derbies could trace their ancestry back to Eclipse.

Anyone wishing to view Charles Vial de Sainbel's work can see Eclipse's skeletal remains at the National Horseracing Museum in Newmarket.

Sir Arthur Elvin

Sir Arthur James Elvin MBE, sports promoter, born Norwich 6 July 1899, died 4 February 1957.

Had it not been for an ambitious tobacco kiosk attendant named Arthur Elvin, there would be no Wembley Stadium today and the 'hallowed turf' would be covered with semis.

Although the near-disastrous 1923 'White Horse Final' and the 1924/5 British Empire Exhibition both attracted huge crowds to Wembley, the Exhibition somehow lost money and the whole 220-acre site was sold to a builder named Jimmy White, who planned to scrap the lot. Wembley Stadium was only saved by the intervention of Arthur Elvin, a kiosk assistant who had fought in the Royal Flying Corps in World War I, spending two years as a POW. Elvin believed he might have escaped had he been able to learn to swim and his ambition was to build a really grand pool.

Though he was only earning £4 10s a week in his temporary job, Elvin had experience in demolition and salvage, and scraped together a little cash by buying and selling the contents of some of the pavilions. Now facing bankruptcy, White offered Elvin the Stadium for a £12,000 down-payment which he didn't have. White's suicide made matters even more urgent and Arthur had just ten days to raise the cash in the City. Having achieved this, he became managing director of Wembley Stadium Ltd. The stadium's only asset was the FA Cup, which promised just £5,000 a year, so Elvin turned to the new boom sports of greyhounds in 1927 and then 'dirt track', hiring Johnny Hoskins to run a speedway team for him from 1929. With its clubs and bars, Wembley was luxurious in comparison to most other sports venues and its good transport links and car parking were soon drawing big crowds for floodlit evening sports. Elvin was able to expand Wembley's sporting offering, opening his dreamed-of Empire Pool and Sports Arena (now Wembley Arena) just in time for the 1934 Empire Games.

The largest span ever constructed, the reinforced-concrete Arena was built in under a year by stadium engineer Sir Owen Williams and seated between 8,000 and 11,000 to watch swimming and diving or, with the pool boarded over, boxing, cycling and tennis. One of the first indoor multi-sports venues, it featured the first indoor athletics meeting in 1934 and was soon being copied by new stadiums such as the Harringay Arena. Wembley also helped revive ice hockey in Britain by fielding two teams, the Lions and Monarchs – mostly made up of imported Canadian stars.

After the war, Wembley was still selling out, but a stinging entertainment tax hit greyhounds, speedway and ice hockey hard, and Elvin shifted to staging ice shows instead. After hosting the first indoor Olympic swimming and diving competition in 1948, the diving pool was permanently closed eight years later, hiting the sport hard. To improve sporting venues in Britain, Elvin and the FA's Stanley Rous suggested a 'Unity Pool', but Fred Howarth of the Football League distrusted Rous and was opposed to 'tainted' gambling money, so British stadiums remained tatty, obsolete and often lethally dangerous.

Elvin died on a cruise in 1957. Wembley remained a greyhound stadium first and foremost, even cancelling a 1966 World Cup fixture that clashed with the dogs. Though the stadium has been rebuilt, the Grade II-listed Arena, which staged the first indoor international track meeting in 1962, still remains. Had British sport been more open to Arthur Elvin's ideas, who knows how many other fine new stadiums might have been built and how many lives saved?

Manfred Ewald

Manfred Ewald, sports administrator, born Podejuch, Germany 17 May 1926, died 21 October 2002. Chairman East German State Committee for Physical Training 1952–60, chairman DTSB sporting and LSK Achievement Federations 1961–88. SED (Politburo) Member for Sport 1963–90. German Olympic chef de mission 1964. Chairman East German National Olympic Committee 1973–90.

For over 25 years Manfred Ewald was 'Mr Sport' in East Germany. Under his control, a nation of just 17 million amassed 157 Olympic gold medals plus countless other sporting prizes.

A tailor's son, Ewald joined the Hitler Youth at 12 and within two years had left school to work as an administrator, posing as a communist to infiltrate the German resistance to the Nazis. After losing two fingers fighting in the war, Ewald made a skilful political transition to become a sincere and full-time communist, studied in Moscow and by 1963 was a Politburo (SED) member, masterminding perhaps the best-resourced sports programme in the world. In 1985, to help keep East Germany in the Seoul Olympics, he was awarded the Olympic Order for the 'perfect ideal of sport and humanity' by IOC president Juan Antonio Samaranch.

Manfred Ewald is best known as the driving force behind the East German doping programme, known as State Planning Theme 14.25, which from 1970 onwards supplied 'supportive means' (i.e. steroids and stimulants) to an estimated 10,000 athletes. The mainstay was oral Turinabol, a state-manufactured steroid known to be linked to heart and liver damage at high doses. As an Olympic insider, Ewald master-minded the regime's shift to less detectable testosterone in the late 1970s and only one major GDR star – shot-putter Ilona Slupianek – ever tested positive.

Despite the collapse of the East German regime in 1989 and a mass of published evidence dating back to 1972, Ewald only came to trial in 2000. That any case was brought at all was due to the persistence of Professor of Molecular Biology Werner Franke and ex-West German field athlete Brigitte Berendonk. Despite intrusive and humiliating questioning, a series of athletes testified to the drugs they had been fooled into taking and the damage caused. It was revealed that athletes as young as 14 had been paralysed, killed or forced out of sport due to health problems. Among older ones there had been a series of premature deaths, plus a high frequency of birth defects in their children. Charged with 142 counts of causing harm, Ewald received a 22-month suspended sentence.

After the verdict Ewald pointed out that over 1,000 of his 'friends' had helped administer 14.25. As for the numerous prizes won under the policy, no medals were reclaimed or records cancelled. From this perspective Manfred Ewald remains perhaps the most successful sports administrator in history.

'Felix'

Nicholas Wanostrocht, cricketer, born Camberwell 5 October 1804, died 3 September 1876. First-class career: Kent 1834–45, Surrey 1846–52, 149 matches, 4,556 runs (18.15).

As a bowler for the MCC, All England, Kent and later Surrey, Nicholas Wanostrocht, or 'Felix' as he was always known, made a huge contribution to the game of cricket – particularly by modernising its dress and equipment to make it safer and easier to play.

Felix, who inherited his father's Camberwell school at the age of just 19, used his pseudonym to avoid any bad publicity for it. A classical scholar and inventor, he also wrote, painted and played music. Having learned his cricket at the East Surrey ground, he moved the school to the local sporting centre of Blackheath in 1832 and began regular appearances for the great Kent side that included Alfred Mynn and Fuller Pilch. Credited with bringing fast footwork and wristwork to cricket in place of the old bludgeoning style, he was regarded as the father of the cut – slapping the ball to send it in the region square or backward of square on the off side. It was said that his cut 'hit the palings as soon as she left the bat'. Training as a fencer may have helped his mastery of this, the wristiest of batting strokes, and he combined 'backward' strokes like this with forward drives – the first batsman to do so, although it was <u>W.G. Grace</u> who popularised the style.

Felix believed cricket should be 'a lively and amusing as well as a scientific game' and produced a series of books – notably *Felix on the Bat* (1845), which is regarded as the first cricket manual. He also designed the first bowling machine or 'catapulta' and encouraged a shift to more practical clothing. His checked woollen deerstalker was the prototype of the cricket cap and led to the abandonment of the impractical topper, which was prone to fall and knock down the wicket. Other sensible changes included the replacement of braces with belts, and well-worn shoes fitted with spikes for speed and comfort. He also embraced new technology in the form of vulcanised rubber, first invented in 1839. Back in 1800, 'Long Jack' Robinson of Surrey had invented some wooden pads, but these were impractical and Felix's team-mate

Mynn had came close to having a leg amputated because of cricketing injuries. Felix was the first to recommend 'longitudinal padded socks' or pads, plus tubular rubber gloves to protect the hands. From 1848, his patent gloves were on sale, and were popularised by W.G. Grace in the 1860s. They helped make the game safer and more appealing, even though cricketers were still doing without gloves as late as the 1920s.

From 1846, Felix began to appear for Surrey as well as the touring All England sides and also helped the Gentlemen beat the Players on equal terms for the first time in twenty years. In 1854, paralysis forced him to quit first-class cricket having scored two centuries – a massive score in an era of bumpy wickets – and benefits were held for him in 1858 and 1866. After retirement, he moved to Brighton to paint, remarried and moved again to Wimborne Minster, where he died in 1876. His tomb lies close to that of fellow cricketer, Jack the Ripper suspect Montague Druitt.

Enzo Ferrari – 'the Commendatore'

Enzo Ferrari, racing driver and team owner. Born Modena, Italy 18 February 1898, died 14 August 1988. Drivers championships 1952, 53, 56, 58, 61, 64, 75, 77, 79. Champion constructor 1961, 64, 75, 76, 77, 79, 82, 83. Overall record: 93 Grands Prix victories, 106 pole positions, 103 fastest laps, 13 world sports car titles.

With his hooded eyes, dark glasses and carefully cultivated mystique, Enzo Ferrari was the Godfather of Grand Prix – except that plenty of *mafiosi* killed far fewer people than Enzo did in his 70-year pursuit of speed at all costs. Throughout this time, he would plot a course between talented engineers, fearless drivers and wealthy sponsors and manufacturers, and his name would become the most famous in motor sport – perhaps in all sport – synonymous with speed, glamour, sex and death. Fans, journalists and film-makers worldwide would be enthralled by the supposed genius behind the shades – the master driver turned master engineer, sending out his champions in their blood-red chargers, bearing the sign of the prancing black horse.

Inevitably, reality falls short of myth, and for his harshest critics Ferrari was no more than a small-town car dealer. As a driver from 1920 onwards, he certainly showed ability and determination. Born in the metal-working town of Modena, he hoped to be a journalist or opera star but proved unable to spell or sing. Instead, after wartime service shoeing mules, he joined the CMN team, coming fourth in his first race, and then joined the more prestigious Alfa Romeo. He once won three races in a row, and his greatest victory was the 1923 Targa Florio, where he braved the wolves and terrible rutted roads of Sicily's Madonie mountains. Five years later, he would still be tenth in the prize-money stakes, but the most important race in his career was probably the 1924 French Grand Prix from which he suddenly withdrew. This withdrawal, which Ferrari would later rather unconvincingly blame on ill health, set him off on a new course – the running of his own racing team, or *scuderia*.

Ferrari ran Alfa's team until 1929, when he launched the Scuderia Ferrari, racing Alfa Romeo cars and Rudge and Norton motorbikes.

It would not be until just before World War II that Ferrari, then aged 49, would actually start making cars. He would remain a product of this heroic age, looking for the same qualities in all his future drivers. The ability to drive beyond the capability of the machine was what Enzo most admired and his favourite drivers were those, like Gilles Villeneuve, who risked all – even if they destroyed his cars while competing for minor places. More calculating drivers, however skilful, were never so popular. At its best, this policy attracted great talents and added to the legend, but it also meant that drivers were sent out in obsolete cars or reconditioned wrecks, and the Ferrari death rate was notable even by the knuckle-scrapingly low standards of the sport.

Ferrari was not the first to come up with the idea of a team – more famous racers such as <u>Tazio Nuvolari</u> and Emilio Materassi had done so already, but they lacked Enzo's talent for intrigue and his ability to attract wealthy individuals and companies as sponsors. (Nuvolari ended up driving for Ferrari, while Materassi ended up dead, crashing at Monza in 1928.) It was this commercial sponsorship that enabled Ferrari to survive in a dangerous and turbulent sport where so many other companies – and individuals – crashed and burned. From the very first his team relied on Alfa for cars, money and engineering expertise and soon also allied with Shell, Bosch, the carburettor manufacturer Weber and the tyre-makers Engelbert – names prominently displayed on the team lorries. In many respects, this was Ferrari's best single idea and the one that enabled his team to survive – even though it could sometimes shackle the scuderia to inferior or obsolete products. The backing of rich car companies and wealthy amateur drivers who pay to drive has funded the sport throughout most of its history, and even with today's TV cash, sponsorship still provides 80 per cent of the income.

Though he termed himself *Ingegnere*, Ferrari wasn't an engineer, although he had some strong and stubborn prejudices. From the beginning, the team's success was dependent on the engineering ability of others, starting with Fiat's talented young designer Vittorio Jano who, according to Ferrari, he succeeded in persuading to join Alfa Romeo – although Jano remembered the facts rather differently. Enzo's strengths were, as he expressed it, as *'un agitatore di uomini'* – an agitator of men, operating behind the scenes.

After Vittorio Jano transformed Giuseppe Merosi's single-seater P1 into the supercharged eight-cylinder P2, Alfa had a winning car. Although they officially withdrew from racing from 1926, they still made the cars available to Ferrari, and the following year the scuderia pulled off eight victories to establish itself as major force in Italian racing. The year after that, they began competing outside Europe too, before gaining more success with Jano's new supercharged P3. Despite the wins, money was tight. Hard bargaining with drivers would always be a Ferrari characteristic. Later champions like Phil Hill risked their lives for little more than board and lodging, while others' wages would be 'recycled' into paying for a discounted car.

Another Ferrari characteristic was conservatism in design. The 1930s depression made creating new cars unaffordable and caused Alfa to withdraw completely from racing in 1933, leaving the way open for Mercedes and Ferdinand Porsche's innovative mid-engined Auto Unions. Ferrari refused to copy them. 'The ox pulls the cart' was the comment of a man who always remained in his native city, later building a racetrack around his farmstead. In 1935 Nuvolari, who had quit for better machines elsewhere, returned and secured a single triumph over the Germans, brilliantly piloting an obsolete P3 around the Nürburgring, but otherwise the team remained outclassed. Ferrari's response was to increase the power, quitting Grand Prix for the no-holds-barred Formula Libre and, under the supervision of Jano, the team yoked together two P3 engines in a giant 'bimotore'. In years to come, Ferrari would continue to make do and mend, often cannibalising old cars or wrecks for new machines. The preference was clear – a reliance on power, talent and instinctive judgement, although without German-style science and resources to test those judgements, the instincts could be very wrong.

Already by the 1930s Enzo Ferrari was staying away from the tracks – building his reputation and disassociating himself from failure, but also removing himself from reality, as he relied on the second- and third-hand reports phoned through to him. In years to come, his reliance on racing managers would often leave him ignorant of what was going on – a point forcibly made by Niki Lauda, a future double world champion for his team. Soon after Alfa returned to the sport in 1938, Ferrari was sacked as their racing manager and set up his own company, which in 1939 finally made his first car, the 815, which was pretty much a souped-up Fiat 508C. During wartime, the factory would churn out engines and gearboxes, but though this was profitable, Enzo soon reverted to racing again. Throughout the rest of his life, Ferrari and his company would remain dedicated to the sport. Though rivals Mercedes withdrew after a disastrous crash at Le Mans in 1955, the Ferrari team carried on through a Mille Miglia crash that killed five children and 11 adults, plus another 15 deaths after their likely world champion Wolfgang von Trips crashed at Monza in 1961. While Mercedes raced to advertise their cars, Ferrari sold cars to fund their racing and nothing – not a four-year judicial inquiry nor even condemnation by the Vatican – would deflect them. Never a good Catholic (he maintained two families), Enzo shrugged off the criticism and carried on. His favourite car, he declared, was the next.

Given their undoubted engineering skills and racing heritage, it might be imagined that Ferrari would dominate the new World Championship, which started in 1950. In fact, during Enzo Ferrari's lifetime, they won it less than one time in four and late starters like Colin Chapman's Lotus would overtake their total number of GP victories. The first Ferrari F1 victory was at the 1951 British Grand Prix, when Froilán Gonzáles drove a 375 to victory. Ferrari's compact and rigid 12-cylinder design, specifically built for the formula, defeated the antiquated, gas-guzzling Alfettas, and the following 1952 and 1953 championships were made easier by the withdrawal of Alfa, the injury of their star driver Juan Fangio and the failure of <u>Raymond Mays</u>'s BRM to even turn up. This forced the authorities to revert to the old Formula Two, and Ferrari, with cars built to suit, cleared up with nine wins in a row for driver Alberto Ascari. However, in 1954, in a repeat of the 1930s, Ferrari were blindsided by the re-emergence of Mercedes, whose engineering excellence dominated the sport until their withdrawal after the Le Mans disaster.

Although buoyed by a booming luxury car market, manufacturing both sports and racing cars was a struggle and in the years before TV money came into the sport, cars were often suddenly sold – sometimes to competing teams like Vanwall – leaving the Ferrari drivers to compete in under-tested prototypes or reconditioned wrecks. Driver Jean Behra later quit in protest at this, having punched out team *Directore Sportivo* Tavoni for good measure. In the mid-1950s, Ferrari came close to collapse, and were only saved because Enzo, the master schemer, persuaded Fiat to buy up his rival Lancia and hand over both their cars and drivers. The Lancia D50 was rebadged as a Ferrari and Fangio, aged 45, took a fourth title for the team. Typically, Enzo replaced the D50's innovative fuel tanks with something more conventional.

Throughout this period, Ferrari struggled to attract or retain the best drivers. On top of a terrifying fatality rate – Mike Hawthorn lost four co-drivers in one year – Ferrari's offhand treatment of him put Stirling Moss off for good, while Juan Fangio, the other great driver of the age, heartily detested the atmosphere at Maranello and stayed for only a single season. Ferrari, already the 'Old Man', couldn't forgive Fangio for using an agent to negotiate with him and after a fierce row about alleged sabotage, Fangio quit for Maserati, producing a passionate 'Ferrari-style' drive at the German Grand Prix to knock 24 seconds off the Nürburgring track record and catch the Ferraris of Mike Hawthorn and Peter Collins. Although Fangio's sportsmanship was impeccable, Ferrari got his revenge in his 1964 book *My Terrible Joys*, accusing him of selfishness. From then on, Ferrari showed a strong preference for talented young foreign drivers who were more biddable and whose deaths would create less bad press at home.

With Fangio gone, Ferrari began losing out to a new wave of British teams, including Vanwall, whose first cars they had supplied. Though dismissed by Ferrari as mere *'garageistes'* (which most were), new teams like Cooper and Lotus were led by engineers rather than team managers and were unencumbered by the Ferrari tradition of building from the engine out. Instead, they bought in or modified existing engines and concentrated on cutting weight and developing innovative designs such as the rear engine, fibreglass in place of aluminium and disc brakes instead of drums. Once the Coventry Climax engine enabled the Brits to match the power/weight ratio of the Ferraris, they started winning regularly and once the sport left the street circuits for purpose-built tracks, these 'runway racers' would start winning championships too. Ferrari, often paralysed by paranoia and infighting, stuck to a front-engine approach and it was a driver, Peter Collins, who installed the first disc brakes.

By 1960, the only Ferrari victory was at Monza, which the Brits boycotted in protest at the state of the track. Ferrari had now finally accepted the logic of the rear-engine design, and they won the champion-ship again in 1961, the British teams being caught flat-footed by the shift to a 1.5-litre formula. With only Ferrari really ready, Wolfgang von Trips piloted his shark-nosed Dino 156 to a string of victories before crashing fatally. The title passed to Phil Hill, who was rewarded with a pay cut.

Success was fleeting, and once Lotus and BRM matched Ferrari's power, the driving of Jim Clark and the engineering innovations of <u>Colin Chapman</u> began to dominate. Ferrari's wife's interference in team affairs prompted a mass walk-out which was followed by the arrival of talented young designer Mauro Forghieri and driver John Surtees, who helped the team adapt to the newish technology of fibreglass and win the 1964 championship. Once again, the team sabotaged itself, as team manager Eugenio Dragoni undermined Surtees, who left during the 1965 season. Ferrari would remain outclassed for the rest of the decade. Despite Forghieri innovating with the first wings and a transverse gearbox, the cars were usually overweight and under-prepared. Even though the formula had shifted to greater power, the Brits' adoption of Ford Cosworth engines meant that their lightweight 'kit cars' stayed ahead. Henry Ford, who had been rejected by Enzo as a potential purchaser, had vowed to 'kick his ass' and kick it he did. Ferrari only gained financial stability when Fiat bought a 50 per cent stake in 1969.

Shunned by safety-minded champion <u>Jackie Stewart</u>, Ferrari only regained the world champion drivers' title in 1975, though their myth had continued to grow, often fostered by film directors in love with the Ferrari style. The renaissance began in 1972 with a new flat-12 engine and the hiring of Nikki Lauda, though in 1973 performances lapsed again. Lauda complained that Enzo was ignorant of the state of his own team and was caught up in intrigue. Forghieri left and returned and Luca de Montezemolo instilled better team management, leading to an improved performance in 1974. The following season brought Forghieri's masterpiece, the 312T, which used a monocoque sourced from an English manufacturer to carry Lauda to the 1975 championship. However, the following season brought a return to traditional Ferrari form, with slanging matches between Enzo and Lauda who, after injuring himself at the beginning of the season, suffered a blazing crash at the inherently unsafe Nürburgring – against which he had been campaigning. Ferrari's first question on watching the blaze on TV was 'Who will replace him?' Almost unbelievably, Lauda returned after just 33 days to race again until, with his burns still weeping and eyelids raw, the tipping rain at Japan's Fuji circuit caused him to withdraw. Having been pilloried by the unforgiving Italian press, he won the championship the following year and, having already signed for <u>Bernie Ecclestone's</u> Brabham, quit Ferrari with a splendidly casual 'Ciao Enzo'.

In the late 1970s, the major innovations came from other teams –
notably Lotus's ground-effect cars and Renault's turbocharger. Ferrari's
answer was the heroics of Gilles Villeneuve, the 'Prince of Destruction',
who fought wheel to wheel with René Arnoux for second place and
once finished a lap on three wheels. After Gilles allowed Jody Scheckter
to win the 1979 championship, Ferrari's performance again dropped
like a stone and Villeneuve only ever won six races.

Ferrari followed Renault's example by 'turning turbo' and the sport
became polarised both off and on the track between the power-dominated
continental grandees like Enzo and the British aerodynamicists. Ultimately,
this led to boycotts of events by the British-dominated Formula One
Constructors' Association that threatened to split the sport. The 1981
126C suffered from particularly bad handling and 'turbo-lag', and the team
turned to British expertise to produce a McLaren-style carbon-fibre
monocoque.

FOCA's boycott of San Marino in 1982 provided Ferrari with a rare
winning opportunity, but the traditional Ferrari reluctance to issue team
orders led to a dispute between Villeneuve and Didier Pironi, which
wrecked the Canadian's concentration and contributed to his fatal crash
at Zolder. In what was meant to be a slowdown lap, he shot into a
cloud of spray containing Jochen Mass's March. When Pironi slammed
into Alain Prost, shattering his leg and ending his own driving career,
Enzo's comment was a laconic 'Arrivederci Mondiale'. So it proved.
Despite the creation of a UK satellite office and the hiring of John
Barnard to build a new seven-speed automatic gearbox, there wasn't to
be another championship in Enzo's lifetime. At the time of his death,
Fiat had dismissed Enzo's son Piero and were installing new directors
on the board.

Despite these failures, Enzo's successes, combined with concerted
mythmaking, had made Ferrari F1's most valuable brand in a new era
of global TV, the only team able to command a fanatic following. (Their
rivals thought that Ferrari often got an easy ride from the judges as a
result.) After Enzo's death, Fiat increased their stake to 90 per cent.
At first, the team culture remained much the same and Nigel Mansell
became the latest champion to quit the snake pit in 1990. The following
season Alain Prost, a master of driving politics, also left in disgust after
dismissing the latest 643 as a 'truck'. However, with support from Shell,
the team was able to hire the best and in 1996 Michael Schumacher

secured what it had never had before – domination of the sport, with joint drivers' and constructors' championships between 2000 to 2004.

Enzo Ferrari claimed not to like monuments, but of course his team is his monument. Even so, it is striking that Ferrari only achieved consistent success when Il Commendatore was safely dead and buried.

Bernard Marmaduke Fitzalan-Howard

Bernard Marmaduke Fitzalan-Howard, 16th Duke of Norfolk, Earl of Arundel and Surrey KG GCVO, GBE, TD, PC, Earl Marshal and Hereditary Marshal of England, born Arundel 30 May 1908, died 31 January 1975. Jockey Club steward 1966–8. Vice-chairman Turf Board, chairman Sussex CCC.

As well as being the premier duke and earl in the kingdom and organiser of the coronations of both George VI and Queen Elizabeth II, the 16th Duke of Norfolk was also the Queen's representative at Ascot and for some odd reason the 1962/3 Ashes tour manager. He also made two crucial interventions in horse racing – both of which we now take for granted.

The first change, in 1961, was to allow trainers to declare openly that a horse had been doped or 'got at'. Until then, trainers were liable for any doping, however it was administered, and had their licences withdrawn if it was proved to the Jockey Club's satisfaction. The result was a series of likely miscarriages of justice with innocent trainers deprived of their livings, often on very questionable evidence. Many other cases went uninvestigated – either covered up by the trainers themselves or by sympathetic stewards. The duke's recommendations immediately proved their value when the Ascot Gold Cup winner Pandofell was discovered dazed and bruised, having been doped with phenobarbitone. Though the culprit was never caught, the horse's trainer was able to declare the matter openly and Pandofell, though he missed Goodwood, gained a consolation win in the Doncaster Cup.

Four years later, the duke chaired a Committee on the Pattern of Racing, intended to organise the sport's chaotic schedule. As well as national and international fixture clashes, another concern was that French racing might become closed to English horses, whose low winnings gave them an unfair advantage under the French system. The duke's committee proposed a new pattern of Group races, assessed as tests of speed and stamina rather than ranked by prize money. Group One races were championships and classics run on a weight for age or sex basis, but not handicaps. Group Twos were other important races of international standing with some penalties and allowances. Group Threes were domestic races – often tests for Group One and Two races. Below these were 'listed races'.

The new system was designed to encourage two-year-olds to be brought on through five- to eight-furlong races and have adequate preparation time for the classics, before staying on to race as four-year-olds. Critics disliked the downplaying of handicaps and the bias towards shorter 'classic' distances, but the system helped international agreement and the fair comparison of horses. From 1971, it was accepted by the French and Irish and has since been adopted by most major horse-racing nations. (The National Hunt racing committee, of which the duke was also a member, also set up a similar system.) In 1985, the Holland-Martin committee went further by setting criteria for all group races and checks on their quality – further boosting the international growth of the sport.

In 1973, the five-furlong Ascot New Stakes was renamed the Norfolk Stakes in the duke's honour. Since 2006 it has been a Group Two race.

Dick Fosbury

Richard Douglas Fosbury, high jumper, born Portland, Oregon 6 March 1947. Olympic champion 1968, NCAA champion 1969. US Athletic Hall of Fame 1992.

In 1968 Dick Fosbury was glad simply to be in the Olympic high jump finals. Only a year before he had been ranked 48th in the world, despite adopting a new style in which he went over the bar on his back, rather than side- or face-on. Despite gaining six inches in height with his new style, he remained well off the pace – and nowhere near the 2.28 metres reached by 1964 Olympic Champion Valeriy Brumel.

Fosbury had switched because he was unable to master the complexities of Brumel's straddle – the dominant high jump technique at the time. With his new approach, he had combined elements of two antiquated styles – the curved run of the 'eastern cut-off' or 'scissors', which he had been using before, and the 'back lay-out' employed a century before by the Victorian jumper Marshall Brooks. Fosbury's curved run, launching from the outer foot, gave him greater speed, while his arched body enabled him to pass his centre of gravity underneath the bar, while jumping over it.

By the time of the Mexico City Olympics, Fosbury had four advantages: 1) no Brumel, who had injured himself in a motorcycle crash; 2) a high-altitude games that favoured explosive events; 3) a new training programme developed at the University of Oregon to build his strength; 4) the first PVC foam mats – in place of the sand and sawdust on which he had already compressed a couple of vertebrae.

In the finals, Dick found himself in a three-way contest between compatriot Edward Caruthers and Valentin Gavrilov of the USSR. On his third attempt at 2.24 he almost timed out, but looped over to become an instant hero, thanks to the 'flop' that was named after him by a local reporter.

Far from this being an instant revolution, the following Olympics was again won with a straddle. It was 1973 before Dwight Stones set a world record with the flop and the early 1980s before it became universal. Despite this, no one would deny the brilliance of Dick Fosbury's idea. Out of contention as early as the 1972 games, he became an engineer, but remained involved with track and field, his fame secure forever.

William 'Fatty' Foulke

William Henry Foulke, goalkeeper and cricketer, born Dawley, Shropshire 12 April 1874, died 1 May 1916. Playing career: Sheffield United 1894–1905 (league champions 1898, FA Cup 1899, 1902), Chelsea 1905–6, Bradford City 1906–7 (Division Two champions 1908). England 1897, 1 cap. Cricket career: Derbyshire 1900, 4 matches.

As his nickname would suggest, William Foulke is most famous for his weight, which increased from 12 to over 22 stones. However, he also deserves to be remembered for giving rise to the use of ballboys and altering the rules on penalties.

Despite his weight, the very limited film that survives of the 6 foot 2 inch Foulke shows an agile and springy keeper, credited by the press as cool, clever and steady and unfortunate to get only one international cap. His ball skills were good enough for first-class cricket, which he quit because of the risk to his hands.

An ex-miner who was signed by Sheffield United for just £5, Foulke was an immediate success with the fans, both for his shot-stopping ability and his natural ebullience. Strong enough to kick from goal line to goal line, he could play like an extra back, running far from goal to break up attacks, and could punch to the halfway line – a valuable skill, as until 1902 a keeper holding the ball could be charged into the net for a goal. Foulke also used his size and speed to race off the line at penalties. Although from 1905 keepers were restricted to their own line, his reputation as a stopper grew, saving ten penalties in one season.

Many colourful press reports surround Foulke, who broke crossbars with his weight, could pick up the ball single-handed, dangled Liverpool's George Allan upside down by his legs and once threw a Port Vale forward into his goal. There was also a famous naked rampage after the 1902 FA Cup final in which referee Tom Kirkham had awarded an offside goal to Southampton. Credited with high spirits, Foulke played up to his star billing and appeared on music hall stages. The six-month-old Chelsea Football Club, which needed big crowds to fill its vast new Stamford Bridge stadium, signed Bill for £50 and were soon the best-supported club in the league. Chelsea's use of young lads to retrieve lost balls and highlight the size of their keeper was the first use of the ballboy. At Bradford City, another new and struggling club, Foulke once again drew big crowds and secured promotion. He is also a possible source for Bury FC's 'Shaker' nickname. After a loss to the team, Foulke was reported to have told Bradford trainer George Waller that City had been 'shaken'.

Foulke retired in 1907, probably due to cartilage injuries, and is often said to have ended up on a Blackpool beach saving shots for coppers. Happily, there is no truth in this – it was a seaside lark blown up out of all proportion. In fact, he enjoyed a fairly comfortable retirement as a publican and illegal bookmaker and later a shopkeeper, living to see his nephew score in Sheffield United's 1915 FA Cup final victory.

C.B. Fry

Charles Burgess Fry, cricketer, footballer, rugby player, sprinter, long jumper, javelin thrower, boxer, swimmer, sculler, tennis player and golfer, born Croydon 25 April 1872, died 7 September 1956. First-class career: Oxford University 1892–5, Sussex 1894–1908, London County 1900–2, Hampshire 1909–21; 30,886 runs (50.22), 166 wickets (29.34); 26 Tests 1,223 runs (32.18). Football career: Southampton 1900–2, Portsmouth 1902–3. England 1901, 1 cap.

A quick glance at the above will show why John Arlott termed the debonair Charles Fry the 'most variously gifted Englishman of any age'. Primarily a cricketer, Fry had a strong defence and a powerful drive, topped the county averages five times and retired with a first-class average second only to his Sussex team-mate Ranji. (Fry joked that he had one shot which he could play to ten different places, although that number increased in the telling.) Gaining extra power from his early backlift, Fry set records with 13 centuries in 1901 and seven in succession ten years later. With his fast-medium bowling he once took 6 for 78 and twice took a hat-trick at Lord's. After Jim Phillips called him three times for throwing in 1898, Fry offered to bowl with his arm in a splint, but it still earned him the 'C.B. Shy' tag.

A natural athlete, Fry was reportedly able to jump backwards off the floor to land on the top of a mantelpiece and his long jump equalled the world record of 23 feet 6½ inches. Always an individualist, he appeared on the track for the first international athletics meeting in 1894 but insisted on starting with one leg dangling over the line. As a footballer he reached the FA Cup final with Southampton and played rugby for Blackheath and the Barbarians.

Said to be able to talk about one subject while writing on another, Fry's other contributions included books, journalism and his own magazine, and he was later credited with developing running commentary as a style of cricket reporting. Narrowly defeated three times in parliamentary elections, he represented India at the League of Nations, taught, founded a training ship and in 1939 recalled being offered the throne of Albania at the 1920 Geneva Convention – although there is no direct historical evidence for this. In his seventies, he claimed to be becoming interested

in racing as a new challenge. 'As what, Charles?' asked his friend Denzil
Batchelor. 'Trainer, jockey or horse?' For all his talents, Fry never got quite
the recognition he deserved. Though he was nearly a quadruple blue at
Oxford, a breakdown caused Fry to slip from a first in Moderations to a
fourth in his Finals. In middle age, he became prone to ever-more eccentric dressing and behaviour, and as well as a growing enthusiasm for
Nazism, also developed a strange fear and hatred of Indians, including his
old friend Ranji.

Fry's most lasting impact on sport was probably in killing off
old-fashioned underarm lob bowling. As late as 1909/10 G.H. Simpson-
Hayward was taking 6 for 43 against the South Africans with this style
and averaged one wicket per 18 runs. However, while playing against
Oxford in 1912, Fry moved to a double century against lob bowler and
future MCC president H.S. Altham by playing the bat croquet-style
between his legs. It seems fitting that Fry is probably the only man to
have changed sporting history through mockery.

Masaru Furukawa – 'The Human Submarine'

Masaru Furukawa, swimmer, born Hashimoto, Japan 6 January 1936, died 21 November 1993. Olympic Champion 200 metres breaststroke 1956. International Swimming Hall of Fame 1981.

Between 1954 and 1956, Masaru Furukawa was pretty much uncatchable in the swimming pool. He was also pretty much unseeable and unjudgeable, as he exploited the rules to swim underwater, which he and other Japanese swimmers had realised was much faster than a surface stroke. Having already twice broken the 200 metres record, on 1 October 1955 Furukawa set four world-record times in a single afternoon. In the 200 metres and 200 yards, he took his first breath at 25 metres, his second at the turn and only three each on the other lengths. In his world-beating 100 metres/100 yards he took just five breaths.

After he won the 1956 Olympic 200 metres title in a near record time, FINA (the international swimming authority) decided that the style was dangerous, dull to watch and impossible to officiate and redefined the breaststroke – although Furukawa's records stood, and it was to be six years before his long-course times were broken. Today there is a stroke judge stationed at the 15-metre line to check that the swimmers' heads are above water and prevent them doing a Furukawa.

Dave Gallaher

David Gallaher, rugby hooker and wing forward, coach, selector and author, born Ramelton, Co Donegal 30 October 1873, died 4 October 1917. Playing career: Ponsonby, Auckland 1896–1909. New Zealand 1903–6, 36 international caps, 6 Tests. Coach and selector 1906–16.

On 30 July 1905, Dave Gallaher's 'Originals' set sail from New Zealand with 27 players plus three half-frozen stowaways on a world rugby tour. When they returned home they were greeted by a crowd of 30,000, having played 35 matches and lost just one, shocked British rugby to the core and established New Zealand as the nation to beat.

Gallaher, a six-foot Boer War veteran, was by no means an obvious choice as captain. Having missed the preliminary tour in Australia, he found the team split between regional factions and risked a vote to reappoint him captain. The team he led weren't the first New Zealand rugby tourists, or the first to wear black or perform the haka. Seventeen years earlier a Maori team had completed an epic 107-game world tour, winning 49 out of 74 British matches and beating Ireland. However, not even they could match the impact of Gallaher's 'Slaughterers' – and not just because full back George Gillett played wearing a sunhat. Gallaher's 'Maorilanders' were bigger than most British sides and wore light boots, shin guards and reinforced jerseys that were rumoured to be made of eelskin to make them harder to grab. They lined up differently too. Otago coach Jimmy Duncan had split the halfbacks' roles, using a wedge-shaped formation in which the fly half and inside centre stood in front of the three-quarter line. (This pair were named 'five-eighths' – either by vice captain Billy Stead or lock George Nicholson.) Above all, Gallaher's men played rugby as the Brits had never seen it before.

The New Zealanders attacked from the first whistle and instead of the usual division between 'donkeys' at the front and 'derby winners' at the back, their forwards attacked the line as well, with Frank Glasgow scoring eight tries. At line-outs their hooker threw in – rather than the British style of using a halfback – and they deliberately missed out jumpers and split the line to score direct, racking up 33 tries this way.

Their seven-strong scrum, with a two-man front row, packed down fast and used their driving wedge shape to get the ball out quickly. Meanwhile, Gallaher played as a 'roving wing forward' – in effect a second scrum half, attacking his opposite number if the ball was lost. Some opponents complained that he was offside and obstructing play, although Wales's captain Gwyn Nicholls thought the tactic perfectly fair and the New Zealanders managed to beat Cardiff without Gallaher. Rather than lying on the ball in the British style, Dave's men aimed to draw opponents into a ruck and dig it out fast – a cornerstone of New Zealand rugby success for decades to come. The forwards' cover defence was also new in the northern hemisphere and it was seven games before their line was even breached. In total, they conceded just eight tries in 35 matches.

The New Zealand backs were another revelation. Rated 'three yards faster' than the opposition, they included world 120 yards hurdles champion George Smith. Behind him was Billy Wallace, the first attacking full back ever seen and a scorer of 246 points, while the mazy runs of five-eighth Jimmy Hunter produced another 132. The New Zealanders kicked with both feet and prided themselves on their handling abilities. In one game, they dropped the ball just once. Plays were practised beforehand and analysed afterwards and included scissor and miss passes, dummy runs and reverse passes that had never been seen before in Britain. (The Welsh only beat them after plotting their own secret move – a reverse pass and a sudden attack on the blind side.) Other teams were no match for the tourists' combined team play and individual brilliance, which drew 70,000 to Crystal Palace for the England game, with tickets selling for six times face value. For the first time, rugby eclipsed football in popularity and the team made nearly £15,000 for the NZRFU – although the players were on just three shillings a day expenses.

Despite barracking before and during the fierce Welsh encounters, the two worst incidents were against Surrey at Richmond, when the RFU's William Williams tried to stop them by blowing his whistle every 30 seconds for undisclosed offences, and at Inverleith, where they beat Scotland and their old adversary 'Darkie' Bedell-Sivright, who had already lost gracelessly to them back in Wellington. The Scottish RFU exceeded themselves in pettiness and vindictiveness – attempting to cancel the fixture, leaving the pitch unprotected and refusing to attend the post-match dinner. The match wasn't even granted international status, and when the next New Zealand touring party arrived in 1924/5, the Scots would deny them a match. Elsewhere, however, the team were heroes, and Billy Stead and Gallaher somehow cranked out 80,000 words in a week to compose *The Complete Rugby Footballer*. The first technical work on rugby, it explained how their various 'ruses' were designed to operate in two or more different ways. The pair were paid £100 for 322 pages that were later also translated into Spanish for Argentinian players.

After returning in triumph by way of France and the US, Gallaher soon ended his playing career and became a coach and selector. Despite being exempt from service by reason of his age and the death of two brothers, he went back to war with his old regiment, the Mounted Rifles, and was killed at Passchendaele.

After the 1905 tour some British clubs such as Bristol immediately set out to adopt the New Zealanders' approach, but the Scots rejected it as 'bad for the game' and most sides ignored the simple message of C.B. Fry – that the tourists had won through better organisation. The New Zealanders' return in 1924/5 was marked by long rows about the two-man front row, which was penalised and banned the year after. It would be the late 1960s before their use of codes, attacking full backs and hookers throwing in began to be adopted in British rugby and another decade before blanket support from forwards was normal. As for a try-scoring front-row forward, that was considered quite laughable until the 1980s.

Today Dave Gallaher is commemorated by an Auckland club cup and the Dave Gallaher Trophy, which is contested between France and New Zealand. In 2005, Dave Gallaher Memorial Park in Letterkenny, Ireland was opened by Tana Umaga's national side, who still use the name the *Daily Mail* coined for Gallaher's 27 men – the All Blacks.

Mike Gatting

Michael William Gatting OBE, cricketer, born Kingsbury 6 June 1957. First-class career: Middlesex 1978–98, 551 matches, 36,549 runs (49.52); 79 Tests 1978–95 (captain 23 tests), 4,409 runs (35.55); 92 ODIs, 2,095 runs (29.50). Wisden Cricketer of the Year 1984.

A Test player from the age of 20, Mike Gatting was a determined batsman who scored England's highest single-day total in India, a great fielder who took two crucial catches at the fabled 1981 Headingley Test and an occasional bowler, once taking 2 for 26 in a rebel Test. As England captain, Gatting was the last to win an Ashes tour in Australia, where his fielding helped win one match in under three days. Despite all this, his most lasting impact on cricket was the row that led to the long-delayed introduction of neutral umpiring in Tests.

This historic change followed Gatting's much-publicised showdown with Pakistani umpire Shakoor Rana at the second Faisalabad Test in 1987. It ended the tradition of home sides providing the umpire – a tradition that stretches back to the very earliest days of cricket, when umpires were mere hired hands. (As late as the 1950s, umpires were either being 'supported' or 'not supported' by cricketing grandees.)

The Faisalabad incident was an accident waiting to happen – the culmination of years of ill feeling and accusation. As early as 1951, an MCC tour of Pakistan produced not a single successful lbw appeal, and five years later friction between the two nations plus 'high spirits' resulted in umpire Idris Begh having a bucket of water tipped on him. Although Pakistani officials like A.H. Kardar were calling for neutral Test umpires in the early 1970s, nothing happened. In 1978, Rana had incorrectly given Gatting out and also had a row with Sunil Gavaskar, but it was in the mid-1980s that tension really increased and Rana, a railway engineer from an old cricketing family, was often at the heart of it. During their 1984/5 tour, the New Zealanders nearly quit the field in protest at his decisions, with Bruce Edgar throwing his bat away in disgust at Karachi. The following year Jeff Thomson kicked the stumps in frustration and the Australians also nearly quit.

The fuse was lit at the first Test in Lahore when Chris Broad refused to leave his wicket after Shakil Khan had ruled him out. With Rana stoking the fire by wearing a Pakistani sweater and cap, a bat-pad catch off Ijaz Ahmed was rejected, and Bill Athey's 'The sooner we get out of this fucking country, the better' came ringing through the stump mic. England tour manager Peter Lush publicly queried the quality of umpiring, but Gatting was more forthright, stating that nine out of 20 dismissals had been unfair – eight of them coming from Rana.

Having lost the first Test, the powder keg finally went off in the second. With Pakistan on 106 for 5 and chasing 292, Gatting was adjudged to have moved fielder David Capel behind Saleem Malik's back, although he claimed he was actually stopping him from moving. Though the microphones picked up the row that followed, it was never clear who swore first, but Rana, allegedly egged on by captain Javed Miandad, demanded an apology for foul and abusive language. The 65-hour stalemate that followed cost a day's play, with the Pakistanis sitting contentedly in the pavilion, until the Foreign Office and TCCB leant sufficiently hard on Gatting to force him to scribble the following: 'Dear Shakoor Rana, I apologise for the bad language used during the 2nd day of the Test match at Fisalabad [sic]'. Because the TCCB didn't demand the reinstatement of the lost day's play, the match was drawn, but Mike and his team-mates were given a £1,000 sweetener. After further disputes in later matches, the need for neutral umpiring became impossible to ignore, especially after the Pakistani paper *The Nation* spoke out against 'puppet umpires'.

If the Faisalabad row had echoes of bodyline, with straightforward players being first supported and then undermined by the administrators at home, this was confirmed by the aftermath. After six months, Gatting (like Douglas Jardine before him) was replaced – the pretext being an off-pitch encounter with a barmaid. In an echo of bowler Harold Larwood's treatment, he was also fined £5,000 for going into print with an unapproved version of events. The immediate result for England was three changes of captain in one summer and four defeats by the West Indies. Both Gatting and Broad, who had helped win the 1986/7 Ashes, were ruled out of the 1989 series (lost 4–0) and went on a rebel tour to South Africa instead. After he returned to Test cricket, a Gatting century helped secure the only win of the next Ashes series. Now a coach and commentator and ECB committee member, Gatting has written of his regret over the whole affair, though few would argue that the change it produced wasn't a good thing.

Rana himself was stood down from Test cricket before bouncing back after four years to help award a record 14 lbws in a single Test. Struck off for a refusal to attend a refresher course, he soon returned to the game.

Spencer Gore

Spencer William Gore, tennis player and cricketer, born Wimbledon 10 March 1850, died 19 April 1906. Wimbledon singles champion 1877. First-class career: Surrey 1874–9, 5 matches, 75 runs (9.37).

The first Wimbledon singles champion, all-round sportsman Spencer Gore developed volleying in the game, which in turn led to the invention of the lob to defeat him.

When the first lawn tennis championships were held in 1877, Gore, who had played football and rackets at Harrow, captained the school cricket XI and occasionally appeared for Surrey CCC, was one of the 22 gentlemen to chip in his guinea fee. After five days' play he reached the final, which was postponed once to avoid a clash with the Eton v Harrow match at Lord's and then for four days due to rain. When Gore finally met William Marshall, it was expected that the distant service line and high drooping net would favour the real tennis style, playing corner to corner. Instead, Gore left the baseline to volley at the net. Serving at shoulder level, he employed his round-arm serve for extra 'cut', making the ball bounce low and keeping it hard to return. With Marshall unable to drive down the line due to the high net, Gore had the match wrapped up within 50 minutes. In front of a crowd of 200, either standing on the ground or seated in their carriages, he won 6–1, 6–2, 6–4 and collected 12 guineas and a cup. (Soon after this, the service line would be moved nearer the net, the net lowered and the balls made heavier.)

The following year, A.T. Myers pioneered the overhead serve and Gore, who complained that he found tennis rather boring, returned as champion to meet challenger Frank Hadow, a Ceylon planter who had also played rackets at Harrow. During the course of the match, there was a lot of bad feeling about Gore's volleying, especially when he leant over the net, and this was made illegal the following year. During the contest, Gore's dominance at the net encouraged Hadow to try the first lob to defeat him and, despite a terrible headache, he won in straight sets. The following year, with Hadow absent, John Hartley won with very similar tactics, confirming the lob as an important stroke in the game, although the patient baselining it encouraged made it rather dull to watch.

E.M. Grace – 'The Coroner'

Dr Edward Mills Grace, coroner, cricketer, born Bristol 28 November 1841, died 20 May 1911. First-class career: Gloucestershire 1862–96 (county champions 1873, 76, 77, 80), 314 matches, 10,205 runs (18.66), 305 wickets (20.37); 1 Test, 36 runs (18.00).

From the 1860s better wickets, overarm deliveries and greater pace and intensity all increased the bowling threat in cricket, but batting remained in the grip of a rigid orthodoxy that rated playing the 'correct' stroke more highly than actually scoring any runs. These correct strokes were believed to exist for every delivery, and batsmen kept their back feet fixed and played at every ball. Above all, off-side balls were played to the off, with no pulling or hooking across the wicket. At its most extreme, off-theorists like Nottinghamshire's Alfred Shaw would bowl exclusively to the off stump, with batsmen virtuously ignoring the unguarded leg side.

The man who drove the biggest coach and four through this orthodoxy was E.M. Grace, the older, smaller, bewhiskered brother of W.G. By the time he was 17, his cricket-mad mother Martha was recommending him for inclusion in the All England side and by 20 he was playing for the Gentlemen. (Martha, who once crossed the Avon attached to a huge box kite, was also the only woman to get a *Wisden* obituary.) According to W.G., it was playing with a large bat at a young age that encouraged E.M.'s pulling tendencies and he scandalised the cricket purists by carting the ball from outside off stump to the leg side, letting the fielders redistribute themselves and then sending the balls through the gaps they had left behind. Not only was the coroner an outstanding fielder who terrorised batsmen by closing in at point, he was also a good lob and round-arm bowler. In 1862, while appearing for the MCC against Kent, E.M. took ten wickets in an innings and scored 192 runs – part of a career total of over 10,000 wickets at every level of the game. One of his tricks was to drop the ball directly on the wicket from a great height, leaving the batsman virtually powerless.

As a 22-year-old medical student, E.M. Grace became the first high-profile 'amateur' to tour Australia with leg hitter George Parr, attracted by £500 expenses and the lure of cheap gold. He also played at the first Oval Test. As Gloucestershire's secretary from 1871 to 1909, E.M. ran the show, setting the entry price, keeping track of the subs by recall alone and raiding the cash box pretty much as he pleased. (Against Surrey he once claimed £20 expenses – four times what a visiting team got.) One 1873 club meeting note read 'Present: E.M. Grace and that's all.' Early on in his career, he responded to a dubious lbw by taking the stumps home with him and once, when heckled from the crowd, he chased the barracker from the stands, returning some while later to report, 'He's still running.' On another occasion, convinced he was about to get the opposing batsman out, he insisted on an extra delivery and had him stumped. Grace's Gloucestershire were unbeaten at home for seven years in the 1870s and he played until 1896, when lameness ruled him out, although he remained an effective lob bowler. Reputedly the life and soul of the party, it was considered a great shame that he never wrote a memoir.

Gradually other batsmen also became more aware of opportunities to the leg side, especially after 1884, when Walter Read, the Surrey and England shamateur, saved England at the Oval, sending the crowd into such a frenzy that they invaded the pitch and <u>Lord Harris</u> threatened to abandon the match. Despite this, the purists continued to regret that Grace 'with all his great qualities, never played with a straight bat', and brother W.G. claimed to be a late convert to leg hitting. From 1905, Jack Hobbs began facing the bowler more directly to take account of leg-side opportunities and, though criticised by some as a 'two-eyed Jack', his style became the new orthodoxy. Even so, as late as the 1920s Walter Hammond was being reprimanded for leg hitting and the prejudice only really died out after the first bodyline test in 1932, when hooking the ball became the only possible means of making runs, as Australia's Stan McCabe showed with a masterful 187.

W.G. Grace – 'The Champion'

William Gilbert Grace, doctor, cricketer, athlete, lawn bowler and sports promoter, born Downend, Bristol 18 July 1848, died Mottingham, Kent 23 October 1915. First-class career: Gloucestershire 1865–99 (county champions 1873, 76, 77, 78), London County 1900–4; 869 matches, 54,896 runs (39.55), 2,876 wickets (17.99). Test record: 22 matches, 1,098 runs (32.29), 9 wickets (26.22).

Still the most famous name in cricket, 'Gilly' Grace, as he was known to his family, had not one but two great cricketing careers. From 1869 until 1880 he topped the batting averages ten times, once scoring nearly twice as many runs as the nearest contender. As well as the first twin centuries in a match, Grace recorded the first 200+ and 300+ scores and was the first to score 2,000 runs in a season. In his 'second career' in the 1890s, the great competitor rose to the challenge of the Australians, playing in the first nine home Tests and winning eight out of 13 matches and four out of five series. In this second flowering 'The Doctor' became the first to score 1,000 runs in the 'bowlers' month' of May. Forty-three years of first-class cricket left him the all-time fifth in runs scored and sixth in wickets taken. Much the most famous sportsman in Britain, he was drawing crowds of 25,000 by the 1870s and was second only to Queen Victoria and perhaps Prime Minister Gladstone in national fame.

The eighth of nine children born to cricket-mad parents, Grace's arrival on the cricketing scene coincided with Edgar Willsher's overarm bowling, which some found easier to 'sight', as well as the heavy rolling of wickets, which replaced the lumps and bumps that had limited scores before. Both changes favoured the talented batsman over the previously dominant bowler. A big lad who carried a small bat, Grace scored 170 and 56 not out against the Gentlemen of Sussex when aged just 15, and at 18 scored an unbeaten double century for England. His success was based on huge physical strength and energy, combined with great concentration. In terms of fitness, he was an all-round athlete, breaking off from the England match to win the quarter-mile hurdles at the National Olympian Festival. He was a master of terrible wickets, and even spectators who could remember Fuller Pilch and <u>Felix</u> had to admit that Grace was streets ahead, with his combination of forward and back play. In 1869 he made an unprecedented 1,320 runs and 6 centuries, and within two years was 'The Champion' with 2,000+ runs in a season. *John Lillywhite's Cricketers' Companion* identified him as 'the most wonderful cricketer who ever held a bat'.

Though he gained weight in the late 1870s, Grace began the decade by setting new standards of fitness. On the pitch he was so strong that he could throw a cricket ball 116 yards (106 metres) or drive a ball to the boundary despite striking a fielder's hands en route. His energy was such that he could score a double century after a night at a patient's bedside and his phenomenal concentration kept him going when others had lapsed, producing great scores on terrible wickets. Before long, his domination of the game was becoming a problem. In 1873 he not only made over 2,000 runs but also took over 100 wickets. 'He is ruining cricket in first-class matches,' complained the *Sporting Gazette*. 'He demoralises fielders and breaks the hearts of bowlers.' Three years later, Grace scored the first triple century followed by another two innings later. Meanwhile, his county Gloucestershire were in the middle of a seven-year run in which they were never beaten at home.

As a batsman, Grace was one of the first to appreciate the value of going in first, before the bowlers had settled, and set out to score as soon as possible, taking each ball on its merits. 'The first duty is to make runs,' he declared, and make runs he did. Though not an innovator in terms of new strokes – he claimed not to have pulled a ball across his wicket until his forties – he did break with the old tradition of defending with front-foot strokes and scoring off the back. Instead, he scored with either, playing around the ground and relying on timing and power rather than the wristy cuts of other, more elegant batsmen. Credited with spreading the popularity of tubular rubber gloves, Grace took on and mastered medium-pacers, off-theorists and eventually even the new Australian speed merchants. ('The faster they are, the better I like 'em,' he claimed.) He only faced one recorded bouncer, and yorkers were trapped under his big brown boots, though he was said to be vulnerable to the googlies introduced late in his career. One stroke he was indirectly responsible for was the reverse sweep. Once, when he and his brother <u>E.M.</u> were fielding and busily trying to distract Sir

Timothy O'Brien of Middlesex, O'Brien unexpectedly swept the ball into his guts as revenge and Grace threatened to call the police.

The flipside of Grace's extreme competitiveness and will to win were complaints of petulant and often not particularly clever behaviour. Gamesmanship and exploitation of the rules were part of his game. He was perhaps the first sportsman to cheat a coin toss – crying 'The lady!' as a sovereign, with Queen Victoria on one side and Britannia on the other, spun through the air. On another occasion, he and brother E.M. simply ignored the whole tossing business and just marched out to the crease. W.G. was once caught using an over-large bat, and was famously reluctant to leave the crease 'while there was a stump left standing'. As a fielder at cover point or long leg he enjoyed catching the ball then hiding it behind his back to give the batsman a moment's false hope, and at the 1882 Oval Test he enraged Australian bowler Frederick Spofforth by luring Sammy Jones from his crease to stump him – the result being that the fired-up Spofforth won the match with 7 for 46 and the *Sporting Times* published its famous obituary for English cricket. As a captain, Grace once declared with the ball in the air to avoid being caught.

W.G. took over 7,000 wickets in all competitions, but was less feared as a bowler and kept to a round-arm style when most had switched to overarm. At first a quick bowler, he gradually slowed down, relying on good length and line but only moderate spin. It was said that his reputation suggested a guile he didn't actually possess and some players reckoned he offered an easy hit every four balls or so. Grace usually aimed for lbw and leg-side catches, and his crossing of the wicket made it harder for the umpires to judge – or refuse – the great man's appeals. Another trick was to fool the batsman into staring into the sun and temporarily blinding himself. Once, when an opponent admitted over dinner that he should have been out last ball, Grace appealed first thing the following morning.

In any other age, Grace's domination of the game might have changed the rules of cricket. At the time, these greatly favoured the batsman and there was some talk of making the wicket larger, but instead the tactical response was 'off theory', led by Alfred Shaw, the Nottingham professional who had the best record against Grace, bowling him 20 times and having him caught 29 more. From 1870 Shaw dropped his speed and concentrated on accuracy, bowling slow off breaks and varying his flight, pace and length to try to lure W.G. into trouble. Shaw, who bowled more balls than he conceded runs, was so successful that most bowlers copied him, leaving England defenceless when the pacy and aggressive Spofforth arrived.

Off the pitch, Grace played along with the establishment, without being part of it. A doctor's son who had come into the game when it was a means of earning a living, he was notoriously grasping, demanding a staggering £3,000 for a tour and all expenses met at home. Lord Sheffield is supposed to have founded his all-Australian cricket competition because it was a cheaper way of encouraging cricket than sending the Doctor out. Though he made his money from the game, from 1865 Grace was a regular for the 'amateur' Gentlemen against the Players and single-handedly turned the tide against the pros. In the 14 years before he joined, the amateur Gentlemen had lost 22 games and won only once, but with him they won 24 and lost only four.

In the emerging County Championship, Grace's Gloucestershire won the title three times in the 1870s and, though he was born too early for a full Test career, as a selector he helped get team-mate and admirer Ranji – the first non-white English Test cricketer – into the side.

When cricket allowed, Grace was reportedly a good doctor, and famous for not billing his poorer patients. Another who had reason to be grateful for his medical skills and strength was team-mate Arthur Croome, whose life Grace saved after he was accidentally impaled on Old Trafford's pitchside railings. Though he screwed every shilling he could get out of the game, Grace once donated a benefit match's proceeds to Alfred Shaw. Above all, he brought a huge popularity to cricket at a time when many other rival games such as hockey and lacrosse might have threatened its supremacy. 100,000 subscribed a shilling each to the *Daily Telegraph*'s testimonial fund. After he retired from cricket, Grace shifted to golf, achieving a 9 handicap, and promoted indoor bowls at the Crystal Palace, captaining the first England v Scotland international. Famous for his high-pitched West Country burr, he yelled defiance at the wartime airships that passed over his south London home and died shortly after a zeppelin raid.

There have been Grace gates at Lord's since 1923 and his bust remains a fixture in the Long Room. On the one occasion that it was removed, a member present remarked 'it must be war'. It was 1939 and he was right.

Clarrie Grimmett – 'The Scarlet Pimpernel'

Clarence Victor Grimmett, cricketer, born Dunedin, New Zealand 25 December 1891, died Adelaide, Australia 2 May 1980. First-class career: Victoria 1917–23, South Australia 1923–36, 248 matches, 1,424 wickets (22.28); 37 Tests, 216 wickets (24.21). Wisden Cricketer of the Year 1931. Australian Cricket Hall of Fame 1996.

Clarrie Grimmett was not only the first Test bowler to claim 200 wickets, but also the first slow bowler to reign supreme, proving that leg breaks and googlies could be both effective and economical. He also invented some entirely new deliveries – notably the flipper, which is still used today.

It took Grimmett until he was 33 to become Australia's best spinner, for the very good reason that he started his career as a fast bowler in New Zealand. After emigrating in 1918, his inelegant, almost round arm, delivery and subtle style held him back, and it wasn't until the final match of the 1924/5 Ashes series that he made his Test debut against Arthur Gilligan's MCC, full of confidence after their win in Melbourne.

Grimmett was an unlikely debutant – 33 years old, prematurely bald, wiry and wizened. However, his impact was immediate, as he took 5 for 45 followed by 6 for 37. His chief weapon was an exceptionally accurate and economical leg break, with endlessly varied length and flight – an elusive ball that earned him his 'Scarlet Pimpernel' tag. The other arrows in his quiver were a fairly obvious googly, used for tactical purposes, and a lethal top-spinner delivered out of the back of the hand, which sped on with extra bounce and pace. Endless practice also produced the flipper. Bowled with the same wrist rotation as a leg break, it was squeezed out of the front of the hand, between the thumb and fingers, bouncing halfway down the pitch and skidding through fast and low. He disguised the tell-tale, joint-wrecking click by snapping his other fingers.

Clarrie proved to be even more effective on soft English turf. Along with his partner Arthur Mailey, he took over 100 wickets on the 1926 tour and exposed the weakness of even the best English batsmen. Walter Hammond described him as a 'real horror'. Grimmett's variety allowed

him to thrive despite the over-prepared wickets of the day and he was
pivotal in Australia's 1928/9 and 1930 Ashes victories. Although <u>Don
Bradman</u> gained the plaudits, 1930 Test captain Vic Richardson was
insistent that they 'couldn't have beaten the blind school without Clarrie
Grimmett'. After taking 33 wickets against the West Indies in 1930/1,
Grimmett struggled in the 1932/3 bodyline series, but in partnership
with fellow spinner Bill O'Reilly took 44 wickets against South Africa
in 1935/6 at just 14.59 apiece. This was to be his last Test appearance,
although as late as 1938 his omission was being described as 'sheer
lunacy' by batsman Bill Ponsford.

Throughout his career, Grimmett continued to experiment and even
developed a 'wrong wrong 'un' – a ball that looked like a googly, but
broke from the leg side. He kept turning his arm over until he was 70.
During the 1990s leg spin renaissance, Grimmett's flipper helped turn
<u>Shane Warne</u> into the world's best bowler, while Anil Kumble's top-
spinner helped win the 1993 series against England for India.

Walter Hagen – 'The Haig'

Walter Charles Hagen, golfer, born Rochester, New York 21 December 1892, died 6 October 1969. Wins include: British Open 1922, 24, 28, 29, US Open 1914, 19, USPGA 1921, 24, 25, 26, 27, Ryder Cup 1927, as non-playing captain 1931, 35, 37. Golf Hall of Fame 1974.

Walter Hagen was a golfing revolutionary. A superstar during the 1920s 'golden age of sport', he was the first modern touring pro, the first to switch press attention from the gilded amateurs, the first to earn $1 million from the game and the first to make big money from endorsements. Along the way, he also bequeathed us the tee and the 14-club limit and cemented the status of the Ryder Cup and the US as the world's leading golfing nation.

The son of a German-American blacksmith, Hagen was golfing on the family cow pasture at the age of five. At first a caddy, then a humble club pro at Rochester, by 1913 he was already finishing fourth in the US Open. His great strengths were his short iron shots, 6 to 12-foot putts and, in an era before the sand wedge, the ability to get out of trouble with a thin-bladed club. He was also one of the first to deliberately overshoot the pin and spin back. His main weakness was his wayward driving and, although this improved during his career, he only once shot a hole-in-one. On the other hand, he was able to pull off sensational recovery shots and could switch his concentration off and on, chatting to the crowd between shots and putting any failures behind him. In an era of hickory shafts, dusty greens and ragged fairways, he would establish a series of stroke-play records, including four consecutive PGA wins and 22 consecutive wins over 36 holes or more.

From 1914, when he won his first US Open with a course record 68, Hagen looked like what he was – a star rather than a shabby servant. Copying fellow pro Tom Anderson, he dressed immaculately in pressed plus-fours, bright jumpers and two-tone shoes and was the first sportsman to make the US best-dressed list. He soon gained a better paid and more independent role at Detroit's Oakland Hills club, and from 1920 broke the social barrier in US golf when the Inverness Club invited him into the clubhouse.

From 1920 'The Haig' took his star style to the UK, where the prize money was pitiful and the pros were treated as hired hands and still banned from all clubhouses. At Deal for the 1920 Open, he turned up with a valet and a Daimler to change in rather than the tent provided, and later that year he and George Duncan threatened to boycott the French Open if they weren't allowed to use the locker room. Though he was only 53rd at Deal, by the following year Hagen was sixth at St Andrews and in 1922 he won at Royal St George's. Second in 1923, he refused to enter the Troon clubhouse, from which he had been banned, and instead took his admirers off to the pub. In 1924 he won again, despite a first round of 77, wowing the crowds on the last green by striking the ball and turning his back on it before it had dropped in. In 1928 his friend the Prince of Wales indicated that Royal St George's wouldn't remain 'royal' much longer unless Hagen was admitted to the clubhouse, and the revolution was complete. The following year Walter confirmed the new supremacy of US golf by winning in terrible conditions at Muirfield. If one includes Hagen's wins at the Western Open – a 'major' in its day – only Jack Nicklaus has exceeded his haul of top tournament victories.

Walter had a reputation for being the last to leave a party, though he was a master at hiding his drinks, and played up to his legend by deliberately arriving for tournaments in 'last night's tuxedo'. At the 1922 Open, he was reminded that his rivals had long since gone to bed. 'Yeah,' replied the Haig, 'but they ain't sleeping.' To quote *Times* writer Bernard Darwin, Hagen had a 'shrewd eye for weaknesses and how to exploit them'. In 1927, the Brits were unable to keep pace with the apparent drinking rate of the US Ryder Cup team – which contributed to their 9½–2½ drubbing and a lasting American enthusiasm for a contest Hagen captained five times. Other examples of his gamesmanship and psychology included waiting until rival Mike Brady was present before holing a putt to secure a play-off with him. Against Leo Diegel at the 1925 PGA, he repeatedly conceded putts before forcing him to take a final crucial one, which Diegel of course fluffed. An expert on the rules, Hagen got round a terrible lie at the 1919 US Open by exercising his right to lift and 'check that the ball was his'.

A master of match play, Hagen trounced <u>Bobby Jones</u> at a 1926 challenge match and was always keenly aware of the need for a current title as a 'selling commodity'. He also employed Bob Harlow as his agent, booker and PR man – another first for the sport. As an endorser of clubs, Hagen soon had so many deals that a 14-club limit was established to save the caddies' backs. From 1924, with steel shafts legalised, he promoted his own range of Wilson-made clubs. Paid $2,500 to publicise William Lowell's wooden tees – in place of the traditional pile of earth – he usually played with one tucked behind his ear. Though after a fatal accident he never drove fast again, he criss-crossed America in his limo, guest-starring at some 200 US golf clubs, many of them praised as 'a racy little course'. He once added to his legend by playing a hole in pitch blackness 'from memory alone'. Little did his opponents guess that he had already planted a series of balls along the hole to 'discover' by torchlight.

Having originally earned just 10 cents a round as a caddy, Hagen earned large sums from tuition and appearance fees, and had a unique ability to blow $10,000 on a trip, put it all behind him and go out for another big win. In his autobiography he stated, 'I never wanted to be a millionaire – just live like one.' Eventually, he abandoned tournament golf for exhibitions – playing an estimated 1,500 in total. He was also president of Florida's Pasadena Club, charming potential members with his charisma and a blonde secretary who played the ukulele.

In 1930, with his powers waning, Hagen and his partner, trick-shot expert Joe Kirkwood, set off on a final great adventure – a round-the-world tour, in which they fought off baboons and lions, taught the shimmy to various undressed native girls, picked up malaria and a baby elephant, and even created a 24-hour ceasefire during the Siege of Shanghai so that bodies could be removed from the course and they could demonstrate their skills.

Careless with money, Walter was lucky that Wilson's club sales and Bob Harlow's business sense enabled him to live a quiet and well-lubricated retirement in Minnesota. In 1966, a celebratory dinner was held in honour of the man who had turned professional golfers from servants into millionaires. Arnold Palmer, whose hard-charging style was often compared to Hagen's, flew in to tell him that 'if it were not for you, Walter, this dinner tonight would be down in the pro shop, not here in the ballroom.' In 1969, the year he died of throat cancer, Hagen was the fourth American to be made an honorary member of the Royal and Ancient. He went straight into the 1944 and 1971 Golf Halls of Fame. Harlow's successor, Fred Corcoran, had already pinpointed his appeal as 'living the life lesser men dream about'. Though some of the stuffier British clubs might have disagreed, fellow pro Chuck Kocsis said simply, 'Everybody loved the guy. He was a lot of fun.'

Wyndham Halswelle

Lieutenant Wyndham Halswelle, sprinter and middle distance runner, born London 30 May 1882, died 31 March 1915. Olympic 400 m champion 1908.

Wyndham Halswelle, the only winner of an Olympic walkover, was at the centre of one of the games' first great judging controversies, which led to major changes in the running of international sport.

A London-born Scot, Halswelle first came to sporting prominence at the age of 22 after returning from fighting in the Boer War with the Highland Light Infantry. He was setting British 440-yard records from 1904, but his greatest exploit came two years later at the Scottish Championships at Powderhall when, in a single afternoon, he won all four races between 100 yards and 880, and set two more national records. Running in the 400 and 800 metres at the 1906 Athens games, he won silver and bronze and his 1908 440-yard British record would last a quarter of a century.

At London in 1908, Halswelle set an Olympic record in his 400 metres heat, but in the final, running on an unmarked track, he was blocked by a diagonal run and an elbow from the American John Carpenter. The umpire, on the lookout for a practice that was accepted in the US but which broke British (and therefore Olympic) rules, cut the tape to void the race and another American competitor, John Taylor of Pennsylvania, had to be forcibly removed from the track. The Amateur Athletic Association, the British body who were judging the event, bungled the resulting inquiry, and refused even to interview the US runners, who boycotted the rearranged final in which Halswelle, under duress but warmly applauded by the crowd, ran a slowish solo 50 seconds.

This row, on top of other disputes about dipping flags to the king, racing on Sundays and alleged bias in the boxing, led not only to marked tracks in future Olympics, but also to the formation of the International Amateur Athletics Federation to agree and judge events on its own independent rules. This helped remove accusations of bias and became a template for most international sporting events, although it has sometimes left the Olympic 'brand' at the mercy of corrupt sporting organisations.

After the debacle, Halswelle lost his taste for athletics and returned to the military. In 1915, during the battle of Neuve Chapelle, he returned to his post despite a bullet wound – only to be killed outright by the same sniper who had struck him earlier. Today, the Scottish under-20 400 metres champion is awarded a trophy in his honour.

Frank Hancock

Francis Escott Hancock, rugby player, born Wiveliscombe, Somerset 7 December 1859, died 1943. Clubs: Somerset, Cardiff 1884–6; Wales 4 caps.

Frank Hancock was the English-born captain of Wales whose talent helped create rugby's modern four-man three-quarter line.

At the time Hancock played, rugby tactics were slowly evolving from the original school game of long drawn-out scrummages, with the ball only occasionally fed out to one of two 'wings', each comprising a half-back, three-quarter and full back, who were charged with running it in. The exception were the Scots, who from 1877 risked a single full back and four years later also began to employ a 'work-shy forward' to form a three-man three-quarter line.

The four-man line was a result of the skill of Frank Hancock. A county captain at just 17, he was one of four rugby-playing sons of a Somerset brewer who later moved to Wales in search of thirsty miners and dockers. In 1883, young Frank came into the Cardiff first team as a replacement and greatly impressed the selectors with two tries that showcased his pace and creative thinking. Rather than lose him, Cardiff dared to field just eight forwards and four three-quarters and by 1885/6 had appointed Hancock captain for what was to be an undefeated season, with 131 tries scored. So successful was Cardiff's handling-based style that most Welsh clubs followed suit – except Newport, where star centre Arthur Gould refused to give up his solo splendour. In 1886, the national squad dared to field both men at centre, but went back to a three-man line after a single muddy defeat. Two years later, in Gould's absence, they risked it again and were finally converted when they beat a touring Maori side. The Welsh three-quarter system swept the home nations – especially after they won their first Triple Crown in 1893. (This may not have gone down entirely well in the Hancock family, as one brother played for England.) The main exception to this formation was in the southern hemisphere, which developed its own variant – the use of players between the halfbacks and three-quarters known, logically enough, as five-eighths.

Alan Hardaker

Alan Hardaker OBE, centre forward and sports administrator, born Hull 29 July 1912, died 4 March 1980. Playing career: Hull City 1929–39. Administrative career: assistant league secretary 1951–6, league secretary 1957–76, chief executive 1977–9, director general 1979–80.

Memorably but unfairly referred to as 'Lytham's answer to Idi Amin', Alan Hardaker's appearance was rather more in the Nikita Khrushchev/Charlie Drake mould. He was the Football League's fourth secretary and by far its most capable, dynamic and influential leader. As the League's modernising 'dictator/enforcer', Hardaker was a full-time professional in charge of a competition managed by warring part-timers. League president Joe Richards claimed that he had never met anyone who got into or out of more trouble.

During his quarter century in charge, Alan Hardaker turned the hidebound League into something like a modern entertainment industry, slowly adapting it to a more complex era of jet travel, European football and star salaries that threatened to tear it apart. Along the way, he set up the League Cup, changed the promotion system, brought in the first TV and sponsorship income and pioneered changes to the game that were later adopted worldwide. However, he never enjoyed enough power to transform the League as he wanted to, and the eventual result would be the floating off of the top division a dozen years after his death.

A former Hull City reserve who was offered professional terms (probably so that he could be flogged off to Bradford Park Avenue), Hardaker was a lord mayor's secretary who in wartime rose to become a naval lieutenant commander. He joined the Football League in 1951 at a time when reform was increasingly urgently needed. A loose confederacy of 88 (later 92) rival clubs all run by various local wheeler-dealers, the League was supposed to be run by its management committee, but the controlling influence was its work-shy secretary Fred Howarth. Howarth, a Freemason who had inherited the secretaryship, ran the League as a family business, with a staff of six operating out of a terraced house in Starkie Street, Preston. Old meeting notes were dumped in the attic and Howarth, who usually limited his role to arranging the fixtures, ruled by telegram, though phone calls were cheaper. There was no European football and no TV or sponsorship revenue and the clubs pursued their own commercial interests. The three-quarters majority required for change was a colossal handicap, made far worse by Howarth's control of the agenda. Comments he disliked never made it into the minutes and no committee member was allowed to leave with a scrap of paper in his hands.

Typical of the League's parochialism, complacency and short-termism was the decision, after just 15 minutes' debate, to refuse Chelsea's request to play in the new European Champion Clubs Cup, as being 'not in the best interests of the League'. The following season, the League was outflanked by Manchester United and Stanley Rous's FA. After the League turned their backs on Europe, it was Rous's fledgling UEFA that seized control of what would become the Champions League, also creating the Cup Winners' Cup and transforming its own Fairs Cup into the UEFA Cup. It wasn't until Hardaker took over that the League began to communicate with its European opposites.

The League's main income was still the traditional 4 per cent levy on gates, plus just £1,000 in advertising revenue. Having failed to break the pools companies in the 1930s, Howarth's 'family firm' refused any share of the 'tainted money' that dwarfed their gate receipts. Nor was there any TV income, the League having set its face against live broadcasting back in 1931. Though they softened their stance towards radio, an Anglia TV deal that would have compensated clubs for any loss of earnings collapsed as Spurs ignored the management committee's decisions and the pros pressed for a few more shillings' appearance money.

Having rowed with Howarth after his first five minutes in the job, the former lieutenant commander spent most of the 1950s dry-docked, as Howarth clung on to power. Without so much as a desk at first, Hardaker described himself as a 'salaried outcast' stuck in what he termed 'a machine covered in rust and cobwebs'. With no meaningful tasks or power, he studied the minutes piled up in the attic to become the expert on the League's history and machinations. It was 1957 before he finally took over. Though he recognised that what was needed was a US-style commissioner with executive powers, the clubs would never have agreed to such a thing and he had to work through the occasionally fractious management committee. In 1963, his 'Pattern for Football' proposed a five-division League to allow more European football, a later season for better weather, and four-up-four-down promotion and relegation to increase the thrills, but the committee failed to back him and the plan was rejected by just eight votes. Instead, the clubs voted for yet more fixtures, in the form of a League Cup. Hardaker's original idea had been an early-season home-and-away competition to boost the smaller clubs' gate receipts, but without the other changes he wanted, it dragged on until the following season, was boycotted by many larger clubs and became known as 'Hardaker's Folly'. Only a Wembley final and a UEFA Cup place would eventually bring in the bigger teams. In years to come, a 1971 plan for League reorganisation as well as the reforming 1968 and 1981 proposals from Sir Norman Chester, would all be ignored or rejected.

Hardaker had more success with finding better premises and raising cash. Though he claimed that he really preferred Leamington Spa as an HQ, the League ended up in Lytham St Annes, right next door to his own house. In 1959, he went out on a limb to copyright the fixtures list and bring a test case against the pools companies. The deal that followed increased League revenues to £250,000 p.a., eventually rising to £2 million. With up to two-thirds of its clubs losing money and gates declining, this gave the League financial security for the first time, and when Harold Sutcliffe, who compiled the precious tables, died, Hardaker was round to collect his data sheets the day he was buried. With improving finances, the League's staff would expand from six to 30, and in the 1970s, Hardaker would use revenues from the untaxed 'Spot the Ball' competition to part-fund the ground improvements demanded by the 1975 Safety of Sports Grounds Act.

As secretary, Hardaker was at first required to support a 'retain-and-transfer' system that he knew to be indefensible and a maximum wage he felt to be too low. Personally he favoured a 'realistic' £30 maximum, with unlimited bonuses. Jimmy Hill's Professional Footballers' Association ran rings around the sclerotic League and a final attempt to fix an unofficial maximum wage soon collapsed, ushering in what Hardaker termed 'a chronic state of financial ill-health'. The League was still trying to reimpose this in 1968.

As for the retain and transfer system, League president Joe Richards reneged on the reforms he had agreed, and Newcastle United's William McKeag refused to let Hardaker intervene in a case against the dogged

George Eastham, which eventually brought an end to the worst of the hated system. In 1978, Hardaker helped hammer out the agreement that finally established freedom of contract for footballers. This exhausting process saw off the terrifying prospect of EEC interference in British football and led to better bonuses and better contracts, but fewer deals done overall. The effort involved in doing this deal may well have shortened his life.

Before the end of the maximum wage, miserly pay had encouraged corruption and led Hardaker to conduct investigations into illegal payments, 'insurance betting' against lost win bonuses and outright match fixing. However, it was the *People's* investigation into fixer Jimmy Gauld that finally enabled him to bring the cases to court and drive corruption out of the game.

As early as 1958, the 'new broom' Hardaker was actually rescheduling matches to help the TV companies, and despite the opposition of clubs such as Everton, Arsenal and Burnley, and the BBC and ITV's unwillingness to compete strongly for football rights, he helped set up the 1964 deal that produced *Match of the Day*. As TV revenues rose five-fold in five years, he would also introduce the Sunday-afternoon *Big Match*. Later, the clubs' intransigence, unrealistic expectations and insistence on cumbersome group negotiation, plus unhelpful interference from Stanley Rous's FA, would lead to TV blackouts and a complete loss of revenue from time to time. Hardaker's other money-making schemes included the first sponsored competition – the pre-season Watney's Cup. Another innovation was the use of substitutes in League matches from 1965. At first replacements were for injured players only, but injuries were easily faked and free substitution soon followed – although it was 1986 before the clubs felt wealthy enough to afford a second man on the bench.

From 1966, Hardaker introduced the *League Review* as a mouthpiece for the League and, by extension, himself. At first, it was poorly designed and written but it padded out clubs' flimsy teamsheets into proper programmes and came to offer a rare source of serious coverage of football – though still prone to tirades against such 'abominations' as Alf Ramsey's 4-4-2.

Overall, relations between the FA and the League deteriorated as Hardaker fought a series of battles against Rous, who he believed wanted to increase the FA's power over the League. The first serious row, over payments to amateurs, led to a short-lived mass resignation from the

FA in 1965. Relations sank to a new low after the FA forced the League to accept a poor deal on TV, and in 1972 Hardaker announced a 'state of war' between the two bodies. Inevitably, these bad relations spilled over into international football. Although Hardaker built and strengthened the League's ties with UEFA, he found Alf Ramsey difficult and refused to help the international side by shifting fixtures. From 1966 onwards, fewer players were released for international duties and fewer matches rescheduled to help the England team. Although Hardaker took firm action when League sides like Don Revie's Leeds fielded weakened teams, he was less concerned about the national squad and baldly stated that the failure to qualify for the 1974 World Cup 'would be forgotten in six weeks'.

Under Alan Hardaker, the League used its independence to pioneer the independent assessment of referees, a totting-up system for offences, the introduction of red and yellow cards, the first move against the tackle from behind and a more liberal offside rule – the last two being later followed by the FA and FIFA. From 1969, the League also began moving towards a formal non-league pyramid, and automatic relegation rather than the old haphazard system of re-election. In 1973, Hardaker asked for four-up-four-down promotion and relegation in order to get a three-up-three-down compromise from the distrustful clubs – the first change since 1905. In 1976, an Arsenal-sponsored proposal replaced goal averages with goal difference.

Throughout his time in office, Alan Hardaker had to cope with a frequently hostile press that either misquoted or selectively quoted him, including claims that he 'wouldn't hang a dog' on the word of a professional footballer. Recession, inflation and stock-market collapses all caused problems – plus the runaway spending on wages that resulted from the collapse of the maximum wage. With 80 per cent of revenue going straight out of the door as wages, grounds grew increasingly run-down and prone to hooliganism. Hardaker demanded stiffer sentences at a time when the problem wasn't being addressed by the government. He also called for penning to keep warring fans apart – a move which would later prove to be fatally dangerous – but really wanted safer all-seater stadiums, funded by a pools levy. If the Royal Commission on Gambling hadn't rejected this, many deaths might have been prevented. Instead, it took the Hillsborough disaster and Lord Justice Peter Taylor to bring it about.

Promotion to director general in 1980 was supposed to allow Hardaker to retire gracefully, but like Fred Howarth before him, he hung on, restricting his successor Graham Kelly to a side room while the DG laboured over his plan for 'Football in the 1980s', until his death that March.

Lacking the powers that he knew were needed and confronted with 'devious, ruthless and selfish' clubs and managers, Alan Hardaker played a bad hand as well as possible. Ultimately, the weakness of the League's structure, the greed of the big clubs and the FA's desire to muscle in would all result in the spinning-off of the League's top division as the Premier League – a title first suggested by Hardaker back in 1964. Ironically, it was the League's ambitious plans for football that would finally scare the FA into sanctioning the breakaway Premiership, in order to ensure that it still had a role in the game. Since this trauma, the League has strengthened its management and sharpened up its presentation in a way that Hardaker would certainly have approved of. An award in his name is still given to the man-of-the-match at the League Cup final.

David Harris

David Harris, cricketer, born Elvetham, Hampshire 1755, died 19 May 1803. Career: 1778–98, 79 known appearances.

According to his Hambledon and Hampshire team-mate, star batsman William 'Silver Billy' Beldham, the genial but devastating David Harris was 'always first chosen of all men in England'.

The first bowler to achieve sharp lift and relentlessly accurate length, Harris would begin his action 'erect as a soldier' then, to quote John Nyren, 'with a graceful and elegant curve, he raised the fatal ball to his forehead, and drawing back his right foot, started off. Woe be to the unlucky wight who did not know how to stop these cannonades.' Harris's whirling action, unleashed at chest height, gave him complete freedom of movement and the ball he delivered went fizzing across the wicket, gaining pace off the pitch and making a leap at the batsman's ungloved fingers. To make matters worse for 'unlucky wights', he could also spin the ball with his strong potter's fingers. Having pioneered winter training by practising in his barn, he was accurate enough to wear a bare patch on a wicket, and the new standards of skill he set led to the first rules on pitch preparation and new balls.

Unlike his predecessor <u>Lumpy Stevens</u>, Harris preferred rising ground for a wicket and deployed his fielders with care – going for catches, even though bowlers weren't credited for them in those days. Although most early records are missing, seven or eight runs was considered a good score against the affable bachelor. Even notorious blockers such as Tom 'Old Everlasting' Walker struggled against him – once making just one run from 170 balls. Described by John Nyren as 'masculine, erect and appalling', Harris forced batsmen to come forward to defend for the first time. 'Silver Billy' began tackling length bowling by leaping out beyond the crease to smother rising deliveries, and William Fennex of Buckinghamshire is credited with developing a more elegant stretch.

Even when he was wracked with gout and forced to use crutches, Harris remained a lethal weapon. 'He was of strict principle,' wrote Nyren, 'high honour, inflexible integrity, a character on which scandal or calumny never dared to breathe.' Eventually, Harris was forced to sit on a chair between deliveries in 'simple grandeur and repose'. After his retirement, no one could match him and batsmen regained the upper hand in the game. Gradually, to restore the balance, the wicket had to be doubled in size and the faster round-arm bowling pioneered by John Willes allowed. The Reverend John Mitford considered Harris 'the finest bowler whom the world ever rejoiced in when living, or lamented over when dead'.

Lord Harris

George Robert Canning Harris, 4th Baron Harris, cricketer and cricket administrator, born Trinidad 3 February 1851, died 24 March 1932. First-class career: Eton 1868–70, Oxford 1871–4, Kent 1870–1911 (captain 1875–89), MCC 1871–95, 9,557 runs (27.31). Test career 1879–84: 4 matches, 144 runs (29.00). Administrative career: Kent president 1875, secretary 1875–80, MCC president 1895, MCC trustee 1906–16, treasurer 1896–1932.

George Harris ruled Kent CCC for 60 years and dominated the Lord's Long Room for 40. It was written of him that 'no man has exercised so strong an influence on cricket for so long'. This influence was usually geared towards defending the status quo, but cricket would be a very different game today if not for him.

The son of the governor of Trinidad and president of Kent CCC, Harris was born into political and sporting prestige. Though he was being coached at Lord's from the age of 11, he only gradually emerged as a good player of fast bowling, who coolly advised a fellow player whose teeth had just been knocked through his lips 'not to put his head where his bat ought to be'. Though he insisted on cricket's status as a 'high moral and educational medium', Harris was unrepentant about carrying out a sneak run-out – a 'mankad' – at the 1870 Eton v Harrow match and always had a fiery temper. (He later recommended pawpaws as a treatment for dyspepsia.) At Kent, he was a player and committee member from the age of 20, captain at 25 and played until his mid-thirties. Under him, the county became part of the first rank in cricket, although their glory years, with four championships between 1906 and 1913, came after he stopped playing regularly.

At Kent, Harris played in a quasi-league with no relegation or promotion and a voluntary fixture list of matches played between sides that varied from the largely professional to the almost entirely amateur. Harris saw nothing wrong with this and was credited with keeping good relations between the counties and the MCC, which grandly 'reigned, but did not rule'. The first ephemeral County Cricket Council formed around him, but it didn't survive his departure for India as Under-Secretary of State, and a plan for a three-division championship was scotched by vested interests. In 1904, nine years after his return from India, an Advisory Cricket Committee would form at Lord's and in 1911 Harris would oppose Yorkshire and Lancashire's plan to ditch perennial also-rans Derbyshire, Northants, Essex, Somerset and Worcestershire.

Having failed in his 1886 bid to implement a 12-month residency qualification, Harris became a stickler for the game's rather illogical rules. In 1896, after he questioned Ranji's eligibility for England and failed to select him, both Lancashire and Surrey picked England's first non-white international, quite possibly just to spite Harris. Within two years, the MCC would take over responsibility for selecting all home Test sides, and the first five-Test series was held in 1899. In 1920, when Walter Hammond preferred to play for Gloucestershire, where he had grown up, rather than Kent, where he was born, Harris compared his choice to 'Bolshevism' and kept Hammond out of first-class cricket until 1923. In response, Worcestershire president Lord Deerhurst congratulated Harris on having 'buggered the career of another young cricketer'. (Later, Harris's MCC would also fail to select Ranji's nephew Duleepsinhji.)

As far as the rules of the game were concerned, Harris campaigned long and hard against throwing. At one point he favoured unpaid amateur umpires, who he thought would be less sympathetic to the 'chuckers'. After this proved impractical, he supported umpire Jim Phillips's 1890s crusade, fired two of his own bowlers and boycotted the Lancashire pair of George Nash and Jack Crossland – though Crossland had bowled unchallenged at Lord's. As an amateur batsman, Harris regarded batsmen's interests as paramount, and blocked an 1897 amendment that would have made lbw less restrictive. As a result, batsmen continued to remorselessly pad balls away, amassing giant scores on wickets that were now being protected from the weather. In 1926, he finally began addressing the imbalance between batsmen and bowlers, but his new rule on 'snicks' proved impractical. It took five years to get a voluntary agreement on a larger wicket and Harris was in his grave before the lbw law was liberalised. In the meantime, drastic measures such as bodyline bowling would be needed to get the more stubborn batsmen out.

As for the illogical divisions between amateurs and professionals, Harris claimed there was an 'agreement' between the two sides, implying that professionals were happy to be called by their surnames only, to never captain sides, get worse accommodation and food, receive low wages and (usually) retire in penury. At Lord's he gained the new power to pick and choose Test captains – sometimes successfully, as with his protégé Pelham Warner, sometimes disastrously, as when Percy Chapman was deposed. A lasting result of Harris's reign was the 1896 deal that added both Headingley and Trent Bridge to the Oval, Lord's and Old Trafford as Test venues, as part of the new five-Test set-up. In 1919, he rejected the rather odd suggestion that left-handed play be banned and oversaw a brief experiment with two-day county matches, which allowed far too little time to get a result on protected wickets.

Internationally, Harris is often credited with helping the spread of cricket, claiming that it had 'done more to consolidate the Empire than any other influence'. In fact, his first brush with international cricket provoked a riot and a boycott. Eternally status-aware, Harris had led the fifth touring party to Australia, billed as 'The Gentlemen of England with Ulyett and Emmett' – the two Yorkshire professionals given bowling duties. After a crushing defeat in Melbourne at the hands of <u>Fred Spofforth</u>, Harris provoked a riot in Sydney in 1879 when Melburnian umpire George Coulthard gave him a second 'life'. After a pitch invasion, Harris accepted a grovelling apology from the Australians, then made a lengthy complaint in the *Daily Telegraph* and used his influence to have Billy Murdoch's Australian tourists frozen out when they came to Britain. Harris emerged a hero after <u>Charles Alcock</u> persuaded him to captain England at the Oval, though the five-wicket victory might not have been possible had Spofforth not been disabled by some 'questionable bowling' (*The Times*) at Scarborough.

In India, where he served as governor of Bombay, native peoples had been playing cricket since the 1830s, and Harris instituted the first official inter-racial matches between the Presidency and a Parsee side. However, he generally preferred playing against other expat Europeans, and it was his protégé <u>Lord Hawke</u> who led the first tour. Surprised by the Parsees' victory over Hawke, Harris resisted local efforts to create more cricket grounds in the city and in 1893 was away playing cricket during nine days of sectarian rioting – only returning to play another match. It was well after he left India that the majority Hindu population were allowed to join in the Presidency matches. Back in England, Harris formed the Imperial Cricket Council, a whites-only talking shop that lacked the power to impose rules on Test cricket. An unsuccessful triangular tournament followed three years later, which was boycotted by several Australian professionals in a row over pay, and the ICC didn't meet again for six years. Although Harris considered the 1926 West Indies side overrated, he did allow the expansion of the ICC to give them, the New Zealanders and the Indians Test status.

Harris continued to play cricket for the MCC until he was 78 and there is a garden in his name at Lord's. Ironically, he is best known from the Australian TV series *Bodyline*, where he was shown selecting <u>Douglas Jardine</u> as captain. That's a little unjust, as he died some months before the appointment.

Coburn Haskell

Coburn Haskell, inventor and businessman, born Boston 31 December 1868, died 14 December 1922.

In 1936, looking back on the ten-fold increase in the popularity of golf over the last 30 years, *Golf Illustrated* concluded that the rubber-wound ball had done for the sport what the pneumatic tyre had done for the car.

As chance would have it, it was at B.F. Goodrich's tyre-making plant in Akron, Ohio that businessman Coburn Haskell, while waiting for his golf partner Bertram Work, first rolled up a bit of rubber thread into a ball and bounced it. After this proto-powerball hit the ceiling, the two men had the idea of rolling a thread around a central core to make a revolutionary new golf ball – though one that was still covered with traditional gutta-percha. Patented in 1899, the early Haskell models tended to duck and swerve, but from 1901 bramble (bump) markings on the cover and a machine to wind 20 metres of rubber under tension produced a ball that allowed new levels of spin, control and 'feel', and even produced a decent result from a mishit. That year a Haskell ball was used by Walt Travis to win the 1901 US Amateur title and Coburn's US sales were off and flying. However, the more conservative UK remained suspicious of the 'bounding billies', which were felt to be too hard to control on the green – not to mention eight times the price of a solid 'gutty' ball. Even when Sandy Herd won the 1902 Open with a billy, not all were convinced. (Herd had made a last-minute decision to play with the ball, which survived four rounds, although by the time he finally secured his great triumph, beating <u>James Braid</u> and <u>Harry Vardon</u> by a stroke, the ball's innards were already poking out.) Matters weren't settled until 1914 when, at the Sandy Lodge course, Braid, Vardon, <u>J.H Taylor</u> and George Duncan carried out a trial in which the Haskell ball won by nine holes, outdistancing the gutty by over 25 metres.

While Haskell prospered, at least 200 rival makers experimented with cores of mercury, ball bearing, lead and cork, as well as covers marked with moons, squares and triangles – until dimples were found to maximise lift and minimise drag. The new rubber-wound balls helped reduce scores so that the 'bogie', which had represented the 'spirit' or likely number of shots per hole, came to represent one *over* par. The slang word 'birdie' – meaning 'good' – came to mean one under par and 'eagle' and 'albatross' represented ever-rarer birds and scores. (Not a 'partridge' because, as the old joke has it, you can't have a partridge on a par three.) Ball sizes were standardised in 1921 and in the years to come the ability of the Haskell ball to take punishment would help bring about the modern world of hard-headed clubs and steel shafts.

By 1917, Haskell had sold his patents to the Spalding Company and retired rich. In fact, the rubber revolution might have begun 30 years earlier, when a Scottish ex-naval captain and inventor named Duncan Stewart had the same idea. However, although Stewart persevered with it, local golfers rejected it, due mainly to the lack of the familiar 'click' when it was struck.

João Havelange

Jean-Marie Faustin Goedefroid de Havelange, swimmer, water polo player and sports administrator, born Rio de Janeiro 8 May 1916. President Confederação Brasileira de Desportos/Futebol 1958–75, IOC member 1963–. FIFA president 1974–98. FIFA president of honour 1998–.

At Frankfurt on 10 June 1974, a new sporting era began as the intense and charismatic João Havelange replaced Stanley Rous as the president of FIFA. Soon Havelange would transform FIFA from a modest sporting association, overwhelmingly concerned with match scheduling, to a politically aware marketing-led business – a transformation so successful that most other international sporting bodies, including the Olympics itself, would soon copy it.

The lawyer son of a French-speaking Belgian, Havelange swam at the 1936 Berlin Olympics, played water polo at Helsinki in 1952 and was chef de mission at the following games. From 1958 he was also president of the Brazilian Sports Confederation (CBD), credited with organising the Brazil side that won its first World Cup that year. He also had profitable business interests in buses, insurance and chemicals.

In the run-up to the 1974 FIFA presidential election, Rous, an ex-referee who worked virtually for free, concentrated on modest reforms and plans for new coaching projects, relying on his own reputation plus a slim leaflet detailing his achievements. Against him, the multilingual Havelange had $6 million from the renamed CBF to spend and lobbied face to face in 86 countries – often with Pelé in tow – winning over many developing nations. Unlike Rous, Havelange was politically astute, promising more World Cup berths for poorer nations and a youth World Cup, which they might have a hope of hosting. After his election, he increased his popularity among his supporters by expelling apartheid South Africa, sidelining Taiwan and Israel and opening FIFA up to China. He also expanded the World Cup to first 24 and then 32 nations. (In 1990, it took 24 matches to eliminate just eight teams.)

Havelange funded his enlarged World Cup by teaming up with Horst Dassler and Patrick Nally to create a modern system of sponsorship deals and TV rights. Fuelled by booming global TV audiences, Dassler and Nally's company sold the first large FIFA sponsorship to Coca-Cola for an unknown amount, before setting up today's system of 'partners', in which global corporations supply cash, goods and favours in return for exclusive advertising and promotional rights, seats and impressive-sounding awards for their bosses. (Today the FIFA World Cup brand is applied to 8,000 products.) Havelange's new approach helped build FIFA into a \$4 billion organisation, able to dole out favours to members and member bodies worldwide. Again, both the Olympics and UEFA would follow suit.

As FIFA president, Havelange kept close to his supporters, whoever they were. The Argentinian generals, who threw their gagged political opponents into the sea from planes and tortured them within earshot of the national stadium, kept the 1978 World Cup despite protests and the assassination of organiser General Omar Actis by rival army factions. Havelange was also a favoured guest of the Nigerian generals who carried out the botched execution of ecological protester and human-rights activist Ken Saro-Wiwa. Such was his power and influence that his subsequent re-elections went uncontested – a pattern to be followed by many other international sports federations.

Keen to boost his own fortune and that of his family, Havelange was reported to be involved in the 1994 plan to set up a FIFA lottery, though this was scuppered when the main movers were killed in a helicopter crash. His son-in-law Ricardo Teixeira was also placed on the France 1998 organising committee, despite repeated allegations of misconduct at the Brazilian Football Federation of which he was president.

To his supporters, João Havelange not only made FIFA bigger but more representative and better able to develop the game worldwide. To his detractors, he helped make sport venal, corrupt, undemocratic and soulless.

In 1998, the election of Sepp Blatter as the new FIFA president was seen as a vote for 'more of the same'. Havelange remains FIFA's honorary president, with an estimated \$125,000 pension, travelling expenses, FIFA credit card and chauffeur-driven Mercedes – although he has yet to receive the Nobel Prize for which the Swiss government lobbied. The Brazilian football championship cup and the 2007 Pan-American Games stadium were both named after him, as is the Centre of Football Excellence on Trinidad – an unlikely location for such a thing, but the home of his supporter Jack Warner.

Lord Hawke

Martin Bladen Hawke, Lord Hawke, cricketer and administrator, born Willingham, Lincolnshire 16 August 1860, died 10 October 1938. Playing career: Cambridge University 1882–5, Yorkshire 1881–1911, captain 1883–1910 (county champions 1893, 96, 98, 1900, 01, 02, 05, 08), 633 matches, 16,749 runs (20.15); 5 Tests 1896–9, 55 runs (7.85). Wisden Cricketer of the Year 1909. Administrative career: Yorkshire president 1898–1938, MCC president 1914–18, MCC selector 1899–1911, 1933.

Yorkshire's captain for 17 years, the tall and strong Lord Hawke was a significant influence on cricket for half a century. As well as helping to form the County Championship, he established Headingley as a Test venue, turned Yorkshire from 'a team of ale cans' into cricket's strongest county and helped the MCC take over the selection of Test and touring sides.

Pretty obviously the 7th Baron Hawke wasn't chosen for his playing abilities alone, but he was a good attacking batsman who made some important innings, and was often forced to give up his wicket to achieve a victory – although, as his South African-based Test figures show, he wasn't much use on matting wickets. On the other hand, Hawke's social prestige gave the warring Yorkshire clubs a figure to unify around and he was credited with improving discipline and team loyalty when he followed Surrey's example by offering winter pay. Hawke usually favoured changes that added to his own prestige and, as well as a retirement fund, he instituted a bonus system of personal cash handouts to his team-mates. Those players who failed to kowtow or who slipped below his expected standards were never forgiven and he lost much popular support in the county after the sacking of local hero Bobby Peel for drunkenness in 1897.

Hawke's Yorkshire commanded the best players from seven cities and countless big towns and from 1893 onwards they dominated the championship in a way that even he occasionally worried about. Having supported the inclusion of minnows Essex, Derbyshire, Worcestershire and Leicestershire in 1894, he was suspected in 1911 of involvement in a plot to expel five 'weaker' counties, including Yorkshire's bogey side

Somerset. Meanwhile, as Yorkshire piled up titles, their secretaries M.J. Ellison and Fred Toone were able to invest in a special railway carriage and the first all-weather training facilities. In 1898, Hawke helped get their new Headlingley ground, in which he was an investor, established as a Test venue.

A doer rather than a thinker, Hawke liked attacking cricket and plenty of it, and lost championships by playing everyone in sight rather than cherry-picking the most winnable matches, as the rules of the day allowed. Rather than reform these rules, he criticised captains like Ranji of Sussex who used them to contain the white rose county and make the most of their more limited resources. Early on in his career, Harris showed signs of mild progressiveness, supporting W.G. Grace's effort to make the championship a true all-play-all league and Ellison's idea of reforming the out-of-date lbw rule. In both cases, the overbearing Lord Harris overrode the reformers, keeping the championship thoroughly unequal and leading to an epidemic of defensive pad play. Hawke's plans for an experimental timed match in 1904 were never even put into operation. Generally, his instinct was to enhance the MCC's prestige and thus his own.

When it came to touring abroad, not even the shadows of Paul Kruger's field guns could dissuade Hawke from cricketing in the run-up to the Boer War. In India, he played a non-white Parsee team for the first time, as well as a mixed-race side, and when he toured the West Indies was impressed by the black fast bowlers Archie Cumberbatch and Joseph 'Float' Woods. However, Hawke's arrogance over claiming players for his own foreign touring sides twice led to him competing for crowds with rival 'England' teams. In 1901/2 he even refused to release Yorkshire players to tour Australia. Within two years, the MCC was choosing all representative touring sides and Hawke was to be a selector for ten years.

Once his playing days were over, Hawke grew increasingly out of touch and his hypocrisies became harder to forgive. For example, while he banned his county players from writing for the newspapers and sacked them for 'disloyalty', he felt free to criticise Yorkshire captains in print himself. A stickler for county qualifications, it was occasionally pointed out that he himself had been born in Lincolnshire – although he had strong residential qualifications. As a selector he was uneven at best. Having failed to spot the potential of home-grown players like

George Hirst, he resigned after a series of inept and panicky decisions, one of which caused *Wisden* to comment that the selectors had 'finally touched the bounds of lunacy'. A poor speaker who never addressed the Lords, Hawke struck a bum note (even for 1925) when he declared 'Pray God no professional ever captains England' at a Yorkshire AGM. Professional Herbert Sutcliffe was too wise to accept the poisoned chalice of the county captaincy. As Hawke fell out of public favour, his memoir *Recollections and Reminiscences* – which had sold out all three of the previous editions – sold only 37 copies of the fourth. Returning to Test selection just five years before his death, Hawke played a minor but characteristically unhelpful role in the bodyline scandal.

Howard Head

Howard Head, inventor, born Philadelphia, Pennsylvania 31 July 1914, died 3 March 1991.

Since World War II, many innovations in sports equipment have been due to ex-aerospace engineers, learning from an industry where vast amounts of money are sunk into creating better-performing materials. Of these, the best known and most influential is Howard Head, who reinvented first the ski and then the tennis racket.

In 1947 Head, a US aircraft designer, was growing increasingly frustrated by his inability to ski. Like a bad workman, but a good engineer, he blamed his tools – in this case heavy, twisting, warping laminated wooden skis, not much changed since the 1880s. Head decided to redesign the ski, using the techniques, materials and new flexible cements with which he built strong, lightweight aircraft floors. In 1947, he quit his job and supported himself through poker games while he created the first in a series of prototypes. His first model used an aluminium sandwich with plywood sidewalls and a honeycombed plastic interior – an idea that followed in the footsteps of a trio of Chance Vought aero-engineers. Head repeatedly made and tested skis, aiming for lightness and strength, but though he reached the strength he needed, the aluminium bottoms still collected snow and the edges dulled. Instead, he created a plywood core with a plastic base and an integral hard steel edge. Though heavier than planned, his new skis didn't warp or scratch and were so much stronger and more flexible than wooden ones that after they went on sale in 1950 they were nicknamed 'cheaters'. After complaints of 'chattering' at high speed, a professional model was produced in 1959 that added rubber to the mix. By the following year, these metal skis had taken half of the market, making skiing easier to learn and fuelling a global boom in winter sports.

Head's next great sporting enthusiasm was tennis, where he once again struggled to master the game. In the early 1970s he joined Prince, who had made an improved ball-throwing machine, and turned his attention to the racket where, as with skis, heavy, warping, laminated wood was being replaced with steel and aluminium. Even so, the weight of metal needed to make a strong enough racket limited the size of the head, and thus the sweet spot – the area that returns the best hit. Head's idea was to use honeycombed aluminium to make a racket that was 50 per cent bigger but would still handle like a traditional one. His 1976 Prince Classic resisted twisting from off-centre hits and gave much more power. Reviewers praised it for volleys, ground strokes and overall confidence-boosting and it sold 76,000 in its first year – but mostly to amateurs. Although in 1978 Pam Shriver used one to become the youngest US Open finalist to date, other professionals claimed that it distorted, led to elbow strain in fast rallies, was too soft and didn't serve well. From 1979, the Prince Pro removed the 'trampoline' effect with a stiffer frame and sales leapt ahead. By the early 1980s, oversized heads and composite graphite frames dominated the professional game. Appropriately, given their aero origins, Martina Navratilova described the new larger rackets as the '747s of the sport'.

In skiing, Head's ideas were an unqualified success, but in tennis his success was two-edged. The misnamed 'graphite' rackets favoured power over finesse, and as a result the first-ever limits on head size had to be agreed. Up until the early 2000s, when players like Roger Federer introduced new levels of skill to the game, there were regular calls for head sizes to be reduced to make the game more skilful.

Sonja Henie

Sonja Henie, ice skater, tennis player, swimmer, horse rider, born Oslo 8 April 1912, died 12 October 1969. Olympic champion 1928, 32, 36, world champion 1927, 28, 29, 30, 31, 32, 33, 34, 35, 36, European champion 1931, 32, 33, 34, 35, 36. World Figure Skating Hall of Fame 1976.

At the 1924 Chamonix International Winter Sports Week, (only later credited as the first Winter Olympics) skating champion Herma Planck-Szabo was not impressed by the late entry of a tiny 11-year-old child – even if Sonja Henie was already the Norwegian national champion. Henie kept breaking off her routine to ask her coach what to do next and finished last. Although Sonja later regretted attending Chamonix, she created a sensation that helped make these experimental winter games permanent. The future of skating would also belong to her as, over the next 12 years, she wowed judges and crowds, won 1,473 titles and trophies and transformed skating. Instead of 'minor stunts and figures' performed to a random music track, Sonja was inspired by ballerinas such as Anna Pavlova to dance on the ice, adding form and flow as well as spins on flat skates and double revolution jumps. A technical genius for her time, she mastered 19 spins, some with up to 80 rotations. Her short, fur-trimmed skirts were a sensation and allowed jump spins, while her head tossing, dimpled smile and *joie de vivre* made skating a popular smash in the US. By 1947, 15 million Americans had watched her shows and nearly 200 rinks had opened nationwide.

Sonja Henie was a fascinating paradox. A spoilt little rich girl, her wealthy father Wilhelm was an ex-double world cycling champion who owned the first private car and then the first private plane in Oslo. Sonja swam, played tennis, rode and later raced cars, but never lost her fierce passion for skating, training for at least five hours a day. Her father transformed her into a star, and they pioneered the first ice spectacles – making use of underused sports halls in the tough times of the Depression. The dimpled smile was combined with a fierce temper, a competitive spirit that allowed her to skate with broken ribs and a keen business sense. Though an 'amateur', she commanded 'appearance fees' and her father's favourite ruse was to tell a promoter exactly how much he would lose to him at cards the night before a show.

At the next Winter Olympics in 1928, Sonja triumphed, thanks partly to a block vote of Norwegian judges, which led to the decision that in future there was to be no more than one judge per country. In Lake Placid in 1932 she won handsomely, while in Garmisch four years later she won only narrowly, after 15-year-old Briton Cecilia Colledge was wrong-footed by having the incorrect music played.

After retiring at just 22, Sonja skated in her own choreographed revues, the first major one being at Chicago in 1937. A perfectionist, she once hired her favourite skate sharpener to travel from New York to Chicago for just two minutes' work. On film, she first appeared in *One in a Million* and was soon charging between $125,000 and $300,000 per picture, briefly becoming Hollywood's third-biggest draw after Clark Gable and fellow moppet Shirley Temple – despite her thick Norse accent. Maddened crowds tore her trademark white ermine off her back and on one occasion even pushed through a glass window to get to her. A smart businesswoman, she charged producer Darryl Zanuck $25,000 to complete *Sun Valley Serenade* after she came out of contract, and was careful to keep very quiet about her affair with heavyweight champ Joe Louis. Despite being the youngest holder of the Royal Norwegian Order of St Olav, she was less of a heroine in Norway, especially after the Nazi invasion. On first-name terms with Joseph Goebbels, she had once heiled Hitler on ice and her family property remained protected while other sportspeople were being tortured and a national sporting boycott was one of the few ways of fighting back. Decried as an 'American Quisling', she later claimed to have donated to the Norwegian war effort, although this is doubted.

In total, Henie accumulated $47 million and endorsed numerous products, although, unusually for the times, she drew the line at cigarettes. Her vast jewel and fur collection led to frequent robberies and she increased her wealth through kleptomania and back-street currency deals. After falling out with manager Arthur Wirtz, she began managing her own tours and despite a seating collapse in Baltimore and playing some tiny venues, she turned her fortunes around for a triumphal European tour between 1953 and 1955 – though one a year later in South America was disastrous. By now drinking heavily, Sonja's homicidal rages included one aimed at her family and another at the nurse looking after her mother for calling her 'dear'. Other exploits included suing her brother for a share of his own ranch, whipping the jewels off her mother's body straight after her death and completely stripping a soon-to-be-ex-husband's mansion. Her final movie, *Hello London* (1958), wasn't released and she ended her career in 1960, although she looked forward to staging a TV spectacular. She died in her third husband's arms aged 57, while on a flight to Norway in search of a treatment for her leukaemia.

Helenio Herrera – 'The Magician'

Helenio Herrera, footballer, coach and manager, born Buenos Aires 17 April 1910, died 9 November 1997. Managerial career: Puteaux 1944–5, Stade Français 1945–8, Real Valladolid 1949, Atlético Madrid 1949–52 (champions 1950, 51), CD Malága 1952, Deportivo la Coruña 1953, Sevilla 1953–6, Belenenses 1956–8, Barcelona 1958–60 (league champions 1959, 60, cup winners 1959, Fairs/UEFA Cup 1959, 60), Internazionale 1960–8 (league champions 1963, 65, 66, European Champions Cup 1964, 65, Intercontinental Cup 1964, 65), AS Roma 1968–73 (Italian Cup 1969), Internazionale 1973–4, Rimini 1978–9, Barcelona 1979–81 (cup winners 1981); France 1946–8, Spain 1959–62, Italy 1966–7.

A minor player, but the winner of 16 major titles as a coach, the tall, cadaverous and suspiciously black-haired Helenio Herrera is often credited as the inventor of the ultra-defensive football tactic known as 'catenaccio' or 'door bolt', using a fifth defender to mark space and sweep up any trouble. In fact, this isn't quite true. Catenaccio was in use in Italian football well before Herrera took over at Inter. What *is* true is that he became an expert in its use and also became the first modern 'star manager', using all means fair and foul to improve his team and get paid his due. In doing so, he made 'La Grande' Inter Europe's number one club and himself the godfather of Italian football.

The Argentinian-born Casablancan-raised son of Spanish anarchists, Herrera never liked the 'Magician' or 'Sorcerer' tag, preferring to stress hard work, perfectionism and the lessons learned as a journeyman player. Though he claimed to have invented the idea of the extra defender in France around 1945, credit is usually given to <u>Karl Rappan</u>, who used a fourth defender to help semi-pro Servette and an outgunned Swiss national side compete with stronger rivals. In Italian football, the extra defender was introduced by minor side Salernitana before being embraced at Inter by Alfredo Foni and at Milan by Nereo Rocca, whose European Cup win over Benfica marked the end of Spanish and Portuguese dominance of the game. Gianni Brera's *Gazzetta dello Sport* also championed the ultra-defensive style, and pioneered player ratings, detailed technical analysis and a new vocabulary to describe the precise function of every player.

Hired by Inter owner Angelo Moratti as his twelfth coach in five years, catenaccio suited Il Mago's dictatorial style and obsession with the analysis of players. Whereas Rocca had merely interfered with the lives of his players, Herrera took them over, cocooning them away from the world in the style that still typifies Italian football. To judge from the doping scandals of the early 1960s, it also seems to have given him more opportunity to dose his men with amphetamines, and subsequent scandals have shown the scale of Italian teams' chemical arsenals.

Herrera's libero, or sweeper, employed behind a man-marking back four, gave defensive resilience and allowed a counter-attacking trap to spring – either through the libero himself or via the first attacking wing-backs like Giacinto Facchetti, who were allowed to overlap the wingers in front of them.

The volatile Herrera, whose office wall bore a single crucifix – though he claimed to be a Buddhist – also had a mass of superstitions, including the ritual spilling of wine before a game. He demanded passion – suspending players who talked of 'playing' rather than 'winning' matches – and all-out effort ('Who doesn't give all gives nothing'). A pioneer of the prematch huddle, Herrera's other mantras included 'Taca la bala' ('attack the ball') and the creation of spaces to exploit.

Herrera is also credited with being the first manager to use the crowd as a twelfth man. His encouragement of travelling support – a new idea in Italy – helped give rise to its sometimes violent travelling ultras. In the semi-finals of the 1965 European Cup, Bill Shankly's Liverpool decided to try a little crowd psychology of their own – whipping up the Kop by parading the FA Cup before winning 3–1. On the return leg, Inter's tifosi kept the Liverpool team awake in their hotel, before filling the San Siro with sirens, smoke bombs and fireworks and raining bottles down on the visitors. This put Bill Shankly off European football for good, and it was followed by another Herrera trademark – a series of more than suspect decisions from the referee. One goal was scored direct from an indirect free kick and the other was kicked from goalie Tommy Lawrence's hands. Liverpool's Tommy Smith was so outraged that he threatened to punch the official and Shankly was convinced he had been 'got at'. In domestic football, the courting and bribing of referees by fixers such as Inter's Italo Allodi was notorious, and despite defending deep in the box, Inter went 100 games without a penalty decision against them. A 1967 match against Venezia was particularly infamous. Il Mago's famed ability to forecast results in advance was perhaps not entirely due to second sight, and writer Brian Glanville reported on a web of corruption surrounding him and Allodi.

Helenio's Inter finally destroyed itself on 25 May 1967 as, chasing a third European title, they met Jock Stein's Celtic in Lisbon. Stein made a mockery of 'cocooning' by running an open house to keep his young players relaxed, and then unsettled Herrera by stealing his bench before the kick-off and having his staff heckle him throughout. At least eight exhausted Inter players were vomiting with nerves before the match and most secretly wanted to lose. Having brought along their own travelling support – a first for British football – Celtic went down to a Sandro Mazzola penalty, and Inter shut up shop as usual, but the attacking was relentless and after Celtic had hit the bar twice, Tommy Gemmell scored. Finally, a deflection gave a first European Cup to a northern European side. 'Celtic deserved to win and their win was a victory for the sport,' said Herrera afterwards.

Helenio's style remained anathema to 'venturesome' British clubs ('Defensive rubbish that nearly killed off the game' was Matt Busby's verdict), but remained influential in the new 'Italian style', in which the libero was usually a converted inside forward. Herrera, who had insisted on top wages at Inter and prided himself on earning proper pay and recognition for managers, went to Roma for 100 million lire a year in the days when 100 million lire was really worth something. As for Inter, they returned to their extraordinary managerial roundabout of 42 changes in 50 years.

George Rowland Hill

Sir George Rowland Hill, rugby administrator, born Greenwich 21 January 1855, died 25 April 1925. RFU secretary 1881–1904, president 1904–7.

While football had <u>Charles Alcock</u> to guide it through the problems of allowing professional players, rugby was stuck with George Rowland Hill. 'An amateur of amateurs, and a Tory of Tories' was *The Times*'s obituary writer's verdict on the telegraph engineer turned civil servant who ruled the sport for nearly three decades. A less generous verdict would be that he set the game back for ever.

Throughout his administrative career, Hill showed a rare ability to start a fight in an empty room. A simple scoring dispute with Scotland soon escalated into a six-year boycott of England by the rival home nations, who refused to recognise the RFU's supreme authority. After this was patched up, with the founding of the International Rugby Board in 1886, Hill masterminded an even more ruinous split, whose consequences live on today. At issue were the six shillings per week to which working players felt entitled as compensation for a lost half-day's pay. These men, who made up 11 of the 15 who in 1892 shut out the other home nations without conceding a point, might have made up the whole team, had the London-based RFU not insisted on an unofficial quota of southern backs. Although there were no rules against professionalism, and Hill himself made his money from the sport, he expressed the great fear that 'a man might make a living from the game', setting the RFU on a collision course with the more successful northern clubs.

Matters came to a head in 1893 when the northern clubs travelled down to the RFU's AGM to debate the issues and discovered that Hill had stitched them up. Extra votes had been given to wealthy and privileged Oxbridge colleges to ensure an anti-broken-time vote, although it seems that these weren't actually needed on the day. Having defeated the northern clubs, the RFU immediately passed a series of by-laws, which had nothing to do with the game itself but banned professional players from it. Through the structuring of the committees, Hill also prevented any future discussion of the issue. The FA's policy of running the game but allowing leagues, clubs and competitions to decide whether or not to allow limited professionalism simply never occurred to the RFU. Instead, they set off on a course of inspecting/spying on every player and club, regulating expenses, gifts, medals, prizes and testimonials and handing out bans to any players or clubs they deemed guilty. Crazily, they even handed out £20 bonuses to anyone prepared to grass on a professional who might have received far less. For fear of creeping professionalism, competitive leagues and cups were discouraged, which meant infrequent, meaningless contests between clubs, a lack of top-level sport for the best players and no relegation or transfers to keep a competitive balance between teams. On the other hand, neither the RFU nor most of its clubs published accounts and £1,000 could easily disappear in 'expenses' after a big match.

Hill's man in the North was the Reverend Frank Marshall, who handed out various fines and bans and within two years had driven many of the biggest northern clubs from the game. In 1895, fearing the loss of their best footballers to the booming soccer clubs, they formed a rival Northern RFU, later the Rugby League.

From the point of view of spreading the game, the decisions that Hill's RFU made were as dumb as a sack of hammers. Its total of 481 clubs shrank to 244 and the two best sides, Bradford and Wakefield Trinity, both left. With no representation at all in some big cities, rugby union became most weakened in its strongest counties – Lancashire and Yorkshire – where cup matches had once pulled in bigger crowds than the FA Cup final. With the loss of their best forwards, England's international performances dived. Having won 34 of the previous 54 matches, they won just ten of the following 49 and didn't win another Home Nations Championship until 1910.

In such a strictly amateur game, only the rich could afford to play at the highest level. Very few spoke out, although star three-quarter Ronnie Poulton complained that the game was being limited to the public schools, Oxbridge and the services. 'Rugby is too good a game to be confined to a particular class,' he declared.

There were frequent disputes with the very few touring sides that could afford to travel. Even the three-shillings-a-day expenses paid to Dave Gallaher's 1905 All Blacks and the 1908 Australians caused ructions. Many nations would struggle to find enough wealthy amateurs to tour abroad – especially in hard times. In the 1930s, South African captain Bennie Osler had to spend all his savings on the entertaining expected of a visiting captain. British touring sides rarely represented the country's full playing strength – consisting only of those who could afford a long unpaid holiday plus a substantial donation to the social fund. While rugby hobbled along, soccer boomed, giving it a lead that it has never lost.

Union's war with rugby league continued, so that even playing the 13-man code still as an amateur could get you driven from the game for life. Union players were also banned for such Orwellian crimes as 'discussing the advantages of rugby league', and clubs were forbidden even to share facilities for fear of contamination. In the 1980s, a string of star players such as Bill Beaumont, Gareth Edwards and Fran Cotton were all banned for the crime of writing a book and 'profiting from rugby'. Even intending to write one was an RFU crime. Unable to bend to the wind of change – partly because of the structures Hill had helped put in place – rugby broke in the 1990s, as the players revolted over working like professional athletes for just £20-a-day expenses. The game ran slap-bang into unlimited professionalism, leading to the needless ruin of some fine old clubs.

Hill had been honoured back in 1926 with the first-ever knighthood for services to the game, and after his death a plaque was set up outside the Twickenham gates. Perhaps there should be one outside Wembley too, as he helped ensure soccer would be Britain's number one sport.

Jimmy Hill

James William Thomas Hill OBE, footballer and manager, born Balham 22 July 1928. Playing career: Brentford 1949–53, Fulham 1953–61. Managerial career: Coventry 1961–7 (Third Division champions 1963/4, Second Division champions 1966/7). Head of Sport LWT 1967–72.

Perhaps it began with the beard. As the owner and operator of the only facial hair in the Football League, Brentford wing half Jimmy Hill was transformed into a 'beatnik' or 'Mephistopheles' – depending on which newspaper you read. While Jimmy might not always have been aware of the crowds around him (he famously failed to notice that Craven Cottage was booing him), he was very well aware of the power of the press and unusually confident in dealing with it. He was a fizzing source of ideas, and his confidence, energy, belief in a professional approach in football, political skills and broad entrepreneurial streak were to transform British soccer.

Having seen <u>Ferenc Puskás</u>'s Hungarians destroy England, Hill became a convert to inter-passing and the creation of space rather than the English tradition of using speed, strength and skill to beat your man. After fellow halfback Ron Greenwood fell out with the Brentford management, Jimmy signed for relegation-bound Fulham, where as a part-time MC he was a natural choice as the club rep on the Association Football Players and Trainers Union. After initially defending AFPTU chairman Jimmy Guthrie on the very reasonable grounds that if the League chairmen didn't like him he must be doing something right, Jimmy was chosen to replace him in 1957. Faced with the latest illegal-payments scandal at Sunderland, Hill proved his resourcefulness and energy by collecting the signatures of 250 other players who had received such payments and miraculously rescued David Hickson and Colin Webster from foul-play charges. Hill also ditched the cumbersome AFPTU title for the Professional Footballers' Association. Guthrie had wanted parity with clerks and bus drivers, but Hill saw that professional footballers could be as well paid as the showbiz stars he mixed with and the new working-class talents emerging on TV.

Hill's PFA tackled the two outstanding issues that players had been fighting against since 1904. The first was the maximum wage. This was probably against the common law, but the courts wouldn't rule on FA matters. The greater injustice was the retain and transfer system which meant that players could be suspended without pay. This historic battle would go all the way to parliament, but was mostly played out on Jimmy's home ground – the TV and the press.

Most footballers' greatest hours come on the pitch, but Hill's came in a pub. On 9 December 1960 he faced the press alone at a suddenly arranged press conference. The League had just done what they always did during pay negotiations – offer minor concessions and refuse to discuss the substantive issues. Earlier on, a £30 maximum wage might have bought off the players, but the chairmen's refusal to discuss the crucial issues had caused the pros to rally round Hill – especially when the League backed out of agreements reached after government arbitration. Even Stanley Matthews supported the strike threat, while Jimmy Greaves promised that the stars would stick by the lower-division players. Although the press and many players seemed to think the latest offer reasonable, Jimmy nailed his colours to the mast, identifying two freedoms that all workers other than footballers enjoyed – the right to be paid your worth and the right to leave on fair terms at the end of your contract. This tipped the headlines in his favour and ultimately led to a victory that would change soccer.

In parliament Conservative MP Philip Goodhart described the players' contract as something 'a 15th-century apprentice would look twice at' and Hill's membership of a Labour Commission on Youth secured crucial TUC support for any strike, with an offer to boycott 'blackleg' League games and take action against any players who appeared in them. A surprise ally was the FA, where Hill had been a fervent supporter of Stanley Rous's coaching revolution. Even his pals in the 'Showbiz All-stars' offered to support the strikers, and to the increasing concern of the League and pools companies, the strike threat grew. Hill even mooted the idea of alternative 'non-League' matches between the striking pros – 'Manchester Rovers v Chelsea United' – while League secretary Alan Hardaker threatened to field amateur sides and hinted that a mysterious 'Mr X' was behind it all. (By this he meant Hill's sports agent, Bagenal Harvey.) Cracks developed in the interpretations offered by Hardaker and League president Joe Richards and 'final offers' came and went before Burnley chairman Bob Lord spoke out and the minimum wage was finally abandoned. With their usual rat-like cunning, the League chairmen planned to ditch an illegal system in favour of an unofficial cartel to be agreed at the Café de Paris, but this was kiboshed when Hill's own chairman, Tommy Trinder, paid his big star Johnny Haynes £100 a week.

The players still stood firm on retain and transfer and the League mooted bringing the first 'strike Saturday' matches forward to Friday, a sneaky wheeze that further alienated the press. After an eleventh-hour agreement was reached at the Ministry of Labour, the hated system was ditched – or so it seemed. In practice, the League Management Committee 'finessed' its report, and by March it was clear the League would still not ratify it. 'The Day the Football League Died of Shame,' read one headline, and at the League AGM, the representatives slow-handclapped the reporters present. Jimmy finally ended nearly 60 years of injustice by taking George Eastham's case to court and winning, although the lengthy judgment gave the clubs wiggle room until 1978, when a tribunal deal was brokered by – you guessed it – J. Hill.

Hill's brand of reasoned argument played well in the press and in years to come he helped form both the Cricketers' Association and the Stable Lads' Association – the latter after a bitter TGWU-led strike. By the time of the Eastham case, Hill had quit playing through injury and his next move was a shock appointment as manager of lowly Coventry City, where his predecessor Billy Frith and all his staff were removed in one day. 'Union man' Hill stated, apparently without irony, that he needed loyalty to the club, and went on a not entirely successful spree, spending £2,500 on Bobby Laverick to replace Scottish international Stewart Imlach. Laverick lasted just four games and when Imlach's journalist son Gary quizzed Hill about this, he was unable even to recall the player who had scored seven goals for him.

Jimmy always believed in a professional approach and at Coventry he proved his case, transforming a club as only Herbert Chapman had before. Blue and white-striped Coventry became all-over sky blue, and instead of charging three shillings to watch in cold, wet misery, Hill marketed a club for the first time. Early innovations included the best programmes seen so far, 'crisp and pop' parties for young supporters and hospitality packages, and soon there was a Sky Blue Stand with 5,000 plastic seats. The hymn-like 'Eton Boating Song' was rewritten as the 'Sky Blue Song' and a Sky Blue Club set up. Dog-handling displays and netball matches were staged as prematch entertainment and Coventry introduced pop music to football with its Sky Blue Radio. (Perhaps oddly, it was former England wicketkeeper Godfrey Evans who manned the wheels of steel.) A Sky Blue Express with a special catering coach ferried the fans to away matches until the costs proved prohibitive. As well as the first electronic scoreboard, Coventry pioneered CCTV coverage of away matches and the ground was built up, thanks in part to a Rover Cars-sponsored tour of Europe. Crowds more than doubled, and while Hill kept up his *News of the World* column, Charles Harrold was hired as the first dedicated PR man. Even the players were now allowed to speak to the press, though none were stupid enough to say anything very controversial.

On the pitch results improved steadily, although Hill recognised that players lost their resale value from their mid-twenties and was remorseless in weeding out his squad. After reaching Division One in 1966/7 and being refused the ten-year contract he felt entitled to, he embarked on his third football revolution, as head of sport at London Weekend Television. Hill had long been a champion of a televised Friday-evening match and had been a natural choice to present the 1966 World Cup, declaring that <u>Alf Ramsey</u> didn't have a prayer of winning. At LWT his new task was to build up the weekend sports operation, despite the apathy of the other regions and a light entertainment culture that was more interested in soaps and game shows than sport. (A classic example was the Gillette Cup final where after covering the play all day, LWT cut away with just five balls left to bowl.) As an astute politician and friend of the stars, Hill thrived despite successive management coups, becoming deputy controller of programmes and even manned the cameras during an electricians' strike. The Sunday afternoon *Big Match* appeared with the first HS100 instant-replay cameras and 'Cedric' – a computer that was supposed to be able to forecast results. LWT closed the ratings gap on the BBC and overtook it at the 1970 World Cup, where Hill brought in the first expert panel – whose bar bills were said to have comfortably exceeded their appearance fees.

1972 brought yet more shocks. Having once ditched his commentary duties at Highbury to run the line, Hill moved to the BBC to present *Match of the Day* – Britain's first big-money 'media transfer'. Until 1978 Jimmy would combine both presentation and analysis, with lyrical, if not always logical, comments and pungent criticism of foul play and play-acting. (On the evening that British Summer Time ended, Jim advised viewers to 'make sure they put their cocks back'.) He remained a BBC analyst before moving to Sky in 1998.

Hill kept a foot in both soccer camps as an FA Council member and a League representative. Having narrowly failed to get the League to adopt a more exciting four-up-four-down system in the 1960s, he joined Matt Busby and Bobby Charlton on a panel to modernise the League and encourage more attractive, attacking play. Having already persuaded the Isthmian League to adopt three points for a win, the League followed their advice. Other ideas included rules to discourage back passes and time-wasting by goalkeepers, plus a relaxation on offside from throw-ins and goalkeepers' kicks. After being initially rejected by FIFA, all of these would become part of the game, although they didn't go for the panel's suggested option on 'last-man' professional fouls – a penalty from the 18-yard line.

From 1975, the hyperactive Hill was back in action at Coventry as managing director and later chairman, pioneering hot-water under-pitch heating and the first big sponsorship deal, as the club extracted £80,000 from car-maker Talbot. Another cunning wheeze was kicking off a relegation battle against Bristol City ten minutes late – knowing that a draw would be enough for survival, the players could safely pass the ball around for the final minutes. A name change to Coventry Talbot was mooted and this idea has since been adopted by teams like Wales's TNS, but the big breakthrough was shirt sponsorship. Approval of Coventry's big 'T' shirt design unleashed a flood of new deals. Having suffered its share of violence and vandalism, the club also went all-seater and all-ticket in 1978, but most seats were uncovered and the move was unpopular with the fans. The club suffered from falling gates and the spiralling wages first unleashed by J. Hill Esq. To Jimmy's disgust, the terraces were reinstated and he quit with the club heavily in debt.

Internationally, Hill had interests in the newly rich Arab world and also attempted to create a sister club for Coventry in another motor city – Detroit. Unfortunately, the US league was based on using tax-deductible investments to attract highly paid stars to vast stadiums where most of the tickets were given away and, although Hill's Detroit Express attracted a steady 14,000 fans, he had to bail out.

Back in England, Hill was to have a lasting influence on two more clubs at a low ebb in their fortunes. As a director at Charlton, he backed the first major ground-share with rivals Crystal Palace. Outraged Addicks fans claimed that the essential maintenance had been deliberately neglected and the costs of repair exaggerated to force the move and it took a stubborn seven-year fight to return Charlton to The Valley. This epic struggle was matched at Fulham, where in 1987 Hill became the front man for a rescue bid which soon turned into a prolonged six-way battle between the new management, developers Cabra, who owned Craven Cottage, the fans, the council and various MPs and interest groups. As Fulham haemorrhaged money, Hill earned a 'Judas' tag for suddenly rejecting a fan- and council-backed rescue plan. Having done a deal with Cabra and negotiated a ground share with Chelsea, he had to hear his own words read out against himself in court and showed his 'cloth ear' by trying to arrange a 'celebration' of the club leaving their home. At the eleventh hour, Fulham were saved by the collapse of the commercial-property market and the new freeholders' unwillingness to antagonise football supporters across Britain.

Despite a relatively modest playing career, no footballer has had more of an impact on modern British football than Brentford's Mephistophelean wing half – after whom Coventry fans named a bar at their new stadium. Like it or not (and Charlton and Fulham fans certainly didn't), football now lives in a Jimmy Hill world.

Bernard Hinault – 'Le Patron'

Bernard Hinault, cyclist, born Yffiniac, Brittany 14 November 1954. Major races and champion-ships: Tour de France 1978, 79, 81, 82, 85, green jersey 1979, king of the mountains 1986, 27 stage wins. Giro d'Italia 1980, 82, 85, Vuelta a España 1978, 83, world champion 1980, Grand Prix des Nations 1977, 78, 79, 82, 84, Paris–Roubaix 1981, Dauphiné Libéré 1977, 79, 81, Liège–Bastogne–Liège 1977, 80.

In the late 1970s and early 1980s, Bernard Hinault was the boss of the Tour de France. By the age of 22, he was beating Tour favourites in the Dauphiné Libéré, despite a crash, and the following year he won his first Tour, wearing the colours of a national champion. He would dominate cycling for over 12 years, winning 200 races, including 13 time trials, and became the first cyclist to reach 60 kph. Tour wins in 1980, 83 and 84 were only missed because of injury, and in 1980 Joop Zoetemelk refused to wear yellow the day after Le Patron quit.

Hinault's second nickname, 'Le Blaireau' ('the badger'), name-checked an animal which the French claim never lets go of its prey – a tribute to the ferocity with which Bernard rode. Pushing big gears, which prob-ably led to his knee injuries, he battled through snow to win the 1980 Liège–Bastogne–Liège and won the 1985 Tour despite two bad falls and a broken nose. In that year's Paris–Nice he even fought his way through striking shipyard workers.

By 1984, Bernard Tapie had made Hinault the first highly paid profes-sional cyclist and he stamped his personality on the entire peloton, ordering them to take it easy if a hard day was in the offing. Combined with his prickly yet remote personality, this did not always play well with the fans, but as Hinault said, 'I race to win, not to please people.' His main legacy to the sport was an end to the exhausting split stages, in which the peloton raced twice in one day, disrupting their sleeping routines. After Hinault led a strike against them at Valence d'Agen on his first 1978 Tour, they were never heard of again. Another innovation in road racing was the first use of an aerodynamic teardrop-shaped helmet.

Bernard Hinault quit cycling in 1986 after a Tour that was supposed to be an elegant handover to team-mate <u>Greg LeMond</u>, who felt he had been cheated out of a victory the year before. Such was Hinault's competitiveness that he led by five minutes and took LeMond almost to breaking point, as he became the first French rider to lead the Tour over Alpe d'Huez and quit with the polka-dot jersey.

After retirement, Hinault developed a new clipless pedal and joined the Tour organisation. In 2008, he tackled a protester who climbed onto the podium at the end of stage three. The badger still bites.

'Judge' Roy Hofheinz

Roy Mark Hofheinz, businessman and politician, born 10 April 1912, died 22 November 1982. Mayor of Houston 1953–5.

Judge Hofheinz, a Houston dance promoter turned FM radio pioneer, businessman, county judge and mayor at just 23, was the driving force behind the first completely covered sports field in history – the Houston Astrodome.

As early as 1952, Hofheinz, a big baseball fan, had grown fed up with cancellations due to Houston's unpredictable, subtropical weather and envisaged a giant indoor park, especially after a visit to the Colosseum in Rome, where he heard how giant shades, or velaria, had sheltered the crowds. By 1960 he had attracted a major league baseball franchise to Houston, and commissioned a structure 200 feet wider than any span ever built, abandoning plans for the first air-conditioned shopping mall to concentrate on the Astrodome. Delivered six months ahead of schedule, it was one of the first 'customer-centric' sports venues, with Hofheinz declaring that the near-circular, 48,000-seater, 9-acre, 18-storey high dome was 'not just a place, but a way of treating people'. As well as air-conditioning, Hofheinz's dome had uniformed Triggerette (later Spacette) hostesses, bars, restaurants and padded tip-up seats that could be more or less configured for both baseball and football. He also pioneered branding in US sports, renaming the Colt .45s the Astros, and setting up an Astroland theme park nearby. The Astrodome also had the first animated electronic scoreboard, with 20,000 lights and 1,200 miles of wiring. After the grass beneath the Lucite roof panels died off, it also became the first major venue to use Chemgrass – soon to be known as AstroTurf.

Over 20 years, the Astrodome hosted 2,750 events and attracted 74 million visitors who marvelled at its architecture and gathered to watch the first indoor American football (1965) and soccer (1968) matches. As the only indoor baseball venue, it was known as a 'pitcher's park' where home runs were hard to get and special rules had to be developed for hits against the giant overhead speakers. Record attendances were set for boxing and basketball matches, and the Astrodome also hosted <u>Billie Jean King</u>'s 1973 tennis Battle of the Sexes.

Both Hofheinz's dome design and use of artificial turf were hugely influential in sport and inspired a series of larger domes, although the fashion has since swung towards moveable-roof stadiums that allow natural grass to grow – such as Houston's neighbouring Reliant Stadium. Gradually, the Astrodome became the smallest and least profitable NFL venue and it proved difficult and expensive to expand. Renovations cost it some of its good looks and it eventually lost its professional and college teams to other cities and venues. Today it is deserted.

Though Hofheinz's creation might not have made as much money as air-conditioned malls, his Texan can-do had ushered in a new era of sports architecture.

Jimmy Hogan

James Hogan, inside right and coach, born Nelson, Lancashire 16 October 1882, died 30 January 1974. Playing career: Nelson, Rochdale, Burnley, Fulham 1905–8 (Southern League champions 1906, 07), Swindon, Bolton. Coaching career: Dordrecht 1910, Austria 1914, MTK Hungary 1916–7, Young Boys Berne 1921–4, Switzerland 1924, Lausanne 1925, 1933–4, Fulham 1934, Austria 1936, Aston Villa 1936–9 (Second Division champions 1938).

Jimmy Hogan's speech to the Germans wasn't going well. Summoned to a conference to justify employing him as a national football adviser, he struggled to make himself understood. With titters breaking out in the audience, he left the stage, returned in his Bolton Wanderers kit, took off his boots and socks and unleashed a barefoot strike that cracked a wooden panel. He trapped the rebound, shot with his other foot and broke the panel. The point was made and soon he was coaching thousands of continental footballers, starting at 5.30 a.m. to fit in all the requests for his help.

Considered to be the father of German, Austrian and Hungarian football, Hogan was not a star player, but his relative failures made him think harder about what he was doing and try to do it better. Having rejected the Catholic priesthood as a career, he had started at Nelson, improving his fitness with a home-made prototype exercise bike and honing his skills until he could trap a ball 18 different ways and kick it through a small hole eight times out of ten. Jimmy's greatest playing success was at Fulham, where the team's 'Scottish' inter-passing style brought two Southern League titles, but the club still adhered to a basic 'hit and hope' style with little attention paid to ball control or tactics. Jimmy developed a passionate belief in the need to 'keep it on the carpet' – controlling and passing quickly and accurately into space. From 1910 he was Britain's youngest coach, working in Dordrecht in Holland, where the Dutch players, unlike the British, thought it was their job to get fit and the coach's to teach them skills. While in the UK training consisted of endless runs, big meals and two ball sessions a week maximum, Hogan pioneered skills training, chalkboard tactics and a more careful diet. After being suddenly interned during the war, he eventually returned to his family in Britain and made the mistake of asking <u>Sir Frederick Wall</u> for financial help. Wall, who considered him a traitor, presented him with three pairs of army socks. Hogan never again lost his distrust of the FA.

Shunned at home, Jimmy returned to the continent to coach national and club sides, while players like Dori Kürschner and Béla Guttman, who had learned under him, spread his ideas throughout South America and to southern European sides like Porto and Benfica. Back home, Hogan's 'foreign' approach was regarded as lacking directness, mainly because the home nations boycotted the 1924 and 1928 Olympics, which showcased some very direct play indeed. In 1931, the Hogan-coached Austrian *Wunderteam* came close to beating England at Stamford Bridge ('Our Visitors Show us How to Play' – the *Daily Herald*) and beat the Scots 5–0, but the value of coaching still wasn't appreciated. At Fulham a player revolt had Jimmy out after just 31 games, the club concluding that training was for juniors only.

Though <u>Stanley Rous</u> employed him for a few FA coaching sessions, he regarded Hogan as disorganised, but at Aston Villa Jimmy helped the club return to the top division and later worked as their youth coach, taking his charges to watch the Hungarian *Aranycsapat* ('Golden Team') thrash England 6–3 – ending any illusion of British superiority over the 'continental' style Jimmy had taught.

Gustáv Sebes, Hungary's manager, said, 'When our football history is told, his name [Hogan's] should be written in gold letters.' Journalist Brian Glanville was driven to write of British football history as one of 'vast superiority sacrificed through stupidity, short-sightedness and wanton insularity . . . a story of shamefully wasted talent, extraordinary complacency and infinite self-deception.' Press calls to instate Jimmy as England coach were turned down on the grounds that he was now too old. Although protégés like Helmut Schoen (Dresden), Ron Atkinson (Aston Villa) and Tommy Docherty (Celtic) all sang Hogan's praises, domestic recognition was limited to being guest of honour when Burnley won the 1972 Division Two championship.

On the issue of patriotism Jimmy Hogan was very clear: 'I am a British coach. I still maintain we have the best players, but it is our style of playing that has gone wrong.'

Nettie Honeyball

Nettie Honeyball, footballer and administrator, born 187?, died 19??.

On Saturday, 23 March 1895, over 12,000 people laid siege to Crouch End Athletic's north London grounds, fighting their way in to watch the first women's football match to be organised by the British Ladies Football Club. BLFC secretary and 'new woman' Nettie Honeyball had whipped up controversy with a poster and PR campaign, arguing in the press that since women were now playing competitive sports like tennis, there was no reason why they should not play football too. One of her more famous soundbites was that she wanted her fellow players to show that 'a manly game could be womanly as well' and that women were not 'ornamental and useless creatures'. She added that she looked forward to a time 'when ladies may sit in Parliament and have a voice in the direction of affairs'.

With the crowds already four to five deep around the ropes, other spectators climbed trees and fences to catch a glimpse of the players, who emerged to 'a hearty roar of welcome (*Daily News*). There had been much anticipation of what the 'new women' might wear. In the end, most opted for the 'rational dress' style of dark serge knickerbockers and a blouse, topped with a tasselled cap, while a few also added a short skirt over the top. The *Daily News* was won over by the new dress, declaring, 'It has been stated that feminine grace without a skirt is an impossibility, but truth to tell, they looked remarkably well.'

After playing 30 minutes each way with a lighter ball, the final result was 7–1 to the North. The press were unanimous that the result could have been the other way around had it not been for the North's Scottish goalie Miss Graham, who was praised for her punting and picking up. 'Worthy of a League club custodian,' said the *Sunday Times*. It was never likely that the press were going to be won over by a single game between inexperienced players, and the teams were reported to have played most of the match in a schoolboy scrum. The spectators who had piled into the single grandstand had also refused to make way for the gentlemen of the press and many journalists got their revenge after the game by dismissing it as a 'farce' or a 'travesty'.

Despite this mixed reception, the BLFC pressed on with a series of charity matches across the country, but the crowds declined and the BLFC soon ran out of steam. However, growing numbers of working women began to form teams, especially during World War I, when many women were recruited into factories for the first time, and mixed-sex or women-only matches raised funds for wartime charities. Preston's Dick, Kerr tram works team attracted crowds of up to 53,000. By 1920, they were also playing international matches, but in December 1921 the English and Scottish FAs banned women's football from their members' grounds, using as their excuse medical claims that the game was 'unsuitable for females' and some unproven claims of financial irregularities. The English Ladies Football Association was limited to park pitches and rugby grounds. It was 1969 before the formation of a Women's Football Association and 1971 before the FA ban was lifted. However, today there are two million women footballers, all of whom owe a small debt to Nettie Honeyball and her 21 pioneers.

An intriguing question is who Nettie Honeyball actually was. Efforts to track her down in census returns have been unsuccessful and she seems to vanish from the historical record. Perhaps she never existed as such. 'Nettie' and 'ball' certainly suggest a soccer pseudonym and many sportswomen of the time played incognito – such as the 'Original English Lady Cricketers' who toured five years before that first north London match.

George Horine

George Leslie Horine, high jumper and baseballer, born Escondido, California 3 February 1890, died 28 November 1948.

The history of the high jump might have been quite different had George Horine not had such a small back yard at his new home in Channing Avenue, Palo Alto.

Until this time, the 19-year-old Horine had been practising his jumping using the scissors style – the least worst technique in an era in which the jumper needed to get his legs back underneath him before he crashed down into a shallow pit of hard, wet sand. At the time, the long-standing record was 1.97 metres, dating back to 1895, when Michael Sweeney had used his own variant – the eastern cut-off – which involved attacking the bar from the right, taking off from the outside foot and lying back over it to raise the hips and lower the centre of gravity.

With little room to manoeuvre in his yard, Horine was forced to approach the bar from the left and discovered a new style in which he took off from his inside foot, approached the bar side-on and rolled over. Using his Horine or western roll, he shattered the world record while at Stanford University and even beat the 2-metre barrier by a centimetre – only to be placed a disappointing third at the Stockholm Olympics, where he also appeared in an exhibition baseball tournament.

After World War I, Horine's style was used by jumpers such as Harold Osborn, who attracted controversy by holding the bar – with the result that the bar supports were turned to face inwards rather than out. The western roll was considered an illegal dive by some judges and there was a series of disqualifications, including that of the multi-talented Babe Zaharias, who lost an Olympic gold in 1932. After 1938, the rule restricting 'dives' was lifted and the Soviets dominated for 30 years with the straddle style, rotating around the bar. At first they were helped by thick soles, which were banned at the end of the 1950s. This style dominated until 1968, when Dick Fosbury revolutionised the sport with his backwards flop.

Len Hutton

Sir Leonard Hutton, cricketer, born Pudsey, Yorkshire 23 June 1916, died 6 September 1990. First-class career: Yorkshire 1934–55 (county champions 1935, 37, 38, 39, 46); 513 matches, 40,140 runs (55.51). Test record 1937–55: 79 matches, 6,971 runs (56.67), captain 23 times.

The scene is Headingley. Alf returns to his seat, having nipped home to fetch the sandwiches.

Alf: 'Ah've bad news for thee, Jim. Thi' house is burnt down, thi' wife's run off wi' lodger and left thi' kids i't' street cryin' their eyes out.'

Jim: 'Aye. And I've bad news for thee. 'Utton's out.'

For twenty years Len Hutton was the mainstay of English batting, often shoring up a weak side. In a move that signalled the eventual ending of the nonsensical amateur/professional divide in cricket, he was the first pro to be appointed captain by the MCC, though their support for him was often less than wholehearted.

Hutton showed his skill and concentration as early as his second Test appearance, when he scored a century, and the following summer, aged just 22, he spent 13½ hours at the crease to break <u>Don Bradman</u>'s Test record with a 364 that also secured a record victory over the Australians. (On a hopeless wicket for bowlers, wrist-spinner Leslie 'Chuck' Fleetwood Smith recorded a worst-ever 1 for 298.) In the years to come, Hutton would show his mastery of any wicket and any bowler – from the speed of <u>Ray Lindwall</u> to (eventually) the spin of <u>Ramadhin</u>. Thanks to his batting, Yorkshire dominated the late 1930s and in 1938 Hutton showed his nous by kicking a ball over the boundary to keep a weak batsman on strike. Unfortunately, this was spotted and five runs awarded. Hospitalised by fast bowling in South Africa in 1938/9, his doggedness and self-discipline was often contrasted with that of his contemporary, the swashbuckling southerner Denis Compton. This did a disservice to both men – Compton was a fine defensive player, while Hutton, a private man with a waspish sense of humour, had a fine cover drive and was well capable of attacking when he could afford to.

Despite a wartime injury requiring three bone grafts that left one arm two inches shorter, Len remained England's outstanding Test

batsman, though under-appreciated by the MCC. As a late addition to
the 1947/8 West Indies touring party, he proved vital. The following
summer's visit by Don Bradman's 'Invincibles' was, as the name suggests,
a disaster for an MCC side ineffectively led by Norman Yardley, and
after Hutton, injured and in pain, dodged a couple of high-speed deliveries from Lindwall, the selectors replaced him with George Emmett,
who scored ten runs and was never chosen again. In 1950, Hutton
made half the runs against the West Indies at a rainy Oval, but another
'officer-class' amateur, Freddie Brown, was selected to lead the following
winter's tour of Australia – after which Hutton's average was twice that
of the next best man. Finally, in 1952 he was tentatively picked as
captain for a single Test against a weak Indian side. The Indians were
beaten 3–0 in the series and in the coronation year Len led England
against the Australians, unbeaten in an Ashes series since Bodyline in
1932/3.

For no obvious reason, the selectors deprived Len of both Brian
Statham and Fred Trueman for the first rained-off Ashes Test, during
which all the England batsmen bar the captain were dynamited – mostly
by Ray Lindwall. Despite his performance, a whispering campaign began
against Len, and ex-skipper and selector Freddie Brown made bad worse
by choosing himself as twelfth man for the second Test. After Hutton
dropped three catches and went off injured and in silence, Brown swept
down to supervise the mopping-up of the tail-enders. The following day,
facing crushing pressure, a difficult wicket, a target of 346 and two
notorious speed merchants in Lindwall and Keith Miller, Hutton played
the innings of his life, eventually totalling 145. This preserved his
captaincy, though it was Willie Watson and Trevor Bailey who ground
out a draw in the second innings, scoring just 71 in 4½ hours. Though
the next two matches were also drawn, a final win at the Oval secured
the Ashes for the first time since bodyline. In the 1953/4 winter tour
of the West Indies, Hutton averaged 96, ignored a hail of flung bottles
on the grounds that 'we want another wicket or two this afternoon', and
played a 16-hour innings in extreme heat to draw the series from being
2–0 down. It was an out-of-form Hutton who drew the 1954 series
against Pakistan, whose fourth Test victory marked their coming-of-age
as a cricketing nation. In 1954/5 his men retained the Ashes 3–1 against
a full-strength Australian side, despite having been 0–1 down. Though
it was regarded as British cricket's greatest post-war achievement, the

slow over rates used to achieve it would reduce the entertainment value of cricket in the years ahead.

Up to 1955, when he retired from Test cricket due to illness and a bad back, Len Hutton never lost a series. After him, the amateur captains who were expected to restore 'panache' proved that his tactics had been right, as they too stuck to winning, though often tedious, strategies such as light appeals, delayed over rates, bowling wide of the leg stump and a reliance on seamers and the new ball – now available every 55 overs. It was the Cambridge-educated Peter May who took the 'safety-first' approach to its furthest extremes at the first Test in Brisbane in 1958, when Trevor Bailey, sent in to wear out the wicket for Jim Laker and Tony Lock, crawled to 68 in 458 minutes. Even the English press were pleased that their side lost – courtesy of a final-day run chase led by Norman O'Neill.

Having become the second cricketing knight after Jack Hobbs, Len was to become an MCC member and a mid-1970s selector, and the gates at Headingley are named after him. Though he retired with the professional cricketer's usual modest income, the amateur/professional division was soon dropped, undermined by the talent of Len Hutton.

Ludwig Jahn – 'The Father of Gymnastics'

Friedrich Ludwig Jahn, gymnast and author, born Lanz, Brandenburg 11 August 1778, died 15 October 1852.

Why is it that European football stadiums tend to have running tracks around them, and thus a worse view of the game? The reasons for this lie, oddly enough, in the 1806 Battle of Jena-Auerstedt, during which Napoleon's forces – particularly those led by Marshal Davout – defeated the outnumbering Prussians and marched on to Berlin. This shock defeat led to a major upheaval in the Prussian army, with its opening-up to new talent as well as the state-wide introduction of gymnastics to build up its people.

One of those who witnessed the battle and was inspired to join up was Friedrich Ludwig Jahn, a theological student turned teacher who saw in gymnastics the chance to build a new German nation, that would be *'frisch, fromm, fröhlich und frei'* ('hardy, pious, cheerful and free'). Abandoning the Latin word 'gymnastics', he created the German *turnen*, establishing the first open-air *Turnplatz* in Berlin in 1811 as a place for group exercises run by a *Turnverein*, or gymnastic association. Jahn pioneered the beam and wooden vaulting horse – at first simply a model horse – as well as the parallel bars, horizontal bars and rings. By 1817, there were 100 *Turnplatzen* in place and Jahn had led a volunteer battalion of German gymnasts – the Lützow Free Corps – as well as working for the secret service.

In peacetime, Jahn's democratic ethos became a danger to the political order. Considered a dangerous liberal – despite his organised book burnings and xenophobic and anti-Semitic outbursts – he was arrested in 1819 and the *Turnplatzen* were temporarily closed. Freed after six years, he was twice exiled. It was only in 1840 that he was awarded the Iron Cross and he was elected to parliament eight years later.

Jahn and his followers saw *Turnen* as an alternative to individualistic, club-based sports such as football, which was labelled 'the English disease' in Germany as late as 1898, and soccer had to be given a new vocabulary and a false German ancestry to become acceptable. *Turnen* also heavily influenced the Olympics, which <u>Pierre de Coubertin</u> set up to encourage his own brand of French nation-building after defeat by Jahn's Prussia. As well as more conventional kit, the first 1896 Olympics included a 45-foot rope to be climbed with the legs held in an L-position – something that only two competitors could manage, while 'fancy' diving evolved from Jahn's practice of doing riskier gymnastic moves over water. Even today, government-funded sports parks – descendants of the *Turnplatzen* – are common across Europe, although they now usually have a soccer pitch in the middle. The one in Berlin is named after Jahn and there is also a monument to him in his hometown of Freyburg.

Carwyn James

Carwyn James, fly half and coach, born Cefneithin, Wales 2 November 1929, died 10 January 1983. Playing career: Llanelli, Wales 2 caps. Coaching career: Llanelli (Welsh Cup 1973–6), British Lions 1971, Rovigo. Rugby Hall of Fame 1999.

Asked what he would do if he had his time again, Carwyn James, the mastermind behind the British Lions' first and only winning tour of New Zealand, replied that he would like to be a football coach, able to pick his own team without interference from selectors.

James used soccer in his training programmes and the closest parallel to his impact on rugby is probably that of Arsenal's <u>Herbert Chapman</u> in football – a manager who, like James, proved the value of new thinking off the pitch with unprecedented success on it.

Though a miner's son and as Welsh as leeks, James was a surprising figure, a cultured multilingual internationalist who played in Russia, personally boycotted matches against apartheid South Africa, turned down an OBE and was probably on Special Branch's files. Described as 'the best and most original thinker in rugby' by <u>J.P.R. Williams</u>, he collected only two caps at fly half – largely because he, like fellow coach Ray Williams, was competing with Cliff Morgan – but he coached Llanelli to four Welsh Cups. An obvious candidate as a national coach, he was scuppered by Welsh rugby's turbulent and reactionary politics. In fact, it wasn't until 1965 that the idea of coaching the national squad was first mooted, after a thrown-together side had suffered a worse than usual humiliation by the visiting Springboks. Even then it was 1968 before <u>Clive Rowlands</u> was able to start putting together the side that would dominate domestic rugby. However when Wales toured New Zealand, technical inferiority and the usual suicidal tour schedule led to two heavy defeats by the All-Blacks. And yet within two years James would lead the British Lions – featuring many of the same players – to victory.

James's achievement was astonishing given the Lions' bad and worsening record against the Springboks and All Blacks. In the 1950s they had achieved three wins and a draw in 12 tests, dogged by selections so bad that the opposition laughed when they saw them and by the

RFU's 'sink or swim' attitude, which saw the chairman of selectors berating one captain for daring to do a prematch team talk. After 1961 the jet age simply made the Lions' problems worse, as there was even less time for the team to gel than in the old days of leisurely sea crossings. In twelve Tests in the 1960s, they managed just two draws and lost the rest. Players didn't know each other or what their team-mates might do, lacked clear objectives on the field and, having played nothing but friendlies, weren't even used to having to win. (The RFU, never the clearest thinkers, encouraged competition between school and hospital sides, but not the big clubs who supplied the national players.) Though the RFU did appoint John Robins as an 'assistant manager' in 1966, Lions captain Mike Campbell-Lamerton thought that any coaching infringed his own duties, side-lined Robins and duly lost all four Tests.

Under Carwyn James it was all very different. Like Herbert Chapman at Arsenal, he had learned from bad playing experiences – in his day Llanelli had 13 selectors – and realised the need for a single shared vision in a team. Rugby sides, he said, should be run as a dictatorship. Again like Chapman, James understood the need for rest and time off and for treating players as responsible adults, capable of sorting out their own rules. His 1971 tour was marked by a lack of the cliques and homesickness that usually beset touring teams, and although the core came from captain John Dawes's London Welsh, James forbade them from rooming together. Recruitment was simply of the best available and when Willie John McBride was chaired off from what most thought was his last match, he was carried by four national captains. Benched players were involved by getting each to study a particular phase of the game and report back on it. Specialist coaching of the forwards was handed over to Ray McLoughlin and, despite conceding seven stones to the All Black pack, the Lions out-scrummaged them to a 9–3 victory in the first Dunedin Test. Attention to the individual meant allowing 'moaners to moan' and 'cocky blighters' to remain so. 'He worked harder on the individual than any other coach,' said Lions forward John Taylor.

Another parallel with the 'Napoleon of football' is that both he and James realised the implications of recent law changes intended to open up their respective games. In James's case this meant the new laws on offside and kicking into touch. He had his wings take over the full back role when needed and used full back J.P.R. Williams to introduce variety into attacks and counter-attacks. He had an especial contempt for the 'flat-footed' crash-tackler beloved of the All Blacks. While much of 1960s rugby had been a kicking contest, James had once ordered a team not to kick at all. Where the laws were an unworkable tangle – notably at the line-out – he got the referees to agree that 'compression' was allowable and organised a mass 'stepping-in' by his forwards that was impossible to punish. He remained a voice for simplification of the laws and when they were disputed, he trained with a ref present to blow up and get players used to his interpretation.

Another similarity between Chapman and James was that each could be thoroughly pragmatic. Just as Arsenal relied on hard-hitting defenders, so the Lions turned to ten-man tactics to win the day. At the line-out, the wingers threw in so that as many forwards as possible could be deployed. As for James's famous 'get your retaliation in first' line, this recognised the need to combat players like Colin 'Pinetree' Meads, who broke jaws and wrenched limbs – 'the essence of competition,' said James. Carried on into the 1974 Lions tour of South Africa, these tactics were often blamed for an increased thuggishness spreading through the game.

Like Jimmy Hogan, another prophet of coaching, James insisted that it was just about doing simple things well in realistic situations. His players always trained against opposition – a far cry from the PE-based training then prevalent. By concentrating on simple skills such as fast hands, he encouraged players to vary and adapt new tactics – and to make mistakes. 'Adventure and error go together,' he said. An analytical thinker, he could see past scorelines and said he was only convinced of a series victory in New Zealand after his side lost the second Test. Like Chapman he was media-friendly, writing a column for the *Guardian*, touring with a newsreel of the 1971 tour and writing – along with various squad members – a book on how the victory was achieved. This was followed up in 1979 by a general history of the game.

When the All Blacks arrived back in Britain in 1972/3 for the last of the long tours, James's Llanelli and the core of his touring side playing as the Barbarians inflicted their only two defeats, with Llanelli's 9–3 win commemorated as 'The Day the Pubs Ran Dry'.

The 'Bard among bricklayers' died in Amsterdam in 1983 aged just 53 and was buried after a service at the Cefneithin Tabernacle, into which players and sporting journalists packed. His legacy lives on in rugby, and such high-profile coaches as Graham Henry of the All Blacks have acknowledged him as a major influence. Many of James's sayings are still referred to in sport – not least his prematch mantra 'Think! Think! Think!' There are many sporting gurus, but Carwyn James, the chain-smoking eisteddfod-loving, Plaid Cymru-supporting polymath, remains sport's only arch-druid.

John Jaques

John Jaques II, businessman and inventor, born London 1823, died 1898. World Croquet Hall of Fame 2007.

To be the inventor of Ludo, Tiddly-Winks, Happy Families and Snakes and Ladders *and* the maker of the first modern chess set would seem to be enough fame for any man, but not for John Jaques II, whose family firm is Britain's oldest sports and games manufacturer. It was he who also helped create the boom in croquet, 'The Queen of Games', with lasting consequences for many other British sports.

John Jaques was the third boss of a family firm founded in 1795 by Thomas Jaques, of Huguenot descent but Wiltshire-born, who set up in London crafting hardwood, ivory and bone. These skills were well suited to the creation of croquet balls and mallets, which required hard, dense woods like turkey boxwood or lignum vitae.

After Edwin Beard Budding's lawnmower enabled the creation of the first suburban lawns, Jaques won a gold medal for his products at the Great Exhibition of 1851. Croquet itself emerged from Ireland as 'crooky', 'crokey' or 'crocky'. It was first mentioned in *The Field* in 1858, and within days Jaques had issued his own *Rules and Directions for Playing Croquêt – A New Outdoor Game*, no doubt adding the accent to posh it up and make his version appear unique. Croquet (the accent was dropped by 1875) lured wealthy Victorians out of their stuffy parlours and into the fresh air for the first time. As a mixed-sex game, 'crinoline croquet' enabled women to compete with men, display their finery and indulge in some mild banter and flirtation while retrieving lost balls from the rhododendrons. 'Only tobacco smoke spread faster,' said one commentator of the croquet boom.

During this craze there were many rival rule- and equipment-makers and matters reached a head in 1864, when the Earl of Essex was successfully sued for plagiarism by the extraordinary Captain Thomas Mayne Reid, an Irish ex-slavemaster and buffalo hunter. Jaques jumped in with his own *Croquet: The Laws and Regulations of the Game* – which ran to 100,000 copies in 15 editions and was published in both London and Boston.

It was another entrepreneur, Walter Jones Whitmore, the author of *Croquet Tactics*, who staged the first championships near Evesham in 1867 and inspired the formation of an All England Club at Wimbledon in 1868. However, the club soon fell out with Whitmore and a protracted croquet war was fought between the two. In the same year, badminton emerged as a new lawn game, but the big winner in this 19th-century turf war was 'Sphairistike' or 'Lawn Tennis', the 1873 invention of <u>Major Walter Wingfield</u>. Tennis offered more obvious thrills than croquet and even the All England Club switched emphasis to the new sport. When <u>Reggie and Laurie Doherty</u> reignited interest in tennis in the 1890s, Wimbledon's croquet players were finally packed off to the Hurlingham Club.

During the great sports boom they had helped create, Jaques's firm supplied kit for all sorts of games. Its present-day survival as a family firm is probably a better tribute to John Jaques than this crappy poem by some unknown hand:

> *Whence croquet sprang to benefit the earth?*
> *What happy garden gave the pastime birth?*
> *What cunning craftsman carved its graceful tools?*
> *Whose oral teaching fixed its equal rules?*
> *Sing, Jaques, thou apostle of the game!*

Douglas Jardine – 'The Iron Duke'

Douglas Jardine, cricketer, born Bombay 23 October 1900, died 18 June 1958. First-class career: Oxford University 1920–3, Surrey 1921–33; 14,848 runs (46.83), 48 wickets (31.10); 22 Tests 1928–34 (captain 1931–4), 1,296 runs (48.00). Wisden Cricketer of the Year 1928.

Douglas Jardine, England's tall Scottish captain, put together two existing cricket tactics and produced something so powerful that it not only won the 1932/3 Ashes and defeated the greatest batsman in history, but changed the rules of the game – and at one time seemed about to split the British Empire itself. Jardine termed it 'fast leg theory', but the name given to it by Hugh Buggy of the *Melbourne Herald* was 'bodyline'. The neatest summation came from fast bowler Bill Voce: 'If we don't beat you, we'll knock your bloody heads off.'

The tactics Jardine combined were the 'death trap' of four leg-side fielders, which had been used to great effect in the 1911/12 Ashes series, (as he planned his campaign, Jardine consulted with Frank Foster, a veteran of that series) and the non-stop pace attack used by Warwick Armstrong's 1921 Invincibles. The result was fast short-pitched bowling with a ring of fielders to make defence risky. At best, it meant attacking the leg stump. At its worst, it meant drawing a bead on a batsman like Vic Richardson, even when he was standing 18 inches clear of the wicket.

The general problems that underlay bodyline were the excessive pitch preparation, pad play and restricted lbw that favoured the batsman over the bowler. The particular problem was getting out <u>Don Bradman</u>, who had averaged 139 in the previous 1930 Ashes series. During 1928/9 Jardine had toured Australia as vice-captain to Percy Fender and had been roundly abused by the Australian fans, who didn't like his snooty appearance or habit of wearing a club cap as a badge of status. When Patsy Hendren remarked on the hostile reception, Jardine replied that the feeling was 'fucking mutual'. Jardine had regarded the Australians as an 'uneducated unruly mob' since Armstrong had deliberately denied him the sporting chance of a century when playing for Oxford. Jardine's solution to the Bradman problem was a result of seeing him briefly struggle at the Oval against the fast bowling of Harold 'Lol' Larwood, the 'Nottinghamshire Express' whose 90 mph deliveries left his knuckles skimming the turf. Larwood, along with fellow fast bowler Bill Voce, would be the main bowling strike force in Australia.

During the 1932/3 series there were a total of 25 'incidents' on the fast hard pitches, with Bill Woodfull struck seven times in four matches and Bill Ponsford six times in three. Although Bradman missed the first Test, bodyline had an immediate impact on cricket as Stan McCabe hooked his way to a masterful 187 – an innings that was credited with finally killing off any lingering prejudice against striking across the wicket. Having lost on a slow wicket that didn't suit his tactics, Jardine was vindicated in the following Test as Bradman was bowled first ball, causing the England captain to dance an involuntary jig of delight. Though his second innings produced 103 not out, 'the little bastard', as Jardine instructed his men to call him, would average only 56 across the series. By the third Test in Adelaide passions were running high, with 40,000 enraged Aussies chanting 'Bastard', but Jardine, who had dropped the Nawab of Pataudi after he protested at the tactics in the first Test, was not to be deflected. It was this Test that brought the two most notorious incidents. The first was a ball that struck Woodfull so hard it was heard in the grandstand and the second when Bert Oldfield fractured his skull after edging the ball. In neither case was the leg trap in operation, but Jardine's 'Well done, Harold' and calling-in of the field ratcheted up the tension, with mounted horse in attendance and umpires Hele and Borwick prepared to defend themselves with stumps if necessary.

After the match, the team stood by their captain, who had offered to quit if they wanted him to, while tour managers Pelham Warner and Lionel Palairet strolled round to the Australian changing room and attempted to find out who had been swearing on the pitch. They got a terse reply from the outraged Woodfull and his comments about the tactics soon leaked. Telegrams and press revelations shot back and forth between the outraged Australian Board of Control and the MCC, which was relying on a handful of evening press reports and had very little idea of what was going on. In the fourth Test, Larwood was applauded by the crowd and this seemed to lift the tension, while the *Melbourne Argus* praised Jardine's 'triumph of tactics and generalship'. Afterwards, the players were greeted back in England as returning heroes.

Commentators were divided on their tactics and only gradually was it admitted that the Australians had a point.

In the summer of 1933, Jardine showed his ability to take what he dished out when he scored 127 in five hours against the West Indies' Learie Constantine and Manny Martindale, during a series in which Walter Hammond's jaw was broken. Similar tactics were in use in the tour of India after which Jardine stepped down. He later became the *Daily Telegraph*'s cricket correspondent, before returning to active service in the war and then dying relatively young of a tropical disease.

After Jardine's retirement as captain, the MCC grudgingly invited Australia to tour. Both Voce and his captain Arthur Carr, a Jardine supporter, were dropped after they used bouncers against the Australians. Larwood, who refused to apologise for using techniques he felt to have been essential to win, was kept away. As a result, the Australians destroyed a below-strength national side, winning by 562 runs in one match. After pressure from the Australians and *Wisden*, persistent bowling at the batsman 'standing clear of his wicket' was banned, but dangerous bowling continued – often from the Australians themselves. Denis Compton would be forced onto his stumps in 1948 and Ray Lindwall was bowling at injured batsmen in 1951/2. Today, several near-deaths later, bouncers are limited by number per over and the skill of the batsman.

A more complex character than the Australians were ever likely to give him credit for, Jardine had interests in Chaucer and Eastern mysticism. Possessed of an un-English determination to win at all costs, he was the wrong man at a time when Australians were suffering badly from the effects of the Depression. However, he was not blind to the quality of their players. Though he and Bradman never exchanged more than one or two words, he later admitted, 'The little man was bloody good.'

Sanath Jayasuriya

Sanath Teran Jayasuriya, cricketer, born Matara, Sri Lanka 30 June 1969. International record: Sri Lanka 1991– (captain 1999–2003), 110 Tests, 6,973 runs (40.07), 98 wickets (34.34); 432 ODIs, 13,114 runs (32.70) (World Cup 1996). Wisden Cricketer of the Year 1997.

Not even the riots, organisational chaos and bloated scheduling of the 1996 Cricket World Cup could disguise the fact that Man of the Series Sanath Jayasuriya had changed the game. Since then it has become clear that Jayasuriya, helped by his partner Romesh Kaluwitharana, has shifted the game from a bowling to a batting-dominated one.

Jayasuriya stood cricketing orthodoxy on its head. Instead of slowly playing himself in, as openers traditionally had, he blasted through the first 15 overs, aiming to put the game beyond reach while fielding restrictions were still in place. A short, shy but powerful man, his trademark was a mighty shot over point. *Indian Cricket* termed his style 'a curious mixture of science, magic and madness, based on quickness of hand and eye and a willingness to do what is pretty dangerous and dirty work.' So extraordinary was he that cricket had to borrow the term 'pinch-hitter' from baseball to describe him. After winning the 1996 trophy, Jayasuriya became the one-day international (ODI) master, the first to play 400 games and the second-highest ODI scorer. Especially dangerous on the slower, less bouncy wickets of the subcontinent, he set records for the fastest 50 (off 17 balls), 100 (48 balls) and 150 (95 balls). It's all a long way from the first ODI at Melbourne back in 1971, when Geoff Boycott scored just 8 off 33 deliveries.

Jayasuriya's daring free-hitting strokes have spread throughout cricket. His lofted drive and reverse sweep were followed in 2001 by Sachin Tendulkar's late cut over the slip cordon. Another modern master is Indian opener Virender Sehwag, while Western Australia's wicketkeeping batsman Adam Gilchrist also demonstrated the new aggression after his Test debut against Pakistan in 1999. Coming in at 126 for 5 and chasing a total of 369, Gilchrist and Justin Langer added 235 in just 265 minutes. Australia went on to win 41 out of 57 Tests and by 2001 had won 16 on the bounce, before being stopped by the counter-attacking flair of India's V.V.S. Laxman and Rahul Dravid.

Jayasuriya captained Sri Lanka for five years until he resigned in 2003 and in 2007 supposedly retired from Test cricket with a final 78. In retrospect, he ushered in a new golden age of batting with fewer draws, and many Tests over in three days, though critics have pointed out that figures are boosted by the presence of weak sides, excessive pitch preparation and pace bowlers worn out by ever-expanding schedules. The new batting dominance has caused bowlers to sacrifice sheer speed for millimetre accuracy – as exemplified by Australia's Glen McGrath – while fielders have had to show more speed and aggression.

Knud Jensen

Knud Enemark Jensen, cyclist, born Arhus, Denmark 30 November 1936, died 26 August 1960.

Knud Jensen, a Danish time-trialler, collapsed during the sweltering 1960 Rome Olympics, fracturing his skull and being declared dead soon afterwards. (Two team-mates in the 175-kilometre trial were also lucky to survive.) The autopsy on Jensen revealed amphetamines and nicotinic acid – though whether he knowingly took the drugs is uncertain – and this set in train the first official drug-testing regimes in sport.

Amphetamines had been in use in the Olympics since World War II, when vast numbers had been produced to boost soldiers' energy and aggression. In elite cycling, their use was common and there had been a number of near-fatal incidents when cyclists had been unable to cool their stressed and dehydrated bodies.

After Jensen's death, cycling became the first sport to test for drugs, though this was largely a matter of searching for unexplained needle holes or blue-tinged urine samples. The first positives were detected in 1965 by Raymond Brooks, when it was estimated that 40 per cent of Italian cycling pros and 88 per cent of their top footballers were taking amphetamines. The following year's Tour de France was the first to run tests. Internationally, Austria was the first nation to outlaw drugs in sport, followed by France, Belgium and Italy, while in 1963 the Council of Europe launched its own investigation.

As for the Olympics, the year after Jensen's death, the IOC formed a Medical Commission under Lord Porritt. Three years later, a Swedish delegate recommended compulsory blood-testing, but Porritt preferred just to condemn drug use, demand sanctions against drug-abusing athletes by National Olympic Committees and require athletes to both agree to testing and make a personal declaration against drugs. However, even this watered-down measure was rejected. In any case, there were no effective tests for amphetamines or steroids, whose performance-boosting effects were still being debated.

Tom Simpson's death in the 1967 Tour de France led to the first compulsory drug-testing at the following Olympics, but the tests were so crude that the single positive result was for alcohol. Until the 1980s, the IOC Medical Commission would remain a club of interested doctors, scientists and administrators who jockeyed for Olympic lab accreditation and the inclusion of their own 'pet drugs'. Some, such as Manfred Höppner of the GDR, even used their insider status to assist vast doping programmes. There was very little logic behind the commission's banned list and no clear sense that drug-taking was simply wrong. The project received little political commitment or funding from presidents Brundage, Killanin or Samaranch and Olympic drug use tended to be regarded as a political embarrassment to be solved through diplomacy, rather than straightforward cheating. The code was later described by vice-president Dick Pound as 'the written musings of a selection of medical commissions and subcommissions that would have been impossible for anyone to enforce properly'.

Ben Johnson

Ben Johnson, sprinter, born Falmouth, Jamaica 10 December 1961. Victories include Commonwealth 100 m and 4 x 100 m 1986, World 100 m 1987 (disqualified), Olympic 100 m (disqualified) 1988. AP Athlete of the Year 1987. Member of the Order of Canada. Lou Marsh Trophy 1987.

On 26 September 1988, Ben Johnson, the 100 metres world record holder and world and Olympic champion, became the biggest sports star to be publicly busted for drugs.

Perhaps the fastest sprinter in history, Ben was repeatedly cut from his school track team, but persevered and carried on running after moving to Canada at the age of 12. Here he joined Charlie Francis's Scarborough Optimists team. Despite bad facilities, very little money and little assistance from the top-heavy Canadian sports bureaucracy, Francis's sprinters came to dominate national track, thanks to an unusual policy of low-volume, high-intensity, individualised training. From 1981 the team, like its major competitors, also used steroids. Francis believed that low, infrequent doses helped protein synthesis and muscle contractions, building the fundamental strength and speed needed to qualify for IAAF times and government funding. He argued that at these doses steroids – usually furazabol – posed no significant health risks.

Ben bulked up considerably and could eventually bench-press over 335 lb, but his great strength was his focus and concentration at the start. 'When the gun go off, the race is over,' he declared. He leapt up from the start, generating 3,000 watts, more acceleration than a Lamborghini and enough power to rip his starting blocks from the tracks. His 0.0997-second reflexes were so fast that at the 1988 Seoul semi-final they were simply not believed, although the machinery indicated nothing wrong. By taking three steps before the opposition had completed one, Ben got vertical sooner than his opponents. Racing on his toes, his 'middle surge' meant that he could complete more than five strides and 40 feet per second.

In 1985, Ben overtook champion – though not world record-holder – Carl Lewis, and at the 1987 Rome World Championships promised

9.85 seconds and delivered 9.83. ('Yah. I don't talk shit,' he told the watching TV millions.) Meanwhile, Lewis implied that Ben took drugs. In 1988, despite hamstring injuries, Ben ran a world record 9.79 in the Olympic final before his 'A' sample result was leaked and the media storm closed in. He remained remarkably calm, commenting, 'Nobody's died.'

Rather than the Olympic or athletic authorities, it was the Canadian government that commissioned the 91-day Dubin Inquiry into drug use in sport. This heard from drugs tester Manfred Donike about extensive US, Soviet and East German drug use and that 80 per cent of track and field athletes had shown abnormal testosterone levels at Seoul. It also noted that many previous positives had been ignored by the authorities – perhaps because the nations concerned were more influential than Canada. The inquiry concluded that the last 16 years of official testing had largely been a waste of time. One practical result was the introduction of the out-of-competition testing Raymond Brooks had been calling for back in 1973. In the US, out-of-competition testing was also introduced, although major loopholes existed in it.

As for Ben, as well as losing his Olympic title, he and fellow Optimist Angella Issajenko, who had also confessed to taking drugs to the commission, both lost their world titles – despite the fact that Ben had tested negative at Rome and that the beneficiaries of the Isajenko decision were athletes from the drug-soaked GDR. IAAF boss Primo Nebiolo's message to the public was 'We're acting on this.' The coded message to athletes was 'Stay quiet or you'll lose everything.'

Ben returned to competition after the standard two-year suspension but two further busts, for testosterone in 1993 and diuretics in 1999, led to a lifetime ban. The actual cause of his Seoul positive remains a mystery. According to Charlie Francis, Ben's last furazabol injection, 26 days before competition, should have cleared his system, and he actually tested for recent use of stanozolol. Ben, who has trained and coached in Italy and Canada, still blames sabotage.

A final uncertainty is how fast Ben Johnson might have run. At Seoul he was pulling up from 80 metres, expecting to run faster in future. Had he matched his Rome pace, it might have been 9.74, had he improved on it, perhaps 9.71. Had his career continued on better tracks, maybe 9.5 was conceivable.

Jack Johnson – 'The Man They All Dodge'

Arthur John Johnson, boxer, born Galveston, Texas 31 March 1878, died 10 June 1946. Heavyweight champion of the world 1908–15. Overall record: 124 fights, 89 wins (49 KOs), 2 losses, 12 draws, 9 no-contests. Boxing Hall of Fame 1954.

After his funeral, Jack Johnson's widow Irene was quoted as saying, 'I loved him because of his courage. He faced the world unafraid. There wasn't anything or anybody he feared.'

Transferred to the boxing ring, Jack Johnson's courage and skill should have made him a national hero at a time when boxing was the sporting expression of American dominance over Britain and the rest of the world. After beginning professional boxing in 1897 for a prize of $1.20 minus expenses, Johnson suffered two early KOs and a defeat by Marvin Hart that flattered his opponent, but thereafter he was the best heavyweight around. Nat Fleischer of *The Ring*, who watched every heavyweight champion for decades, had no hesitation in naming Jack the best for his craft, speed and elusiveness. Johnson was a careful counter-puncher whose attack usually took the form of waiting for opportunities and then striking. So swift were his reactions that he could pick off or deflect most punches and lean backwards away from the few that got past his guard – a boxing no-no which <u>Muhammad Ali</u> also made work. In Johnson's case the 'train never arrived' and he retained his brains, skills and reactions. A ready wit, generous and free-spending, Johnson paraded his wealth with fine cars and fine clothes, eschewing the champion's traditional black shorts for fetching pink, and was a fund of tall tales, including fighting off a 23-foot shark and developing a cure for TB. Also a musician, inventor and entrepreneur, he founded what would become the Cotton Club, managed himself and made money from endorsements – refusing to be ordered about by organisations like Britain's National Sports Club, which usually rode roughshod over fighters' wishes.

Though his behaviour was not always faultless, what limited Johnson's popularity was quite simply his colour. As the first black heavyweight champion, he came to fame at a time when American sport, like American society, was becoming more deeply divided, with black athletes banned from baseball, cycling and racing, and growing moves to do so in boxing. Though there had been black champions since bantamweight George Dixon in 1890, many boxers such as <u>John L. Sullivan</u> drew the colour line – refusing to fight a black opponent. Though Johnson was the Coloured Champion after 1903, when he beat 'Denver' Ed Martin, it took him over a decade of fighting to get a crack at the title, pursuing Tommy Burns to Sydney, where on Boxing Day 1908 he became the first black heavyweight champion, after a TKO. Throughout his reign, Johnson had to cope with staggering levels of abuse – from fans who chorused 'Kill the nigger', bands who played tunes like 'All Coons Look Alike to Me' and a press who depicted him as sub-human and wrote of him as an amoral menace or translated his words in an 'Uncle Remus' style that bore no relation to his real recorded voice. ('De Big Coon Am A-Comin' was the headline in the *Sydney Truth* before the Burns fight.) Even the newsreel cameras cut away from the moment of Burns's defeat and films of later fights were banned from performance. In such polarised societies, Johnson's craft and guile, which would be admired in a white fighter such as James Corbett, were regarded as cowardice. Fearful of their champion's defeat by a black man, the British Home Office prevented him fighting Bombardier Billy Wells. In the US, his record $101,000 fight against ex-champion Jim Jeffries, billed as a racial grudge match, was ended when Jeffries's corner called it quits in the 15th to prevent him being KO'd. In a nation where lynchings were commonplace, coast-to-coast celebrations of the victory by black Americans resulted in 23 deaths. Soon afterwards, Johnson jumped bail and fled the country, having been charged with a law that was aimed at preventing the trafficking of prostitutes.

Exiled from the US, Johnson returned to serve a year in jail after losing his title in controversial circumstances to Jess Willard in Cuba. Johnson's version of events was that he threw the fight for a pay-off and the expectation, encouraged by promoter Jack Curley, that his sentence would be commuted. The alternative version was that Johnson was out of condition and that fighting another counter-puncher in blazing heat in the last scheduled 45-round contest was too much for him. Footage of the fight and a photo of the KO'd Johnson apparently shielding his eyes from the sun have been argued over ever since. After his release from prison, some boxing authorities banned him from the ring by reason of his age, while champions Willard and Gene Tunney still drew the colour line and promoter Tex Rickard discouraged Jack Dempsey from fighting him.

Johnson himself was largely blind to racial divisions and tried to live his life as though they didn't exist. He refused to recognise the racial segregation within US cities, living where he chose. Like George Dixon and light- and welterweight champion Joe Gans – the first recognised black world champion – Jack had various 'wives' and companions, both black and white, but unlike the others he made no secret of this. (Jack is supposed to have attributed his remarkable sexual potency to 'jellied eels and distant thoughts'.) However, he certainly wasn't the saint that blacks or liberal whites might have liked. His abusive relationship with white socialite Etta Duryea ended in her suicide, and while enlightened people railed against the battles royal in which black contestants fought en masse for the entertainment of whites, Jack wasn't above presiding over one himself. As for advancing the cause of black boxers, he carefully avoided Sam Langford, who along with Sam McVey and Joe Jeannette was easily a match for the white challengers he fought. Johnson even drew a gun on Langford after he challenged him to a fight. In the cause of making the rematch a bigger draw, Johnson agreed to let a fight against Stanley Ketchel, the 'Michigan Assassin', go the whole way. However, when Ketchel ratted on the deal and felled Johnson, Jack picked himself up and struck a blow so powerful it bowled both of them over and led to Ketchel receiving the last rites. Two of Ketchel's teeth were found embedded in Jack's glove.

On his enforced retirement from championship boxing, Johnson remained unmarked, with his powers intact. Though he suffered reverses such as the takeover of his club by gangsters, he was too resourceful and determined to be ground down. The shadow he cast over boxing was so long that the next black champion, Joe Louis, was deliberately kept away from Jack and schooled not to act like 'Little Arthur'. Louis's coach, the razor-scarred killer Jack Blackburn, kept the 'fool nigger' Johnson away from Joe's camp and Johnson retaliated by becoming a fierce critic of Louis, reportedly tipping off his German opponent Max Schmeling about a weakness in Joe's guard and then celebrating his winnings in the face of Joe's disappointed black supporters.

The end of this 'deep and colourful' personality, as Jack once described himself, came after the last of a thousand slights and humiliations – being denied use of the restaurant counter at a diner in Raleigh, North Carolina. Johnson's fatal crash led to a well-attended burial next to Etta in Chicago's Graceland cemetery. The grave, bearing only his name, is close to that of another heavyweight champion and former opponent, Bob Fitzsimmons.

Since his death, Johnson has been commemorated many times in films and stories and many legends have grown up – including the tale that he was refused a ticket for the *Titanic*. When he was being persecuted for his opposition to the Vietnam War, Muhammad Ali often drew on the story of Jack Johnson, who both he and Joe Frazier regarded as one of the two best fighters of the past. In moments of drama, Ali's trainer Drew Bundini would call from the corner, 'Ghost in the House! Jack Johnson's here!' Today 41st Street in Galveston is named after Johnson and in September 2008 the US Congress passed a motion, supported by John McCain, calling for a posthumous presidential pardon for him.

Robert Trent Jones Snr

Robert Trent Jones Snr, golf architect and writer, born Ince, Cheshire 20 June 1906, died 14 June 2000. Notable courses include: The Dunes (1947), Oakland Hills (1951), Baltusrol (1954), Pevero (1972), Valderrama (1985). World Golf Hall of Fame 1987.

The cherubic Robert Trent Jones was probably the first person to set out in life to become a golf-course architect. He transformed golf design, creating over 500 of his muscular courses worldwide, and probably inflicted more misery on golfers than any other man. After winning the 1951 US Open on Jones's remodelled Oakland Hills course, Ben Hogan celebrated bringing 'this monster to its knees'. Hogan later told Jones's wife that if Robert had to play the course for a living rather than design it, he'd soon be on the breadline.

A scratch golfer at a young age, Jones quit golf after developing an ulcer and went to work as a draughtsman until a chance meeting with golf architect Donald Ross inspired him to become a course designer – even creating his own programme of study at Cornell. However, when he left college, depression-era America was building very few courses and his work was limited to a few public ones and a handful in Canada.

After the war, Jones announced his new style with The Dunes in South Carolina (1947), where he made use of natural hazards such as trees and water, as well as fairway bunkers and massive multi-level greens to make achieving par harder than ever before. Engaged in what he described as a 'fair fight' with golfers, Jones used the new technology of earth-moving and crushing to fight back against improved clubs and balls. Regarding an easy sub-par score as a 'fraud', he declared that every hole should be a 'hard par but an easy bogey'. The following year, he cooperated with Bob ('Bobby') Jones at Peachtree in Georgia and later remodelled two holes at Augusta. To reduce the natural confusion between them, he adopted the middle name Trent.

Jones the designer really hit the headlines in 1951 with his remod-elled Oakland Hills course, complete with narrow fairways, punishing rough and 100 large bunkers, all of which demanded exact landings from a number of different tee positions. The greens were again multi-level and up to 30 feet above the level of the tee, and Jones was soon much in demand as a 'course doctor', starting work at Baltusrol in New Jersey the following year. To prove that a much-criticised hole was 'eminently fair', he once shot a hole-in-one. His more dramatic courses lent themselves particularly well to the new era of televised golf, and during the 1960s and 1970s golf boom, he exported golf to places that had seemed incapable of supporting it. In Dorado Beach in Puerto Rico he built on sand, in Florida he sculpted hills where none had existed, at Mauna Kea in Hawaii he made soil from crushed lava, and at his scenic masterpiece, Pevero in Sardinia, he blasted away tons of granite.

As well as creating over three dozen championship courses in 35 nations, Jones also created new golf 'theme parks' such as the 54-hole Robert Trent Jones Trail in Alabama, and built holes or greens at the White House and Camp David. His sons Robert Junior and Rees both followed in his footsteps and collaborated with their father, whose last course was completed posthumously. Towards the end of his life, he awoke in hospital to be informed he'd had a stroke. 'Do I have to count it?' he asked. Today the Cornell University course, where his career started, is named after him.

Bob ('Bobby') Jones

Robert Tyre Jones, golfer, born 17 March 1902, died 18 December 1971. Wins include: US Open 1923, 26, 29, 30, US Amateur Championships 1924, 25, 27, 28, 30, British Open 1926, 27, 30, British Amateur Championships 1930. World Golf Hall of Fame 1974.

Bob Jones is perhaps the most written-about and mythologised figure in golf. As well as being one of the five giants of American sport in the 1920s, alongside Babe Ruth, Bill Tilden, Red Grange and Jack Dempsey, Jones was the man who bequeathed us Augusta and the 'Masters' tournament – a title he never much liked.

Jones was an early talent. The son of a golf-loving lawyer from Atlanta, he began playing at five and despite poor health was defeating boys nearly twice his age by the age of nine. Five years later he reached the third round of the US Amateur Championship, beating a former champion, and after graduating from Georgia Tech in 1922, he missed the US Open title by just one stroke. The following year he embarked on what he called his 'fat years', winning five out of seven US Opens and 13 out of 20 majors. Great professionals like Walter Hagen and Gene Sarazen were regularly beaten by an amateur with movie star looks, who fitted golf around his legal studies, played only about 100 rounds per summer and concentrated on a few major championships each year.

Jones was renowned for the ease and rhythm of his swing and was supreme with long woods and irons. His legendary sportsmanship added to his myth, especially after he penalised himself and narrowly lost the 1925 US Open, though no one else had seen the offence. This was in part a reaction to his early youth when he had sworn, hit a spectator with a flung club and torn up his card at the 1921 St Andrews Open, abandoning a losing match. (In private, he never lost the cursing, smoking or drinking habits.)

After becoming the first American to win both the British and US Opens and getting a ticker-tape parade in 1926, Bob announced his intention to leave the game at the end of 1930. The crowds bothered him and the stress of competition caused him stomach problems.

Championships, he explained, were like cages. 'First you are expected to get into them and then you are supposed to stay there. But of course nobody can stay there.'

1930 brought a momentous Grand Slam, winning both the US and British Open and Amateur titles. In the fourth round of the British Amateur, Cyril Tolley missed a 12-foot birdie putt and Bob won after a perfect stymie – placing his ball exactly between Tolley's and the hole, as the rules then allowed. (This British Open was the first broadcast over American radio.) On his way to the US titles, Jones survived an incredible series of mishaps. Almost hit by a runaway car and a lightning-struck chimney, he nearly injured himself badly by instinctively grabbing a falling razor. Despite all this he won through, receiving another ticker-tape welcome in New York and quitting at the top.

Throughout his playing career, Bob was funded by the USGA, for whom he played in five Walker cups and lost just one match. He had planned for his retirement with a series of 12 star-studded instructional films called *How I Play Golf*, lent his name to an early set of matched clubs, and wrote some well-received books on the game.

Augusta, his lasting gift to golf, arose out of his chain-smoking nervousness and dislike of crowds. Having admired Alister MacKenzie's Cypress Point course, Bob worked with him and financier Clifford Roberts to create a private course on an ex-fruit nursery. This boasted a mild winter climate, plenty of mature trees and a naturally varied landscape on which they created the first 'strategic course'. In essence, it was an inland adaptation of the links courses Jones had (eventually) learned to love. Rather than penalising shots that deviated from the approved route, Augusta lured golfers into trouble by encouraging them to be over-ambitious. As Jones said, 'There isn't a single hole out there that can't be birdied if you just think. But there isn't one that can't be double-bogeyed if you stop thinking.' Augusta was distinguished not just by its beauty and cunning, but also by its lack of rough and having just 29 bunkers, making use instead of the naturally undulating ground. It also featured the first ropes to hold spectators back and the first scoreboards around the course.

MacKenzie didn't live to see the completion of the course and in 1935, two years after its rainy opening, Bobby Jones reversed the sequence of the first and last nine holes. Otherwise it remains pretty much intact. For championship golf, the tees are placed well back from the members'. Later, Bob combined with his namesake <u>Robert Trent Jones</u> to design the Peachtree course in Atlanta.

After his retirement, Bobby Jones resisted the temptation to return to competitive golf and this only increased his mystique – especially in Scotland. Having at first firmly stated his dislike of the Old Course and then learned to love it, Jones delighted the crowd in 1927 by asking for the Open trophy to remain in the town. In 1958, he was elected a Freeman – the first American to receive the honour since Benjamin Franklin – and when he played a final round there thousands gathered. By this time, Bobby Jones was suffering from a spinal disease, which eventually paralysed him. One honour he did not collect was the presidency of the Royal and Ancient, since he had so obviously made money from the game. Today, clubs are still sold under his name and he is commemorated with scholarships and the USGA's sportsmanship award.

Michael Jordan

Michael Jordan, basketball shooting guard and small forward, baseballer and team owner, born Brooklyn 17 February 1963. All American High School player 1982, Freshman of the Year 1982, College Player of the Year 1984, Olympic gold medallist 1984, 92. Professional career: Chicago Bulls 1984–93, 1995–8 (Defensive Player of the Year 1988, NBA champion 1991, 92, 93, 96, 97, 98, NBA MVP 1988, 91, 92, 96, 98, Finals MVP 1991, 92, 93, 96, 97, 98), Washington Wizards 2001–3. ESPY Athlete of the Century. Baseball career: Birmingham Barons 1994 (.202), Scottsdale Scorpions 1994 (.252).

Michael Jordan, the greatest basketballer of his time and probably of all time, is also the most marketed sporting star ever – as popular among advertisers and sponsors as he was with Chicago Bulls fans.

Having nearly ended his career before it started by almost chopping off his toe with an axe, Michael Jordan developed into an all-round athlete. Having been dropped from his high-school basketball team because he was too short, he grew four inches in one summer and never looked back. He came to national prominence in his freshman college year with a sensational last-second score at the 1982 NCAA final – the start of his reputation as a 'clutch' player, at his best in a tight spot. Drafted third overall by the Chicago Bulls, who had lost $5 million and 109 games in the previous two seasons, he filled the arena and gained an ovation for his first away game against the Celtics. Thereafter he was credited with doubling attendances wherever he played.

'Only' 6 feet 6 inches tall, but able to jump 44 inches into the air, Jordan could slam-dunk from the free-throw line and his speed and athleticism in the air created the impression that he could fly. 'Not human' was how one Spanish coach later described him. His fade-away jump shot alone was a lethal weapon, getting around opposing blockers and helping him to ten NBA season scoring records. The second player to 3,000 points in a season, after Wilt Chamberlain, Jordan's hand speed made him an unusually effective defender and rebounder for a shooting guard, setting records for steals and blocked shots – though his spectacular jumps and slam-dunking ability led fans to ignore his all-round game. As well as his ability to score 'from the hot dog stand' – to quote the Detroit Pistons' coach Chuck Daly – he also drew a high rate of fouls with his drives to the basket. Detroit's special 'Jordan rules' were soon circulating between NBA teams, showing how strong-arm tactics and double-teaming could keep him out of the game. However, from 1990 to 1991, Jordan was picking these tactics apart with the accuracy of his passing and went on to lead the Bulls to two sets of three consecutive titles, interrupted by a less successful foray into baseball, his first sporting love.

Jordan was part of basketball's commercial world as early as his appearance in the McDonald's All-American High School game and attracted the attention of star agent David Falk, rated the second most important man in basketball after the NBA Commissioner. Falk went out and sold Jordan as a star to companies that had been wary of African-American athletes. Nike, who had bought Frank Rudy's idea of shoes with air pockets but were in dire financial straits, paid him an initial $500,000 but a potential $2.5 million, dependent on sales and an All-Star appearance – an offer *Fortune* magazine thought ridiculously generous. Nike hoped to earn $3 million over 3–4 years from their 'Primetime' boots. Instead, 'Air Jordans' – the name Falk preferred – sold $100 million worth in one year alone and made $20 million for Michael. Despite an initial NBA ban, the black and red shoes became so desirable that people were robbed in the streets for them. Air Jordan turned into a brand and a string of shops, outselling entire rival makes to become the most successful endorsement in sporting history. In 1992, when Jordan's US 'Dream Team' were criticised for staying away from the Olympic Village and he refused to have a Reebok logo on his shirt, a vast billboard of him dominated Barcelona.

Other major sponsors included Gatorade, for whom he made over 20 commercials, Quaker, Hanes, McDonald's, Chevrolet and Coca-Cola. The Nike 'Hare Jordan' commercial co-starring Bugs Bunny turned into the 1996 movie *Space Jam*, and two years later Jordan was able to turn down $300 million of endorsements in just four months. Falk bought him out of standard league endorsements and was also instrumental in the 1995 and 1998 lock-outs over wages, arguing for a Hollywood-style star system rather than the wage-capped NBA, which paid Jordan a mere $30 million a year.

Today part owner of the Charlotte Bobcats, Jordan has promoted the team rather than his own name. As a player, he is commemorated by a statue outside Chicago's United Center and, more obscurely, by a bacterium named in his honour – Salmonella mjordan.

Duke Kahanamoku

Duke Paoa Kahinu Mokoe Hulikohola Kahanamoku, swimmer and surfer, born Waikiki, Hawaii 24 August 1890, died 22 January 1968. Winner Olympic 100 m freestyle (1912, 20), 4 x 200 m (1920). Swimming Hall of Fame 1965, Surfing Hall of Fame 1966.

Duke Kahanamoku was not only the man who introduced the crawl to swimming, but also the first great populariser of surfing as a sport.

Duke's first name was a tribute to his father, who had been named after the visiting Alfred, Duke of Edinburgh, Queen Victoria's second son. Baptised in the Hawaiian way, by being thrown into the surf, Duke had to be a swimmer from the start and remained so all his life, helped by vast hands and feet that were supposed to be big enough to steer a canoe. It was in 1911 that he came to prominence in his first official swimming contest in Honolulu harbour, setting a world record of 55.4 seconds for 100 yards, using an overarm stroke with scissoring feet and a flutter kick. He was so fast that for a long time the American Athletic Union refused to accept his record.

To judge from ancient wall paintings, overarm strokes date back to antiquity, but when they were first demonstrated in Europe in the mid-19th century they were regarded as 'grotesque' and compared to 'crawling' through the water – although they were demonstrably faster. From 1873 the 'Trudgen' overarm stroke copied that used by native South Americans, but the Europeans still stuck with a frog-leg kick. Even the new style developed by the Australian Frederick Cavill only 'fluttered' from the knee down. The crawl (officially still just part of a 'freestyle' anything-goes contest) wasn't seen until the 1912 Olympics. Having swum 100 metres in 60 seconds in qualification, Duke and two other Americans missed a semi-final they hadn't been informed about and only reached the final after insisting on an extra race against the clock. In the final itself, Duke used his full leg action to set a new world record and chop two seconds off the existing Olympic record – despite taking a look round before he finished. In the backstroke, Harry Hebner's alternating-arms style – effectively a reverse crawl – hacked three seconds off a 100 metres record set with a frog-style kick. Despite protests, it was agreed there was nothing in the rules against it.

In the 1920 Olympics, Duke returned to win again in the muddy waters of an Antwerp canal, nearly breaking the minute barrier, and then winning a rerun final after a complaint about blocking in a race staged without lanes. However, the following year he ducked a challenge to compete against the high-riding crawl style of <u>Johnny Weissmuller</u>, claiming indigestion. Weissmuller won at Paris in 1924, the first games with a proper pool, with Duke in second place. At the age of 42, Duke was still swimming as fast as ever and was present at the 1932 games as a water polo reserve.

As well as giving swimming demonstrations, Duke also popularised surfing, a sport that Europeans had at first frowned on. Riding a giant traditional 114 lb, 16 foot, skeg-less board, he introduced first Californians and then Australians to the sport and to his cry of 'Coming down!', founding the first official surf club at Waikiki in 1920. Based in LA, he worked as a character actor and lifeguard, and in 1925 rescued eight men from a capsized boat in heavy surf, which led to the wider use of surfboards among lifeguards.

Inducted straight away into both the Swimming and Surfing Halls of Fame, Duke is commemorated by statues in Hawaii, California and Australia, and various surfing championships, clubs and restaurants still name-check him. His board can be seen in the Honolulu museum.

Ben Johnson's positive drugs test brought about the first out-of-competition testing.

Flying V: Jan Boklöv's new ski-jumping style (*left*). Tiger Wood's upper body strength (*below*) – plus new club designs – helped make him more accurate at longer distances than anyone before.

Michael Jordan (*right*) was the first athlete to be as popular with advertisers as sport fans. Greg Louganis (*below*), one of the first openly gay athletes, came back from this crack on the head to win again.

'Captain' Martin Becher inspired the Grand National and first made steeplechasing a popular sport (*left*). Long fellow, short leathers: Lester Piggott's exceptional size (*below*) and control helped make him flat racing's king of the big occasion.

Billie Jean King (*right*) beat Bobby Riggs in the 'Battle of the Sexes' and set up the first professional sports competition for women. Ed Moses' unbroken stride pattern (*below*) put him a country mile ahead of other 400 m hurdlers.

Muttiah Muralitharan created a new bowling style and changed the rules of the game.

Annette Kellerman – 'The Million-Dollar Mermaid'

Annette Marie Sarah Kellerman, swimmer, diver, author, lecturer, stage and movie star, born Sydney 6 July 1887, died 6 November 1975. International Swimming Hall of Fame 1975.

When Annette Kellerman was born with rickets, her mother blamed herself, believing that it was because she had swum during her pregnancy. In fact, swimming would not only build up Annette, but would allow her to – quite literally – bring swimming to the world stage, leading to a minor revolution in women's dress and attitudes to exercise and sport.

Sydney, where Annette grew up, had had a swimming culture since the 1850s and she swam and dived behind the shark-proof netting of Cavill's Floating Baths, run by the family that had developed the Australian crawl. Wearing what would elsewhere he considered a man's knee-length costume, she became the first woman to swim ten miles, and set an all-comers' record for the mile aged just 15. Though she aspired to the theatre or ballet, hard times forced her and her father to stage swimming shows at the Melbourne Aquarium and in 1904 they travelled to London in search of a living.

Annette needed to hit the headlines fast, and risked a 26-mile swim down the polluted Thames to become an overnight sensation. When she was down to her last halfpenny, the *Daily Mirror* sponsored her in a series of coastal swims, followed by an attempt on the Channel, which hadn't been swum for 30 years. Smeared in porpoise oil, she was defeated by the tides and rough conditions, and the cocoa she was promoting made her sick, but she was soon appearing on stage with a swimming and diving act that even drew the Duke and Duchess of Connaught. To protect their sensibilities, Annette adopted a close-fitting full-length swimsuit with a tunic or skirt – a huge advance on the elaborate costumes worn by most female swimmers.

As the 'Cooo-ee Girl' she entranced Dave Gallaher's touring All Blacks, who greeted her with a lusty Maori cry, and she survived a high dive into a dirty and unexpectedly shallow pool that left her

permanently scarred. In Paris she drew a long-distance race in the
Seine with Tom Burgess – the second cross-Channel swimmer in
history – and in the icy, turbulent Danube was 45 minutes ahead of
rival Baroness Isa Cescu.

Invited to appear in America, Kellerman became a huge Vaudeville
star. In New York her swimming in a glass tank was credited with starting
off synchronised swimming. Her arrest on a beach for 'indecency' while
wearing one of her short costumes did her publicity no harm and she
graduated to films, doing her own stunts as she dived off waterfalls and
into tanks of crocodiles. She became the first swashbuckling heroine –
a new image of female independence at a time when women were still
pursuing the right to vote. Her seventh movie, *Neptune's Daughter*
(1914), set attendance records that weren't broken until 1955. Women
read her keep-fit books and attended lectures on achieving the 'body
beautiful' through exercise rather than corsets. (She always referred to
her own body in the third person.) For men, much of her appeal was
straightforward ogling of a figure that Dr Dudley Sargent of Harvard,
who had measured 10,000 other female forms, declared to be 'perfect'.
Annette's next film, *Daughter of the Gods*, was the first $1 million-
budget movie, with tinted frames and the snappiest editing ever seen,
and Annette became the first movie star to be filmed naked, although,
despite the evidence, she claimed to have worn a body stocking. One
Ohio moviegoer who watched the film three times in a row almost paid
for it with his life after his jealous wife attacked him with a potato
masher.

Though her professional status barred her from the Olympics,
Annette's graceful style inspired others to take up the sport and helped
the international swimming federation FINA's early recognition of
female athletes. By 1912, women swimmers were competing at the
Olympics – 16 years ahead of track and field. Annette's role was belatedly recognised in 1975 when, shortly before her death, she was
inducted into the Swimming Hall of Fame.

Billie Jean King

Billie Jean King (née Moffitt), tennis champion, coach, promoter, publisher and administrator, born Long Beach, California 22 November 1943. Grand Slam singles wins: Wimbledon 1966, 67, 68, 72, 73, 75, US Open 1967, 71, 72, 74, Australian Open 1968, French Open 1972. Women's doubles wins: Wimbledon 1961, 62, 65, 67, 68, 70, 71, 72, 73, 79, US Open 1964, 67, 74, 78, 80, French Open 1972. Mixed doubles wins: Wimbledon 1967, 71, 73, 74, US Open 1967, 71, 73, 76, Australian Open 1968, French Open 1967, 70. International Tennis Hall of Fame 1987. Sports Illustrated Sportsman of the Year 1972.

In 1990, when *Life* magazine rated the 100 most important Americans of the 20th century, only three were sportspeople – <u>Muhammad Ali</u>, <u>Michael Jordan</u> and Billie Jean King. Of the three it is probably Billie Jean who has had the most lasting impact – a social phenomenon who, through sheer willpower and hard work, built tennis into the first major professional sport for women and created an example for other female athletes and other sports to follow.

Few stars can have overcome so many obstacles to reach the top and stay there. Though her family were athletic and her brother pitched for the Giants, Billie Jean herself was only 5 foot 4½ inch tall, suffered from chest and sinus problems, had poor eyesight and underwent several knee operations. (She said she chose tennis because golf was too slow, swimming too scary and nothing else offered any advancement.) Without family wealth, she trained on public courts for a sport whose culture favoured the well-off. On the plus side, she had great speed, a hard-hitting net-rushing game, a full range of spins, chops and smashes, a crunching high backhand volley and ferocious determination – particularly at crisis point. Of the 13 championship games in which the score was 5–5 in the final set, she won 11. 'Winning,' she declared, 'is fleeting. Losing is forever.'

Ranked fourth in the world at 17, she became Wimbledon's youngest doubles champion and the following year beat champion Margaret Court, who had been 30–15 up and leading 5–3 in the third set. In 1966 she won her first Wimbledon singles title, while officially earning just $100 a week as a playground instructor. In practice, she was receiving $4,000 a year in unofficial payments, but unlike most athletes she spoke out against this 'shamateurism' in 1967 and encouraged Herman David's shift to open tennis at Wimbledon. A triple champion in 1967, she won the first open Wimbledon in 1968 with a new metal Wilson T2000 racket.

After Jack Kramer's 1970 Pacific Southwest tournament offered the women just $7,500 prize money – as opposed to $50,000 for the men – Billie Jean and eight other female pros paid $1 each to Gladys Heldman to start what became the Virginia Slims tour, taking on the USLTA, which at first banned the new Women's Tennis Association, of which Billie Jean became president. Solidly backed by Joe Cullman of the Philip Morris tobacco company, the WTA prospered through Billie Jean's hard graft in a variety of claustrophobic winter venues. Like her opposite number Kramer, she would tutor her rivals while also trying to wipe them off the court. The tour was soon worth $100,000 a year and saw off a USLTA-led rival, and in 1971 Billie Jean became the first woman to earn $200,000 in a season. This often meant two matches, two clinics and two broadcast appearances in a single day. With her husband Larry, she also set up *WomenSports* magazine and the Women's Sports Foundation, and campaigned for Title IX, a federal law requiring equal state funding for female and male athletes. When passed, this helped boost the number of girls playing high-school sport from 300,000 in 1970 to two million seven years later – though it was also blamed for a decline in the number of female coaches, as men muscled in. Later she founded World Team Tennis, where, as coach of the Philadelphia Freedoms, she became the first female coach of professional male athletes and inspired a song by her friend Elton John. She also led a campaign to get equal prize money for women at the US Open, 34 years before Wimbledon followed suit.

At the time, Billie Jean's rivalry with Margaret Court became a social and political phenomenon as well as a sporting one. Court was quoted as saying, 'If you worry too much about money you become hard like a man. I don't think women should be paid the same as men, even outside tennis.' Of the Slims tour she said, 'I can make as much on my own. I would hate to play the same women time after time.' To add extra edge, Court also played in front of segregated audiences in apartheid South Africa.

Ironically, it was thanks to Margaret Court that Billie Jean King played the most famous tennis match in history. In the 1973 'Mother's Day Massacre', Court accepted a $10,000 challenge to play renowned hustler Bobby Riggs, a former Wimbledon champion who, though old, had great speed, ball control and self-belief. Court played badly – her second service was particularly weak – and lost 6–2, 6–1. Having previously avoided what she saw as a demeaning contest, Billie Jean agreed to play Riggs in 'The Battle of the Sexes' in front of 30,000 fans in the Houston Astrodome with 40 million watching worldwide. With the hype cleverly built up by self-proclaimed 'chauvinist pig' Riggs, people even paid to watch their practices. On the night itself, with dancing midgets in attendance, Riggs made his entry drawn by a bevy of tightly sweatered 'bosom buddies', while Billie Jean was borne in on a Cleopatra-style litter. The press corps was betting two to one in favour of Riggs, but King, whose main concern was being dropped off the litter, had taken advice from Court and knew that Riggs's backhand was his weakness. Reckoning that a loss would set women's sport back fifty years, she won 6–4, 6–3, 6–3 after the legendarily nerveless Riggs choked at 5–4. Even at US colleges, the home of 'jock' sports, marching bands played 'I am Woman' and spelt out her initials on the pitch.

Billie Jean took her 20th Wimbledon title in 1979, but 1981 brought a new battle, when her lover and secretary Marilyn Barnett sued her for a share of earnings. Much of Billie Jean's prize money had been spent on new enterprises and campaigns. As she became the first openly lesbian sports star, her sponsors took fright and she lost $2 million. This meant that she had to continue playing competitively, reaching the Wimbledon semi-finals in 1983 and playing doubles until 1990. Never happy at being labelled a 'gay athlete' – though she was a fundraiser for Aids charities – she said she found this her greatest struggle.

Described by Margaret Court as 'the greatest competitor I've ever known', by the mid-1990s Billie Jean was a Federation Cup captain and US Olympic coach, as well as a commentator and trustee of the new American National Sports Museum. Now showered with awards, both the US National Tennis Centre at Flushing Meadow and the Women's Sports Federation awards are named after her.

Don King – 'The Ghetto Einstein'

Don King, boxing promoter, born Cleveland, Ohio 20 August 1931.

At 6 feet 3 inches, plus several inches of Aqua Netted hair on top, Don King is the most identifiable sports promoter of all time, the man who since the 1970s has used the power of global satellite TV to fund some of the most famous boxing matches in history, including the 1974 Foreman v Ali 'Rumble in the Jungle', the 1975 Frazier v Ali 'Thrilla in Manila', and in 1980 the record $11 million 'Brawl in Montreal' between Roberto Duran and Sugar Ray Leonard. Since then, King has dominated fight promotion and managed or promoted as many as nine of the top ten heavyweights at any one time.

King himself has attributed his rise to 'grit, wit and bullshit'. As well as the ability to talk the hind leg off a donkey and to entrance journalists and TV presenters, he has out-thought rival promoters, managers, organised crime and national governments and been credited with thinking five moves ahead of his opponents – whoever they might be.

In terms of first-hand experience of the ring, King fought only four amateur bouts. He first came to attention in 1954, as 'Donald the Kid' when he was running a 'numbers' or illegal lottery operation and was cleared of murder on the grounds of justifiable homicide. Twelve years later he stood trial for second-degree murder after kicking to death a smaller man named Sam Garrett over a $600 debt, but in a closed session the judge decided to downgrade the offence to manslaughter, and after serving four years, King, who had been a model prisoner, was released. It was then that he entered boxing promotion by persuading Muhammad Ali to stage an exhibition bout in aid of a local hospital. Though he knew a few fighters, King went into a short-lived partnership with Don Elbaum, who controlled a stable of local boxers. As early as 1973, King was rising to prominence at a Foreman v Frazier fight held in Jamaica for the benefit of US CCTV audiences.

King neither invented nor named the 'Rumble in the Jungle' (Ali came up with it), but it was the making of him, as he showed a masterful ability to manage the promotion, the clashing egos, the creation of a stadium from scratch in the jungle in six months and the tensions created by a delayed contest under the dictatorial eye of the backer President of Zaire, Mobutu Sese Seko, or, as he had just renamed himself, Mobutu Sese Seko Nkuku Ngbendu Wa Za Banga ('The all-powerful warrior who, because of his endurance and inflexible will to win, goes from conquest to conquest, leaving fire in his wake'). Even the anticipated rains held off as King emerged $20 million richer and pre-eminent in his field.

This rise to fame was easier than it would have been in other sports. As the 'red light district of sport' or 'showbiz with blood', US-based boxing has never had effective federal control or an NFL-style commissioner – so power rests with local officials and various fractured and warring governing bodies. At the time King entered the sport there was also something of a power vacuum and he exploited these weaknesses with a brilliant campaign of 'creative destruction', producing multiple champions – 20 in eight years – while also being paid millions of dollars by cable channels to reunite the titles. The downside for the sport was crowds in the low hundreds for supposed 'big name' fights and a growing lack of public interest in who all the rival 'champions' actually were. Don could use his influence with the WBC to have Leon Spinks stripped of his title, and after James 'Buster' Douglas defeated his man Mike Tyson, he almost succeeded in having both the WBA and WBC disregard a clear knockout, until press and public outrage stopped them.

King also profited by blurring the roles of promoter, manager and agent. Able to bill a manager's fee as well as a promoter's, he could also take or demand shares – sometimes secret ones – in fighters including Larry Holmes and Tim Witherspoon. His ability to attach himself to fighters at will was obvious from the first Jamaican fight, when he arrived at ringside as part of Joe Frazier's entourage and left with the victorious Foreman's. Since then he has shown a remarkable ability to separate boxers from their managers and promoters, even when they have offered more cash and greater loyalty. This was particularly the case with Mike Tyson, where King gatecrashed Tyson's ex-manager's funeral to make his move. Though he has frequently used race and ideas of racial solidarity and prejudice to his advantage, King also promoted white fighters (including Chuck Wepner, the inspiration for 'Rocky'), and on occasion paid them more than their black opponents. Though he pitched fights as racial armageddons and promoted in apartheid South Africa, Don, as fast on his feet as any boxer, was able to command support from America's black press and later appeared alongside Nelson Mandela. Larry Holmes's verdict was that he 'looks black, lives white and thinks green' [in the dollar sense].

King has also proved pretty nimble in his dealing with two grand juries and the tax authorities. In 1980, an assistant took the rap for tax evasion and three years later Don was cleared of charges by a state governor, having backed both parties before the election. (In 2004, he was a strong supporter of George W. Bush.) The following year, when King was confronted with 23 counts of tax fraud, the judge suddenly changed the rules of evidence, and after acquittal King flew the jury to the Witherspoon v Bruno flight – billing the expenses to Witherspoon. When questioned about any underworld links in 1992, he took the Fifth Amendment, while a Justice Department prosecution three years later led to a retrial and acquittal in 1998.

King has always been acutely aware of the power of hard cash to get fighters to give away lifetime shares, sign blank contracts or to agree to drop legal actions, and it was the simple promise of $5 million each that drew Ali and Foreman to Zaire. Despite this awareness of the power of money, King's expressed intention to create a black entertainment and sports empire has largely failed to materialise. The simplest reason, given by former champ Tim Witherspoon, was that King 'prefers a dishonest quarter to an honest dollar'. It is believed that the hospital, for whom his first Ali exhibition was staged, received little money from the fight and since then King has often been accused of scamming his fighters by making high charges for training or simply trying it on with deductions that might go unnoticed. In 1981, after he promoted Muhammad Ali's final return to the ring, he was even reported to have scammed 'The Greatest', extracting an extra $1.17 million from a fight that most observers felt Ali was in no condition to contest. Even after a beating from Ali's affiliates, King is said to have got away with paying him just $50,000 cash, rather than the full amount demanded. At least one of King's heavyweight champions found that he was fighting for one-tenth the purse of his untitled opponent. Those fighters who have sought redress have found that King refuses to release documentation, and in the case of Witherspoon it took him six years of effort to reclaim just $3 million of the $25 million he believed he was owed. When Mike

Tyson sued King for $100 million, he got approximately a tenth of that amount.

A classic King scam was the excellent idea of staging a grand US championship, which could be held on a variety of dramatic federal locations, such as a battleship. This brilliant idea foundered when it was discovered that he had falsified fighters' records, bribed boxing magazine *The Ring* to back his story and was demanding that competing fighters sign up with him as manager. As a consequence Marvin Hagler, an obvious championship contender, kept well away and the deal with Roone Arledge's ABC collapsed. Another reason to avoid Don is a reputation for bad organisation. Mike Tyson's loss to James Douglas was partly blamed on an under-prepared corner that lacked basic equipment, and King's management of him was disastrous. The 'ghetto' positioning of Tyson helped turn him from one of sport's most exciting prospects to one that no sponsor would risk association with. Other fighters have often been denied payment of medical bills and some later champions such as Lennox Lewis carefully kept their distance.

Boxing has always been a poorly regulated game, based on pain and deception, that attracts criminals and the most desperate, so Don King's activities are hardly unprecedented. He's the symptom, not the disease.

'Bart' King

John Barton King, baseballer and cricketer, born Philadelphia, USA 19 October 1873, died 17 October 1965. Career: Tioga, Belmont and the Gentlemen of Philadelphia 1892–1916. First-class career: 2,134 runs (20.52), 415 wickets (15.67).

It might seem odd that one of the greatest and most influential bowlers in cricket was an American, but in fact it is entirely logical. John Barton King was born in Philadelphia, where baseball and cricket were competing summer games, the US and Canada having played the first international cricket match back in 1844. During the first 15 years of his life 'Bart' played baseball, where the use of swerve and dip had recently become part of the game, but from 1889 he began to introduce the same techniques to cricket, flicking his fingers to spin the ball backwards and keep the seam upright. A tall, strong-shouldered lad, his one concession to baseball pitching was to hold the ball in both hands during his delivery, but there was never any criticism of an otherwise classic fast-bowling style.

In his first season for the Tioga club in 1889, Bart took 37 wickets for 99. His basic ball was an outswinger that moved at the last instant. Even more confusing for the batsman was the occasional inswinger or 'angler' that moved in the opposite direction. Historically, pace bowlers had restricted themselves to a bit of spin or 'cut' off the grass rather than changing direction through the air. The regular use of swing or drift was something quite new and wickets toppled fast.

King made his first international appearance in 1892. Aged just 18, he took 19 wickets over three games against Ireland at an average of just 13.53. The following year, the Australians disembarked from a rough crossing on their way back from an Ashes series and the Philadelphians shocked the cricketing world by defeating them by an innings and 68 runs. Bart took 5 for 78 and Aussie captain <u>Jack Blackham</u> classed the team alongside England's best. Despite this, it was not until 1897 that the Gentlemen of Philadelphia first toured England. Though they won only two of their 15 first-class matches, the big news was their defeat of Sussex, during which Bart bowled

Ranji first ball, took 7 for 13 and had the county out for 46 in the first innings.

The next tour didn't depart America for another four years, by which time Bart had taken 8 for 78 against an MCC touring side. British bowlers like George Hirst began to pick up on the new technique, steering the ball through the air to attack the wicket from various unlikely angles, and in 1906 he broke the record for a season with 208 wickets. In 1903 both Lancashire and Surrey were defeated by the Americans, which led to a series of offers for Bart to take up residence and play county cricket. To support him financially, one side was even supposed to have lined up a willing widow with an income of £7,000 p.a. Instead, he returned to the US to play for the Belmont club and collect three batting and four bowling cups in five years, racking up the first triple century in America, a US record of 344 and over 2,000 wickets at an average of 10.47 runs.

The 1908 tour was Bart's last, taking 87 wickets at an average of 11.01 over ten matches – the best bowling average for forty years until another 'king of swing', Les Jackson of Derbyshire, bettered it with 10.99. Perhaps most impressively, in 1909 Bart bowled all 11 Gentlemen of Ireland for 53 – including one man bowled with a no-ball. The following year he polished off Trenton single-handed, taking the last of their wickets with only a single fielder to assist him. Two years later, aged nearly 40, he took 9 for 78. A great raconteur with a dry wit, he became an MCC member and saw his innovation become standard in the sport, as bowlers like Hirst and Sydney Barnes developed all kinds of swerves, dips and sudden straightening-ups. In response, batsmen adopted a more 'eyes-front' style and fielding patterns also changed, with the leg side attracting more attention.

The MCC's Pelham Warner, who had played Bart King, described him as 'undoubtedly one of the finest bowlers of all time'.

Phil 'Buck' Knight

Philip Hampson Knight, runner and businessman, born Portland, Oregon 24 February 1938. Co-founder and chairman of Nike.

As a miler, Phil Knight's best time was 4.10, but his lasting impact on sport was as founder of the company that he and his University of Oregon coach Bill Bowerman formed in a handshake deal. Nike, as it would eventually be named, not only made Knight very rich, but also revolutionised the world's athletic shoe markets and created a new star system in sport, recruiting and managing outstanding players and teams. In 1999 it was revealed that Nike were even controlling player selection and fixtures for the Brazilian national football squad. In one *Sports Illustrated* poll, Knight was listed as the most influential figure in sport.

Nike is best known for its name, 'swoosh' tick, 'Just Do It' slogan, smart ads and Air Jordan shoes – none of which Knight had much to do with. Founded as Blue Ribbon Sports – a name allegedly inspired by Pabst Blue Ribbon beer – 'Nike' was dreamt up as a brand name by Knight's first employee, Jeff Johnson. 'I don't really like any of them, but I guess that's the best of the bunch,' said Knight, who was pushing for 'Dimension Six' instead. The tick was drawn for $35 by art student Carolyn Davidson, with Knight commenting, 'I don't love it, but I think it will grow on me.' As for 'swoosh', that was a term first used by Johnson to describe a nylon-topped Tiger shoe that Blue Ribbon imported from Japan. The association with Jordan and the creation of Nike's first TV campaigns were down to executive Rob Strasser, who signed his memos 'just do it'.

Unlike those of his great rival <u>Adi Dassler</u>, Knight's innovations were financial rather than technical. His big idea, first mooted in a Stanford Business School paper, was to import low-cost Adidas copies from the Far East. After importing Onitsuka Tiger shoes, Bowerman and Johnson improved the product with new ideas like the waffle sole and cushioned midsole. Despite the success of models like the Cortez, Blue Ribbon didn't actually have a shoe that was superior to Adidas until the mid-1970s, when it developed its own research facilities and bought in ideas like Frank Rudy and Bob Bogert's air-cushioned soles. (Air soles were to revolutionise the market, but the first 'Tailwind' prototype flopped after its metallic paint ate through the uppers.)

At first combining retail, wholesale and mail-order sales, Knight soon focused on wholesale, using self-employed agents to do the selling. After falling out with Onitsuka, he negotiated with Nippon Rubber to make Blue Ribbon's own designs, while the Japanese conglomerate Nissho provided finance. From there he diversified supply, seeking out low labour costs, high production standards and protection of Nike's trade secrets. Profit margins were soon 40 per cent compared to Adidas's typical 25 per cent, and Knight's US-style willingness to lobby government and to go to law also helped the company thrive and survive, despite occasional exposés of workers' conditions. In 1997, Vietnamese workers were receiving $10 a week for six 12-hour days in unhealthy conditions – something that Nike has repeatedly promised to address.

As a culture as well as a business, Blue Ribbon combined a Far Eastern work culture with West Coast self-indulgence. Knight apparently once offered a manager $50,000 not to get married, while Nike's 'frat boy' antics included restaurant-wrecking parties and tequila fountains. Senior managers were 'buttfaces' and the top two officers Delbert Hayes and Rob Strasser were known as 'Doomsday' and 'Rolling Thunder'.

From the early 1970s, Blue Ribbon's new designs transformed the hitherto protected US market, in which chemical and tyre companies had made cheap rubber shoes unchanged in a generation. Despite the running boom, Blue Ribbon struggled with finance and supply until sales manager Jim Moodhe invented 'Futures', in which retailers made firm financial commitments to get guaranteed deliveries. By the mid-1970s the Nike brand had 'clicked', fuelling 85 per cent year-on-year sales increases. The company moved from white-dominated track sports into mainly black basketball, where a larger number of players wore their shoes out faster, and attracted star endorsees through a royalties deal. At the same time, white suburban Americans began wearing Nike trainers to the bar or supermarket as an affordable 'label'. Although Blue Ribbon's sartorially challenged male founders failed to produce any attractive or well-made sports clothing, Nike grew fast and chaotically. Separate product development and marketing facilities slowed down innovation, and a jumble of promotion and advertising deals meant that up to 2,000 athletes were receiving money or free shoes.

As Blue Ribbon increased the amount paid to star athletes, a new generation of agents racked up the cost of their signatures to $100,000 and the company also made payments to college players and coaches, openly offering $50,000 in road race prizes and forcing the US track and field authorities to allow trust-fund payments, which helped end purely amateur athletics. At the 1984 LA Olympics, a quarter of the US squad were members of the Nike-funded 'Athletics West' squad – although their medal haul was smaller than hoped and Carl Lewis was less than a hit with the crowd.

By this time Nike, as they were now officially named, had been blind-sided by the decline of the jogging fad, and Reebok was riding the new aerobics boom with softer women's shoes that Knight dismissed as 'shit'. It was Rob Strasser who helped turn Nike around with the 'ambush marketing' of the Olympics – using ads to suggest that Nike was supporting an event even if it wasn't. Abandoning the old policy of supporting thousands of athletes, Strasser copied Converse by focusing on a few high-profile stars and even allowed Adidas to take over sponsorship of the University of Oregon track team. His deal with Adidas fan Michael Jordan, combined with the improved Air shoes he pushed through the company, became the most successful endorsement in sports history, with the NBA eventually being forced to allow their new star to wear Nike's non-standard black and red footwear. For the first time, sports promotion was paying an athlete more than the game itself, and Nike now also diversified into sports agenting.

Since then, Nike has innovated with Shox hi-spec foams and moved into soccer. (At first they had to pay teams to 'spat' their shoes, sticking Nike logos onto other superior boots.) At Atlanta in 1996, the Olympic vice-president Dick Pound forced them to pull their 'You don't win silver, you lose gold' campaign – the antithesis of Pierre de Coubertin's beliefs – but the differences were soon overcome and the company stepped in to sponsor the 2000 Sydney games after Reebok withdrew.

As for Phil Knight, his distant and enigmatic style was apparent from the early days of Blue Ribbon. It was five years before he worked full-time himself, relying instead on Bowerman to promote the shoes and Johnson to build the company and design the product. Later he preferred to sit back, allowing his senior 'buttfaces' to fight it out while he absented himself. Brendan Foster, who briefly held the thankless position of president under Knight, described him as a 'black hole' sucking in ideas and expressing nothing. Having once confessed that he didn't much like people or saying what could be left unsaid, Knight often preferred to hide behind his black spectacles. After the buttfaces gradually departed, he resigned as CEO in 2004, but remains the chairman and major shareholder.

Bill Koch

Bill Koch, cross-country skier, born Brattleboro, Vermont 7 June 1955. Winner Cross Country World Cup 1982.

Bill Koch was both the first American and the first non-European to win a cross-country skiing medal, but his main contribution to the sport was his later development of the revolutionary 'skating' style.

In 1976, when Koch collected an Olympic silver medal behind the Red Army's Sergei Savelyev, he was still using the classic 'stride and glide', with skis kept parallel except on the turn. A favourite for the following games, he suffered from asthma and the stress of excessive media attention and performed badly, only to bounce back with an entirely new style. Influenced by speed skaters, he now skated with his ski tips turned outward, pushing off the inside edge. The new technique added 10 per cent to his speed on the flat but, as so often in sport, it was seen as either ridiculous or unacceptable. At first, attempts were made to rein him in with steeper courses where the technique wouldn't work, but progress couldn't be held back forever. Cross-country formally adopted the new style in 1982 and three years later both the biathlon and Nordic Combined events followed suit. Today most events offer 'classic' and freestyle options.

Koch, who carried the US flag at Albertville in 1992, has had various US skiing festivals and leagues named after him and now resides in the less than likely state of Hawaii, specialising in sand skiing.

Alvin Kraenzlein

Alvin Christian Kraenzlein, hurdler, sprinter and long jumper, born Milwaukee 12 December 1876, died 6 January 1928. Olympic champion 60 m, 110 m hurdles, 200 m hurdles, long jump (1900).

'You've got to be in it to win it' is a sporting truth that was never better proved than at the chaotic 1900 Paris Olympics. On hearing that some events were to be run on the Sabbath, most of the college athletes representing America refused to compete, except for five University of Pennsylvania jocks who between them carted off eight first places – and one of them wasn't even an American. Of these five, the most famous was dental student and American Athletic Union champion Alvin Kraenzlein, who won four individual track and field golds – an all-time Olympic record. He also revolutionised the hurdles with his modern straight-leg style.

Hurdling traces its history back to imitation horse races, where runners bunny-hopped over heavy wooden sheep hurdles staked firmly into the ground. Although earlier British hurdlers such as <u>W.G. Grace</u>'s Gloucestershire team-mate Arthur Croome experimented with a straight leading leg, these mini five-bar gates didn't encourage a faster 'skimming style'. Instead, this developed in the US, where lighter, inverted 'T'-profile hurdles were introduced. These could be safely knocked over and enabled the event to move from the field to the track, where the faster straight-leg style emerged. At Paris in 1900, the French wouldn't allow a cinder track on the Bois de Boulogne, so Kraenzlein ended up winning both hurdles races on grass, setting a 200-metre record that would last until 1923. More controversial was the long jump, where he broke a gentleman's agreement with leading jumper Myer Prinstein not to compete on a Sunday. After bettering Prinstein's jump by just one centimetre, he refused a jump-off the following day. The enraged Prinstein had to be restrained from attacking Kraenzlein, who was now promenading around Paris in a cravat, cap and Eton collar. (Prinstein got his revenge at the 1904 and 1906 games.)

Kraenzlein retired in 1900 with six world records and by 1910 was a professor of physical training, producing an Olympic champion in

Ralph Craig, who took two sprint titles at the 1912 games. On the back of his coaching success, Kraenzlein was hired at a reported salary of $50,000 to train the German track and field team for the planned 1916 Berlin games. On the eve of war he took a squad to the US, where he signed up as an Army physical training instructor. Before his early death he also coached in Cuba.

Jack Kramer

Jack Kramer, promoter and tennis player, born Las Vegas 1 August 1921. Wimbledon singles champion 1947, doubles champion 1946, 47, US Open singles champion 1946, 1947, doubles champion 1940, 41, 43, 47. Davis Cup winner 1946, 47. International Tennis Hall of Fame 1968.

As the world's best player during the late 1940s, the tall and slim Jack Kramer is credited with popularising a consistent serve-and-volley style as well as 'percentage tennis'. He was also to change tennis history as a promoter and advocate of open competition between professionals and amateurs.

Kramer's 'percentage tennis' meant protecting one's serve, playing for survival on opponents' first serves and attacking suspect second serves. Taken to its extreme, percentage tennis holds that a good enough player need win only 18 games to take a match.

With a family to feed, Kramer didn't have the moneyed background of many amateur tennis stars and he wasn't willing to be a 'social gigolo', sucking up to the tennis authorities in return for under-the-counter payments. After coming out of the coastguard at the end of the war, he planned to win both major titles and turn pro. In fact, he was thwarted at Wimbledon by blisters, but returned the following year to drop just 37 games over the fortnight and record the fastest ever win in a men's singles final, at only 45 minutes. (He was also one of the first to wear shorts, which he reckoned to be the single greatest advance in equipment during his whole career.)

Having turned professional in what was officially an amateur game, Kramer toured with champion pro 'Pancho' Gonzales, playing some 123 matches in all kinds of venues, often on a temporary canvas court. The weakness of this 'star system' was that it could only tour once before the crowds fell off. More seriously, a slight edge would produce lopsided scores over time and Kramer's 96 wins over the series seriously damaged Gonzales's prospects. Against speedy 1939 Wimbledon champion Bobby Riggs, Kramer took over $250,000 at Madison Square Garden and developed his 'big game', routinely following up every service to the net in a way that had never been done before. The success of his serve-and-volley tactics encouraged other less talented players to adopt them and they were blamed for the sport's post-war decline in popularity.

A natural leader, who had led a players' strike aged just 20 in protest at inadequate accommodation, Kramer organised a series of gruelling individual and team tours. His 'circus', as it was derisively known, travelled constantly and he might have had to give up the game through injury, had he not been one of the first players to use cortisone injections. During the late 1950s, he signed Australian stars Lew Hoad, Ken Rosewall and Rod Laver and at one time had seven players earning $50,000 p.a. – more than any other professional sport. Having 'lost' their best stars to him, official tennis fought back by setting up 'wedding funds' or buying businesses for players such as Frank Sedgman. Scare stories also circulated that Jack was planning a similar coup in swimming, another popular amateur sport.

In 1959, tennis nearly accepted the inevitable by going open, but an ILTF vote narrowly failed, with the decision being made while one supporter with plenty of votes to cast was in the toilet. Kramer was demonised by the tennis establishment and in 1963 opted to withdraw from the game, arguing that his presence was holding up progress. In 1967, when Herman David's Wimbledon opted to go it alone with an open tournament, it was to Jack that they turned to line up the stars. Its success prompted the first open championship, after which the ILTF finally accepted open competition too. In the carve-up that followed, Arthur Ashe lobbied for Kramer to lead the newly formed Association of Tennis Professionals in 1972, and he also organised the players during their showdown with the ILTF, whose member federations still claimed the right to use or suspend players at will.

Kramer's Pacific Southwest tournament also sparked off the creation of the Women's Tennis Association. When the female players rebelled over being offered just $7,500 in prize money, his long-standing enemy Gladys Heldman encouraged the women players to form their own organization.

George Lambton

The Hon George Lambton, racehorse trainer, born Fenton, Northumberland 23 December 1860, died 23 July 1945. Champion trainer 1906, 11, 12. Wins include: 2000 Guineas 1926, 1,000 Guineas 1916, 17, 18, 23, Derby 1924, 33, Oaks 1896, 1906, St Leger 1910, 19, 23, 33.

In 1892, after a crashing fall in a steeplechase at Sandown Park, George Lambton turned to training – at the time an extraordinary decision for an aristocrat, however horse-mad. (Lambton was said to have found Eton rather too close to Ascot, and Cambridge too close to Newmarket.) As the fifth son of the 2nd Earl of Durham, he was well positioned to attract wealthy, aristocratic owners and within a year was private trainer to the Earl of Derby, remaining so until 1933. During his long career, the elegant Lambton defied bad health to train 13 classic winners, starting in 1896 with Canterbury Pilgrim and ending in 1933 with his most popular winner, the small and lazy Hyperion, later an important sire of broodmares.

For all his success in the classics, Lambton's most influential victories were in 1903, when he deliberately and publicly doped five of his worst horses to highlight the use of drugs in racing. At the time cocaine, a recent chemical discovery, was widely used in the US, where horses were doped for stamina to compete again and again in long drawn-out race meetings. Owners such as barbed-wire magnate John Warne 'Bet-A-Million' Gates were believed to have brought the practice to Britain, whose he and fellow playboy John Drake won an estimated £2 million. Their trainer Enoch Wishard was a near neighbour of Lambton in Newmarket. With the Jockey Club unwilling to act, Lambton's public doping brought him four first places and one second. Spurred into action, the Jockey Club amended its Rule 76 to make trainers responsible for any doping. This poorly conceived law meant that trainers were reluctant to reveal horses which had been 'got at' for fear of losing their own livelihoods, and led to some terrible miscarriages of justice, until the <u>Duke of Norfolk</u>'s committee came up with a more sensible policy in 1961. (The first accurate saliva test came in 1910, with the first 'positive', Bourbon Rose, detected two years later.)

After being 'retired' by the Earl of Derby in 1933, Lambton lost control of Hyperion, who turned up for the Ascot Gold Cup only half-fit and finished third. Lambton now set up as a public trainer at the unlikely address of Kremlin House, Newmarket. Having campaigned for the continuation of racing in wartime, he died just two days after his official retirement. Today there is a road named after him in the town.

Marie-Reine Le Gougne – 'The French Judge'

Marie-Reine Le Gougne, ice skater and sports administrator.

Marie-Reine Le Gougne, an ex-figure skater and skating judge, was the key figure in the Winter Olympics' greatest sporting scandal to date – one that led to a complete change in the way the sport was marked.

As it's an artistic, judged event there have always been controversies over the scoring in figure skating. Partly these are due to genuine differences of opinion, but the sport made matters worse with its tangled and illogical rules and 'protocol judging', which allowed judges to witness practice sessions, so that they marked final performances according to their expectations rather than what actually happened on the ice. Another problem was that judges were appointed by their own national federations rather than the International Skating Union, which meant they could favour their own athletes and trade votes between themselves. The ISU had stopped having multiple judges from single countries since the days of <u>Sonja Henie</u>, but block votes persisted and judges who rocked the boat often found themselves out of the game. Even when the highest and lowest votes began to be stripped out, unfairly low or high scores could still shift the averages.

Within this rotten state of affairs, Marie-Reine Le Gougne was a reformer who, despite the sport's notorious sexism, was an international judge by the age of 25. However, at the 2002 Salt Lake City Olympics, she was plunged into controversy after Canadian world champions Jamie Salé and David Pelletier were placed second to Russians Elena Berezhnaya and Anton Sikharulidze. In the run-up, Berezhnaya had over-cooked herself on a sunbed, the pairs had collided in practice and a last-second slip in their short programme had placed the Canadians second, but after a shaky long programme from the Russians and a crowd-pleasing display from Salé and Pelletier, there was a storm of protest when the 'Eastern bloc' – plus Le Gougne – voted for the Russians.

With broadcasters NBC on the warpath and the whole games overshadowed by the controversy, Le Gougne, who was trying to get onto

the ISU Technical Committee, broke down and publicly told referee
Sally Stapleford that she had been leant on to swap votes with the
Russians, who would in turn support French skaters Marina Anissina
and Gwendal Peizerat. Against a backdrop of threatening phone calls
to waitress Salé and hot-dog salesman Pelletier, Le Gougne soon retracted
her claims, but they had also been made in an official briefing meeting.
ISU president Ottavio Cinquanta hoped to ride out the latest scandal
until confronted by new Olympic vice-president Dick Pound, who
declared, 'You've fouled up our festival, now sort it out. This is a contrived
situation, not a random error.'

Fortunately, a precedent existed from the 1992 Olympics, when
synchronised swimmer Sylvie Fréchette was awarded gold after a judging
error was unfairly manipulated. Accordingly, the Russian pair, who had
very sportingly offered a skate-off to decide, found themselves joint gold
winners with Salé and Pelletier. (One bonus was that the controversy
led to lots of offers of exhibitions by the two pairs.) Subsequent investigations identified crime figure Alimzan Tokhtakhounov, who was said
to have fixed Russian beauty contests in the past.

For Le Gougne and French federation president Didier Gailhaguet,
the result was a three-year suspension from the sport, while, under IOC
pressure, the ISU shifted to a new scoring system, with nine judges
chosen randomly from a panel of 12 and the top and bottom scores
stripped out. However, as the judges' individual scores were now to be
kept secret, the new system also ensured that any future corruption
would remain secret.

Archibald Leitch

Archibald Leitch, engineer and architect, born Glasgow 27 April 1865, died London 25 April 1939.

Archibald Leitch was the Scottish draughtsman, engineer and architect who built and designed nearly all of Britain's major sports stadiums. During the football boom of the early 20th century, he planned and built between 46 and 51 major projects, transforming Victorian fields with twee pavilions, tumbledown sheds and muddy banks into scientifically designed stadiums, the best of which boasted electric lighting, laundries, baths, running tracks and massage and billiards rooms for the players, plus bars, tip-up seats and car parks for the spectators and overhead press boxes for the journalists.

Though he worked in an era of picks, shovels, barrows and carthorses, Leitch used lightweight prefabricated steel to build his stands, and from 1906 was also using the new 'wonder material', reinforced concrete. At Ibrox in 1902 he also pioneered wood and steel lattices to carry the terraces of an 80,000-capacity stadium – the largest in the world – but a disastrous collapse on 5 April 1902 caused them to give way, with 26 people falling to their deaths and 516 injured. Thereafter, his terraces were supported by banks of spoil or, at Roker Park, Sunderland, reinforced concrete.

Terraces were the major source of income for clubs, since, as Archie pointed out, 'two could stand where one could sit'. He copied the sunken lateral and radial aisles that Alexander Blair pioneered at Hampden Park, which encouraged crowds to fill the whole terrace rather than cluster round the entrances and exits. He also developed his own cheap and effective method of moulding steps, used patented crush barriers for safety and dug down the front of terraces to improve visibility and pitch drainage and reduce the costs of banking-up. Starting at John Davies's Old Trafford (1908), he abandoned the old 'racecourse style' stand with a flat paddock in front, in favour of a dug-down pitch that gave everyone a better view, and the United pitch is still well below ground level today. At Anfield (1906), Leitch created a gigantic 132-step Kop, and when his firm came to remodel Hampden Park in 1927, they would build the world's largest stadium, with a capacity of 149,000. Many Leitch terraces were left open to the skies and if covers were added, they were of steel latticework. It would be continental European architects who would first experiment with reinforced-concrete roofs.

Leitch's methods allowed grounds to be built fast and cheaply and he fuelled the football boom by building for speculative clubs such as Chelsea, or those like Bradford City and Huddersfield, who were seeking election to the League. (At Selhurst Park, he campaigned unsuccessfully for the return of the FA Cup to south London.) New stands were crammed into awkward or poorly accessed sites like the Dell, Highbury and Fratton Park, and at some grounds chevron-shaped stands had to be used to fit into awkward sites. The use of reinforced concrete also allowed him to build on tricky slopes such as Bradford City's Valley Parade (1908), although the ill-fated main stand was not his design.

Instead of building pavilions that were separate from the stands, Archie favoured a cost-saving 'integrated' design, with seats above and changing rooms below, although at Craven Cottage lack of space forced the creation of a final Victorian-style pavilion. (His Grade II listed 'Cottage' would save Fulham from the developers during the 1980s property boom.) Generally, decoration was limited to a central gable and the painted criss-cross ironwork that became his trademark, but when given the opportunity, time and budget, he produced an elegant brick façade at Craven Cottage, stained glass and mosaic detailing at Villa Park and terrazzo marble and oak at Ibrox – the three most stylish grounds in the country, until Highbury was rebuilt in the 1930s. Though it was Everton's architect Henry Hartley who built the first double-decker stand, Leitch soon learned to cast larger concrete decks and built the biggest ever seen – the towering 'Mauritania' stand at Goodison Park (1908), a ground which by 1938 would be the first to be double-decked on all four sides. He also built a 'two-way' stand between the cricket and football pitches at Bradford Park Avenue.

Though Leitch's early grounds were often intended for multiple use – such as athletics and football at Stamford Bridge – most later commissions were football-only, giving rise to the British tradition of small urban grounds with spectators packed close to the pitch. Only John Davies's Manchester United dared to move to a large open site, which would allow them to expand easily. Here the basic Leitch plan has survived massive rebuilding, including the removal of one of his dangerous, old-fashioned multi-spanned stands – a design he also inflicted on Wolves and Arsenal.

During the pre-World War I football boom, a series of rushed jobs led to rows and arguments with clients, including missed completion dates at Highbury (1913) and a serious collapse at Hillsborough in 1914, when 75 were injured. However, the true value of Leitch's expertise was shown when he *wasn't* used. In 1923, Wembley Stadium was 'designed' by the almost criminally thoughtless Maxwell Ayrton, and without proper gates or terracing produced 1,000 injuries during the near-disastrous White Horse final.

As late as 1966 all the club venues for the World Cup were Leitch grounds – of which only Old Trafford had been substantially remodelled. Many clubs cut corners on safety, which led to a series of accidents, at Ibrox (1971), Valley Parade (1985) and Hillsborough (1989). Although these grounds were now out of date – and in the case of the multi-spanned stands, dangerously slow to evacuate – the first minimum standards for safety, set out in 1975, compared closely to those by which Archie Leitch worked.

The financial and building boom of the 1990s has wiped out most of Leitch's architectural legacy, but some works still remain. There is a Leitch stand still in use at Craven Cottage and his masterpiece – the Ibrox Main Stand – survives today as the Bill Struth Stand, with a new layer built over the top. Today most new football stadiums still follow the basic plan of Leitch's Old Trafford design, with their stands close to the pitch on all four sides but rounded at the corners. Over a century after he first defined the look of a British football ground, Archie Leitch's influence is still felt.

'Cecil' Leitch

Charlotte Cecilia Pitcairn Leitch, golfer and author, born Silloth, Cumbria 13 April 1891, died 16 September 1977. British Ladies' Amateur Golf Champion 1914, 20, 21, 26. American Golf Hall of Fame 1967.

A record-breaking amateur golf champion, Cecil Leitch was the first woman to play a high-profile game against a man and the first to regularly give the ball a bloody good whack.

One of five sisters – all golf champions – 'Cecil' first emerged aged just 17 as a semi-finalist at the 1908 British Ladies' Amateur Golf Championships. Although women had been recorded playing golf as early as 1792, it was only in 1867 that they were officially allowed to play and the 'no arms above shoulders' rule, intended to keep women's golf lady-like, restricted them to a pitch-and-putt style with few holes longer than 80 yards. The first to break with this and fire the ball further, though still in a ladylike fashion, was Lady Margaret Scott, who won the first three championships, which from 1893 were organised by the new Ladies' Golf Union.

It was Cecil Leitch, with her characteristic flat swing, who first wound up and gave the ball a smack and in 1912 she was good enough to play Harold Hilton, the US and UK amateur champion. Though the event was handicapped, with Cecil receiving half a stroke per hole over 72, the point was made that women could play a physical sport on near-equal terms with men.

Though her career was interrupted by war, Cecil won three championships in a row, plus five French Opens and one Canadian, and her duels with Joyce Wethered made the front pages. After her final Open victory in 1926 she continued to promote the game, supported the YWCA and National Playing Fields Council and became an honorary member of 25 clubs and five associations. 'Cecil Leitch' matches are still held in her honour.

Greg LeMond

Gregory James LeMond, road racing cyclist, born Lakewood, California 26 June 1961. World champion 1979, 83, 89. Tour de France 1986, 89, 90. *Sports Illustrated* Sportsman of the Year 1989.

After three weeks and 2,025 miles, Greg LeMond won the 1989 Tour de France by just eight seconds – the narrowest margin in history – despite starting the final day's 25-kilometre time trial 50 seconds behind leader Laurent Fignon. Making up two seconds per kilometre was judged impossible before the race, but Fignon, who had dreaded this time trial, was feeling unwell, and Greg LeMond was a different rider from previous champions.

As well as all the usual attributes – a great cardiovascular system and a willingness to train and suffer – Greg was unusually consistent and had great powers of recuperation, as well as being a better-than-average sprinter. The first non-European winner of the Tour, he was also an outsider, bringing new ideas on training, dieting and business practice into a hidebound sport.

At first a skier, LeMond won a world junior road race title aged 19, and began studying nutrition and physiology. As well as overturning many old cycling superstitions about diet and alcohol, he introduced interval training and played indoor sports to stay fit through the winter. Instead of relying on team sponsors, he created his own commercial outlet, Team LeMond, and in theory became the first $1 million bike rider, when he joined Bernard Tapie's La Vie Claire team as successor to <u>Bernard Hinault</u>. He might have beaten Hinault in 1985 had the team not misinformed him about his time on the road.

LeMond also embraced new technology. Like Fignon, he went into the 1989 time trial using the disc wheel first demonstrated by Francesco Moser five years before, but went further still by using a teardrop-shaped aerodynamic helmet and the triathlon handlebars he'd used in the preceding Tour de Trump. Invented by Boone Lennon, they put the racer in a more aerodynamic tucked position and LeMond even hired Lennon to advise him on their use.

The 1989 victory was all the more remarkable as it was only his second win since a shooting accident which would have claimed Greg's life, had a helicopter not happened to be in the vicinity. After losing four quarts of blood, he also missed the 1987 season thanks to an emergency appendectomy. Still with 30 pellets lodged in his body, including two in his heart, he was out of contention at the 1989 Giro d'Italia before he diagnosed himself as needing iron injections and returned to form.

After retiring, LeMond's name was licensed to Trek. Since his retirement he has been drawn into conflict with the two other Americans to win the Tour – Lance Armstrong and Floyd Landis – and has also spoken about the impact of childhood sexual abuse on him.

Greg's three injury-interrupted Tour wins were a watershed between the first three great Tour champions – Jacques Anquetil, Eddy Merckx and Bernard Hinault – and two later ones – Miguel Indurain and Lance Armstrong. Because of injury and team tactics, all five overshadowed him in terms of Tour wins, but it was Greg's scientific and technical approach that showed how to triumph in a new era.

Suzanne Lenglen – 'La Divine'

Suzanne Rachel Flore Lenglen, tennis player, born Compiègne, France 24 May 1899, died 4 July 1938. Major championships: Olympics 1920, French Open 1914, 21, 22, 23, 25, 26, Wimbledon 1919, 20, 21, 22, 23, 25. International Tennis Hall of Fame 1978.

Suzanne Lenglen dominated tennis for seven dramatic years of scandal, illness, tears and brandy stiffeners. Through it all, she found winning a necessity and missing a shot, let alone a match, was intolerable to her. Her brilliance and charisma, displayed in a series of momentous matches, made her the first great female sports star and changed tennis for ever.

Perhaps the greatest of her matches began at 11.15 a.m. on 16 February 1926 as the attention of the world focused on the ramshackle Carlton Club in the south of France where Suzanne was to play twice-US Champion Helen Wills. The club was so badly sited that a morning start was necessary to keep the sun out of the players' eyes, the seating was still being constructed on the morning of the match and the changing room measured just 11 x 17 feet. The club was soon under siege as spectators fought to get in, climbed trees, perched on bus roofs and stripped the tiles off nearby houses to peer down from the roofs. Special broadcasts were set up and in Wills's home state of California people stayed up all night to catch the result.

Most money was on Wills, who was younger and bigger, while Suzanne had endured a sleepless night after rowing with her father and coach. Despite the noise and distraction, being close to collapse and having a shot called out after she thought she'd won, she triumphed 6–3, 8–6. It was a typical display of flamboyance, drama and triumph over adversity.

Having first played tennis as a means of overcoming her asthma, Suzanne reached the French Championship final aged just 14 and soon won the World Hard Court Championship, which as an open tournament was a better guide to form. War interrupted her progress, but in 1919 she first appeared at Wimbledon and created a sensation. Playing in a light calf-length dress with bare arms, no petticoats and plenty of stocking on show, her graceful leaps around the court were a revelation, as was her accuracy, said to have been built up by training exercises such as hitting a handkerchief laid in the opposite court. After reaching the final without dropping a set, she came up against seven-times champion Dorothea Lambert Chambers in her old-fashioned ground-skimming skirt. In front of the King and Queen and just one-tenth of all the people who had applied for tickets, Suzanne won 10–8, 4–6, 9–7. The following year, she would return with bobbed hair and a silk bandeau to beat Dorothea easily, and also claimed the Olympic title after dropping just four games.

With Suzanne and <u>Bill Tilden</u> claiming the headlines, the All England Club felt able to move to Church Road, more than doubling its capacity, before introducing seeding and finally doing away with the old challenge round in favour of a straight knockout. Official international rankings were introduced in 1925, with Suzanne at the top. In total, she would win 81 championships, 31 with Grand Slam status and seven without dropping a game, but none were in the US. In 1921, after a stormy crossing, she expected to play an exhibition charity match but found herself scheduled for a championship game against a fired-up Molla Mallory. Suffering from whooping cough, Suzanne broke down in front of the jeering crowd, defaulted and never returned – though she got her revenge by walloping Mallory 6–2, 6–0 at Wimbledon the next year and 6–0, 6–0 at a tournament in Nice.

More drama occurred in 1924 when she missed a season due to jaundice, and in 1926 she inadvertently left Queen Mary waiting for her – after hearing of which Suzanne fainted. The All England Club wanted to default her, but the other players rallied to her cause. After being booed on court she withdrew, never to return, and became the first great tennis star to turn professional. As promoter Charles C. Pyle arranged a series of exhibition matches against US champion Mary Browne, Wimbledon stripped her of her honorary membership. In her defence, Suzanne pointed out that she had made millions for them, but was herself threatened with poverty. 'Under these absurd and anti-quated amateur rulings, only a wealthy person can compete,' she wrote. 'The fact of the matter is that only wealthy people do compete. Is that fair? Does it advance the sport? Does it make tennis more popular, or does it tend to suppress and hinder an enormous amount of tennis talent lying dormant in the bodies of young men and women whose names are not in the social register?'

Suzanne earned about $100,000 on her tour and it would have been far more had she not beaten Browne every time in what *New York Times* writer Allison Danzig termed 'a masterly exhibition of court generalship'. After this she published books and ran a tennis school that gained national status, but in 1938 was diagnosed with leukaemia and died soon afterwards. Today there is a Suzanne Lenglen Cup on the women's seniors' tour and a Court Suzanne Lenglen at Roland Garros.

Walter Lindrum – 'The Bradman of Billiards'

Walter Lindrum OBE, billiards player, born Kalgoorlie, Australia 29 August 1898, died 30 July 1960. World billiards champion 1933, 1934–50.

Many great players have dominated their sports, but perhaps only Walter Lindrum killed his off through sheer brilliance.

In 1907 Tom Reece of Oldham had proved that a billiards master could ruin the game by scoring 499,135 points with endless anchor cannons, which eventually had to be banned. The next player to take the game to its limits was Walter Lindrum, a third-generation champion who by the age of five had already survived a tree crashing into his bedroom and being swept away by a flood. After losing a fingertip in a mangle as an infant, he played left-handed and was regularly made to practise for seven to eight hours a day, spending six months hitting a single ball. This left him with phenomenal concentration and amazing ease and speed around the table – but perhaps unsurprisingly, the first non-English world champion was something of an odd fish. 'His mind was so full of billiards there was no room for anything else,' said one contemporary.

With his miraculous eyesight, mastery of the all-round game and a great close cannon, Walter was recording four-figure scores by 17 and in 1929 played what he regarded as his best game against British champion Willie Smith. Despite playing with his spare cue while his girlfriend Rosie Coates was lying mortally ill nearby, Walter still made the first 2,000-plus break.

After Rosie's death, Walter toured Britain twice, clocking up a 3,262 break despite a new rule limiting the number of cannons. As the 'Bradman of billiards', his mastery won the admiration of the Don as well as the King, who presented him with a pair of cufflinks he always wore afterwards. The tap tap tap of his play allowed him to amass scores faster than ever before and he set an unofficial record of 100 points in 27 seconds. In 1932, he recorded a 4,137 break with 1,900 consecutive scores over 2 hours and 50 minutes, and a new baulk line rule had to be invented to disrupt him. Though he got round that restriction, his 4,137 figure remains the world record, never seriously challenged since. As he composed massive heartbreaking scores and repeatedly beat Willie Smith and <u>Joe Davis</u>, even a 7,000-point start wasn't enough to beat him and he made one four-figure break while the tip was hanging off his cue. He once even played a game on grass, just to prove that he could. The lack of any really effective competition left the way open for snooker, a game with real duelling qualities whose possibilities were soon being explored.

In 1933, Lindrum returned to Australia as world champion and demanded that any challenger come to him, though when Joe Davis did, he discovered that the wayward Lindrum had organised nothing and was left stranded for six months before he could raise his fare home. Walter would retain his title unopposed for 16 years until 1950 and retired with a total of 771 1,000-plus breaks. Later on in life he refused to teach and getting him to shave or agree appearance deals became increasingly difficult. Close friends attested to a likeable side, but he left debts unpaid, would endorse anything and displayed zero loyalty to many who tried to befriend him. Despite depression and lethargy, his play remained fluent and to help keep track of his breaks, scores began to be announced while in progress, rather than at the end of them.

Lindrum died suddenly in 1960, having collected an OBE for his wartime charity work. By now billiards was in severe decline, with dwindling attendances and internecine strife, and in 1968 the Billiards Association actually melted down their trophy to pay the bills. In Melbourne he is commemorated by the Hotel Lindrum, while his grave in the city's General Cemetery is well worth a look – it is shaped like a billiard table.

'Atomic' Ray Lindwall

Raymond Russell Lindwall MBE, cricketer, born Mascot, New South Wales 3 October 1921, died 23 June 1996. First-class career: New South Wales 1941–54, Queensland 1954–60; 228 matches, 5,042 runs (21.82), 794 wickets (21.35); 61 Tests 1946–60, 1,502 runs (21.15), 228 wickets (23.03). Wisden Cricketer of the Year 1949. Australian Cricket Hall of Fame 1996.

When Harold Larwood appeared at Sydney for the first 'bodyline' Test in 1932 and took ten wickets, fast bowling briefly dominated over batting. Watching from the stands was an 11-year-old boy who not only resembled Larwood, with his short height and good looks, but whose fast bowling – rated the best ever by Richie Benaud – would also change the game.

Ray Lindwall lost his mother at the age of seven and lived in relative poverty, but was a natural athlete. Able to run 100 yards in 10.6 seconds, he also played as a full back and kicker in rugby league, reaching two grand finals. He dated his hatred of batsmen to 1938 when as a young bowler he beat Test opener Jack Fingleton four times – only for Fingleton to claim he was simply jaded from travel. After volunteering to fight in World War II, Ray was lucky not to be killed in action in New Guinea, but was unlucky enough to contract malaria, dengue fever and hepatitis. After this, he gradually built up his bowling speed and strength, working on a low skidding delivery and a combination of outswingers, yorkers and bouncers. He was probably the first to use photography to perfect an action so smooth that when he saw himself he was astonished at how relaxed he looked. His accuracy was comparable to a medium-pacer and his late outswinger was devastating with a new ball on any pitch. From 1948, the rules gave him a shiny new ball every 55 overs and 20 per cent of the wickets he took were clean-bowled.

Lindwall's home Test debut was in the 1946/7 Ashes series, during which he took three wickets in four balls, knocked Denis Compton's bat from his hands and scored Australia's second fastest 100. With Don Bradman's 1948 Invincibles, he helped win four Tests despite injury and his 6 for 20 in the first innings at the Oval had England all out for 52 – their lowest score of the century. Forty-three of his deliveries completely beat the batsman and the devastation he caused encouraged the MCC to switch the captaincy from the amateur Norman Yardley to the steelier <u>Len Hutton</u>, who rated Lindwall highly.

Despite Australia's mid-1950s decline, Lindwall remained a Test fixture, adding more control and swing to his deliveries and once captaining an illness-ravaged side in India. He was so accurate that six immaculate, unplayable deliveries persuaded the ICC to permanently abandon an experiment with a smaller ball. Another feature of Lindwall's play was a throat-height bouncer, which he 'normalised', once delivering 25 out of 40 balls with no complaint from the umpires. Though he didn't use it against tail-enders, he knocked out both Frank Tyson and Denis Compton and also used it against the West Indies' injured Everton Weekes. Another problem for cricket was that the sheer pace of his deliveries could carry him undetected past the crease, cutting the batsman's reaction time, until the Australian Board of Control cracked down on 'dragging' in 1958.

Dropped for the 1957/8 series against South Africa while just short of <u>Clarrie Grimmett</u>'s Test wicket record, Lindwall rejected a lucrative offer to switch to journalism and played his way back into Test contention, compensating for a slight loss of speed with greater variety. He claimed the record and was still bowling in Tests aged 38.

Later a selector, MCC member and Australia's most celebrated florist, Ray Lindwall brought on the country's third great fast bowling generation by mentoring future record holder Dennis Lillee. Not only had Ray established fast bowling as the main form of attack for years to come, he also left his mark on cricket in a more literal sense: while the Australian Board laundered the trousers, the players had to get their own shirts washed, and Ray, at his wife's insistence, became the first cricketer to routinely shine the ball on his flannels.

Per Henrik Ling

Per Henrik Ling, fencer and writer, born Ljunga, Sweden 15 November 1776, died 3 May 1839.

Physical education in schools, netball and sports centres can all trace their ultimate origins back to Per Henrik Ling, a minister's son, fencing master and university professor who became fascinated by Chinese martial arts and the idea of combining exercise and health. After building up his own body through exercise, Ling studied as a doctor and developed a holistic approach to health, establishing a Royal Gymnastic Central Institute in 1813. Despite opposition from doctors, he gradually gained credit for his ideas, and after his death 'medical gymnastics' began to be taught in Swedish schools, as well as the first exercises for women – sometimes intriguingly referred to as 'gynaecological gymnastics'. Ling's exercises were less stressful, perilous and expensive to stage than those of the German Ludwig Jahn and were widely incorporated into cost-conscious British schools in the 1900s, when the first concerted efforts were made to improve children's health. From 1899 the first physical education college for women – Madame Osterberg's College of Physical Training – was set up in Dartford, from where it pushed the Ling agenda and trained the first female PE teachers.

Unlike Jahn's followers, Ling's were not opposed to games in principle and from 1901 the Ling Association published the first netball rules, remaining in charge of the sport until 1946. Another lasting influence was the association's 1930s press officer Phyllis Colson who, while walking in Upper Woburn Place, had a vision of a national umbrella organisation promoting sport for all young people. At the time 90 per cent of 14- to 16-year-olds left school to work in jobs with no paid holidays, no limits on hours or pay and no health insurance or dole. Working from a dingy office in Doughty Street with practically no money, Colson helped forge the Central Council of Physical Recreation, which later set up sports centres such as Bisham Abbey, Lilleshall and Crystal Palace and through the 1960 Wolfenden Report influenced the government to set up the first sports centres.

Clive Lloyd – 'Supercat'

Clive Hubert Lloyd CBE, cricketer, born Queenstown, Guyana 31 August 1944. First-class career 1966–86: Lancashire 1968–86 (Gillette Cup 1970, 71, 72, 75), 490 matches, 31,232 runs (49.26), 114 wickets (36.00); 110 Tests 1966–85 (captain 1974–85), 7,515 runs (46.67); 87 ODIs, 1,977 runs (39.53) (World Cup 1975). Wisden Cricketer of the Year 1971. Administrative career: ICC match referee 2001–6, ICC Cricket Committee chairman 2008–.

It was during the drought summer of 1976 that cricket tactics in Britain changed for good – or, as some might argue, bad. The man responsible for the new, potentially lethal, 'anything goes' style was West Indies captain Clive Lloyd.

Clive Lloyd didn't look much like a cricketer. He seemed too big, stooped and slow-moving and wore thick glasses – the result of a child-hood injury while breaking up a fight. In practice, he was a natural athlete who combined vast reach with murderous power, his signature stroke a ferocious drive with a heavy bat. Batting right-handed, bowling left and catching with either hand, he gained his nickname for his agility and cool. Though not at first a very consistent scorer, he always had the knack of playing great innings at crucial moments.

After starting his Test career in 1966 with knocks of 82 and 78, he was recruited to Lancashire, where he raised his family. A young team was built around him, and though they never won the County Championship, victory in the 1972 Gillette Cup final cemented the popularity of the one-day game, as Lloyd drove Bob Willis et al for a dazzling 126. Three years later, as captain of the West Indies, he would do much the same at the first World Cup final. From 50–3 down, Lloyd rescued his team with a fantastically powerful 102 from just 82 balls. As a Test captain he would make his big impact the following year.

The West Indies side was perennially short of cash, and Lloyd recalled having to beg for an extra man for a long tour. Their reputation was for 'Calypso Cricket', a tag Lloyd regarded as synonymous with reckless batting and sudden collapses. A fractious 1975/6 tour to Australia culminated in 5–1 defeat and seemed to confirm the reputation, but instead it became a turning point for cricket. Having been ground down by the

Aussie pacemen, Lloyd gave his three spinners a last chance at Port of Spain, setting them the task of surviving the day or bowling out India for 403 runs. After they took just two wickets, Lloyd reasoned that 'nice guys never rule the world' and set out to emulate the Aussies with such success that other nations copied him too. Even his cousin Lance Gibbs was jettisoned as he opted for a four-pronged bowling assault based on pure speed – what Bob Woolmer termed 'constant, unrelenting blitzkrieg'. This was not a completely new tactic in cricket, but what was different was the sheer pace and ferocity. In the 'war' that followed, the team bowled multiple bouncers at India's Sunil Gavaskar, who accused them of 'barbarism', and forced captain Bishan Bedi to declare simply to save his spinners from injury. After the tour many of the Indians went home in bandages. It was the start of two decades of West Indian cricketing dominance, during which Lloyd would lead his side to a record 27 Tests unbeaten and 14 out of 15 series wins.

The next to reap the whirlwind were the English, whose captain Tony Greig had suggested they would make the West Indians 'grovel'. From the first match the fired-up Windies were knocking caps from heads and bats from hands, leaving Dennis Amiss, who had averaged 82 in the previous drawn series, spattered with his own blood. Choosing any four from Wayne Daniels, Bernard Julien, Andy Roberts, Vanburn Holder and Michael 'Whispering Death' Holding, Lloyd's men won the 1976 series 3–0. Victory was not just about pride. The 1975 World Cup had paid only £350, and the fee for an entire winter's tour was just £500. Lloyd, who had been supporting his family since he was 16, made a record £950,000 from the big crowds, insisted on hard cash for publicity appearances and argued for the introduction of central contracts. When Kerry Packer's World Series Cricket emerged, he and most of his team signed up and in 1978 he briefly resigned the captaincy when WSC players were excluded from the official side.

Lloyd's successful weathering of the WSC storm was typical of his astute handling of tricky situations. Unlike previous captain Gary Sobers, who briefly visited and played in Rhodesia, Lloyd spoke out against apartheid and even addressed the UN. In Britain, he attacked Enoch Powell in measured terms and offered to serve on a race relations board if requested. He held together a multinational side, which for West Indian immigrants to Britain was a source of pride at a time when most sports were unwelcoming and TV shows such as *Love Thy Neighbour* normalised racism. During the tours of 1984 and 1985/6, morning-to-evening shouts and tin-can rhythms would unsettle English batsmen already having to deal with non-stop 90 mph deliveries, and two years later the England team would get through four skippers in one series.

As for Lloyd's impact on cricket, opinion was, to put it mildly, varied. 'Boring' was a frequent comment about the non-stop attack that killed off spinning, while run-ups launched from the sightscreen lowered the over rates. Far more serious was the sheer danger. The most notorious example occurred at Old Trafford during the 1976 tour when openers Brian Close and John Edrich (combined age 84) were sent out at twilight to defend a cracked wicket on which judging a bouncer was impossible. Journalist Frank Keating termed it 'sadistically terrifying', and after this heroic stand neither Close nor Edrich played Test cricket again. Lloyd excused the barrage, arguing that it was within the rules, that conditions were the same for both teams and that England had selected their openers. The closest to an apology was an admission that the 'boys got carried away'.

Leading by example and inspiration, Lloyd scored 12 of his 19 Test centuries as captain and, despite knee injuries that confined his fielding to the slips, his batting grew more consistent, peaking in the early 1980s before he signed off in 1984 with the 5–0 'blackwash' of England and a 3–1 series win over Australia. The team reigned supreme until 1994 when the Australians regained their dominance. As a team manager Lloyd had the difficult task of managing a new generation of stars who were also holding out for more cash, plus a relative decline in West Indies cricket as more young athletes turned to sports such as basketball, and he resigned in 1999. Now a match referee, Clive Lloyd can truly be said to have defined an era – albeit at times a pretty brutal one.

Greg 'God' Louganis

Gregory Efthimio Louganis, diver, born El Cajon, California 29 January 1960. Victories include: Olympics 3 m springboard (1984, 88), 10 m platform (1984, 88), world champion springboard (1982, 86), platform (1978, 82, 86), Pan-American champion springboard (1979, 83, 87), platform (1979, 83, 87). ABC Athlete of the Year 1988.

On the 10-metre diving board at the 1988 Seoul Olympics, Greg Louganis performed the most difficult and dangerous dive in the book to claim victory by just 1.14 points from China's Xiong Ni and add a fourth gold to his collection. His victory was even more impressive if you knew the full background – which only a handful of people did. Louganis was HIV positive and taking life-saving medicines every four hours at a time when it was far from certain that the games would continue to admit HIV+ athletes.

Louganis's dive – the last of his competitive career – was the reverse 3½ somersault 'death dive', which he had seen kill Sergei Shalibashvili at the 1983 World University Games and which had nearly claimed his own life four years earlier. Greg had already gashed his head after hitting the springboard in the 3-metre competition when completing a reverse 2½ pike – normally one of his best dives – but still went on to win gold with his last two dives. Despite his injured head, he added the ten-metre title by sacrificing a safer outward jump for a higher one, closer to the board.

With his strength, grace and control, Louganis had dominated diving for over ten years, completing perhaps 180,000 30 mph dives, despite an impressive collection of personal disadvantages. Adopted by a heavy-drinking and unsympathetic father, Greg stuck at his sport despite suicide attempts, drug abuse, detention in Junior Hall, depression, frequent injury and an abusive relationship with his manager, to record 29 national titles, complete the first perfect dive in 12 years and earn the soubriquet 'God' from the rest of the team.

Though it was generally recognised that Greg Louganis was gay, this was a period in which there was a tremendous fear of Aids, and it was only after playing a gay character in a Broadway play that Greg finally came out at the first Gay Games, which attracted more contestants than Seoul itself. He also campaigned against staging any 1996 Olympic events in Cobb County, Georgia, the one place in America that had passed a law attempting to forbid homosexuality.

After Louganis came out, there was no great rush of athletes to follow his example and it was 2007 before the first major-league sportsman – basketballer John Amaechi – did so. However, Louganis's record and his recovery from the springboard accident proved to the world that gay athletes were as tough, determined and focused as straight ones.

Joe Louis – 'The Brown Bomber'

Joe Louis Barrow, heavyweight boxer, born Lafayette, Alabama 13 May 1914, died 12 April 1981. World heavyweight champion 1937–49. Overall record: 72 fights, 69 wins, 55 KOs, 3 losses.

Still rated the best puncher in heavyweight boxing history by *The Ring*, Joe Louis was the longest holder of the title, with the greatest frequency and number of defences, 23 out of 27 of them being KOs. Only Tommy Farr, Joe Walcott and Arturo Godoy went the distance with him, and the last two were knocked out in later bouts. (Farr later claimed that he only had to read Louis's name and his nose started bleeding.)

After the two-fisted Joe had been hooked by the lure of the gym while on the way to violin lessons, his razor-scarred trainer John 'Chappie' Blackburn taught him to use an energy-saving shuffle, softening his opponent up before releasing deadly jabs and crosses 'like light bulbs going off in your face', to quote ex-champion James Braddock. Aware that refs would favour a white fighter in any points decision, Joe's manager John Roxborough told him to end fights early and let 'his right hand be the referee'. He helped get Joe into contention for a title fight by schooling him to 'live and fight clean', which at the time meant showing no triumph in victory, avoiding nightclubs and not being seen with white women, although he did have affairs, including one with 'Queen of the Ice' Sonja Henie. All of this was intended to prevent him evoking memories of the first black champion, Jack Johnson – or, as Blackburn termed him, 'that fool nigger'. Louis's poker face intimidated most opponents, and crowds danced in the streets in his hometown Detroit after he beat former champions Primo Carnera and the seemingly impregnable Max Baer.

In the end, it was promoter Mike Jacobs, a protégé of Tex Rickard, who persuaded champion James Braddock to fight Louis by offering him $300,000 and a cut of Louis's future earnings. After Joe had knocked Braddock out in round eight, Jacobs used Joe's popularity to sidestep the power of Madison Square Garden and establish his 20th Century Sporting Club as the power in boxing promotion. Among Joe's most famous quotes during his 11 years as champion were 'He can run, but he can't hide' (of Billy Conn, who took him closest to defeat), and 'Everyone has a plan until they've been hit.'

Louis's greatest triumph was one of his easier fights, against Max Schmeling, the only fighter to have beaten him on his rise to the top. Before this fight, Joe was seen as the champion of black Americans, competing in a sport that had usually denied them a shot at the big titles, but by fighting Hitler's 'future world champion' he united white America behind a black sporting champion for the first time. The fight was soon over, as Schmeling succumbed to what he claimed was an illegal kidney punch, throwing just two shots before spending a long spell in hospital. Joe's popularity increased further in wartime when he was recruited into a still-segregated army, but he refused to spar in front of segregated audiences. His popularity as a champion helped lead other American sports to drop their colour bars, as Woody Strode and Ken Washington appeared in pro football in 1946, Jackie Robinson broke into major league baseball a year later and Charles Cooper played basketball for the Boston Celtics from 1950.

After Jacobs fell ill, James Norris's International Boxing Club managed Joe's post-war return. Joe retired in 1949 – officially undefeated, but lucky to get a points decision over Jersey Joe Walcott in the US's first major televised fight. Though his powers were waning, financial pressures forced Joe back into the ring, as the IRS went after him for unpaid taxes – even on money that he had donated to the war effort. Heavy involvement from organised crime meant that he received only $71,000 for his return fight, and after losing to Ezzard Charles he was pounded through the ropes by Rocky Marciano. Forced to turn to TV appearances and wrestling, Joe was in the ring as late as 1972, while addiction and mental illness led to him smearing windows with Vaseline and blocking vents with paper in the belief that the IRS were trying to kill him. Max Schmeling proved to be a better friend than Uncle Sam, and helped him out in hard times.

Eventually, Joe worked as a greeter in Las Vegas, often appearing ring-side, although after multiple strokes he was confined to a wheelchair. After his death, he was buried in Arlington Cemetery and awarded a posthumous Congressional Medal. Today a Detroit stadium, an American Legion post and a New York street all bear his name.

Oddly enough, Joe was also on the books of Liverpool FC – he signed as a publicity stunt in 1944.

Spiridon Louis

Spiridon 'Spiro' Louis, runner, born Marousi, Greece 12 January 1873, died 26 March 1940. Winner 1896 Olympic marathon.

In 1896 <u>Pierre de Coubertin</u> staged the latest in a series of attempts to revive the Olympic Games. Previous 'Olympic' contests had been held in Much Wenlock in Shropshire, Canada, Sweden, Poland and three times in Greece itself, but it was these Athens games that would end in triumph, laying the foundation for the world's greatest sporting festival. However, it might all have been very different had local hero Spiridon Louis not won the marathon.

Louis, a water carrier from Marousi, near Athens, had passed on the chance of an education in order to help out his impoverished family, but distinguished himself during military service by running 20 kilometres in under two hours to retrieve a sword he had forgotten. He qualified as one of the 13 Greek contestants in the marathon – the idea of IOC member <u>Michel Bréal</u>, who wanted to recreate the ancient athlete Pheidippides' run from the battlefield at Marathon to Athens.

After a five-hour journey by cart to get to the start of the race, Louis began race day with wine, milk and eggs and a warm-up trot around the village square in the new 25-drachma shoes donated by his home village. He and the 16 other contestants set off along the dusty road, pausing only for more wine at Pikermi. The accompanying mounted police officer fired shots into the air as Spiridon outstripped the field, including the 800 metres and 1,500 metres winner Edwin Flack of Australia, who was accompanied by the British embassy butler riding a bike and wearing a bowler hat, and Albin Lermusiaux of France, who had set too fast a pace. When he entered the Panathenaic Stadium, Louis created the most extraordinary scene de Coubertin ever witnessed. Having been disappointed at not gaining a single track or field title, the packed crowd leapt to its feet crying 'Hellas! Hellas!' The military band played, women threw jewellery at Louis's feet and the two crown princes, George and Constantine, jogged with him to the finish. The goodwill generated would be enough to sustain the

Olympics through two shambolic episodes at Paris in 1900 and St Louis in 1904.

For Louis the result was fame and donations of a new horse and water cart from the royal family, plus the offer of his daughter's hand in marriage by organiser and sponsor George Averoff – although Louis was already betrothed to a local girl named Heleni.

Louis's triumph also anticipated some of the problems the Olympics were to encounter later. For a start, the games were supposed to be about international brotherhood, but it was beating the foreigners that whipped up the crowd and continues to do so today. Then there was the problem of who was allowed to compete. Carlo Airoldi, who would probably have beaten Louis, had walked 700 miles from Italy to enter, only to be disqualified as a professional – despite the fact that the amateur Louis was allowed to keep presents of jewellery and a small-holding, plus meals and clothes. Another issue that was ignored was the basic sexism of the games, after local girl Stamata Revithi completed the same distance as Louis, but was kept out of the stadium. Nor was there any clarity as to who was to set the rules for events. It was 1924 before the Olympic marathon distance was standardised, and it was near being dropped in 1921 in favour of mountaineering. Yet another theme to reoccur in Olympic history was the suspicion of trickery in poorly supervised events. Third-place man Spiridon Belokas had his singlet ripped off him when it was suggested that he had hitched a lift en route, and in 1964, long after Louis's death, a witness reportedly confessed to Olympic historian Harold Abrahams that Louis had also hitched a lift on a cart.

Having set the Olympics on its muddled but triumphant way, Louis lived quietly as a farmer and policeman until 1926, when he was held in jail over charges of falsifying documents. Released after a public outcry, he remained a hero, attending the 1936 Olympics as a guest of honour. After his death, many Greek sports clubs were named after him, as was the 2004 Olympic stadium and the road outside it. He lives on in the Greek language too – to 'become Louis' means to make yourself scarce.

Hank Luisetti

Angelo 'Hank' Luisetti, basketballer, born San Francisco 16 June 1916, died 17 December 2002. Playing record: Stanford University (1936–8) 1,596 points. Helms College Player of the Year 1937, 38. All-American selection 1936–8. Basketball Hall of Fame 1959.

The single-handed shot, dribbling behind your body, jumping for a rebound and the high-speed counter-attacking 'full court press' all seem like natural basketball moves today, yet all were invented by one man – Hank Luisetti.

Unable to outscore taller opponents, Hank, a restaurateur's son from San Francisco's Telegraph Hill district, developed his single-handed style and used it to win the city's high school championships before moving to Stanford, where he turned round a losing college team. On 30 December 1936 he brought Madison Square Garden to its feet after Stanford beat the previously all-conquering Long Island University 45–31, and on 1 January 1938 against Duquesne he became the first player to score 50 points in a game – more than whole teams scored in the days before three-pointers (1979 in the NBA) and shot clocks to speed up the action. Hank's college record still stands today.

Luisetti lost his amateur status for a year after appearing opposite Betty Grable in *Campus Confessions*, a movie and an experience he hated, and suffered a knee injury before spinal meningitis threatened his career. After serving in the navy, he preferred the travel business to the newly formed NBA, but in 1951 coached the Stewart Chevrolet club to the AAU title. By this time, even the most reluctant coaches had been forced to accept the Luisetti style. Today there is a bronze statue of him in Maples Pavilion, home of the Stanford University team.

Sir Arnold Lunn

Arnold Henry Moore Lunn, skier, sports administrator and author, born Madras, India 18 April 1888, died 2 June 1974.

Arnold Lunn, the skier who created the first modern slalom and downhill events, had the best possible introduction to the sport. His father, Methodist minister Henry Lunn, had organised a conference on Christian unity at Grindelwald in Switzerland and discovered an aptitude as a travel agent, setting up the Public School Alpine Sports Club and opening new English-only resorts at Klosters and Mürren.

When Lunn junior began skiing, the sport, like the British skiers themselves, was still finding its feet. The Brits had at first come to Switzerland for summer mountaineering and initially skiing was seen simply as a fast and enjoyable means of descent. It was 1902 before downhill races were first staged in Davos, and the following year a Ski Club of Great Britain was formed. Their first cup competition combined skating and tobogganing with skiing round a flat field, which was all the visiting Brits were thought to be good for, but by the following year Lunn had become the first champion in a genuine downhill contest, writing that it was 'the nearest approach to flying'. This set the Alpine skiers against the Nordic cross-country tradition, which regarded downhill runs mainly as a chance to catch one's breath.

Lunn set up an Alpine Ski Club in 1908 as a more open and progressive body and soon began organising downhill races, despite a mountaineering accident in 1909 that shortened one leg by two inches and left him in continual pain. The highlight of the club's year was the Roberts of Kandahar race, which consisted of a three-mile traverse of the Plaine Morte glacier, followed by a 4,000-feet descent on wind-blown crust and a final zigzag race through the tree line.

Lunn, as editor of the *British Ski Yearbook*, praised downhill as 'the finest and most conclusive test of skiing'. In 1922 he named the run through the trees a 'slalom' (from the Nordic *slalåm*) and set up a light-hearted race against the clock through artificial stick gates in the grounds of Mürren's Palace Hotel. This 'pure slalom' proved so popular that by winter 1924 he was publishing rules for the new Kandahar Ski Club while also making the first ski descent of the Eiger. (The first Ladies Ski Club was also set up that winter.)

The Scandinavians, who dominated the newly formed International Ski Federation and later the Olympics, regarded spectacular Alpine plunges as 'not skiing' or too dangerous, but Lunn was more outgoing than most Brits and from 1924 was staging open contests with Walter Amstutz's Swiss University Ski Club. Four years later, the Kandahar Club staged an open event with the Austrian maestro Hannes Schneider's Arlberg Club. This forced the international ski federation to accept Lunn's rules as a basis for competition, but their reluctance to fully embrace alpine events led him to stage a first alpine world championships in 1931. Though alpine skiing was introduced at the 1936 'Nazi' Olympics at Garmisch – which Lunn opposed – it would be 1948 before they finally had equal status with Nordic cross-country.

A famous controversialist and a prolific/repetitive writer, Lunn converted to Catholicism and cheerfully disputed the idea that truth was preferable to falsehood and much else besides. After all his battles with the FIS and IOC, he was knighted in 1953 for services to Anglo-Swiss relations and is commemorated with a monument at Mürren. His family name also lives on in the Lunn Poly travel agency.

Mark McCormack

Mark Hume McCormack, businessman and author, born 6 November 1930, died 16 May 2003. Founder, chairman, president and CEO of International Management Group (IMG). Golf Hall of Fame 2006, Tennis Hall of Fame 2008.

Seen either as a visionary or a corrupter of sport, Mark McCormack built the world's most successful sports management and marketing company, turning sportsmen and women first into brands and then into multimillionaires. Identified as the 'most powerful man in sports' by *Sports Illustrated* in 1990, he also originated the world ranking system in golf. Based on money won, this existed from 1967 but was officially adopted in 1986.

It was in 1960 that McCormack, a Cleveland-based lawyer and golf nut, offered to manage the affairs of a college golf opponent named Arnold Palmer. Palmer, who had won one major in 1958 but had a disappointing following season, 'wasn't interested in taxes, in opening his mail or filling out forms or contracts'. As for McCormack, the results of a childhood car accident had diverted him from football to golf. Good enough to play in the US and UK amateur championships, he became a lawyer and decided to try to combine his business and sporting interests. After an initial deal with Wilson Sporting Goods worth $5,000, Palmer's income soon grew to $300,000 p.a. and he was followed into the IMG stable by Jack Nicklaus and South African 'man in black' Gary Player. McCormack's choice of golfers was as good as his timing. His 'big three' won every Masters from 1960 to 1966 and by the end of the decade they had collected 20 majors. In the booming TV market of the time, more and more companies were willing to pay for the instant status and recognition created by a famous endorser – whether they sold golf products or not. IMG became the first company to vertically integrate sports marketing, promoting first its athletes, then the events at which they appeared, then all kinds of sporting events, and eventually music and cultural events too. From 1968, just as worldwide colour satellite broadcasting was becoming a reality, IMG could begin to guarantee coverage through Trans World International, the tautologically named broadcaster that became the biggest independent maker and distributor of sports programming.

As tennis opened up to professionalism that year, McCormack moved into another sport with identifiable heroes and heroines such as Rod Laver and Margaret Court. After getting a contract to produce a film for Wimbledon, IMG took over the commercial side of the operation. Prizes and profits ballooned as it invented a new logo and IMG managed the sponsorship, hospitality and broadcasting rights. Later the Royal and Ancient would do a similar deal. IMG also worked for major corporations, devising sporting events and competitions that would suit their needs.

As managers – rather than mere 'agents' – IMG not only looked after their stars' needs and whims, but created brand images for them that could be aligned to corporate marketing strategies. IMG also maintain their fame through seniors or 'legends' events, and clients such as Jackie Stewart came to transcend their sport. Some, like Palmer, were still top-ten earners in their dotage and many stars who left IMG later returned – including Nicklaus, Ray Floyd and Nick Faldo. In golf, IMG had a lock on major events such as the World Match Play Championships, which it started in 1964, deciding who was and wasn't to be invited, and although players might leave IMG control, they were usually careful not to badmouth it. However, in other sports IMG were outflanked by Patrick Nally and Horst Dassler's ISL, which during the 1970s actually went into international sports federations and repackaged them from the inside, eventually capturing the Olympics and World Cup.

IMG was clearly the right idea at the right time and grew to a turnover of $900 million p.a. Now representing sports broadcasters and models as well as sportspeople, it also made successful moves into financial planning (i.e. investment and tax avoidance). TV sales for sporting events and the staging of performing arts and public ceremonies were another growth area. Perhaps their most spectacular sporting star was Tiger Woods, talent-spotted at 12, after which IMG got round the amateur regulations by paying his father. Tiger had $60 million in sponsorship behind him before he even began his professional career. However, in team games, where the stars were less identifiable and the leagues and competitions better established, IMG never had quite the impact it did in more malleable and individualistic sports such as tennis and golf.

Like his biggest stars, McCormack's personal success was based on hard work, long hours and ruthless timetabling as he scribbled 'to do' lists on his ever-present yellow A4 pads. His 'judicious application of common sense' translated into the huge-selling book *What They Don't Teach You At Harvard Business School*. Although creative in dreaming up positionings for his stars and new events for them to compete in, he was narrow-minded in what could be sold and his judgement that <u>Muhammad Ali</u> had 'spoilt his value' is questionable, given that Ali later sold his image rights for $50 million.

Nicknamed 'Mark the Shark' by his detractors, McCormack once asked, 'Have I ever done anything bad for golf or sport?' For some, the answer was 'yes', and his sporting legacy was an endless treadmill of grandly named 'silly season' events plus 'classics' such as the US Open tennis that were structured entirely around TV viewers rather than athletes and spectators. On the other hand, IMG helped keep great events alive in the new big-money era – and it certainly kept athletes out of the poorhouse. In 2003, McCormack left a $750 million fortune and an award in his name is now presented to the number one world-ranked golfer.

Bill McCracken – 'The Offside King'

William McCracken, defender, born Belfast 29 January 1883, died 20 January 1979. Newcastle United 1904–24 (FA Cup 1910, league champions 1905, 07, 09); Ireland 1902–23, 15 caps. Manager Hull City 1923–31, Millwall 1933–6, Aldershot 1937–50.

It was Bill McCracken, Newcastle United's dark-haired Northern Irish defender, who perfected the offside trap, bringing about the single most important change to football's laws.

Strange as it may sound, Newcastle's 0–0 draw against Bury in February 1925 was to be one of the most significant games of the century. It was United's sixth goalless draw of the season, and the game was once again compressed into a narrow central strip in a contest dominated by endless free kicks for offside. With the crowds declining, the FA acted with uncharacteristic boldness by changing the three-man offside rule.

Offside itself dates from Eton's 'no-sneaking' rule, and was adapted by the FA in 1866 to require three players – usually a goalkeeper and two defenders – to be between the attacker and the goal when he received a pass. As early as 1910, the little and large combo of Herbert Morley and Jim Montgomery of Notts County (aka 'Weary Willie and Tired Tim') had had the idea of a move up the field to catch an opponent offside, while still retaining cover behind. However, it was McCracken and his partner, England international Frank 'Old Surefoot' Hudspeth, who perfected the staggered sweep. Against Everton, United sprang the trap 43 times in a single match. The old joke among teams pulling into Newcastle station and hearing the guard's whistle was 'Are we offside already?'

To stop these constant interruptions to play, the FA tried an experimental 40-yard limit on offside, but rejected it in favour of the present two-man offside rule, which was also adopted by the Scots and the International Board in time for the 1925/6 season. The FA's intention was to smooth the passage of play, but the surprise result was that full backs, deprived of their risk-free offside trap, became susceptible to fast-breaking forwards. In the first day of play under the new rule, both

Sheffield United and Manchester City scored 11 goals. By the end of the season things had settled down, but it still produced an extra goal a game (from 2.54 on average in 1924/5 to 3.44 in 1925/6) and was judged a great success. In the longer term, football moved from 'frills to thrills' as the old style of long passes and mazy individual runs was replaced by teamwork and speed.

The first forward to really profit from the new rules was Boro's George Camsell, who scored 59 goals in 1926/7, but the following season he was pipped by Everton's superstar Bill ('Dixie') Dean. The 5 foot 10 inch Dean could do a standing jump onto a billiard table and, although he had silver plates in his head after fracturing his skull, remained a fearless powerhouse header. His 60 goals in 39 appearances still stands as a league record today – part of a total 82 in all competitions that season. In 1937, he overhauled Steve Bloomer's overall league tally.

After Arsenal suffered a 7–0 mauling at Newcastle, McCracken's new offside rule inspired Charles Buchan and Herbert Chapman to create their own 'three-back' defence which proved hugely successful, although many blamed it for a culture of caution and negativity in the British game. As for McCracken himself, he reached the FA Cup semi-finals as manager of Hull – thanks partly to a new offside trap in which the back line stepped up as one. This was to become a standard tactic until the end of the century, with Wimbledon using it 22 times in one 1986 match. As an Arsenal trademark, it also inspired the dance routine in the film *The Full Monty*.

After leaving Hull, Bill McCracken managed both Millwall and Aldershot before becoming Newcastle's chief scout. He is credited with being the first to spot the talent of fellow countryman Pat Jennings.

William McCrum

William McCrum, footballer, rugby player and administrator, born Milford, Armagh 1870, died 13 December 1932. Playing career: Milford Everton.

No single footballer has had a greater impact on the rules of the game or the pitch itself than Irish goalie William McCrum, inventor of the penalty.

The son of a linen millionaire, McCrum was instrumental in setting up the first Irish soccer league, and played in goal for Milford Everton, a team that represented the model village his father and grandfather had founded. 'Master Willie' probably wasn't selected purely on ability, since during the team's 1890/1 debut season in the Irish League they lost every match and he shipped 62 goals. On the other hand, he got to observe plenty of foul and rough play. Until 1890 the only sanction available to the referee had been an indirect free kick, but McCrum persuaded the Irish FA to adopt a penalty kick, which punished any fouls within 12 yards of the goal with a free kick from anywhere along that line. (This was the first direct free kick in the game.) It is tempting to believe that McCrum's love of chess and theatrics may have contributed to the idea of a man-against-man showdown.

When put to the FA that same year, the 'Irishman's motion' or 'death penalty' was rejected by players and administrators such as <u>C.B. Fry</u>, who objected to the very suggestion of ungentlemanly play as 'a standing insult'. However, attitudes changed after another season of mayhem, especially after the 1891 FA Cup quarter-final between Notts County and Stoke, in which County's Hendry deliberately handled on the line to deny a goal and the resulting indirect free kick was scrambled away.

Though a few diehards refused to contest them, penalty kicks were generally adopted that year. It was agreed that the other players should be kept back the usual six yards and Renton's Alex McColl scored the first. The following year it was further agreed that the penalty-taker couldn't dribble in towards goal and from 1902 there was an 18-yard box around the penalty spot, which FIFA, never content to leave well alone, now calls a 'penalty mark'. Disputes over goalkeepers such as

William Foulke charging out of goal were settled in 1912 when they had to remain on the line, although players like Billy Meredith had learnt to chip over the heads of onrushing keepers.

The inspiration for Law 14, the penalty spot and the box, William McCrum lived high on the hog until 1932, but saw his fortune wiped out by gambling debts and the Wall Street crash, losing his mansions in London and Armagh and the model village, complete with its pitches and clubrooms. There are plans to commemorate him with a specially commissioned bust and memorial park.

William McGregor – 'The Father of the Football League'

William McGregor, team owner and sports administrator, born Braco, Perthshire 13 April 1846, died 20 December 1911. Director Aston Villa 1886–95. Chairman League Management Committee 1888–92. FA president 1892–5, life member 1895–1911.

In the late winter of 1888, William McGregor, a director of Aston Villa Football Club, had a serious problem. Even Villa, the FA Cup holders, were struggling to bring in the crowds. They had been paying out regular wages since 1885, when McGregor had publicly backed <u>William Sudell</u>'s campaign for open professionalism, and McGregor, a draper by trade, was not a rich man. The problem was the fixture list – or rather the lack of one. Villa had had to scratch five matches in a row and were now edging close to bankruptcy. Team after team either failed to turn up or sent weak sides that produced mismatches no one enjoyed. Between national, local and city cup competitions, friendlies, tournaments and exhibitions, the season was a mess and no one knew what was happening. McGregor reasoned that what was needed was 'fixity of fixtures', a regular competition like the cricket County Championship, but one that would increase the gate money and use promotion and relegation to ensure fewer mismatches. Working from the available gaps in the season, he reckoned that 10 to 12 teams, all playing home and away, could form an 'Association Football Union'. In fact, it was to become the Football League.

Though a keen street footballer as a boy, William McGregor was never more than a reserve keeper at Aston Villa, the club he joined after moving to Birmingham to set up his shop in the tough neighbourhood of Summer Lane. The handsomely bearded 'Genial Mac' was a popular man and a natural leader, a Methodist and Liberal who would hold every office at Villa and once even traced and reclaimed a piano that had been stolen from the club.

With a classic Lancashire v Midlands FA Cup final in the offing, McGregor wrote to the finalists Preston and West Brom, plus Blackburn and Bolton, suggesting a 'friendly conference' on 23 March, the night before the final. When the teams met in Anderton's Hotel in Fleet Street, it soon became clear that southern clubs weren't interested and that Sudell's Preston were playing hard to get, but on 17 April the northerners met again at the Royal Hotel in Manchester to hammer out a plan. A balance of leading Lancashire and Midlands sides would produce plenty of crowd-pulling derbies and make travel easier, though there were a few odd choices, such as preferring Everton FC to the far larger Bootle. It was further agreed that gates would be split – although this didn't last and was soon replaced with a £15 minimum guarantee for the visitors. The only significant part of McGregor's plan to be rejected was the name 'Association Football Union', which it was feared might annoy the Rugby Football Union. Instead, they chose Sudell's suggestion – the Football League. McGregor disliked this, as it reminded him of the radical Irish Land League, and he kept the word 'English' off the title as he hoped to attract Scottish clubs at a later date.

The first League season began on 8 September 1888, with the first fixtures chosen by ballot and the rest left to the clubs to sort out themselves. The first goal was scored by either Jack Gordon or Fred Dewhurst of Preston – opinions vary – and the League rapidly became a great success, largely because Sudell and McGregor insisted that clubs give priority to League fixtures. (Without this rule, the rival Football Combination soon failed.) To start with, only the fixtures were listed in the press, but soon there were match reports and by Christmas the crowds had reached 10,000.

At first, two points were awarded for a win, and after a few weeks, the League narrowly voted for J.J. Bentley's proposal that there be one point for a draw. The first season was dominated by William Sudell's Preston side, and a new elite was established. After this first season, only half a dozen non-League teams would ever again reach the FA Cup semi-finals, and by 1889/90 League clubs were getting exemptions from the early rounds. Preston also won the following season and suggested a cup for the winners, rather than the flag the League had been planning. They were pipped twice in the following two seasons as the contest became more equal and exciting.

Despite rowing clubs and a rather wayward secretary in Harry Lockett, by 1892 there was a second division in place and McGregor's league had spread to Cheshire, Yorkshire and the north-east. It would be another six years before automatic promotion and relegation were agreed.

Writer Charles Edwards noted that the League was already defining the sporting year in Lancashire and the Midlands, a 'passion rather than a recreation' that aroused more interest than politics and racing. The players were starting to become bigger celebrities than local MPs and were followed by big crowds in all weathers. Already the League's eight months a year didn't seem enough and McGregor got on the football bandwagon by endorsing footballs and boots laced to the toe, which he claimed contributed to greater safety in games.

Local clubs that couldn't get into the League formed their own Alliance and Conference, which joined the expanded Football League in 1898, and the Scots formed their own league in 1893. However, it was another two years before the League had a London outpost in Woolwich Arsenal, and 1920 before it became truly national by taking over the entire Southern League.

By cultivating friendly relations with the FA, joining its committee and not threatening its authority, McGregor sorted out a power-sharing deal between the London-based rulers of the game and the independent Lancashire-based League. As FA chairman Charles Clegg neatly put it, the FA represented the public schools and the League the public houses. McGregor's unofficial deal would last over a century, until 1992, when the FA skimmed off the top teams and cut free from the League as the Premiership. McGregor himself quit the League management committee in 1893 and left the Villa board the year afterwards, but remained League president and a life member, as well as a staunch defender of the League against its detractors.

As the League boomed, 'Genial Mac' became more famous through his writings. Very presciently, he spoke out against the ridiculously low £10 fee which football planned to pay to transferred players and which would lead to years of corruption and resentment. McGregor pointed out that Villa had already paid some players five times that amount.

As late as 1910, William McGregor was still being mooted as a future League chairman. When he died, he was buried without any great fanfare or epitaph in St Mary's, Handsworth. The *Birmingham Post* said, 'We do not believe he ever made an enemy. He certainly never lost a friend.' The Father of the League was commemorated with a fountain and portrait at Villa Park and a statue is now being planned.

Dr Alister MacKenzie – 'The Course Doctor'

Dr Alister MacKenzie, golf architect, born Wakefield, Yorkshire 30 August 1870, died 6 January 1934. Notable courses include: Alwoodley (1907), Ganton (1920), Royal Melbourne (1931), University of Michigan (1931), Cypress Point (1928), Pasatiempo (1929), Augusta (1932–4).

Though never a particularly good player, Alister MacKenzie is frequently rated the greatest golf architect in history, with ten of the top 100 courses. During his career he changed the whole idea of golf-course design, away from punishing those who deviated from a set line and towards a strategic approach, in which golfers of varying abilities could take different routes to the pin. This was most famously seen at Augusta, of which his partner <u>Bob Jones</u> commented that every hole could be birdied – or double bogeyed if you stopped thinking.

A Yorkshire-born doctor though he played up his Scottishness and was never an enthusiastic medic – MacKenzie became convinced of the value of golf as healthful exercise for his patients, and his stated desire as a course designer was to create 'the maximum enjoyment for the greatest number'. After serving in the Boer War as a surgeon with the Somerset Infantry, he gained an appreciation of the enemy's talent for concealment, which he would go on to use in both golf and in World War I, when he was employed by the Royal Engineers as a camouflage expert. He even risked a court martial by criticising them in print.

MacKenzie's first major course was Alwoodley in Leeds, where he at first collaborated with designer Henry Colt and then took over the project. In 1914 he won a high-profile competition judged by Charles Blair MacDonald, in which he worked five different approach routes into a single hole. After the war, the 'Doctor', as he liked to be called, published *Golf Architecture*, in which he spelt out his 13 general principles of course design. These included a short walk between the green and following tee; an emphasis upon natural beauty rather than artificial gimmicks; a course that was enjoyable for the weaker player and challenging for the stronger one; minimal searching for lost balls in heavy rough and the need to use every club in the bag. He added optimistically that golf could help 'counteract discontent and Bolshevism'.

Working without heavy earth-moving equipment, MacKenzie wrung the maximum variety out of the landscape, using tiered greens to increase the challenge of shorter holes, and he claimed to be disappointed when his layouts created admiration rather than controversy.

From 1926, MacKenzie toured the world, building and designing courses such as California's Cypress Point, whose 16th hole is often rated the most photogenic in the world. After playing it, Bob Jones invited him to build his masterpiece on the site of the Fruitlands Nursery near Augusta. MacKenzie never lived to see its completion, but it remained almost unaltered until <u>Tiger Woods</u>'s 12-stroke victory in 1997 forced some remodelling. This would have pleased the Doctor, who believed frequent alterations were a sign of 'faulty design'. Though nearly broke when he died, MacKenzie is still revered for his ability to create characterful courses that stretch golfers to their limits, and he still has his own appreciation society.

James 'Jem' Mackie

James Mackie MP, rugby player and politician, born Kirkcudbright, Scotland 1821, died 28 December 1867.

To judge from first-hand reports, it appears that it was Rugby School's Jem Mackie who 'invented' the game of rugby, by first picking up the ball and running with it. Before this time a player catching the ball was allowed to retreat and take a kick at goal, but actually running at the line was regarded as a suicidal tactic, until the big Scottish lad made a success of it in the 1838/9 season. By Mackie's time Rugby School's football was already famous enough to have attracted the attention of Queen Adelaide and was also being practised at Cambridge University. His 'running-in' tactic was formally agreed at the school three years later, the main restriction – other than the hideously convoluted offside laws – being that the ball had to be caught in the air rather than picked up off the ground. This 'picking-up' prohibition would linger on until 1958, when players were finally allowed to pick up the ball directly from a tackle, rather than first playing it with the foot. As for Mackie, after leaving school and university, he would become a rather inactive Liberal Member of Parliament for the Stewartry of Kirkcudbright, known for his friendly smile, athletic build and penchant for country sports.

Unfortunately for Jem, William Webb Ellis, a schoolboy at Rugby some years before him, overshadowed his sporting claim to fame. When in 1895 a committee of Old Rugbeians set out to prove that the code had originated at their school – which it certainly had – they chose the earliest possible date, based on the claims of a deceased anti-quarian named Matthew Holbeche Bloxham. Fifteen years earlier, Bloxham had recorded an incident dating back to 1823, in which Ellis was supposed to have picked up the ball and run. Bloxham himself had left the school before this date and his hearsay report appears to have originated from his brother. Rather suspiciously, no one else could recall this momentous event and Ellis, like Mackie, was long dead. Ellis's contemporary Thomas Harris had no recollection of the event and stated that no right-thinking player would have attempted 'running in' in his day. The committee's other major witness was Thomas Hughes, author of *Tom Brown's School Days*, who stated that the Ellis tradition was unknown in his day and credited Mackie, 'fleet of foot and brawny of shoulder', as the first to successfully run with the ball. Although other authors, including the RFU's own Frank Marshall, had made no mention of Ellis in their published works, the committee opted for the earlier date and it is Ellis's name that has been attached to the Rugby World Cup trophy. While hearsay evidence and wishful thinking made Webb Ellis world-famous, the truer inventor of rugby's essential feature died suddenly aged just 46, was buried at Minnigaff and generated no coverage beyond the *Kirkcudbright Advertiser and Galloway News*.

Graham McNamee – 'The Father of sports broadcasting'

Graham McNamee, broadcaster, born Washington DC 10 July 1888, died 9 May 1942. National Sports Broadcasting Hall of Fame 1984.

'Good evening, ladies and gentlemen of the radio audience. This is Graham McNamee speaking.'

Today it is almost impossible to imagine a world without broadcasting. Or to think of great sporting moments without the commentator's voice to bring them alive. Or to imagine the impact of live sports coming into quiet and lonely homes for the first time. The man who acheived all this was Graham McNamee.

McNamee was not actually the first sports broadcaster. Those honours go to Harold Arlin of KDKA in Pittsburgh and Tommy Cowan of WJZ Newark, while Hal Totten in Chicago was the first ball-by-ball announcer in an era in which stations wandered off their frequency and microphones had to be tapped to shake up the powdered carbon inside. However, it was McNamee who first brought radio sports to life by conveying sights and sounds, excitement and 'colour', rather than just scores and stilted reports. A slim-faced man with a rich baritone voice, McNamee started off as a singer until he wandered into WEAF New York on a whim and was hired on the spot. In 1923, his World Series coverage, direct from the New York Polo Grounds, drew 1,700 fan letters from a station with only a 100-mile reach. By 1925, he was receiving 50,000 letters a year and an envelope with only his name on it could reach him from anywhere in the US. Two years later, when he broadcast the Gene Tunney–Jack Dempsey fight, 50 million Americans listened in coast-to-coast and at least five of them died of excitement.

For 19 years, the fledgling NBC worked Graham McNamee into the ground, covering at least ten different sports as well as political conventions, news events and pretty much everything else. Sitting in an ordinary box seat, he covered every World Series until 1934, but ended his career as an advertising voice-over artist and straight man to Ed Wynn on *The Texaco Hour*. He is still remembered by a very few for his sign-off: 'This is Graham McNamee speaking. Goodnight all.'

Ray 'Boom Boom' Mancini

Raymond Michael Mancini, lightweight boxer, born Youngstown, Ohio 4 March 1961. WBA light-weight champion (1982–4). Overall record: 34 fights, 29 wins, 23 KOs.

In an unguarded moment, world middleweight champion Alan Minter once commented that there had been deaths in boxing – 'but none of them serious'. That was before 13 November 1982, when Ray Mancini made his second WBA title defence outside Caesar's Palace. Known for his spectacular whirlwind style, Mancini was, to quote promoter Bob Arum, 'never the same again' after this bout. And neither was his sport.

Ray's opponent that day was Orient and Pacific champion Duk-Koo Kim, a southpaw who had won 17 of his 20 fights – eight by KOs. However, Kim had never been out of Korea and his record flattered him, as many of his opponents had never fought a left-hander before. Certainly Kim had never met a fighter like Mancini and had only twice before fought the full 15 rounds. In the match itself, the already dehydrated Kim gave a good account of himself early on, but by round 13 Mancini was in control, striking Kim 39 times in a row. Only a couple of weak punches from Kim discouraged referee Richard Green from ending the contest. After the fight was stopped in the following round, Kim collapsed and died five days later – followed by the suicide of his mother and referee Green himself. With CBS's live coverage of the fight and a *Sports Illustrated* cover, this was one boxing death that couldn't be ignored.

The WBC immediately cut contests to 12 rounds, eliminating the final three where weary competitors were less able to defend themselves. The WBA and WBO followed suit in 1988 and the IBF in 1989. More ropes around rings and better pre-fight health checks were introduced and a mandatory eight count was later brought in to give fighters a chance to recover from a knock-down – plus a standing eight count for a fighter in trouble on the ropes.

Mancini defended his title for two years and then made two spirited attempts to regain it. Having taken good financial advice, he profited from his time in boxing and went into movie production and fight analysis.

'Oubass' Markötter

August Friedrich Markötter, rugby halfback, coach and selector, born Haarlem, Eastern Cape 10 June 1878, died 1957.

Oubass Markötter loved the game whose tactics he would revolutionise. When first asked to play for his university side, Stellenbosch, he didn't even have to change – he had been wearing his kit under his ordinary clothes in the hope that he might be picked. By 1903, he had led the first provincial team to beat a touring Test side and was captaining Stellenbosch – often as a 'donkey' halfback, whose role was to grab the ball and hang on to it, whatever happened to him. It was claimed that opposing players broke their boots on his head.

Ironically, it was cricket that ended his playing career. Having been good enough to play against an MCC side, he wrenched his knee and had to turn to rugby coaching instead, running the team from his own home. Over the next half century, the 'Alpha and Omega of South African rugby' would make it the joint strongest rugby nation on earth.

As fearless a coach as he had been a player, Markötter was renowned for never giving praise, booting errant players up the backside and beating them with his stick or a branch ripped from a nearby bush. One was even given sixpence to buy rope to hang himself. Nor were referees safe as Markötter, sometimes the worse for drink, ventured onto the pitch to berate them too. When he was stopped without a ticket at one Test he declared 'Newlands belongs to me!' and stormed through the gate.

Irascible he may have been, but Markötter was no fool. Within three years his Stellenbosch University side contained 11 Springboks, and although he had an array of maxims and principles, he recognised genius when he saw it and the need to allow players to develop their own moves.

Markötter's big idea was the new 3-4-1 scrum formation developed by South African international Paddy Carolin. This supplied more power to the props and thus more ball, but Oubass went further by deliberately wheeling the scrum and using André McDonald as the first specialist number 8 to pick up and break, attacking the opposing backs. This put South Africa decades ahead of northern-hemisphere opponents and Oubass once simply telegraphed a touring team 'SKRUM SKRUM SKRUM'. Perhaps recalling the batterings of his own playing days, he encouraged his protégé Danie Craven to dive to get the ball away fast.

Off the pitch, Markötter had the intelligence to keep out of party politics and rose to be virtually the sole national selector. In 1938, the touring Lions, already 2–0 down, actually asked him to pick their team – and won the final Test 21–16. As a German sympathiser, Markötter fell out with the rugby authorities during the war over a plan to donate funds to POWs. He died in 1959 and is commemorated by the Markötter/Craven Rugby Museum at Stellenbosch University.

Leonard Maton

Leonard James Maton, rugby player and administrator, born Devizes 1845, died 15 April 1933. Clubs: Oxford University, Wimbledon Hornets. President Rugby Football Union 1875–6.

There is a certain inevitability to the fact that the man who wrote the first rugby rules did so while suffering from a bad playing injury.

Leonard Maton, the sturdy captain of Wimbledon Hornets, was one of three rugby-playing London lawyers who in 1871 were asked to put together the first set of laws by the newly formed RFU. Progress was slow until Maton broke his leg, and while laid up at his home, Elmshurst Lodge, he drafted the rules, having been promised limitless tobacco as a reward by the other two – Edward Holmes and Algernon Rutter. (For many years it was thought that RFU Presidents Edwin Ash and Arthur Guillemard had done the work, and it was only much later that the rules were revealed to be Maton's.)

As might be expected of an ex-Rugby School lawyer, Maton's rules stuck largely to those of his old haunt and were massively complex, comprising six definitions, a long introduction and 37 rules that were later converted into 59 'laws'. These were accepted by the RFU that year, ending some of the chaos that had marred the previous March's England v Scotland fixture.

Apart from reducing the complexity of scoring after a 'try at goal', Maton's major innovation was to get rid of hacking and tripping of the player with the ball – a crusade that the Blackheath and Richmond clubs had begun five years earlier. This made a profound change to the game, as banning hacking made it safer and allowed it to spread from testosterone-crazed public schoolboys to respectable men who couldn't afford to lose a limb on the field. However, without hacking to dig the ball out of the 40-man scrums, massively long forward battles became the norm and the game was grinding to a halt by 1875, when Maton became RFU president. In response, both the Scots and the universities pioneered 15 players per team rather than the traditional Rugby 'Bigside' 20 and, although it was 1892 before it was in the rules, 15 soon became the norm. With fewer forwards on each side, the game opened up, and allowing tries as a decider in drawn matches also encouraged more 'running in'. From 1878, the ball had to be put down after a tackle, rather than having a scrummage form around it, and this greatly speeded up the game. Within two years, heeling the ball from the scrum, inter-passing within the team and routinely passing the ball before being tackled were all regular tactics, and with a three-man three-quarter line in place, the game was becoming comparable to the modern one.

Despite all the extra tobacco, Maton outlived both Holmes and Rutter, though his part in history was only revealed in a letter to the *Morning Post* after his death.

Raymond Mays – 'Mr Motor Racing'

Raymond Mays CBE, motor racing driver and team owner, born Bourne, Lincolnshire 1 August 1899, died 6 January 1980. British hill climbing champion 1947, 48.

During the 1930s, 1940s and 1950s Britain's answer to Maranello was . . . Eastgate House, Bourne, Lincolnshire, the lifelong home of Raymond Mays, the man who inspired Formula One car design in the UK.

The son of a prosperous fellmonger (skinner) and wool dealer, Mays served in World War I and was given his first racing car, a Hillman, while at Cambridge University. His first race was also his first win, one of hundreds in a career that lasted until 1949. While driving Bugattis and Vauxhalls, he conceived of an English Racing Automobile – a purpose-built car to compete in the smaller 1.5-litre 'voiturette' class. From 1934 he charmed the equivalent of £6 million from backer Humphrey Cook and converted a series of single-seater Rileys that were fitted with superchargers designed by his Oundle schoolmate Amherst Villiers. After starting with a conventional works team, Mays had the idea of offering his ERAs for general sale to a series of British racers, including future star Dick Seaman. After a win at the Nürburgring in 1935, it was two years before the next, and even the famously charming Mays, a friend of film and stage stars, was unable to persuade Cook to pile in more cash. At the Crystal Palace track in 1939, Mays anticipated modern racing tyres by doubling up the back wheels on his ERA, but this was also the year that he and Cook finally fell out.

In 1949, Mays went a step further and created the British Motor Racing Research Trust, with a view to entering a British-made Grand Prix car. Inspired by his involvement, thousands of UK racing fans and hundreds of engineering companies contributed to a car designed by his partner Peter Berthon. An innovative design combined oil and air suspension, a Mercedes-style chassis, a diagonal drive shaft to keep the driver low, and a new 16-cylinder engine equipped with an experimental centrifugal supercharger. The whole thing was expected to deliver undreamt-of power from a tiny intricate engine turning at up to 12,000 rpm. In practice, the BRM was a nightmare of chaotic management and overambitious engineering. Stirling Moss, who drove an early BRM, considered the chassis and driver's set-up 'out of the ark'. The super-charger overstressed the minute engine parts and delivered vast power in a very narrow rev band, which made the car hard enough to drive in a straight line. On corners it was, to quote Moss again, 'simply dreadful'.

Though it put in an appearance at the 1950 British Grand Prix, the BRM's driveshaft broke on the grid at that year's International Trophy race, and fifth place in the following year's British Grand Prix was as good as it ever got. The following year, Mays preferred tinkering in Bourne to actually turning up for the Turin Grand Prix and the whole formula had to be suspended for two years, being dominated by <u>Enzo Ferrari</u>, who had ditched supercharging as too stressful for the engine and requiring too many fuel stops. BRM's backer Tony Vandervell lost patience and started his own team, at first racing bought-in Ferraris. Over the next ten years, BRM was nursed along by its new backer, Alfred Owen, who in 1962 finally threatened the team with closure unless they won at least two Grands Prix. Instead, Graham Hill drove the car to a world championship.

Having disappointed and embarrassed so many race fans, it was 1978 before all was forgiven, and 'Mr Motor Racing' got his CBE. Today Mays is commemorated with a room at the Bourne Heritage Centre.

Gus Mears's Scottish Terrier

Born 1900(?), died 1907(?).

We know only one thing about developer and sports fan Gus Mears's terrier, and that is that in autumn 1904 it bit London Athletic Club member Fred Parker and drew blood. However, this single vengeful act was to shape London football forever.

At the time of the fateful nip, Mears was meeting Parker to break the news that their plans for a grand football and athletics stadium at Stamford Bridge had fallen through. The idea had been to build an arena on the lines of Glasgow's Ibrox, Celtic Park or Hampden Park, and perhaps even capture the FA Cup final from the isolated and primitive Crystal Palace. Unfortunately, the intended guest club, Fulham FC, had pulled out of the deal after their shareholder Henry Norris rejected the attractive terms Mears had offered. Then, with the Bridge about to be turned into a coal yard, the Scottie suddenly intervened.

After the bite, the unapologetic Mears merely said, 'Typical Scotch terrier, always bites before he speaks,' while the remarkably forgiving Parker replied that Mears was the 'coolest fish he had ever met'. Parker's measured response encouraged Mears to think that this was a man he could do business with, and he decided to press on with their sporting plans anyway. Within days, Mears was in touch with Ibrox architect Archibald Leitch, who crammed a vast but basic stadium into a site close to Walham Green (later Fulham Broadway) tube station. After rejecting the names 'Stamford Bridge', 'Kensington' and 'London FC' for their planned team, they settled on 'Chelsea', justifying this by the nearby Chelsea and Fulham railway station – just as Spurs had named their ground after White Hart Lane station. As press commentators pointed out, the location really had as much to do with Timbuktu as it did with Chelsea.

By creating London's first grand athletics and football stadium, Mears and Parker influenced other clubs across the capital. Although Fulham also hired Leitch to rebuild Craven Cottage and compete with the Bridge, they never enjoyed the good tube access that Chelsea had or their ability to use a vast stadium to secure a prestigious Football League place from the start. In south London, Crystal Palace responded to the booming football market and the new competition by creating its own club side, which, like Chelsea, joined the League in 1905.

Eight years later, having fought a losing battle with Chelsea to attract the west London crowds, Fulham's Henry Norris was thwarted in his plan to gain Division One status for the team by merging them with his other side, Woolwich Arsenal. In response, Norris 'did a Mears', building a new stadium at Highbury, near what was then the far end of the Piccadilly line. This meant that Spurs, who had ruled the roost in north London, suddenly found themselves with a new Football League side just three miles from their front door, which soon led to a passionate, all-consuming rivalry. The Arsenal move meant that south-east London was now without a League side and in 1921 Charlton's Edwin Radford was able to persuade the League to let them in, on the basis that they, like Chelsea, also had a vast new stadium to fill. Just two years previously, Charlton had been a local league side going round with a collecting tin, and after having borrowed massively to pay for The Valley, they would remain cash-strapped for decades to come.

By the time of Charlton's elevation to the League, Chelsea had finally secured the prized FA Cup final, but Gus Mears had died in 1912 and his brother Joe regarded both Chelsea FC and Stamford Bridge as 'cash cows'. The Bridge's high ticket prices, lack of seats and uncovered terraces meant that it would soon lose out to the planned new stadium at Wembley. For another sixty years, the Mears family would retain an interest in the Bridge and Chelsea would be cursed with endless disputes because they didn't own their ground. And all because of one Scots terrier.

Ian Meckiff – 'The Count'

Ian Meckiff, cricketer and Australian rules footballer, born Mentone, Victoria 6 January 1935. First-class career: Victoria 1956–63; 778 runs (11.27), 269 wickets (23.35). Test career 1957–63: 18 matches, 154 runs (11.84), 45 wickets (31.62).

'It was as if an atomic bomb had hit the place,' said one witness. The place in question was the suddenly silent Gabba ground in Brisbane, where Australia's favourite bowler Ian Meckiff had just been 'called' for throwing against the South Africans. Not only was this the first time in 70 years that such a thing had happened in Australian Test cricket, it also marked the end of a period that might have changed the game forever.

The main issue at stake was throwing. For reasons lost in time, cricket had decided that a bowler should release the ball with a straight arm, but in practice the arm nearly always straightens during the delivery – hence over a hundred years of controversy. However, by the late 1950s it seemed that cricket was on the cusp of a new 'baseball bowling' style. Umpires had been turning a blind eye since Trent Bridge in 1951 when the MCC's Pelham Warner informed Frank Chester, who wanted to no-ball South African Cuan McCarthy, that he wouldn't be 'supported' by the lawmakers. In consequence, the use of a bent arm grew, though England's Tony Lock, who had practised his style in a room with a low ceiling, was no-balled against the West Indies. A related issue was 'dragging', as the sheer speed of bowlers like Ray Lindwall and Frank Tyson carried them well past the crease. In the 1958/9 Ashes series, the 6 feet 5 inch Gordon Rorke's delivery took him almost to the batsman's feet as he claimed eight wickets in two Tests. In the case of the handsome Meckiff – known as 'The Count' or 'The Lord Mayor' to the crowds – a permanently bent arm, whippy wrists and a degree of double-jointedness helped him make the ball swerve and jag. During the 1958/9 Ashes whitewash, his unusual front-on delivery claimed the wickets of Peter May, Colin Cowdrey and Tom Graveney plus three others for just 38 runs, with 9 for 107 in one match. Two years later, he would be run out by the

West Indians to produce a tied Test, a result that created a huge new burst of enthusiasm for the game.

In 1960, the ICC had met and passed a characteristically hard-to-define law that banned 'straightening at the instant of delivery', plus a new 'front-foot rule' which declared that the bowler's foot, whether grounded or not, had to be behind the popping crease when the ball was released. A secret hit list was issued to umpires and 16 bowlers were called over the next four years – five of them Australians. Cricket being cricket, there were inconsistencies. The West Indian Roy Gilchrist was sent home from India for dangerous bowling, but Charlie Griffith, whose javelin action nearly claimed the life of India's captain Nari Contractor, was never called. One umpire who refrained from blowing the whistle on Griffith and endangering a highly profitable Test series was praised for his 'discretion'. In Australia, <u>Sir Don Bradman</u>, who ruled the game, was inclined to discount British press criticism of his bowlers until high-speed photography revealed that the 'chuckers and draggers' did indeed contravene Law 24 and that their deliveries were too difficult and dangerous for batsmen to pick up.

The main sacrificial victim was Geoff Griffin of South Africa, whose arm had been permanently bent by an injury. Having been called at three county matches but also taken an historic hat-trick at the second Test at Lord's, Griffin was no-balled 11 times by umpire Lee and four times by Syd Buller during an exhibition match. When he switched to underarm bowling, he was penalised yet again for changing his action unannounced. Griffin didn't want to go to court and was later officially cleared, but his Test career was over. At least one umpire had sleepless nights over what he had done.

In 1963, with Rorke injured and suffering from hepatitis, the big question was what would happen to the recalled Ian Meckiff, who had missed the 1961 series due to a torn ligament. Once four of his deliveries had been no-balled by umpire Colin Egar, captain Richie Benaud took him off. After this humiliation, outraged fans booed Egar and Benaud and chaired Meckiff off the pitch. Both they and the press suspected that he had been deliberately set up – especially because the team had selected a spare fast bowler. Meckiff himself blamed his thin wrists and a change of action when tired. Though he later sued Benaud's successor Bob Simpson for libel and got an out-of-court settlement and apology, Meckiff refused to be embittered by the event – as he showed

20 years later at a charity match, when Colin Egar no-balled him again for old times' sake.

In theory, cricket had saved its soul, but in practice dangerous bowling continued, arms still straightened during deliveries and many just felt that the latest rule changes had brought more artificiality to the game.

Eddy Merckx – 'The Cannibal'

Edouard Louis Joseph, Baron Merckx, road and track cyclist, commentator and administrator, born Meensel-Kiezegem, Belgium 17 June 1945. Professional record (1966–77): 525 wins including: Tour de France 1969, 70, 71, 72, 74, Giro d'Italia 1968, 70, 72, 73, 74, Vuelta a España 1973, world championship 1967, 71, 74, Liège–Bastogne–Liège 1969, 71, 72, 73, 75, Milan–San Remo 1966, 67, 69, 71, 72, 75, 76, Paris–Roubaix 1968, 70, 73.

Until Eddy Merckx came to fame, it was believed that road racing was a balance of individual and group effort in which no man, however strong, could expect to win everything. However, Eddy did not recognise this. While other champions would take part in a breakaway but gracefully concede the stage win for the sake of overall victory, Eddy would go for the line and the sprinter's points too. He showed that you really could have it all. It was this insatiable desire to win and unwillingness to let anything get in his way that earned him his 'Cannibal' nickname.

He made a sensational start in the big races, winning his second Giro aged just 23, and was leading the 1969 race before he received a 28-day suspension for a doping offence he still vehemently denies. Recognising that they had a phenomenon on their hands, the Tour authorities let him ride anyway and Eddy won all three jerseys – overall champion, King of the Mountains and points (sprints) winner. If there had been a young rider's white jersey he would have won that too. This sensational performance has never been repeated, although Eddy came close to it the following year, coming second in the points competition and winning the others. His 1972 hour record would stand for 12 years and was only bettered by Francesco Moser on a high-tech superbike. He retired with record wins both for a single season and overall.

Merckx's record is all the more amazing for the pain and adversity he had to overcome. Always troubled by his stomach, he also had bad pelvic and back injuries after a 1969 crash which killed his pacer Fernand Wambst. Merckx claimed he was never as good after this, and was frequently seen adjusting his saddle – even on 70 kph descents. In 1970, he needed oxygen to revive him on Mont Ventoux, but still became a hate figure in France where they resented his success, being stoned and spat at the following year. In 1974, he rode away from the peloton despite shorts soaked with blood from an injured perineum, and in 1975, after aiming for a historic sixth Tour victory, finished in triple second place after fracturing his jaw and getting a punch in the kidneys from a French spectator.

Awarded the Légion d'honneur by France and made a baron in his own country, Eddy's popularity transcended even Belgium's notorious linguistic divide, with both the Flemish and Walloons voting him to high places in a 'Greatest Belgians' poll. Today his bike is on display at the metro station named after him. He now owns a bike factory and works as a commentator and race adviser.

'Dally' Messenger

Herbert Henry Messenger, rugby union and league player, cricketer, canoeist and sailor, born Balmain, New South Wales 12 April 1883, died 24 November 1959. Playing career: Warrigals 1900–5, Easts 1905–7, Eastern Suburbs 1908–13; New Zealand 1908, Australia 1908–10.

Of the three southern-hemisphere rugby giants, only Australia is deeply divided between league and union. The reason for this can be traced back to one man – the free-scoring centre Dally Messenger, Australian rugby league's first and greatest hero.

On 16 August 1907, Australian rugby and cricket star Victor Trumper and his backer James Giltinan persuaded the elusive Messenger to abandon the union code, under which he had played against the All Blacks, and accept £180 to play rugby league against their touring 'All Golds'. A crowd of 20,000 formed for the first league Test on Australian soil, and another two matches were hurriedly scheduled. Messenger's earlier successes as a union player were wiped from the record book by the authorities and he joined Trumper's team on a league tour of England, in which he scored 100 more points than any other player and was even offered £1,500 to play soccer for Spurs.

When Dally (so named because of his childhood resemblance to state premier W.B. Dalley) returned to New South Wales, a rugby league premiership was soon established. The union authorities' refusal to insure their players against injury encouraged many to switch to the league code, but Messenger was the big attraction, able to demand £150 per match in Tests against New Zealand. Like W.G. Grace in cricket, his presence in the team was advertised outside the grounds before matches. The laws even had to be changed to cope with his tricks, such as punching the ball into the air to catch and score, and a dummy kick at goal that turned into a chip, catch and try. In one interstate game, he was actually restricted to his own half to even up the contest.

Messenger also captained the national side – known as the 'Kangaroos' or 'Pioneers' – in two Tests against Great Britain, drawing the first, kicking all the points in the second but missing the third through injury. He ended this tour nearly 100 points ahead of his nearest team-mate, having kicked one goal from his own 25-yard line – a record for many years to come. The banning of union players who competed in Kangaroos v Wallabies charity matches caused more to switch to league, which became established as the New South Wales game, with union restricted to a small middle-class following.

After having his best-ever season in 1911, Dally retired in 1913, running hotels and later a plantation without great success. Though his home life was not happy, he remained hugely popular within the sport and his portrait, hanging in the NSW Rugby League HQ, is simply captioned 'The Master'. The best league player of the year now receives the Dally M Medal and there is a life-size statue of him outside the Sydney Football Stadium.

Rinus Michels – 'The General'

Marinus Jacobus Hendricus Michels, striker and coach, born Amsterdam 9 February 1928, died 3 March 2005. Playing career: Ajax 1946–58 (league champions 1947, 57); Holland, 5 caps. Management career: JOS 1960–4, AFC 1964–5, Ajax 1965–71 (league champions 1966, 67, 68, 70, cup winners 1967, 70, 71, European Cup 1971), Barcelona 1971–5 (league champions 1974), Ajax 1975–6, Barcelona 1976–8 (cup winners 1978), LA Aztecs 1978–80, FC Koln 1980–4 (cup winners 1983), Bayer Leverkusen 1988–9; Holland 1974, 84–6; as technical director 1986–8, 90–2 (European champions 1988). Dutch Manager of the Century 1999.

Declared 'Coach of the Century' by FIFA in 1999, Rinus Michels ended the 1960s era of negative football, outwitted blanket defences with massed attacks and created the greatest tactical flexibility ever seen. While other coaches had blended attack, midfield and defence and even let players switch from left to right, Michels's *Totaalvoetbal* was the first system in which players changed their roles depending on the position they found themselves in on the pitch – so that attackers might play as defenders and vice versa.

An easy-going man away from football but a disciplinarian at work, the lantern-jawed Michels believed in technique, openness and honesty in team discussions. At Ajax he took over from Vic Buckingham at a time when the team lacked even a massage table, and were threatened with relegation. The employment of the gritty Velibor Vasovic in defence helped stop the rot and Michels sought new talent, including stadium cleaner's son Johan Cruyff. Four training sessions a day built up extraordinary fitness and understanding within the team, which combined remorseless attack and hounding defence of the player in possession. By having his team-mates fill in for him, a player didn't have to track back vast distances – although amphetamines, painkillers and relaxants were also handed out to the players to keep them going.

In attack, Ajax aimed to expand the playing space with wingers and attacking full backs, but to reduce it in defence, with a high defensive line and close-packed ranks to limit the other side's room for manoeuvre. From 1970, they shifted from a traditional 4-2-4 to a 4-3-3 in which a defender could move up to boost the midfield. This made it easier to regain possession than with four forwards, and the pattern is still common in Dutch football today. Ajax unpicked the meanest defences, won the first of three successive European Cups, and vanquished Inter, the masters of defensive play.

After Michels left for Barcelona, the players briefly thrived under the more relaxed regime of Stefan Kovacs, but in 1974 the team fell apart, though many of them reunited under Michels to reach the World Cup final. During a virtuoso display, they – to quote Johnny Rep – 'forgot to score the second goal' and lost 2–1 to West Germany. Revenge came 14 years later, with Germany defeated on the way to a European Championship title.

For many, Michels personified the Dutch character – thrifty, clever, hardworking and with a taste for practical jokes and unconventional tactics. 'Professional football,' he declared, 'is something like war. Whoever behaves too properly is lost.' After his death in 2005, the Ajax board declined to rename their new home, the Amsterdam Arena, after him, so the fans created a large home-made banner reading 'Rinus Michels Stadion', which they hung out for every home game. There is also a Rinus Michels Award for the best Dutch manager of the season.

Mick the Miller – 'The Wonder Dog'

Mick the Miller, greyhound, born Killeigh, Offaly 24 June 1926, died 5 May 1939. 51 wins including: Greyhound Derby 1929, 30, 31 (first running), Cesarewitch 1930, St Leger 1931.

Mick the Miller may not have been the fastest dog in history, but he was the smartest and most famous, and he cemented the popularity of his sport in Britain.

Mick's owner, Irish priest Martin Brophy, named him after his house Millbrook and trainer Michael Greene. He was one of the weaker dogs of his litter and was brindled, which in the bad old days had been regarded as sufficient reason to have a dog put down. Long in the back, Mick was not particularly big or well proportioned, but he had good shoulders and haunches. As a youngster, he survived an attack of distemper and later acquired a scar through a fight.

Mick graduated from hare coursing to the new sport of greyhound racing, shortly after the first track was built in Ireland. He clocked 36 mph and could run 12 times his own body length in a second, but what impressed most was his judgement, using his tail as a rudder to gain position round the curves. Though scientists claim that dogs are merely instinctive reactors, those who saw Mick race believed him to be twice as clever as any other dog, able to win from any position and virtually unbeatable if drawn on the rails.

Brophy, who rated Mick's brother Macona more highly, was continually on the lookout to sell him, and would have packed him off to the US had the prospective owner's kennels not been blown away by a tornado – which the man took as a message from the Almighty to stay off the tracks. Brophy finally unloaded Mick in 1929, after he had won his first Derby. Mick went on to set nine track records and six world records from 500 to 700 yards and was the first to break 30 seconds for the Derby distance of 525 yards. During his series of 19 wins in a row, Mick drew crowds of 70,000 and the press revealed titbits such as his dislike of thunder and of dog-coats. Meanwhile, the numbers attending tracks leapt from 400,000 in 1926 to 17 million in the early 1930s.

After back-to-back Derby victories, Mick won a third, only for it to be declared invalid simply because there had been a bad bump. Owner 'Phiddy' Kempton allowed herself to be pressurised by Alfred Critchley and his Greyhound Racing Association into re-entering Mick, but this fourth Derby proved too much, and after his results tailed off, smart punters turned their back on him. However, in a final tilt at the St Leger over the unfamiliar distance of 700 yards, Mick ran a masterpiece of tactics and bravery to snatch a final victory.

Retired to stud and publicity duties, he opened stores, met royalty and appeared in the comedy *Wild Boy*. Though he was only on-screen for a third of the film, Mick was much the best thing in it. He easily out-acted co-star Sonnie Hale, yawning on cue, looking both ways when crossing the road and even racing through traffic in one action sequence.

After his death, Mick was stuffed and mounted in the central hall of the Natural History Museum, alongside Eclipse, St Simon and Brown Jack, but has since been relegated to the Walter Rothschild Museum in Tring. Although this museum has a unique charm, Mick is now treated like any other animal exhibit, rather than a sporting hero. However, when a virtual dog track was created for computerised betting in 2003, the name chosen was Millersfield.

Alice Milliat

Alice Milliat, rower and sports administrator, born Nantes, France 1884, died 1957. Treasurer Fédération Française Sportive Féminine 1917. Secretary Fédération Sportive Féminine Internationale (FSFI) 1921–36.

'I declare open the first women's Olympic Games of the world!'

These words, spoken by Alice Milliat in 1922, were just part of her 16-year campaign to gain women the right to compete in track and field – the heart of the Olympic Games. Though often left out of Olympic histories, Alice is the main reason why women gained that right, as she and her colleagues fought a war with the never welcoming and often duplicitous International Olympic Committee – a war that a less determined woman would never have won.

Though Olympic founder <u>Pierre de Coubertin</u> was a supporter of women's education and was impressed by stars like <u>Suzanne Lenglen</u>, he was opposed to women's involvement in the Olympics, claiming – quite incorrectly – that the 'only role of women at the Olympics was to hand out the garlands, as they had in Ancient Greece'. (In fact, Ancient Greek women would have been pitched off a mountaintop if they had so much as shown their faces at Olympia.) It was only after de Coubertin quit the organising committee for the 1900 Paris games that the first 12 female competitors took part. Women competed in swimming from 1912, but remained banned from track and field and restricted to 'aesthetic' sports such as archery or ice skating – although the inclusion of physically exhausting swimming made nonsense of the 'no exertion' rule.

Ironically, it was in de Coubertin's home nation that the first women's sports clubs were set up, and Alice Milliat came to prominence as a rower and administrator. After being rebuffed in her attempts to get women's track and field included in the 1920 Antwerp games, she organised an all-female international track and field meeting at Monte Carlo, which she provocatively announced as 'Les Premières Olympiades', and used her skills as a translator to form an international federation in October 1921. When both the IOC and International Amateur Athletic

Federation refused to allow women's track or field at the 1924 Paris games, Alice set up a rival single-day Women's Olympics in Paris. This was attended by athletes from five nations, who broke eight world records in 11 events in front of 20,000 spectators.

While the IOC complained of Milliat's 'abuse and excess' and the IAAF claimed authority over women's sports without allowing them to participate, Alice planned a far bigger 1926 Women's Olympics. Finally, both organisations agreed to allow ten women's track and field events at the 1928 Amsterdam games – provided that Milliat drop the name 'Olympic' in favour of the 'World Women's Games'. Alice kept her side of the bargain, but the IOC ratted on theirs, holding only five athletic events at Amsterdam, compared with 13 at the FSFI's games, which were held in front of royalty in Gothenburg, Sweden. Although some female athletes preferred competing in female-only meetings, the British Women's Athletic Association were so outraged by the IOC decision that they carried out the only feminist sporting boycott in history, with founder Lady Mary Heath publicly rebuking de Coubertin's successor Baillet-Latour.

To make matters worse, after Jeannie Thomson of Canada fell at the finish of the 800 metres, the press reported that all the 'sobbing girls' had collapsed. The *Daily Mail* even used pictures from the 100 metres to illustrate this fiction. Claiming that athletics caused 'irreversible premature ageing' of women, Baillet-Latour got women's athletics voted out of the Olympics the following year – only for the 1932 LA games organisers to threaten to cancel the whole games unless women were admitted. Even after Mildred 'Babe' Zaharias showed what female athletes could do, future IOC president Avery Brundage still continued to dismiss them as 'ineffective and unpleasing'. Yet another vote to remove women from the 1936 Olympics was only narrowly defeated, and there was only one extra women's event at Berlin.

By this time, the FSFI's 1930 Prague games had attracted 15,000 fans to watch 200 athletes from 17 nations, and in 1935 the FSFI demanded that the IOC and IAAF finally make up their minds – either admit women or let the FSFI take over. Instead, the IOC decided that it could give the IAAF the formal right to rule women's athletics, and the FSFI's 1934 London games were its last. The FSFI never met again, although Alice was formally thanked by the IOC and the records set at her meetings were ratified.

IOC President Avery Brundage, who later recalled Milliat as having 'made quite a nuisance of herself', was still attempting to ban women athletes as late as 1952, and the IOC kept restricting the number of events women could enter. There was no 800 metres until 1960, no 1,500 metres until 1972, and it was another nine years before the first female IOC member was finally admitted. It wasn't until the 2002 Salt Lake City winter games that women could compete in as many events as men.

It has been said of Alice Milliat that if she had been more diplomatic in her dealings with the IOC, then women athletes might have progressed further and faster. The alternative view is that if she had been more diplomatic, women might have had to wait even longer to get onto the track.

François Mingaud

Captain François Mingaud, billiards player and inventor, born Le Cailar, Nîmes 1780(?), died Rotterdam 1847.

Few have made such a small yet significant contribution to sport as François Mingaud, inventor of the rounded cue tip.

In Mingaud's day, billiards – a French word which may derive from *bille*, meaning a stick, and/or *pila*, the Latin for a ball – had evolved from a medieval game played on grass to a tabletop game played on a grass-like green cloth with a shovel-headed mace, shaped like a mini-golf club. In 1469, when the French King Louis XI played it, the object was to get your ball through various targets, such as a miniature arch and a port, while avoiding a queen and a kingpin. The cushions were simply slats to keep the ball on the table and the pockets were hazards to knock your opponent's ball into. From the late 16th century, ivory balls replaced wood and players began using the 'queue' or tail of the mace. By Mingaud's time, French players were using the tail alone to play various games, with or without pockets and with up to 15 balls. (As late as 1900 the ball could still be played with the butt end of the cue.)

By the early 18th century, flax and cotton-stuffed cushions had replaced wooden boards and allowed rebound shots, while the pockets had become targets. To get better control, players roughened their cue tips against walls and ceilings and even added leather tips to them. However, it was Mingaud who invented the rounded tip, or *pomerans*, in 1807, while imprisoned either for debt or his political beliefs – reports vary. This tip allowed him to strike the cue ball above or below the centre to get it to roll on or come back, and he developed new effects with a raised cue and glancing blows. After release he played professionally, became a champion and in 1827 wrote *Le Noble Jeu de Biliard*, which detailed his own 40-shot programme and was translated into English three years later. In 'artistic pool' a number of trick shots are still named after him.

Though Mingaud can claim credit for the tip, the notion of using chalk seems to have come from Jack Carr of Bath, who developed a profitable sideline selling special 'twisting chalk', until it was discovered that any old chalk would do. The use of 'side' is credited either to Carr or his contemporary John Bartley and is still known as 'English' by American players.

Sheikh Mohammed

Sheikh Mohammed bin Rashid al-Maktoum, ruler, politician, businessman and racehorse owner and breeder, born 22 July 1949. British champion owner 1985, 86, 87, 88, 89, 91, 93, 97. As partner in Godolphin Stables: 1996, 97, 98, 99, 2001, 04, 06, 07. Wins include: Preakness Stakes 2006, Prix de l'Arc de Triomphe 1994, 2001, 02, Irish Derby 1989, 95.

Asked why he loved thoroughbreds, Sheikh Mohammed, now the ruler of Dubai and Prime Minister of the United Arab Emirates, simply replied, 'We invented them.' Since 1994 he has been the driving force behind Godolphin – an organisation named after the Yemeni-born Godolphin Arabian, one of the pillars of the thoroughbred breed, while his Kentucky stud is named after another, the Darley Arabian.

Having seen Nijinsky in action at Newmarket while studying at Cambridge University, Sheikh Mohammed bought his first horse, Hatta, in 1977 and soon began building up a stock of broodmares, buying Newbury's Gainsborough Stud in 1981. His spending at the US Keeneland sales rose from $2.4 million in 1980 to $41 million in 1984, fuelling a boom in prices as he and his elder brothers Hamdan and Maktoum competed in the bidding with <u>Robert Sangster</u>'s Coolmore Stud. Even the $10.2 million spent on the infertile Snaafi Dancer was only 'a bump in the road', but in 1985 a meeting was held with Coolmore at which a settlement seems to have been reached and afterwards, Sheikh Mohammed overtook Sangster as the leading owner. Following their first Group One win with Awaasif in 1982, Godolphin dominated flat racing as never before. Between 1994 and 2000 they won 66 Group One races – more than double the nearest rival. Though purchases were cut back in the 1990s, they took off again when the Sheikh began to tackle US dirt-track racing in earnest.

Many rich men have poured money into racing, but Sheikh Mohammed is something else – and not only in terms of the sheer size of his spending. A horseman himself, he has a different perspective on the sport since he (like his subjects) doesn't gamble. Instead, he can afford to 'breed to race' – investing huge amounts for the satisfaction and challenge of winning. Godolphin's global perspective was shown in

2000 when they won major races on both sides of the Atlantic in a single day. Another difference is that Sheikh Mohammed wants to succeed on his own terms, through winter training and prep races in Dubai. His Al Quos stables are air-conditioned and boast a 250-metre pool, backed up by an equine hospital, the Zabeel training centre and the Al Sheba racetrack, where he can stage night races in the cooler season. The first conspicuous success of the system was his brother Maktoum's record-setting Derby-winner Lammtarra, who was prepped in Dubai and raced abroad only once as a two-year-old.

In the very different world of American racing, the operation has struggled to achieve similar levels of success. Since buying Worldly Manner for an estimated $5 million in 1997, it is claimed that Sheikh Mohammed has spent $1 billion on his US racing operation, but has yet to win the Kentucky Derby. (Although only one $1 million+ horse has ever done so.)

What is very clear is the Sheikh's determination to use sports to promote Dubai, of which he has been the ruler since 2006. The only deep-water port on 400 miles of coast, Dubai has always been outward-looking and today is being transformed into a winter resort and a bridge between East and West. At first, the Sheikh's best horses simply had 'Dubai' inserted into their names, but in 1996 he followed the example of John Gaines, who set up the Breeders' Cup in 1982, and began to make Dubai a racing centre through the Dubai World Cup, which lured owners with luxurious facilities and a record $15 million in prize money for a single day's racing. Today the Dubai World Cup, increased to 1½ miles to steal a little of Kentucky's thunder, is the starting point for a World Series of 12 races across ten nations. Dubai's Sport City is also a staging post for the vastly expanded 'European' Golf Tour, and since 2005 it has been the home of the International Cricket Council. Having revolutionised horse racing and training, Sheikh Mohammed is now well on the way to changing the face of sports globally.

Old Tom Morris

Thomas Morris, golf course designer and Custodian of the Links (1865–1908), born St Andrews 16 June 1821, died 24 May 1908. Open champion 1861, 62, 64, 67.

Old Tom Morris, the senior partner in sport's greatest father–son combination, has had more influence on golf's rules, competitions and course design than any other man.

The second-youngest son of a St Andrews weaver, Tom was a street golf ('sillybodkins') champion who at 14 was apprenticed to ball- and club-maker Allan Robertson, the first full-time golf professional. Morris became Robertson's foursomes partner and the pair were so good that for the first time it was the standard of play, rather than the social eminence of the players or the size of the stake, that drew the crowds. In 1851, having fallen out with Robertson over the superior new guttie ball, Tom was lured to Prestwick, where for 15 shillings a week he built the course and worked as the club pro.

Having helped Robertson lay out Carnoustie, Tom developed a talent for imaginative course design, creating deliberate obstacles to be avoided rather than simply leaving natural hazards across the fairway. Without heavy earth-moving equipment, he was limited to going with the lie of the land, but was the first to actively create and manage a golf course. At 'Car-nasty' he showed a talent for using natural hazards such as fast-running streams, while the holes repeatedly changed direction to make the wind more of a challenge. At Prestwick an otherwise compact course began with a 578-yard monster, and Tom coined imaginative names like the 'Alps' and 'Himalayas' for the hills and 'Purgatory' and the 'Sahara' for an area of rough and a large bunker. He was the first to brush and top-dress greens to prevent a thick disease-prone thatch forming.

Prestwick's patron, the Earl of Eglinton, who had already sponsored prizes for curling and bowls, was so proud of his course and his club professional that in 1860 he held a contest for a silver belt to see if anyone could match Tom. (The silversmith who made the belt depicted a golfer swinging a club with no head.) After Willie Park beat Morris by two strokes to win the title he proudly declared it 'open to the world', though in practice it was only his fellow Scots who were in contention. Morris had the consolation of a £3 cash prize and went on to win the next two Open titles – the second by 13 strokes and 17 holes, the largest margin in the sport until Tiger Woods won the 2000 US Open by 15 strokes. This new contest shifted the focus of golf from four-somes to individual play and five years later Tom became the oldest-ever Open winner. Today the tournament he inspired is the most valuable event in a packed golf calendar.

From 1865, Tom was back at St Andrews, in those days a scrubby area of common land frequented by cows, strolling couples and wash-erwomen. The fairways through the gorse were no wider than streets and the shared greens and teeing areas were so crowded that some players tried to play at night with lanterns. Tom transformed this mess into golf's great archetype. Not only did the 18 holes and sandy depressions (bunkers) become standard, but so did his idea of a standard-sized hole. After shoring up the crumbling High Hole with a metal collar, all the rest were lined with 4½-inch diameter pipes from the Kincaple brickworks and this became the accepted width. Another big idea was marking the holes with red flags, initially cut from members' old coats. Other innovations included separate teeing areas and the use of sleepers from the nearby railway to reinforce bunker walls. As for the enduring challenge of the course, Arnold Palmer once said that God himself would have to throw the ball out of some of the bunkers, while Mark James claimed that the commonest mistake at St Andrews was 'turning up'.

As golf boomed from seven societies in 1800 to 2,330 in 1900, many new designers were directly influenced by Tom, including Charles Blair Macdonald, Alister MacKenzie (who titled his book on course design *The Spirit of St Andrews*), Henry Colt and Albert Tillinghast. Tom carved out a reputation as a travelling course designer, initially charging just £1 a day. The scope for building courses increased from 1872, when he introduced mowing machines to St Andrews, and these allowed the spread of inland courses, away from the rabbit-cropped dunes. Other Morris courses included Royal Dornoch (1886), a design that became very influential in the US golf boom. At County Down (1889) Tom built the first course with two loops of nine holes leading back to the clubhouse and at Muirfield (1891) he laid out no fewer than 160 bunkers.

With his great beard, morning dips in the freezing North Sea and banning of Sunday golf, Tom became the conscience of the game. As St Andrews' walking rule book, he judged on balls lodged in rabbit holes and even stuck in thick beards like his own. In 1873, a particularly soggy Open gave rise to the 'pick and drop' rule for unplayable lies. It was only in 1892 that the club formally took over the rule-making from him.

It helped that Tom retained his powers for so long. In middle age, he became cursed with the 'yips' – such that he received post addressed to the 'Misser of short putts' – but his putting improved in later life and he shot an 81 when aged 64. His life-long rivalry with Willie Park was such a draw that they virtually invented the idea of seniors' golf. Tom's natural diplomacy and deference enabled him to play and chat with princes and prime ministers – a far cry from his youth, when St Andrews members had had no compunction about beating errant caddies with their clubs.

Morris outlived virtually his whole family, including his talented son Young Tom, and eventually even became an honorary member of the R&A. This was no small matter for a club that had once balked at buying a £20 trophy for the Open, with the result that it became shared with other clubs. Tom met his end after a tumble down some clubhouse steps. By that time he had already turned down a request to create a Tom Morris Golf Club in the town, although naturally enough he enjoyed his iconic status, which he still retains today. At St Andrews, the 18th hole is named after him and his bust sits in the clubhouse with his shop nearby. In 2004 he appeared on a Scottish £5 note and recently the golf world was abuzz with the rediscovery of a lost Morris course at Askernish on South Uist.

Young Tom Morris

Thomas Morris Jnr, golfer, born St Andrews 20 April 1851, died 25 December 1875. Open champion 1868, 69, 70, 72.

The famous son of a famous father, 'Young Tom' or 'Tommy' Morris was the first touring golf professional, making a decent living from his playing skill without having to caddy and maintain courses as well. While his father Old Tom tore out gorse bushes by hand and knelt to tee up balls for aristocratic club members, Tommy was invited to big-money events with travel and accommodation paid.

Tommy's ability to draw a crowd was based on his bold, imaginative play. His swing was said to be powerful enough to break a hickory shaft without any contact and he was the first to curve the ball through the air at will or close the club-face at the last instant to send it screaming through at chin-height, below the worst of the wind. Using a rut iron – a forerunner of the sand wedge – he developed backspin to stop the ball dead and was a superb putter, confident enough to turn his back on a ball before it had dropped. He was a battler too, winning his last Open by three strokes after being five strokes behind his great rival Davie Strath with 12 to go.

Born in soggy St Andrews 'with a golf club in his hand and webbed feet', Tommy was named after his father and an older brother who had died in infancy, and by 13 was winning boys' competitions with scores that would win a pro tournament. In 1868, at the age of 17, he won his first Open title by eight strokes, and went on to become the permanent possessor of the trophy, a red leather belt. Across his four wins he averaged nine strokes lead over the field – a margin only matched since by Tiger Woods. After Tommy claimed the belt, there was a gap of a year before Prestwick, St Andrews and Musselburgh agreed to share the modest cost of a new trophy – a claret jug that no winner would be allowed to keep.

At St Andrews, Tommy set the course record for 20 years to come and was the first to regularly average fewer than four strokes per hole. Another record was the first official hole-in-one at the 1868 Open in

Prestwick, achieved on the Station Hole that his father had built. This helped open the door to more lucrative offers, despite his occasionally rebellious nature. In St Andrews, he once caused a scandal by refusing to doff his cap to a wealthy club member and it took a lot of his father's famous diplomacy to smooth this over. Together Tommy and Davie Strath changed the game as they teed off further and further from the previous hole, until separate teeing areas were established.

Tommy's death was sudden and tragic, following the death of his wife in childbirth and a marathon match in freezing conditions. His father, usually careful with his cash, spent £100 on a fine funeral which half the town attended, and a monument was set up to Tommy in the cathedral graveyard, attesting to his 'amiable qualities'. Though the cause was a pulmonary embolism, many claimed that he had died of a broken heart. Old Tom, who outlived his son by 33 years, used to say that 'If that were true, I wouldn't be here.'

Tommy's red leather belt, donated by his father, is on display at St Andrews. Both his 149 at Prestwick and record of four consecutive Opens remain unequalled.

Ed Moses

Edwin Corley Moses, hurdler and bobsledder, born Dayton, Ohio 31 August 1955. Winner Olympic 400 m hurdles (1976, 84), World Championships 400 m hurdles (1983, 87). Winner Jesse Owens Award 1981, James E. Sullivan Award 1983, US Track Athlete of the Year 1984, *Sports Illustrated* Sportsman of the Year 1984. US Track and Field Hall of Fame 1994.

If there is one athletic record that should stand until the crack of doom it is Ed Moses's 122 races unbeaten in the 400 metres hurdles – a span of 9 years, 9 months and 9 days for an athlete with a 9 foot 9 inch stride.

Until the 1970s, when Moses burst onto the scene, the 400 metres had a reputation among its detractors as a refuge for the moderate quarter-miler. Traditionally, 400-metre hurdlers changed down from 15 to 17 strides between the hurdles as the race took its toll, until South African Gert Potgieter began alternating his lead leg – a style that John Akii-Bua of Uganda used to win Olympic gold in 1972, changing down from 13 to 14 strides. Deciding at what point to do so is a crucial part of this complex, killing race.

The notion of keeping an unbroken stride pattern going the whole way round was unheard of until 20-year-old Ed Moses, an almost unknown physics and engineering student, lined up for his first major international meeting – the 1976 Montreal Olympics – and won it in world-record time with the largest margin in Olympic history. Moses, who had only been training seriously for six months, kept up a 13-stride pattern that in years to come would win top-notch races by up to a second and set four world records. Coaching himself, he eventually got down to 12 strides for the early part of the race.

Moses's dominance lasted until 1987 and one could have bet one's life on him winning the 1980 Olympic title had it not been for the US boycott, against which he spoke out strongly. Along with his serious demeanour and 'mechanical' style, this didn't endear him to some US sports fans. He also upset the expectations of some coaches who had considered pure speed, rather than technique, to be the province of black runners. However, in 1984 Moses was chosen to take the Olympic oath and did so rather haltingly, because the autocue had suddenly failed. His world-record time was finally beaten in 1992 – something many hurdlers thought they might not live to see.

Off the track Ed Moses campaigned against under-the-counter payments and helped persuade IOC president <u>Juan Antonio Samaranch</u> to move to a more open system of payment for athletes, with trust funds being OK'd in 1981. Less popular with his fellow athletes was his late-1980s campaign for regular out-of-competition drug testing in track and field. Since winning a bronze in the bobsleigh World Cup, he has reached the top of two important sports organisations and there is a street named after him in his hometown.

Max Mosley

Max Rufus Mosley, racing driver, owner, manager and administrator, born Surrey 13 April 1940. Co-owner March Racing 1969–77, president Fédération du Sport Automobile (FISA) 1991–3, president Fédération Internationale de l'Automobile (FIA) 1993–, Chevalier de la Légion d'honneur.

Max Mosley is a unique paradox – a man with all the legal, diplomatic and leadership skills to be a successful politician, but virtually disqualified from birth because his father was the founder of the British Union of Fascists. Having fought (literally) for his father's post-war party, the Union Movement, he chanced on the more accepting world of racing. Though he was active in the Conservative party in the early 1980s, his future turned out to be in sporting rather than party politics, becoming one of the two most important men in motor racing, alongside Bernie Ecclestone.

When Mosley stood for the presidency of FISA in October 1991, he was almost comically well qualified. An independently wealthy, multilingual physicist turned barrister with a specialisation in patents and trademarks, Mosley had a personal interest in safety, having raced for Frank Williams's team in 1968 and 1969, two of the most dangerous seasons in the history of the sport. A competitor in the Hockenheim race in which Jim Clark died, he had also seen team-mate Piers Courage killed. After retiring as a driver, he became part of the new wave of teams as the commercial and legal representative, and later race engineer, for March. (Mosley was the 'M' followed by Alan Rees, Graham Croaker and Robin Herd.) After winning the Spanish GP in 1970 with Jackie Stewart, Mosley took full charge as the team achieved two third places in the overall constructors' championships and continued to duck and dive in the low-prize-money world overseen by the Commission Sportive Internationale – which in 1978 became FISA. March won two more GPs with BMW and Alfa engines and raised its profile with four-wheel-drive and six-wheeler designs as well as a sixth place for Lella Lombardi at Montjuich in 1975. However, they had more success manufacturing for other formulas.

From 1971, Mosley allied with Bernie Ecclestone and began transforming the Formula One Constructors' Association from a glorified
travel agency for racing teams into a body capable of wringing a better
deal out of the race promoters. After 1976, when March quit F1, Mosley
worked as FOCA's legal representative, often in conflict with FISA's
bombastic president, Jean-Marie Balestre. Battle lines were drawn up
both on and off the track between the British aerodynamicists and the
continental 'grandees', with their more powerful turbo engines. From
1979 to 1981, Mosley and Ecclestone led the often perplexed British
teams into a series of battles that culminated in FOCA's own alternative 'World Federation of Motorsport' South African GP in January 1981.
Ecclestone and Mosley threatened a rival series of races and bluffed
FISA into surrendering the commercial rights and revenue distribution
in return for official control of the sport. Though the main deal was
done in a nightclub, the official 1982 negotiations dragged on near
FISA's offices in the Place de la Concorde in Paris and the deadly secret
Concorde agreements have underpinned the sport ever since. These
battles also created the 'Piranha Club' – the close but ferociously
competitive teams who were to dominate the sport in the years ahead.

From 1986, Mosley returned to the sport to become a joint owner
of Simtek Research and president of FISA's Manufacturers'
Commission, where the continental power blocs often stymied him.
Balestre's disqualification of Ayrton Senna after a collision with Alain
Prost at the 1989 Japanese Grand Prix was the trigger for Mosley
standing against him in 1991 – an election he won convincingly. Re-
elected the following year, from 1993 he also headed up the FIA and
was able to merge the two organisations. In charge not just of Formula
One but also rallying and touring car races, he was able to award the
vastly profitable commercial rights to FIA vice-president Ecclestone.

Mosley helped clean up the sport's image by bringing in new manufacturers in place of the old wheeler-dealer team owners. In the cause
of making F1 more competitive and attractive to TV, active suspension,
traction control and braking 'gizmos' were banned in 1993. This levelled
the playing field somewhat, although it brought Mosley into conflict
with owners like Ron Dennis, whose view was that the sport was all
about winning, not helping out the also-rans.

More dramatic moves on car and circuit safety followed the deaths
of Ayrton Senna and Roland Ratzenberger – whose funeral Max attended

– and the near-fatal crash of Karl Wendlinger. In the aftermath, Mosley set up the Expert Safety Advisory Committee and F1's safety requirements have steadily increased to 21 pages of data, including 15 load and impact tests that have grown ever tougher. Having already reduced engine capacity and power and altered aerodynamics and tyre regulations to slow cornering speeds, they brought new composite helmets in 2007 and even higher cockpit sides the following year.

From 1996, Mosley's FIA also took a more public lead on safety by forcing through the creation of the European New Car Assessment Programme (ENCAP) safety tests, despite the opposition of many motor manufacturers. A new Concorde deal was also forced through and in 1997 Tony Blair was persuaded to offer a stay of execution on F1 tobacco sponsorship until 2006, though this was later brought forward a year.

Mosley made another historic change to the sport after the 2002 Austrian Grand Prix, when Rubens Barrichello followed team orders to give the race to Michael Schumacher. Team orders had always existed in the sport, but this came in the middle of a series of processional victories for Ferrari and Mosley had such obvious tactics banned in time for the 2003 season. Two years later, he weathered calls for his resignation after the American Grand Prix, in which only six cars raced after the course was judged unsafe for those with Michelin tyres. He also came through another storm – the exposure of his private life by the *News of the World*. Mosley came out fighting and secured a vote of support plus £60,000 in damages and legal fees.

Mosley's most recent interventions have included a cost-saving ten-year freeze on engine and tyre development to stop the steady reduction in the number of teams willing to tip money into the F1 money pit – or rather pits. Greater use of standardised machinery and limits on wind-tunnel testing are all part of a plan to reduce team budgets by up to 80 per cent and make F1 affordable for independents. A switch to environmentally friendly kinetic energy-recovery systems is also intended to make F1 of more practical value to motor manufacturers and more attractive to sponsors wary of such an environmentally destructive sport. This move from high revs to high technology, combined with limits on team budgets, could be the most fundamental change to the formula in a century – and may be essential if it is to have a long-term future. In the summer of 2009 he appeared to have prevented a breakaway championship by agreeing not to stand again as FIA president.

Albert Mummery

Albert Frederick Mummery, mountaineer, born Dover 10 September 1855, died 24 August 1895.

More than any other man, Albert Mummery transformed mountaineering from a pastime for the well-to-do into a true sport, whose essence was 'not ascending a peak, but struggling with and overcoming difficulties'. In Mummery's day mountaineering was an activity in which any reasonably brave and resilient man could buy sporting fame. A typical example was the tubby, short-sighted Reverend W.A.B. Coolidge, a bitchy Oxford don who was shepherded up the mountains by his Swiss guides to record the first official winter ascents of the Wetterhorn, Jungfrau and Schreckhorn, and went on to produce a series of arse-achingly dull monographs on the subject.

Since 1854, mountaineering had been organised and publicised by the Alpine Club, which declared that its members Blackwell and Wills's conquest of the Wetterhorn that year marked the first 'sporting climb'. In doing so they ignored Swiss and French climbers like Father Placidus a Spescha, who over nine seasons had climbed the Stockgron, Rheinwaldhorn, Güferhorn, Oberalpstock and Piz Urlaun and, aged 70, led the successful conquest of the 11,000-foot Tödi.

The Alpine Club was a social rather than a sporting club, dominated by wealthy lawyers and academics who blackballed anyone they didn't like. In the spirit of the times, some claimed a scientific value for their climbs, while others, such as John Ruskin, were admirers of the scenery who regarded mountaineers as despoilers of the landscape. Others were most interested in the historical or religious background of the 'playground of Europe' or saw climbing as a means of spiritual revival, away from the industrial filth from which their fortunes so often derived.

Though it was exclusively British, and trumpeted its members' successes in its *Alpine Journal*, the club professed to deplore 'nationalistic' and 'competitive climbing', and from 1870 set its face against climbing without guides, as well as 'acrobatic' climbing, dismissed by some members as 'monkey tricks'. The use of rubber shoes, ice axes and pitons were all regarded as not being fair play and the club would later oppose the use of oxygen and ski mountaineering. This all helped lead to the formation of a separate Alpine Ski Club by <u>Arnold Lunn</u>, without a 'social' membership rule.

Mummery, who became Professor of Logic and Metaphysics at King's College London, broke with convention by climbing without guides, pioneering difficult routes for their own sake and mountaineering in the Caucasus and Himalayas – peaks which most Alpine Club members had no interest in. Despite successful first ascents of the Grépon, Grand Charmoz, Dent de Requin and the Zmutt ridge of the Matterhorn, Mummery was at first blackballed by some club members. As well as being envious of his new athletic style, many club members were also hostile to his ideas – in *The Physiology of Industry* he had been one of the first to argue that intervention was necessary to stabilise an economy. Another pretext was that his father, a successful tanner and Mayor of Dover, was 'in trade'. Some members resigned over Mummery's exclusion and a degree of subterfuge was needed to eventually get him in. There were further waspish comments over his book *My Climbs in the Alps and Caucasus*, now regarded as a classic, shot through with adventure and humour. Sayings attributed to Mummery include his assessment that every Alpine climb was at first 'impossible', then 'the most difficult' and then 'a good day out for a lady'. (This has been used to suggest that Mummery was a terrible sexist, which seems unlikely as he climbed with his wife and female friends.)

Albert Mummery and two Sherpa companions met their deaths on Rakhiot, the icy west face of Nanga Parbat, the world's ninth-highest mountain, having climbed 7,000 of its 8,000 metres. A human bone was later found there by another climbing legend, Reinhold Messner, who 'adored' Mummery and kept it as a souvenir. Today Mummery is commemorated by a mountain, creek and glacier in British Columbia and a famous fissure on the Grépon. In 1992, Chris Bonington restaged Mummery's ascent of this mountain for BBC TV.

Muttiah 'Murali' Muralitharan

Muttiah Muralitharan/Muralidaran, cricketer, born Nattarampotha, Sri Lanka 17 April 1972. Playing career 1989–: Tamil Union 1991–, Kent 2003, Lancashire 1999–; 224 matches, 1,343 wickets (19.13); 125 Tests, 769 wickets (21.95); 329 ODIs, 505 wickets (22.74) (World Cup 1996). Wisden Cricketer of the Year 1999.

Muttiah Muralitharan is a true sporting revolutionary. As well as creating a new genre – the wrist-spinning off-spinner – his short run-up and whirling 'helicopter' ball-release has broken all records for Test bowling, changed the Cricket Laws to allow wrist flexing and rotating and even caused the game to re-examine its past.

At first mistaken for a leg-spinner, Murali reinvented off spin, traditionally a finger-spun style, which heavier bats, fitter batsmen and shorter boundaries had seemed to threaten. After his debut in 1992, he made a slow start in Test cricket, even though he was capable of making a ball leap two feet across a wicket. It took him 27 Tests to reach 100 wickets, until in 1994 the trauma of having six sixes scored off his off-break and top-spinner combinations caused him to change his length. By 1999, he had also perfected his doosra – a top-spinning ball that goes from leg to off – and completed his transformation into the most effective Test wicket-taker.

Murali has averaged almost six wickets per Test and was the first to 1,000 in internationals. On his English Test debut in 1998, he took 16 wickets at the Oval for Sri Lanka's first win in the UK. Eight years later at Trent Bridge, an eight-wicket haul levelled a series for the first time, and at the following year's World Cup he took 23 wickets. His record is unmatched and he has 22 ten-wicket bags.

Throughout his career, the pop-eyed Murali has been compared with his leg-spinning rival Shane Warne who, like him, could conjure spin from any surface and matched him for consistency, control, guile, competitiveness and willingness to suffer – both men having undergone shoulder surgery. Both also had their portraits up in Lord's while still playing and vied for the title 'The Don Bradman of Bowling'. Though it took Murali 29 fewer matches to break the Test wicket record, critics pointed to the large number of wickets taken against weaker nations such as Zimbabwe and Bangladesh, although against the expert batsmen of India Murali shades it, with best figures of 5 for 23. The contrasts were obvious – Warne the tabloid-friendly ex-surfer, Murali the first member of the minority Tamil community to play Test cricket for a divided island. Although his family have been attacked by majority Sinhalese, Murali's endless competitiveness has made him a national hero, and after the 2004 tsunami he personally funded and supervised relief convoys, and was honoured by the national legislature in 2008.

Murali's extraordinary delivery, based on a congenitally bent arm, has both made and dogged his career, having first been 'called' by umpire Darrell Hair against Australia on Boxing Day 1995 and again the following January. Backed by Don Bradman himself, Murali's action was studied and ruled legal by the ICC in 1996 and again in 1999 after further 'callings', during which even the Australian prime minister voiced his opinion. It was found that his arm remained as straight as he could make it and he only appeared to throw. The result, in 2000, was the latest in cricket's long history of unworkable laws – one that allowed a 'maximum flexing' of 5 degrees for spinners, 7.5 for medium-pacers and 10 for fast bowlers. Unsurprisingly, this proved impossible to enforce. In 2004, match referee Chris Broad once again questioned Murali's doosra, after which a TV crew proved that he could still spin the ball with his arm in a brace. In 2005, Law 24 was amended to allow a 'flat rate' of 15 degrees – simpler, if not much easier to measure – and yet another flurry of tests revealed that Murali's 'mean elbow extension' was within this limit. Another investigation had suggested that 99 per cent of bowlers past and present 'threw' or straightened their arms, and cricket was left to reflect on a long history of bans, wrangles and even suicides created by a law that hardly anyone seems to be able to obey.

The result of all this science is that Murali is 'cleared', although controversy rumbles on. The man himself has been honoured as Wisden's greatest ever Test match bowler and Sri Lanka and Australia now compete for the Warne-Muralitharan Trophy. How far his action can be replicated remains to be seen – Harbhajan Singh is the most noted contender. It may be that Murali's impact will be greater on cricket's past than its future. Now that *is* pretty revolutionary.

James Naismith

James Naismith, gymnast, inventor and author, born Ramsay Township, Ontario 6 November 1861, died 28 November 1939. Honorary president International Basketball Federation. Founder member Naismith Basketball Hall of Fame.

James Naismith is the only man in history to have single-handedly invented a major sport from scratch. A stocky McGill University footballer, gymnast and lacrosse player turned theology student – sometimes also credited as the inventor of the football helmet – Naismith was working at the Springfield YMCA International Training School in 1891 when Superintendent Luther Gulick asked him to create a winter game to amuse a snowed-in class of 18 'incorrigible' students, bored with gymnastics.

After failed experiments with American football and soccer had nearly wrecked the hall, Naismith started again from first principles, eliminating violent tackling by having no running with the ball. The ball itself, he reasoned, should be soft and large enough not to be hidden, and the goal small and high, so that large crowds of players couldn't block it. It would also be horizontal, so that an accurate lob was needed, rather than a violent pitch or whack. James's first idea for the goal was a box, but Mr Stebbins, the college caretaker, only had a couple of tapering peach baskets, which were nailed to the gym balconies. Meanwhile Miss Lyons, the college secretary, typed out James's 13 rules. (It is sometimes claimed that ancient American games were the inspiration for Naismith, but in his own writings he credits 'duck on a rock', a game he had played as an orphaned boy in Ontario.)

The first nine-a-side match was held on 14 December 1891 and despite a few fouls was an immediate success. After he laughed off player Frank Mahan's idea that it be called 'Naismithball', James went with his second suggestion 'Basket Ball'. Influenced by football, scores were at first awarded for 'field goals' and defenders were named 'guards'. Once a system of fouls and free throws was worked out, the value of a goal was increased from one to three points. In his original game the throw-in went to the first team to touch the ball, but the resulting scrambles led to a change to the present system.

As the game attracted spectators, a screen, later replaced by a back-board, was put up behind the basket to stop spectators interfering, and the players, using coal dust on their palms for better control of the leather ball, began playing off it. Soon holes were cut in the bottom of the baskets so that the ball could be poked out with a stick, then closed nets were used with a pulley to pull the ball out, until bottomless nets were finally adopted. After experiments with up to 50 players, five a side became standard in 1897 and the following year new rules were developed for a women's game. Naismith was an early champion of women's basketball, although at first some girls tried to play in long skirts and bustles.

Having left Springfield in 1895, Naismith taught PE and medicine in Denver and from 1898 was at the University of Kansas. Though he preferred gymnastics and wrestling and doubted that the basketball could be coached, it spread fast and was demonstrated at the 1904 St Louis Olympics. Other coaches developed the court markings and it was not until 1903 that the playing area had to be rectangular and straight-sided.

Naismith's rule that a running player who caught the ball had to stop 'as soon as possible' was replaced by one that allowed pivoting, but the big innovation was dribbling, which he had not anticipated. At first dribblers were not allowed to score, but that ended in 1908. A lost skill is the 'overhead dribble', throwing the ball up and catching it while running along. Two other innovations, both of which Naismith opposed, were the end of the jump-off between the two centres to start play after a score and the introduction of a ten-second clock. This was brought in to overcome a five-man defence around the basket, which once led to 343 consecutive passes and 19 minutes' play without a score. It was the ancestor of the modern shot clock.

By 1932 Naismith had seen the first international basketball match and his game had become the dominant US college sport, particularly because it lent itself to smaller schools and could be played in any weather. At the 1936 Berlin Olympics, Naismith was guest of honour and handed out the first basketball medals.

In his posthumously published book *Basketball: Its Origins and Development*, Naismith makes no hint of the problems in his life. With five children to raise, his wife lost her hearing due to typhoid, and a losing record caused him to be edged out of his coaching position at Kansas in 1907, although he remained a professor and athletics director and saw many of his students become big-name coaches. Though he never made a cent from his invention, his main emotion was wonder at the new skills of the players and their fascination with his simple game. Today, James Naismith is commemorated by various college courts, roads and nine sporting halls of fame – one of which bears his name. Of his 13 original rules, 12 are still in force.

Patrick Nally

Patrick Nally, businessman, born Braintree, Essex 16 August 1947.

Patrick Nally practically invented modern sports marketing and in doing so changed the character of sport, ushering in a new world of sponsored tournaments and contests, often timetabled to suit the TV advertising sales market and presided over by executives made rich and powerful by the great torrent of cash.

As a young man Patrick Nally started off working in advertising and PR for clients such as Littlewoods Pools, before becoming involved in sporting promotions. This happened just as the television advertising of cigarettes was being banned, creating a new source of sponsorship cash. Nally joined up with Peter West, a well-connected BBC sports journalist, and began creating and running new events such as cricket's Gillette Cup. As well as dreaming up sponsorship ideas for companies like Ford, Kraft and Green Shield Stamps, West and Nally worked with ramshackle amateur-run sports organisations to develop the new ideas of legal and merchandising rights and to persuade journalists, photographers and broadcasters to respect these rights and feature the sponsors' names. (At this time, even Mark McCormack's IMG group were more interested in representing individual stars than packaging events for sports federations and organisers.)

The idea took a quantum leap in the mid-1970s when the dashing, enthusiastic Nally joined up with the fabulously well-connected and driven Horst Dassler, the man Nally called 'the puppetmaster of the sporting world' and who later created ISL. Set the task of raising £12 million in global sponsorship to support João Havelange's 1978 World Cup, they landed Coca-Cola after 18 months of tortuous negotiations – no mean feat, given that the Argentinian host government had recently conducted a coup and were now engaged in a bloody war against their own population. Until this time, all sponsoring companies had operated market by market – even Coke, whose dummy astronauts had been squirting free fizz at the 1968 Olympics. However, FIFA were so skint and ill-adapted to money-making that only the promise of an extra 15 million Swiss francs from Coke helped them take full control of their own World Cup. In return, Coke gained the rights to 'clean' ad-free stadia, and which brown fizz got drunk inside them.

From this first deal arose the idea of sports offering sponsors exclusive global tie-ins – an idea that virtually created international marketing. The timing was good. Where Coke led, others followed. Set the challenge of raising three times the 1978 total for João Havelange's expanded 1982 World Cup, Dassler and Nally recruited a series of new Japanese manufacturers who operated worldwide under single brand names. The Olympics, Formula One, the relaunched Davis Cup, Adriaan Paulen's 'Golden' athletics events and World Championships and the Commonwealth Games would all soon take this route. Along the way, Nally gained a reputation as a host and fixer, meeting the numerous strange demands of organisers, including sourcing 67,000 pairs of jeans for the 1980 Moscow Olympics. For FIFA and UEFA he created the Intersoccer 4 rights programme, which embraced not just sports events but training programmes, promotional events and meet-and-greet sessions with the athletes – whether or not they liked being herded around and forced to play at odd times of the day. In the case of especially generous 'donors' such as Coca-Cola, the company president would gain an Olympic Order and the 1996 games would be held in their hometown.

Nally split with Dassler after being muscled out by Dentsu – a huge Japanese advertising agency fearful of losing influence with its sponsoring clients. Although Nally had developed Intersoccer, Dassler had the greater political clout and was gifted the rights to market the Olympics as well as the World Cup and international athletics – although large profits were slow to come through, as FIFA, the IOC and IAAF spent as fast as they earned. Nally remained frozen out of many sports before Dassler's death and ISL's collapse, and has been quoted as saying that his business only really picked up afterwards.

Sarfraz Nawaz

Sarfraz Nawaz Malik, cricketer and commentator, born Lahore, Punjab 1 December 1948. First-class career: Lahore, Northants 1967–85, 299 matches, 5,709 runs (19.35), 1,005 wickets (24.62); 55 Tests 1969–84, 1,045 runs (17.71), 177 wickets (32.75); 45 ODIs, 221 runs (9.60), 63 wickets (23.22).

Until the big and burly Sarfraz Nawaz reinvented it, everyone in cricket thought they understood swing – the lateral movement of the ball through the air – especially the Australian batsmen who faced him at Melbourne in 1979. Thirty-three fast-medium deliveries and one run later, seven of them had lost their wickets to an entirely new type of swing – the so-called 'reverse' or 'super' swing.

Conventional swing, first used in cricket by ex-baseballer John Barton King, usually comes into operation after 10 to 15 overs, when the ball is battered enough to create useful 'border effects' in the air. With the correct angle of delivery and one side kept shiny by polishing, the ball can swing towards the rough side. As an 'outswinger', it will move away from the batsman, encouraging an outside edge and a catching chance. Switching to an 'inswinger' that might hit the inner edge of the bat is tricky, so bowlers tend to stick to one style and vary their line, trying to catch the batsman out with late swing until the ball is too worn to respond. Most swing bowlers are medium-pacers bowling at about 70 mph – which an article in *Nature* proved to be the optimum speed.

Although widely used, conventional swing has mysterious qualities, and is supposed to be easier in humid conditions, although science has never proved this. It relies on the bowler's speed and action as well as the ball's angle and pattern of wear, although experts such as Ian Botham and Craig McDermott believe the delivery is more important than the ball, as even a new one can be made to swing.

What no one suspected until Nawaz struck was that a totally different form of swing could be created when a more worn ball is bowled at over 80 mph and different 'border effects' cause it to swing towards the *shiny* side. This reverse swing is more accurate and produces more deviation, especially in hot, dry conditions. It was no great surprise that

it originated in Pakistan, where lifeless wickets require the bowler to
do his tricks in the air. (In some cases, the ball can even trace an
S-shape.) After his success in 1979, Nawaz passed the skill on to Imran
Khan, who used it brilliantly against India in 1982, and in turn taught
Wasim Akram and Waqar Younis. During the 1980s, they reversed the
tendency towards fast, short deliveries in favour of fuller ones pitched
at the batsman's feet. More recently, Andrew Flintoff has been a famous
exponent and has generated reverse spin after just 15 overs.

As Ian Chappell has pointed out, reverse swing is easy to understand
and replicate and less 'mysterious' than the old sort. However, there
have often been claims of ball-tampering to bring it on early, and in
1999 Younis became the first player to be suspended for ball-tampering.
Hair wax and lip gloss are both supposed to have been used to smooth
balls, while roughening can be achieved with bottle tops, nails, grit, dirt
and sugary spit. Suspicions are often raised if reverse swing sets in
before the 40/50-over mark, and matters came to a head at the fourth
Test between England and Pakistan in 2006, when allegations of
tampering led to its historic abandonment.

As for Sarfraz Nawaz, since his stormy Test career ended, he has
married the actress Rani and was a Pakistani MP for three years. When
Pakistan coach Bob Woolmer was discovered dead, Nawaz was one of
the first to advance the theory that he had been murdered.

Miklós Németh

Miklós Németh, javelin thrower, inventor, promoter and trainer, born Budapest, Hungary 23 January 1943. Olympic gold medallist 1976.

Until 1976 Miklós Németh was known, if at all, as the less successful javelin-throwing son of 1948 hammer champion Imre. That all changed at the Montreal Olympics when Miklós's first throw flew two feet past the world-record mark. Part of the reason was his use of a rotational style, using the muscles of his torso to add impetus. His throw, which beat his personal best by 10 feet, so demoralised the field that no one got within 6.5 metres of it and his record stood until 1980. After setting this record, Németh would add another twist to the tale – or rather tail – of the javelin with a design that would be banned by the authorities and wiped from the record books.

Unlike a shot, hammer or discus, the javelin is a 'non-standard' item that can be tweaked and improved. Although now fixed in weight at 800 grams for men, it has a long history of innovation, dating back to Greek times, when the military olive-wood javelin was replaced with lighter cornel wood. The type of javelin that Németh threw in 1976 was pretty much unchanged since the 1950s, when brothers Dick and Bud Held had replaced the straight tube with a cigar shape that flew 3 to 6 metres further. (They went even further when thrown with a life-threatening rotational style that was banned in the mid-1960s.)

In the early 1980s, it was found that with the centre of gravity shifted back, a precisely thrown javelin could go 20 metres further, but by the time the record had reached 104 metres, they were shooting through crowds of steeplechasers and even at the judges' tent at the 1984 Olympics. The design was banned and a new nose-heavy formula was used to decrease distances by about 10 per cent. Németh, now an inventor as well as a promoter and trainer, fought back with a new rough-tailed composite model, whose greater tail drag actually increased overall distance by keeping the nose up. Others tried to copy the effect with paint, holes or dimples in the tail, but all such designs were banned in 1991 and javelins must now have smooth tails. Previous records were wiped out by this ruling and world-record holder Steve Backley had the strange experience of losing his current world record to his old one, but then reaching an even greater distance – 91.46 metres – with a new legal model.

Jack Nicklaus – 'The Golden Bear'

Jack William Nicklaus, golfer and course designer, born Columbus, Ohio 21 January 1940. Wins include: USPGA 1963, 71, 73, 75, 80, US Open 1962, 67, 72, 80, British Open 1966, 70, 78, Masters 1963, 65, 66, 72, 75, 86. World Golf Hall of Fame 1974.

Voted 'Golfer of the Century', Jack Nicklaus helped ignite the sport's TV boom and became both the most popular player and the most successful golfer-businessman, bringing course design into the TV age.

A pharmacist's son, Nicklaus broke 70 aged 13 and won five straight state junior championships and two US Amateur Championships before turning pro in 1962. The crew-cut college boy collected a US Open title in his first season, going up against the people's favourite Arnold Palmer. It was the start of what golf writer Henry Beard termed 'a thirty-year lucky streak'. Unkindly labelled 'Ohio Fats' by some of 'Arnie's Army', the young Nicklaus had to endure occasional cries of 'miss it', but he could concentrate non-stop throughout a round and apart from a single altercation with a referee, his sportsmanship was never in doubt. With two majors in 1963 and consecutive Masters wins, he soon became a popular hero and his rivalry with Palmer did the viewing figures no harm. During the mid-1960s he pulled ahead of Palmer and also conceived the idea of creating a 'home course', just as Bob Jones had at Atlanta.

Over 26 years on the PGA tour Nicklaus averaged 70.78, based on long hitting, intense concentration and practice, and intelligently calculated putting. Strangely for such a big hitter, he has rather small hands and uses an unusual interlocking grip. He was also one of the first golfers to take care of his diet and was a noted banana eater.

By 1986, Nicklaus was being described in the Atlanta press as 'done, washed up and through', but he defied eyesight and back problems (the lot of so many professional golfers) to pick up six shots in the last nine to secure a sixth Masters win. The following day there were 5,000 orders for the Response ZT putter he used and $5 million worth were sold. Though many golfers had promoted products and designed courses before, Jack made and endorsed different ranges of clubs for different budgets and from 1969 lent his name and skills to new courses such as Harbour Town, which helped 'anchor' new developments. Later, he formed a company to both create and manage courses. At the last count this operated 299 courses in 25 countries – nearly 1 per cent of the global market.

Nicklaus's designs included the first 'stadium courses' created for the needs of the crowd and the TV audience as well as the golfer. The most famous are Glen Abbey and his home course of Muirfield Village near Columbus – named in honour of the Scottish course, though it bears no real relation to it. Glen Abbey in Ontario, his first solo project, is the home of the Canadian Open and the Royal Canadian Golf Club. This was a redesign with wide spaces along the fairways for crowds to gather and natural amphitheatres around the greens, six of which are within just 100 yards of the clubhouse. At Muirfield Village a fortune was spent on a variety of water hazards, despite agent Mark McCormack's warning to Nicklaus that he was 'tearing up $100 bills'. In fact, it attracted PGA Tour events within a short time of opening. Like the equipment business, the courses showed an intelligent appreciation of 'segmenting the market' – challenging for the pros, but still able to be enjoyed at a lesser level by ordinary golfers. Muirfield was also the venue for the first post-war US Ryder Cup defeat on home soil – befitting a sport that, as Nicklaus has pointed out, teaches you how to lose as well as win.

After nearly 15 years on the seniors ('Champions') tour, Nicklaus quit competitive play in 2005 at St Andrews, sinking a 15-foot birdie putt and receiving a ten-minute ovation. To mark the occasion, he appeared on a Scottish banknote – the only living non-royal to have done so, and just the second sportsman, after Old Tom Morris the year before.

George Nissen

George P. Nissen, gymnast and inventor, born Blairstown, Iowa 1 February 1914. NCAA Gymnastics Champion 1935, 36, 37. Founder US Tumbling and Trampoline Association 1971.

It was George Nissen who first brought weightlessness to mankind – two seconds at a time.

Inspired by circus athletes bouncing on their safety nets, gymnast and diver Nissen had the idea of a device specially built for jumping on, and in 1934 he and coach Larry Griswold fashioned one from angle iron, rubber tyres and tent canvas. They soon discovered that a circular design was easiest to manufacture, but disorientating for the user, and opted for a space-efficient rectangle instead. The invention was a huge hit at a summer camp and Nissen and two friends went on tour as the 'Three Leonardos' performing throughout the US and Latin America, where the invention was compared to a diving board or *trampolin*. From 1941, Nissen was manufacturing his own 'trampolines' in Cedar Rapids, Iowa. Though he feared that war might close the business, trampolining boomed as training for airmen and wartime nylon webbing improved the product. Nissen continued to promote his invention after the war. As well as being photographed in temporary flight alongside a kangaroo, he counted future President Richard Nixon among his 'backyard bouncers'. A UK factory opened in Brentwood in 1956 and led to a strong trampolining presence in the area. Meanwhile Nissen toured the Eastern bloc and Latin America, where, to avoid confusion, trampo-lines were known as 'Nissens'.

In the early 1960s, a boom in unregulated jumping centres with inferior equipment led to a series of accidents, so Nissen set up the US Tumbling and Trampoline Association and promoted a safe bouncing game named 'Spaceball', plus 'rebound track' as an alternative to running in a circle. In 1980, a spectacular demonstration of mass trampolining at the 1980 Moscow games was lost to US viewers because of their government's TV blackout and Nissen's company ceased manufac-turing. However, he continued to create new inventions such as padded benches for sports fans and even an exercise bike for air travellers.

In 2000, George Nissen saw his sport gain Olympic status and also attended Beijing in 2008. A Nissen Cup competition exists in trampolining and the Nissen-Emery award is presented to the top American college gymnast.

Sondre Norheim

Sondre Norheim, skier and inventor, born Morgedal, Norway 10 June 1825, died 9 March 1897.

In 1868, in snowy Oslo – then named Christiania – a group of athletic young men and one middle-aged one lined up for the national skiing contest. In turn, each of the young bucks made tentative jumps and stepped turns on the shallow slopes as they schussed down the hillside on heavy, wooden skis, steered with a single pole ridden like a witch's broomstick. (*Skid* is the early Norwegian for 'split timber'.) Of those watching, few would have recognised Sondre Norheim, a 42-year-old carpenter and farmer from the distant backwater of Telemark. Only aficionados would have known that Norheim held the jumping record with an extraordinary 30.5 metres, had won a regional meeting two years earlier and had been renowned for his daredevil leaps ever since, as a boy, he threw his ABC book into the fire and took to the slopes.

Norheim was a sensation. His sweeping 'Christiania' curves down the steepest slopes and tight braking uphill 'Telemark' turn proved that, to quote a local paper, 'a new era has arisen in skiing.' The simple reason was that the Telemark skiers, of whom Norheim was the most daring, had replaced the solid pine plank with shorter, lighter laminated skis, which were bowed and cambered to spread the skier's weight and float across the snow. Birch or willow bindings across the toes allowed long leaps without leaving the skis behind. In fact, Norheim had gone even further, creating a waisted ski that flexed rather than skidded through turns and allowed the first slalom runs. He became not just a sporting star, but a symbol of Norwegian identity itself, as the nation pressed for independence from Sweden.

Norheim's neighbours Torjus and Mikkel Hemmestveit soon set up the world's first ski school and by 1884, when Norheim emigrated to North Dakota, the first laminated hickory skis were already in production and there was a national skiing association in place. Inspired by Sondre's designs, new skis went into production and four years later Fridtjof Nansen publicised the Telemark style worldwide through his polar explorations. In years to come, the Norwegians' fierce protectiveness towards 'their' sport would lead to years of argument with the speed-happy Alpine plungers led by <u>Arnold Lunn</u>. Nordic skiers still stuck to Sondre's 'arms out' style as late as the 1930s.

As for Sondre, he found himself stranded on the freezing flat plains of North Dakota, still with a pair of skis propped by his cabin door. After he died in 1897, his grave remained unmarked, but was redis-covered in 1965 and statues of him have been erected in both the US and Norway. Today, not only is a turn with the skis held parallel still called a 'Chrissie', but since the 1970s the Telemark style, using a free heel and staggered skis, has enjoyed a revival. Alpine skiers have also rediscovered Norheim's side cut – a tribute to the man whose skill and inventiveness created the modern world of skiing. Since 1924, the winter games' Olympic torch has been lit at his hearth no fewer than four times.

Henry Norris

Colonel Sir Henry George Norris MP, businessman and team owner, born Kennington 23 July 1865, died 30 July 1934. Chairman Fulham FC 1903–8, Woolwich Arsenal/The Arsenal FC 1912–27.

With a face somewhere between an Easter Island statue and a walrus, Henry Norris was a tough nut with a big ego. Arsenal Manager Leslie Knighton declared, 'I have never met his equal in logic, invective and ruthlessness against all who opposed him.' Football's first knight did more than any man to create the soccer map of London and, for good measure, pulled off the greatest scam in Football League history.

Born into a modest home, Norris worked in a solicitors' office before entering the house-building trade, putting up 2,000 houses in Fulham alone. Renowned as an astute politician, he was a senior Freemason, a local mayor from 1909 to 1919, a Coalition Unionist MP for four years after the war and a personal friend of the Archbishop of Canterbury, from whom he bought land for development. After taking a share in Fulham FC in 1903, he refused to agree to move the team to Gus Mears's larger, better-connected Stamford Bridge stadium and instead had Craven Cottage rebuilt in a more elegant, safer style. Fulham won two Southern League championships and got into the Football League in 1907, but neighbours Chelsea outstripped them in popularity. In 1910, hoping to achieve instant Division One status, Norris flouted the FA's rules by attempting to merge Fulham with his second side, the near-bankrupt, hard-to-reach, but still top-division Woolwich Arsenal, which was nominally run by his cat's paw, a diminutive Putney metal dealer named William Hall. When the FA refused the merger, Norris hatched a new plan – to copy Chelsea's success by building a new stadium with good tube links that might even host the Cup final itself. With Arsenal now relegated, Norris found his site at the other end of the Piccadilly line, in the grounds of St John's College of Divinity, and the archbishop signed a contract selling the ground for £20,000. Despite fan protests, Arsenal were moved from Plumstead to Highbury, and Norris employed his Craven Cottage architect <u>Archibald Leitch</u> to cram a stadium into this residential neighbourhood, persuading Islington

Council to ignore the local complaints about such a 'vulgar project'. Spurs' and Orient's long and loud objections ensured that no League club would be so free to move again. Another legacy was tighter rules on having a controlling interest in more than one club – rules which later club owners like Robert Maxwell would still be able to skip around.

Highbury was far from ready for the first match against Leicester Fosse. With his architect virtually in hiding from him, the vengeful Norris was confronted with no gates, no roofs, no kitchens and only a milk cart to transport any injured players to the local hospital. In despair, he went off to an Italian restaurant but returned to find a large and patient crowd waiting outside. Despite big attendances, Arsenal ended the 1914/15 season £60,000 (perhaps £1.3 million today) in debt and in fifth position in Division Two. Having been knighted for his service to the War Office, Norris pulled off his greatest stunt when play resumed after the war in 1919. With two extra berths in the expanded First Division, logic suggested that relegation candidates Chelsea and Spurs should be allowed to stay up, and Preston and Derby both be promoted, but Norris had other ideas. He had influence through William Hall, now on the League management committee, and fellow mason John McKenna of Liverpool FC, and had earned credits by paying his League subs through the war as well as making sure the wartime London Combination didn't become a permanent rival to the League. As a result, Spurs were relegated while Arsenal leapt ahead of Wolves and Birmingham to grab the last promotion spot – officially on the entirely irrelevant grounds of League seniority. Though Spurs bounced back the following season, they neither forgave nor forgot.

Though he managed to land the first 'non-home nation' soccer international against Belgium in 1923, Norris's Arsenal continued to struggle as he interfered in team selection and refused to pay the going rate for new players. (He twice failed to persuade the League to cap transfer fees.) Manager Leslie Knighton was sacked after Norris refused to pay his bonus and although new manager Herbert Chapman was to transform the team, Norris is said to have regretted the decision. However, once again he showed his deal-making ability when he hired veteran forward Charlie Buchan – not for the £4,000 that Sunderland wanted, but for £2,000 plus £100 per goal in his first season. Though Norris lost £100 on the deal, he gained far more as crowds gathered to watch the '£100 a goal' man.

Norris lost his chairmanship to the more respectable Samuel Hill-Wood after a long series of disputes, offences and libel cases against the *Daily Mail* and the FA that included under-the-counter payments to secure Buchan, illegal payments to players, billing his chauffeur to the club and making £125 from the sale of the team bus. Spurs chairman Morton Cadman was one of those who got his revenge and Norris was banned from the game. In the summer of 1934, with Arsenal now the leading club in the land and having just collected their fifth League Championship, Henry Norris, their destroyer and saviour, died.

Northern Dancer

Northern Dancer, stallion by Nearctic (son of Nearco) out of Natalma. Foaled Windfields Farm, Ontario 27 May 1961, died 16 November 1990. Winner of 14 races out of 18 including: Kentucky Derby 1964, Preakness Stakes 1964, Flamingo Stakes 1964, Florida Derby 1964, Blue Grass Stakes 1964, Queen's Plate 1964. Champion sire (UK) 1970, 77, 83, 84.

There is really only one certainty in racing and that is that the blood-line of dark bay stallion Northern Dancer will dominate it for years to come. Owned and unfashionably bred by Eddie Taylor, Northern Dancer was 'a rough little guy' who tried to throw his riders at every opportunity and didn't make his CAN$25,000 reserve. After winning five out of seven races at home, he won by eight lengths at Aqueduct in New York but still wasn't favourite for the Kentucky Derby, which he won in the record time of two minutes dead, beating the big Californian Hill Rise by a quarter of a length. Still second favourite for the Preakness Stakes, he beat Hill Rise by a bigger margin but failed to stay in the Belmont Stakes – the final race of the Triple Crown. After retiring with an injured tendon, he became the first horse in Canada's Sports Hall of Fame, but was still only the 43rd biggest North American winner.

Northern Dancer became the 20th century's most successful stallion when Robert Sangster and Vincent O'Brien, who admired his battling qualities, paid a record $84,000 for his gorgeous-looking son Nijinsky, who won the first Triple Crown since 1935. Others from Northern Dancer's first crop of foals included Derby winner The Minstrel, double Arc winner Alleged and champion sire Be My Guest. By 1970, Northern Dancer was the first North American horse to become Champion Sire in Britain and his legend grew as Nijinsky sired the winners of 1,000 races. As Sangster and O'Brien repeatedly raided the sales, the world record price for a yearling rose from $170,000 in 1965 to over $10 million for Northern Dancer's (useless) son Snaafi Dancer in 1983. However other offspring like Nureyev, Sadler's Wells and Storm Bird all proved their value as sires – making Northern Dancer the most reliable source of racing and breeding ability around. Today his bloodline dominates in Europe – with every Arc winner since 1994 – as well as in America, South Africa, India, Australia and Japan.

From being syndicated for just $2.4 million, Northern Dancer's covering fee rose to $900,000 with no guarantee of a foal – and it must be said that he enjoyed his work, prancing out on his rear legs and freaking out if it became apparent that a mare was destined for another stallion. It was only in the mid-1980s that he lost a little of his zip, and in 1990 this 'feisty, gutsy, complex character' finally had to be put down. He was commemorated with a stamp, a statue at the Woodbine track in Ontario, two roads and three races. In total, he had produced 635 foals, averaging $620,000 each when sold. Of the 12 highest-priced yearlings of all time, eight were his sons and three were grandsons by Nijinsky.

Today an estimated 75 per cent of thoroughbreds can be traced back to Northern Dancer and the number is rising, thanks to the success of Sadler's Wells, Champion Sire for 14 years between 1990 and 2004, and more recently to Northern Dancer's grandson Danehill.

Tazio Nuvolari – 'The Flying Mantuan'

Tazio Georgio Nuvolari, racing driver and team owner, born Castel d'Ario, Italy 16 November 1892, died 11 August 1953. Victories include: Rome GP 1927, Tripoli GP 1928, Mille Miglia 1930, 33, Targa Florio 1931, 32, Monaco GP 1932, Italian GP 1932, 38, Coppa Ciano 1931, 32, 33, 35, 36, Le Mans 1933, German GP 1935, Vanderbilt Cup 1936, Milan GP 1936, 37, British GP (1938).

Tazio Nuvolari, the first master of the four-wheel drift, was the greatest motor racing star of the pre-World Championship era and possibly of all time.

Though he was to become famous driving works Alfas for <u>Enzo Ferrari</u>, Nuvolari made an unpromising start at Monza in 1925, the year in which he became European 350 cc motorcycle champion. After crashing his Alfa P2 and having to be extricated from a nest of barbed wire with a lacerated back, he was told by designer Vittorio Jano, 'You're an idiot. You will never be a racing driver.' In fact, he was back racing six days later, beating Britain's Wal Handley to claim the Grand Prix des Nations.

The short, urchin-like Nuvolari was the son of a respectable Mantuan family with a car dealership and a reputation as motorbike champions. Prophetically, young Tazio started racing on a black horse without a saddle or bridle, before moving on to bikes, a home-made glider that he crashed and a rebuilt biplane that struck a haystack and burst into flames. (Later Tazio would be one of the first sports stars to routinely pilot himself.) After wartime service as a courier, he began racing cars in 1921, though it was ten years before he gave up motorbike racing altogether.

Nuvolari set up his own *scuderia*, or racing team, paired with his great rival, the ice-cool Achille Varzi, but he lacked Ferrari's talent for business and after a failed attempt to create a new car in 1929, began racing for Enzo, securing his first win at the 1930 Trieste-Opicina hill climb. He demonstrated his skill at the 1930 Coppa Ciano by twice cutting a corner and sending his car through a filling station forecourt with centimetres to spare, and his resourcefulness was shown in that year's Mille Miglia road race, taking the lead in the last three kilometres by driving without lights to catch Varzi unawares. In a Bologna time trial, his racing mechanic was shaken out of the car and hauled back in before Tazio fixed his broken accelerator with a belt and descended 'like a hawk' to win in an underpowered car. (To lower the centre of gravity – or perhaps because he was terrified – another mechanic named Mabelli spent the entire 1932 Targa Florio beneath the dashboard.) Keenly aware of the risks, Tazio once laughed at Ferrari, who had bought him a return rail ticket to a race, saying that Enzo was a bad businessman because he might not be coming back.

It wasn't until 1931 that Ferrari discovered Tazio's mastery of the four-wheel drift. Turning the car into the bend early, with the right gear selected and the accelerator floored, Nuvolari could achieve a controlled skid in which centrifugal force turned the car while the drive from its rear wheels kept it on the road. 'Brakes are no good,' Nuvolari explained. 'They just slow you down.' He added to his legend and rapport with the fans by trying to push his blazing car over the line at Monaco in 1933. At that year's Tripoli Grand Prix, the Mercedes Benz team manager Alfred Neubauer claimed that Tazio threw the race with unnecessary pit stops to allow Varzi to win, but in 1934 he set a record time for the 'flying kilometre' on the Avus track in Germany and even came fifth in a race there, despite having a leg in plaster. Having spent two years with Maserati, he returned to Ferrari to win the 1935 German Grand Prix at the Nürburgring in an ageing, underpowered Alfa P3. Tazio entered what he termed *'in bocca al lupu'* ('the jaws of the wolf') to seize a stunning victory by sheer driving skill, despite a disastrous final pit stop. In the 1936 Tripoli GP, he survived a 120 mph crash that threw him from his car and was back racing the following day – this time in a plaster corset. He also won that year's Vanderbilt Cup in the US, after which he turned down an offer of $50,000 to appear on the radio, preferring instead to race at a dirt track to help out a poor Italian immigrant who had staked his reputation on his ability to produce the great man. Two years later, he quit the out-gunned Ferrari for Auto Union and recorded a win on the day war broke out.

Nuvolari carried on racing into his fifties, despite the advice of his friends, and trusted in his lucky mascots – the yellow of Modena, a wallet with portraits of his family and the tortoise emblem given to him by the poet Gabriele d'Annunzio. With his lungs wrecked by car fumes and his son Alberto now dead, his penultimate drive was the 1948 Mille Miglia, in which he secured his legend, driving a Corsa Spider without mudguards or engine cover and hardly any rear brakes. Perched on a sack of fruit because his seat had also come free, he was 29 minutes ahead of the field when the car finally broke in the closing stages. He was too ill to complete his final race and died in 1953, after which 20–50,000 Mantuans gathered for his funeral.

Of all drivers Ferrari rated Nuvolari the greatest, stating that while the others were equal partners with the car, Tazio was 75 per cent of the combination. Varzi called him the 'the boldest, most skilful madman of us all'. Dr Ferdinand Porsche went further: 'The greatest driver of the past, present and future.'

Vincent O'Brien

Dr Michael Vincent O'Brien, racehorse trainer, born Churchtown, County Cork 9 April 1917, died 1 June 2009. Wins include: Epsom Derby 1962, 68, 70, 72, 77, 82, 2,000 Guineas 1968, 70, 83, 84, 1,000 Guineas 1966, Oaks 1965, 66, St Leger 1957, 70, 72, Prix de l'Arc de Triomphe 1958, 77, 78, Washington DC International 1968, Breeders' Cup Mile 1990, Grand National 1953, 54, 55, Cheltenham Gold Cup 1948, 49, 50, 53, Champion Hurdle 1949, 50, 51. Champion trainer 1966, 77.

Voted both the greatest flat racing and National Hunt trainer of the 20th century, it was no surprise that Vincent O'Brien was also chosen as the greatest figure in horse racing overall by a *Racing Post* poll, collecting nearly 30 per cent of the vote. He is credited with training nine of the 35 best horses of all time, two of which came close to breaking Mahmoud's (hand-timed) record for the Derby – one being Nijinsky, the only Triple Crown winner since Bahram in 1935. The success of O'Brien's Ballydoyle operation is credited with having put Ireland in the first rank of horse-training nations, while its sheer scale and commercial acumen changed the whole business of racing.

What makes MV so significant is not just his success, but also his record as an innovator in a conservative sport. Neither a great ex-jockey (though he rode a few winners) nor a member of the traditional horse-breeding aristocracy, he was the fifth son of a small-scale breeder and trained single-mindedly to win, often relying on his betting at a time when even the Irish Derby was worth only about £6,000. Though he later concentrated on more profitable flat racing, to start with O'Brien trained hurdlers, jumpers and flat racers and early horses like Knock Hard moved between the styles. Tough and smartly dressed, O'Brien had energy, total concentration, high standards, a retentive memory and a thoroughness that was often the difference between success and failure. Of his six Epsom Derby winners, the Minstrel might have been spooked had his ears not been stuffed with cotton wool, while the highly strung Nijinsky might have bolted from the paddock had O'Brien not stationed three stable lads to head him off. Famous for his ability as a judge of a yearling, his horses came in all shapes and sizes, but most were renowned for their good looks.

424   Vincent O'Brien

From 1951, O'Brien's outsider status was confirmed when he
eschewed the traditional base at the Curragh for a new complex at
Ballydoyle, where he could train in privacy. Here he offered top pay for
top performance, and a carport soon replaced the traditional bike shed.
Ballydoyle gave O'Brien the space to pursue new ideas in racing, such
as peat tracks to avoid jarring in summer, cinder tracks for the winter
and Ireland's first covered track. Padded boxes and screens at gallops
to stop horses spooking each other were installed, while the variety of
turns and gradients led to the false belief that he had replicated Epsom's
Tattenham Corner. In terms of training style, Ballydoyle aimed for
patience, understanding and the pursuit of speed without rough treatment – Lester Piggott's use of the whip in training was said to drive
O'Brien crazy. To get horses used to travelling, they were rewarded for
riding in the horsebox, and from 1949 they were the first in Ireland to
be flown to races. Jumpers were trained over low fences to gain confidence and were given a 'come-down' outing after a demanding race like
the National.

After winning the Irish Autumn double with Dry Bob and Good
Days in 1944, O'Brien first ventured to Cheltenham in 1948. Having
dominated the meeting in the early 1950s, he shifted his attention to
the flat and cemented this new success with the US-owned Ballymoss,
who won the St Leger, Irish Derby and Arc in 1957/8 and was regarded
as the best Ireland had produced. Sudden success brought suspicion
and he was summoned to face the Irish Turf Club stewards six times
between 1949 and 1953, with a three-month suspension for inconsistent running the following year. 1960 brought a threatened 18-month
suspension plus the libellous claim that he had doped Chamour. Public
support for O'Brien's decision to contest the libel case led to a reduced
suspension and a deal on the steps of the court, where he wisely
decided against asking the Turf Club for damages. It is probably this
case that led to the Duke of Norfolk changing the laws on dope testing
and negligence, but it was 1999 before O'Brien was finally invited to
join the Irish Turf Club.

In the 1960s, O'Brien instigated the system of freelance rather than
retained jockeys when he employed Lester Piggott, even though trainer
Noel Murless thought Piggott had a verbal agreement with him. An
admirer of US racing, O'Brien hired one of the first overseas jockeys,
Braulio Baeza, to set a record at York, and also recognised that US

owners might be tempted to train in Europe by lower costs and the prestige of the races. His first Derby winner, Larkspur, was bought at a record price for a US owner, and O'Brien was adept at managing sometimes awkward American owners so that their horses remained on this side of the Atlantic as long as possible. An expert on US bloodlines, he was one of the first to sell yearlings on their breeding as well as their racing potential and invested heavily in the Canadian-born Northern Dancer, then unproven as a sire of sires. Thanks to the syndicate O'Brien formed with owner Robert Sangster and breeder John Magnier, Northern Dancer remains the dominant influence on thoroughbred breeding. With business interests worldwide, O'Brien also pioneered the wintering of animals abroad – despite an early scare when Sir Ivor, stabled near Pisa, developed a foot infection and nearly bolted into a dyke.

In 1968 Sir Ivor's Washington DC International victory was the first high-profile 'foreign' win in US racing and O'Brien's position was soon strong enough for him to become the first British or Irish trainer to take a percentage of a stallion's syndication rights. In the 1980s, the busting of the bloodstock boom, competition from Arab owners and viruses in his yard all contributed to a falling-off in performance, but Royal Academy's win in the 1990 Breeders' Cup mile under the 54-year-old Lester Piggott was a final great hurrah for both O'Brien and his star jockey. Today Ballydoyle has been taken over by Aidan O'Brien (no relation), but MV's influence still runs through racing – notably through Sadler's Wells, 14 times champion sire.

Inevitably MV's sixth sense occasionally let him down and he holds the unenviable record of having helped spend $13.1 million on Seattle Dancer, who registered just two Group Two wins. Proof perhaps that the only one who knew a horse better than Vincent O'Brien was the horse itself.

Kerry Packer

Kerry Francis Bullmore Packer, sports promoter, born Sydney 17 December 1937, died October 1990 and 26 December 2005.

Australia's richest man, the pugnacious, sports-loving Kerry Packer didn't set out to revolutionise cricket, but he did. At first, all he wanted was the right to showcase a game that had gained hugely in popularity with the success of Ian Chappell's national side and the advent of colour TV in Australia in 1975. However, after the Australian Cricket Board refused to accept his $1.5 million offer and went for the state broadcaster instead, he delivered on his promise to put the ACB through the 'meat mangler', walking out on further talks, successfully challenging their monopoly of the sport and staging his own World Series Cricket. After 23 months of warfare, everything in the game would change, including the finances, rules and how the game was presented on TV. It was the beginning of the modern 'showbiz' age for a most traditional sport, bringing it into line with tennis and golf, which Packer had already showcased.

The ACB and the International Cricket Council had severely underestimated Kerry Packer's determination and love of a fight – which really was no secret at all. Once, attending a particularly savage rugby match, a shuddering Packer employee said how glad he was not to be out there. 'I'd *love* to be out there,' said Kerry. The Packer family already had some 'previous' in this regard. In 1932, Kerry's father Frank, the second in the Consolidated Press dynasty, had defied the authorities by hiring <u>Don Bradman</u> to write for his *Sydney Sun*. At the end of the great Kerry Packer schism, a secret deal with Bradman would finally settle matters as official Australian cricket not only agreed to hand over ten years of TV rights but also accepted many of WSC's innovations – to the great irritation of other countries that had been fighting anti-Packer crusades on their behalf.

For the players, the most obvious change was in rates of pay. Before 1977, even England captain Tony Greig, Kerry's first recruit, was paid just £5,000 p.a. as captain of Sussex, while Tests offered – but didn't guarantee – £210 for five days' play. Official offers of more money were too little, too late. It was the same in Australia, where Rod Marsh earned just $66 per Test per day and pointed out that even the blokes who shifted the sightscreens earned more. Even on the vague promises that they could make, Packer's lieutenants Austin Robertson and John Cornell had no difficulty signing up 35 players – including all but four of the Australian national squad – by offering fixed £25,000 contracts. So many West Indians signed up that the planned Australia v The World series became a triangular contest – although Clive Lloyd's West Indians refused to play apartheid-era South Africans, which kept some major talents out. As well as better pay, WSC changed the legal status of players and brought in a new world of contracts and stability. No longer would cricket careers end with cap-in-hand trawls round pubs, poverty and even suicide.

Instead of merely banning WSC players from Test squads, the TCCB and ICC ignored wiser heads such as the West Indies' Jeff Stollmeyer and attempted to ban WSC players from the game completely – thus depriving them of their right to work and encouraging them to break their contracts. 'We've been accused of betraying the game because we are playing for what we think we're worth,' explained Greig. Packer spent £250,000 on a court case, including the cost of 'parking' the ten best barristers so that they weren't available to represent the ICC. Mr Justice Slade's decision in favour of Greig, John Snow and Mike Procter meant that WSC players could carry on playing official Test and county cricket.

As for the game itself, WSC was forced to start virtually from scratch. Groundsman John Maley pioneered the craning in of pre-prepared wickets into football stadiums, while electronic scoreboards and flood-lighting meant that even staid English country grounds took note of what was possible and began to improve their offerings. WSC majored on one-day internationals, which were to become the bread and butter of international cricket, and deliberately restricted defensive fielding positions to ensure a more dynamic game. Day/night matches were particularly popular and eventually made a success of the WSC's provincial games – after a fairly disastrous start.

In terms of media presentation, Packer's Channel Nine also rethought the game. Obvious innovations included yellow and then white balls in floodlit stadiums, more colourful commentary and on-screen graphics that included Daddles the Duck, who followed departing scoreless batsmen across the screen. Almost unbelievably, Channel Nine were also the first to have a camera at each end of the wicket – sparing viewers the sight of the batsman's backside half the time. Most famously, the limited-over 'pyjama game' teams also had different colour uniforms to separate them, although 1970s Aussie sporting couture did leave something to be desired. (Like different uniforms.)

Another reason for WSC's success was the quality and aggression of the cricket, as the cream of the game played with clear financial incentives to win. Tail-enders, previously protected from the likes of Dennis Lillee and Jeff Thomson, found themselves in the firing line and helmets became normal for the first time. Overall, Colin Cowdrey reckoned that the number of bouncers trebled in this ferocious new era.

Despite the need for change and the willingness of top players to sign up, WSC would not have succeeded without Packer. He stuck by his players, personally driving the wounded David Hookes to hospital. (Years later, he founded an organ-transplant association in Hookes's name.) The first season was a minor disaster, but the tide turned the following year, with 44,000 packing the floodlit Sydney Cricket Ground to which the state premier had been persuaded to give Packer access. This was twice the attendance at the official Tests. 1979 also brought a profitable tour of the West Indies, while the official Ashes tour back home lost money, forcing the authorities to parley. Even WSC's country matches, which started off drawing just a few hundred fans, attracted 20,000+ as advertising and promotion improved. By year three, it looked as if there would be a Pakistan side too and New Zealand was also keen to invite the circus to town. In total Packer spent perhaps $30 million – a vast amount for the times – but generated 600 hours of TV and endless headlines.

With both sides losing money and 50 Australian players now under WSC contracts, a deal had to be done and Channel Nine was granted ten years of rights. Many of the WSC innovations on rules and dress were accepted and the Super Tests became the World Series Cup, although traditional Test matches still continued to dominate the game overall.

Post-WSC, Packer even attempted to secure the 1980 Moscow Olympics. In later life, he remained famous for his unwillingness to pay tax, his heavy gambling (one $28 million loss was the biggest in history) and a series of heart attacks. One in 1990 left him dead for six minutes and it was sheer luck that the ambulance that arrived had a defibrillator. After reporting, 'The good news is there is no devil, the bad news is there is no heaven,' Packer paid half the cost of installing 'Packer whackers' state-wide and was able to face a 1991 inquiry into his control of the press. Asked to state his name and the capacity in which was attending, he replied, 'Kerry Francis Bullmore Packer. Reluctantly.' His lifestyle finally caught up with him in 2005. His death was marked by a minute's silence at the MCG and a state-funded funeral for the great tax avoider himself.

Arnold Palmer – 'The King'

Arnold Daniel Palmer, championship golfer and course designer, born Latrobe, Pennsylvania 10 September 1929. Wins include: US Masters 1958, 60, 62, 64, US Open 1960, British Open 1961, 62, PGA 1964, 68, 70. World Golf Hall of Fame 1974.

Arnold Palmer, golf's first millionaire, was the player who brought golf out of the country clubs and into mainstream consciousness, making it the hugely valuable business it is today.

Like many players, Palmer came from a golf family, his father a pro at the modest Latrobe Country Club in Pennsylvania, and first broke 70 aged just seven. While attending Wake Forest University, he met future IMG founder Mark McCormack and, after enlisting in the coast-guard for three years, won the 1954 Amateur Championships, turned pro and won the Canadian Open in his first season on the tour.

In 1960, having won the US Masters two years earlier but had a modest 1959, Palmer signed up as McCormack's first client in a deal that was to be vastly profitable for both of them. With 29 wins over the next four years, Palmer would become the popular hero of golf's new TV age. For a start, there was his barrel-chested he-man appeal and good looks, plus his modest upbringing, which brought a new crowd – 'Arnie's Army' – into golf. In a sport in which concentration and strict rules of etiquette encourage dullness, Palmer let his emotions show. Above all, he was exciting to watch. Though in control, his furious lash of a swing didn't look that way and he played an all-out attacking game. In that year, he cemented his appeal with two charges to victory to catch Ken Venturi in the Masters and Ben Hogan and Jack Nicklaus in the US Open. Lee Trevino later declared that Palmer 'would go for the flag from the middle of an alligator's back'. Another notable trait was his obsessive trouser hitching. A fan once counted 345 hitches in a single tournament.

The new TV age led to many changes in golf. In the past, tournaments had been held midweek so that pros could scurry back to their clubhouses for the weekend and start doling out clubs for their members. Now, matches were played over the weekend, with the leading pair going out last. Stroke play replaced the less exciting match play in which the game could be settled many shots from home. Another significant new development was the jet plane. At a time when most US pros stayed at home, Palmer embraced the radically different seaside links courses of Britain and, despite the low prize money, flew over to win consecutive second, first and first places in the British Open from 1960 to 1962. His victories were credited with reviving the event – the second acheived in foul weather.

After this victory, there was only one more major – the 1964 Masters – but Palmer remained in the top ten of earners and in 1967, after 13 seasons, became golf's first millionaire. This was thanks both to his furious work rate and his strong appeal to advertisers and sponsors. He also helped establish the success of the World Match Play – a new event devised by IMG to highlight their showcase of golfers, which now included Jack Nicklaus and Gary Player. In 1971, Palmer experienced a revival, winning four events and buying the course on which his father had worked. The following year, he set up his own course-design company, and in 1980, his 'marquee name' helped make a success of the new Seniors golf tour. By 1987, he was said to be earning £675,000 a year and as late as 1994 was the fourth highest earner in sport, earning $13 million from the Seniors Tour and endorsements. Among other business interests, he has set up his own invitational tournament, founded a TV golf channel and negotiated the deal to build the first course in China.

Arnold Palmer finally retired from golf in 2006, having transformed prospects for the talented player. Arch-rival Jack Nicklaus reckoned every successful golfer owed him a cut.

Adriaan 'Adje' Paulen

Colonel Adriaan Paulen, athletics administrator, runner, footballer, motorcyclist, rally driver, born Haarlem 12 October 1902, died 9 May 1985. President European Athletic Association 1964–76, president IAAF 1976–81. Congressional Medal of Honour. Order of King Willem.

Adriaan Paulen held the world record for the then-popular distance of 500 metres and beat Eric 'Chariots of Fire' Liddell in the semi-finals of the 1924 Paris Olympics, but his big impact was as a tireless and popular athletics administrator who built up the IAAF almost from scratch, founded the World Athletics Championships and laid the foundations for modern professional track and field.

Paulen had helped organise the 1928 Amsterdam Olympics, but when he came to the IAAF in 1948, his authority rested not just on his athletics career and organising ability but also on his wartime record in the Dutch resistance. With one cell operating from his running club, Paulen sent reports to the Dutch government in exile and ran 20 kilometres of escape route for downed Allied airmen. As a mining engineer, he would blow up rail lines at night then the following morning explain to the Nazis why he was unable to shift the coal they so desperately needed. His protection of his miners led to him being imprisoned and repeatedly threatened with execution, and after his release he had to sleep on the roof in case he needed to escape. (This left him with a remarkable ability to sleep on floors or roadsides.) During liberation, he fought with the US 2nd Armored Division and was made an honorary US colonel. He remained fearless ever after, once ordering the King of Sweden off an athletics field, and racing and crashing motorbikes into his sixties.

When Paulen joined the IAAF, it employed just one secretary in a two-room office near Victoria, and as late as 1956 it was unable to pay her fare to the Olympics. However, the IAAF began staging and televising international athletics matches, which stoked up interest in track and field. With the arrival of live international coverage in the late 1960s, Paulen saw the need to manage the new money that would come into the sport, to prevent it breaking up into commercially-backed 'circuses'.

Unlike the purists at the IOC or his predecessor as IAAF president, Lord Burghley, he saw the need to regulate rather than ban appearance money outright, and to deal with outsiders such as <u>Horst Dassler</u> and Middle Eastern entrepreneurs eager to showcase events. At the 1972 Munich Olympics, he was also briefly caught up in controversy about the US vaulters' new poles which were judged illegal on the shaky grounds that, while they didn't break any rules, only the Americans had them. As well as overseeing the first World Cup team competition at Düsseldorf in 1977, Paulen created the first 'golden' event, the Golden Mile, which was inserted into an existing meeting the following year. In 1979 he staged a sensational Golden Mile in Oslo, where Seb Coe beat a glittering field and shattered the world record. Paulen also devised the first World Championships, scheduled for Helsinki in 1983.

Wanting to stand for a second term to oversee the Helsinki games, Paulen would undoubtedly have won the 1980 election had it not been postponed due to the Moscow Olympic boycott. The following year only Primo Nebiolo stood against him, backed by Dassler, who had found Paulen too independent. ('Once you are bought you are not free any more,' Adriaan had said.) Probably misrepresenting the members' voting intentions and certainly misrepresenting themselves – Nebiolo campaigned against 'commercialism' – the two plotters persuaded Paulen to step down, seized power and claimed credit for the structures he had put in place.

Pelé – 'O Rei do Futebol'

Edson Arantes do Nascimento KBE, striker/playmaker and politician, born Três Corações, Brazil 23 October 1940. Playing career: Santos 1956–74 (Intercontinental Cup 1962, 63, state champions 1958, 60, 61, 62, 64, 65, 67, 68, 69, 73, cup winners 1962, 63, 64, 65, Copa Libertadores 1962, 63), New York Cosmos 1975–7 (NASL champions 1977). International career: Brazil 1957–71, 91 appearances, 78 goals (World Cup 1958, 62, 70). South American Footballer of the Year 1973. Minister for Sport 1994–7. FIFA Player of the Century. IOC Athlete of the Century.

The first global sports star from the developing world, Pelé burst onto the international scene at the televised 1958 World Cup. As part of Brazil's first victorious national squad, he was the youngest player ever to play in the finals, scored two hat-tricks and was the star of the final itself, chesting down a pass, back-heeling and then heading a goal from the return pass.

Having signed with club side Santos aged 15, Pelé was their top scorer by 16 and the *artilheiro* – the league's highest scorer – the year afterwards. By now he was already playing for the *seleção*, or national squad. With virtually no playing weaknesses, his club coach Lula claimed he was the only striker to pick and hit a precise spot whenever he shot. His jumping ability, control with his chest and thighs and ability to play-off his toes amazed the TV-watching world, and his agility allowed him to cover as a goalie when needed. He could also freeze while taking a penalty to send the keeper the wrong way – a move that is now illegal. Most impressive of all were his strength and stamina. In all, Pelé is believed to have scored a record 1,280 goals in 1,363 games, often playing over 100 games a year in multiple tournaments. Though most of his goals weren't recorded on film, his *'gol de placa'* was commemorated with a plaque at the Marcanã, although he thought he scored a better one two years later. Pelé remains Brazil's highest scorer, with a unique record of three World Cup wins, though he was injured for all but two of the 1962 games.

Pelé and his team-mates believed in an attacking style, reasoning that defensive long-ball play risked losing possession and led to more injuries through uncontrolled tackles. 'One cannot win games by not losing,' he said.

Declared a national treasure to prevent him being sold to a European club, Pelé was the perfect national icon. Having been born into poverty, his first ball was made of old newspapers and his team wore old flour sacks as shirts. As a black Brazilian, 'O Rei', or 'The King', could become a natural focus for the whole nation and its rulers, and in 1962 both his second World Cup win and Santos's World Club Championship were celebrated with national holidays, after which Santos ruthlessly exploited his value with exhausting tours. At the 1966 World Cup – which the team management were disastrously over-confident and badly prepared – Pelé was hacked out of the tournament, and swore never to play international football again. However, he kept touring with Santos and in 1967 even the vicious Nigerian–Biafran civil war stopped so that both sides could watch the match.

Unflappable on the field and unfailingly polite off it, Pelé remained an emissary for Brazil and swung votes behind the Brazilian Football Federation president João Havelange when he won the FIFA presidency from Stanley Rous. (Pelé was no doubt pleased, as he blamed Rous for tolerating the vicious tackling in the 1966 finals.) His legendary status was confirmed in 1969 with his 1,000th goal (O Milesimo) which was dedicated to the poor children of Brazil and commemorated by a poem read in Congress. His return to international football in 1970 brought a third World Cup for a Santos-dominated team. In Mexico, he helped unpick England's defence, and in the final set up the iconic fourth goal, gently rolling Jairzinho's pass into the path of the onrushing Carlos Alberto. 'I thought he was just a man of skin and bones like everyone,' said Italian defender Burgnich. 'I was wrong.' With the tournament being watched by 900 million worldwide – ten times the 1966 audience – Brazil's ruling generals organised massed celebrations and even talked of replacing the globe on their flag with a football. After Pelé retired from international football in 1971, 40 million petitioned for his return. Unfortunately, the Jules Rimet trophy he won outright was later stolen and probably melted down.

Having twice come close to bankruptcy thanks to unreliable business partners, Pelé signed a $3 million deal with Warner Brothers to join the New York Cosmos achieved 25,000 lockouts at the ramshackle Downing Stadium and drew 77,000 to Giants Stadium. His trademark bicycle kick even introduced soccer to the opening credits of <u>Roone Arledge's</u> *Wide World of Sports*, but home-grown players failed to come through. After Pelé retired in triumph in 1977 and the 1986 finals were lost to Mexico, ABC pulled the plug on US soccer and only five teams were left playing.

By 1995, Pelé's commercial interests allowed him to bid to televise the anarchic Brazilian domestic season. His refusal to pay bribes caused him to go public on the corruption, severing his links to the CBF – the Brazilian football federation – and Havelange, who refused to invite him to the 1994 World Cup draw. Instead, he was appointed Minister for Sport and took on the 'robber barons' of the CBF with a Pelé Law intended to bring openness and fairness to contracts, team accounts and the running of the league and cup competitions. This law, though watered down by vested interests, was passed in 1998.

Early on in his career, Pelé had trademarked his name and was one of the first players to employ an agent, which led to endorsements, appearances on TV and film and a contract with Pepsi to promote football worldwide. So great was his influence that Adidas and Puma agreed not to engage in a ruinous bidding war for his name – until 1970, when Puma broke ranks and were rewarded with big sales for their 'King' and 'Black Pearl' boots. (Pelé carefully tied his laces before kick-off to ensure that the eyes of the world were on his feet.) Vying with <u>Muhammad Ali</u> as the world's best-known athlete, he was said to hold more honorary citizenships, to be more photographed and more serenaded in song, with over 90 tunes, than any man on earth.

Ironically, his childhood nickname Pelé has absolutely no meaning. Edson – originally 'Dico' to his friends and family – disliked it so much that he punched the kid who invented it.

'La Divine': Suzanne Lenglen liberated women's tennis and became the first great female sports star.

Track and film star Mick the Miller's sport briefly overtook football as Britain's most popular (*left*). Old Tom Morris (*below*), creator of the modern 18-hole golf course.

Riding high: Johnny Weissmuller's new-style crawl made him almost unbeatable (*above*). The multi-talented 'Babe' Zaharias (*below*) beat whole teams single-handed. Her medal-winning 'dive' changed the rules of high jumping.

Tazo Nuvolari (*left*),
the first master of the
four-wheel drift. Jarno
Saarinen (*below*) was
the first rider to routinely
hang off his bike to keep
it more upright and
faster through turns.

After a near-fatal crash at the Belgian Grand Prix, Jackie Stewart (*above*) fought
a long crusade for better F1 safety. Clive Rowlands' kicking helped bring about
profound changes in the rules of rugby (*below*).

By ignoring training orthodoxy, distance runner Emil Zátopek did what no one else has before or since – win triple Olympic gold in the 5,000 m, 10,000 m and marathon.

Fred Perry

Frederick John Perry, table tennis and tennis player, broadcaster and businessman, born Stockport 18 May 1909, died 2 February 1995. Championships include: US Open 1933, 34, 36, Wimbledon, 1934, 35, 36, Australian Open 1934, French Open 1935. Davis Cup winner 1933–6. International Tennis Hall of Fame 1975.

Fred Perry was not only the most successful British tennis player of the 20th century, but also its first modern sports/media star – at his best, bright, hardworking and shrewd; at worst, egotistical and selfish.

'There was never a champion in sport who looked more of a champion than Fred Perry,' said fellow champ and tennis promoter Jack Kramer. But, although Fred looked like a matinee idol, smoked a pipe and drawled 'very clevah!' to drive his opponents nuts, he was not a typical British tennis player. Rather than an Oxbridge-educated public schoolboy, he was a northerner, the son of a cotton spinner who became Labour MP for Kettering, and gained a reputation as being something of a rebel. 'I didn't aspire to be a good sport – champion was good enough for me,' he later declared. Fred confirmed this 'un-Englishness' by marrying an American, moving to California and touring as Britain's first big-name professional player – which got him banned from all the major tournaments.

Even Perry's entry into tennis was unusual. He first came to prominence as a world table tennis champion at Budapest in 1929, a training that gave him sharp reflexes, lightning speed and great footwork. After switching to tennis at 18 he mastered his trademark shot – a freakish snapping forehand that took the ball early on the rise as he ran forward to volley. His overhead was good, but his backhand was weak and his volley not highly rated – although he was fast enough to pick off the return. His relentless attack and speed made the 26-year-old the first player to achieve a career grand slam – although he probably wouldn't have been if Ellsworth Vines hadn't turned professional.

At the 1934 Wimbledon final, Perry achieved the first of three straight-sets victories but recalled a committeeman pointedly congratulating his Australian opponent Jack Crawford instead of him. There was (as usual) no trophy presentation and his honorary member's tie and £25 Mappin and Webb voucher were left on a chair. Fred felt more at home in the US, where he began his professional career in 1937 after a handshake deal with Vines. They and <u>Bill Tilden</u> went on the road, playing on canvas courts in halls across America and Europe and becoming the first players to earn over $50,000 in a single night. After earning $91,000 from a 61-date tour, Perry and Vines bought the Beverly Hills Club.

Kramer rated Perry one of the half-dozen greatest players, though not as good as Vines, who he claimed had 'carried' Fred on occasion. Both Kramer and Tilden accused 'the world's worst good player' of throwing the occasional match – which Perry denied.

Reinstated by the All England Club after the war, Fred never missed a day at Wimbledon until 1983. He part-invented and sold the first sweatbands, and launched his own range of tennis kit. He rejected his first idea of a pipe as a logo on the very sensible grounds that 'girls wouldn't go for it' and instead chose the laurel wreath, which has sold very well ever since. In 1948 he confirmed his reputation as an opportunist by siding with a promoter in a court case against his fellow pros, and as broadcasting boomed in the 1950s, became a TV and radio commentator. By now part of the tennis mainstream, when the professionals struck against the ILTF in 1973, Perry used his newspaper columns to side with the authorities. Today there are Perry gates and a statue at Wimbledon and a Fred Perry Way in Stockport, but his greatest monument is that since he quit the amateur game in 1937, Britain has neither regained the Davis Cup nor had a men's singles champion.

'Dimboola Jim' Phillips

James Phillips, cricketer, coach and umpire, born Stawell, Victoria 1 September 1860, died 21 April 1930. First-class career 1885–99; 124 matches, 1,827 runs (12.59), 355 wickets (20.00).

In the 1890s, traditional 'straight-armed' bowling seemed to be going the way of round-arm and underam bowling, as increasingly large numbers of 'chuckers' let fly at the wicket in any way they saw fit. This was especially the case with wealthy amateurs such as Charles Kortright of Essex, who could hire and fire umpires at will. In 1897, fast bowler Frederick Spofforth even suggested in the *Sporting Life* that there should be a free-for-all to allow matters to sort themselves out. However, at this point there appeared – of all things – a crusading umpire, who stopped the game taking this path.

'Dimboola Jim' Phillips had been a medium-pace all-rounder and took ten wickets in a match on seven occasions. From 1895 he umpired 24 Tests in England, Australia and South Africa, becoming the first truly international umpire. Cheered on by *Wisden*, he went after the 'shyers' with a vengeance, starting with the great amateur C.B. Fry himself. After heading off on the 1897/8 Ashes tour with Andrew Stoddart's team, he also 'called' Australian bowlers Ernest Jones and Tom McKibbin – with Jones becoming the first bowler to be pulled up for throwing in a Test. Other umpires were inspired to follow suit and in 1900 the county captains met and agreed to drop nine suspect players, although the MCC were characteristically reluctant to act and hired one of the banned chuckers – Lancashire's Arthur Mold – whom Phillips called 16 times in a row, ending his county career. (There were suspected suicides among some suspended players.)

Despite the human cost, other officials were inspired by Phillips's example and umpires West and Sherwin also called Fry, who amended his technique to a slower, legitimate one. In 1901, the MCC threatened some fairly non-specific action against offenders and the problem went away for 50 years.

Having saved the game, as he and his supporters saw it, Phillips carried on umpiring until 1905, when he set off to North America to work as a mining engineer. Having been mocked by the patrician Fry for carrying his textbooks in his pocket, he is believed to have prospered in his new job.

Today Jim Phillips's principle is debatable, as modern testing has revealed that almost all bowlers straighten their arms during a delivery and acceptable tolerance limits have had to be agreed. Nevertheless, an open 'free-for-all' would be dangerous for batsmen, so his influence does still live on.

Lester Piggott – 'The Long Fellow'

Lester Keith Piggott, jockey and trainer, born Wantage, Oxfordshire 5 November 1935. Career (1948–85, 90–5): 4,493 wins including 1,000 Guineas 1970, 81, 2,000 Guineas 1957, 68, 70, 85, 92, Derby 1954, 57, 60, 68, 70, 72, 76, 77, 83, Oaks 1957, 59, 66, 75, 81, 84, St Leger 1960, 61, 67, 68, 70, 71, 72, 84, Prix de l'Arc de Triomphe 1973, 77, 78, Breeders' Cup Mile 1990, Washington DC International 1968, 69, 80. Champion jockey 1960, 64, 65, 66, 67, 68, 69, 70, 71, 81, 82.

Lester Piggott owes his unusual first name to Lester Rieff – another great jockey who also fell foul of the racing authorities. It proved a good choice for a man who, despite repeated run-ins with owners, trainers and other jockeys – not to mention the racing authorities and HM Government – saddled over 4,000 winners in a 47-year career and was champion jockey 11 times, with a record 29 Classic wins. As the 'house-wives' favourite' he broadened the appeal of the sport and was the first jockey able to go freelance and get valuable syndication rights for the great horses he rode to victory.

Lester was the product of two racing families – the Piggotts and the Rickabys; his father, a National Hunt trainer, had ridden the 1939 Champion Hurdle winner, while his mother twice won the Newmarket Town Plate – the only race open to women riders of her day. He won his first race at 12, already displaying the judgement, daring, cool and courage that would mark his career. The exceptional height of 5 feet 7½ inches threatened to divert him into steeplechasing, before the Long Fellow embarked on a 40-year battle to stay 1½ stone below his natural weight. 'Losing the habit of eating' was how he described it.

As a reward for this effort, Piggott was able to use his size to exert a greater authority and control over horses. This might mean the strength to keep a wilful one on course or to speed up another, but usually it meant the ability to maintain control, constantly adjusting to balance the animal in a way that a lighter jockey, piloting more dead weight, simply couldn't. (During the 1960s, Lester followed riders such as Edgar Britt by riding with shorter and shorter leathers.) His strength also enabled him to come through some horrible accidents. In 1977 he came close to being killed at the start of the Oaks, but still won the final race of the meeting. At Epsom in 1981 his mount plunged under the stalls, stripping Lester's skin and almost detaching his ear. After coming back from retirement, he survived two horrible tumbles at the 1992 Breeders' Cup and at Goodwood two years later.

Lester has been quoted as saying that his motivation was not winning, but competing. As well as battling his own body, he fought his fellow jockeys on the course for victory and off it for rides, becoming notorious for 'jocking' them off. On the track, he used his whip to give rival Doug Smith a crack, grabbed Alain Lequeux's whip at Deauville and shoved a rival horse away at Sha Tin. At least one jockey even claimed that Lester forced him over the rails. Perhaps this desire to compete rather than to win also insulated him from the effects of defeat. It certainly brought a series of brushes with authority, starting in 1954 when, having already won his first Derby, he was banned by the Jockey Club's Duke of Norfolk for dangerous riding at Ascot. This, his tenth ban, saw him removed from his father's yard for six months – later reduced to three, after which he won the first race on his return.

Renowned as a great judge of horses and a believer that you can't be both good and careful, Lester drove trainers like Vincent O'Brien mad by giving their cosseted steeds a smack to see what they could do. (A man of robust opinions, Lester once claimed that the best cure for a horse that persistently hung to the left was a shotgun.) In a tight race his skill, varied tactics and quick-fire use of the whip to grab victory made him exceptionally valuable in a sport in which a marginal winner can be worth ten times the horse in second place. By the mid-1960s, he was the highest-paid sportsman in the land and, supported by Vincent O'Brien, broke a verbal agreement and left Noel Murless's stables to become the first freelancer. He would go on to ride four Derby winners for O'Brien on a course that is one of the most dangerous in racing, and was able to negotiate a share of the syndication rights for winners including Alleged, Nijinsky, Sir Ivor and The Minstrel. O'Brien said that 'the real beauty about having Lester riding for you is that it gets him off the other fellow's horse'.

From 1971 Lester rode more selectively, chopping and changing and 'jocking off' other riders from their expected mounts. In 1984, a row with owner Daniel Wildenstein cost him a ride on Arc winner All Along, leading to a parting with trainer Henry Cecil and a move into training, in which he produced 34 winners.

Given Lester's 'careful plus' attitude to money, it was a shock but hardly a surprise that large amounts of untaxed income were found in a series of accounts. The immediate cause was the leaking of a secret letter circulated by Cecil, detailing the percentages and bonuses that the jockey required. The result was a record bail amount and a year in jail after a trial in which he demonstrated his amazing powers of recall. An understandably tetchy HM Government removed his OBE and the near-certainty of a knighthood, but this didn't dent his popularity with racegoers. Despite five years out of the saddle, he was still considered to be worth 5 to 7 lb in a race by Vincent O'Brien and ten days after his return to riding he won a sensational 1990 Breeders' Cup Mile – perhaps the greatest comeback in sport. His last race could have been at Haydock Park, where he had won his very first race on The Chase, but he preferred Nottingham, where they offered him £1 per spectator. Which was very Lester.

Lester Piggott retired in 1995, and his only real rival as the greatest flat racing jockey in history is Sir Gordon Richards, his predecessor at Noel Murless's yard, who won 4,870 races and 26 championships, though 'only' 14 classics. Experts considered them equals for strength and determination, although the Richards era was one in which trainers were more demanding and the standard of jockeying (arguably) higher. Racing was also a rougher game, with no camera patrols and starting stalls, fewer meetings and harder travel. On the other hand, Lester had to clock up 300,000 miles a year while riding 800 winners in 36 countries and, had he not been so selective in his rides, he would certainly have exceeded 11 championships. With 29 classics, he is certainly the undisputed king of the big occasion and the annual jockey awards are named after him.

Martin Pipe

Martin Pipe CBE, racehorse trainer, born 29 May 1945. Champion trainer 1988–93, 95–05. 4,183 winners, including Grand National 1994, Champion Hurdle 1993, 97.

Martin Pipe, the most successful jump-racing trainer in history, was also something of a radical by racing's standards. In the 1980s, when athletics coaches were learning to boost human performances with individual training and low volumes of high-intensity exercise, Pipe was doing the same with his equine athletes and was credited with turning his sport from 'an amateur run-around into a sleek profession'.

Rather than being born into the sport and apprenticed at Lambourn or Newmarket, Pipe originally planned to be a bookmaker like his father, until his father sold his chain of shops. Being a 'totally and utterly useless jockey' (his words) who won just one race and broke his hip, he turned to training, starting from scratch in Devon. With just one winner in his first season, it took him 14 years to become champion trainer, but once there he dominated the sport with his fitter, lighter horses. He was to win the title for 14 out of 16 years, sending out up to ten runners in the Grand National, though he won it just once with Miinnehoma.

What the self-taught Pipe lacked in racing tradition he more than compensated for in openness to new ideas, favouring short, sharp canters rather than long drawn-out gallops and installing all-weather gallops, indoor tracks, a solarium, a horse walker and pool – all new departures for this very traditional sport. Most radical of all, he studied veterinary science and learnt the value of regular blood tests and temperature checks, installing his own laboratory on site. The presence of this lab helped raise suspicions about the operation and there was a Jockey Club raid in 2002, in which all the samples tested negative for controlled substances. Other scrapes included the perhaps inevitable questions over supposed non-triers and a heavy fine for avoiding the official blood-sampling unit. The yard also attracted accusations of cruelty from investigative reporter Roger Cook. Pipe was also implicated in the betting coup when Le Saadien, rechristened There is No Doubt, won in 2004, but no rules were found to have been broken.

Awarded the CBE, Martin Pipe accompanied the Queen Mother in the royal carriage at Ascot, where he had won six of his 256 flat race victories. After making an emotional retirement announcement live on TV in 2006, he handed over to his son David who, in contrast to his father's slow start, won the 2008 National with Comply or Die. Cheltenham racecourse – where Pipe had won 32 races, though bizarrely never a Gold Cup – also held a meeting in his honour.

Dick Pound

Richard William Duncan Pound OC OQ, swimmer and sports administrator, born St Catharine's, Ontario 22 March 1942. Gold medallist 110 yards freestyle and 110 yard relay 1962 Commonwealth Games. Canadian Olympic Association secretary general 1968–76, president 1977–82. IOC member 1978–2001, executive member 1983–2001, vice-president 1987–91, 1996–2000. President World Anti-Doping Agency 2001–7.

In 1980, the Olympics were down to their last $250,000, had no reliable TV revenue or sponsorship programme and had no effective drug controls. Twenty years later, they had survived a potentially ruinous scandal to remain the greatest brand in sport, do TV deals worth over $2 billion, run the most effective sports sponsorship programme in history and helped set up a World Anti-Doping Agency. The main mover behind all of this was vice-president Dick Pound.

A tax lawyer and Olympic swimmer at Rome in 1960, Pound was an IOC member at the tender age of 36, and once Juan Antonio Samaranch was appointed IOC president, became the most senior Anglo-Saxon administrator in world sport, given responsibility for Olympic TV negotiations from 1981 and sponsorship from 1985.

In the past, the IOC hadn't bothered to brand, promote or archive its TV coverage, which was controlled by Roone Arledge's ABC. As a passive partner, the IOC took whatever it was given – even though this represented 95 per cent of its meagre income. The near-ruinous Moscow boycott concentrated some minds, as did the LA organising committee's decision to suddenly withhold the IOC's expected share of $125 million. Pound replaced the abrasive Monique Berlioux as negotiator and insisted on open auctions with pre-signed contracts and only the final amount to be filled in. Despite interference from the US Olympic Committee, who regarded any money as theirs by right, not to mention the unrealistic hopes of some host cities and Samaranch's willingness to sell the European TV rights for a pittance, this led to a huge increase in TV rights. The decision to stagger the winter and summer games, rather than have them compete for the same year's advertising spend, also helped. In Pound's last deal, $2.3 billion from NBC guaranteed $700 million for Athens and financial stability for the IOC and the sporting federations that depend on it. Without this money, many sports would simply implode.

From 1985, Pound was also in charge of sponsorship. In the past, the Olympics' complex structure had required sponsors to negotiate with organising committees, National Olympic Committees and the IOC, knowing that someone would probably rat on them and do a deal with a competitor. Instead, Pound employed <u>Horst Dassler</u> and <u>Patrick Nally</u>'s ISL to offer exclusive global sponsorships – an idea carefully sold to an unenthusiastic Olympic movement that was only partially under the IOC's control. The Olympic Programme (TOP) took a while to get going, but proved an outstanding success, with revenues rising from $95 million in 1988 to $700 million in 2004. While building and maintaining good relationships with existing sponsors, Pound had to slap down those like Mars that bent the rules, as well as parasitical marketers like Amex who tried to profit from the games without contributing. Another bugbear were host city governments like Atlanta's, which contributed nothing to the games but flooded the streets with aggressively sold tat. Pound, chairman of the Atlanta Coordination Committee, stated that many thought the best view of the city was in their rear-view mirror as they left. Even Nike, whose 'You don't win silver, you lose gold' campaign attacked the Olympic ideal, were persuaded to desist and became an official sponsor. While there were complaints about the commercialisation of the games, none of the alternatives – rich athletes only, taxpayer-funded games or a complete reliance on host cities – were achievable or desirable. With Dassler's death and a decline in ISL's management and finances, Pound managed to extricate the Olympics before the company collapsed – a trick neither tennis nor football pulled off.

Unlike many in the IOC – for whom ethics often appeared to rank between carbon paper and paper clips in importance – Pound had a strong moral sense and was not afraid of criticising unfair judging practices. He personally intervened when <u>Ben Johnson</u>'s start was unfairly penalised at Seoul and defended him during his positive drugs test. At Salt Lake City in 2002, he also intervened on the part of Canadian skaters Jamie Salé and David Pelletier, deprived of gold by backstage manipulations involving <u>Marie-Reine Le Gougne</u>.

The Salé and Pelletier case followed another scandal over the bribes taken by IOC members to vote for Salt Lake City's 2002 Winter Games bid. This PR disaster could have been a financial one too, had the US removed the tax advantages that underpinned the Olympics' vital sponsorship deals. Pound's investigation was only one of many, but he succeeded in identifying the main culprits, and bringing the right (leaked) charges, so that the IOC had to act, with ten of those on the take either leaving or being forced out.

On the issue of drugs, which had been ineffectively dealt with in the past by various groups of Olympic scientists and administrators, Pound identified the need for a clear and focused policy with an ethical dimension, arguing that this was a problem to be tackled, not an embarrassment to be smoothed over. In 1999, meetings in Lausanne and Copenhagen established an independent World Anti-Doping Agency with an agreed list of substances and sanctions, standard testing procedures and a recognised appeals process.

In 2001, Pound stood as Olympic president and was understandably vexed to receive fewer votes than the better-funded Kim Un-Yong, who had come close to dismissal over the Salt Lake scandal and was subsequently charged with bribery and corruption. Fortunately, new IOC president Jacques Rogge persuaded Pound to take charge of WADA and chair the Olympic Games Study Commission, which attacked Olympic 'bloat' by limiting accreditations and trying to reduce the number of white elephants left behind.

WADA not only investigated new areas such as genetic doping, but took the battle to professional sports, most of them highly litigious 'entertainment businesses' with very limited drug-detection programmes. It even managed to get support from the US administration, which took an unusually forthright view on sports drugs and brought the first prosecutions of coaches. The outspoken Pound was involved in a number of spats – particularly with cycling – and Lance Armstrong pushed unsuccessfully for his removal.

William Prest and Nathaniel Creswick

Lieutenant Colonel William Prest, footballer, athlete, cricketer and administrator, born York 1 April 1832, died 10 February 1885. Founder Sheffield FC 1857. Cricket career: Yorkshire 1852–62, 16 matches, 286 runs (10.21). Colonel Sir Nathaniel Creswick KCB, born Sheffield 31 July 1831, died October 1917. Co-founder, secretary and treasurer Sheffield FC 1857–62.

The names of Sheffield wine merchant William Prest and solicitor Nathaniel Creswick are missing from many football histories, but there is a strong argument that in the late summer of 1854 these two young cricketers and part-time soldiers became the true fathers of the game.

After choosing football as good out-of-season training, Prest and Creswick braved the ridicule usually attached to it to found Sheffield FC, the first official club. The club first met formally on 24 October 1857 at their friend Harry Waters Chambers's house. At first, Sheffield FC was based in a spare greenhouse and matches were played by surnames A–M versus N–Z. To begin with, football seems to have played second fiddle to the athletics at which Prest excelled, but the club committee on which both he and Creswick sat soon produced their first rules – based on Cambridge University's – and a first inter-club match followed against Hallam in 1860. Two years later, both men played in a return match that turned into a general riot.

When the London-based FA first met the following year, it was the burgeoning Sheffield clubs who pushed for less handling, which helped lead to the split with rugby. The Sheffielders' rules were already far closer to modern soccer than the FA's, which at the time allowed catching and handling and even rugby-style marks and touchdowns instead of corners. The FA also had line-outs instead of throw-ins, no mention of goalies and two posts instead of a modern-style rectangular goal. As with rugby, you couldn't even pass forward. It wasn't until 1866, when they first played a Sheffield side, that they made catching illegal and caught up with Sheffield, who had allowed forward passes since 1863.

Although Prest was, like many of the London FA, an ex-public schoolboy, Sheffield football attracted a broader middle-class support that helped bring in more players. During the 1860s, Sheffield became a much stronger footballing centre than London, although it was 1867 before a formal association was formed. While the London FA numbered just three or four teams, Sheffield had at least 14, stretching from the Trent to the Tees, and held the first cup competition – the Youdan Cup – four years before the Londoners' FA Cup. In 1868, Sheffield pioneered corners rather than touch-downs (four years ahead of London) and two years later added crossbars to the goal and abandoned their old system of 'rouges' – near-misses that settled a goalless game – in favour of an eight-yard goal. The Sheffield Association began allowing passes to any player who hadn't sneaked past the goalie – which also made them the first to mention goalkeepers in their rules. A modern two-man offside rule soon followed. Free kicks were yet another Sheffield invention of the early 1870s, though you couldn't score directly from them – hence indirect free kicks today. Another first was extra time, dating from a match between Wednesday and Heeley in 1877.

In the 1870s, the Sheffielders played a series of 16 matches against the London FA, demonstrating new tactics such as deliberately passing to team-mates, crossing the ball and even heading it into goal. This bold strategy worked so well that the southerners shed their team caps and switched to Sheffield-style coloured jerseys. In 1878, a first floodlit game at Bramall Lane attracted thousands more fans than the FA Cup final, and after a player ran over a quarry edge in pursuit of the ball, they also started the first insurance scheme.

It was only in 1877, when Sheffield and London finally merged their rules, that football as we know it today really began. This led to the 90-minute game with no handling except by goalies, modern goal sizes and the angled throw-in, which merged Sheffield's angled kick-in from touch with London's straight throw. In return, the London FA got the goal height dropped to eight feet from Sheffield's nine and their own three-man offside rule remained in force until 1925, when they went back to Sheffield's two-man rule – which is what we still use today. In fact, most of what we take for granted in football should be stamped 'Made in Sheffield', but as the FA expanded nationwide South Yorkshire's role became downplayed. As passionate defenders of amateurism, the Sheffield Association missed the boat when professional clubs created the Football League and Prest and Creswick became better known for local politics and the Hallamshire Rifle Volunteers. After Prest's death, thousands of mourners gathered, but the bust that his family had presented to his old regiment was gradually forgotten and spent many years in a junk room, until Nathaniel Creswick's great-great-nephew identified it in 2001. In 2007, it was presented to Sheffield FC and unveiled by Sepp Blatter.

Ferenc Puskás – 'The Galloping Major'

Ferenc Purczeld, footballer and manager, born 2 April 1927, died 17 November 2006. Playing career: 1943–56 Kispest – from 1949 renamed Honvéd – 341 appearances, 352 goals (league champions 1949, 50, 52, 54, 55), Real Madrid 1958–66, 182 appearances, 157 goals (league champions 1961, 62, 63, 64, 65, cup winners 1962, European Cup 1959, 60, 66, world club champions 1960). Hungary 1945–56, 85 caps, 84 goals (Olympic champions 1952), Spain 1961–2, 4 caps.

Until Wednesday, 25 November 1953, British football reckoned that individual speed and strength would always win out over foreign guile and team tactics. It was Ferenc Puskás's Hungarians who ended that belief by scoring within two minutes of kick-off on a foggy winter's afternoon. A strong English side found themselves – to quote *The Times*'s Geoffrey Green – 'Strangers in a strange world of flitting red sprites' as Puskás led his team to a 6–3 victory. It was England's 'twilight of the gods', the first loss at home to continental opposition. The loss of their assumed footballing supremacy would be confirmed by a 7–1 drubbing in Hungary – still their worst international performance. Green concluded, 'England can be proud of its past, but must awaken to a new future.'

For all their speed and strength, England, in their baggy kit and clod-hopping boots, were thrown together and slotted into <u>Herbert Chapman</u>'s 30-year-old WM formation to become Hungary's latest victims in an undefeated 32-match run. Afterwards, the obvious cause of defeat was the superior skills displayed by the visitors and especially Puskás, who scored twice – part of the total of 84 goals that he would score in 85 appearances. His left foot was lethal at all ranges and angles and he could stop a ball dead in the air, bounce it 200 times or drag it back and shoot – a move that the match commentator struggled to even describe. 'Sheer jugglery,' wrote Green in *The Times*. With the occasional assistance of his right foot, Puskás could dribble with his head up, and alongside him Sándor Kocsis headed 75 goals in 68 matches, and centre forward Nándor Hidegkuti's feint and shot led to that first goal.

However, there was more to the Hungarians' success than skill on the pitch. Behind the team was 'Uncle Guszti', aka Minister of Sport Gusztáv Sebes, who had taken over the team after an embarrassing loss to Czechoslovakia. Sebes set up a national system of coaching, complete with a new national stadium and a stable side that included players from three club sides who all trained together in midweek. Knowing and trusting their colleagues, they learned to share defensive and attacking duties. While Gyula Lóránt was the 'stopper' in defence, the two full backs counter-attacked, and even centre forward Hidegkuti had marking duties. To his left and right, inside forwards Puskás and Kocsis could attack or break up attacks. Sure of their places, the players were allowed to experiment. Goalie Gyula Grosics became a virtual sweeper, the inside forwards swapped positions, the wingers overlapped and Hidegkuti might start up front but then withdraw. At Wembley, Blackpool's centre half Harry Johnston simply didn't know where to go.

A shrewd political and sporting operator, Sebes knew the prestige victory would bring, and kept his players from playing the 'English idiots' in the preceding FIFA v FA match. However, he did take home some heavy English balls to practise with on pitch conditions that matched Wembley. On the pitch, however, Puskás was in charge. After Uncle Guszti's peroration before the England game, he told the team to forget it all and just play.

Such a set-up was a far cry from England, where ex-Grimsby fish merchant and FA selector Arthur Drewry picked the team, and the players were simply thrown together. At Wembley, Tom Finney was dropped and at the rematch Portsmouth's Peter Harris and Fulham's Bedford Jezzard replaced Stanley Matthews and Stan Mortensen. Only skipper Billy Wright and Jimmy Dickinson played at all well.

Afterwards, some progressive British players and clubs adopted some of what they had seen, though not the national side. Don Revie adapted Hidegkuti's withdrawn centre forward role to win the 1956 FA Cup final for Manchester City, and Manchester United were the first to copy the Hungarians' slim-fitting kit and lightweight boots.

Expected to win the 1954 World Cup for Hungary, Puskás should have been put out of the tournament by German centre half Werner Liebrich's hack at his ankle in the early rounds, but he insisted on playing in the final and also had outside right Laszlo Budai dropped. Kept awake the night before the match and jostled on the way to the stadium, Hungary lost to an inferior team that many believed were dosed up on amphetamines. In heavy rain, they went 2–0 up but couldn't put the game away, losing 3–2 after conceding two soft goals – one after an unpunished foul – and having Puskás's equaliser disallowed.

Two years later, Honvéd's tour of Spain coincided with the violent suppression of a national revolt by the Russians and Puskás chose to stay away from Hungary. After his two years' suspension from the game – because of his defection – during which Manchester United were interested in signing him, Real Madrid took a chance on the stocky 31-year-old and Puskás rewarded them with a hat-trick in his second appearance, before guiding the team to a fourth European Cup final, which he missed due to injury. In 1960, in Real's fifth European Cup final in as many years, he dazzled the 127,000 packed into Hampden Park by scoring four times to beat Eintracht Frankfurt 7–3. A hat-trick in the 1962 final against Benfica wasn't enough to beat a team coached by fellow ex-Hungarian international Béla Guttmann. Although Puskás, second only to Pelé as an international goalscorer, qualified for Spain, he never scored for his second international side. After Spain ended up bottom of their 1962 World Cup group, non-Spaniards were banned from the team, but at club level, he played on for Real until 1966, when a younger side triumphed with a sixth European Cup win.

As a coach Puskás never scaled the same heights, though he took Panathinaikos to the 1971 European Cup final and South Melbourne Hellas to the 1991 Australian title. Welcomed back to a newly democratic Hungary, he briefly managed the national side but died in 2006 after suffering from Alzheimer's disease – so often the fate of the professional footballer. He was buried with full honours, his body taken from the national stadium that now bore his name, given a military salute befitting his honorary majorship and buried beneath St Stephen's Basilica.

'Sonny' Ramadhin

Ramadhin (later K.I. Ramadhin), cricketer, born St Charles, Trinidad 1 May 1929. First-class career: Trinidad, Lancashire and Lincolnshire 1949–65, 184 matches, 1,092 runs (8.66), 758 wickets (20.24); 43 Tests, 361 runs (8.20), 158 wickets (28.98). Wisden Cricketer of the Year 1951.

As the first East Indian to play for the West Indies, 'Sonny' Ramadhin was launched into Test cricket aged just 20 after only two trial games. On tour in Britain, wearing his sleeves long to disguise a suspect action, he subtly varied his line and length and bowled leg or off breaks or straight balls from the back of his hand, so that neither his wicket-keeper nor the poor batsman knew what was coming. At the second Lord's Test he secured the West Indies' first win on foreign soil, bowling 70 maidens and taking 11 wickets for 152, while fellow spinner Alf Valentine picked up another seven wickets. The West Indies won by 326 runs, part of a 3–1 Test series win in which the 'spin twins' took 59 wickets and set their supporters – mostly new immigrants to Britain – dancing in the stands.

Was there no answer to this unreadable spin? There was, and it revealed itself seven years later at Edgbaston as Colin Cowdrey joined Peter May, with England 288 runs behind the West Indies, to face Ramadhin, who had figures of 7 for 49 from the first innings and 2 for 34 so far in the second. Together May and Cowdrey used the restrictive lbw law to kick away any ball that pitched wide of the wicket. Cowdrey took almost eight hours to reach three figures. With Valentine absent and Roy Gilchrist and Frank Worrell injured, Ramadhin was bowled into the ground, delivering a record 98 overs in the innings. In total, an estimated 100 lbw appeals were turned down.

Pad play itself had existed since the 1880s, when what had been intended as protection for batsmen began to be used to kick the ball away, but although the MCC had issued condemnations, no effective changes had been made to the rules of the game to curb it. This record-breaking monument to tedium and negativity, which deprived the West Indies of victory, is mysteriously absent from Cowdrey's ghosted auto-biography, but it proved a significant match. For a start, Ramadhin, though he played Test cricket until 1960, was never the same force again. Meanwhile, the pad-play epidemic gradually built up the demand for more exciting Test and then limited-over cricket. Pressure increased still further after the following year's Brisbane Test, when May ordered Trevor 'Barnacle' Bailey to stay put until the wicket was worn enough for spinners Jim Laker and Tony Lock – Bailey crept to just 68 in over seven and a half hours. Ultimately pad play would lead to changes in Law 36, which finally allowed umpires to award lbw appeals when the batsman made no effort to play the ball. So Sonny Ramadhin's effort was not entirely in vain.

Sir Alf Ramsey – 'The General'

Sir Alfred Ernest Ramsey, footballer and manager, born Dagenham 22 January 1920, died 28 April 1999. Playing career: Portsmouth 1940, Southampton 1943–9, Tottenham Hotspur 1949–55 (Second Division champions 1949/50, First Division champions 1950/1); England 1948–54, 32 caps (captain 3 times). Management career: Ipswich Town 1955–63 (Third Division South champions 1956/7, Second Division champions 1960/1, First Division champions 1961/2), England 1963–74 (World Cup 1966), Birmingham City 1977–8.

'Look at them – they're finished! You've beaten them once, now you've got to do it again!' Thus Alf Ramsey lifted his team to beat Germany in extra time at the 1966 World Cup final. A great communicator when he had to be and famed for his spirited rendition of 'Maybe it's Because I'm a Londoner', Ramsey hated public speaking, was a grumpy old cuss in public and, necessarily, remained quiet about his team selection and tactics. As a result, his innovations in football have often been lost in a fog of patriotism and anecdote.

As a player Ramsey broke, or at least stretched, the mould. In his day, many full backs aimed to do little more than clear their lines, but Alf, who made his league debut at 26, attacked out of defence, compensating for his lack of pace with great anticipation and positional awareness that sometimes resulted in spectacular goals and produced an England call-up while still in Division Two. In Arthur Rowe's double championship-winning Spurs side, the ice-cool 'General', backed by Bill Nicholson, combined with Sonny Walters, a winger who drew back to receive better passes in more space and attack an opposition full back who didn't know where to go. Tottenham's fast-passing 'push and run' side won consecutive Second Division and First Division titles – scoring more goals and conceding fewer than ever before. It was perhaps the beginning of Ramsey's big idea – pulling back and then even doing without wingers in a football culture that fetishised them.

Miraculously, Alf managed to copy Spurs' achievement with Ipswich Town, his first managerial berth. When he first arrived in this backwater, cattle strayed onto the pitch, the office was a Nissen hut, the

ambulance was his own Ford Anglia and the changing room had rough
bare boards. Making the best of what he had, Ramsey encouraged his
players to do 'the easy thing well' with simple, quick and accurate
passing. Ramsey used the aged-looking Jimmy Leadbetter as a withdrawn left winger, turning their 4-2-4 formation into a twisted 4-3-3.
He also used Roy Stephenson as a deep-lying right winger, feeding accurate passes to 'poacher' Ray Crawford and Ted Phillips, whose shots
were considered hard enough to kill. It was the beginning of 4-4-2 in
Britain. Promoted to the First Division, Ipswich stuttered at first, gaining
only one point from three matches, but then 'Ramsey's Rustics', assembled for just £30,000, roared into life with the front two scoring 40 and
30 goals each to secure an extraordinary championship. In a TV-less
era, defenders were flummoxed by facing two centre forwards rather
than the expected one, but by the following season Town had been
rumbled, and with the front two man-marked, they won just two out
of 15 matches before Ramsey accepted the England job.

England 'management' truly was a poisoned chalice, with Walter
Winterbottom driven from it after 16 years of dealing with capricious
and ignorant selectors who filled the standard 'WM' berths with their
favourite players, regardless of the opposition. Having been refused
Jimmy Adamson by Burnley, and turned down by Bill Nicholson of
Spurs and Wolves' Stan Cullis, the FA hired the fiercely patriotic Ramsey,
who even took a pay cut. By the following May, he had full control of
team selection and team formation – for which the ex-selectors never
forgave him.

Ramsey, a football obsessive with an incredible recall of the game,
gradually assembled another tight-knit squad of players that many other
managers wouldn't have considered – plus the first (unpaid) team doctor,
taken on after Peter Swan had nearly died on national duty in 1962.
An initial loss to France in the European Nations Championship was
followed by a honeymoon period of improving results, which ended with
the 'mini World Cup' and defeats in Brazil and Argentina. Ever since
he had played in the 1950 World Cup, Ramsey had hated Latin America,
having been stationed in a mining camp, a long and perilous journey
from the baking prison-like stadium in which England lost to the USA,
while a 1953 tour had brought a brush with dysentery and more 'wild-
eyed negroes'. (On the other hand, these early experiences do seem to
have inspired him to get his own full backs to overlap.) Defeat to

Argentina seems to have persuaded Ramsey of two new facts: 1) that against four defenders, the winger lost his space and potency; 2) that while four attackers worked well against inferior opposition, they struggled to regain the ball against better sides. Against European Champions Spain, with his hand forced by injury, Ramsey played a 4-3-3 with fast running midfielders who attacked down the middle instead of the wings and tracked back better in defence. From 1965 he also had his secret weapon – a 4-1-3-2 with a stopping midfielder to cancel out any particular danger man.

Having predicted that his side would win the World Cup, Ramsey constantly experimented which kept the squad on their toes but produced an unconvincing series of results. The use of players like Nobby Stiles, whose eyesight was so bad he once tackled the wrong man, led Jimmy Hill to declare that 'no one could win with this lot'. However, after a training camp at Lilleshall, the team won four games in a nine-day European tour, although midfielder Martin Peters was a very late entry and it wasn't until the quarter-finals that Ramsey settled on his winning XI.

In front of the back four, Stiles broke down attacks, man-marked crucial opponents and provided 'enforcement', and Ramsey staked all by standing by him after a horrible tackle on France's Jacques Simon. Afterwards, Nobby cancelled out both Argentina's Ermindo Onega and Portugal's Eusébio. (When told to mark the latter, Stiles asked, 'During the match, or for life?') Alan Ball did the work of a winger and midfielder combined and ex-winger Bobby Charlton also kept the opposition pre-occupied. Having experimented with nine centre forwards in three years, Ramsey's chosen front two were Geoff Hurst, who was inexperienced but strong in the air and could hold up play, and Roger Hunt, a hard-running attacker with a knack of scoring in crunch matches.

Despite confident predictions that they couldn't win, they did. Not even Hurst's winning goal could disturb Ramsey – 'Sit down,' he ordered trainer Harold Shepherdson, who had leapt up, spoiling his view of the goal. In return, the FA paid him a bonus of just £6,000 and even a set of commemorative place mats was reserved for the blazer brigade. Alf's salary remained below that of some Third Division managers and his training staff numbered just two.

England's road to glory had included a vicious conflict with Argentina, whose undeniably skilful players resorted to punching, tripping, shirt-pulling and spitting – while they in turn protested at the English team's crunching tackles. After the outraged Argentinians had hammered on the England dressing room and pissed against the walls, Ramsey was said to have described them as 'animals'. In fact he referred to bad behaviour generally as teams who 'act as animals'. Despite a subsequent apology, the misreported comment was never forgotten and it boded ill for the Mexico finals in 1970. There, Ramsey's plan to cocoon the team with their own food resulted in the team's fish fingers being burnt on the quayside as a 'health measure', and their hotel became a focus for noisy protests. FIFA's decision to schedule the matches at midday to catch the European evening TV viewer led to matches in 110-degree heat, and the players might have collapsed without the help of Charing Cross Hospital professor Hugh De Wardener, who provided them with experimental salt tablets. Other prematch distractions included the presence of some players' wives – paid for by the press – and the framing of Bobby Moore for the theft of a bracelet. Most seriously, on the eve of a crucial match against Germany, keeper Gordon Banks suffered food poisoning which, according to one theory, was engineered by the CIA, keen to eliminate England and keep the Brazilians happy despite their repressive government. (That might seem far-fetched, but remember this *is* the CIA we're talking about.) In the match itself, England were winning 2–1 when Germany struck twice. Ramsey's supporters blamed two howling errors by stand-in keeper Peter Bonetti, but Alf himself admitted his mistake in taking off Bobby Charlton and thus releasing Franz Beckenbauer.

Back home, Ramsey received little help for the 1974 qualifying campaign. Matt Busby put the phone down when he tried to secure Nobby Stiles for a match, future England manager Don Revie refused to release Norman Hunter and Brian Clough claimed that his players were injured, before fielding them just 48 hours later. 'Cheating clubs and managers' was Alf's comment. He got just as little cooperation from League secretary Alan Hardaker who, preoccupied with his all-unimportant Texaco Trophy, disregarded the 'whims' of international management and the need to rest players.

At a time of growing defensiveness (Spurs won the 1961 title with 115 goals, Leeds the 1969 one with just 62), many writers and players didn't like the elimination of old-fashioned crowd-pleasing wingers and blamed Ramsey for a general trend. Persecuted by the press for his 'cautious and joyless' teams and his refusal to choose flair players such as Peter Osgood, Alf, in his trademark tracksuit and shiny brogues, struck an increasingly isolated figure amid the non-achieving flash Harrys of the 1970s. Worse, he seemed to go out of his way to alienate his few loyal supporters such as the *Mirror*'s Frank McGhee. Even the 1966 victory was now being attributed to home field advantage – despite the fact that no other host nation had won the World Cup since the war. As the Ipswich experience suggested, Alf was better at retaining players than replacing them and took little interest in scouting or developing junior teams. Alan Hudson was reported to have refused a call-up to play under Ramsey, and by the time new recruits such as Trevor Brooking were brought in, it was all too late, although the overall record was impressive: won 69, drawn 27, lost 17, 224 goals for, 99 against.

Denied World Cup qualification by the amazing and amazingly lucky goalkeeping of Polish keeper Jan Tomaszewski, it was clear that teams like Germany and Holland had progressed beyond Ramsey's England. The executioner was FA vice chairman Professor Sir Harold Thompson CBE, MA, DSC, FRS. An ex-Oxford blue and founder of the elite amateur side Pegasus, 'Tommy' Thompson was notorious for his cigar-smoking around the players and sexual harassment of women, and habitually called Sir Alfred and his players by their surnames. 'That bloody man', as Alf termed him in private, gave him an £8,000 pay-off, after Alf had passed on £250,000 worth of commercial offers to serve his country. With his Ramsey's FA pension amounting to just £25 a week, his main source of income was a ghosted column for the *Daily Mirror*.

With most clubs put off by his reputation, the best offer was to go on the board at Birmingham City, and as caretaker manager he won four out of five matches before he left over the transfer-listing of Trevor Francis. A coaching appointment at Panathinaikos lasted only one year before a change of regime. Having been dismissive of his Ipswich successors Jackie Milburn and Bobby Robson, he was unwilling to help Robson when he succeeded him as England manager, although Robson later paid Alf's nursing-home bills. Two years after his death, his memorabilia had to be sold – not including a winner's medal, which the FA had also denied him.

Articulate and popular with his core players and passionate about the game, Ramsey never resonated with England supporters. Though Ipswich fans funded a statue of him, the new Wembley stadium, which could have been named after him, wasn't. When the supporters were given the opportunity to name at least a bridge after the man who brought the nation its finest sporting achievement, they opted instead for Billy – the white horse who helped clear the pitch in 1923. His players knew better. 'You did it, Alf,' a tearful Nobby Stiles had said. 'We'd be nothing without you.'

Ranji

His Highness Kumar Shri Sir Ranjitsinhji Vibhaji Maharajah Jam Sahib of Nawanagar, cricketer, born Sarodar 10 September 1872, died 2 April 1933. First-class career: Cambridge University 1893-4, Sussex 1895-1920; 307 matches, 24,692 runs (56.37); 15 Tests 1896-1902, 989 runs (44.95). Wisden Cricketer of the Year 1897.

'The most brilliant player of cricket's most brilliant period' was contemporary Gilbert Jessop's verdict on Ranji, who not only created a new stroke – the leg glance – but also became England's first non-white sporting captain and hero.

A member of a relatively hard-up branch of a noble Rajput family who had never played much organised cricket, Ranji first came to attention at Cambridge University in 1890. With his great eye and strong and flexible wrists, 'Smith', as he was nicknamed, could defend solidly on the back foot or drive powerfully off the front and was said by his friend C.B. Fry to have 'three strokes for every ball'. Excluded from the university side for three years – probably because of his race – he played his cricket for local teams and used his wealth to hire England players for bowling practice, developing lightning reactions that served him best on bad pitches. Having scored three separate centuries in one day, he became too good to ignore, and played for the university before moving to Sussex to score a double century in his first match and top the county averages. Even his defensive moves had an attacking force of their own, and he solved the problem of scoring off a good ball on the leg side by pivoting and glancing it to the boundary. Striking through the line of flight of the ball with a crooked bat required immaculate timing.

Along with Fry, Ranji dominated cricket for ten years, but this wasn't enough for the MCC's Lord Harris, who questioned his eligibility for the 1896 Lord's Test against Australia and kept him out of the side. Fortunately, Lancashire were still selecting the Old Trafford Test sides and picked Ranji for the second Test – quite possibly to spite Harris. He scored 62 and 154 not out – only the second debut Test century since W.G. Grace. In 1897/8 Ranji also toured Australia with A.E. Stoddart and Archie MacLaren's side and made another great start, overcoming tonsillitis to score 175 in the first innings at Sydney.

In 1899, with a full Test series now increased to five matches, Harris's MCC gave themselves the power to select players for all Tests and once again attempted to drop Ranji, despite him becoming the first batsman to score more than 3,000 runs in a season. However, W.G. Grace was also a selector. Ranji had swelled the gate for Grace's London County side and both he and Fry had fulsomely praised Grace in their *Jubilee Book of Cricket*. The Doctor insisted on Ranji's inclusion and even had Fry made a selector.

Despite suffering from hay fever and coming close to bankruptcy, Ranji was Sussex's captain from 1899 until 1903 and led an MCC tour in 1899 – the first non-white captain for a representative national side. Though he played much less after 1904 and lost an eye in a hunting accident in 1915, he carried on playing for 27 years, though he grew rather portly. In 1934, India's first inter-provincial trophy was named after him, and his nephew Duleepsinhji also played for Cambridge, Sussex and the MCC. Less helpfully, Ranji established the notion of Indian sides being captained by nobility. Inevitably, there was a shortage of nobles as good as he.

Karl Rappan

Karl Rappan, footballer and coach, born Vienna 26 September 1905, died 2 January 1996. Playing career: SV Donau Vienna 1922–4, SC Wacker 1924–8, Austria Vienna 1928–9, Rapid Vienna 1929–30 (league champions 1930); Austria 2 caps. As player-coach: Servette FC 1931–5 (league champions 1933, 34). As manager: Grasshopper Zurich 1935–48 (league champions 1937, 39, 42, 43, 45, cup winners 1937, 38, 40, 41, 42, 43, 46), Switzerland 1937–8, 42–9, 53–4, 60–63, Servette 1948–57 (league champions 1950, cup winners 1949), FC Zurich 1958–9, Lausanne 1964–8. As technical director: Rapid Vienna 1970–1.

Football has always been a balance between wanting to score and not wanting to concede goals, but it was Karl Rappan who first prioritised defence over attack.

In 1931 Rappan, a league championship-winning forward at Rapid Vienna, became player-coach of Servette in Switzerland, a lowly semi-pro team that couldn't hope to match the big guns in fitness or skills. Instead, Rappan bulked up the traditional two-man defence by pulling back both wing-halves. Rappan's 'T-shaped' defence, with the two new centre backs staggered, ensured that there would always be a spare man – a system that the local press termed the *'verrou'*, or bolt.

A bigger defence meant fewer men up front and Servette became masters of dogged defending, winning two low-scoring championships thanks to occasional counter-attacking breaks. Promoted to national coach, Rappan reached the World Cup finals three times, and in 1938 beat both England and a combined German-Austrian side.

Though regarded as a sign of weakness, the tactic spread to Italy after the war as Gipo Viani's Salernitana briefly reached Serie A. The style was also taken up at Inter, where full back Ivano Blason was used as a *'battitore libero'*, or 'free hitter'. The ferocious Blason was famous for drawing a line beyond which attackers dared not tread, then launching his 'mortar shells' forward or into the crowd, and the iron-clad Inter won the 52/3 championship with less than half the usual number of goals. Local rivals Milan also used this *catenaccio*, or 'door-bolt', system, which would reach its peak under Inter manager Helenio Herrera, who claimed to have invented it independently of Rappan. The libero was to become a more elegant player, often a left half working with a back four that included an attacking wing-back or *tornante* – a template for defensive-minded Italian football for years to come.

The softly spoken and dignified Rappan combined football management with running a café, kept up a mystique-building silence about his techniques and stayed in the game until retirement age. An enthusiast for a European league, he helped set up the Intertoto competition with the Swiss pools company in 1961.

John Rattray – 'Captain of the Goff'

John Rattray, golfer and archer, born Blairgowrie, Scotland 22 September 1707, died 5 July 1771. Winner of Royal Company of Archers' silver bowl 1732, 35, 40, 42, silver arrow 1735, 44, Company of Gentlemen Golfers' silver club 1744, 45, 51.

Most people would probably guess that the Royal and Ancient in St Andrews created the rules of golf. In fact, the main author was most likely John Rattray, an Edinburgh surgeon who in 1744 signed them off for the first-ever open competition, which he won three times in a career interrupted by the 1745 Jacobite rebellion.

In March 1744, Rattray and the rest of the Company of Gentlemen Golfers petitioned the Edinburgh council to provide a silver club as a trophy, in line with the silver bowl and arrow that he won six times for his archery. The following month, Rattray beat nine competitors to become 'Captain of the Goff', and was charged with keeping up the course and settling disputes. He won again the following year, before being swept up in volunteering for Bonnie Prince Charlie's 1745 rebellion. He accompanied the invading army south to Derby, then retreated to Culloden, where he surrendered before spending time in prison and being released in an amnesty. (That fellow club member Duncan Forbes was Lord President of the Court of Session probably did him no harm.) Rattray won again in 1751 but by 1759 his playing days were over and he described himself as a 'cripple', though he carried on his doctoring for another seven years.

As an Episcopalian, John Rattray's burial went unrecorded and even his written rules were lost until they were rediscovered in 1937. Although a small monument was put up to him in 1984, the 13 rules themselves are his greatest legacy, establishing most of the basic principles of the game. As late as 1888, it was stated that they were really all you needed to know.

Of the rules, one was purely 'local', relating to the in-bounds area on the five-hole Leith links. The first two seem oddest today. In the days before separate greens and teeing areas, they required teeing off within a club's length of the previous hole, while tees of earth or sand had to be placed 'on the ground' – i.e. not at height, a principle that remains in force. On the crowded and messy common land, Rattray's rules dealt with obstacles and outside interference and are also roughly those we use today. Broken clubs were commonplace, so the rules dealt with them and also defined what constituted a stroke. Split balls were also part of the challenge. Players had to struggle on with them, and even today, one still can't change balls during a hole or (sometimes) during a round. Two soggy balls lying together in a rut or hole were another common occurrence on the Leith links, leading to the principle of playing 'furthest first' and removing a ball lying within six inches of another. Rules for lost balls and against 'marking the green' (i.e. treading down obstacles) are also similar to today's and there was a dropped-stroke penalty for a ball in water or 'wattery filth'. The principle of going for the hole rather than your opponent's ball is also spelt out. A major difference is that one could usually pick up and re-tee a shot at the cost of a stroke.

Rattray's 1744 rules lasted for 14 years and were copied word for word by the St Andrews golfers when they set up their club – although they altered one of them to take account of their drier conditions. As rival clubs set up, they made their own rules and in 1807 a dispute with the Bruntsfield Club over the 'stymie' or blocking shot was so acrimonious that two years of vicious correspondence was ordered to be burnt.

Rattray's club – later the Honourable Company of Edinburgh Golfers – became troubled by crowding on the Leith links and actually closed between 1820 and 1836, before moving to Musselburgh and then Muirfield. As a result, by the mid-19th century they had lost pre-eminence to the R&A. The St Andrews club was formally recognised as the rule-making body in 1897, although their international status was only confirmed in 1919 – a quarter of a century after the US Golf Association formed.

Today's golf rules, definitions, subsections and cases histories could – and do – fill a book, but the 'Captain of the Goff' had done most of the job in half a page.

Willie Renshaw

William Charles Renshaw, tennis player, born Leamington Spa 3 January 1861, died 12 August 1902. Wimbledon singles champion 1881, 82, 83, 84, 85, 86, 89, doubles champion 1880, 81, 84, 85, 86, 88, 89. International Tennis Hall of Fame 1983.

With his twin brother Ernest, Willie Renshaw won 14 Wimbledon titles, invented the smash and is often credited as the father of the modern game.

The tennis Renshaw first encountered at Wimbledon in 1879 was a well-mannered pat-a-cake, usually played from the baseline with soft and irregularly bouncing balls. The main aim was simply to return the ball after the bounce, and rallies of 80 shots were not unknown. William and his brother took this game by the scruff of the neck and turned it into modern tennis. Both played hard, flat and fast, replacing the wristy flicks of rackets and the heavy cuts of real tennis with a new, more aggressive style that by 1885 was drawing 3,500 spectators to Worple Road.

By far the Renshaws' most dramatic tactic was the smash, defeating the lob by taking it early, but they also volleyed more aggressively than ever before. Willie was the first to routinely serve overarm, with lots of kick or twist to make returns difficult. In his ground strokes he used a slight undercut to make the ball skid on the surface with a fast low hop that left his opponent with little time to react. The result was that he won the 1881 championship 6–0, 6–1, 6–1, the most crushing victory for over 50 years, and went on to win the next five championships (as champion he went straight through to the final). After Willie lost in 1887, Ernest won his sole singles title the following year and Willie won the year after that, eventually winning the Wimbledon trophy outright. After being drawn against each other in 1893, Willie dropped out in favour of his brother in what was to be their final appearance. After his death, the Wimbledon men's singles winner was also presented with a commemorative Renshaw Cup.

Carlos Ribagorda

Carlos Ribagorda, basketballer, born Spain 1974.

No player has had a greater impact on disability sport than Spanish basketballer and journalist Carlos Ribagorda, whose revelations about the Sydney 2000 Paralympics changed the games for good.

On 31 October 2000, Ribagorda, a quietly spoken member of Spain's gold-winning Paralympic basketball squad, flew back to Madrid with his victorious team-mates after an unusually high-tempo 87–63 win over Russia in the final. At the airport the team, who had won in the intellectual disability (ID) section, were seen to be behaving rather strangely. Many had grown beards, while others wore sunglasses or hid behind caps and hats.

There was already a suspicion that two of the players exceeded the 75 IQ limit set by the International Sports Federation for Persons with an Intellectual Disability (INAS-FID). Before the games, the team had flown out separately from the main body of physically disabled athletes and two of them had already been identified by a local paper as having no significant handicap. However, it was Ribagorda's low-key report in the magazine *Capital* that blew the doors off.

In his article, Ribagorda revealed that he had gone undercover to expose the use of non-disabled 'ringers' in ID games. He had joined the squad the year before, when it had already won a world championship with four non-disabled squad members – after which coach Jordi Clares resigned in protest. For Sydney, a total of ten non-disabled basketballers were selected. Not only were there no tests of intellectual ability, but it was made clear to these men, who included a lawyer and an engineer, that their objective was to win medals and gain grants. They were assured that there was no testing and no chance of being rumbled. All but Ribagorda were happy to play along, enjoying the trip and slowing the tempo of their play to avoid detection. Most shunned the two genuine ID players on the squad – Juan Pareja and Ramon Torres. During the games, Ribagorda soon came to suspect that the problems extended well beyond Spanish basketball. He noted that all four of the

ID teams he played against seemed to be fielding non-disabled athletes, while the Spanish squad included non-disabled competitors in track and field and table tennis, as well as two swimmers.

After the article came out, Fernando Martin Vicente, the high-rolling president of FEDDI, the Spanish federation for disability sports, denounced Ribagorda's exposé as 'lies' from 'a handicapped person who had gone mad', but the truth was out and Vicente was expelled from the Spanish and International Paralympic Committees before quitting as president of INAS-FID. During the court case that followed, it became clear how open the system was to abuse. One American claimed that dyslexia was seen as sufficient grounds for inclusion in ID teams.

Since January 2001, the International Paralympic Committee has restricted its games to athletes with physical disabilities. Pointing out that 69 per cent of Sydney's ID athletes came from countries with no proper verification process, the IPC suspended the category and it remains suspended until what they term a 'thorough, transparent and fair evaluation and verification system' is implemented. In response, the IOC has backed a Special Olympics for ID athletes robbed of their chance to compete.

Viv Richards – 'The Master Blaster'

Sir Isaac Vivian Alexander Richards, cricketer and footballer, born St John's, Antigua 7 March 1952. First-class career: Leeward Islands 1971–91, Somerset 1974–86, Queensland 1976–7, Glamorgan 1990–3; 507 matches, 36,212 runs (49.40). Test record 1974–91: 121 matches, 8,540 runs (50.23); 187 ODIs, 6,721 runs (47.00) (World Cup 1975). Wisden Cricketer of the Year 1977. Wisden Cricketer of the Century.

Like <u>W.G. Grace</u> a century before him, Viv Richards turned the tide against fast bowlers by taking them on and shattering their confidence, both ending and defining an era in the game.

One of three cricketing sons of a successful fast bowler, Viv Richards was also one of the first Antiguans to play Test cricket. He showed his ability early; at just 17 his disputed dismissal provoked a riot at a local match and a two-year suspension. With his boxer's shoulders, power and timing, the 23-year-old Richards's batting was one of the better things to emerge from the West Indies fairly disastrous 1975/6 tour of Australia. Despite receiving a crack on the jaw, he faced down both Dennis Lillee and Jeff Thomson and made good scores in the final two matches. After this, he would never again be on the losing side in a Test series. The following summer, he made two double centuries against England and, despite glandular fever, set a record for runs scored in a calendar year.

With all the usual shots, plus some new ones, Richards delighted both the purists and the lovers of big hits with his trademark shot through midwicket and mighty hooks. Like W.G. Grace, he defied ortho-doxy and set out to score from the off, setting records for the fastest Test and one-day centuries. Even a mishit might fly for a six and on one occasion he skied a ball so high that he had scored two runs before the wicketkeeper caught it. As captain of the West Indies during the 1980s he never lost a series – leading the only team of fast bowlers who hadn't been treated like medium-pacers by I.V.A. Richards. A bouncer limit and a change to the ball itself were needed to curb the team's successes and excesses, and Richards's 1991 retirement marked the beginning of the end for West Indian cricketing supremacy.

In county cricket, Richards helped turn Somerset from also-rans into the kings of the one-day game, winning both the Gillette Cup and John Player League in a single weekend. Proud of his race, he once jumped the barriers at Weston-super-Mare to tackle racists in the crowd and refused to join rebel tours of apartheid South Africa at any price. In World Series Cricket – 'some of the hardest, meanest cricket I've ever played' – he stood out among the newly helmeted batsmen by going bareheaded and relying on a hard stare and a ferocious hook.

The latter years of Viv Richards's career were successful but controversial. In 1986, he was sacked by Somerset, then languishing at the bottom of the championship table, who later made amends by naming some gates after him. His appeal against England's Rob Bailey at Barbados in 1990 and refusal to recall Dean Jones to the wicket the following year were worthy of W.G. at his least sporting.

Because he so obviously punched the ball (and once invited Australian captain Allan Border to duke it out behind the SCG), the 'Master Blaster' was often compared to heavyweight boxers like Floyd Patterson and 'Smokin' Joe Frazier. However, for his mastery of the game, flouting of convention, confidence, ruthless intelligence, power, principles and pride, the obvious comparison is to The Greatest himself. Which makes Sir Vivian Richards cricket's <u>Muhammad Ali</u>.

Jackie Robinson

Jack Roosevelt Robinson, second baseman, born Cairo, Georgia 31 January 1919, died 24 October 1972. Playing career: Kansas City Monarchs 1945, Montreal Royals 1946, Brooklyn Dodgers 1947–56 (National League Rookie of the Year 1947, MVP 1949, pennant winners 1947, 49, 52, 53, 55, 56, World Series 1955); 1,518 hits, 137 home runs (.311). Baseball Hall of Fame 1962.

Jackie Robinson, a talented all-round athlete and baseballer, made his major league debut for the Brooklyn Dodgers on 15 April 1947 and played for the 'Boys of Summer' for ten seasons, during which time his outstanding fielding and base-running took them to six pennants and one World Series win.

Except that that doesn't tell the story at all – Jackie Robinson was the first black major league player in 57 years and had to cope with extraordinary hopes and pressures. The son of a Georgia sharecropper, Robinson was a UCLA graduate who represented his college in baseball, basketball, football and track, and a US army lieutenant who had faced court martial on trumped-up charges after 'doing a Rosa Parks' and refusing to sit at the back of a bus. (This may have influenced President Truman's decision to integrate the US military in 1948.) After enduring the grind of playing for the Kansas City Monarchs in the Negro leagues, Robinson was selected by the Dodgers' general manager, Branch Rickey, for his Montreal Royals 'farm team'. Rickey had detected not just Robinson's sporting ability but also the 'guts not to fight back'. Attacked on the road but welcomed by the home fans, Robinson was a success, and backed by Commissioner Happy Chandler and National League president Ford Frick, Rickey moved him to the Dodgers. When the news was announced, Frick faced down the St Louis Cardinals who had threatened to strike, saying, 'I don't care if it wrecks the National League for five years. You cannot do this, because this is America.'

A week into his Dodgers career, thrown at by pitchers and spiked by runners, Robinson received such abuse from the notorious Phillies that it was said to have united his team-mates behind him – although only Dodgers captain Pee Wee Reese made any public gesture (a year later), and the most visible support came from Pirates star Hank

Greenberg who, as a Jewish player, had suffered similarly. Hate mail, kidnap threats, biased umpiring and deliberate spikings continued until Robinson emerged as 'Rookie of the Year' and the second most popular man in America after Bing Crosby. Despite this, there was still pressure not to select him. Dodgers manager Leo Durocher put the issue in clear terms: 'I do not care if the guy is yellow or black, or if he has stripes like a fuckin' zebra. I'm the manager of this team, and I say he plays. What's more, I say he can make us all rich. And if any of you cannot use the money, I will see that you are all traded.'

As his batting improved, Robinson became the Dodgers' best-paid player, with a film biography and a comic book featuring his exploits. On the road, the Dodgers overcame the colour bar at hotels and restaurants and opened the door for other black baseballers. During the 1950s, there were seven black Rookies of the Year, including fellow Hall of Famer Satchel Paige, but the American League was more resistant, with only six black players by 1960. Meanwhile, the Negro Leagues were ruined as the crowds left to see the stars play in the majors. The integration of other sports followed, as Robinson's UCLA team-mates Woody Strode and Kenny Washington played for the LA Rams, while in basketball the Celtics were the first to sign a black player, Charles Cooper, in 1950.

Although his powers were on the wane, Robinson won the 1955 World Series and quit to become a match analyst and vice-president of Chock Full O'Nuts Lunch Counters – the first black VP of any major company. By now, he was credited with changing both US sport and society and paving the way for white acceptance of the civil rights movement. Robinson became the first black Hall of Famer and founded an African-American bank and a company to build homes for low-income black families. As a columnist and TV presenter, he was also an active supporter of Dr Martin Luther King. Suffering from heart disease and diabetes, he never lived to see the first black baseball manager, as Frank Robinson (no relation) took over the Cleveland Indians two years after his death. Jackie received numerous honours, many posthumously, and the UCLA Bruins stadium is now named after him. On the 50th anniversary of his first game, his number 42 was retired across all teams. Ten years later, 200 pro ball players wore his number for the day.

Leigh Richmond Roose – 'Yr Ercwlff synfawr hwn' ('This wondrous Hercules') 'Gwr o Athrylith' ('Man of Genius')

Lance Corporal Leigh Richmond Roose MM, footballer, born Holt, North Wales 27 November 1877, died 7 October 1916. Playing career: Aberystwyth Town 1895–1900 (Welsh Cup 1900), Druids 1900, London Welsh 1900–1, Stoke City 1901–4, Everton 1904–5, Stoke City 1905–7, Sunderland 1908–10, Celtic 1910, Port Vale 1910, Huddersfield Town 1910–11, Aston Villa 1911, Woolwich Arsenal 1911–12; Wales 1900–11, 24 caps (Home International champions 1907).

Once rated the best goalkeeper on earth by the *Daily Mail*, Leigh Richmond Roose was directly responsible for the 1912 change to Law 8, which limited goalkeepers to handling in their own penalty area, rather than anywhere in their own half.

The tall and robust Roose made his debut against professional opposition in 1895 and soon distinguished himself with his daring and courage, being chaired off the field after Aberystwyth Town's 1900 Welsh Cup triumph. Supposedly able to alter his dives in flight, Roose had fast reflexes and sharp eyes beneath his trademark twin-peaked cap, never conceding more than two goals in a game. Even by the standards of the day, he was ultra-physical, shoulder-charging Irish international Harry O'Reilly so violently that he was knocked unconscious. Roose's sweeper-style runs to the halfway line and monstrous kicks were as famous as they were unusual, and during one international he actually 'doubled up' for a missing full back.

A renowned man-about-town and snazzy dresser off the pitch, Roose once had a fling with Marie Lloyd and was volatile and entertaining, playing to the crowd and performing gymnastics on the crossbar during lulls in play. Almost as likely to punch the player as the ball, he was suspended for two weeks for laying out a Sunderland director and also offended the England selectors with his ripe language. An irresistible comparison is with Liverpool's keeper Bruce Grobbelaar – especially as Roose, like Grobbelaar, used 'wobbly legs' to put off a penalty taker when playing for Everton against Manchester City. Another bit of kiddology was a fake bandaged hand before the 1909 international against Ireland.

As an amateur, Roose played for expenses only, although these could be steep, and he is believed to have billed Stoke for £31 for a special train to take him to a match. Usually, he wore his old green and black Aberystwyth jersey and a pair of unwashed shorts which, to quote March 1904's *Bolton Cricket and Football Field*, 'carried about them the marks of many a thrilling encounter'.

In World War I, Roose served first as a doctor on the Western Front and at Gallipoli. Then, despite being officer class and having seen the horrors of war at first hand, the 39-year-old Roose enlisted in the Royal Welch Fusiliers as a private and won the Military Medal after his first action at the Battle of Pozières. The location and manner of Roose's death in the Battle of the Somme is uncertain – most likely near Thiepval, a fortified village that lay before three German redoubts. His body was never recovered but his name, misspelt 'Rouse', can be seen on the Thiepval Memorial to the Missing.

Sir Frederick Wall credited Roose with 'the eccentricity of genius'. His own written verdict was that 'A good goalkeeper, like a poet, is born not made.'

Admiral Rous

Vice Admiral the Honourable Henry John Rous MP, racing trainer, breeder and administrator, born Wangford, Suffolk 23 January 1795, died 19 June 1877. Public handicapper 1855–77. Jockey Club steward 1838–77.

Today horse racing still works to a handicapping system first devised over 150 years ago by Admiral Henry Rous.

Rous, the second son of the 1st Earl of Stradbroke, had to go out and seek his fortune rather than stay home and inherit it, and opted for the navy at the age of 13, winning medals for various actions, expeditions and adventures. His most notable was his last in 1834 when, having run the 36-gun frigate *Pique* aground off Labrador, Rous brought her home across the Atlantic despite having lost her keel, rudder, pumps and most of her foremast and taking in 23 inches of water an hour.

After being acquitted by the court martial, Rous stayed on dry land and was eventually promoted to admiral in 1846. He had already imported horses and organised regattas when stationed in Australia, and from 1838 became a Jockey Club steward as well as managing the Duke of Bedford's Newmarket stables. Rous was to become more famous for his energy and integrity than the horses he trained, and as senior steward he would track horses across the Heath with his telescope, roaring at any non-triers.

In 1850, Rous published his masterpiece, *The Laws and Practice of Horse Racing*, bringing some clear thinking to handicapping, which until then had been a black art. Rous's weight-for-age system put aside old ideas based on the size of the horse and grasped the fundamental connections between weight, age and distance so that, for example, a three-year-old racing a two-year-old over five furlongs in the second half of March should concede 31 lb. As Public Handicapper, Rous based his assessments on 'observation, price, stable and hearsay'. His masterpiece was the 1857 Cesarewitch, a tie between El Hakim, Prioress and Queen Bess.

Under Rous's energetic reign, the Rules of Racing were reissued in 1858, 1861 and 1871 and jockeys were forbidden to bet. He also built up the Jockey Club's reserves so that they could invest in more land around Newmarket and were able to seize complete control of British racing in the years after his death. Rous is buried in Kensal Green cemetery and was commemorated by a Memorial Stakes.

Sir Stanley Rous

Sir Stanley Ford Rous CBE, footballer, referee and administrator, born Mutford, Suffolk 25 April 1895, died 18 July 1986. FA secretary 1934–61. Co-founder and vice-president UEFA, FIFA president 1961–74, honorary president FIFA 1974–86, life president QPR.

The rules of football, youth teams, the penalty arc and sports centres are just four of the achievements that can be traced back to the hyper-active 6 feet 3 inch tall Sir Stanley Rous, for nearly forty years the ruler of first British, and then international football.

As a boy of 15, Rous played in goal, organised a local side and regu-larly cycled 50 miles with two other lads on the back of his bike to watch Norwich City. He kept up this organising ability and incredible energy throughout his life. As well as running the FA and then FIFA, he was a local councillor, a magistrate, an organiser of the Duke of Edinburgh Award Scheme, a patron of Homes for the Blind, an organ-iser of the 1948 Olympics and a founder of the Central Council of Physical Recreation – which helped bring about the creation of public sports centres, the Sports Council and specialist centres such as Crystal Palace, Bisham Abbey and Lilleshall.

After a wrist injury from a Turkish shell while serving in Palestine, Rous switched from amateur goalkeeping to refereeing while also working as a schoolmaster in Watford. All four influences – goalkeeping, mili-tary service, refereeing and schoolmastering – would inform his approach to football. As a keeper he had never even been taught to narrow the angle and became a convert to coaching, which at the time was regarded with suspicion in British football. Teaching convinced him that junior football was the bedrock of the game, at a time when it was so badly taught that many schools were drifting to rugby. Military service strength-ened his belief in discipline, loyalty and sportsmanship and refereeing confirmed the need for control and authority. From 1927 it also exposed him to international soccer. Most Brits simply ignored the game over-seas, and the FA had been in and out of FIFA like a fiddler's elbow, leaving whenever it didn't like its decisions – whether over playing the defeated powers, recognising Eire or allowing broken-time payments to amateurs. Rous, who had a French wife, studied the game abroad and imported new ideas such as the diagonal refereeing system that he had seen in use in Belgium. Here the referee and linesmen worked as a team, with the ref patrolling a diagonal strip, while the linesmen manned the two stretches of line furthest from him. Despite opposition from the League, who threatened to remove him from their referees list, Rous demonstrated the system at the 1934 FA Cup final and it soon became standard.

In 1934, Rous became the FA's sixth secretary – beating the League's Fred Howarth, which helped ensure poor relations between the two men thereafter. The FA that Rous had taken over was a micro-bureaucracy of five employees with a total wage bill of £2,000. Its aged president Charles Clegg was deaf and outgoing secretary Frederick Wall, who had eked out his salary by making the sandwiches for FA meetings, still wore a top hat and frock coat to matches. On retiring, Wall refused to shake Rous's hand. His handover briefing was: 'The job's straightforward. You can read up the files. There's nothing more I can tell you.'

At the FA, Rous produced *First Steps in Playing Football*, the first coaching manual the organisation had managed to create in 65 years, and continued to adopt new ideas such as the Italian system of a penalty arc to keep players back from the spot and boards showing substitutes, which he had seen in use at a Malaysian youth tournament. In 1938, Rous rewrote the flowery and illogically presented rules of the game. His new rules, which remain largely intact today, also helped the FA to settle refereeing disputes – in the past their lack of helpfulness had been legendary. Having been injured at the dangerously overcrowded 1923 FA Cup final, he wrote another guide to staging the FA Cup, and would later write a similar handbook for the 1966 World Cup that even detailed the six different types of souvenir on offer. Though it remained a low priority in British football, Rous's FA actually closed a stadium on safety grounds. Ironically, this was The Nest, the home of Norwich City. Having refereed the first match to be televised in Italy in 1933, Rous overcame the FA's reluctance to broadcast by pandering to the egos of FA president William Pickford and councillor Charles Sutcliffe, encouraging them to broadcast 'talks' on the BBC.

Though not in FIFA, England continued to play internationals, partly in the hope that sport would break down barriers between nations. This policy of playing potential enemies led to a lasting change in 1936, when a misunderstanding about team numbers before a match against Germany led to Mrs Rowland, the FA's housekeeper, being asked to sew numbers onto both team's jerseys – an idea which the League had resisted in domestic football, but which soon became standard. In his memoirs, Rous claimed that his instruction to England's players to do a Nazi salute when they played Germany in 1938 was simply to keep the crowd happy, and when Aston Villa failed to do so before playing a combined German-Austrian team, they were booed throughout the game. In wartime Rous set up a system for national sport, arranged a 15,000 limit on crowds in the interest of safety and organised a mass of charity matches and events, buying up the prizes cheaply from bomb-damaged shops and raising £3 million for the Red Cross. In 1940 he temporarily lifted the FA's ban on Sunday football in the interests of national morale and fitness. His work was rewarded with a knighthood in 1949.

Rous's first great post-war success was to get the home nations back into FIFA and able to win or host a World Cup. He was also one of the first to bring Germany back into international football, through youth sides that were untainted by the Nazi past, and this helped establish the idea of under-23 and youth teams. The first such tournament was held in 1947 and the idea soon spread to other sports. In 1955, Rous also began promoting the Inter-Cities Fairs Cup and became an enthusiast for a European league – which also set him against the Football League. The first contest took three years to complete, but soon became more streamlined and began attracting club sides rather than strange citywide amalgams of teams. By now Gabriel Hanot of *L'Equipe* had come up with the idea of a midweek Champion Clubs' Cup and this was taken over by UEFA, which, despite the reluctance of FIFA president Jules Rimet, Rous helped form as a counterweight to the growing number of non-European footballing nations. After Howarth's Football League discouraged Chelsea from entering the first tournament in 1956, Rous, who had recommended Manchester United's manager Matt Busby as a manager for both the Army and Olympic teams, encouraged him to ignore the League and enter anyway.

The eventual success of the Fairs Cup and UEFA's takeover of Hanot's Champion Clubs' Cup raised fears of a European League in the minds of the Football League, who had missed their opportunity to take charge.

Most within the League were quite convinced that Rous wanted to take them over too, and when he invited League members to visit the 1958 Sweden World Cup and to join the FA's Management Committee, this only increased their dark suspicions. Rows continued over the League's reluctance to release players for international duty or home internationals. One irony was that some of the fixture congestion that caused the problems was the result of the League Cup – an idea first suggested by Rous as a consolation prize for teams out of the FA Cup. Another source of disagreement was over the plan for a National Pools, which Rous and Wembley owner Sir Arthur Elvin had come up with in 1947. This could have funded ground and coaching improvements throughout sport, but was rejected by the FA, who had set their faces against 'tainted money' back in 1908 and saw no reason to change their minds. Naturally, Howarth at the League also said no. Despite these knock-backs, Rous remained a progressive within the English game, pushing for a winter break, artificial pitches where necessary and the use of TV replays to judge contested goals. All were opposed by the ever-suspicious League.

At international level, Rous's lieutenant and England's first director of coaching, Walter Winterbottom, also became the first national manager, though he remained shackled by a ridiculous selection system, which Rous was unable to replace. At best, the FA selectors bickered and fought as they argued for the team position by position – usually destroying any continuity, team spirit or possibility of tactical innovation. At worst, a single selector such as ex-fish merchant Arthur Drewry could select the entire team which lost to the US in 1950. The selectors wouldn't give up their power to hire and fire until Winterbottom quit and Alf Ramsey insisted on full control. (Drewry also ended the career of inside forward Eddie Bailey, after he discovered him mimicking him.) Rous repeatedly warned that British football was falling behind and was proved right in 1953 when the team was dismembered by Ferenc Puskás's Hungary.

From 1961 Rous was president of FIFA, helping to transform another poverty-stricken micro-bureaucracy by adding more continental associations in the UEFA mould and setting up committees to run the international game – including one that began the first crude and ineffective drug testing, introduced at the 1966 World Cup. The awarding of this tournament to England was testimony to Rous's popularity within FIFA at the time. After England's quarter-final bust-up with Argentina, Rous encouraged chief referee Ken Aston's idea of red and yellow cards to eliminate misunderstandings on the pitch. These were first used at the 1968 Olympics and 1970 World Cup, though Rous felt they were unnecessary in domestic football. He was also an enthusiast for soccer in the US, ever hopeful that the game would finally break through.

With the dismantling of empires, the numbers of nations in FIFA rose fast and, thanks to the Cold War, South African apartheid, the creation of Israel and the revolution in China, political and ideological arguments increased within football. Rous, already at retirement age, stuck to the FA policy of 'keeping sport out of politics' by recognising federations rather than nations. Accordingly, China was refused admittance because it insisted that Taiwan be removed from FIFA. Though South Africa had been suspended from the African Cup of Nations since 1957 and from FIFA in 1961, Rous was reluctant to throw out the wartime allies who had funded Bisham Abbey. Ignoring the facts of apartheid, his 'investigative' commission spoke only to those sporting organisations that supported the status quo and dismissed others as 'communists' who 'desired to hinder and act contrary to government policy' – which of course they did. Having cheerily pointed out that some non-white stadiums were as good as white-only ones, he even managed to get the FIFA ban lifted for a year, but his patronising approach towards the 'younger associations' eroded support for him, especially when the 1966 World Cup finals he organised offered the whole of Africa and Asia just one place. This caused Kwame Nkrumah's Ghana to lead a boycott of the finals. As late as 1973, Rous was trying to get approval (through a postal ballot) of a proposed multiracial sports event in South Africa.

During the late 1960s and early 1970s, Rous continued his schoolmasterly tickings-off about corruption, bribery, poor refereeing and bad crowd control. In 1974, Russia refused to play a World Cup qualifier in Chile, where a democratically elected government had been overthrown in a CIA-backed coup. To make matters worse, the proposed venue was the National Stadium where music had been played at full volume to cover the screams as Pinochet's torturers went about their work. (A favourite wheeze was to torture couples in front of each other to maximise their agony.) Rous's commission managed to miss all the evidence. The idea of playing in another stadium came too late and Rous lost support from the Russians and their allies. The East Germans got another ticking-off when they compared staging the event to having a kickabout in Dachau.

In 1974, although hoping for another two-year term, Rous was replaced by <u>João Havelange</u>, who though he himself came from a repressive regime, represented the non Anglo-Saxon world and, more tellingly, the promise of extra cash. Money had always been one of Rous's blind spots. Living 'over the shop' at Lancaster Gate, he carried out his reforms on a shoestring budget and never put in for a pay rise or copyrighted his laws. Naturally, he had little sympathy for players such as England's Neil Franklin, who wanted better pay, and suspended him for bringing the game into disrepute after he played for a club in Colombia. Never an entrepreneur, as late as 1968 a single Carnaby Street shop could buy a quarter of the hoardings at the World Cup. Domestically, relations with <u>Alan Hardaker's</u> Football League worsened dramatically after the FA volunteered to pay tax, rather than use its income to fund ground improvements for struggling clubs. The FA also overruled the more experienced League representatives to strike a very poor deal on TV rights. For six months, neither Hardaker nor Rous would speak to the other.

Rous's defeat by Havelange was a crucial moment in sporting history, as FIFA became a commercial and political organisation rather than a purely sporting one, an example which other sports and the Olympics itself would soon follow. The astute Havelange offered Rous the honorary presidency of FIFA, which he accepted, plus a generous pension and the renaming of the World Cup trophy after him. Rous, who had worked voluntarily for FIFA and didn't approve of trophies being named after individuals, turned down both. The English-Scottish-Latin American Rous Cup was short-lived and today his main memorial is the Rous Stand at Watford.

Arthur Rowe

Arthur Sydney Rowe, centre half, born Tottenham 1 September 1906, died 5 November 1993. Playing career: Spurs 1929–38 (201 games), England 1933, 1 cap. Managerial career: Chelmsford City 1940–9, Tottenham Hotspur 1949–55 (Division Two champions 1950, Division One champions 1951), Crystal Palace 1960–2, 1966.

As manager of Spurs, Arthur Rowe sent shock waves through British football with a new playing style that secured two consecutive championships.

Rowe was Tottenham through and through, a local boy who honed his passing skills against walls and kerbs and rose through Spurs' Northfleet nursery club to become an attacking centre half. Even his one and only international cap was at White Hart Lane, and he never lost his north London accent or his penchant for a pithy phrase, defining peripheral vision as 'seeing out of your arse'.

Inspired by the speedy passing of Huddersfield's Clem Stephenson, who was never caught in possession, and the positional play of Spurs' manager Peter McWilliam, Rowe – who already doubted the value and accuracy of the 30-yard pass – started wondering if a whole team could interpass that well. In 1939, he was forced to retire due to a cartilage injury, but his coaching ability was immediately recognised. Only the war stopped him fulfilling a three-year appointment as Hungary's coach and instead he worked with Matt Busby's Army team, before steering Chelmsford City to the Southern League and Cup double. Here, he encouraged his players to 'make it simple, make it accurate, make it quick'. One significant tactic was overlapping, with the full back advancing up the field to pass directly to the winger.

Recruited by Tottenham, Rowe hired smooth passers such as <u>Alf Ramsey</u>, demonstrating with a stopwatch how faster passing could release players into space. The new tactic did away with the old notion of 'beating your man' and took Division Two by storm. Spurs attracted the biggest crowds in the league as they won the championship by nine points, unbeaten in 22 matches. The top division was equally unprepared as the team achieved their first championship the following season, scoring more goals and conceding fewer than any other side. A second place and an FA Cup semi-final followed, but the 'push and run' or 'give it and go' tactic demanded high levels of fitness, and as the team aged, their results suffered. The stress caused Rowe to have a breakdown in 1954, though Spurs were saved from relegation by the recruitment of Danny Blanchflower.

Using tactics similar to Rowe's, Spurs' Yorkshire-born wing-half Bill Nicholson would lead the side to the first League and FA Cup double in 1961. After a spell scouting for West Brom, Rowe returned as manager of Crystal Palace from 1960 to 1962 and briefly in 1966, staying on as an assistant manager as the club reached the top division for the first time.

Clive Rowlands

Clive Rowlands, rugby player, coach and administrator, born Upper Cwmtwrch 14 May 1938. Playing career: Abercrave, Pontypool, Llanelli, Swansea; Wales 1963–5, 14 caps (all as captain). National coach 1968–74. Lions tour manager 1989. Wales manager 1987. WRU president 1989.

During the early 1970s, it was Wales's youngest-ever coach Clive Rowlands whose national squad sessions, tactical nous and appeals to the *calon* (heart) of his players helped make their brand of attacking rugby supreme in the northern hemisphere. Not only did Wales dominate the Home Nations Championship, but they gave the game a huge lift after years in the doldrums and made up the core of the Lions sides that defeated the two southern-hemisphere giants on their home turf.

The delightful irony is that the thrilling play inspired by Clive Rowlands the Welsh coach might not have happened so soon without the ultra-defensive play of Clive Rowlands the Welsh captain and scrum half. He was already regarded as a negative choice by the press, when in 1963 he and his opposite number Stan Coughtrie of Scotland 'touched bottom', kicking the ball into touch a total of 111 times as Wales won a waterlogged match through line-out dominance alone. (That's one line-out per 45 *seconds*.) 'Completely futile' and 'cynical' read one match report. It was a game that typified the low-scoring, no-thrills play encouraged by unrestricted kicking to touch. 'He had six signals and they all meant kick,' said one spectator, and Rowlands's fellow halfback Dave Watkins was supposed to have passed the ball just five times. It was a winning tactic, but it threw the problems of the game into sharp relief. As Spurs manager Bill Nicholson pointed out, 'There has to be something wrong with a game where you seek to make progress by kicking the ball off the field.' To reinforce the message, the following weekend's England v Ireland match was a scoreless draw.

After this numbing display, rugby did finally change its rules, opening up the game by making the hindmost foot in the scrum the offside line and keeping all players, bar the scrum half, ten yards back from line-outs. Kicking direct into touch outside the 25-yard line was also eventually penalised. Some reckoned that skills such as Rowlands's over-the-shoulder 'box kick' were diminished without the pressure of the other side breathing down your neck, but the result was more open play and more tries. In particular, the full back was freed to adopt a more attacking role – one typified by Wales's own ultra-competitive J.P.R. Williams. By 1971, with the new rules in place – plus new soft boots that allowed players to curve the ball rather than toe-poke it – a rugby renaissance was under way. When Rowlands's Wales played at Murrayfield, the result was a 19–18 thriller, with John Taylor scoring the 'greatest conversion since St Paul'.

'Babe' Ruth – 'The Sultan of Swat'

George Herman Ruth Jnr, baseball outfielder and pitcher, born Baltimore 6 February 1895, died 16 August 1948. Playing record: Baltimore Orioles 1914, Boston Red Sox 1914–19 (World Series 1915, 16, 18), New York Yankees 1920–34 (World Series 1923, 27, 28, 32, All-Star player 1933, 34). 714 home runs, 2,217 RBI (.342). Assistant manager Boston Braves 1935, assistant coach Boston Dodgers 1938. Baseball Hall of Fame 1936.

'Sixty! Count 'em – sixty! Let's see some son of a bitch beat that!' So said 'Jidge' Ruth in 1927 after setting a home-run record that would last until 1961.

Rated the third greatest American athlete ever by ESPN (after Muhammad Ali and Michael Jordan) and a holder of over 40 batting and pitching records, 'Babe' Ruth changed America's national game for ever, turning it from the fast, pitching-dominated 'inside game' to the batting-dominated 'power game' we know today.

Most famous today for his 'Ruthian' big hitting, the Babe first came to prominence as a pitcher. Recruited straight out of reform school by local side the Orioles, he was fascinated by trains, elevators and big breakfasts – none of which he had seen before – and almost decapitated himself while playing with some lift controls. Despite the 'Babe' tag, he wasn't overawed on the pitch or off it, referring to all his teammates as 'kid'. At Boston his fastball set records for the most scoreless innings, but after pitching the team to World Series victory in 1916 he gradually pitched less and less. As a left-hander, like master batter Ty Cobb, he was always a couple of steps closer to first base, but his style was very different. Other batsmen held the bat high, aiming for maximum control and clever placement to 'hit them where they [the opposition] ain't', but Ruth gripped the knob of the bat, pivoted from his ankles, hit hard and followed through. Only Jim Thorpe hit as far as he did. Until then home runs had been regarded as an occasional oddity and Frank 'Home Run' Baker won his nickname with just 12 in a season, but by 1919 the Bambino had slugged 29.

Short of both cash and patience, Boston owner and showman Harry Frazee sold Ruth to the Yankees for $125,000, having tired of Ruth's umpire punching, horseplay, $10,000 salary and occasional side trips to play in better-paying fixtures. After this, the 'Curse of the Bambino' would be blamed for the Red Sox's 85-year wait for another World Series title.

In New York, Ruth made a slow start, playing for a team that had never won a divisional championship, but he hit 54 homers in 1920 – three times more than his nearest rival and more than entire teams. The following season's 59 was twice his nearest rival and might have been 100+ under modern batting conditions. Eventually, batters such as Yankees team-mate Lou 'Iron Horse' Gehrig would close the gap, thanks in part to the accidental death of Cleveland Indians shortstop Ray Chapman, which led to a brighter, safer and livelier ball and the banning of the unpredictable 'spitball' pitch.

Coming after the bribery scandal surrounding Chick Gandil's White Sox, Ruth became a popular hero, admired and envied for his big hits, natural ebullience and high living, so that many of his more lurid exploits were hushed up. Among a host of huge shots, one at Navin Field in Detroit was accurately measured as at least 575 feet. The Sultan of Swat set records for pay (higher than the President) and endorsed every-thing from notebooks to cars, appearing on screen, on the radio and lending his name to ghosted newspaper columns written by his agent Christy Walsh. This was despite being stripped of the Yankees' captaincy in 1922 for throwing dirt at umpires and chasing hecklers into the stands. Off the pitch, commissioner Kenesaw Mountain Landis suspended him for six weeks for an 'illegal' exhibition tour.

Growing crowds enabled the Yankees to build the biggest ballpark in the US, the 60,000-capacity, $2.5 million Yankee Stadium, which opened in 1923, and they would come to dominate the game, with 20 champion-ships in 44 years, eventually driving local rivals the Giants and the Dodgers to the West Coast.

In the mid-1920s Ruth's health suffered as high living, fluctuating weight and (probably) gonorrhoea caught up with him, but he bounced back in 1927 to set a home-run record as part of the 'Murderers' Row' team that included Gehrig and infielder Tony Lazzeri and averaged .307 across the batting line-up. In the early 1930s, Ruth's figures declined with age, though he compensated with a lighter bat and cemented his fame with the legendary 'called shot'. Playing against the Cubs in the 1932 World Series, he was believed to have deliberately allowed two strikes and then indicated where the following home-run would go. In 1933 and 1934, he was still good enough to make the first two All-Star games, and his tour of Japan helped establish the sport in that country, with a professional league forming two years later.

Only the Boston Braves were bold enough to offer the unreliable Ruth a player-coach position in the 1935 season and he rewarded them with the third worst season of all time. Though now so slow that three Braves pitchers refused to play with him in the team, he scored his last homer five days before he quit as a player, clearing the double-decker stand at Pittsburgh's Forbes Field for the first and only time.

Ruth was one of the first into the Hall of Fame and lived to set up a foundation for disadvantaged children like he had been. (Only one of his seven siblings had survived infancy.) After contracting a rare cancer, he became one of the first chemotherapy patients and just lived to see his own 1948 biopic.

Many of Ruth's records have been whittled away since, but the players who have done so have often been compared unfavourably with the Babe. His 'scoreless innings' records as a pitcher remain intact, as do his slugging percentage (0.690) and record of getting 'on base plus slugging'. To be both a great pitcher and a great batsman remains a unique achievement and by changing the whole character of the game he made a bigger impact on baseball than any player before or since. Yankee Stadium, 'The House that Ruth Built', lasted until 2008.

Samuel Ryder

Samuel Ryder, golfer, businessman and philanthropist, born Preston 24 March 1858, died 2 January 1936. Captain Verulam Golf Club 1911, 26, 27. Captain Stratford upon Avon Golf Club 1929, 30.

Samuel Ryder, a seed merchant with a straggly moustache, had two great ideas in his life. The first was to sell his seeds in standard penny packets. His father sold in bulk to the wealthy and could see no merit in the idea, but Sam moved to St Albans, with its good rail connections, and began mailing seed catalogues and packets, sending them out on Fridays so that the working men who bought them could be ready to sow them on their Saturday afternoons off. The success of this venture led to Ryder ruining his health through overwork, until a chance invitation to play golf led to a new passion. Starting at the age of 50, but with the aid of full-time tutor Abe Mitchell, he eventually got down to a single-figure handicap.

Sam's next great idea was that of a Britain v America professional golf challenge, which can be traced back to 1921, when the *Glasgow Herald* sponsored a match before the Open. (In Toledo, Ohio, Sylvanus Jermain, president of the Inverness Club, tried to promote a similar venture.) Ryder was sympathetic to the pros, and after sponsoring a tournament with a generous £5 allowance for all who entered, he backed Mitchell and a partner against two US golfers over 72 holes. After this, he held a 'small friendly lunch party' before the 1926 British Open, where he and US captain Walter Hagen sat down and developed the idea of a biennial contest. The following year, aged 70, Ryder and the Stock Exchange Golf Society sponsored a team that travelled to the US, minus the intended captain Mitchell, who was suffering from appendicitis. With him Sam took a new £250 gold trophy, which weighed four pounds and stood 17 inches tall. The British team suffered a stormy crossing and exhaustion plus lavish US hospitality contributed to a crushing 9½–2½ defeat – which naturally made the Americans very enthusiastic about the contest. Next time out, the Brits won a freezing 1929 return match, which encouraged them to think that the trophy was naturally theirs. Ryder would live to see a further British victory in 1933, with crowds of 15,000 and royalty in attendance.

Samuel Ryder died of pneumonia in 1936, having created a trust to ensure that the Ryder Cup would continue, and was buried at Hatfield Road Cemetery with his 5-iron. Though he could have chosen to put himself on top of the cup, he chose Abe Mitchell, who declared that it was 'more distinction than I could ever earn'.

Jarno Saarinen

Jarno Karl Keimo Saarinen, motorcyclist, born Turku, Finland 11 December 1945, died 20 May 1973. World Champion 250 cc 1972; 46 Grands Prix, 15 wins.

Like Todd Sloan in flat racing and Federico Caprilli in showjumping, motorcyclist Jarno Saarinen took a riding style that everyone accepted as the best possible and showed that it could be improved.

In the case of Saarinen's sport, it was believed that both man and bike should be cranked over at the corners. However, Saarinen, a mechanical engineer who had competed in ice racing in his native Finland, realised that if the rider 'hung off' the bike it would stay more upright and enjoy better traction. He used his new style – later perfected by Kenny Roberts – to win 15 Grands Prix between 1970 and 1973 and give Giacomo Agostini a scare.

Saarinen died at Monza after an inescapable multiple crash in which Renzo Pasolini, who hit a spillage on the track left over from a previous race, also perished. After this his Yamaha team would withdraw from the sport for a year while they, Suzuki and MV Agusta campaigned for better conditions. A further fatal accident happened at the same spot just 40 days later and led to Monza being closed to bike racing for eight years.

Today Saarinen's style is standard. An Italian fan club still exists and there is a cohort of Jarnos named in his honour – notably F1 driver Jarno Trulli.

Arrigo Sacchi

Arrigo Sacchi, footballer and coach, born Fusignano, Italy 1 April 1946. Playing career: Fusignano CF 1964–77, Bellaria 1977–9. Teams coached and managed: Parma 1985–7, 2001, AC Milan 1987–91, 96–7 (league champions 1988, Super Cup 1989, European Cup 1989, 90), Italy 1991–6, Atlético Madrid 1998–9. Director of football Real Madrid 2004–5.

'A jockey doesn't have to be a horse,' said Arrigo Sacchi and the sharp-suited man in the big sunspecs certainly proved it. After an utterly obscure amateur playing career, Sacchi led AC Milan to back-to-back European Cups and came up with what some – particularly Signor Arrigo Sacchi – would argue is the last major innovation in football tactics.

Having guided Parma to Serie A with what he termed a 'collective and harmonious style' that combined attacking football with good defence, Sacchi implemented the same at AC Milan. At the time, Milan had won only a single league championship in 20 years. Backed by club owner Silvio Berlusconi, Sacchi ripped up the conventions of Italian football to embrace a new style. Instead of the traditional libero, Milan employed a flat or arced back four and instead of individual man-marking, the whole team shared defensive duties. Milan moved as one, shifting left and right, up and down, often with just 25 metres between the first and last player. When chasing possession, the whole team had pressing duties, which they used to help win the ball, force errors, control and wear down the opposition, or just give themselves a breather as attackers tried and failed to move through their massed ranks. In attack, Milan flew into action, with the forwards scattering to open up space and passing opportunities, while the back players moved up or filled in for attacking full backs.

Milan won and retained the European Cup – but were disqualified in 1991 after refusing to retake the field against Marseilles – and Sacchi moved on to the national squad. Many coaches since have adopted the defensive elements of his style, although few could match the attacking speed. Back at Milan, Fabio Capello won four championships in five years with a tougher, more defensive approach, built around stars like

Marcel Desailly. Sacchi has argued that this marked a lasting change in European football tactics, which are now more about accommodating stars within sides than building something greater than its parts.

Juan Antonio Samaranch

Juan Antonio Samaranch Torelló, sports administrator, born Barcelona 17 June 1920. Spanish Olympic Committee 1956–70. Minister of Sport 1966–70. International Olympic Committee member 1967–, vice-president 1974–8, president 1980–2001.

When he retired as Olympic president, Juan Antonio Samaranch left the games united, universal and solvent – which they certainly weren't when he took over 20 years before. En route they had changed from a quasi-amateur sports festival run by wealthy part-timers to a commercial enterprise dominated by professional athletes and run by a full-time CEO. Samaranch broke with the traditions of founder Pierre de Coubertin, turning the IOC from a predominantly sporting organisation into a political and financial 'pork barrel', doling out cash and honours to a swelling number of members, commercial sponsors and affiliates.

As a boxer, 'Kid Samaranch' appeared in a few lightweight bouts in his native Catalonia around 1940. However, for him it was sports administration that would provide a route to power, which in a telling moment he explained 'is the glory'. After apparently deserting the Republican forces in the Spanish Civil War, he befriended the daughter of victorious General Franco and in 1951 used part of his family fortune to fund a roller hockey tournament, a rare sporting contact at a time when fascist Spain was isolated from democratic Europe. A home victory provided positive headlines at a time when poverty was rife and strikers were being shot in the streets. Without the trouble of democratic elections, the energetic and ambitious Samaranch was appointed to city and then provincial posts, organised the 1955 Mediterranean Games and eventually rose to be Minister of Sport, or as IOC vice-president Dick Pound preferred to put it, 'a minor government official'. After Samaranch invited like-minded IOC president Avery Brundage to his villa, Brundage bent the rules to have him elected an IOC member. Samaranch's experience in one undemocratic, self-perpetuating semi-secret elite, obsessed with ceremonies and medals, soon transferred to another as he was made Head of Protocol, organising such Olympic niceties as the final parade, where he ordered athletes not to break rank or take pictures. He was on the IOC executive from 1974 to 1978, supported by <u>João Havelange</u> and the omnipresent <u>Horst Dassler</u>.

When Franco finally died, still clutching the withered arm of St Teresa, his government were forced from office and Samaranch, the scourge of communists, took over as ambassador to the USSR, ideally placed to win support in the run-up to the Moscow games. The risk to his candidature caused by the 1980 Moscow boycott was partly overcome when Spain attended anyway and he was elected president in the first round – by one vote less than expected, which led to a minor witch hunt.

As an Olympic leader Samaranch proved to be a masterful tactician, identifying and avoiding trouble ahead. When the Soviet bloc boycotted the 1984 LA Olympics, he used his influence to limit the damage far more effectively than Lord Killanin had in the run-up to the 1976 and 1980 boycotts. By having the IOC, rather than the organisers, issue invitations to the games, he also limited the danger of future trouble. Another diplomatic triumph was his ability to find a form of words that kept both China and Taiwan in the club. On his appointment it had seemed that Taiwan was destined for exclusion, but 'His Excellency' – a title Samaranch encouraged, as it raised his status in dealing with governments – managed to succeed where others had failed. Before the Seoul games, Samaranch's endless patient junketing limited the fourth successive Olympic boycott to a tiny hardcore, despite the presence of massed North Korean troops just 50 miles away, the shooting-down of a South Korean jet and the rounding-up beforehand of 263,000 undesirables in a 'social purification' drive.

Within the Olympic movement, Samaranch increased his powers of patronage by creating new committees and associations which, to paraphrase US president Lyndon Johnson, kept everyone 'inside the tent, pissing out'. He increased his popularity by supporting anti-apartheid statements, appointing the first female IOC members, restoring Jim Thorpe's medals and endorsing organisations such as the Olympic Council of Asia, which sought to exclude Israel on purely political grounds. Though he stumbled over the rule change that allowed him to serve past the previous retirement age, he was skilled in avoiding internal divisions by referring awkward details to committees he could control, allowing no minority reports and limiting votes to avoid any dissenting voices. Though he made sure he had enough yes-men to support him, he also included a number of independent thinkers like Pound. By granting numerous short audiences and carefully attending to smaller nations, he amassed enough political power to avoid any contested re-elections.

In public, Samaranch's skills were less polished. His speeches were generally hollow and bland. Used to the fawning newspapers of fascist Spain, even criticism from a small nation like Norway irritated him and he apparently ordered that it be stopped – seemingly unaware that this was a) impossible and b) counter-productive. After sacking the previously all-powerful Monique Berlioux, who had effectively run the IOC under Killanin and Avery Brundage, Samaranch paid her an unspecified amount to keep quiet.

Financially, the Olympics leapt ahead during the Samaranch presidency, securing the games' future. After setting up a committee to look at new sources of finance, he appointed Dick Pound to take firmer control of television sales and later established the TOP sponsorship programme run by his political sponsor Horst Dassler's ISL. This allowed the IOC to expand its payroll, increase the size of the 'pork barrel' and pay the expenses of members, who no longer had to be independently wealthy. Above all, it freed the games from reliance on wayward organising committees and potentially rebellious local taxpayers. Samaranch also kept the Olympics 'front of mind' by offering cut-price deals to European public broadcasters. For the athletes, the introduction of trust funds from 1981 enabled Westerners to compete with the state-subsidised East and make the games a genuine global contest. The Olympics now shed its historic attachment to amateurism, discovering a convenient new flexi-principle that 'no one should suffer disadvantage through competing'. As a result, professional athletes were allowed to compete, even if the games had little real prestige in their sport. No appearance money was offered – the prestige of an Olympic title was enough – and this brought the modern games into line with the way the ancient ones had operated. To protect the games' own sponsors, athletes were forbidden from advertising and trackside boards within the stadiums were banned to help make TV commercials easier to sell.

The downside of this commercial success was the ever larger bids from more and more potential host cities and an increase in corruption within the IOC. A continental rotation of Olympic venues would have eliminated many wasteful bids, but Samaranch declared it a principle that any nation might hold the games at any time, and this certainly helped him maintain his power of patronage. In theory, an ethical code was in place from 1991, but it wasn't enforced and many IOC members, who refused to let the executive committee choose the venues, lived like boorish kings. This was particularly the case during Winter Olympics bids, where many voting members had no sporting interest in the contest and cash and favours ruled. Though the heavily political IOC never actually chose a disastrous venue, it often came close to rejecting the best candidates in the early rounds. This led inevitably to the Salt Lake City scandal, when it was revealed that IOC members had been on the take to the value of tens of thousands of dollars. The games came close to losing their US tax privileges and His Excellency had to appear in front of a US investigation before the IOC purged itself of most of the wrongdoers.

The other great ongoing scandal was the misuse of drugs. Although Samaranch made ritual statements against drugs, the drug-detectors received limited financial and political support. Drugs were regarded as a potential embarrassment that threatened the popularity and profitability of the games and needed to be smoothed over, rather than an attack on the ideal of sport itself. Some of the biggest drug users, such as Manfred Ewald's East Germans, even used their insider knowledge to avoid detection. Personally, Samaranch seems to have taken the perfectly defensible view that limited doses of steroids were safe. However, when a journalist accompanying him quoted this, the resulting furore led to the creation of WADA, the World Anti-Doping Agency, and a genuine assault on drugs in sport, albeit at the end of his presidency.

Perhaps the least appealing feature of the Samaranch years was the favouring of despots rather than those who worked for sport. Among those who collected Olympic Awards were Ceausescu of Romania, Todor Zhivkov of Bulgaria and Erich Honecker of East Germany. Other cronies included Primo Nebiolo, who covered up cheating in sport, and Mohammad Hasan, later convicted of forestry fraud. As for the biggest award of all, actually hosting a games, Samaranch played his hand subtly enough to bring the games to his native Barcelona in 1992, while his associate South Korean security boss Kim Un-Yong got Seoul (1988), sponsors Coca-Cola had Atlanta (1996), and Turin (2006) was seen as a posthumous victory for Nebiolo.

Overall, the Samaranch years were a triumph of pragmatism over principles – many of them outdated principles that threatened to wreck or sideline the games. They also showed that sporting politics is one of the few direct routes to pure unadulterated power and prestige. Juan Antonio Samaranch is an outstanding example of just how much can be gained through hard work and good political sense, despite a slightly 'tricky' background.

G.H. Sampson

George Henry Sampson, footballer, born Sheffield 1852, died 1896.

Sheffield midfielder G.H. Sampson is the first man known to have headed a football, which he did at the Kennington Oval on 27 January 1872, while playing for the Sheffield FA against the London FA – the biggest and most keenly fought football contest the capital had ever seen.

In earlier times, heading a heavy leather ball would have been a suicidal tactic and only the use of a lighter ball made it something that a sane man might contemplate. To judge from the lack of reaction back home in Sheffield, heading may have already gained some acceptance there as a scoring tactic, but in London there was general amazement and not a few sniggers when Sampson nutted the ball early on in the big match.

A small man with curly black hair and a moustache, Sampson had already distinguished himself by playing in long shorts rather than full-length trousers and by scoring Sheffield's third goal in their 3–1 home victory over London the previous month. Variously described as a forward and a 'short behind' (a proto midfielder), Sampson's terrier-like tackling had attracted the attention of his opponent Charles Alcock, who threw him to the ground in irritation – after which Sampson felled three Londoners in revenge.

The January 1872 match seems to have been just as robust, with very little intervention from the umpires as the smaller but better-trained Sheffielders, with their long-ball tactics, once again took on London. Apart from a solitary own goal by Sheffield's keeper Carr, the other big post-match talking point was Sampson's tactic – helpfully described by the *Daily Telegraph* as 'an ingenious method of "heading" the ball, i.e. stopping it with the head so placed as to make it rebound in the direction it came from.'

Generally, there was high praise for the Sheffielders' commitment and work rate on a slippery and – to them – undersized pitch, while playing to unfamiliar offside and throw-in rules. Sampson and his partner T.C. Willey were especially singled out for praise.

Many important things would come out of this series of matches. These included the idea of a formal 'half-time' – at first to allow two different sets of rules to be played in each half – plus changing ends at half-time and, from 1877, a universal set of football rules, formed by the merger of the two associations' rulebooks. Another legacy was soccer's eternal battle between clever inter-passing (London) and the northerners' long-ball style – or as the *Sheffield Independent* preferred to put it, 'beautiful and judicious crosses'.

The January 1872 game gave a big boost to what was still a fairly obscure sport, and one spectator wrote to *Bell's Life* stating that he had never passed a more pleasurable afternoon in his life – especially because of 'the gallant manner in which he [Sampson] charged the ball full with his head'.

Robert Sangster

Robert Edmund Sangster, racehorse owner, breeder and boxer, born Manchester 23 May 1936, died 7 April 2004. Champion owner 1977, 78, 82, 83, 84.

Wealthy men have always enjoyed buying expensive horses to race for small but prestigious prizes. Robert Sangster was the first to turn this expensive hobby into a profitable business.

Sangster, who inherited a family business empire that included Vernons Pools, dabbled in horse ownership from 1960, started a stud at Swettenham in 1968 and gained his first big success in the 1969 Ayr Gold Cup with Brief Star. Three years later he and Irish trainer <u>Vincent O'Brien</u>, an enthusiast for US horses, formed a breeding syndicate with O'Brien's son-in-law, John Magnier. 'The Brethren', as they became known, had conceived a business plan that would turn Sangster's initial £2 million stake into £100 million at the height of the bloodstock boom they helped fuel.

The idea was to buy US yearlings with strong or fashionable blood-lines for their breeding as well as their racing potential, export them to Europe, where training costs were lower and the races more presti-gious, and, if successful, re-export them to the States. At the time, the value of syndication rights for successful stallions was already leaping ahead. O'Brien's Sir Ivor had fetched $2 million in 1968, but Vaguely Noble reached $5 million just a year later. Improved veterinary science was also altering the economics by allowing stallions to cover more than 100 mares a year rather than the traditional 45.

By bidding for <u>Northern Dancer</u>'s yearlings before his success as a sire was proven, the syndicate captured Derby winner The Minstrel for $200,000 and syndicated him for $9 million, while Alleged's Arc wins in 1977 and 1978 took his price from $175,000 to $13 million. As year-ling prices topped $1 million, Sangster became a 'marked man' at auctions as he attempted to corner the market, but he used other appointed bidders to disguise his intentions. Travelling non-stop, he found bargains such as Assert, bought in Normandy for £16,000, and one Irish Derby win later valued at $28 million.

During the boom of the 1970s and early 1980s, Sangster, once the youngest Jockey Club member, brought money, nerve, stamina, a TV-friendly presence and a well-connected second wife to the business. The first glossy marketing of bloodstock attracted investors, and the syndicate astutely offered top jockeys shares in their success. This helped extract the last ounce of effort in races in which the narrowest winning margin could be worth a fortune. At Sangster's £14 million Manton stables, more was spent on box barns than most men would pay for a house and at his peak he had a stake in 1,300 horses worldwide, winning about three races a day. After an unsuccessful attempt at breeding out of season for the Australian market, Boone's Cabin would be the first stallion flown out to Australia for a further season of his pleasurable work.

As fortunes were made from trading in foals and stallion syndications, Sangster's business model helped insulate prices from actual performance. The quality and promise of his breeding meant that El Gran Senor's second place in the Derby didn't affect his $30 million valuation, while Assert's poor performance at stud simply boosted values for his sire Be My Guest. In 1981, Storm Bird was valued at over $21 million despite achieving no better than one seventh place as a three-year-old, while Shergar, the Derby winner by a mile, was valued at just $10 million because of his less fashionable bloodlines. Of course, the risks rose with the stakes. Bidding against Sheikh Mohammed, Sangster came within an ace of landing the ultimately useless and infertile Snaafi Dancer for $10.2 million, while Seattle Dancer cost $13.1 million but won just two modest races. Reputation was all, and Lester Piggott's dismissal of Monteverdi as 'useless' led to a split between him and the syndicate. The record prices paid for the relatives of successful horses further boosted their value, but increased the suspicion that a false market now existed.

Despite the vast spending of the oil-rich Maktoums, who helped topple Sangster from champion owner in 1982 to seventh in 1985, the market had to fall. Syndication prices were beyond what the yearlings could be sold for. Prizes had never covered outgoings, and in 1984 Sangster's group invested $27 million to win just $50,000 of prize money. (Manton's annual winnings of £14,000 didn't even cover its feed bill.) Prices fell steeply at the end of the 1980s, while Sangster's bargain Derby winner Golden Fleece died of cancer and El Gran Senor and Secreto's progeny never rivalled their parents' achievements.

Reportedly £60 million in debt, Sangster sold the languishing pools business for £90 million in 1988 – before it was decimated by the National Lottery – and sold off 100 Australian mares in a $17 million deal, though no buyer could be found for Manton. Phoenix Park racecourse, in which he had bought a stake, was also sold in 1993. A public company – Classic Thoroughbreds – couldn't buck the market or a run of bad luck and closed after four years, after just one big (shared) win between them and Sangster in the 1990 Breeders' Cup. By rationalising his businesses and training his own yearlings, rather than buying them in, Sangster lifted himself to fifth among owners worldwide by 1990. Though he was never champion owner again, he had changed the business forever – particularly by promoting the now all-conquering Northern Dancer bloodline.

Hannes Schneider

Johannes Schneider, skier, instructor, author and film star, born St Anton, Austria 24 June 1890, died 25 April 1955.

Along with his near-contemporary Arnold Lunn, Hannes Schneider is the joint father of modern Alpine skiing. Born near the Arlberg Pass, Johannes, the son of a cheese-maker, would first create a new skiing technique and then export it around the world.

As a boy, Johannes was taught both the Telemark and stem techniques and by the age of 16 was Austria's youngest instructor, on the way to becoming national champion. In World War I he fought against the Russians and Italians and set up a systematic ski training scheme for soldiers, teaching them in weeks what had previously taken months. After the Austrian army melted away into defeat in 1918, he simply walked home. Instead of being employed by a hotel to teach its guests, he set up as an independent tutor at St Anton, a stop on the line of the Orient Express.

As his business expanded, Johannes organised a military-style cadre of instructors, many of whom became champions in their own right. Strictly disciplined and banned from fraternising with pupils, they taught a method based on the 'stem' or skidding turns first developed by Mathias Zdarsky, so that pupils always felt in control. At its best, the Arlberg crouch, lift and swing allowed an exhilarating *schuss*. As early as 1920, Schneider was helping film *Das Wunder des Schneeschuhs* ('The Wonder of Skiing') and used the stills in a book of the same name. Later he co-starred, with Leni Riefenstahl, as 'Hannes' Schneider in the worldwide hit *Der Weisse Rausch* ('White Ecstasy'). The Arlberg style was exported to America by 1931, and in 1936 Hannes himself demonstrated it on indoor slopes in Boston and Madison Square Garden. He also taught hundreds of Japanese students and by 1932 the style was reported to have reached Mongolia.

Since 1928, Schneider's Arlberg skiers and Lunn's Kandahar Club had joined forces to create the joint Arlberg-Kandahar, which led first the Austrian government and then the Nordic-dominated International Skiing Federation to finally recognise Alpine skiing.

When the Nazis annexed Austria in 1938, Schneider was imprisoned, and blamed ex-co-star Riefenstahl for his predicament, but was released thanks to Lunn's intelligent politicking and the influence of US businessman Harvey Dow Gibson, who installed Hannes and his son Herbert at his New England Cranmore Mountain resort. During the war, Hannes trained US ski troops, many of whom would later establish new resorts such as Vail and Aspen, while Herbert fought with the most famous unit of the lot – the 10th Mountain Division.

Today the Schneiders' method still lies at the root of much ski teaching. A Schneider Meister Skiing Cup is still held in the US, with past and serving soldiers of the 10th Mountain Division in attendance.

Irving Scholar

Irving Scholar, team owner, born London 1947. Chairman Tottenham Hotspur FC 1982–91 (UEFA Cup 1984).

It was Irving Scholar, the sharp-suited chairman of Tottenham Hotspur, who established British clubs as public companies to be bought and sold, ushering in vast fortunes and vast losses for the investors who followed. At Tottenham, his reign was truly a rollercoaster – full of high-profile twists and turns and occasional peaks, but overall leading relentlessly downward.

Scholar emerged at Spurs as a successful property developer and Monaco-based tax exile. At the time, Tottenham were a 'big five' club, drawing 10,000 more fans than nearby Arsenal. The first to sign new foreign stars such as Ricky Villa and Osvaldo Ardiles, Spurs were soon to be back-to-back FA Cup winners. Scholar offered to help with the rebuilding of the West Stand, which had already caused chairman Sidney Wale to 'resign' in 1980, handing over to the patriarchal 75-year-old Arthur Richardson. The 1980–2 build resulted in one and a half revenue-sapping seasons with a three-sided ground, while Richardson's late decision to override architect Ernest Atherden and install extra boxes rather than more seats led to an awkward, expensive and unprofitable design. Costs doubled and the anticipated sponsorship and box sales failed to materialise.

With the West Stand finally completed, Scholar and Paul Bobroff, who had been brushed off by the board, began amassing supporters' shares, intending to buy Spurs and turn it into a diversified leisure company. Despite Richardson's refusal to register their shares, they won the support of Wale. So parlous were Spurs' finances that despite a £200,000 operating profit, they paid just £500,000 for the club.

The following year the new management gained the support of a pliant FA to publicly list a British football club for the first time – in defiance of Rule 34, which stated that they were clubs first and businesses second. The FA allowed Spurs to skip around this by listing a holding company instead. On 13 October 1983, 3.8 million £1 shares were listed and the offer was hugely oversubscribed, raising cash for new ventures and a new East Stand. British football clubs, like Italian ones, were now available for anyone to buy, whereas in Spain and Germany the members kept a controlling share. Scholar and Bobroff also hoped to profit from a new ITV-backed Super League.

Promising not to repeat the mistakes of the old fossils who had preceded them, Bobroff and Scholar proceeded to make even worse decisions against a backdrop of falling gates, violence and rioting in British football. (On the pitch, a UEFA cup win in 1984 was the high point, although manager Keith Burkinshaw left that year.) The East Stand underwent a tortuous, time-consuming and expensive 'retrofit' and the leak of a planning proposal to install boxes on the stand's 'shelf' further alienated the fans – although planning permission may not have been required. Costs spiralled from an estimated £4.6 million to £8.6 million, leaving Spurs with a stand that still has old-fashioned view-blocking props. Meanwhile, the club poured money into clothing companies, ticketing operations and boxing promotions. With Scholar's hoped-for Super League failing to emerge, Chris Waddle and Paul Gascoigne were both sold off – the latter nearly bankrupting the club after he fell through the West Stand roof while up shooting pigeons in its unused roof-top press box. Another near-disaster was the discovery of a fractured gas main near the club's diesel store.

The end came after a commercial-property bust that nearly bankrupted Scholar, who was secretly borrowing £1 million from Robert Maxwell to fund the acquisition of Gary Lineker. Later, the first Stock Exchange-listed club would be found to have been trading brown bags of cash in hotel car parks to acquire Teddy Sheringham from Forest. With Spurs shares suspended, Alan Sugar and Terry Venables, who bought out Scholar and Bobroff for £7.2 million in 1991, narrowly edged out Maxwell as a buyer. By this time, the club was £20 million in debt and in need of £10 million worth of essential improvements. Though Scholar had been pushing for a Sky and FA-backed Premier League, it was Sugar, on the inside of the deal as Sky's dish manufacturer, who profited from it.

In 1996, Scholar returned to repeat his trick at Nottingham Forest – buying into the last old-fashioned member-owned club and then publicly listing it while its fortunes ebbed away. He quit the board in 1999, accusing it of a lack of 'professionalism'.

Though many clubs have followed Spurs' example, few have retained their market listings, as most clubs have proved to be unattractive investments – either unstable or unprofitable. However, Scholar's innovation has opened the door for a series of investors and speculators to lose and occasionally make vast fortunes – although most of the money still walks out of the door in the players' back pockets.

Ayrton Senna

Ayrton Senna da Silva, racing driver, born São Paulo, Brazil 21 March 1960, died 1 May 1994. World champion 1988, 90, 91; 162 races, 41 wins, 65 poles, 19 fastest laps.

At 2.17 p.m. on 1 May 1994, Ayrton Senna's Williams FW16 shot off the Tamburello curve at Imola and crashed into a concrete wall. No driver's death, not even that of Jim Clark at Hockenheim, comes close to the impact that this had on the public or on motor sport. Like Clark, Senna was the acknowledged master, rated the best ever by Niki Lauda. To quote fellow driver Gerhard Berger, who had crashed at the same spot five years earlier, 'He was so great no one thought anything could happen to him.' Unlike Clark's unseen death in a minor race, the Imola footage (though not the precise moment of impact) was seen around the world. For Formula One, the consequences would be radical and long-lasting, with changes to circuits, rules, cars and safety procedures, as this single instant altered the sport for ever.

Ayrton Senna had already changed the world of motor sport with the unusual aggression of his driving, something he displayed from the very beginning. Having entered the sport by the usual route of karting, his aggression, ability and focus won him three championships in a row before moving to Formula Ford in 1982, where he often drove other drivers off the track to secure 12 wins from 20 starts. With the wealth and political ability to move from team to team and car to car to maximise his chances of victory, he entered the 2-litre class, taking an unfamiliar car to pole position in his first race and winning by 14 seconds – the first of 21 victories from 27 races. In Formula Three, he won his first race by 13 seconds. As well as an unusual depth of understanding of the engineering of cars, which allowed him to talk slip angles and spring rates with his race engineers, he also had perfect recall of what happened to every part of the car at every point in a race. 'Winning,' he said, 'is a drug.'

In 1984, as he arrived in Formula One to race for Toleman, Senna took on the F1 champions in identical Mercedes on the Nürburgring and beat them all, and at Monaco was close to catching Alain Prost when the race was flagged to an early halt. Only Prost had the political and driving abilities to match his own and he was to be Senna's great rival, though in later years Ayrton couldn't even bring himself to utter his name. Having broken his Toleman contract to move to Lotus, Senna showed his skills with two Grand Prix wins in the wet at Estoril and Spa.

Senna would achieve 65 pole positions in 162 Grand Prix starts. He had an unusual ability to drive fast from the start on cold tyres, but his greatest skill lay in overtaking. Keeping his car at the limit of adhesion, he would continually adjust to wring the utmost speed from every curve and was the master of the late braking that provided the best overtaking chances. He also brought his Formula Ford techniques with him, using feints, blocks and deliberate collisions that would have been fatal in the days before thick tyres and safety cells and caused driver complaints from 1985 onwards. At Estoril in 1988, he lunged at team-mate Prost, whose wheels brushed the concrete pit wall at 190 mph, causing the crews to flinch and threatening catastrophe. 'If he wants victory that badly,' said Prost afterwards, 'he can have it,' and Senna edged the championship with eight wins to Prost's seven. The following year, the pair clashed again at Suzuka, where both went off at the first corner. Senna restarted but was deprived of the championship by FISA president Jean-Marie Balestre – an event that led to Max Mosley replacing him. 'Not only unsporting but disgusting' was the verdict from Prost, who left for Ferrari. The following season saw Senna winning another championship after yet another collision at Suzuka, which he blamed on Balestre's siting of pole position.

Off the track, Senna's total war against Prost included slights on his courage and recorded outbursts which he later claimed were 'misinterpreted'. The mind games he played on a succession of team-mates led to what future champion Damon Hill neatly termed 'Senna-phobia'. However, there was no doubting his extraordinary abilities and search for perfection. A religious man, Senna donated over $80 million to charitable programmes and hospitals for street children in Brazil and even created a comic for them to read, based on the adventures of a mini-Senna.

For the two years preceding his death, Senna was kept out of the Williams Renault team, whose engines and active suspension made them the ones to beat. Forced to chase in the responsive but less powerful McLaren MP4/4, Senna was only able to convert his courage, touch and vision into victory in exceptional circumstances – such as the drenched 1993 European Grand Prix where, with the Williams gizmos temporarily neutralised, he carved out an amazing victory.

In 1994, having secured 35 wins in six seasons for McLaren, Senna finally got to drive for Williams, just as the authorities, concerned by the high costs and dull races, banned traction control and active suspension. They also sought to increase the thrills by reintroducing refuelling – banned ten years earlier on safety grounds – and introduced the pace car, a 'safety measure' that bunched up the field and added to the thrills in the event of an accident. Having protested about the pace car, Senna found himself in an FW16 that was far from the magic-carpet ride of previous seasons. The car was uncomfortable, twitchy and seemed scarcely ready to race. Prone to pitch, it lacked grip and had to be fought all the time, especially at low-speed corners. When leading at Interlagos, it jinked and stalled.

Imola started badly as Rubens Barrichello's Jordan took off like a jet in the first day's qualifying, before Roland Ratzenberger was killed the following day at the Villeneuve bend – the first F1 fatality in 12 years. Before the race, Senna was so worried about safety he phoned his girl-friend in tears. J.J. Lehto crashed in the race itself, bringing on the pace car that Senna had worried about. While he was stuck behind it, his tyres cooled and the handling of the car probably altered. After the race resumed, the crash was almost immediate. Though the Tamburello corner presented few obvious challenges, driver error was one theory, another being that debris from the track and those cooled tyres caused the Williams to bottom on the lumpy surface. With the suspension data lost, there was disagreement as to whether a snapped steering column was a result or a cause of the crash. A million São Paulistas lined the funeral route.

After another near-fatal crash at Monaco, both the drivers and authorities acted. The former group re-established Jackie Stewart's Grand Prix Drivers' Association, there were bollards out at the Canadian Grand Prix, and curves like Monza's Lesmo and Spa's Eau Rouge were remodelled – emasculated, said some observers. Max Mosley's FIA acted to slow the cars and protect the drivers better, and from mid-season cars were restricted to pump petrol and 50 mph in the pit lane, with further aerodynamic restrictions and skid blocks fitted underneath. From the 1995 season, cars were limited to 3 litres capacity, with limits on down force, and bodywork now built up to shoulder level to protect drivers such as Michael Schumacher, who used Senna-esque shunting tactics at Adelaide in 1994 and Jerez three years later. The changes remain in place and over a decade after his death, Formula One cars and tactics are still defined by the sport's 'Holy warrior'.

Joseph Sherer

Major General Joseph Sherer, polo player, born Bay of Biscay 1829, died 1901.

In the 18th century, British forces in India helped to almost wipe out the millennia-old sport of polo. However, it was a British Bengal Army officer named Joseph Sherer who revived it and became credited as 'The Father of Modern Polo'.

In 1859, in the wake of the Indian Mutiny, Sherer was posted to Manipur in north-west India as assistant superintendent. By this time, the fortunes of the 'game of kings' (as well as princesses) had gone full circle. From humble origins as a horseback muskrat hunt in Tibet, it had come to be played by Alexander the Great, Darius of Persia and Genghis Khan himself. Like the great Khan, it had conquered Asia, spreading from Turkey as *djerid*, to Japan as *da-kyu*, while at Isfahan in Persia, Shah Abbas even laid out his capital around his pitch, or *maidan*, and defined the goals as eight yards wide – the same distance that soccer later adopted. In the 16th century, India's Mughal Emperor Akbar the Great created the first agreed rules.

By Sherer's time, polo was restricted to a few mountainous regions, such as Ladakh, Gilgit and Manipur, where it was played in the village streets as *kanjai-bazee* or *phulu* – from the Tibetan for a willow root, out of which the ball was made. Inspired by what he saw, Sherer formed the Silchar Club with his senior officer Robert Stewart and seven tea planters and, to avoid injury, they agreed that there was to be no bhang, ganja or liquor consumed before play.

Polo reached Dacca in 1861, and the following year Sherer's Manipuris, billed as the 'Band of Brothers', beat the new Calcutta Club during race week, sold their ponies and departed in triumph. As news of the game spread, Indian royalty joined in again and back in Britain Captain Edward 'Chicken' Hartopp of the 10th Hussars, then under canvas at Aldershot, read a report in *The Field*. Hartopp and his fellow officers were inspired to improvise their own game with walking sticks and billiard balls, and after ordering ponies from Ireland organised a formal match at Hounslow Heath – now Heathrow – which proved a great success. Another officer, John Watson of the 13th Hussars, became 'The Father of English Polo' after he developed the first backhand shots and created new rules for the game. From there it spread to the richer parts of the world, limited by the risk of injury, the five-hectare pitch required and the cost of ponies.

Tom Simpson

Thomas Simpson, road and track cyclist, born Haswell, County Durham 30 November 1937, died 13 July 1967. Wins include Ronde van Vlaanderen (1961), Bordeaux–Paris (1963), Milan–San Remo (1964), World Road Racing Championship (1965), Paris–Nice (1967). BBC Sports Personality of the Year 1965. Bidlake Memorial Prize 1965.

'He destroyed himself – he had the ability to do that.' So said mechanic Harry Hall of Britain's most famous sporting martyr.

Few have cast a longer shadow over their sport than 'Major Tom'. Forty years after the event, one could still argue that the spiritual heart of British road racing is the bare summit of Mont Ventoux, 1,912 metres above the plains of Provence and prone to 320 kph blasts of wind. It was here, on the 13th stage of the Tour de France, that Simpson died – perhaps the only top sportsman in history to have killed himself through sheer effort. 'It's a good rider who can ride himself into the ground,' he once said.

The sixth child of a Durham miner who moved to Nottingham, Tom Simpson had to borrow his first racing bike, but won his first race at 16 and achieved an Olympic bronze and Commonwealth silver in pursuit cycling. As a professional, the whippet-thin 'Four-stone Coppi' (nicknamed in honour of Tour champ Fausto Coppi) won his first championship in 1959. After moving to France, Tom could soon pass as a native and won two stages in his first big race, plus four of the first nine he entered, also becoming the first Brit to wear yellow in the 1962 Tour. The first stage winner would be Barry Hoban, granted a victory after Tom's death.

After his collapse on Ventoux, The *Daily Telegraph* at first reported his death with the suggestion that he'd be 'happy to go the way he has'. A large crowd, including <u>Beryl Burton</u> stood in the rain outside the church at Harworth while the funeral was conducted inside. It was only later that the *Daily Mail*'s J.L. Manning broke the news that amphetamines had been found in his pockets.

This really was a tragedy waiting to happen. There had been numerous drugs scares in previous years, nearly all related to amphetamines, including collapses on the Aubisque the year before and the near death of Ferdi Kübler on Ventoux itself. In the end it was Simpson, spending a reported £800 a year on carefully wrapped Tonedrin, who had driven himself too far. 'If it takes ten to kill you,' Tom was supposed to have said, 'I'll take nine.' He had fallen about 1 kilometre short of the summit, his final words 'Go on, go on'. Afterwards Sid Saltmarsh, absent from the scene but covering the Tour for *Cycling* and the *Sun*, came up with the line 'Put me back on my bike' for the sport's most quotable champion.

Tom's death provoked a tightening of French anti-doping laws, while the Olympic movement also started trying to detect stimulants from the 1968 Mexico games onwards. Less attention was paid to the madness of sending cyclists out in 131-degree heat with rationed water supplies. (Tom hated the heat and Ventoux in particular – 'It's another world up there, with the white rocks and blinding sun.') Still less was said about the trainers who would put any muck into their charges, or the agents who had threatened Tom with reduced appearance fees, as he chased his target of a new Mercedes 280SL.

Despite the great and continuing successes of British road racers since 1967, the story of Tom Simpson still haunts the sport. Today Tom's *stele*, or monument, on Ventoux, paid for by British cyclists, remains a shrine where those who have dragged themselves up the 'Giant of Provence' leave some memento behind. A small museum dedicated to him can also be found in Harworth and Bircotes Sports and Social Club.

Matthias Sindelar – 'The Mozart of Football'

Matthias Sindelar, footballer, born Kozlov, Moravia 10 February 1903, died 23 January 1939. Playing career: Hertha Vienna 1918–24, FK Austria 1924–39 (league champions 1926, cup winners 1925, 26, 33, 35, 36, Mitropa Cup 1933, 36); Austria 1926–37, 43 caps, 27 goals.

Despite the lack of any good filmed footage, it seems that Matthias Sindelar was the first, or at least the first successful, playmaker in football – a centre forward who deliberately withdrew from the front line to elude the defence and control the game.

The son of Moravian immigrants who worked in a grim Vienna brickworks, Sindelar started as a street footballer. At the newly professional FK Austria, he became known as the 'wafer' or 'paper man' because of his slight build and ability to slip through defences – the more so because from 1926 he began replacing the robust Josef 'the Tank' Uridil in the national side. Sindelar was a huge favourite among the footballing intellectuals of Vienna, epitomising skill and tactical awareness unlike the more common 'bull at a gate' number 9. Though he scored on his international debut, he fell out with the authoritarian national coach, Hugo Meisl, who was only persuaded to reinstate him in 1931 by massed lobbying at the Ring Café, the unofficial HQ of Austrian soccer. The returned Sindelar led the *Wunderteam* to a series of wins, including a 5–0 thrashing of Scotland, the supposed masters of the passing game. However, in the 1934 World Cup semi-finals, Italy's Luis Monti kicked and marked him out of the game. Two years later, playing the English in Vienna, he repeatedly dragged the English centre half John Barker out of position – much as Nándor Hidegkuti would when <u>Puskás</u>'s team overcame England at Wembley in 1953.

Sindelar's last game for Austria was against the Germans, who were annexing his country. Having refused to play in Sepp Herberger's combined German-Austrian side, Sindelar toyed with the opposition before scoring for Austria – ruining what is thought to have been intended to be a fixed draw – and celebrated in front of the massed Nazi officials. His death soon afterwards was regarded as thoroughly suspicious, although the evidence seems to point towards a faulty cooker and a blocked chimney.

Voted Austria's sportsman and footballer of the century, the attacking type Sindelar created is still beloved by fans today – recent notables being Eric Cantona and Gianfranco Zola.

Tod Sloan

James Forman Sloan, jockey, born Bunker Hill, Indiana 10 August 1874, died 21 December 1933. Winner 1,000 Guineas 1899, Ascot Gold Cup 1900. US Racing Hall of Fame 1955.

It is a strange thing that the most influential jockey in history should have begun his career scared of horses. Despite this fear, Tod Sloan's small size, poverty and uncaring family marked him out for a career on the turf. Like many unwanted lads, he ended up working in US horse racing, which in the late 1800s was almost unregulated. Most riders were virtual slaves, competing in epic drawn-out meetings held on dirt ovals near city centres, many of which were later built over. (Eight lie beneath the streets of San Francisco alone.) It was in California that Tod first came to prominence, riding in races where deception, false starting and foul tactics were common – not to mention deliberate shocking or the doping of horses with cocaine and heroin.

Tod's lightning start, driving finish and great sense of pace soon marked him out as a star. By 1895 he had developed both an uncanny understanding of horses and the tactical sense to get into the best position undetected. Soon he was winning over 30 per cent of his races in a sport in which the margin of victory is usually less than a length. Often he used the 'Western Style', perched over the horse's withers – the highest part of its back – rather than the conventional upright seat. This lowered wind resistance and gave him a better view and balance. In San Francisco the style was old news, but it was rarer on the East Coast and even more so in Europe, where only Willie Simms had used it before. When in 1897 Tod announced that he would ride in Europe as a freelancer, the *Sporting Life*'s New York correspondent helpfully described the position as being 'like a toy monkey on a pole'.

In England Tod won an unprecedented 12 out of 16 races during 1898, his first full season, and the following year achieved a 31 per cent win rate – though he lost his Derby chance when Holocaust's leg broke beneath him. Within six years Tod's style would be universal. Following in his wake – sometimes because they'd been drummed out of US racing – came more Americans with new ideas about the importance of timing horses, the need for lighter, airier stables and an enthusiasm for doping and heavy betting. Accompanying them was an influx of new horses, all claiming thoroughbred status. Tod, who was close to gamblers such as George 'Pittsburgh Phil' Smith, soon became tainted by association. Although the Prince of Wales warmed to him, the aristocratic Jockey Club didn't like his independence or style and before long the Earl of Durham spoke out against him.

Tod, with his valet and his seven trunks of fine clothes, didn't appreciate the weakness of his position until a thunderbolt struck on 6 December 1900. Based on a casual note in a meeting book and the usual unaccountable in-camera judgment, the Jockey Club used their *Racing Calendar* to advise him not to reapply for a jockey's licence. The club's pretext was a real but relatively minor offence – accepting a present to ride Codoman, who lost the 1900 Cambridgeshire to Tod's preferred ride Berrill.

'A genius on a horse, off one erratic and foolish' was trainer <u>George Lambton</u>'s verdict, and Tod made bad worse when he was deprived of his licence to ride in France for spreading turf rumours. Never a great businessman, he lost money on a car dealership, an illegal bookmaking operation, a tipping service and a billiard hall and sold the Paris club that became Harry's Bar. The US press turned against him and as racing was reformed, he became a symbol of the bad old days. The UK actually deported him in 1915, despite which Tod still volunteered to fight in the trenches. After serving in the Ambulance Corps, he ended up as a greeter at a track in Mexico, but never gave up hope of turning round his fortunes. Before he died of cirrhosis, he was still ordering boxes of cigars and looked forward to striking gold in one of a couple of mines he claimed to own.

As well as establishing a revolutionary new riding style, Tod inspired the show *Little Johnny Jones* – often credited as the first US musical – which featured the hit songs 'Give my Regards to Broadway' and 'Yankee Doodle Dandy'. Tod's independence and riding ability are still part of the language today, through the rhyming slang phrase 'on your Tod' (on your own/Tod Sloan).

O.P. Smith

Owen Patrick Smith, inventor and sports promoter, born Memphis, Tennessee 12 July 1866, died January 1927. Greyhound Hall of Fame 1973.

Though there were attempts at a straight-line greyhound track as early as 1876 and a patent was taken out in 1890, it was Owen Smith, the US-born son of Irish emigrants from the coursing county of Cavan, who created the first circular greyhound track. After ten years of unrewarded effort, he created a boom sport that in Britain would even overtake football in popularity.

In 1909, after Smith had taken a dislike to the bloodthirsty coursing events staged at his South Dakota farm, he set out to stage dog racing on the same basis as horses. After starting out pulling a stuffed hare behind a motorbike, he was soon working with engineer Thomas Keen to create a round track. Supported by his wife Hannah, it was ten years before the first successful venue opened in Emeryville, California, but once the sport was established as a betting medium it boomed, with Smith becoming Commissioner of the International Greyhound Racing Association.

In 1926 US businessman Charles Munn, cement mogul Alfred Critchley and vet Major L. Lyne Dixson formed the Greyhound Racing Association and imported racing into Britain. After starting at Belle Vue in the whippet-loving North-West, the number of courses mushroomed, with the GRA dominating the South while the rival National Greyhound Racing Society ruled the North and Midlands. Both attracted big crowds by bringing evening gambling into the cities. The Tote was finally legalised in 1934 and by 1936 the dogs were attracting 19 million spectators a year. For the first time spectators could enjoy weekday sport as well as such luxuries as seats, trackside restaurants, car parking and, at Wembley, a cocktail bar. The greyhounds were the salvation of under-used venues such as Wembley and Cardiff Arms Park, and there were plans for huge tracks at the Oval and Crystal Palace.

To combat corruption and fixes, the dogs were kennelled near the tracks and the trap release was made automatic. The number racing per heat was reduced from seven to six and in 1939 the sport pioneered the photo-finish camera, with electromagnetic timing from 1946. The following year greyhound racing displaced football as the number one sport – though it was soon hit by a betting tax and the rise of TV, and never recovered its crowd-pulling ability.

Owen Smith died suddenly in 1927 with 17 tracks under his control. Forced to act, Hannah took over the reins and issued a 'carry on' order, becoming the first woman to head an international sporting organisation. In 1931 she took Owen's patent rights to the sport as far as the US Supreme Court, but the judgments went against her.

Tommie Smith

Tommie Smith, sprinter and wide receiver, born Clarksville, Texas 6 June 1944. Olympic 200 m champion 1968. Cincinnati Bengals 1969. National Track and Field Hall of Fame 1978. Black Californian Athlete of the Millennium.

Tommie Smith is forever famous for his Black Power salute on the winner's podium at the 1968 Mexico Olympics, but he wouldn't have been there had he not been the most beautifully balanced runner since Jesse Owens – the only track athlete in history to hold 11 world records simultaneously.

Some of Smith's high-school records still stand, but his talent might have been wasted had he not been recruited by Lloyd 'Bud' Winter at San Jose State, an innovator who believed in low-volume individualised training. At one time Winter's 'Speed City' team had seven men under 9.4 seconds for the 100 yards – a record never matched since. In 1966 Tommie hacked half a second off the straight 220 yards and 200 metres, although in the run-up to Mexico his record on the curve was unofficially bettered by John Carlos, running in 'illegal' brush spikes.

The other side of the story was, of course, political. The seventh child of 12 born to a Texas sharecropper who moved to California, Tommie initially volunteered as a military reservist, but became politicised by Muhammad Ali's stand against the Vietnam War and joined ex-athlete Harry Edwards's Olympic Project for Human Rights. The OPHR campaigned for black representation in US coaching and its Olympic Committee, the removal of IOC president Avery Brundage and an end to the New York Athletic Club's whites-only policy. After Tommie raised the possibility of an Olympic boycott and picketed the NYAC centenary, Brundage turned on the OPHR with such ferocity that they received an unexpected publicity boost, including support from the Harvard rowing eight. In the end, Tommie and San Jose teammates John Carlos and Lee Evans all opted to run.

In the final, Tommie broke 20 seconds for the first time, despite no practice and a strained adductor (groin) muscle, while Carlos's glance across let in Aussie Peter Norman. When Carlos realised he had forgotten his gloves for the planned protest, it was apparently Norman who suggested they split the pair belonging to Tommie's wife Denise Paschal. The iconography of the moment – heads bowed, left and right arms raised in an arch, bare feet, beads around Carlos's neck, open jacket, endorsed Puma Suedes in hand, was complex but unforgettable – especially when <u>Roone Arledge</u>'s ABC zoomed in to beam what Roger Bannister termed their 'dignity and poise' live around the world. 'A gesture not of hate, but of frustration,' said Smith. 'A nasty demonstration against the US flag by negroes,' countered Brundage.

While Brundage and the USOC attempted to remove the pair's medals, John Carlos pointed out the impossibility of divorcing sport from politics in a games that celebrated the triumph of nation over nation. Questioned by ABC's Howard Cosell, who asked him if he was proud to be an American, Tommie, supposedly the less radical and articulate of the pair, came up with the perfect response: 'I'm proud to be a black American.'

With the Feds already on Harry Edwards's tail, both Smith and Carlos endured unemployment and death threats, and the Cincinnati Bengals dropped Tommie after a single season. At one point he was reduced to tutoring Yorkshire schoolkids, before eventually gaining prominence as a track and field coach and sociologist. By the 1984 Olympics both men were being honoured and Carlos was on the organising committee.

Today their Black Power salute is commemorated with a statue at San Jose. The empty silver medallist's plinth is intended to encourage others to take a stand, although some think it would be better if it included Peter Norman, who wore an OPHR badge in support, spoke out against the White Australia policy and was there at its unveiling. Norman's reward was to be vilified by the media and shunned by the Australian track authorities. He was even kept out of the Munich games despite reaching the qualifying time, and was still being denied any recognition as late as Sydney in 2000. At his funeral in 2006 both Tommie Smith and John Carlos were pallbearers.

Edward Smith Stanley

Colonel Edward Smith Stanley, 12th Earl of Derby, 6th Baronet Stanley MP, PC, politician and sportsman, born Preston 12 December 1752, died 21 October 1834. Wins include: Oaks 1779, 94, Derby 1787.

The 12th Earl of Derby was the sporting aristocrat responsible for two of Britain's five classic races. It was in 1778, at a dinner party at his Surrey home The Oaks, that the idea of a sweepstake of the same name was dreamt up. This was to be for fillies, in opposition to the Doncaster St Leger, which was for both colts and fillies. The Oaks Stakes was run the following year on Epsom Downs, where there had been races since 1648 – officially 1661.

After Sam Arnull piloted Derby's filly Bridget to victory, the Earl and Sir Charles Bunbury flipped a coin for the honour of naming a second race – a sweepstake for three-year-old colts or fillies to be run over a mile, for a prize of £1,065 15s. In 1784, the distance would be amended to 1½ miles, although in 1991 some pedant decided it was actually ten yards longer. Though he lost the naming rights, Bunbury had the first winner – Diomed – and it was 1787 before Derby himself won the race, when Sam Arnull won on Sir Peter Teazle.

The Derby meeting, held in the week before Whitsuntide, was a roaring success and in the 19th century became renowned as 'the blue riband of the turf' (Disraeli) or 'our Olympic Games' (Lord Palmerston). Part of its appeal was the easy access from London and the drama of the U-shaped switch-backed course with its 143-foot climb, descent, sharp left turn and 6-foot camber. No course would be built this way today and racing radicals like Phil Bull believed it should be done away with. Although the course design is inimitable, many other racing nations have copied the Derby distance, which represents a test of both speed and stamina – or what in Derby's day they called 'bottom'. The distance is a huge challenge, as it is a very rare animal that has the physiology to run flat-out for so long. (Most horses are destined by nature to be stayers over 2 miles or sprinters up to 1¼.) Peter Burrell, the Director of the National Stud in the 1960s, reckoned that only one horse in 300 that had the breeding could be a serious contender – assuming good training, luck and jockeyship.

A keen sportsman in the 18th-century sense, Derby was renowned for the 3,000 fighting cocks he owned, plus the nation's finest cockpit at Preston. Until his new wife objected, he was not above staging an impromptu 'main' in the drawing room – which may explain why his first wife had an affair with the Duke of Dorset. After the 12th Earl died it was another 137 years before the 17th Earl won the race again, as Tommy Weston piloted Sansovino to victory in 1924.

Karsten Solheim

Karsten Solheim, engineer and inventor, born Austrheim, Norway 15 September 1911, died 16 February 2000. World Golf Hall of Fame 2001.

'That's nice, honey' was Louise Solheim's reaction when her middle-aged husband told her the name he had given his prototype putter, based on its pinging note. A third of a century later there were 1,800 gold-plated putters at the Ping HQ – each marking a tournament won with a design that changed golf.

Karsten Solheim had come to the game late, by way of jobs as a shoe repairer, cookware salesman and defence engineer. Norwegian-born, he had emigrated to the United States aged just three and after his mother's death was shunted around between families. This set back his progress at school, but it soon became clear that he was a genius at crafts and engineering – once fixing a broken car bearing with a piece of bacon rind.

By the time he started playing golf, Solheim had worked on the first US jet fighter, banking computer and portable TV and had moved on to space research, but his big golfing idea was a result of the frustrations of trying to putt straight with a traditional blade putter. Solheim improved the club design by attaching the shaft to the centre rather than the heel and following the perimeter-weighting principles behind a tennis racket – moving the weight to the toe and heel for stability and lowering it to make the ball roll rather than skid off. At first, manufacture was in the family garage and kitchen, where the clubs were heat-treated over the stove. Sales really took off in 1967, when Julius Boros won the Phoenix Open with a Ping. Soon <u>Arnold Palmer</u>, <u>Jack Nicklaus</u> and Gary Player were all customers as the goose-necked Anser putter became the most popular in history.

Despite the shock of having his slightly curved handles banned by the USGA in the late 1960s, Solheim introduced perimeter weighting to irons to make them less prone to twisting and also used more accurate investment casting with the Karsten 1, which replaced the old technique of stamping and then grinding out a club. From 1982, the Ping Eye 2 became the most popular iron ever. Ping's U- rather than V-shaped grooves, legalised in 1984, also kept the behaviour of the head consistent despite uneven wear. Between 1989 and 1993, the now-wealthy Solheim fought a dogged legal action against new USGA and PGA rules that would have made many of his club designs illegal.

It was only when Ping's patents started running out that many other manufacturers caught up and in 1995 his son took over the business – helped by sponsorship of the Solheim Cup, a ladies' version of the Ryder Cup that started in 1990.

Al Spalding

Albert Goodwill Spalding, baseballer, businessman and administrator, born Byron, Illinois 2 September 1850, died 9 September 1915. Playing career: Chicago Excelsiors 1867, Boston Red Stockings 1871–5 (National Association pennant 1872, 73, 74, 75), Chicago White Stockings 1876–8 (National League pennant 1876); average .313. National Baseball Hall of Fame 1939.

Handsome, successful, intelligent and diplomatic, Albert Spalding was not only a great pitcher, but also the player who raised the status of the newly professional ballplayer, took baseball to the world and first built and then helped create and maintain both the National League and a sporting-goods empire, both of which survive today. On the other hand, Spalding did not succeed through ability and charm alone. As a player he triumphed in a rough game, and as a team owner fought just as dirty, denying other players the rights and the income he had enjoyed, and often played fast and loose with the truth.

Spalding first came to prominence in Illinois at a time when Midwestern baseball was just beginning to threaten the East Coast. Pitchers like Albert were required to aim high or low as directed and their only weapon was speed. Hired by the Boston Red Stockings for the National Association's debut season, Spalding's skilful pitching won 55 games out of 60 and in a sport where ERAs (runs surrendered per nine innings) under 3 are good, he managed to average 2.14. By 1875, he was able to negotiate a sky-high $2,000 p.a. and a share of team ownership in return for moving to Chicago with three team-mates and Phillies batsman Cap Anson.

At the time, baseball was renowned for drinking, violence and stealing players – hence the Pittsburgh 'Pirates'. However, Chicago White Stockings owner William Hulbert was planning a new National League that would enjoy a better reputation and more control over players. (Later, Spalding would claim sole credit for the idea.) Together, Hulbert and Spalding seized the moral high ground by banning whisky and Sunday play, and they weakened the rival leagues by only hiring players from their teams, rather than other National League sides. Having recorded his last great season in 1876, and become the first star to regularly wear a glove, Spalding quit playing in 1878 with a win percentage of 79 – the highest ever. After Hulbert's death in 1882, he took over the team, built a new ballpark and continued to expand his sporting-goods business. He got his equipment endorsed by the League and even written into the rules – including the new gloves, which allowed a faster, harder game – and he produced various official-sounding baseball publications.

For the rest of his life, Spalding would defend the National League against all comers, using as his mouthpiece the New York-based *Sporting Times*, which he owned. In 1889 and 1890, a Players League was defeated using all the means at his disposal, and the National League imposed a reserve system that kept players' wages in check until Curt Flood challenged it in the 1970s. The following year, Spalding defeated the rival American Association by co-opting a few of their more successful teams, and in 1902 he returned from retirement to co-opt the American League, creating the present two-league structure and a pattern of teams that would stay unchanged until after World War II.

As well as helping to run baseball at home, in 1888 Spalding took two teams and a balloon trapeze artist on a world tour to make base-ball the 'universal sport of the world'. In reality, this was a small-scale loss-making venture that didn't switch any nations onto baseball, but it kept his name in the papers, helped spread the sporting-goods empire, didn't cost him too much and meant he was welcomed back as a hero. Convinced of the value of big trusts in business, Spalding went on to create a giant American Bicycle Company and even tried to turn the National League into a single company, though the rival owners wouldn't agree terms. He was also on the 1900 US Olympic Games Commission and may have been behind the abortive plan to seize control of the Olympics in 1900 and 1904.

In 1905, Spalding became fed up with press claims that his American game was simply a more macho version of rounders and commissioned League president A.G. Mills to conduct an inquiry into its origin. Mills leapt upon a report that the safely dead Union General Abner Doubleday had sketched out a baseball diamond at Cooperstown in 1839. This was despite the fact that Doubleday had been at West Point at the time and made no mention of such a game. The source for this tale was 'reputable man' Abner Graves, a serial fantasist who was placed in asylums three times and distinguished himself in his eighties by shooting his wife. Spalding publicised Graves's claim in *America's National Game* (1911) – a book that combined history with a cheerleading autobiography. Soon his reputation was so high that he could have become a Republican senator, had he fought a more energetic campaign.

Strangely for such a hard-headed man, Spalding ended his days living in a sculpture-packed white octagon and worshipping the 'Purple Mother' – part of a Theosophy cult his wife adhered to. This 'Barnum of Sport' died praised for his 'transparency, square-dealing and rectitude' (*NY Times*). Today his name lives on in the sporting-goods brand and the Baseball Hall of Fame in Cooperstown – despite the weakness of its claim to be the home of a game that Europeans were playing years earlier as 'base'. Both the brand and the hall are lasting tributes to Al Spalding's talent for ball play, business and bullshit.

Frederick Spofforth – 'The Demon Bowler'

Frederick Robert Spofforth, cricketer, born Balmain, New South Wales 9 September 1853, died 4 June 1926. First-class career: New South Wales 1874–85, Victoria 1885–7. Derbyshire 1889–90, MCC 1896; 155 matches, 1,928 runs (9.88), 853 wickets (14.95); 18 Tests 1877–87, 217 runs (9.43), 94 wickets (18.41). Australian Cricket Hall of Fame 1996.

'Ain't I a demon?! Ain't I demon?!'

On the afternoon of 27 May 1878, a rake-thin 6 feet 3 inch Australian bowler leapt around the Lord's visitors' dressing room making suitably demonic gestures. Fred Spofforth and his Australian team-mates had just brought about the most unexpected, momentous and crushing victory in cricket history.

Only 500 hardy souls had braved the rain to watch the Australians, who had gone down to an innings defeat at Trent Bridge, square up to an MCC side that included W.G. Grace, A.N. 'Monkey' Hornby and four of the Notts professionals who had already defeated them. Even at the end of the day, with the news spreading fast that something extraordinary was going on, there were still only 4,000 present to see the MCC bowled out in their second innings for 19 runs. They had been wiped out in under a day by the penetration and hostility of Harry Boyle (9 for 17) and Fred 'the Demon' Spofforth (10 for 20 – seven of them bowled). Spofforth, the first bowler to deliberately eyeball the batsman, had skittled Grace for a duck in the second innings, leaping two feet in the air and yelling, 'Bowled! Bowled! Bowled!'

That evening the crowds gathered outside the tourists' Tavistock Hotel to see what manner of men could have done such a thing. Spofforth was an instant celebrity, the subject of a *Vanity Fair* cartoon (the highest popular accolade of the day), and the rest of the tour was a huge financial success that helped set up the first great international sporting rivalry. In the longer term, Spofforth's triumph signalled a shake-up in British cricket. Reliance on medium-pacers like Alfred Shaw was clearly no longer enough and the search began for English pacemen. Fielders had to sharpen up, close leg fielding became the norm and English sides even began to copy the bold new technique of setting fields for specific bowlers.

Those who had already seen Fred Spofforth in action were less surprised at his success. A banker's son from Sydney, he had started out as a lob bowler until at 11 he witnessed the pace bowling of George Parr's 1863/4 tourists. He then set about fashioning himself into Australia's finest and fastest bowler. Able to run 100 yards in 11 seconds, by the age of 21 he was appearing for New South Wales against Grace's touring XI.

With greater financial security than most players, Spofforth ruled himself out of the 1877 Test against James Lillywhite's tourists – the first match held on equal terms – in protest at the exclusion of his NSW team-mate Billy Murdoch. With Murdoch reinstated, the 23-year-old Spofforth bowled more overs than anyone else, combining unusual pace and intensity with a characteristic leap at the end to take four wickets. Deadly accurate, he bowled out more than half his victims.

By 1878/9, when Lord Harris's 'Gentlemen of England plus Ulyett and Emmett' appeared in Australia, Spofforth had added to his 'skill set' of speed, cut and swerve and took the first hat-trick in Test history. Having discovered that his off break – with which he had taken seven of his ten Lord's wickets – worked better at lower speeds, he learned to disguise the pace of his delivery and add a greater degree of swerve. The result was that he took 13 wickets for 110 runs to win the first Melbourne Test and was also present at the Sydney game, when an umpire's decision triggered a crowd invasion, the use of mounted police to break it up and grovelling apologies from the Australian cricket authorities. In 1880, when the latest Australian touring party reached Britain and the still disgraced cricketers were finally allowed to play an MCC side, Spofforth was absent, injured by some 'questionable bowling at Scarborough' (*The Times*), which suggests that he was already being targeted. In his absence the tourists lost, although this helped to repair relations and tee up the momentous 1882 Ashes Test at the Oval. On 28 August, 20 wickets fell on the first day and England ended up needing just 85 to win. However, the Demon's blood was up after Grace had run out Sammy Jones in questionable style. 'That will cost you the match,' he told Grace, and declared to his team-mates, 'Boys, the thing can be done.' The thing was done. Though England needed only 36 runs with six wickets in hand, the Aussies took the last eight wickets for just 26 and Spofforth was carried shoulder-high from the field – his figures of 14 for 90 the best for 90 years to come. The following day's *Sporting Times* announced the death of English cricket: 'The body will be cremated and the ashes taken to Australia.' Spofforth had now not only created, but also named the great sporting rivalry.

In three Tests in Australia in 1885 Spofforth took 19 wickets for 16.1 runs apiece, and there was no answer to him until he injured a finger in 1886. He ended his Test career in 1887, still at the top of his game. After this he married, played for Derbyshire and began a successful career in the Star tea company – although even at the age of 43, playing for the MCC, he could still take 8 for 74.

Though he was not an out-and-out fast bowler by modern standards, Spofforth was one of the first to get his bowling arm completely vertical and was rated 'terrifically fast' by Grace, who he bowled seven times. Although he wasn't the first 'demon' bowler – John Jackson had the nickname back in 1850 – it was Fred Spofforth who made the name stick.

Edward Stevens – 'Mr Lumpy'

Edward Stevens, cricketer, born Send, Surrey 1735, died 7 September 1819. Career: 1767–89.

Short, stout, genial and with a rather long nose, Edward 'Lumpy' Stevens is probably the most influential bowler in the history of cricket – one whose bowling helped shape bats, wickets, bowling styles and the lbw rule. He was also the first bowler to be recognised as a match-winner, his name being written into the contracts drawn up before matches.

Stevens probably came from a cricketing family, as two Stevenses are referred to in a 1744 match between London and Slindon, the Duke of Richmond's team. Lumpy himself first comes to light in 1772, on one of the first scorecards to be printed, when he bowled out champion batsman John Small of Hambledon, reputedly the first stealer of singles. Though he appeared for many teams, Edward's main one was Surrey, having been hired as a gardener by the Earl of Tankerville, a local nobleman and cricket fanatic. By the 1770s, underam 'length' bowling was replacing rolling balls and the wicket, which had been low and wide, became a vertical target, measuring about 22 by 6 inches. Although we don't know if Lumpy was the first length bowler, he was certainly a master of pace and direction. John Nyren, our best source on the period, stated that he could send down the 'greatest number of length balls in succession'. Bowling at a brisk medium pace, he once won £100 for Tankerville by hitting a feather at the other end of the wicket four times in succession.

Relatively unconcerned about fielding or catches – for which he wouldn't have been credited – he once kept star batsman John Small pinned down for three hours, scoring only 14 runs. During this match – a five-a-side single-wicket contest played between Hambledon and All England on 22–3 May 1775 – Lumpy sent the ball through the stumps three times without dislodging the bail. Though Small was their man, the Hambledon club agreed that this was 'hard lines' and decreed a third stump, though it was ten years before it became universal.

In response to the new bowling style, Small, who was also a batmaker, created the first straight bat, to defend the new taller wicket. Small's 'new technology', priced at four shillings, replaced the old hockey-style curved bat, which had cost just half a crown for 11.

Another Lumpy legacy was the lbw rule. He was an expert in choosing the right strip of land to set up the stumps, usually on a ridge so that he could shoot low at it. As one poet put it, 'For honest Lumpy would allow/He ne'er would pitch but o'er a brow.' To prevent too much home field advantage, it was decided that the visitors should choose where to place the wicket, which couldn't be moved while the match was in progress. The tactical use of humps and bumps led to the rule that only a ball bowled straight could count as lbw – which was formally recognised from 1788 as 'standing unfair to strike'.

As far as bowling tactics were concerned, length bowling encouraged the first spinners, as the ball naturally moved from leg to off stump. The Hambledon bowler Lamborn is credited with the first off break, which moved in the opposite direction, while Noah Mann, who also played for the club, is said to have discovered swing through the air before suffering an unpleasant death, falling into a fire after a 'free carouse'.

Stevens last appeared for All England at Sevenoaks at the age of 50. After his death the grateful Earl of Tankerville erected a tombstone for him, and Knole House in Kent still has his portrait – the first of a professional cricketer.

Jackie Stewart

Sir John Young Stewart, racing car driver, team owner and marksman, born Dumbuck, Scotland 11 June 1939. F1 driving career 1965–73: 99 races, 17 pole positions, 15 fastest laps, 27 victories. World drivers' champion 1969, 71, 73. Team principal Stewart Grand Prix 1997–9. Winner Coupe des Nations 1955. BBC Sports Personality of the Year 1973. Sports Illustrated Sportsman of the Year 1973. International Motor Sports Hall of Fame 1990.

The 1966 Belgian Grand Prix at Spa-Francorchamps was the first and only serious crash in the eight-year career of triple world champion Jackie Stewart. It also marked a turning point in the history of the sport as Stewart went on to lead an often unpopular campaign for greater safety – something that would change cars, races and circuits for good.

The race itself was a microcosm of everything that was bad, stupid and pointlessly dangerous about racing. Spa-Francorchamps (which, as its hyphenated name suggests, is not terribly close to Spa) is in southern Belgium and was renowned for its pissing rain, which had caused teams and drivers to withdraw in 1963 and 1965. Spa's 14-kilometre circuit consisted of public roads lined with ditches, kilometre markers, road signs, huts and trees, and was large enough for track conditions to vary across the circuit. With no proper marshalling or rescue services, safety had scarcely improved since star racer Dick Seaman was killed there in 1939. In 1960 alone, it claimed the lives of Alan Stacey and Chris Bristow and nearly killed Stirling Moss and Mike Taylor. Jim Clark, the champion driver of the time, declared that if he'd known what it was like beforehand, he'd never have raced on it.

In 1966, Spa surpassed itself as seven drivers left the track on the first soaking corner. (Only five of the field would reach the finish.) The next to aquaplane off at 130 mph was Stewart, who had made a late but meteoric rise through the sport. Though he was brought up around motors at the family garage and his father was an ex-TT racer, Jackie didn't race a car until he was 21, and concentrated instead on clay pigeon shooting, using his excellent eyesight, reactions and powers of concentration. After unexpectedly failing to make the Olympic squad, he turned to racing and competed anywhere and everywhere in club races, quickly gaining experience in a variety of cars. In a Formula Three test for Ken Tyrrell's Cooper BMC, he broke the Silverstone record on only his seventh lap, and with his smooth driving style he won 11 races out of 13 before graduating to Formulas One and Two, while also competing in Can-Am and Tasman races. In his first World Championship season in 1965, he won a point in his debut race, got on the winner's podium in his second and, after a wheel-to-wheel battle with team-mate Graham Hill, won outright at Monza to finish third in the overall championship.

The following season marked an increase in power and speed with the introduction of semi-slick tyres. He won at Monaco, but the second GP, at Spa, was nearly his last. This was not unusual in the sport at the time, as two-thirds of drivers were dying within five years of their track debuts. After losing control, Stewart's BRM struck a ditch, a telegraph pole and a woodman's hut in rapid succession, ending up on a patio with its cockpit bent like a banana and the instrument panel 200 metres away. Stewart had four broken ribs and a broken shoulder, plus a cracked pelvis – none of which would have been so serious had he not been trapped in the cockpit by its fixed steering wheel while its ruptured tanks filled it with fuel. Despite the introduction of fireproof overalls three years before, this was a driver's worst nightmare. With no marshals to help, Stewart spent 25 minutes in his fuel bath, knowing that a single spark would kill him. Rescue came from fellow drivers Bob Bondurant and Graham Hill, who had to borrow tools to free him. After half an hour wrestling with the wheel, there was a ten-minute wait for a pair of ambulances, one of which then got lost, and no proper medical care until he reached the plane to take him home.

Jackie was a new kind of driver – one who believed racing should be a test of skill and concentration rather than bravery. Many racers thought that being flung from a wreck was your best chance of survival, but Stewart installed seat belts and for a while drove with a spanner taped to the dash to get the steering wheel off fast. Though BRM paid for the first basic F1 bus-cum-ambulance, it was Jackie who led the crusade for safety. By 1969 there would be a specialist ambulance, full-face helmets, roll bars, fire-extinguisher systems and rupture-proof fuel tanks, and after a boycott of Spa that year, the circuit was made somewhat safer with chicanes and guard rails. Churns full of fuel were banned from the pits, as were the grass borders that acted like launch ramps. This was all despite apathy and obstruction from the governing body, mockery from some other drivers (Innes Ireland made chicken gestures) and outright opposition from circuit owners and journalists such as Denis Jenkinson, who accused Stewart of 'milk and water' or 'social security' racing.

Stewart's argument was simply that drivers should learn, rather than die, from their mistakes. It helped that he was the master of long and difficult circuits, his powers of recall perhaps compensating for severe dyslexia. The year after the Spa crash, he returned to post his best result of a disappointing season, while the need for seat belts was shown by Mike Parkes's horrible crash – ironically the result of an oil leak from Stewart's own car. The following year, at the 187-turn 28-kilometre Nürburgring – the only circuit larger and riskier than Spa – Stewart drove with his broken wrist in a cast to finish four minutes ahead of the field on new Dunlop tyres. Three championships and 22 wins in five years gave him authority, but so did the dizzying death toll. Though there were 27 'official' F1 deaths in the 1960s, Stewart personally knew of 50 drivers who had met their end while racing or testing.

Each tragedy taught a lesson – usually one that should have been learned long before. For example, Lorenzo Bandini's agonising death at Monaco in 1967 proved that straw bales were not just inadequate but lethal, especially when aflame and fanned by a TV helicopter. The following year, Stewart lost four friends in four months – Mike Spence, Jim Clark, Ludovico Scarfiotti and Jo Schlesser. The death of the master driver Clark at Hockenheim proved yet again that no one was safe racing past unprotected trees, while Schlesser's demise showed the folly of combining unsafe circuits and experimental cars as he crashed at Rouen-les-Essarts, driving a Honda that John Surtees had dismissed as a death trap.

In 1969, the Spanish Grand Prix seemed to take over from Spa as the 'cursed race'. The new aerofoils plus <u>Colin Chapman</u>'s obsession with lightness produced two terrible crashes from Stewart's ex team-mate Graham Hill and friend Jochen Rindt, as their aerofoils buckled under the stress. At the following year's race, held at Jarama, Jackie Ickx's crash left the circuit strewn with debris and foam and reinforced the need for adequate marshalling. However it was only after Bruce McLaren's death later that year that the Grand Prix Drivers' Association formed to lobby for greater safety in car and circuit design. It took the death of Rindt three months later before aerofoils became fixed and standardised. Racing in a horrifyingly unstable Lotus 72, he died after orders to run with the aerofoils off and became the sport's first posthumous champion. After that it took the avoidable death of Jo Siffert at a race at Brands Hatch to get in-car fire extinguishers installed. At Zandvoort, where Stewart clinched his 1973 championship, Roger Williamson died under the gaze of disorganised, ill-equipped marshals and passing drivers, despite the heroic solo efforts of driver David Purley. One improvement that season was the introduction of deformable structures in cars. Introduced at Spa, they proved their value during a massive pile-up at Silverstone.

All in all, it was no surprise that Stewart secretly decided that 1973 would be his last season as a driver. Even his third championship ended in catastrophe as team-mate and apparent successor François Cevert crashed in practice at Watkins Glen. Tyrrell withdrew and Jackie quit on 99 races. The following season, Mike Hailwood would win a George Medal for a solo rescue that should have been carried out by trained marshals. The number of Armco barriers would only slowly increase from one to two to three, and at the 1975 running of the Spanish GP Emerson Fittipaldi refused to race in protest at Montjuich's inadequate railings. (Rolf Stomellen, who did drive, crashed and claimed five lives.)

The legacy of Jackie Stewart's campaigning was a reduction in racing deaths to 'just' 12 in the 1970s. Slick tyres, carbon brakes and compulsory crash testing all cut the death toll. Circuits were slowly upgraded with tyre walls, chicanes, gravel traps and debris fences. First Spa and then Zandvoort were closed, although it would be 1976 before Niki Lauda's near-fatal crash finally shut down the old Nürburgring. From 1978, Bernie Ecclestone invited Professor Sid Watkins to take charge of medical safety and life support systems were installed the following season. As safety improved, 1980 brought the first fast rescue cars, 1981 the FIA Medical Commission and survival cells in cars, and in 1985 the first frontal crash testing was carried out. When Watkins pioneered extractable seats in the late 1990s, the first team to fit them would be Stewart's Grand Prix team.

Today Grand Prix circuits take a pride in their safety facilities and a medical car automatically follows the first and most dangerous lap of the race. Fires are now so well contained that drivers like Jos Verstappen at Hockenheim in 1994 and Michael Schumacher at Austria in 2003 have lived through blazes that would have been fatal before. Without the efforts of Jackie Stewart it would all have happened a lot later.

Adrian Stoop

Adrian Dura Stoop MC, rugby player and administrator, born London 27 March 1889, died 27 November 1957. Playing career: Dover College, Rugby School, Oxford University 1902–4, Harlequins 1901–39, England 1905–6, 1910–12. Administrative career: Harlequins secretary 1906–14, president 1920–49, RFU president 1932–3.

After delays caused by crowds and heavy traffic, the first Twickenham international kicked off on 15 January 1910 as England, who hadn't won the championship since the 1895 split with rugby league, faced the Welsh, the masters of handling and unbeaten in 12 years. The ball was received by Adrian Stoop, Harlequins' renowned fly-half, an abrasive character who had only just been recalled by the selectors – many of whom distrusted his radical approach to the game. On the other hand, Twickenham was Stoop's home turf. The year before, his 'Stoopendous Harlequins' had launched the new Twickenham ground, drawing big crowds with their exciting open rugby and helping to pay for the RFU's great financial gamble.

Stoop, a believer in 'planned surprise', didn't disappoint. He collected the ball and instead of kicking to touch, ran at the Welsh and punted. A loose scrum formed and the ball was spun out to Frederick Chapman on the wing, who scored the first international try at Twickenham, which he then converted. (Chapman also scored the first Twickenham penalty.) The Welsh never recovered the lead and Stoop was chaired from the field. The victory would establish Twickenham as England's stronghold. Over the next two seasons, Stoop was never beaten there and after he retired from international rugby in 1912, there was to be only one loss before the war, to the touring Springboks.

As well as seeing an English rugby resurgence, 1910 marked the new role of the fly-half as a mercurial playmaker and the pivot of attack, plus a new trend in the game for a more open, scientific approach based on fitness and detailed planning. Nearly all of this was Stoop's doing. His approach, dismissed as 'handball' by his critics, was a radical departure for rugby. Halfbacks like Stoop had traditionally been split between left and right, depending on where the ball came out of the scrum.

They often alternated stand-off duties during the match and were usually expected to dribble or fall on the ball. Arguments between rival half-backs were frequent. Although in the 1890s the Welsh had been the first to split the roles, it was Stoop, half Dutch/German, a quarter Scots and a quarter Irish, who really worked out the scrum half–outside half partnership.

Since attending Rugby School, Stoop's fitness had allowed him to spin the ball out of the scrum to either side without needing another player in close attendance. He took his dedication to speed, fitness and the study of the game with him to Oxford University, where he and Pat Munro became the first half-backs to interlink, getting the ball to the backs ASAP and winning 33 out of 43 matches.

When Stoop joined Harlequins, the club were homeless and had less than £50 to their name, but he had a guaranteed income from a marble quarry in the Crimea and was able to concentrate on the club. As secretary for 40 years, he rebuilt their finances and created the 'Stoop system'. For Quins players this meant the first restrictions on cigarettes and beer, lighter studded boots and regular fitness coaching sessions. His new partner Herbert Sibree became the first modern 'scrum half', but Stoop realised how much more there was to learn after a thumping 34–0 defeat while playing for Middlesex against Dave Gallaher's all-conquering All Blacks. Stoop persuaded his backs – traditionally solo speedsters and 'dodgers' – to cooperate, mastering sudden changes of direction, reverse passes, miss-moves and cross-kicks and abandon rugby orthodoxy to attack or counter-attack from all areas of the pitch. Instead of aiming to get the ball to the wings as fast as possible, Quins deliberately drew in defenders and released from the tackle. They also adopted the All Blacks' idea of a front-line 'rover' to attack the opposing half-backs. When their opponents followed suit, Stoop was often the target for their attention.

Despite Harlequins' success, the RFU preferred to parcel out England berths across the clubs, rather than field the strongest national team. The selectors were unpredictable at best and perverse at worst, and their distrust of Stoop's methods kept him out of the side for three years before his sensational return.

After retiring from international rugby in 1912, Stoop would complete a unique double of Harlequins and RFU captaincy and presidency. After being shot in the scrotum while fighting in Mesopotamia, he returned to a club decimated by World War I, the two greatest losses being back-row stars Edgar Mobbs and Ronnie Poulton-Palmer. Stoop established a training ground at Teddington and recruited new talent such as <u>Wavell Wakefield</u>, who arguably would do for forwards what Stoop had done for backs. When the RFU boycotted the 1924 Olympics, Stoop coached the US side to a gold medal and was a selector from 1927, combining this with appearances for Harlequins until the age of 56. Other claims to fame include helping to save the life of ex-Quin Douglas Bader, who he introduced to golf after he lost both legs. (Bader found watching rugby too painful.) Stoop was to lose one son in a car accident and a second in World War II and, perhaps understandably, developed an interest in spiritualism to try to contact the dead.

An outspoken figure in his youth, Stoop declined into occasional windbaggery at RFU dinners and meetings, but his impact on the game was undeniable and he remained a fixture at Twickenham, always standing in the North Stand so he could study the lines of running. In 1959, two years after Stoop's death, G. Carey, who had kicked off that first international at Twickenham, did so again at what was now the Stoop Memorial Ground.

'Major' William Sudell

William Sudell, footballer, team manager and administrator, born Preston 1851, died 5 August 1911. Playing career: Preston North End 1878–89. Manager 1881–93. League treasurer 1889–91, honorary treasurer 1891–2.

The first official history of the Football League contains a minor mystery. Though its other founders are all pictured and eulogised, there is nothing about its first treasurer, William Sudell, player-manager for the most successful league side in history, originator of football professionalism, prime mover behind the setting-up of the League itself and the inspiration for its trophy. The reason for this strange omission? William Sudell was a jailbird.

A handsome member of an old Preston family that seems to have provided many former mayors, Sudell was a maths and business whiz, supposedly able to total three columns of figures at once. From the age of 16 he was also an enthusiastic member of the sports club that met at Moor Park at the north end of the town, playing rugby as well as cycling and swimming. In 1875, he encouraged the North End club to take a lease on a new ground at Deepdale – Preston's home ever since – and by 25 the young cotton mill manager was also the club's chairman.

With a new lease to pay, North End needed crowds, but they struggled to compete with neighbours Preston Grasshoppers and switched to soccer in 1878, making the change permanent in 1881. Within a few years they would be the best club in the country. After a traumatic 10–0 tonking at the feet of local rivals Blackburn Rovers, Sudell became determined to beat them. The reason for Blackburn's success was obvious – they had hired professional Fergie Suter from FA Cup quarter-finalists Darwen. After recruiting many of Blackburn Olympic's 1883 FA Cup-winning side, Rovers would win it themselves the following season.

Although professionalism was against FA rules and resulted in the suspension of Accrington in 1884, Sudell also set about building his own team of pros – mostly Scots, who were the most skilful players and had trounced England in 1880 and 1881. One of the first was playmaker Nick Ross, a centre-back who sprayed the ball around the park and was the first to deliberately pass back to the keeper. As manager of a mill, Sudell was well placed to offer lucrative part-time jobs and eventually had ten Scots on his books, plus Welsh international goalie James Trainer. (A later signing was Arthur Wharton, English football's first black player.) As player-manager, Sudell took his team to Upton Park in 1884, drew 1–1 and was shopped to the FA. To the FA's surprise, Sudell was unrepentant and pointed to the anomalies in their rules: 'Gentlemen, Preston are professionals, but if you refuse to recognise us then we will be amateurs and you cannot prove otherwise.' Preston even withdrew from the FA Cup, taking Burnley and Great Lever with them. To make matters worse for the FA, Sudell was supported by the *Sporting Life*, which thought the exclusion of professionals 'absurd'. Preston and 30 other northern and Midlands sides even debated forming a rival British Football Association, which scared the FA into accepting professional football in July 1885.

Now there was no stopping Preston, and James Trainer was soon able to stand under an umbrella, so rare were attacks on his goal. In the 1885/6 season they won 59 out of 64 matches, scoring 318 goals and conceding just 60. Sudell introduced prematch tactical talks and used chessmen on a billiard table to demonstrate moves, before he brought a blackboard into the changing room. By 1888 Preston were red-hot favourites for the FA Cup and their 26–0 destruction of Hyde led to the idea of bigger clubs entering at later rounds. Before the final, they were so confident they asked to be photographed with 'their' cup, as their kit would be nice and clean. A loss to West Brom came as a total shock. Though Preston had missed the meeting the night before at Anderton's Hotel in Fleet Street, from which the Football League emerged, they joined up for the first season and became the 'Invincibles', carrying off the first championship by 11 points and attracting crowds of over 10,000 as they won 18 matches and drew four. Instead of the flag the League was proposing as a trophy, Sudell wanted a cup and this was agreed, provided the cost was under 50 guineas. Not only did he name the League and work with William McGregor to ensure its success, Sudell also wheeler-dealed with the FA, withdrawing his players from internationals and requesting better payment for FA Cup appearances. As a player, he quit at the top after an FA Cup win that sent all Preston mad with excitement.

The following season brought another League championship, followed by two runners-up places, but by now other clubs were luring Preston's stars away (Derby offered full back Bob Howarth £3 a week) and were also catching up with the Invincibles' tactics. In 1894, Preston were temporarily suspended for fiddling gate receipts and Sudell, who had left the board the year before, had to be replaced as treasurer. A cholera outbreak didn't help matters and relegation threatened. The following year the full truth emerged. Sudell – who had invented his Major rank during the 1880s – was found to have embezzled £5,000 from the mill and was sentenced to three years' imprisonment. Such misery might have broken many men, but not Billy Sudell, who was passionately defended by the *Athletic News*. Aged 52, he left prison and set off for South Africa to work as a journalist, rising to become sports editor of the *South African News*.

Preston never again lifted a major trophy, but the 1889 Invincibles' average of 3.4 goals per match and their 84 per cent win rate remain unmatched. Deepdale, which Sudell helped found, is now the oldest established league ground, home since 1998 to the Football Museum and from 2007 to an Invincibles Pavilion.

John L. Sullivan – 'The Boston Strongboy'

John Lawrence Sullivan, boxer and baseballer, born Roxbury, Massachusetts 12 October 1858, died 2 February 1918. World champion 1882–92. Official record: 42 fights, 38 wins (33 inside time), 1 loss, 1 stoppage, 3 draws. International Boxing Hall of Fame 1990.

John L. Sullivan, the first world champion boxer, was both the last bare-knuckle champion and the first gloved one, ushering in the general adoption of John Chambers's Queensberry Rules. Sullivan became America's first sporting superstar and was the first to gross $1 million. He turned boxing from an illegal, illicit sport into front-page news and made the heavyweight championship the greatest prize in sport.

Born to poor Irish immigrants, Sullivan rose rapidly to become the 'Emperor of Masculinity', a representation of the American dream for those at the bottom of the ladder and an image of national triumph at a time when the West had been won – or more accurately, purchased. He was feted by the papers, forgiven his various crimes and mobbed by crowds. At the end, fans would offer the chance to shake hands with a man who had shaken hands with John L. Sullivan.

Only 5 feet 10 inches tall, but apparently strong enough to lift a streetcar, Sullivan first came to prominence in 1878 at Boston's Dudley Opera House, where champion Jack Swannell offered a prize for anyone able to last four exhibition rounds with him. John L., then working in the Boston sewers, shed his coat, pulled on a couple of mitts and soon sent Swannell crashing into the onstage piano. Turning down the chance to play baseball for the Red Stockings, he fought a first exhibition in 1880 and was soon fighting in New York. Promoted by its *Police Gazette* sporting paper, he offered $50 to any man who could live with him. Few could. His crouch and rush was unsubtle and his defence limited to an iron chin, but he was remorseless and relentless and his right felt like a telegraph pole. 'Win I must and win I shall,' he declared. Wisely, he stuck with gloved boxing, establishing it as the mainstream style. Only in three major fights did he use bare knuckles.

Sullivan claimed the American title after defeating Paddy Ryan in Mississippi City in 1882. With his corner decked in colourful banners, the handsome moustachioed John L. took just ten minutes to defeat Ryan in front of a crowd that included Jesse James. The following year, he suffered his only knock-down from the light and skilful Brummie Charley Mitchell – though Mitchell was lucky that the police stopped the fight after round three. Sullivan turned up too drunk for the rematch and, because boxing was illegal in Britain, the 1887 re-rematch took place in bitter rain behind Lord Rothschild's stables in Chantilly. Mitchell fought a fine defensive battle, which left both fighters too exhausted to carry on.

Sullivan's Queensberry Rules world championship is usually dated from his sixth-round defeat of Dominick McCaffrey in 1885, but his last bare-knuckle prize-ring fight was against the undefeated Jake Kilrain, who had announced himself champion after only drawing an epic 106-round contest with Englishman Jem Smith. Sullivan initially ducked Kilrain, preferring to profit from exhibitions, tours, speechmaking, appearances in the melodrama *Honest Hearts and Willing Hands* ('Mr Sullivan was as good as the play,' commented one ambiguous critic) and appearing in tableaux as 'The Dying Gladiator' or 'Hercules Resting'. One popular part of his boxing act was a punch from Mrs Hessie Donahue, who had once decked him for real. Though he kept his cool in the ring, John L. was notorious out of it. A famous dandy who wore a teal-blue vest and pink and black checked trousers, he would fight anyone, generally butting them into submission, and narrowly avoided death after falling off a train while drunk. 'A son-of-a-bitch of the first water,' said one witness, 'if he ever drunk any.' Wisely, Sullivan refused to take bribes or deal with gamblers, removing any taint from his victories.

The showdown with Kilrain finally came in 1889. Officially banned from New Orleans – although the mayor acted as ref – Sullivan battered Kilrain into submission after 75 rounds of an 80-round contest, held in the woods near Richburg, Mississippi. There were photographers in the trees, and the *New York Times*, which had carried prematch publicity for the first time, declared that 'The Bigger Brute Won'. The law intervened again, and the high cost of defending himself and escaping a one-year sentence led Sullivan to declare that he would never again fight bare-knuckle. He, or more likely his ghostwriter, explained that 'They [the old rules] allow too much leeway for the rowdy element to indulge in their practices. Such mean tricks as spiking, biting, gouging, strangling, butting with the head, falling down without being struck, scratching with the nails, kicking, falling on the antagonist with the knees are impossible under the new Queensberry Rules. Fighting under them in front of gentlemen is a pleasure.' In the same year, the last bare-knuckle fight in Europe ended in disgraceful scenes as Frank Slavin was cudgelled by Squire Abingdon Baird's hired thugs. The disgusted reaction finally killed off the old London Prize Rules.

After the Kilrain fight, Sullivan enjoyed his fame, deploying the old prize-ring trick of setting an unaffordably high price for a fight. He refused to fight the Australian-West Indian Peter Jackson, who was probably his superior, and also the black Canadian George Godfrey, declaring, 'I will never fight a negro. Never have and never will.' This convenient doctrine, known as 'drawing the colour line', not only saved his title but also helped other fighters to do the same for years to come. Sullivan even had a stage production of *Uncle Tom's Cabin* rewritten so he could beat the daylights out of Uncle Tom. When Tommy Burns finally fought the black fighter <u>Jack Johnson</u> for the championship, Sullivan decried Burns's actions in print then claimed afterwards that he had never really been a champion. Johnson's defeat of the previous champion Jim Jeffries he declared to be a fix.

Sullivan's fights caused newspaper sales to increase tenfold and encouraged more sponsored fights. With so much money to be made, boxing became legal again in New York in 1896 and Nevada the year after. By this time, John L. had met his nemesis, in the form of the younger and better prepared Jim Corbett, an ex-bank clerk with a wider range of skills, including boxing on the defence, dodging and weaving. Sullivan's reign ended in 1892 during a three-day extravaganza held under electric lights in New Orleans. Though the 4–1 favourite, Sullivan was out of shape, having not fought for four years, but he was still dangerous and Corbett avoided fighting him, instead picking off his punches, ducking, countering, sidestepping and weaving. Unable to carry on after round eight, Sullivan made a graceful speech which left all present in tears and secured his fame, while Corbett was widely reviled for beating the champion in a new and less heroic defensive style. He only became popular after losing his title and making two brave attempts to regain it.

In years to come, Sullivan would show his punch in one more come-back fight in 1905, laying out Jim McCormick in two rounds when aged 50. He reformed his alcoholic ways, though the damage to his health was done, and toured as an anti-drink evangelist and general celebrity, also reporting from ringside and umpiring baseball matches. He went out with a bang too – the frozen earth had to be dynamited to make his grave.

Today Sullivan's image is still used as the archetypal old-style fighter and his name crops up in steakhouses and computer games. Apparently 'long johns' are named after his stage garb.

Michael Sweeney

Michael F. Sweeney, high jumper, long jumper, sprinter and coach, born Kenmare, Ireland 27 October 1872, died ?. US high jump champion 1892, 93, 94, 95. World champion 1892.

It was Michael Sweeney who made the first major technical advance in the high jump with his 'eastern cut-off' style, holding the world record until it was overtaken by <u>George Horine</u>'s western roll.

Like many great field athletes, Sweeney was an Irish-American. After the Sweeney family left County Kerry for a tearful reunion with their father in New York, young Michael set to work as a painter and varnisher to earn a crust, but his skill as an athlete was soon recognised and, though only 5 foot 8 inches tall, he was national high jump champion by the age of 20. Five years later, in the first international athletics match between the New York and London clubs, he electrified the crowd with a jump of 1.97 metres – a record for 17 years to come.

High jumping had its origins in northern British and Scottish contests in which a variety of jumps were featured. The first well-documented meeting was held in 1840, when heights of about 1.60–1.70 metres were reached. By 1865, the rules allowed three attempts at the bar, no lowering of it and no two-footed jumps. However, the styles were very inefficient, consisting of a basic 'sitting' scissors or a rough side-on roll. This changed in 1876, when Marshall Brooks of Brasenose College, Oxford, the future English champion, reached 1.89 metres with a twisting cat-like jump, technically known as a 'frontal back layout'. This leap, which many professional athletes simply couldn't believe, was to be a university record until after World War II.

Sweeney took the scissors – the most economical style – and improved it by lying back over the bar to lower his centre of gravity and get his body higher. He would have been a favourite for the first two Olympics, but was working at The Hill, a prep school in Pennsylvania, which disqualified him as a professional. In 1900, he won the high and long jump and 100-yard dash at a professional meeting. At The Hill Sweeney taught sports and athletics for forty years with great success, and the gym there is still named after him.

Florence 'Madge' Syers

Florence Madeleine Syers (née Cave), figure skater, swimmer and horse rider, born Weybridge, Surrey 9 September 1882, died 9 September 1917. Great Britain champion 1903, 04, world ladies champion 1906, 07, Olympic gold medallist 1908.

Florence Syers was perhaps the first modern British sportswoman to win on level terms against male opposition.

When the first World Skating Championships were held in 1902, it didn't even occur to the organisers to ban women and they were unable to stop Florence entering. Using Jackson Haines's freer 'international' style, she came second only to the great Ulrich Salchow, inventor of the jump. (Salchow reportedly thought her superior to him and handed her his medal.) After being banned from international competition – partly on the grounds that her long skirts made it impossible to see her skates – Florence moved to a calf-length skirt and beat her husband and coach Edgar into second place at the 1903 UK Championships. Once an International Ladies' Championship was established in 1906, she won the first two titles, also winning individual gold in the 1908 London Olympics and a bronze with Edgar in the pairs. At 27, she would be the oldest Olympic champion and the only skater to win two medals at one Olympics. She was also the last British champion until Jeanette Altwegg in 1952. Poor health forced her to retire in 1908 and she died of influenza, aged just 35.

Maurice 'Chub' Tate

Maurice William Tate, cricketer, born Brighton, Sussex 30 May 1895, died 18 May 1956. First-class career: Sussex and MCC 1912–37, 679 matches, 21,717 runs (25.04), 2,784 wickets (18.16); 39 Tests 1924–35, 1,198 runs (25.48), 155 wickets (26.16). Wisden Cricketer of the Year 1924.

'Maurice, you must change your style of bowling immediately.'

In 1922, a faster delivery that scattered the stumps of his county captain Arthur Gilligan transformed the cherubic Maurice Tate into the best bowler in the world. Before then Tate, like his father Fred before him, had been plying his trade with slow off breaks, but this encouragement from Gilligan and fellow pro Ernest Tyldesley of Lancashire turned him into the first great seam bowler, deriving movement from landing the ball on its stitches and setting records that would last for years. In his next match against Kent, he took 8 for 67 with his new style.

A big strong man who bowled with a remarkably smooth action, Tate used his whole body to turn the ball and eventually had to bowl with a corset under his shirt. His deliveries, which seemed to gain pace off the pitch, could rear up and swing or break in any direction in all conditions. Bowler <u>Sydney Barnes</u> remarked that Tate tried to get a wicket with every ball and was surprised if he didn't. In first-class matches, Tate and his captain Arthur Gilligan were especially feared on hazy mornings at Hove, where the conditions particularly favoured them. On Maurice's 1924 Test debut at Edgbaston, the pair bowled out South Africa for just 30 runs in only 75 minutes. That winter, bowling in great pain on rock-hard grounds, Tate took 38 wickets against the Australians – an Ashes record until Alec Bedser beat it at home in 1956 – and in 1926 he helped England regain the Ashes at the Oval. He was still effective against the young <u>Don Bradman</u> in 1928/9 and bowled him again in 1930, but ended up getting pummelled. With his 'go for the wicket' approach, it never occurred to him or his team to try to contain Bradman with a leg trap. Tate, who probably lost loads of wickets for the want of a man at short leg, wasn't used in the 1932 or 1934 Test series.

Having bowled more than 150,000 balls and seemingly gone on

forever, Tate was dumped by his county aged 42, having made very little provision for retirement, and became a school coach and publican. Later, Sussex made partial amends to their first professional captain by naming some gates after him. Seam bowling remained an English stand-by, but a decision in 1989 to cut the number of strands on the seam from 15 to 9 reduced its effectiveness.

John Henry 'J.H.' Taylor

John Henry Taylor, golfer, born Northam, Devon 19 March 1871, died 10 February 1963. British Open champion 1894, 95, 1900, 09, 13. Non-playing Ryder Cup-winning captain 1933. PGA president 1901.

Along with Harry Vardon and James Braid, J.H. Taylor formed part of the 'Great Triumvirate' that dominated golf before World War I. He was the first to break Scottish dominance of the game and the player most responsible for the creation of the PGA, turning the pros from – to quote golf writer Bernard Darwin – 'a feckless company into a self-respecting and respected body of men'.

A strong and stocky man, Taylor was born near the Royal North Devon's Westward Ho! course which, as common land, was open for general use. After caddying, he became a member of the greenkeeping staff, which helped him in his later career as a course designer. He was renowned for his straight and accurate driving, often delivered with a little grunt, as well as his ability in bad weather. His success often rested on his use of a mashie – usually a chipping and bunker club – for distances as long as 100 yards.

After firing the lowest round of the year in 1893, his breakthrough came in 1894 at Sandwich, the first time that the Open had left Scotland, when he secured the first of five victories. The following year he won at St Andrews, confirming the end of the Scottish stranglehold on the game. As late as 1922, at the age of 52, he was within four strokes of victory and his 1904 Muirfield course record lasted a quarter of a century, before Walter Hagen broke it.

Taylor took leadership of the poorly paid, overworked pros, and when a strike was threatened over the low prize money at Sandwich in 1899, he organised extra funds. Two years later he formed the Professional Golfers' Association and arranged the first £15 contest on Tooting Bec Common. As their leader, J.H. wrote columns and even took speaking lessons to argue better on their behalf. He attracted new money into the sport when the *News of the World* provided £200 for a professional match-play tournament, which he won. He was also in at the creation of the National Association of Public Golf Courses and the Artisan Golfers' Association – a group that represented the clubs' 'second-class' working members.

As well as being club pro for the Royal Mid-Surrey from 1899 to retirement in 1946, Taylor was golf's first all-round sports-businessman, setting up the equipment company Cann and Taylor and writing an un-ghosted autobiography, *Golf: My Life's Work*. In partnership with Fred Hawtree, he designed and redesigned various courses, of which the best known is Royal Birkdale (1931), with its splendid art-deco clubhouse. The Ryder Cup, which Taylor's work had helped lead to, arrived too late in his career for him to play, but he captained the team to victory in 1933. After he retired, he was made an honorary member of the R&A and was later captain of Royal Birkdale and president of Westward Ho! He died in the village of his birth.

Peter Taylor

Peter Murray Taylor, Baron Taylor of Gosforth, judge, born Newcastle 1 May 1930, died 28 April 1997. Lord Chief Justice England and Wales 1992–6.

The transformation of British football stadiums into all-seaters may only have been a small part of Peter Taylor's legal career, but the Hillsborough disaster inquiry he headed was to change the sport for ever.

On his appointment in 1989, the papers made great play of Taylor's credentials as a Newcastle United supporter, but this hadn't blinded him to the failure of most clubs to protect their customers from death and injury. What his interim and final reports grasped was what the previous eight inquiries into safety at British grounds had all failed to recognise – that the game was incapable of regulating itself. As a consequence, 4,000 people had been killed or injured in over 35 serious incidents at 29 grounds since records began. The Taylor Report bit the bullet, put a state agency in charge of safety and forced clubs to upgrade through the very real threat of closure. Though six were allowed an extension to complete works, five were not. For the first time, the report also directed government money into safety works.

Though there were 120 recommendations in the report, the main ones were an immediate reduction in numbers on terraces by 15 per cent (later 13 per cent), while in the top two divisions all terraces were to be replaced by seating by 1994 and in the bottom two by 1999. Spiked fences and any over 2.2 metres were banned and other enforced improvements included the creation of police control rooms and first-aid areas. The government's planned ID card schemes were stopped, as they would slow movement into the stadium and create crushes, but it also became illegal to go onto the pitch.

The scramble to meet the Taylor requirements led to £1 billion being spent, with 40 grounds redeveloped and 30 teams re-sited. The report was also a catalyst for a change in attitudes. The police, who had been obsessed with the threat of violence to the exclusion of all else, began taking fan safety into account and clubs realised that they had to stop treating their customers as criminals. As a result of better conditions and the gentrification of football, violence fell from 7,100 arrests per year in the mid-1980s to less than half that by the 1990s.

Unbeknownst to most football fans, Peter Taylor shook up and modernised the criminal law almost as much as he did football. A famous cross-examiner, he prosecuted corrupt MPs and civil servants, extended legal protection to unborn children and helped bring in a 'diminished responsibility' defence in domestic violence cases. Under him the law began to face up to its bias against women and racial minorities as well as a series of past miscarriages of justice – including Taylor's own prosecution of the innocent Stefan Kiszko. The first judge to hold a press conference, Taylor called for fuller disclosure of evidence and ended the blanket defence of 'national security', which allowed unlimited spying on citizens. The year before his death he strongly attacked what he saw as the Home Secretary's crowd-pleasing attacks on justice. Since his report there has been just one death in a British football ground. There is a bust of him in the Royal Courts in the Strand, though it is often said – perhaps appropriately for the heart of the British legal system – that it doesn't do him justice.

Edward Thring

Edward Thring, educator, born Alford, Somerset 29 November 1821, died 22 October 1887.

Most people would expect a good school to have a gym for all-weather sport, but there were none in Britain until Edward Thring built the first at his school in Uppingham.

Thring, a games-loving Old Etonian priest, found his real vocation when he took over the tiny, struggling Uppingham and transformed it into one of England's most successful and progressive schools. A great believer in broadening the curriculum beyond the traditional maths and classics, he also had the radical idea of trying to help every pupil achieve – not just the most gifted. Thring also knew that what he called 'machinery' was vital to schooling, and not only did Uppingham boast the first continental-style gym (perhaps inspired by Thring's German in-laws), but also a heated swimming pool.

Having built up the roll from just 25 to 300 and escaped a local typhoid outbreak by briefly exiling the school to West Wales, Thring spread his ideas by hosting the first Headmasters' and Headmistresses' Conference at his own home in 1869. He also employed his brother John, who had been at Cambridge in 1848 when their football rules were created, and who in 1862 published 'The Simplest Game', a short series of rules for playing football. The following year these 'Uppingham Rules' would became the basis for the Football Association's.

John Thurston

John Thurston, businessman and inventor, born London 1777, died September 1850.

No equipment-maker can have had a greater impact on a sport than John Thurston, whose family firm created the modern billiard table, spread the rules of the game and created the Match Hall – 'the Lord's of billiards'.

Thurston's was founded in 1799 as the first specialist maker of tables and by 1815 had a patriotically-named Waterloo Billiards Works at Cheyne Walk in Chelsea. Over the next half-century the firm came up with two great innovations that allowed a rise in standards of play. The first was slate beds instead of warping oak, which they introduced in 1826 and which were universal by 1840. The other was a more regular rubber cushion in place of felt or flax. At first these were deemed to be less accurate and too hard at low temperatures, so zinc or copper water pipes were used to warm them up, starting with a model given to Queen Victoria, the third in a long line of monarchs to use Thurston's tables. From 1845, a patented vulcanised rubber cushion meant that the warmers were no longer needed. In 1851, the year after John Thurston's death, his company's tables won a top award at the Great Exhibition and they soon issued a first standard set of rules, written by champion Jonathan Kentfield.

Thurston's continued to innovate, producing the bottomless pocket and rail in 1887, and five years later theirs became the first officially approved table. In 1901, they set up offices and showrooms on Leicester Square as well as the richly decorated and curtained Match Hall. Here the white-gloved and stiff-collared referee Charlie Chambers held court in smoky silence, keeping mental track of scores, hazards, nursery cannons, sequences of minuscule contacts, and periodic crossings of the line. In the late 1930s, J.B. Priestley wrote, 'When the world is wrong, hardly to be endured, I shall return to Thurston's Hall and there smoke a pipe with the connoisseurs of top and side.' Unfortunately, on 4 October 1940 a German landmine wrecked the Match Hall, though the table survived.

After the war the site of Thurston's Hall became the HQ for <u>Joe Davis</u>, the godfather of billiards and snooker. As a company, Thurston's celebrated its 200th anniversary in 1999.

'Big Bill' Tilden – 'The King of the Nets'

William Tatum Tilden II, tennis player, born Philadelphia 10 February 1893, died 5 June 1953. US singles champion 1920, 21, 22, 23, 24, 25, 29, US doubles champion 1918, 21, 22, 23, 27, mixed doubles champion 1913, 14, 22, 23, Wimbledon singles champion 1920, 21, 30, doubles champion 1927, French mixed doubles champion 1930. Davis Cup winner 1926–30. International Tennis Hall of Fame 1959.

The tall, lean 'Big Bill' Tilden dominated men's tennis for seven years and has been rated both the best player of the years 1900 to 1950 and the best US player of all time. Along with fellow champion <u>Suzanne Lenglen</u> (who he disliked), his fame led to him becoming one of the first touring professionals in a hitherto amateur sport. Along with Jack Dempsey, <u>Bobby Jones</u>, <u>Babe Ruth</u> and Red Grange, he was one of the greatest stars in a golden era of sports. His great strength, smoking and steak-eating shook tennis free of its effete, country-club image – which was ironic, because Bill was widely believed to be gay and became increasingly effeminate in later life.

Like Lenglen, Bill Tilden built his game through determination and practice. Blessed with a great physique and long reach. His crucial match was the 1919 US Championships, where he lost to 'Little Bill' Johnson. After this, Tilden rebuilt his backhand to emerge, at the late age of 27, as an unbeatable champion, winning every serious game, and a record seven consecutive Davis Cups.

Famous for his deception and high-speed cannonball service, Bill was once clocked serving at 163 mph, although the alternative figure of 151 seems more credible. (The current record is about 155.) Usually, he spun his serves, producing a vast kick that sent the ball from an opponent's left leg to his right shoulder. Rather than rushing to the net, Bill dominated the baseline with chops, slices, drops and lobs, and his only real weakness was reckoned to be his overhead. A natural entertainer with a highly developed source of honour, he threw away points when he felt his opponent had been badly treated and reputedly even gave away sets to make the contest more of a challenge. He had huge hands, slightly reduced by the loss of a fingertip, and a favourite trick was to hold five balls, serve four aces and lob the spare away.

Like Lenglen, Bill was often at odds with the tennis establishment, which profited from his star status but banned him from even writing about the sport. His feud with Julian 'Mike' Myrick of the USLTA led to a ban from US tournaments and the Davis Cup and such a row with the French that even President Hoover had to intervene.

In 1931, at the age of 37, Bill turned pro – preferring to play for a living, rather than suck up to wealthy fans as what he termed a 'social gigolo'. He would spend the rest of his life criss-crossing the States with players such as Ellsworth Vines, Fred Perry, Don Budge and Bobby Riggs, and even refunded the promoters if he failed to draw a crowd. Although the statistics suggest otherwise, Bill felt he reached his peak in 1934, and aged 52 was still able to hold his own against the 27-year-old Riggs. Free from the USLTA, he wrote *The Art of Lawn Tennis* and *Match Play and the Spin of the Ball* – the latter regarded as a definitive text.

Urbane, well-read and a master of bridge, Tilden maintained a stylish suite at the Algonquin Hotel, but was less successful with his fiction and appearances on the stage and the shows he backed. The consensus view is that deaths in his family and rejection by his father left him lonely and asexual. (Bill makes a disguised cameo appearance in *Lolita*.) Even two offences with minors, for which he served prison time in the 1940s, could not prevent him being voted the player of the half-century, although it hurt him badly in lost tuition and appearances and he was shunned by some clubs and universities. Nevertheless, when he died of a stroke aged 60 his bags were packed for another tournament.

Harry Vardon – 'Mr Golf'

Harry Vardon, golfer, born Grouville, Jersey 9 May 1870, died 20 March 1937. Major wins: British Open 1896, 98, 99, 1903, 11, 14, US Open 1900, PGA Match Play 1912. World Golf Hall of Fame 1974.

In the early spring of 1900, Harry Vardon, a visiting British golf pro, was carrying out an in-store demonstration of this minority sport at the Jordan Marsh department store in Boston. Egged on by an enthusiastic crowd, which included future US Open winner Francis Ouimet, Harry began playing mashie shots around the store, threatening to set off the sprinkler system as he targeted the taps in the ceiling. By the end of the day, Jordan Marsh had sold every bit of equipment they had and America was in the grip of Vardonmania. Even Wall Street closed the day he played an exhibition in New York and by the time he left the US it was estimated that 250,000 new golfers had tried the game and 1,100 new courses opened.

Golf's first international star was born into a poor family far from the game's main centres and at first played with a stick and a stone. After starting work aged 12 as a farmer's boy and gardener, Harry's skill was recognised by his employer Major <u>Spofforth</u> (<u>Fred's</u> brother) and he eventually went to Ripon as a pro and greenkeeper for their nine-hole course. His breakthrough came at Bury in 1891 when he recognised that his right hand was overpowering his left and started interlocking his fingers. 'Golf,' he later declared, 'is a two-handed affair.' In fact, John Laidlay had tried this before, but he was so unconventional that few ever copied him. Harry also replaced the old shallow 'St Andrews' sweep with a more upright and elegant swing, attacking the pin from distance. He made such an impact that the majority of golfers still use his grip or variants on it. His classic swing and mental toughness made him the most consistent striker of the ball, and he was half-jokingly said to be able to land his ball in the divots from his previous round. He was also the first to wear knickerbockers in place of trousers.

Vardon's only significant weakness was his putting, and by 1896 he was Britain's pre-eminent golfer, going on to win a record 14 consecutive events. Despite his success, he was not blind to the problems of humbler pros, driven from the club-making trade by the factories, and working long hours for little over a pound a week. In 1899, there was a near-strike over the inadequate prize money on offer at Sandwich. Vardon, Willie Park and fellow 'triumvirate' members James Braid and J.H. Taylor persuaded their fellow pros not to strike but doubled the money through their own efforts. In 1901, Vardon co-founded the PGA, whose *News of the World* match play prize helped to create a new source of income for professional golfers.

Not only did Harry win more British Opens than any other player in history, but he was also willing to travel and profit from his skills and endorsement value. His 1900 US Tour promoted his 'Vardon Flyer' ball and led to a £900 contract with Al Spalding's equipment company as he played 80 exhibitions for up to $200 each. Even playing against the better ball of two opponents, he only lost two matches. 'No one had any idea that a player could control a golf ball in the masterly way that Vardon did,' wrote golfer Herbert Wind. Copied by future champions Francis Ouimet and Walter Hagen, he carried off the US Open and remained a massive star in the US.

Despite contracting TB in 1902, Vardon still won the following year's Open but later had to retire to a sanatorium, where he wrote *The Complete Golfer*, which sold out 13 editions in two years. It would be 1911 before he won the Open title again. When in 1913 Ouimet beat him on his home course to win the US Open, it was regarded as American golf's coming-of-age. Afterwards, Vardon completed another 20,000-mile tour, this time witnessed by future champion Bobby Jones.

In 1914, George Duncan and the Triumvirate conducted an elaborate test of the gutta-percha ball versus Coburn Haskell's livelier rubber-wound ball. Played at the Vardon-designed Sandy Lodge course, the nine-hole victory for the Haskell ball confirmed it as the best and changed golf forever.

Having lost some of his trophies to a zeppelin raid on his house, Vardon remained a good player into his fifties and at the 1920 US Open, in which he was paired with Jones, was still leading after the third round. As runner-up in that year's British Open, he was also involved in the first international PGA match – the precursor of Samuel Ryder's Cup, for which he made the team selections in 1927. Harry died in

1937, but the Vardon medal, showing his famous grip, is still presented to the lowest average scoring golfer of the season. Bernard Darwin, the first full-time golf correspondent, termed Vardon a 'genius' and wrote that he was 'a natural speaker, a natural fighter and leader who would have made his mark in any walk of life'. A first-round pick when the US Golf Hall of Fame started in 1974, he was rated the 13th best of all time by *Golf* in 2000.

Harry Vassall – 'The Ajax of the Football Field'

Henry Vassall, rugby player, born Tadcaster, Yorkshire 22 October 1860, died 5 January 1925. Playing career: Oxford University 1879–82, England 1881–2 (4 caps). RFU treasurer 1884–94.

Between the 1870s and the 1880s, rugby changed from a senseless shoving match into a constructive game with forwards, halfbacks and backs working together. The man most associated with this was Harry Vassall, whose Oxford team lost only one game under his captaincy.

Vassall was a rugged forward, who at the 1881 Varsity Match tussled single-handedly with his opposite number for five minutes. However, since being captain of the Marlborough School 1st XV, Vassall had always been a schemer – particularly after a bad accident led to a school-wide ban on forwards picking up. This meant that instead of the ball shooting out of the scrum by accident, there was planned heeling to the backs. At Blackheath, Lennard Stokes's side began wheeling the scrum to attack on either side, but Vassall's university team went much further, with planned heeling, wheeling, breaking, short passes and attacking drop kicks. Their all-round attack, with three three-quarters in support, meant that one series of 26 tries was scored by 17 different players.

By 1882, Vassall's side had 11 internationals, including Alan Rotherham, a halfback from <u>Edward Thring</u>'s soccer-playing Uppingham School. Rotherham was another freethinker who became the first effective link between forwards and backs, passing before he was caught and deliberately spraying the ball across the field.

These new ideas made rugby a far more attractive spectacle and fed back into school, university and club sides – particularly Bradford, the leading club side of the time. From 1887, the 'release in the tackle' rule made some elements of Vassall's style universal, although many of his more enterprising ideas were forgotten until the Home Nations were steamrollered by <u>Dave Gallaher</u>'s All Blacks in 1905. Vassall served as RFU treasurer for ten years, wrote *Rugby Football* and worked as a teacher and bursar at Repton School, near to where he is buried.

Willy Voet

Willy Voet, sports physiotherapist, born Hofstade, Belgium 4 July 1945.

At 6.45 a.m. on 8 July 1998, Willy Voet, a *soigneur* (healer) for the Festina cycling team, was driving from Belgium into France on his way to the start of the Tour de France when he opted to take a back route, rather than the E17 motorway. It was to prove a historically bad decision. The road Willy took was used by smugglers and despite driving a Festina team car, he was pulled over near the village of Dronckaert (Flemish for 'drunkard') and found to be driving on a mixture of illegal drugs while banned. To make matters worse, the car was stuffed full of performance-enhancing drugs including narcotics, the blood-booster erythropoietin (EPO), growth hormones, testosterone and amphetamines, for which Willy could come up with no very convincing explanation.

Despite attempts by the Festina management and riders and the Tour authorities to distance themselves from the discovery, further searches led to the most public drugs scandal in Tour history, with seven teams quitting or expelled, sit-down protests, riders dragged from their bikes and the race almost cancelled twice. Though the fines and bans handed out were pretty limited, it marked a new intensification in the fight against drugs in cycling – particularly EPO.

Willy's arrest was to have implications beyond cycling too. Commenting on the record to a Spanish journalist, Olympic president Juan Antonio Samaranch suggested that too many drugs were banned in sport and that only those definitely injurious to health should be restricted. The implication was that anabolic steroids were 'OK'. Coming hard on the heels of the suspicious death of track star Florence Griffith-Joyner, this led to huge furore and a call for concerted action against drugs in sport.

Having seen the Tour brought low, the Olympics' international sports federations were persuaded to adopt a new, more practical and forceful anti-drugs code. After the 1999 Lausanne Conference, with the games on the back foot after the Salt Lake City bribery scandal, the IOC formed the World Anti-Doping Agency (WADA) – the first effective drug control and detection body in international sport.

As for Willy, in 2000 he received a ten-month suspended sentence and a US$4,200 fine. Banned from the Tour, which has since dropped the term *soigneur*, he quit the sport to work as a bus driver, occasionally attending seminars to explain and discourage drug abuse in sport.

Wavell Wakefield

Sir William Wavell Wakefield, 1st Baron Wakefield of Kendal, rugby player, cricketer, athlete, skier, water skier, diver and sports administrator, born Beckenham, Kent 10 March 1898, died 12 August 1983. Playing career 1918–29: RAF, Cambridge University, Harlequins 1919–39; England 1920–8, 31 caps (captain 13 times), Grand Slam winners 1921, 23, 24. President RFU 1950–1. President Harlequins 1950–80. International Rugby Hall of Fame 1999.

Between 1920 and 1927, William Wavell Wakefield revolutionised English forward play and led a resurgent squad to a series of victories.

Despite standing 6 feet tall and weighing 14 stone, 'Wakers' was faster than most backs, an RAF quarter-mile champion who gave Olympic champion Harold Abrahams a scare, and a sporting all-rounder who also won the Kandahar downhill skiing race and played cricket for the MCC. As well as having unusual speed and handling abilities, he was an ace dribbler with the more rounded ball of the day and an innovative tactician. In a pre-coaching era, Wakefield, usually kitted out with a white scrum cap over his fair hair, transformed his fellow back-row forwards from static scrummagers and ball-winners in the loose into fully involved team members, supporting the backs in attack and defence. He declared rugby 'a game for the mentally alert', and after seeking out, moulding and switching around the best talent at Cambridge, defeated Oxford in 1923 by letting them wear themselves out with fruitless possession.

At the time, most teams scrummed down any old way, with any number of forwards jostling for front-row advantage, but Wakefield, who saw the clear advantage of the put-in, defined roles and from 1926 his three-man front row was in the rules. At line-outs he worked out the first patterns of jumping and support, and had a winger throw in so that the scrum half was in place to clear the ball faster and defend if necessary. His forwards added tackling and passing to the old skills of wheeling and dribbling and pioneered deliberate second-phase play – drawing in their opponents, then heeling back fast, with the open-side flanker supporting the three-quarters. These tactics were greatly helped by England's cool-headed Welsh-born fly half W.J.A.

'Dave' Davies, undefeated in 22 games. A favourite wheeze was to swing the ball wide to the winger, who cross-kicked to Wakefield, who then dribbled to the try line and touched down.

When the opposing backs had the ball, Wakefield's forwards had patterns of defence to follow, rather than leaving it all to their own backs. The back-row forwards also tried to intercept the opposing half-backs and backs – the blind-side wing-forward targeting the scrum half while the other two supported the fly half and three-quarters. If the opposition broke free, the number eight had specific defensive 'corner-flagging' responsibilities.

By doing for forwards what fellow Harlequin <u>Adrian Stoop</u> had done for backs and halfbacks, Wakefield nullified Stoop-style attacks from the three-quarters and his 136 appearances for the Quins helped make them England's premier side, taking over from Blackheath. As bigger crowds gathered to watch 'Wakers' and his men, the RFU built up Twickenham to a 74,000-capacity stadium, which, at three shillings a seat, was also Britain's most expensive.

Wakefield's England retained their advantage over other international sides who were slow to copy their tactics. As so often in sport, it was the defensive ideas that were copied first and most easily, and as the number of tries dropped, the game became less attractive. Even so, as late as the mid-1920s the Welsh pack were still packing down any old way and were once out-scrummaged by a better-organised bunch of Cardiff policemen. It was 1928 before they started to copy England's innovations. With no organised coaching, once Wakefield retired, English rugby slipped back.

After his playing days were over, Wakefield pursued careers in business and politics, returning to active service in World War II and becoming head of the Air Training Corps. After the war he helped grass-roots sport through the YMCA and National Playing Fields Association. His record of 31 caps lasted until the 1960s, when Budge Rogers of Bedford finally overtook it.

Frederick Wall

Frederick Joseph Wall, sports administrator, born London 1858, died 1944. Football Association secretary 1895–1934.

When in 1934 Fredrick Wall, the fifth secretary of the FA, handed over to his successor, <u>Stanley Rous</u>, he refused to shake his hand or allow a photograph, commenting only, 'The job's straightforward. You can read up the files. There nothing more I can tell you.' It was another virtuoso display from a man whose complacency had blighted British football and the lives of its professional players for forty years.

Wall, the son of a Battersea nurseryman – or as he preferred to put it, 'of yeoman stock' – was a solicitor's clerk who rose rapidly through the ranks of amateur football administration. Thanks to the FA's system of player registration, from 1895 Wall had power over thousands of clubs and millions of players, proudly boasting that 'no sport was more rigidly controlled'. From 1884, the FA had given itself the power to call in any witness or document it chose to its Chancery Lane offices and to subject its victims to a private grilling without legal representation. Any team or individual might shop their neighbour or rival and, as the FA was protected by privilege, it was above the law, able to fine or ban as it saw fit without any right of appeal. Wall's unaccountable, unreported investigations often included 'fishing expeditions' which went in search of one thing – such as violent play – but turned up something else, such as hearsay evidence of corruption. If you didn't like the system – tough. (Or, as Wall put it, 'You have to trust the FA.')

Wall's FA was firmly in the southern amateur tradition and he pointed out, quite correctly, that the FA represented ten times as many amateur clubs as it did professional ones. Believing that only amateurs had 'no interest but the good of the game', he continued to exclude professional players from all committees and meetings. By being paid wages, they had 'forfeited the right to rule'. Although their 'amateur' rulers might make a tidy living from the sport in salary and expenses, Wall feared football turning from a sport into a business, which would encourage gambling and match-fixing, sharp practice and rule-bending, a neglect of local talent and the gradual supremacy of big rich clubs over smaller ones. As history has shown, he was pretty much spot-on.

Wall's main method of control over the professional clubs was financial. From 1904, club directors were forbidden to earn a salary and dividends were limited to 5 per cent. It would be the 1960s before Louis Edwards of Manchester United (never Wall's favourite club) began to dismantle this system. Wall also did his best to limit any non-gate revenue by banning sponsorship, gambling and most commercial tours and competitions. 'No sane man,' he commented, 'should hope to make his fortune from football.'

The professional players, whose registration the FA controlled, certainly weren't going to get rich. From 1901 the FA set up a £4-a-week maximum wage, which lasted until Jimmy Hill successfully campaigned against it in 1961. Though it offended all principles of natural justice and encouraged the very match-fixing and gambling that Wall decried, the judges wouldn't even hear a case against it. ('We never lost a case' was Wall's version of events.) The FA further strengthened their hand by discouraging bonus payments and preferred regular year-round wages to part-time jobs, a common ruse used to get round the rules on pay. When underhand payments were suspected, Wall dispatched gimlet-eyed bean-counters like Tom Hindle, 'the Hammer of the Pro', to fine and suspend players and directors alike, and in 1904 FA Cup-winners Manchester City were all but destroyed by one such investigation. Failure to cooperate actually resulted in the closure of Herbert Chapman's Leeds City in 1920, with all its players auctioned off. In practice, illegal payments were so common, and the gratitude to City for remaining quiet so great, that a new Leeds side – United – were soon back in the League.

The FA at first opposed transfer fees, but Wall saw their value as another means of control, preventing players 'intriguing for new situations'. (Which was exactly what he had done to get his FA post, his salary supplemented by providing the sandwiches for meetings.) Clubs were now allowed 'compensation for loss of services', although the players' cut was limited to £10. Players' contracts enforced the hated retain and transfer system, which lasted until George Eastham won his case, and meant that footballers and their families could be shunted around like cattle and suspended without pay or even a home if they complained. Wall claimed to dislike this aspect of the policy, but typically did nothing to limit or prevent it. The last vestiges of it would last until the <u>Bosman</u> verdict of 1995.

Wall didn't remain in power for so long without being a bit of an operator. The retain and transfer system helped to maintain the support of what he termed the 'hardy northerners', while southern amateur sides like the Corinthians were waved through to the later rounds of the FA Cup. For those amateur clubs that were unable to defeat the pros, Wall set up special amateur-only cups and internationals and saw off a short-lived rival Amateur Football Association. Generally, he sided with the less-wealthy Southern League clubs, who clung to the maximum wage, fearful of losing players to the bigger northern clubs, but he also reached an accommodation with the Preston-based Football League, wiping the slate clean on previous misdemeanours and giving them control of their own members' finances and the maximum wage from 1910 onwards. This meant that the FA no longer had to settle wage disputes and helped the League freeze out the Players' Union, which between 1907 and 1909 had campaigned for legal rights, freedom of contract, a share of transfer fees and an end to the maximum wage.

Even by the standards of his age, Wall was a hidebound reactionary in his attitude to women's sport. After refusing to referee an experimental women's match in 1895, he ignored any positive press comment and the growing crowds that attended mixed-sex or women-only charity matches. Later, he claimed to have 'discouraged' women's football – in fact, he started off discouraging it and then, when that didn't work, he banned it from all FA members' grounds, citing spurious medical grounds and unproven claims of financial irregularities. The FA didn't relent for fifty years.

Away from football, Wall's supposed ability to control the media led to him being placed in charge of press relations for the 1908 London Olympics. His autocratic style and the arrogance of the British judges led to numerous rows and walkouts, fierce press complaints and a pompous printed rebuttal. His judgement failed again in 1914, when the FA's muddled handling of football after the onset of war created a storm of complaint. Wall himself attended a match at which a pro-enlistment campaigner was given the bum's rush out of Craven Cottage. Afterwards, many schools switched to the more 'patriotic' rugby. In response, Wall co-founded the 17th Service Battalion (1st Football), which raised 600 men to fight with the Middlesex Regiment. After 1918, he tried to make up lost ground by suggesting that all the losing powers be suspended from the international game – plus any team that dared play them. Few nations supported him and the FA quit both FIFA and the Olympics, missing out on three very winnable World Cups, the invitations to which were curtly refused. The boycott of the Olympics has lasted until the present day.

In 1923, Wall's FA financed Wembley's Empire Stadium, whose inexperienced and complacent designer didn't even bother to install gates. After its rushed completion, Wembley was swamped for the 1923 FA Cup final. Luckily for the FA, the debacle was remembered for a policeman on a white horse rather than the cracked ribs and collapses during what could have been a catastrophe. Thereafter, it was greyhounds and speedway that kept Wembley going.

Under Wall's hand, the FA's rules became ever more tangled, illogical and opaque, and the organisation was famously unwilling to offer any help in deciphering them or judging difficult cases. As for rule changes, Wall oversaw more protection for the goalkeeper, though he still hankered after the 'good old-fashioned manly shoulder charge'. After 1925, he was enthusiastic about the new offside rule, which made the game run more smoothly and produced more goals, but disliked the new formations it produced. He was adamantly anti-substitutions, claiming that they would produce 'relays of players', and they remained outlawed from competitive games until 1965, as players battled on through injury, reluctant to 'let the side down', and often did themselves permanent damage. He rejected plans for goal judges or two refs on either side of the pitch, and it took his successor Stanley Rous to pioneer a workable refereeing system.

Among Wall's few progressive notions was a general support for numbered shirts and a more streamlined system for selecting international players – though he managed to achieve neither during his forty years in office. The idea of appointing a full-time national coach or manager like other international sides remained unthinkable and it wouldn't be until 1963 that England had a true manager in <u>Alf Ramsey</u> – the main reason why such a strong and talented footballing nation didn't win a World Cup until 1966.

Unsurprisingly, Wall opposed the Sunday football that would allow working men to play as well as watch, and it took a sustained campaign to finally overcome the FA's opposition in 1960. Indoor and artificial pitches were also dismissed as a 'circus' when they were proposed at Olympia in 1906, and floodlighting was rejected as an 'impossible dream' in 1935 – just a year before Arsenal introduced their own US-style system for training. It was the 1950s before the FA relented and gradually allowed evening matches. In the meantime, football's popularity was overtaken by evening sports such as greyhound racing. With a compulsory 3 p.m. Saturday kick-off, football spectators frequently lost track of the play in the winter gloom.

As a 'club before country' man, Wall allowed teams to block international selections and was content with occasional 'missionary tours' abroad. Despite frequent calls for action, the FA had no desire to lead the game internationally and Wall dealt with Robert Guérin's attempts to create an international football association by holding his head in his hands, ignoring him and not responding to his requests. When Guérin went ahead and set up FIFA anyway, the FA joined but stayed at arm's length. The legacy of this is that football's rules are still decided by an International Board consisting of the home nations plus FIFA representatives. The idea of a British-based World Cup, floated by the ever-entrepreneurial Alfred Critchley, was also rejected. Wall hid behind the claim that football was a mere 'sporting entertainment' rather than an international contest, but he was actually under government pressure to limit end-of-season tours by worn-out, disorganised players, which were felt to be bad for national prestige.

On the rather limited credit side, Wall clearly loved his football, though the highlight of his own playing career was the occasional appearance for the deeply amateur London FA. He preferred to credit gentlemanly sides such as the Royal Engineers with inventing passing or 'combined play' and heading – although most agree they both came from northern and Scottish players. Though he could be enthusiastic about talented pros like winger Billy Meredith, he seemed genuinely puzzled that Meredith often appeared 'none too happy'. Perhaps this was something to do with Billy having been fined, suspended and deprived of a crucial benefit match by Wall's organisation.

In 1931 Frederick Wall was rewarded with a knighthood – four years after he had curried favour with King George V and Queen Mary by having their favourite hymn, the lugubrious 'Abide With Me', performed

at the FA Cup final. He retired with a £100,000 golden handshake –
a figure it would have taken an honest pro fifty years to earn.
Connoisseurs of poorly disguised boastfulness, mock humility, dismissive snobbery and low-grade name-dropping will relish his memoir *Fifty
Years of Football*.

Shane Warne

Shane Keith Warne, cricketer, born Ferntree Gully, Victoria 13 September 1969. Career: Victoria 1990–2007, Hampshire 2000–7. First-class record: 301 Matches, 6,919 runs (19.43), 1,319 wickets (26.11); 145 Tests 1992–2007, 3,154 runs (17.32), 708 wickets (25.41); 194 ODIs, 1,018 runs (13.05), 293 wickets (25.73) (World Cup 1999). BBC Overseas Sports Personality of the Year 2005. Wisden Cricketer of the Year 1994. Wisden Cricketer of the Century.

You don't have to be mad to be a wrist spinner, but it's a definite advantage.

Effective wrist- or leg-spinning depends on combining precisely the right ball speed, length and rotation and landing it just right on the seam. Failure to achieve this, especially on unhelpful wickets, will usually result in the ball getting walloped.

Until 1993 leg-spinning (outside the Indian subcontinent) was regarded as an expensive and antiquated skill – something like being a wheelwright. Most captains and selectors favoured economy over magic and one leg-spinner's Test career lasted just six overs. The man who changed all this was Shane Warne.

Warne's potential was spotted early and he made his Test debut after only seven first-class matches and 26 wickets. Despite high hopes, his figures stood at an Australian worst-ever of one wicket for 346 runs when he was given the ball against Sri Lanka in 1992. With Australia needing four wickets for 36 runs or less, it was a last chance for both Warne and his team. Needless to say, he came through, taking three wickets in 13 balls for no runs. Even so, he remained a marginal player until Boxing Day that year, when he beat Richie Richardson and triggered a 7 for 52 collapse in a West Indies team that hadn't lost a Test series for 16 years. Six months later, his first delivery in his first Ashes Test was the now-mythic 'Ball of the Century', which leapt 18 inches to beat Mike Gatting. Only John Emburey was able to get the measure of him and by the fourth Test Graham Gooch, bowled five times, had resigned as captain. By the end of the series, Ted Dexter had also quit as England's chairman of selectors, as Warne broke Richie Benaud and Clarrie Grimmett's records with 34 wickets. Over the next two years,

Warne, now with a Nike contract, would be the leading bowler in the world, winning six Test series alongside Glen McGrath, the best new-ball bowler since Lillee. Of the world's batsmen only Hansie Cronje, Saleem Malik, Sachin Tendulkar and Mohammad Azharuddin regularly got the better of him.

Why the sudden revival of wrist spin? Simply because Warne bowled it better than ever before, combining massive spin with great accuracy. One secret was his upper-body strength, perhaps dating from when, as a toddler, he broke both legs and had to propel himself around in a cart. With his huge shoulders, arms and hands he was near medium pace, which meant batsmen had just one second to work out which way his fizzing deliveries, often delivered around the wicket, were going to go. The standard, though endlessly varied, delivery was the leg break, but Warne, helped by 'spin doctor' Terry Jenner, had also mastered Clarrie Grimmett's flipper, which shot through fast and low, Bernard Bosanquet's googly and the 'slider', which also looked like a leg break but shot straight on. Other possibilities were the 'zooter', which suddenly loses momentum, and the 'top spinner', which loops, drops short and bounces high. Warne also brought a new aggression to spinning. A firm believer in captain Steve Waugh's policy of inducing mental disintegration, he was fined his match fee for his ferocious dismissal of South African batsman Andrew Hudson. As Hudson's team-mate Graeme Smith put it: 'Warne will call you a c— all day.'

Throughout his career, Warne showed incredible bounce-back-ability. In November 1996, after a serious operation on his spinning finger, he bowled into the marks on the pitch to reach 300 Test wickets in the fourth fastest time. Between 1997 and 1999 his form dipped, Stuart MacGill replaced him as first-choice spinner and he had to have his shoulder screwed together after damaging his rotator cuff – the injury that effectively ended Richie Benaud's career. That was followed by the revelation that four years earlier he had been fined A$8,000 by the Australian Cricket Board for supplying match information to a bookie. Despite it all, in the 1999 World Cup semi-final he took the ball with South Africa on 0 for 43, bowled Herschelle Gibbs and took 4 for 29 to propel Australia to victory. Three years later, having broken his spinning finger, lost the Australian vice-captaincy and suffered another slump in form, he set a new three-Test record against Pakistan. 2003 brought a one-year suspension after the detection of an illegal diuretic that could have been used to mask steroids and some 'vague, unsatisfactory and inconsistent testimony'. The response? To break the 500-wicket barrier and trigger a collapse by the Sri Lankans. In 2005, after a long series of indiscretions – even by the non-monastic standards of Australian touring sides – his wife finally left him, just before an Ashes season in which England were reckoned to have their best chance of victory. Dismissed beforehand by his critics and with a series of unhelpful wickets to bowl on, surely he couldn't do it again? He could. In the most sensational Ashes series in memory, Warne supplied instant pressure and took almost half Australia's wickets on pitches where no other spinner could operate. After victory at Lord's, he brought Australia close to victory at Edgbaston, saved the Old Trafford Test, nearly won at Trent Bridge and frightened the life out of the English at the Oval. 2005 was to be his best-ever year, with 96 Test wickets. After this he and McGrath's final Test series was a crushing 5–0 Ashes victory, once again bouncing back from a bad start at Adelaide, taking his 700th Test wicket and quitting the SCG 15 years to the day after his debut.

Despite countless tabloid headlines, awful TV ads and sundry indiscretions, no one could deny that Warne's estimated 120,000 deliveries brought a new dimension to cricket, not least by killing off the remorseless pace attack of the 1980s and early 1990s. 'The best thing for a long time' was <u>Don Bradman</u>'s verdict. At his final Ashes Test in the UK, even the Warne-baiting home fans broke into a chorus of 'We wish you were English.'

Maud Watson

Maud Watson, tennis player, born Harrow, Middlesex 9 October 1864, died 5 June 1946. Wimbledon singles champion 1884, 85.

The best female player of her day, Maud Watson established women's tennis as a game equal in excitement to the men's and paved the way for athletic sport for women.

Before Maud's Wimbledon victory, it was far from certain that women would be allowed to compete in the game. The All England Club had been keen to promote the sport as 'a training in graceful and charming movements' rather than a serious competitive activity, and only organised its tournament after the London Athletic Club set up their own rival contest. There was much debate about whether the ladies' tournament should even be held in public. The use of a smaller court and a lighter ball or racket as well as a special service point were all debated, until it was decided to apply the same rules as the men's tournament.

Any thought of making tennis easier for women was cancelled by the 19-year-old Maud. Despite being handicapped by petticoats, corsets, an ankle-length woollen skirt, a bustle and a straw hat that got in the way of overhead shots, she impressed all those present as she drove and volleyed to a three-set victory over her elder sister Lillian, winning a 20-guinea rose bowl. (Part of her success was due to having learnt squash from an uncle who had played the game at Harrow.) Maud kept the Wimbledon title the following year and is also credited with establishing white as the natural colour for tennis.

The example of tennis soon led to more competitive sport for women – something that had been tabooed as 'unladylike' in the past. As *The Field* put it in 1885, 'Lawn tennis has taught women how much they are capable of doing and it is a sign of the times that games are actually encouraged at various girls' schools.'

James Weatherby

James Weatherby, racing administrator, born Newcastle 1733, died 1799.

Since 1770, when lawyer James Weatherby took over the job of Keeper of the Match Book for the Jockey Club, his firm have continued to administer British racing and determine which horses are qualified to race.

At the time of Weatherby's appointment, the Jockey Club was only about 18 years old and existed to stage matches and settle bets between its small aristocratic membership. (The first general racing rules had been published a year before its formation, in John Pond's *Sporting Kalendar*.) Supported by steward Sir Charles Bunbury, Weatherby began to combine the roles of Secretary, Stakeholder and Keeper of the Match Book and two years later, after a long legal battle, also began printing the club's officially approved *Racing Calendar*, which listed races, voiced judgments and 'warned off' any owners, trainers or jockeys who had crossed the club or its members. In time, the Jockey Club would move their London HQ from Richard Tattersall's rooms to Weatherby's office in Old Burlington Street.

A new fashion for high-value, multi-horse sweepstakes led to increasing levels of fraud and errors in pedigrees, and in 1791 Weatherby delved into the members' private stud books and race records to put together an *Introduction to a General Stud Book*, listing 387 mares that he believed could be traced back to the Darley Arabian, Godolphin Arabian or Byerly Turk via Eclipse, Matchem or Herod. Two years later, the first *General Stud Book* appeared. By the early 1800s, when the firm had been taken over by Weatherby's nephew, inclusion in the *Stud Book* had become a qualification for racing and the club used both it and the *Calendar* to expand its control of the sport. From 1807, adjudged cases began to be published and in 1816 the club offered to settle disputes between non-members (though few came forward), slowly forcing all those involved in the sport to follow its rules and accept its unchallengeable, in-camera rulings.

Published four-yearly since 1845, the *Stud Book* has been maintained by Weatherbys ever since and many foreign stud books were based on it. Their standards were often questioned by British racing, although the awkward fact remained that foreign outsiders such as 1865 Triple Crown winner Gladiateur occasionally triumphed.

As the independent 'Civil Service of the Turf', Weatherbys now administers horses' names, owners' colours, race details and declarations, horse passports, and the allocation of weights and prizes, and has expanded into publishing and software development, as well as banking and insurance. Despite this, its core purpose is still that established by James Weatherby over two centuries ago – keeping track of the thoroughbred breed – although today it does so through DNA-testing and the micro-chipping of foals. His portrait still hangs magisterially in the boardroom.

Johnny Weissmuller

Peter John Weissmuller, swimmer and water polo player, born Timişoara, Romania 2 June 1904, died 20 January 1984. Olympic 100 m champion (1924, 28), 400 m champion (1924), 800 m relay champion (1924, 28).

In 1920 Johnny Weissmuller, who was trying out welterweight boxing, got KO'd and quit the ring forever – however, as an amateur swimmer, he would retire undefeated.

The son of an immigrant miner turned brewer, Weissmuller began swimming as a treatment for childhood polio and was talent-spotted by Illinois Athletic Club coach Bill Bachrach. Together they created Weissmuller's revolutionary 'high riding' crawl. His six-beat style and unusually high body position defined a stroke that had only been featured in the Olympics since 1912. It has been used by freestyle swimmers ever since.

Having built up his stamina by training away from races and concentrating on separate exercises for arms and legs, Weissmuller burst onto the scene aged 16, setting records in four different distances from 50 to 150 yards. By the following year, his 'freak style' was so feared that even double Olympic champion Duke Kahanamoku ducked the challenge of swimming against him. In total, Weissmuller would set 67 records at distances from 50 to 800 yards – including a backstroke record. The first man to swim 100 metres in under a minute and 400 metres in under five, his record of 57.4 seconds for the 100 metres would stand for 10 years. In 1950, 250 sports writers would vote him the greatest swimmer of the half-century.

In the first-ever Olympic pool, at Paris in 1924, Weissmuller became the first swimmer to dominate a games, beating Duke and the leading contenders, Andrew Charlton of Australia and the 'Swedish Sturgeon' Arne Borg. In a single day, he set 100 metres and relay records and won bronze in the water polo. After two more golds at Amsterdam in 1928 he, like many other stars of the time, fell foul of the Olympics' rules on amateurism, being banned from the LA games in 1932 for accepting $500 to model swimwear.

Having appeared in promotional 'aquacades' and short films, Weissmuller was visiting his friend Clark Gable on the MGM set when he heard that they were casting for a sixth screen Tarzan – the requirements being the ability to 'run, climb a tree and carry a pretty girl'. Weissmuller got the gig, and became the first Tarzan to talk. In total, he shot a dozen movies in a forest north of Hollywood and invented the Tarzan roar (though it was actually recorded by two singers and a hog-caller spliced together). He also came up with the line 'Me Tarzan, you Jane', invented as a private joke with co-star Maureen O'Sullivan. After shooting his last movie, his advice for future Tarzans was 'Don't let go of the vine.'

After making 13 Jungle Jim movies, Weissmuller was caught up in an attempted kidnapping in Cuba, where his ability to roar impressed the rebel soldiers and earned him an escort to safety. He invested in real estate, a chain of pools and health-food shops and also founded the International Swimming Hall of Fame, but lost money on a Tarzan theme park and eventually became a Las Vegas greeter. Suffering from a weak heart, he later fell ill with additional kidney and lung infections. Barred from his retirement home because of his attempts at roaring, he quit hospital 'to die like a man' in Mexico with his sixth wife. He was still attempting the roar – despite having a tube in his throat – when he died aged 79. As he had requested, his body was lowered into his grave to the accompaniment of three lusty yells.

John Willes

John Willes, cricketer, born Headcorn, Kent 1778, died 5 August 1852. First-class career: Kent 1806–22, 5 matches, 9 runs (1.28), 6 wickets.

To quote his tombstone at Sutton Valence, Kentish farmer John Willes was 'a patron of all manly sports and the first to introduce round-arm bowling in cricket'.

In fact, according to the Reverend John Mitford, Tom Walker of the Hambledon club had raised his bowling from hip to shoulder back in the 1780s, but was decried for 'throwing' by the Earl of Winchilsea – who no doubt struggled to cope with the new style.

Willes's sister Christina is said to have been his inspiration for the new style after bowling round her 'voluminous skirts' – however, this was often used as a dig against Willes and not only were the skirts of the time slinky and close-fitting, but his daughter denied the whole story. What is clear is that from 1807, when 23 of Kent played 13 of England at Penenden Heath, John Willes was bowling round-arm – the start of 13 years of cricketing illegality. His new 'overhand' style was faster, more powerful and harder to score against, and the *Morning Herald* noted that 'The straight-armed bowling introduced by John Willes Esq . . . proved a great obstacle against getting runs.' Willes had shifted power to the bowler, especially now that the wicket had been increased to 26 x 7 inches. Though his style was banned by the MCC in a chaotically phrased 1816 law, leading cricketers like Frederick Beauclerk were happy to use round-arm when Willes was on their side. Although his first-class matches were marked by controversy, uproar and pitch invasions, Willes was undeterred. A feisty character, he kept a pack of hounds and once withstood besieging creditors by barricading himself inside his home.

Matters finally came to a head on 15 June 1822, when Willes, then playing for Kent against the MCC at Lord's, was no-balled by an unknown umpire quite possibly taking his instructions from the MCC's William Ward, who had struggled against round-arm bowling. In disgust, Willes mounted his horse and left, never to play a major game again.

With the ban on 'throwing' or 'jerking' still in place, the wicket was again increased in size to try to even up the contest. Over the next five years, the MCC's George Knight, and James Broadbridge and William 'The Nonpareil' Lillywhite of Sussex (the first regular county side) would all champion the round-arm style.

In 1827, Knight persuaded the MCC to play three experimental 'round-arm' matches against Sussex for 1,000 guineas. Ward top-scored in the second match and when the nine England pros refused to play the last match in protest at round-arm, they were all replaced. The MCC won this game in front of a large crowd and Ward was finally converted. Despite this result, the style remained fiercely debated, with Knight pointing out in the press that it was neither 'throwing' nor 'dangerous'. He wanted bowling below shoulder height, but the MCC compromised in 1828 with a 'level with the elbow' rule, which proved impossible to judge or enforce. In 1833 old-stagers were still holding out against 'the rough game' and professional nostalgic John Nyren wrote, 'I am decidedly of the opinion that if the custom be not stopped, the character of the game will be changed.' However, by this time Willes's style was taking over and in 1835, with the 'old bowlers all used up', it finally became legal to bowl level with the shoulder. The faster pace that soon required more protection for the batsman. Two other results of this change were a long-term decline in scoring that lasted a quarter of a century, and a new requirement that an lbw should pitch directly wicket to wicket – a complication that has dogged the sport ever since.

Scores and Biographies reports that Willes lived until 1852 'in fearfully reduced circumstances', the lot of so many early cricketers.

Frank Williams

Sir Francis Owen Garbatt Williams CBE, Chevalier de la Légion d'honneur, motor racing driver, manager and team owner, born Jarrow 16 April 1942. Constructors championship 1980, 81, 86, 87, 92, 93, 94, 96, 97. Drivers championship 1980, 82, 87, 92, 93, 96, 97. Overall record: 113 Grand Prix victories, 125 pole positions, 130 fastest laps.

Debates about Formula One cars are many and endless, but the 'best', or at least most technically advanced, cars ever built may still be Williams Grand Prix Engineering's FW14 and FW15C. Bristling with electronic gadgets, their 'magic-carpet ride' whisked Nigel Mansell to 14 pole positions out of 16 in 1992 and brought another championship for Alain Prost the following season. They were so effective that they had to be banned to create more of a contest and their success has coloured Formula One regulations ever since.

Frank Williams's achievement in creating these cars was all the greater because as late as 1977 he and his chief engineer Patrick Head were out of a job, forced from the racing team they had founded. For Williams this was only the latest episode in a long and colourful association with motor sport, apparently sparked off by a ride in a schoolmate's father's Jaguar. Williams had begun racing in 1961 in an Austin A35 and over six seasons gained a reputation as an exciting, though not faultless, driver. Though he lacked engineering skills, his boundless enthusiasm and some work as a grocery salesman sustained a series of racing ventures, despite apparently insuperable odds. (A second-hand Brabham gave Williams its dark blue livery.) After an experimental magnesium alloy-bodied de Tomaso led to the death of his friend and driver Piers Courage, Williams's first original design crashed on its debut in 1973. At one time he was forced to use a public callbox because the phone was disconnected; on another occasion only £50 from Bernie Ecclestone paid for the fuel to get the team back to the UK from a continental race.

Williams's breakthrough year came in 1979, when rivals Lotus and McLaren both nearly went out of business and Clay Regazzoni won the team's first (British) Grand Prix. Over the following 20 seasons, they would claim over 100 victories.

The immediate cause of the breakthrough was careful studying/copying of <u>Colin Chapman</u>'s ground-effect Lotus 79, which had dominated the previous season's racing. A week's testing in a wind tunnel drastically improved the existing FW06, just as Lotus were setting off in other less successful directions. Sponsorship from the Saudi-financed TAG group allowed Williams to invest in their own wind tunnel, recruit aerodynamicist Frank Dernie and create the FW07B, with its to-be-banned sliding skirts. While the Lotus 80 went off at tangents (in every sense), Williams's pragmatic approach won the 1980 and 1982 drivers' championships for Alan Jones and Keke Rosberg. However, performances dropped after they shifted to Honda turbos in 1983. (The handling of the wayward FW09B would be compared to a bomb going off under the driver's foot.) As for the new carbon-fibre chassis pioneered by Lotus and McLaren, Williams preferred to stick to their tried-and-tested aluminium body until 1985, when the FW10 could be produced economically 'at home'. The stiffer chassis made better use of the Honda engines, and at Silverstone Keke Rosberg set an 18-year lap record, clocking up over 160 mph.

In 1986, Williams abandoned metal-bashing production techniques for computer-aided design and manufacture and won that year's constructors' championship, despite a car accident that left Williams paralysed and unable to cough or laugh. Now living what he termed 'a different sort of life', he was at work within four months rather than the expected twelve. (There was a suspicion that his accident prompted Honda to walk out early on their partnership.)

Once again, the team took their cue from Lotus, who were experimenting with active suspension in their 99T. This was intended to keep a car level by compensating for the effects of cornering and braking. Williams's first attempts were so unreliable that Nigel Mansell refused to drive until fail-safe controls were introduced, but while Lotus only ever achieved two wins, from 1990 Williams had a lighter, faster-revving Renault V10 turbo and had hired designer Adrian Newey. By 1991, Williams's now 200-strong team were assembling a unique package of 'gizmos', including a fully automatic gearbox. Nigel Mansell began to excel in the 1991 season and in 1992/3 Williams's domination was so complete that Max Mosley acted to ban artificial aids, including active suspension, fully automatic gears and the traction control that prevented wheelspin. (Ferrari's version was so hopeless that at Estoril in 1993 it steered Gerhard Berger straight across the path of some very rapidly oncoming traffic.)

Such sudden changes to the regulations led to the creation of the cramped and jittery FW16, in which <u>Ayrton Senna</u> lost his life, leading to a new round of alterations so expensive that the basic engine capacity hasn't been touched since 1995. In 1997, Bernie Ecclestone helped stymie Patrick Head's proposed use of CVT (continuously variable transmission), which would have kept engines working at peak performance, though at a continuous whine.

Although racing teams continued to develop and test 'gizmos' for the auto industry, the emphasis in F1 shifted away from innovative engineering to subtler, harder-to-detect software systems, more scientifically based assessment (and firing) of drivers and the sort of vastly expensive aerodynamic tweaking that demands £50 million wind tunnels. As a result, the early 1990s Williams cars remained the peak of engineering sophistication. Today, the cars that get the drivers to the track can often be more sophisticated than the ones they race.

J.P.R. Williams

Dr John Peter Rhys Williams, rugby and tennis player, born Cardiff 2 March 1949. Playing career 1968–81, London Welsh, Bridgend; Wales 1969–81, 55 caps (Five Nations champions 1971, 75, 76, 78, 79; Grand Slams 1971, 76, 78); British Lions 8 caps.

With long hair and sideburns you could land a plane on, rugby's first great counter-attacking full back was instantly identifiable – although it was a role John Williams never originally intended to play. Williams was the eldest of four brothers, all of whom played for Bridgend, were Welsh junior tennis champions and medical students at St Mary's Hospital, and he wanted to be a fly half or flanker, a position he 'covered' and once played for Wales. (His background was more comfortable than that of many of his team-mates and may have been the reason for proving himself with his shattering tackles, which had to be restricted in training.)

Williams's lack of enthusiasm for the full back role was quite under-standable. In 1960s rugby, it was the next worst thing to being off the team, the main duties being to shiver in the wind, carry out last-ditch tackles and kick for goal. It was particularly miserable in a game domin-ated by forward play and kicking for touch. Although the authorities had opened up the game by requiring that backs be 10 yards behind the line-out or scrum, only a few brave souls, notably at Bristol, dared use their full back as an extra back, overlapping with the wingers and following up. In general, kicking into touch, wherever you happened to be, was the best option. Matters finally changed in 1968 with the general application of the 'Australian dispensation', so that you could no longer kick into touch on the full unless you were inside the 25-yard (later 22-metre) line.

At London Welsh, which pioneered squad training and coaching, captain John Dawes reasoned that you now needed a 'REAL full back' who could combine solid defensive duties with counter-attacking play. With the ball in his hands he could come into the back line, mixing things up with miss-moves, scissors passes, crash balls and overlaps. Such a player would need 'anticipation, courage and concentration'.

Perhaps someone with the ball skills of a junior tennis champion and the guts of an aspirant flanker.

After winning his first full cap in 1969, Williams became a lynchpin of a Welsh side that won its first Grand Slam for 19 years in 1971 and dominated northern-hemisphere rugby, with three grand slams, six triple crowns and 11 wins over England. The first international full back to regularly score tries (five), he was also a vital part of the first victorious British Lions tours of the southern hemisphere. In New Zealand in 1971, Williams secured the series win with a 50-yard drop goal to help tie the last Test, and he was also part of the undefeated side that toured South Africa in 1974. He repeatedly showed his teak-like qualities, sustaining a broken jaw and multiple facial injuries in some very dirty matches, as well as taking hits for more vulnerable players like fly half Barry John. Another player with reason to thank him was All-Black Bob Burgess who lay choking to death, surrounded by head-scratching trainers and stretcher-bearers, until Williams intervened.

As for the biggest favour anyone ever did *him*, in 1973 sprinter John (J.J.) Williams – aka 'The Welsh Whippet' – came into the national side, and Williams's three initials, which he had regarded as a slight embarrassment, became the most famous in rugby – perhaps in all sport. A splendid irony is that Williams, the skeleton-jangling tackler, became an orthopaedic surgeon.

Tom Wills – 'the Grace of Australia'

Thomas Wentworth Spencer Mills, cricketer and Australian rules footballer, born Molongo Plains, New South Wales 19 August 1835, died 3 May 1880. First-class career: Cambridge University 1855, Kent 1856, Victoria 1856–76; 32 matches, 602 runs (12.28), 130 wickets (10.09). Football career: Melbourne, Geelong and Richmond (Champion of the Colony 1859, 65, 72).

Which football association was the first to have agreed rules, a cup competition and a professional league? As all Victorians know, the answer is Australian Rules, a game first devised, played, promoted and umpired by Tom Wills.

Packed off to Rugby School by his politician father, Tom played cricket for the school, the Gentlemen of Kent, Cambridge (as a ringer) and even the MCC before returning home to showcase his controversial overarm bowling style and then organise the first cricketing tour of Britain in 1868 by an aboriginal side, who played 47 games, winning 14 and drawing 19. (Wills's enthusiasm was remarkable given that he had narrowly escaped death when his father's party were killed by a group of Queensland aboriginals.) Wills also regularly sent off rockets to the national sporting press – one of which sparked Australian Rules into life.

On 10 July 1858, in a letter to *Bell's Life in Victoria and Sporting Chronicle*, Tom suggested a rifle or 'foot-ball' club as winter training for Melbourne cricketers. When football was preferred, he umpired a scratch match at Yarra Park near the present MCG Oval and a week later a multi-day 40-a-side schools match. The following May, Wills chaired the new Melbourne Football Club, which declared, 'We shall have a game of our own,' and he helped draft the first rules. Though he regarded himself mainly as a cricketer, Tom was to play in three championship sides before his alcoholic suicide – stabbing himself to death with a pair of scissors.

Aussie Football, later celebrated with the slogan 'One flag, one destiny, one football game', was a game unlike any other, being played on cricket ovals with no offside, but historians have had fun piecing together the influences on it. At first the Irish influence was stressed. The Irish folk game *caid* was certainly played at Geelong in 1858, but modern Gaelic football wasn't formulated until 1884 and has probably been more influenced by Aussie Rules than the reverse.

Wills's own Rugby School heritage was also apparent. The first inter-school game was on a rectangular pitch and in 1865 he tried to introduce rugby-style posts. On the other hand, the rules he helped draft had no offside, throwing, hacking the man in possession, running with the ball or scoring of tries – all features of rugby football in his day.

More recently, links with the Aboriginal game *marn grook* have been emphasised. Tom would certainly have known of this through boyhood contact with the Djap wurrung, and the high jumping and use of the mark may well have influenced him, although *marn grook* uses a small ball and is scored by catches.

By the time of his death, Wills had seen Australian Rules spread beyond Victoria, with an Adelaide club from 1860. He had also helped formalise the 200 x 150 yard (max) oval, fixed duration matches (1869) and the use of umpires (1872). However, his death brought out prejudices against him, especially as his grandfather had been transported for highway robbery. Believers in the 'convict stain' preferred to emphasise the role of Tom's cousin and fellow rule-maker H.C.A. Harrison. Today, however, Wills has regained his standing, with a monument in his hometown of Moyston and statue outside the MCG – although the game's Wills Cup is actually named after the cigarette manufacturers.

By opting for a giant oval, Wills's committee scuppered any chance of the sport spreading to nations with more limited space, but Victorians took it to their hearts. When soccer arrived in the form of the uselessly named South British Football Soccer Association, Melburnians stuck with what they liked and still do so today, with huge crowds for inter-suburban games.

'Ned' Willsher

Edgar Willsher, cricketer, born Rolvenden, Kent 22 November 1828, died 7 October 1885. Playing career: Kent 1850–75; 267 first-class matches, 5,089 runs (12.41), 1,329 wickets (12.78).

On 26 August 1862, Edgar Willsher, a tall, slim, rather mild-looking fast bowler, helped bring about the legalisation of overarm bowling in cricket and the beginning of the sport's modern age.

Bowling actions had been creeping up past shoulder level for 20 years and as early as 1845 the MCC had given umpires the power to stop such illegal actions. Despite this, overarm bowling was tolerated by more and more of them and, as so often in cricket, confusion reigned. The crucial August 1862 match was at the Oval between Surrey and Willsher's All England XI – a high-profile fixture. The umpire was John Lillywhite, the son of the man who had helped get <u>John Willes</u>'s round-arm bowling legalised a generation before. As Willsher deliberately bowled his overarm leg breaks, Lillywhite just as deliberately no-balled him. After the sixth delivery, Willsher and the eight other pros on his team walked off. The match continued the next day without umpire Lillywhite, and Willsher took 6 for 49. Though Lillywhite had forced the issue, it was another two years before the MCC voted 27 to 20 to allow 'high bowling' – with the usual proviso against 'throwing'.

This rule change, along with the first publication of *Wisden*, the first international tours and the appearance of <u>W.G. Grace</u>, is now regarded as the beginning of the modern game – although many bowlers, like Grace himself, stuck with round-arm until the 1880s.

Willsher was apparently reconciled with Lillywhite, appreciating what he'd done for the sport, and even became an umpire himself. He died aged just 56, having played all his cricket with only one lung.

Walter Clopton Wingfield

Major Walter Clopton Wingfield, inventor, born Rueben, Wales October 1833, died 18 April 1912. International Tennis Hall of Fame 1997.

It was cavalry officer Walter Clopton Wingfield who in 1873 first adapted real tennis to British lawns, creating a new and far more popular game.

Having served in China with the first Dragoon Guards and led the Montgomery Yeomanry, the inventive Wingfield began looking for an alternative game to croquet, which was becoming overly complicated and losing some of its popularity. The only real candidate was badminton, or 'Poona', which could only be played on the stillest days. Instead, his thoughts turned to the ancient game of real tennis. This was perhaps in the blood, since an ancestor had been the gaoler of Charles D'Orleans, grandson of Charles VI and a keen real tennis player.

Wingfield tried out his ideas at neighbouring Nantclwyd around Christmastime using small rubber balls, the sagging net and hourglass-shaped court of badminton and real tennis rackets. Having been granted a patent (no. 6875) for his 'new and improved court for playing the ancient game of tennis', he went into production, selling boxed sets for five guineas, with nets from French's of Pimlico, rackets by Jeffries and Mallings and his own short and fuzzy history of tennis, complete with deliberately archaic spelling. The name chosen for it – *Sphairistike* – was Greek for 'ball play'. At best, the name was distinctive and upmarket, at worst, impenetrable and pretentious. Wingfield, who had junked the complexities of real tennis, claimed that it took just five minutes to learn.

Under his rules only the server scored, initially from a diamond-shaped crease, and he used the familiar rackets scoring system in which the first to 15 'aces' won. He boasted that the game was adaptable to all seasons, including days too frosty for shooting, and that it could even be played on ice skates.

'Sticky', as it soon became known, was a great hit, with 1,000 sets sold in the first year, and soon Wingfield was able to point to ringing endorsements from a customer list that included the Prince of Wales and no fewer than 8 dukes. He was exporting too, with sets supplied to the Crown Princess of Prussia and the Tsarevitch. In his second edition he modified the unnecessary side nets and offered extra balls at five shillings for 12 uncovered, 10 shillings covered in kid. By the time of the third edition, standard (£6) or luxury (£10) versions were available and 'Sphairistike' had been dropped in favour of 'Lawn Tennis' – apparently the suggestion of future Prime Minister Arthur Balfour. Though the winter sport aspect didn't take off, Wingfield's enthusiastic promotion – and the need for a lawn – confirmed tennis as a game for the affluent. In years to come, Davis Cup teams would travel first-class, while most sportspeople went third.

Unfortunately, Wingfield was undone by his very success. As early as 1874 *The Field* was debating the scoring system, rules and size and shape of the tennis court. No doubt to Wingfield's relief, the MCC, the authority for real tennis, adopted his hourglass court, although they changed the scoring method, lowered the net and moved the server to the baseline. By the following year 'the Royal Bodyguard', as he billed himself, was forced into a tactical retreat on the rules, while holding out for the hourglass-shaped court on which his patent rested. As rival manufacturers such as Slazenger, Felthams and Ayres began producing better and stronger rackets, he had to go into print to warn against these 'inferiors'. The final straw was when *The Field*, which favoured a rectangular court, staged an All England tournament and their journalist 'Cavendish' came up with a new scoring system. After the MCC fell into line, 7,000 copies of the new rules were circulated, the Wingfield patent lapsed and he fell into obscurity.

When he died in 1912, Wingfield's *Times* obituary made much of his military career and work as a JP and even made passing mention of later ideas such as the 'Bicycle Gymkhana'. However, there was no mention of his role as the inventor of lawn tennis.

Katarina Witt

Katarina Witt, figure skater, born Staaken, East Germany 3 December 1965. European champion 1983, 84, 85, 86, 87, 88, world champion 1984, 85, 87, 88, Olympic singles champion 1984, 88. World Skating Hall of Fame 1995.

Had she been born in West rather than East Germany, Katarina Witt would probably never have become a world-famous, innovative skater and she certainly wouldn't have been the first since <u>Sonja Henie</u> to successfully defend her Olympic title.

Thanks to socialist East Germany and its sporting obsession, Katarina, a farmer's daughter, was able to compete in what is usually a rich kids' sport, and from 1977 was coached by Jutta Müller, who had already trained two Olympic medal winners. Having won her first Olympic long programme by a tenth of a point on a single scorecard, there were none of the usual tours or endorsements on offer, so she went for a second – although she was paid by the state and jumped to the head of the queue for a Russian Lada. Like many GDR athletes, she was spied on as well as being rewarded with privileges.

As 'the beautiful face of communism' (*Time*), politics and sexual politics inevitably overlapped. After one Olympic appearance, she apparently received 35,000 love letters, and she was quite clear that in a judged sport, sexual appeal and the creation of a great moment were as important as grit and athleticism. 'You can skate – or interpret' was her verdict on the sport, and she was the first to embody a role, ditching the traditional skater's dress when it wasn't appropriate. This drew further complaints from competing coaches that she exploited her sexuality. After Katarina defended her title in Calgary, beating fellow world champion Debi Thomas in the 'The Battle of the Carmens' (each had independently chosen to skate to the Bizet score), rival coaches complained about her short showgirl's costume. Afterwards the rules were changed to stipulate 'modest dress' – a rule that few skaters seem to have bothered about since.

After Calgary, Witt was trusted to go on a professional tour with a minder in tow and sold out a Madison Square Garden ice show for the first time in years. Thanks to an International Skating Union power play, she was able to return as a pro to compete at the Lillehammer games. Here she appeared in a tribute to the city of Sarajevo, where she had won her first medal and which was in the process of being blown to bits. Dancing mainly for effect rather than to win, she still came seventh. In 1998, she became the first athlete to appear in *Playboy* – the first sell-out issue since Marilyn Monroe's. (One sports-minded reader's immediate reaction was 'My God – she's got the greatest calf muscles.')

Asked to contribute to the Olympics' official centenary history, Katarina was the only athlete not to dwell on her personal glory, but to concentrate on the value of the games as a demonstration that there can be 'peace in conflict and competition in peace'. As well as business interests and cameo appearances in movies, in 2007 she hosted the German leg of *Live Earth*.

Tiger Woods

Edrick Tont Woods, golfer and course designer, born Cypress, California 30 December 1975. US junior champion 1991, 92, 93, US amateur champion 1994, 95, 96. Wins include: Masters 1997, 2001, 02, 05, US Open 2000, 02, 08, PGA 1999, 2000, 06, 07, British Open 2000, 05, 06. Sports Illustrated Sportsman of the Year 1996, 2000. PGA Player of the Year 1997, 99, 2000, 01, 02, 03, 05, 06, 07.

No golfer has yet won the modern 'impregnable quadrilateral' of the PGA Championship, Masters and US and British Opens in one calendar year. Ben Hogan came closest in 1953, but was prevented from winning all four by a calendar clash. However, in 2000 Tiger Woods, golf's first non-white star, came within a couple of shots of adding the Masters to the other three.

Tiger changed the face of golf in many ways. For a start, he was a child prodigy, beating ten-year-olds when aged three, pitching as far as an adult at five and leading championships at 13 – by which time he already had a sports psychologist and the backing of Mark McCormack's IMG group – the story being that his father Earl was employed, not Tiger. Thanks to this, Woods Jnr started his career with $60 million in the bank – perhaps the first sportsman ever to begin his career already financially secure. IMG's faith was fully vindicated when Tiger won the Masters in his debut season as a professional. After four bogeys in the first nine holes, he had the skill to adjust his swing to win by a record 12 strokes and 18 under par. Within 42 weeks of turning pro, he was ranked number one – the fastest ever ascent of the rankings.

Woods's success was, as usual in golf, due to relentless focus and good technique, but he coupled this with other less usual attributes – his mother's Buddhist faith and his Vietnam veteran father's physical and mental training. Named the 'fittest athlete in the world' by US health magazines, he added 20 lb of muscle to his upper body, arms and shoulders. With his torso coiled like a spring, Woods's club-head speed could reach 130 mph. Helped by the best golf balls money could buy, the heaviest, springiest club-heads and more consistent, faster fairways, he now drove 50 yards further than Jack Nicklaus in his prime.

Having learnt on ultra-fast Californian greens, Tiger could drop a ball straight down and put backspin on it at will and had amazing control of the club-face. After rebuilding his swing in his 1998 'slump' season – during which he remained ranked number one most of the time – his control at distance improved and his putting rose from the 147th to 24th best on the tour. During his 2000 assault on golf's holy grail, he avoided every bunker at St Andrews and never once three-putted at Pebble Beach, where he won the US Open by 15 strokes – the biggest margin since Old Tom Morris. St Andrews and Augusta have both had to be 'Tiger-proofed' since – adjusted to cope with a golfer who could get onto a green 575 yards away in just two shots. In the US, more yardage has been added, but at historic St Andrews a moveable out-of-bounds line had to be introduced in 2005 and it was joked that the first tee might soon have to be moved into the dining room.

Woods's impact on golf was all the greater as the first non-white star in a sport that has symbolised sporting racism in the past. Back in 1948, the PGA changed its charter to become a members-only club and keep Bill Spiller, Madison Gunther and Theo 'Rags' Rhodes off the tour. It was 1961 before Charlie Sifford was allowed to compete, enduring constant hostility as he went on to win the LA and Hartford Opens. The Masters repeatedly changed its rules of entry to keep Sifford out and, until Lee Elder got an invitation in 1975, only whites played and only blacks caddied at Augusta. Lee Trevino boycotted the locker room because he disliked the atmosphere so much, and Tiger was only the fourth non-white player to play there. (When he arrived on the PGA tour, Jim Thorpe was the only black player on it.) Woods's debut 'Hello world' commercial for Nike claimed there were courses he couldn't play on because of his colour – which was probably untrue – but there certainly were clubs that wouldn't have had him as a member, and Augusta had only just accepted its first two black members. Woods's great golf and final-round charges in his trademark red shirt allowed both golf and golf sponsors to feel good about themselves, while scape-goating Fuzzy Zoeller who had made an offhand, off-colour remark. That Tiger belonged to all-male clubs didn't seem to matter. Although a few off-colour remarks of his own offended feminists, gay rights activists and the moral majority, they generally increased his appeal among the fans. Understandably, he has been much more circumspect with the press ever since.

From the off, Tiger got the highest appearance money in golf, but more than justified it with the big crowds and TV numbers he attracted. He blew the traditional NFL season preview off the front cover of *Sports Illustrated* and even overtook *Monday Night Football* in the TV ratings. Like Muhammad Ali and Michael Jordan, he extended his appeal beyond traditional fans and even beyond sport itself. Nike, who had paid an initial $40 million for him, stumped up more than twice as much in 2000. Up to 16 swooshes have been spotted on Tiger at any one time and Nike have become the leading golfwear company. Other sponsorships and endorsements, his book *How I Play Golf*, video games and, since 2006, course design have all made Tiger the highest-paid athlete in history – now likely to be the first-ever sports billionaire. He has also campaigned to be paid for Ryder Cup appearances, although he wanted the money for his own charitable golf clinics and scholarships.

Tiger suffered a temporary slump in 2003/4 when he changed his swing, swing coach and clubs – with the exception of his putter, a veteran of 11 major victories. Though his driving accuracy is supposed to have declined slightly, his iron, bunker and recovery play and putting under pressure still lead the way. Although the arm pumping and final-day attacks catch the eye, his success is based on consistency and caution. By preparing better for fewer events, he has achieved a 29 per cent win rate in PGA events and made 142 cuts in a row. After winning the 2008 US Open in obvious pain, he quit for cruciate ligament surgery.

Babe Zaharias

Mildred Ella, Zaharias (née Didrikson) sportswoman, born Port Arthur, Texas 26 June 1911, died 27 September 1956. Olympic champion javelin and 80 m hurdles (1932), US women's amateur golf champion (1946, 47), UK ladies' amateur golf champion (1947), LPGA champion (1948, 50, 54). LPGA Hall of Fame 1967, PGA Hall of Fame 1976, World Golf Hall of Fame 1974. AP Greatest Female Athlete of the Century and Half-Century.

'The most flawless section of muscle harmony, of complete mental and physical coordination, the world of sport has ever seen' was US sports-writer Grantland Rice's verdict on Babe Zaharias. The first female track and field star, the first long hitter in women's golf and co-founder of the LPGA, she firmly established women in both sports, though she excelled in at least 17 others.

The daughter of a Norwegian ship's carpenter who survived ship-wreck and a mother who was a skiing and skating champion, Mildred was only 5 feet 5 inches tall, but inherited talent, determination and immaculate timing. In baseball she could throw a ball 313 feet and once struck five homers in a match – hence the 'Babe' nickname, after Babe Ruth. As well as setting basketball throwing records and winning three national titles in the sport, she was an excellent footballer and handballer and was counted good at lacrosse, tennis, fencing, shooting, skating, swimming, diving, cycling, bowling and billiards. How good a boxer she could have been is uncertain as she gave up the sport at 18. (She also typed fast, was a sewing champion, played a mean game of cards and was a recording artiste.)

Having set javelin records by the age of 15, Didrikson's club Employers Casualty entered her as a one-woman team for the 1932 AAU Championships – the de facto Olympic trials. On 16 July at Evanston, Illinois, she single-handedly beat teams of 22. As well as achieving five first places, one tie and one fourth place in just 2½ hours, she set a javelin world record and tied the high jump with her western roll against Jean Shiley's scissors style. Though aged 20, she claimed to be 18, aware that a teenager would be more of a sensation.

Although the LA Olympics featured six women's track and field events, the rules only allowed her to enter three. 'I'd break 'em all if they'd let me,' said the Babe, who by now had set world records in discus, pole vault, long jump and shot put. At LA she took a unique triple of throwing, running and jumping medals. In the javelin she pulled a muscle and was well short of her personal best, but still broke the Olympic record and, after a false start, narrowly beat Evelyne Hall in the hurdles, though photos later showed she had tied with her. After matching Shiley in the high jump, Didrikson's western roll was suddenly judged a dive by one judge – although more photos showed it wasn't. Rather than being disqualified, she was awarded silver and was still credited with an Olympic record – an irrational decision that led high jumping to abandon its 'feet first' rule.

Perhaps predictably, Didrikson soon fell foul of athletics' strict and illogical rules on amateurism and turned to a profitable Vaudeville show and mixed-sex basketball and baseball exhibitions, during which she once struck out Joe DiMaggio. As there was no money in tennis, she took up golf and claimed that she got down from 95 to 83 after three lessons. Although her big hits equalled most men's, pure athleticism wasn't enough and though she practised until her hands bled, she was often beaten by the willowy Englishwoman Joyce Wethered. Earnings in other sports led to her being expelled from amateur golf in 1935 and again she turned to promotional tours, organised by her agent Fred Corcoran, in which she competed against male golfers as good as Gene Sarazen. US pro Byron Nelson said he knew of only eight men who could outdrive her. In 1938 she married wrestler and promoter George Zaharias, billed in those pre-PC times as 'the crying Greek from Cripple Creek'.

Restored to the amateur golf ranks in 1943, the Babe won 17 straight titles, including the US and UK championships – the first American to do so – before co-founding the new Ladies PGA and releasing a series of 'how to' films. In the course of her golf career she won 31 titles, led the rankings for four years and beat the English champion Leonard Crawley on equal terms – a first for women's golf. Needless to say, there was a continual barrage of hostile and sexist comment, with US sports writer Joe Williams opining that 'It would be much better if she and her ilk stayed at home, got themselves prettied up and waited for the phone to ring.' Babe particularly antagonised sports journalist and former athlete Paul Gallico by beating him in a race.

Often regarded brash and arrogant (she once told a male opponent, 'You play first – it's the only time you will'), her dress sense was also sometimes considered unacceptable in golf, but she remained a huge draw for the struggling women's game with her big hits and sensational recovery shots and achieved a ladies' grand slam in 1950 with the US and Western Opens and Titleholders Championship. After a late diagnosis of colon cancer, she spoke out about the disease and returned from operations to win two All-American titles and one US Open. She died two years later, in 1956, commemorated by the *Guardian* as the 'World's Greatest Sportswoman'. Since then both Associated Press and ESPN have rated her the best woman athlete of the 20th century. Today there is a Babe Zaharias Park and Museum in Beaumont, Texas and a course in Tampa. Today she is still a heroine of the lesbian community, and a musical about her life is reported to be in the offing.

Emil Zátopek – 'The Czech Locomotive'

Emil Zátopek, distance runner, born Koprivnice, Czechoslovakia 19 September 1922, died 22 November 2000. Victories include Olympic 5,000 m (1952), 10,000 m (1948, 52), marathon (1952), European 5,000 m (1950), European 10,000 m (1950, 54).

The Finns love their running, so it was fitting that it was at the 1952 Helsinki Olympics that 68,700 of them saw Emil Zátopek complete the greatest feat of distance racing in history, as he won the marathon, having already achieved the double of the 5,000 and 10,000 metres.

Zátopek was a runner of two halves. Hunched and in apparent agony, his tongue lolled 'like a man who'd been stabbed in the heart' and he joked that he wasn't good enough to run and smile at the same time. However, his legs kept a perfect cadence as he revolutionised distance-running techniques and won 10,000 metres races by over a minute.

A natural runner who raced the family geese as a boy, Zátopek was discouraged from athletics by his father and sent to work in a shoe factory. Pressured to run in a local 1,500 metres contest, he ran in borrowed tennis shoes and came second out of 100, loved the applause and by 1944 was setting national records. Instead of the recommended summer-only training at a steady pace, Emil tortured himself year-round with a simple but brutal method of interval training, alternating fast and slow 200 metres with 400 metres fast and 200 slow. These methods were not entirely new, having been used in the 1930s by coach Woldemar Gerschler and before him by the Finn Lauri Pikhala and American George Orton. What was new was the sheer volume of work Zátopek put in, even running in his army boots when conscripted.

In 1946, in his first overseas competition, Zátopek was fifth behind the great British runner Sydney Wooderson – a race that he said taught him the need to combine bursts of speed with tactical awareness. Two years later, still considering himself a novice, he ran the legs off the 10,000 metres field at the London Olympics. Keeping up a steady 71 seconds per lap, he lapped ten runners and so confused the timekeeper that he rang the bell a lap early. The 5,000 metres heat was just two days later and Zátopek was over-competitive, but even 'running for bronze' in the final, a last-second surge almost took him to victory.

Thereafter Zátopek was supreme, winning 38 10Ks in a row and breaking the world record five times. By the following Olympics he had suffered illness and defeat and looked older than his 30 years, but looks were deceptive. Once again he thrashed the 10,000 metres field before winning his greatest race, the 5,000 metres final, in which he was over-taken on the final lap by three runners, only to fight back with a raging sprint to win by a metre.

Major Zátopek now made a last-minute decision to run his first marathon, which the 100-mile-a-week man judged a 'straightforward test of control'. At the tape he was two minutes outside Jim Peters's record time, but Peters himself had long since dropped out. After setting a scorching pace, he had found himself matched by Zátopek, who perhaps innocently asked if they should be going faster. Seeing Peters looking 'a little tired', Emil left him behind and was still chatting with his police escort when he swept into the Olympic Stadium to set an Olympic record, raise the roof and be chaired off by the victorious Jamaican relay squad. (That afternoon his wife Dana won gold in the javelin.)

By the 1956 Olympics, Zátopek's records were being dismantled as runners such as Vladimir Kuts built on his training methods. Running two weeks after a hernia operation, Zátopek managed sixth in the marathon and congratulated the winner, his old foe Alain Mimoun, who judged his words 'as good as a medal'. Emil's Olympic treble has only been seriously threatened once – by double gold medallist Lasse Viren, who achieved fifth place in the marathon. In this modern era of special-isation, it is almost inconceivable that it could ever be equalled.

Though quiet and unassuming, Emil Zátopek was never cowed. At London he broke team orders to attend the opening ceremonies and sneaked into the girls' camp to show Dana his medal. Before Helsinki he ignored doctor's orders not to run, nursing himself back from injury with tea and lemons, and defied his government by refusing to attend the games unless 1,500 metres runner Stanislav Jungwirth could do so too. (Jungwirth's father was a political dissident.) Still greater acts of heroism followed in 1968, when Zátopek signed the reformist President Alexander Dubcek's manifesto and stood against the invading Russian tanks on Wenceslas Square. He even dared call for the Soviets to be suspended from the 1968 games. For this act of defiance he was stripped of all privileges and was quite literally sent to the mines. Fortunately he lived to see the Czech Republic regain its independence and get some measure of the credit he was due – although the Olympics, so keen to award tyrants and rich businessmen, only gave him a special award posthumously.

Mathias Zdarsky – 'The Father of Alpine Skiing'

Mathias Zdarsky, inventor, skier, author, teacher and artist, born Kozichowitz, Czech Republic 25 February 1856, died 20 June 1940.

A 'crazy cockerel' was the verdict of one contemporary on Mathias Zdarsky, the Van Gogh lookalike who first adapted skis for sharp Alpine descents.

Growing up in German-speaking Moravia, Zdarsky was inspired by the cross-country exploits of Nordic skiers such as explorer Fridtjof Nansen, but found that their long skis were unsuited to steep alpine slopes. Having moved to Lilienfeld in Austria, he developed shorter skis and, after developing some 200 prototypes, created a secure steel binding that allowed skiers to venture into the mountains and use a stem turn, which enabled gate runs or *Torlauf* – the ancestors of modern-day giant slalom. However, when it came to ski poles, Zdarsky was a traditionalist, favouring a single pole ridden hobbyhorse style. He also had an irrational dislike of ski goggles.

Zdarsky was more interested in fitness, style and managing obstacles than pure speed, although after staging the first steep descent of the Schneeberg, he did win an experimental contest in 1905. Later that winter, he staged another carefully arranged trial against the Nordic style of skier Hassa Horn, which proved that his style was faster on steeper slopes. Horn was open-minded about the new approach, but skiers became divided between Zdarsky's more athletic style, Scandinavian cross-country racing and the new British passion for plunging down mountainsides with two poles to steer by. British skier Vivien Caulfield dismissed Zdarsky's style as that of a 'zig-zagging crawler' and Arnold Lunn regarded his own shorter, more demanding 1922 race as the first true slalom.

During his life, Zdarsky tutored an estimated 20,000 skiers and produced 17 editions of his 1897 guide *Lilienfelder Skilauf-Technik*. Though not the first skiing guide, it was by far the clearest and the most widely translated. At the age of 60, he was still fit and determined

enough to return to skiing after an avalanche that fractured or dislocated 80 bones. Though he stuck to his style, most skiers preferred the
two-pole method with its faster turns and Zdarsky was seen as more of
an eccentric uncle than the supposed 'father' of their sport. He was
awarded a gold medal for his training of skiing soldiers, and there is a
mountain named after him in Antarctica.

John 'Montana Jack' Ziegler – 'The Father of Dianabol'

Dr John Bosley Ziegler, coach and weightlifter, born 1920, died 1983.

John Bosley Ziegler was the US doctor and weightlifter who intro-duced Western athletes to steroids – the first strength-producing drugs. After his promotion of Dianabol in the early 1960s, steroid use boomed in many sports, performances soared and athletes bulked up massively. It was the mid 1970s before steroids could be detected in-competition, and many more years before serious out-of-competition detection began.

Though Ziegler was a strapping Midwesterner from a medical family, he preferred to be thought of as a westerner and encouraged the nick-names 'Tex' and 'Montana Jack'. After being injured fighting with the US Marines in the Pacific, Ziegler began working part-time for Ciba Pharmaceuticals, who were using the steroid drugs first developed in Nazi Germany to treat burns victims and kidney patients. A restless, eccentric character and a keen bodybuilder, Ziegler experimented on himself and on power athletes such as former 'Mr America' Jim Park – the most notable effect being that for a whole week Park got an erection every time he saw a woman. Although he knew that the Soviets were using testosterone at the 1954 World Weightlifting Championships, Ziegler abandoned drugs for 'isometrics' – the 'Charles Atlas' muscle-building method.

In 1958, Ciba brought out the steroid Dianabol as a treatment for geriatric and post-operative patients, but the US weightlifting establish-ment stuck with traditional methods of strength-building such as barbells – which was how many of them made their money. It was now that Ziegler's enthusiasm made a lasting impact on sport. Despite his ambi-tions to create what he termed 'SUPERMEN!', Tex was, to quote lifter Jim George, 'certainly no researcher and worked in totally uncontrolled settings'. From 1959, Ziegler tried out Ciba's little pink pills on various lifters and in 1960 he dosed his entire Olympic squad, but adminis-tered his 'supplements' so late and so randomly that they had no obvious effect. Afterwards, he sent consignments to athletes, including Louis Riecke, a previously undistinguished lifter who soon reached Olympic standard. Every time Ziegler supplied the pills, Riecke's performance rose, but neither doctor nor patient could seem to see the correlation. Ziegler saw the steroids simply as 'supplements' and continued to experiment with isometrics, 'Christian Yoga', sleep tapes, 'positive thinking' and a home-made device called the Isotron, which was supposed to 'duplicate muscle signals'. During his short career, Riecke displayed all the classic signs of steroid use – rapidly increasing muscle bulk and strength, elation, repeat injuries, plateauing of results, dependency and mood swings – none of which registered on Ziegler. It was only when *Iron Man* magazine ran an article on steroids in 1962 and named names that lifters and athletes could get their own supplies – freed from reliance on Ziegler, who continued to remind these 'simple-minded shits' that 'I'm the doctor.'

In 1967, having seen various cases of prostate trouble and atrophied testicles, Ziegler publicly condemned steroids in sport, but the genie was out of the bottle. In 1968, it was reckoned that one-third of US track and field athletes were using steroids and by the following Olympics an estimated two-thirds were. Detection only became possible from the 1976 games after Manfred Donike developed a test, and as late as 1987 there were still only eight approved labs worldwide. To avoid the tests, many athletes shifted to testosterone in the weeks before competition – the drug Ziegler had ignored 30 years before. Ziegler himself died in 1983 of a weakened heart, which he blamed on the drugs he had taken. Commemorated by a group of steroid-users called the John Ziegler Fan Club, he came to be credited as the 'Father of Dianabol'. Perhaps a more accurate assessment was that offered by lifter Jim George – 'He was a god-damned nut.'

Bibliography

Abt, S. *Greg LeMond* (1990) London: Stanley Paul

Allen, E. 'The British and the Modernisation of Skiing', *History Today*, Volume 53 (4) (2003)

Alliss, P. *Golf: A Way of Life* (1987) London: Stanley Paul

Allis, P. *100 Greatest Golfers* (1989) London: MacDonald

Arledge, R. *Roone* (2003) New York: HarperCollins

Arlott, J. (ed) *The Oxford Companion to Sports and Games* (1976) Oxford: OUP

Arlott, J. *John Arlott's Book of Cricketers* (1980) London: Readers Union

Armstrong, L. and *l'Equipe The Official Tour de France Centennial 1903-2003* (2003) London: Weidenfeld and Nicolson

Arnold, P. *History of Boxing,* (1985) London: Deans International

Arnold, P. and Mee, B. *Lords of the Rings: The Greatest Fighters Since 1950* (1998) London: Hamlyn

Arnold, P. *All-Time Greats of Boxing* (1987) Leicester: Magna Books

Barber, R. *The Broadcasters* (1970) New York: da Capo

Barend, F. and van Dorp, H. *Ajax Barcelona Cruyff* (1999) London: Bloomsbury

Barrett, J. *Wimbledon: Serving Through Time* (2003) London: Wimbledon Lawn Tennis Museum

Barry, P. *Spun Out: Shane Warne: The Unauthorised Biography of a Cricketing Genius* (2003) London: Corgi

Bickerton, B. *Club Colours,* (1998) London: Hamlyn

Birley, D. *Sport and the Making of Britain* (1993) Manchester: Manchester University Press

Birley, D. *A Social History of English Cricket* (2000) London: Aurum

Boddy, W. *The History of Motor Racing* (1977) London: Orbis

Bodleian Library *The Rules of Association Football 1863* (2006) Oxford: Bodleian Library

Booth, K. *The Father of Modern Sport: The Life and Times of Charles W. Alcock* (2002) Manchester: Parrs Wood

Booth, L. *Armball to Zooter: A Sideways Look at the Language of Cricket* (2007) London: Penguin

Bose, M. *Sports Babylon* (1999) London: Carlton

Bowen, R. *Cricket: A History of its Growth and Development throughout the World* (1970) London: Eyre and Spottiswoode

Bowers, C. *Fantastic Federer* (2007) London: John Blake

Bracegirdle, H. A. *A Concise History of British Horseracing* (1999) Derby: English Life

Brearley, M. *The Art of Captaincy* (1985) London: Coronet

Brondfield, J. *Rockne* (1975) New York: Random House

Brown, C. *Wimbledon Facts, Figures and Fun* (2005) London: AAPPL

Bryson, B. *Made in America* (1994) London: Minerva

Buchan, C. *A lifetime in Football* (1956) London: Sportsman Book Club

Burleigh, R. *Home Run* (1998) San Diego: Voyager

Busby, M. *Soccer at the Top: My Life in Football* (1973) London: Sphere

Campbell, M. *The Encyclopedia of Golf* (1991) London: Dorling Kindersley

Chapman, K. *The Rules of the Green* (1988) London: Virgin Books

Christopher, M. *Babe Ruth* (2005) Little Brown: New York

Clary, J. *Tiger Woods* (1997) Wilton: Tiger Books

Clavin, T. *Sir Walter: The Flamboyant Life of Walter Hagen* (2005) London: Aurum

Coe, S. *More Than a Game* (1992) London: BBC Books

Coe, S. *The Olympians: A Century of Gold* (1988) London: Pavilion

Coldham, J. *Lord Hawke: A Cricketing Legend* (2003) London: Tauris Parke

Collings, T. and Sykes, S. *Jackie Stewart: A Restless Life* (2004) London: Virgin Books

Collings, T. *The Piranha Club* (2002) London: Virgin Books

Conn, D. *The Football Business* (1997) Edinburgh: Mainstream

Considine, B. *The Unreconstructed Amateur* (1962) San Francisco: Amos Alonzo Stagg Foundation

Cook, K. *Tommy's Honour* (2007) London: HarperSport

Cooper, H. *Henry Cooper's 100 Greatest Boxers* (1990) London: Queen Anne

Cooper, I. *Immortal Harlequin: The Story of Adrian Stoop* (2004) Stroud: Tempus

Cox, R., Russell, D. and Vamplew, W. (eds) *Encyclopedia of British Football* (2002) London: Cass

Critchley, A. *Critch!* (1961) London: Hutchinson

Crombac, G. *Colin Chapman: The Man and his Cars* (1986) Wellingborough: PSL

Cronin, M. and Holt, R. 'The Globalisation of Sport' *History Today*, (2003) Volume 53 (7)

Daniels, S. and Tedder, A. *A Proper Spectacle: Women Olympians 1900–1936* (2000) NSW: Walla Walla

David, R. *Robert Sangster: Tycoon of the Turf* (1991) London: Heinemann

David, R. *Lester Piggott: Downfall of a Legend* (1989) London: Mandarin

Davies, H. *Boots, Balls and Haircuts* (2003) London: Octopus

Davis, J. *The Breaks Went My Way* (1976) London: W.H. Allen

Dawes, J. (ed) *Thinking Rugby* (1979) London: George Allen

Dawes, R. (ed) *World Horse Racing* (1989) London: Marshall Cavendish

Devlin, J. *True Colours: Football Kits 1980 to the Present Day* (2005) London: A&C Black

Disraeli, B. *Lord George Bentinck* (2007) Teddington: Echo

Dillon, P. *The Tyne Oarsmen* (1993) Newcastle upon Tyne: Keepdate

Dimmock, P. (ed) *Sports In View* (1964) London: Faber and Faber

Dizikes, J. *Yankee Doodle Dandy: The Life and Times of Tod Sloan* (2000) New Haven: Yale

Dobson, P. *Doc: The Life of Danie Craven* (1970) Cape Town: Human and Rousseau

Dodd, C. and Marks, J. *Battle of the Blues* (2004) London: P to M

Donohoe, T. and Johnson, N. *Foul Play* (1986) Oxford: Blackwell

Duncanson, N. *The Fastest Men on Earth* (1988) London: Thames

Easton, G. *Determined to Win* (1966) London: Sportsman's Book Club

Edmonds, P. *100 Greatest Bowlers* (1989) London: Queen Anne Press

English, A. Sunday Times *Sporting Century* (1999) London: Willow

Evans, R. *Tales from the Tennis Court* (1983) London: Sidgwick and Jackson

Everton, C. *The Story of Billiards and Snooker* (1979) London: Cassell

Fair, J. 'Isometrics or Steroids? Exploring new Frontiers of Strength in the Early 1960s' *Journal of Sport History*, Volume 20 (1) (1993)

Farnsworth, K. *Sheffield Football: A History, Vols 1 and 2* (1995) Sheffield: Hallamshire Press

Fitzgeorge-Parker, T. *Vincent O'Brien: A Long Way from Tipperary* (1974) London: Pelham

Fortin, F. (ed) *The Illustrated Encyclopedia of Sport* (2000) Montreal: Aurum

Francis, C. *Speed Trap* (1990) Toronto: Lester and Orpen Dennys

Gelman, T. *Young Olympic Champion* (1964) New York: Scholastic

Genders, R. *The Encyclopedia of Greyhound Racing* (1982) London: Michael Joseph

Gibson, E. *The Original Million Dollar Mermaid: The Annette Kellerman Story* (2005) Australia: Allen and Unwin

Glanville, B. *Matt Busby: A Tribute* (1996) London: Virgin Books

Glanville, B. *England Managers: The Toughest Job in Football* (2007) London: Headline

Glendenning, R. *Just a Word in Your Ear* (1953) London: Stanley Paul

Goldblatt, D. *The Ball is Round* (2006) London: Viking

Goodwin, B. *Spurs: A Complete Record* (1993) Derby: Breedon Greenberg

The Guinness Book of Sporting Facts (1982) London: Guinness Superlatives Ltd.

Greenberg, S. *Whitaker's Olympic Almanack* (2000) London: A&C Black

Greene, B. *Hang Time* (1992) New York: St Martin's Press

Greene, B. *Rebound: The Odyssey of Michael Jordan* (1995) London: Penguin

Greyvenstein, C. *The Bennie Osler Story* (1970) Cape Town: Howard Timms

Griffiths, J. *What is a Loose Head? The Mysteries of Rugby Explained* (2007) London: Robson

Haigh, G. *The Big Ship: Warwick Armstrong and the Making of Modern Cricket* (2002) London: Aurum

Hamilton, I. (ed.) *The Faber Book of Soccer* (1992) London: Faber and Faber

Hamilton, M. *Frank Williams* (1998) London: Virgin Books

Hardaker, A. *Hardaker of the League* (1977) London: Pelham

Harding, J. *Football Wizard: The Story of Billy Meredith* (1985) Derbyshire: Peak Press

Henderson, J. *Best of British: Hendo's Sporting Heroes* London: Yellow Jersey Press

Henry, A. *Grand Prix Motor Racing* (2000) Richmond: Hazleton

Herbert, I. (ed) *Horse Racing* (1980) London: Collins

Hill, J. *Striking for Soccer* (1961) London: Sportsman's Book Club

Hill, J. *The Jimmy Hill Story* (1998) London: Hodder and Stoughton

Hislop, J. and Swannell, D. *The Faber Book of the Turf* (1990) London: Faber and Faber

Hobbs, M. *50 Masters of Golf* (1983) Ashbourne: Moorland

Hodgkinson, D. and Harrison, P. *The World of Rugby League* (1981) London: Allen and Unwin

Holden, J. *Stan Cullis: The Iron Manager* (2000) Breedon: Derby

Holt, R. 'Race to Glory' *Oxford Today*, Volume 18 (1) (2005)

Houlihan, B. *Dying to Win* (1999) Strasbourg: Council of Europe

Hoult, N. (ed) Daily Telegraph *Book of Cricket* (2007) London: Aurum

Howett, B. and Howarth, D. *1905 Originals* (2005) Auckland: Harper Collins

Huggins, M. *Horseracing and the British 1919–1939* (2003) Manchester: Manchester University Press

Huggins, M. 'Going to the Dogs' *History Today*, Volume 56 (5) (2006)

Imlach, G. *My Father and Other Working Class Football Heroes* (2005) London: Yellow Jersey Press

Inglis, S. *League Football and the Men who Made It* (1988) London: Willow

Inglis, S. *Football Grounds of Britain* (1996) London: Collins Willow

Inglis, S. *Sightlines: A Stadium Odyssey* (2000) London: Yellow Jersey Press

Inglis, S. *Engineering Archie* (2005) London: English Heritage

Inglis, S. *A Lot of Old Balls* (2005) London: English Heritage

Jacobs, N. *Speedway in London* (2001) London: Tempus

James, C. *Focus on Rugby* (1983) London: Stanley Paul

Jennings, A. *Foul: The Secret World of FIFA* (2006) London: HarperSport

Johnson, M. *Rugby and All That* (2000) London: Coronet

Kimmage, P. *Rough Ride* (2001) London: Yellow Jersey Press

Kowet, D. *The Rich Who Own Sports* (1977) New York: Random House

Kramer, J. *The Game: My 40 Years in Tennis* (1979)

Laidlaw, R. *Golfing Heroes* (1989) London: Century Hutchinson

Lamster, M. *Spalding's World Tour* (2006) New York: Public Affairs

Law, D. *The King* (2003) London: Bantam Press

Lenahan, K. *A Little History of Golf* (1996) Belfast: Appletree

Levin, J. *From the Desert to Dubai* (2002) New York: DRF

Lewis, M. *Moneyball* (2004) New York: WW Norton

Lipsyte, R. and Levine, P. *Idols of the Game* (1995) Nashville: Turner

Lott, C. *Michael Jordan* (1993) New York: Scholastic

Louganis, G. *Breaking the Surface* (1995) London: Orion

Lovesey, J. and Mason, N. and Taylor, E. (ed) Sunday Times *Sports Book* (1979) Tadworth: Windmill

Lunn, A. *Switzerland and the English* (1944) London: Eyre and Spottiswoode

Lynam, D. *Sport Crazy* (1999) London: Arrow

McCormack, M. *What They Don't Teach You at Harvard Business School* (1986) London: Fontana

McKinstry, L. *Sir Alf* (2007) London: HarperSport

McNab, T. *The Complete Book of Athletics* (1980) London: Ward Lock

McWhirter, N. *Book of Millennium Records* (1999) London: Virgin Books

Marlar, R. *The Story of Cricket* (1979) London: Marshall Cavendish

Martin-Jenkins, C. *The Complete Who's Who of Test Cricketers* (1980) London: Orbis

Matthews, R. *The Age of the Gladiators* (2003) London: Arcturus

Miller, D. *Athens to Athens: The Official History of the Olympic Games and the IOC* (2003) London: Mainstream

Moore, G. (ed) *The Concise Encyclopedia of World Football* (1998) Bath: Paragon

Moore, T. *French Revolutions* (2002) London: Vintage Books

Naismith, J. *Basketball: Its Origins and Development* (1941) New York: Association

Nawrat, C. and Hutchings, S. Sunday Times *Illustrated History of Football* (1994) London: Hamlyn

Nawrat, C., Hutchings, S. and Struthers, G. Sunday Times *Illustrated History of Twentieth Century Sport* (1995) London: Hamlyn

Neufield, J. *Only in America: The Life and Crimes of Don King* (1995) New York: William Morrow

Oborne, P. *Basil D'Oliveira: Cricket and Controversy* (2005) London: Time Warner Books

O'Brien, J. and Herbert, I. *Vincent O'Brien: The Official Biography* (2005) London: Bantam

Odd, G. *Kings of the Ring: 100 Years of World Heavyweight Boxing* (1985) London: Newnes

Onslow, R. *Great Racing Gambles and Frauds* (1991) Swindon: Marlborough

O'Sullevan, P. *Calling the Horses* (1989) London: Stanley Paul

O'Sullevan, P. *Horse Racing Heroes* (2004) Newbury: Highdown

Pelé *My Life and the Beautiful Game* (1977) London: New English Library

Perry, J. *Rogues, Rotters, Rascals and Cheats* (2007) London: Sun

Philips, C. (ed) *The Right Set: The Faber Book of Tennis* (1999) London: Faber and Faber

Phythian, G. *Colossus: The True Story of William Foulke* (2005) Stroud: Tempus

Piesse, K. *Cricket's Greatest Scandals* (2001) London: Penguin

Piggott, L. *Lester* (1996) London: Corgi

Plumptre, G. *Back Page Racing* (1989) London: Queen Anne Press

Pound, D. *Inside the Olympics* (2004) Canada: Wiley

Powell, W. *Wisden Guide to Cricket Grounds* (1989) London: Stanley Paul

Puskas, F. *Captain of Hungary* (1955) London: Cassell

Quercetani, R. *A World History of Track and Field 1864–1964* (1964) Oxford: OUP

Quirke, P. *The Major: The Life and Times of Frank Buckley* (2006) Stroud: Tempus

Radford, P. *The Celebrated Captain Barclay* (2001) London: Headline

Rait Kerr, R. *The Laws of Cricket* (1950) London: Longmans

Rayvern Allen, D. *Cricket Extras* (1988) Enfield: Guinness

Rayvern Allen, D. *More Cricket Extras* (1992) Enfield: Guinness

Reason, J. ed. *How We Beat the All Blacks* (2005) London: Aurum

Reason, J. and James, C. *The World of Rugby* (1979) London: BBC Books

Rendel, M. *Blazing Saddles: The Cruel and Unusual Story of the Tour de France* (2007) London: Quercus

Remnick, D. *King of the World* (1998) London: Random House

Rice, J. *Start of Play* (1998) London: Prion

Richards, H. *A Game for Hooligans* (2006) Edinburgh: Mainstream

Riffenburgh, B. and Clary, J. *The Official History of Pro Football* (1990) London: Hamlyn

Roberts, P. *A Pictorial History of Cars* (1978) London: Octopus

Rosaforte T. *Tiger Woods: The Championship Years* (2000) London: Headline

Ross, M. *Baseball* (1988) London: Hamlyn

Rous, S. *Football Worlds: A Lifetime in Sport* (1978) London: Faber and Faber

Rubinstein, W. 'Jackie Robinson and the Integration of Major League Baseball' *History Today*, Volume 53 (9) (2003)

Simson, V. and Jennings, A. *The Lords of the Rings; Power Money and Drugs in the Modern Olympics* (1992) London: Simon and Schuster

Samuels, C. *The Magnificent Rube: The Life and Times of Tex Rickard* (1957) New York: McGraw Hill

Seddon, P. *Steve Bloomer: The Story of Football's First Superstar* (1999) Derby: Breedon

Seth-Smith, M., Willett, P. and Lawrence, J. *The History of Steeplechasing* (1969) London: Michael Joseph

Smit, B. *Pitch Invasion: Puma, Adidas and the Making of Modern Sport*
   (2008) London: Penguin
Smith, E. *What Sport Tells us About Life* (2008) London: Viking
Smith, M. (ed) Daily Telegraph *Book of Sporting Obituaries* (2000)
   London: Pan
Starmer-Smith, N. *Rugby: A Way of Life* (1986) London: Hutchinson
Stotts, S. *Curly Lambeau: Building the Green Bay Packers* (2007)
   Wisconsin: Badger
Strait, R. and Henie, L. *Queen of Ice, Queen of Shadows: The Unsuspected
   Life of Sonja Henie* (1985) Chelsea: Scarborough House
Strasser, J. and Becklund, L. *Swoosh: The Unauthorised Story of Nike
   and the Men who Played There* (1991) London: Harper Business
Studd, S. *Herbert Chapman: Football Emperor* (1981) London: Souvenir
Sumner, T. *Karsten's Way* (2000) Chicago: Northfield
Swanton, E. *Barclays World of Cricket* (1980) London: Collins
Synge, A. *Cricket: The Men and the Matches that Changed the Game*
   (1988) London: Century Benham
Tanner, M. *The Legend of Mick the Miller* (2004) London: Highdown
Thomson, G. *Ten: The Best of the* Observer *Sports Monthly's Tens* (2003)
   London: Yellow Jersey Press
Tibballs, G. *Great Sporting Failures* (1993) London: Collins
Tibballs, G. *Great Sporting Eccentrics* (1998) London: Robson
Tibballs, G. *Great Sporting Scandals* (2003) London: Robson
Ticher, M. *The Story of Harringay Stadium and Arena* (2000) London:
   Hornsey Historical Society
Titley, U. and McWhirter, N. *Centenary History of the Rugby Football
   Union* (1970) London: RFU
Todd, T. 'Anabolic Steroids: The Gremlins of Sport' *Journal of Sport
   History*, Volume 20 (1) (1987)
Tossel, D. *Grovel!: The Story and the Legacy of the Summer of 1976*
   (2007) London: Know the Score
Trelford, D. *Len Hutton Remembered* (1992) London: Witherby
Tremayne, D. *The Science of Speed* (1997) Sparkford: Haynes
Ungerleider, S. *Faust's Gold* (2001) New York: Thomas Dunne
Vamplew, W. 'Reduced Horse Power: The Jockey Club and the Regulation
   of British Horseracing' *Entertainment Law*, Volume 2 (3) (2003)
Venables, T. *Terry Venables' Football Heroes* (2001) London: Virgin Books
Viney, N. and Grant, N. *An Illustrated History of Ball Games* (1978)
   London: BCA

Voet, W. *Breaking the Chain* (2001) London: Yellow Jersey Press

Walker, M. and Taylor, S. *Murray Walker's Formula One Heroes* (2000) London: Virgin Books

Wall, F. *Fifty Years of Football* (2006) Cleethorpes: Soccer Books Limited

Wallechinsky, D. and Louck, J. *The Complete Book of the Winter Olympics* (2006) London: Aurum

Walton, J. 'Football, Fainting and Fatalities' *History Today*, Volume 53 (1) (2003)

Ward, A. *Soccerpedia* (2006) London: Robson

Ward, G. *Unforgiveable Blackness: The Rise and Fall of Jack Johnson* (2004) London: Pimlico

Warren, V. *Tennis Fashions* (1993) London: Kenneth Ritchie Wimbledon Library

Webber, R. *The County Cricket Championship* (1957) London: Phoenix Sports Books

Wheatcroft, G. *Le Tour* (2003) London: Simon and Schuster

Wigglesworth, N. *The Evolution of English Sport* (1996) London: Routledge

Wilde. S. *Number One: The World's Best Batsman and Bowlers* (1999) London: Victor Gollancz

Williams, J.P.R. *JPR* (1979) London: Collins.

Williams, R. *The Death of Ayrton Senna* (1995) London: Viking

Williams, R. *Racers* (1997) London: Viking

Williams, R. *Enzo Ferrari* (2001) London: Yellow Jersey Press

Wilson, B. *Googlies, Nutmegs and Bogeys* (2006) Thriplow: Icon

Wilson, J. *100 Greatest Racehorses* (1987) London: Queen Anne

Wilson, J. *Inverting the Pyramid: A History of Football Tactics* (2005) London: Orion

Witt, K. *Only with Passion* (2005) New York: Public Affairs

Wright, G. *Olympic Greats* (1980) London: Queen Anne

Wright, H. *Bull: The Biography* (1995) Halifax: Timeform

Yates, R. *Master Jacques* (2001) Norwich: Mousehold

Young, P. *Football in Sheffield* (1964) London: Sportsman's Book Club

Index by Sport/Profession

Athletics

Robert Barclay Allardice
Fanny Blankers-Coen
Michel Bréal
Avery Brundage
Don Catlin
John Graham Chambers
Pierre de Coubertin
Adi Dassler
Horst Dassler
Manfred Ewald
Dick Fosbury
Wyndham Halswelle
George Horine
Ben Johnson
Phil Knight
Alvin Kraenzlein
Spiridon Louis
Alice Milliat
Ed Moses
Miklós Németh
Adriaan Paulen
Dick Pound
Juan Samaranch
Tommie Smith
Michael Sweeney
Babe Zaharias
Emil Zátopek
John 'Montana Jack' Ziegler

Baseball

Jackie Robinson
'Babe' Ruth
Al Spalding

Basketball

Michael Jordan
Hank Luisetti
James Naismith
Carlos Ribagorda

Billiards/ Snooker

Neville Chamberlain
Joe Davis
Walter Lindrum
François Mingaud
John Thurston

Boxing

Muhammad Ali
Robert Barclay Allardice
John 'Jack' Broughton
John Graham Chambers
Jack Johnson
Don King
Joe Louis
Ray Mancini

Cricket

Charles Alcock
Sydney Barnes
Jack Blackham
Bernard Bosanquet
Don Bradman
Mike Brearley
William Clarke
Brian Close
Basil D'Oliveira
'Felix'
C. B. Fry
Mike Gatting
E. M. Grace
W. G. Grace
Clarrie Grimmett
David Harris
Lord Harris
Lord Hawke
Len Hutton
Douglas Jardine
Sanath Jayasuriya
John Barton King
Ray Lindwall
Clive Lloyd

Ian Meckiff
Muttiah Muralitharan
Sarfraz Nawaz
Kerry Packer
Jim Phillips
'Sonny' Ramadhin
'Ranji'
Viv Richards
Frederick Spofforth
'Lumpy' Stevens
Maurice Tate
Shane Warne
John Willes
Tom Wills
Edgar 'Ned' Willsher

Croquet

John Jaques II

Cycling

Jacques Anquetil
Beryl Burton
Tullio Campagnolo
Henri Desgrange
Bernard Hinault
Knud Jensen
Greg LeMond
Eddy Merckx
Tom Simpson
Willy Voet

Diving

Ludwig Jahn
Greg Louganis

Football

Charles Alcock
Franz Beckenbauer
Carlos Bilardo
Jean-Marc Bosman
Amadeo Carrizo